WITHD

BREWERS
QUOTATIONS

BREWER'S QUOTATIONS

A PHRASE AND FABLE DICTIONARY

NIGEL REES

CASSELL

A CASSELL BOOK

First published 1994 by Cassell
Wellington House,
125 Strand, London WC2R 0BB

First published in paperback 1996

Distributed in the United States by
Sterling Publishing Co., Inc.
387 Park Avenue South, New York, New York 10016–8810

British Library Cataloguing-in-Publication Data
A catalogue record for this book is available from the British Library

ISBN 0-304-34832-5

Typeset by Colset Private Limited, Singapore

Printed and bound in Great Britain by
Mackays of Chatham PLC, Chatham, Kent

Contents

'He was a learned man, of immense reading, but is much blamed for his unfaithful quotations.'

ANON., of the Puritan pamphleteer William Prynne (1600-69)

'He would forget to eat dinner, though he never forgot a quotation.'

ANON., of Richard Porson (1759-1808), Regius Professor of Greek at Cambridge

'With just enough of learning to misquote.'

LORD BYRON, *English Bards and Scotch Reviewers* (1809)

'Next to the originator of a good sentence is the first misquoter of it.'

R.W. EMERSON, *Letters and Social Aims* (1876), 'Quotation and Originality' (misquoted)

'It is bad enough to see one's own good things fathered on other people, but it is worse to have other people's rubbish fathered upon oneself.'

SAMUEL BUTLER, *Notebooks* (c 1890)

'Quotation: The act of repeating erroneously the words of another. The words erroneously repeated.'

AMBROSE BIERCE, *The Devil's Dictionary* (1906)

'Misquotation is . . . the pride and privilege of the learned. A widely-read man never quotes accurately.'

HESKETH PEARSON, *Common Misquotations* (1937)

'Misquotations are the only quotations that are never misquoted.'
   ibid.

'Famous remarks are very seldom quoted correctly.'
   SIMEON STRUNKSY, *No Mean City* (1944)

'It [is] gentlemanly to get one's quotations very slightly wrong. In that way one unprigs oneself and allows the company to correct one.'
   LORD RIBBLESDALE, quoted in Lady Diana Cooper, *The Light of Common Day* (1959)

'The price of pedantry is eternal vigilance.'
   OLIVER MASON, in a letter to the *Independent*, 28 January 1987

Introduction

This is not the usual kind of dictionary or anthology of quotations so, to begin with, several words of explanation are necessary. It is neither a 'dictionary', boldly aiming to provide a source for any quotation that the reader might wish to know about, nor is it an 'anthology', proffering quotable lines on various themes. What *Brewer's Quotations* does contain is the most commonly misquoted, misattributed, misascribed, misremembered and most disputed sayings that there are. It also contains sayings that are frequently unattributed, unascribed, misunderstood and misapprehended, or words whose authors might wish to reconsider them. To put it another way, and at its broadest, these are the sayings about which there is something more to be said. As such it follows naturally in the tradition of Dr Ebenezer Cobham Brewer whose original *Dictionary of Phrase and Fable* singled out words and phrases 'with tales to tell' and did not attempt an unachievable comprehensiveness.

The need for this new type of dictionary of quotations seems to be incontestable. Most, if not all, quotation reference books currently available fail to provide contextual notes. And, even if they provide material on sources, there is seldom sufficient editorial commentary. Hence the fact that this dictionary is, if you like, made up entirely of the notes and footnotes missing from the other books.

In consequence, I have had to ponder long and hard the question of how to describe the contents of this book in its title. Should it be 'Proper Quotations' or 'Correct Quotations' or even 'Difficult Quotations'? Finally, I have settled, simply, for 'Quotations'. What it is not is a dictionary setting out to be the ultimate authority or in any way comprehensive. There are plenty of other dictionaries of quotations which may put in shaky claims to be either or both of these things. What it may be, is the quotation dictionary of last resort, though perhaps it will become the first.

Many is the time I have been approached by people saying 'I have looked in all the obvious places' when trying to trace a 'lost' quotation (by which they mean an elusive source). Indeed, a good number of the quotations in this book were drawn to my attention through this kind of query and, I have to admit, that some are included not because there is much to be said about them but because, for a time, their sources proved particularly elusive.

In several cases, also, the source has yet to be found. I take no pleasure in having to put 'untraced' or 'unverified' in any of these entries, but I feel it may provide a useful service to present the evidence that has been gathered to date in attempting to crack these hardest of quotation nuts.

I do this, proceeding on the principle that someone, somewhere knows the answer or, having been alerted to the fact that someone is interested, may soon stumble upon the answer. Please help if you can and your diligence or serendipity will be reflected in future editions.

The vagueness is all

I think it was George Bernard Shaw who said, 'Only fools use quotations'. In fact, I know Shaw never said anything of the kind. I am merely following the custom adopted by so many who are called upon to speak or write. The names Oscar Wilde, Winston Churchill, or Mark Twain, Abraham Lincoln and (for a time, not so long ago) Orson Welles, may be substituted for Shaw's, but the form remains the same.

Notice particularly the use of 'I think'. This is inserted to give the speaker the air of a man who is familiar with everything worth quoting but does not wish to appear too effortlessly knowledgeable. In all probability the speaker had no idea that Shaw, Wilde, Churchill, Lincoln, Twain or Welles ever said any such thing until, shortly before standing up to speak, he opened a dictionary of quotations. No matter. He decided to start with a quotation to lend his theme dignity and himself with a whiff of erudition. The choice of Shaw is instructive, however. He is an 'O.K.' name to quote. So much so that even if Shaw never uttered anything remotely similar it is possible to get away with quoting remarks he never made.

Hence, *Rees's First Law of Quotation*: 'When in doubt, ascribe all quotations to George Bernard Shaw.' The law's first qualification is: 'Except when they obviously derive from Shakespeare, the Bible or Kipling.' The corollary is: 'In time, all humorous remarks will be ascribed to Shaw whether he said them or not.'

Why should this be? People are notoriously lax about quoting and attributing marks correctly, as witness an analagous process I shall call *Churchillian Drift*. The Drift is almost indistinguishable from the First Law, but there is a subtle difference. Whereas quotations with an apothegmatic feel are normally ascribed to Shaw, those with a more grandiose or belligerent tone are, as if by osmosis, credited to Churchill. All humorous remarks obviously made by a female originated, of course, with Dorothy Parker. All quotations in translation, on the other hand, should be attributed to Goethe (with 'I think' obligatory).

Shaw, Churchill, Wilde, Lincoln and Twain are, in fact, fixed in the popular mind as practically the sole source of witty and quotable sayings. But what is alarming is the way in which almost any remark not obviously tied to some other originator will one day find itself attributed to one of these five.

The pedantry police

Having written all this, I am only too aware that I am open to *Rees's Second Law of Quotation*: 'However sure you are that you have attributed a quotation correctly, an earlier source will be pointed out to you.' For example, in my *Quote . . . Unquote* book (1978) I also stated that Somerset Maugham took the title of his novel *Cakes and Ale* from Shakespeare's *Twelfth Night*. In no time at all, I received a letter from a reader pointing out that the phrase also occurs in a papyrus dated *c* 1000–900BC: 'Grant ye cakes and ale and oxen and feathered fowl to Osiris.' I was duly mortified – but I have a strong suspicion that Maugham didn't know that either.

Even when a quotation has become firmly yoked to a particular source, there is always someone to put you right about it. Again in that first *Quote . . . Unquote* book I included Churchill's description of Clement Attlee as, 'A sheep in sheep's clothing'. Later I discovered that Churchill himself had corrected this – he claimed he had said it about Ramsay Macdonald (rather more to the point, be it said). Then along came another phrase-detective who asserted that even if Churchill *had* expressed the sentiment about either gentleman, he had been taking unto himself a phrase originated by J.B. Morton, alias 'Beachcomber'. Without re-reading the whole of Beachcomber – a pleasant enough task, to be sure – I am unable to say if this is so. But it seems quite feasible, even if that would make it more a case of Churchillian Grab than Churchillian Drift.

It stands to reason that when a *bon mot* is first uttered, a lot depends on the hearing and memory of those present – or on the public relations skills of the man who disseminates his own *bons mots* (Oscar Wilde must have been a dab hand at this). Yet even when words are broadcast on radio or television, audible to millions, error is likely to creep into the quoting of them.

In fact, strictly speaking, one ought to append to every quotation a covering note of deliberate and vague periphrasis: 'I am not saying it *was* Shaw/Wilde/Twain who said this . . . I am merely suggesting that sources would support the view that thingummy is one of a number of possible options as to who might have been associated with the above remark at one time or another.'

Monarchs of all we survey

After presiding over almost two decades of *Quote . . . Unquote* on the radio, I like to think I have a pretty fair idea of the average person's knowledge of quotations or lack of it. An opportunity to test this idea scientifically presented itself when Public Attitude Surveys Ltd of High Wycombe offered to carry three sets of questions about quotations and advertising slogans on one of its regular omnibus surveys (of 1,851 adults throughout the UK in May 1992).

Firstly, what did the Great British Public know about its greatest single cultural asset, the plays of Shakespeare? It was, I suppose, reasonably reassuring that 78.3 per cent of those interviewed managed not to suspect a trick question and correctly identified 'O, Romeo, Romeo! wherefore art thou, Romeo?' as coming from *Romeo and Juliet*. The 0.3 per cent who thought it was from *Julius Caesar* are, I hope, statistically insignificant.

A reasonable 38.3 per cent correctly placed 'Friends, Romans, countrymen, lend me your ears' in *Julius Caesar* while 3.7 per cent put this (no doubt mischievously) in *Richard III*. Half the respondents said they hadn't a clue. A fair 31.5 per cent knew that 'A horse! a horse! my kingdom for a horse!' came from *Richard III*, whilst 14 per cent managed confidently to place it wrongly elsewhere.

I am not sure whether to be amazed or depressed at this level of knowledge, or lack of it, but when only 28.4 per cent know that 'Alas, poor Yorick' comes from

Hamlet, and only 36.6 per cent that 'To be or not to be: that is the question' comes from the same play, you do begin to wonder about our educational system.

Turning to the second group of questions, it is possibly not so surprising that political quotations—albeit all from the last fifty years or so—were generally better known. A very respectable 70.6 per cent knew that it was Winston Churchill who said, 'Never in the field of human conflict was so much owed by so many to so few', though almost 28 per cent appeared not to have a clue. Of more recent sayings, 54 per cent knew Margaret Thatcher's mighty line 'U-turn if you want to—the lady's not for turning'. But what is one to make of the fact that only 24 per cent connected George Bush with 'Read my lips—no new taxes'? It was not generally reported in the British press when he said it in 1988 (not even in the quality papers), so this is possibly not too bad a showing.

On the other hand, only a meagre 11 per cent volunteered that it was John F. Kennedy who said, 'Ask not what your country can do for you—ask what you can do for your country'. Does this result betray a lack of interest in foreign affairs among the British—the sort of thing of which Americans in their turn often stand accused? Only a comparable survey in the US would give a pointer to what might be considered a reasonable level of awareness on this question.

Knowledge of advertising slogans is, of course, engineered by the agencies. A cleverly constructed slogan either incorporates the name of the product or insists on your thinking of it. This was probably borne out by the results of our survey, though the relative amounts currently being spent on the different campaigns must also be a factor. With the product name detached from the slogan, only 46 per cent managed to conclude that Carlsberg is 'Probably the best lager in the world'. Almost 10 per cent guessed that it was Heineken, however, despite the fact that Carlsberg has been coupled with this line since 1973. As for Heineken, which has been famous for 'refreshing the parts other beers cannot reach' since 1975, 57 per cent knew that.

Guinness has been promoted over the years with all kinds of memorable slogans. It used to be said that if you stopped a member of the British public in the street and said, 'Name an advertising slogan', the one volunteered would be 'Guinness is good for you'. Recently, however, Guinness has been heavily advertised in rather an oblique, allusive way with the line 'Pure genius'. I suppose, 'genius' sounds a bit like an anagram of Guinness, and that may have helped 62 per cent to make the connection—though this was the only one of our four slogans that, in its full form, does not include the product name.

The clear winner was 'I bet he drinks . . .' Nearly 70 per cent of our respondents were aware that this line was for a considerable period completed with the brand name '. . . Carling Black Label'. Heavily advertised though this beer may have been, the slogan obviously had clawed its way, if not 'into the language', at least into the mass consciousness.

How to use this book

This being the kind of dictionary it is, the location of quotations under the names of specific people (REAGAN, SHAKESPEARE) or in the ANONYMOUS SAYINGS category or under one or two institutional headings (*THE TIMES*) is a touch on the arbitrary side. I have sometimes been faced with the problem of whether to put a quotation under the name of the actual originator (if known) or under the name of someone to whom it is frequently and mistakenly ascribed.

But I have not lost too much sleep over this. The main consideration was that the quotation should be easily located *somewhere* in the book. Hence, the way to find what you want should always be *through the Index*. Look for the quotation's key word or words in the Index and that will refer you to a numbered quotation on a particular page. In many cases, where a quotation is popularly misremembered the quotation will be found indexed under both the correct and the misquoted wording.

Acknowledgements

I am grateful to the many people who have posed questions about quotations that have puzzled them and to the many people who have contributed helpfully to solving these queries. Since January 1992 these searches have been conducted in the pages of *The 'Quote . . . Unquote' Newsletter*, published quarterly in Britain and the United States, as well as on the BBC Radio programme *Quote . . . Unquote*, which is broadcast on Radio 4 in the United Kingdom and on BBC World Service.

For helping me with my investigations, or just for being there, my thanks are due to these people (with apologies for any omissions): Roy Alexander; Dr Eric Anderson; Frank Atkinson; Paul Beale; H.E. Bell; Peter Black; Stephan Chodorov; Professor Denis J. Conlon; David Cottis; Barry Day; T.A. Dyer; Susan Eden; David Elias; Peter Effer; Charles G. Francis; Ian Gillies; W. Eric Gustafson; Celia Haddon; Raymond Harris; Jenny Hartland; Donald Hickling; Michael Holroyd; Sir David Hunt; Arthur Illes; W.W. Keen James; Sir Antony Jay; Martin Knapp; Oonagh Lahr; Michael R. Lewis; R.P.W. Lewis; Malcolm Macdonald; Frank Loxley; Henry B. McNulty; David Mather; Leonard Miall; Professor Wolfgang Mieder; Tony Miller; Jan Morris; Michael and Valerie Grosvenor Myer; John Julius Norwich; Charles Osborne; Derek Parker; Philip Purser; Steve Race; Claire Rayner; David E.T. Read; Betty Reid; Derek Robinson; Adrian Room; William Shawcross; Anthony W. Shipps; Godfrey Smith, *The Sunday Times*; Thomas Sutcliffe; Michael Swan; Kevin Thurlow; Nelson and Pat Tomalin; Horst Vey; Martin Walker; Bill Watts; Barbara Wild.

To which I would add my gratitude for the institutional help I have received from David Evans, Michel Petheram and other staff of the BBC Radio Research Library, London; the staffs of the British Library Newspaper Library, Colindale, and the London Library.

I am grateful to Barry Lee, Managing Director of Public Attitude Surveys Ltd of High Wycombe, for allowing me to reprint the extracts from the quotations awareness poll.

NIGEL REES

Abbreviations

Bartlett	*Bartlett's Familiar Quotations* (15th ed.), 1980, (16th ed.), 1992
Benham	*Benham's Book of Quotations*, 1907, 1948, 1960
Bible	The Authorised Version, 1611 (except where stated otherwise)
BDPF	*Brewer's Dictionary of Phrase and Fable*, (13th ed.), 1975, (14th ed.), 1989
Burnam	Tom Burnam, *The Dictionary of Misinformation*, 1975; *More Misinformation*, 1980
CODP	*The Concise Oxford Dictionary of Proverbs*, 1982
DNB	*The Dictionary of National Biography*
Flexner	Stuart Berg Flexner, *I Hear America Talking*, 1976; *Listening to America*, 1982
Mencken	*H.L. Mencken's Dictionary of Quotations*, 1942
Morris	William and Mary Morris, *Morris Dictionary of Word and Phrase Origins*, 1977
ODMQ	*The Oxford Dictionary of Modern Quotations*, 1991
ODP	*The Oxford Dictionary of Proverbs* (3rd ed.), 1970
ODQ	*The Oxford Dictionary of Quotations* (2nd ed.), 1953, (3rd ed.), 1979, (4th ed.), 1992
OED2	*The Oxford English Dictionary* (2nd ed.), 1989, (CD-ROM version), 1992
Partridge/ Catch Phrases	Eric Partridge, *A Dictionary of Catch Phrases* (2nd ed., edited by Paul Beale), 1985
Partridge/ Slang	Eric Partridge, *A Dictionary of Slang and Unconventional English* (8th ed., edited by Paul Beale), 1984
PDMQ	*The Penguin Dictionary of Modern Quotations* (edited by J.M. & M.J. Cohen), 1980, 1993
Pearson	Hesketh Pearson, *Common Misquotations*, 1937
Safire	William Safire, *Safire's Political Dictionary*, 1978
RQ	*Respectfully Quoted* (edited by Suzy Platt, Congressional Reference Division), 1989

A

Acheson, Dean
American Democratic politician
(1893–1971)

1 *Great Britain . . . has lost an Empire and not yet found a role.*

Acheson was a former Secretary of State (under President Truman) and the son of a British army officer who went to Canada. The home truth was thus all the more painful when Acheson, speaking at the Military Academy, West Point, on 5 December 1962, went on to say: '[Britain's] attempt to play a separate power role — that is, a role apart from Europe, a role based on a "special relationship" with the United States, a role based on being the head of a "Commonwealth" . . . this role is about to be played out . . . Her Majesty's Government is now attempting, wisely in my opinion, to re-enter Europe.'
   Lord Chandos, President of the Institute of Directors, protested that such words coming from one of President Kennedy's advisers were 'a calculated insult'. Prime Minister Harold Macmillan quietly observed that, in any case, the general drift of world affairs was against Britain or any other country trying to play 'a separate power role'. Thirty years later, one can see that Britain's European 're-entry' is all but accomplished.

2 *Present at the Creation.*

The title of Acheson's memoirs (1969) came from a remark by Alfonso X, the Wise (1221–84), King of Castille, on studying the Ptolemaic system: 'Had I been present at the Creation, I would have given some useful hints for the better ordering of the universe.'
   Thomas Carlyle had earlier quoted the remark in his *Life of Frederick the Great* (1858–65). In Bishop Berkeley's *Three*

Dialogues Between Hylas and Philonus (1713), Philonus says: 'Why, I imagine that if I had been present at the Creation, I should have seen things produced into being; that is, become perceptible, in the order described by the sacred historian.'

Acton, Lord
English historian (1834–1902)

3 *All power corrupts, and absolute power corrupts absolutely.*

In the correct form, 'Power tends to corrupt and absolute power corrupts absolutely', Acton's dictum appeared in a letter to Bishop Mandell Creighton, dated 3 April 1887 (published 1904). It is often quoted without the 'tends'. Acton had been anticipated by William Pitt, Earl of Chatham, speaking in the House of Lords on 9 January 1770: 'Unlimited power is apt to corrupt the minds of those who possess it.' In 1839 Lord Brougham had written in *Historical Sketches of Statesmen of the Time of George III*: 'Unlimited power corrupts the possessor.' A.J.P. Taylor questioned the accuracy of the remark in a *New Statesman* article, *c* 1955, calling it, 'Windy rot . . . many an engine-driver is not corrupted' (which misses the point, surely?)

Adams, John
2nd American President (1735–1826)

4 *All great nations inevitably end up committing suicide.*

What Adams wrote, precisely, in a letter to John Taylor (15 April 1814) was: 'Remember, democracy never lasts long. It soon wastes, exhausts, and murders itself. There never was a democracy that did not commit suicide.'

1

Adams, Samuel
American revolutionary politician
(1722–1803)

1 *What a glorious morning for America!*

Thus is it usually quoted, but what Adams most likely said on hearing the sound of gunfire at Lexington (the opening battle of the War of American Independence) on 19 April 1775 was, 'What a glorious morning is this'.

Adams, Mrs Sarah Flower
English hymnwriter (1805–48)

2 *Nearer, My God, To Thee.*

The title of a hymn first published in 1841. This is often said to have been what the ship's band was playing when the *Titanic* sank in 1912. In the song 'Be British', written and composed by Paul Pelham and Lawrence Wright in the year the ship sank, there is a tear-jerking 'recitation after 2nd verse' enshrining the belief that the band played the hymn 'Nearer My God To Thee' as the ship went down. According to Burnam (1980), however, the band played ragtime until the ship's bridge dipped underwater, and then the bandmaster led his men in the Episcopal hymn, 'Autumn'. This information was based on a reported remark of the surviving wireless operator in the *New York Times* (19 April 1912). According to Walter Lord, *A Night to Remember* (1955), the 'Nearer My God To Thee' version was one of many rumours circulating within a few days of the ship's sinking.

Adamson, Harold
American songwriter (1906–80)

3 *Coming in on a Wing and a Prayer.*

This was the title of a song popular in the Second World War (published in 1943), which derived from an alleged remark by a real pilot who was coming in to land with a badly damaged plane. Adamson's lyrics (to music by Jimmy McHugh) include the lines:

Tho' there's one motor gone, we can still carry on
Comin' in on a wing and a pray'r.

A US film (1944) about life on an aircraft carrier was called simply *Wing and a Prayer*.

Addison, Joseph
English essayist and politician (1672–1719)

4 *And pleas'd th' Almighty's orders to perform,*
Rides in the whirlwind, and directs the storm.

Written about the 1st Duke of Marlborough in *The Campaign* (1705), a celebration of the Battle of Blenheim (1704), Addison's second line has become a figure of speech. Alexander Pope repeated it with comic effect in *The Dunciad* (1728). Henry Buckle in his *History of Civilisation in England* (1857) had: 'To see whether they who had raised the storm could ride the whirlwind.' Nowadays it simply means to deal with an extremely difficult situation: 'With his overall Commons majority already down to 18 and his Government fighting on several other damaging policy fronts, Mr Major is riding a whirlwind' (*Daily Mail*, 21 May 1993).

5 *He who hesitates is lost.*

What Addison actually wrote in *Cato*, his neo-classical tragedy (1713), was, 'The *woman* that deliberates is lost'. In fact, most early uses of the phrase were about women. The *CODP* has not found an earlier citation of this proverb.

Adler, Polly
American brothel keeper (1900–62)

6 *A House is Not a Home.*

Adler was a notable New York madam in the 1920s and 1930s. She finally closed her bordello in 1945 and spent part of her twilight years writing memoirs, which were published in 1954. Then: 'One day I happened to be spraying a rose-bush in my back yard, and Dora [Maugham] . . . was profoundly impressed by this spectacle of suburban domesticity.
' "I wonder what the cops would say," she mused, "if they could see you now".
' "Oh," said I, "probably they'd be disappointed that my home is not a house." Dora's reaction to this remark was so unusual . . . "Eyeow!" she squealed. "Hold everything! . . . Turn that around and you've got it!"
' "What on earth are you talking about?"
' "The perfect title for your book . . . "
'So far as I was concerned, I told her, it was the most inspired piece of thinking

anyone had done in a garden since the day Isaac Newton got conked by an apple.'

Of course, 'house' here means 'brothel'. When the book was filmed (US, 1964), there had to be a theme song incorporating the title, which managed coyly to avoid any suggestion as to what sort of 'house' was being talked about.

Agate, James
English drama critic (1877–1947)

1 *A professional is a man who can do his job when he doesn't feel like it; an amateur is one who can't [do his job] when he does feel like it.*

From *Ego* (1935; entry for 17 September 1933). The context was a lunch with the actor Cedric Hardwicke, who said: 'My theory of acting is that it is so minor an art that the only self-respect attaching to it is to be able to reproduce one's performance with mathematical accuracy.' The above was Agate's concurrence. Hardwicke added: 'It shouldn't make a hair's breadth of difference to an actor if he has a dead baby at home and a wife dying.'

There have been several other attempts to define the difference between amateurs and professionals, beyond the acting profession: 'Amateurs [musicians] practice until they can get it right; professionals practice until they can't get it wrong' (quoted by Harold Craxton, one-time professor at the Royal Academy of Music); 'Professionals built the *Titanic*; amateurs built the Ark' (Anon.)

Akins, Zoë
American playwright (1886–1958)

2 *The Greeks had a word for it.*

For seemingly so venerable a phrase, it may come as a surprise to learn that this dates back no further than 1929, when the words were used as the title of a play. Although, as Akins said, 'the phrase is original and grew out of the dialogue', it does not appear anywhere in the text. Akins told Burton Stevenson that in dialogue cut from her play the 'word' was used to describe a type of woman. One character thinks that 'tart' is meant but another corrects this and says that 'free soul' is more to the point. Nowadays the phrase is used a trifle archly, as when one wishes to express disapproval and say, 'There's a name for that sort of behaviour'.

Alden, Robert
American theologian (1937–   )

3 *There is not enough darkness in all the world to put out the light of even one small candle.*

So attributed by *The David and Charles Book of Quotations* (1986). On the other hand, Bernard Levin describes this in *Conducted Tour* (1981) as 'an ancient proverb'.

Alexander, Mrs C.F.
Irish poet and hymnwriter (1818–95)

4 *The rich man in his castle,*
The poor man at his gate.

An omission rather than a misquotation. Indeed, the enormously popular hymn, 'All things bright and beautiful', written by Mrs Alexander in 1848, is in danger of becoming known as the hymn from which a verse had to be dropped. Causing all the trouble is the third verse, with its apparent acceptance of an unacceptable (to modern ears) *status quo*.

In Barbara Pym's novel *No Fond Return of Love* (1961): 'Dulcie sang in a loud indignant voice, waiting for the lines

'The rich man in his castle, the poor man at his gate,
God made them, high or lowly, and ordered their estate.

'but they never came. Then she saw that the verse had been left out. She sat down, feeling cheated of her indignation.'

Most modern hymnbook compilers omit the verse. *Songs of Praise Discussed* (1933) calls it an 'appalling verse . . . She must have forgotten Dives, and how Lazarus lay "at his gate"; but then she had been brought up in the atmosphere of a land-agent on an Irish estate. The *English Hymnal* led the way in obliterating this verse from the Anglican mind.' The verse remains in *Hymns Ancient and Modern* (Standard Edition, reprinted 1986), but it has disappeared from the *Irish Hymnal*. The authors of *The Houses of Ireland* (1975) note that by the present century 'the ecclesiastical authorities had decided that God's intentions are not to preclude movement within the social system. However, few of her contemporaries doubted that Mrs Alexander's interpretation was correct.'

Born in Co. Wicklow, Mrs Alexander was the wife of a Bishop of Derry and Archbishop of Armagh.

Algren, Nelson
American novelist and short-story writer
(1909–81)

1 *Never eat at a place called Mom's.
Never play cards with a man called
Doc. Never go to bed with a woman
whose troubles are greater than your
own.*

This comes from a *A Walk on the Wild Side*
(1956) but Bartlett (1992) finds it only
in H.E.F. Donahue, *Conversations with
Nelson Algren* (1964). ODQ and ODMQ
both cite a *Newsweek* report (1956) rather
than the book itself.

Allingham, Margery
English detective novelist (1904–66)

2 *Once sex rears its ugly 'ead it's time to
steer clear.*

From *Flowers for the Judge* (1936). The
ODMQ (1991) gives this, suggesting that
Allingham coined the expression, but 'sex
rears its ugly head' has been current since at
least 1930 when James R. Quirk used it in
a *Photoplay* editorial about the film *Hell's
Angels*. It is used both as an explanation for
people's behaviour (like '*cherchez la femme*')
and as a complaint of the intrusion of sex
into books, TV programmes and so on,
where the speaker would rather not find it.
    And how curious. Why? Because the
penis rises? If so, then why ugly? A very
odd usage, except that the construction 'to
raise/rear its ugly head' was used about
other matters before sex. Anthony Trollope
in *Barchester Towers* (1857) has: 'Rebellion
had already raised her hideous head within
the [bishop's] palace.' The image is presumably of a Loch Ness-type monster, perhaps,
emerging from the deep.

Amery, Leo S.
English Conservative politician (1873–1955)

3 *Speak for England, Arthur!*

On the eve of war, 2 September 1939, Prime
Minister Neville Chamberlain appeared
in the House of Commons and held out
the prospect of a further Munich-type
peace conference and did not announce any
ultimatum to Germany. When the acting
Labour leader, Arthur Greenwood, rose
to respond, a Conservative MP shouted,
'Speak for England, Arthur!' For many
years, it was generally accepted that the MP
was L.S. Amery and, indeed, he wrote in
My Political Life (Vol. 3, 1955): 'It was
essential that someone should . . . voice the
feelings of the House and of the whole country. Arthur Greenwood rose . . . I dreaded
a purely partisan speech, and called out to
him across the floor of the House, Speak for
England.' (Note, no 'Arthur'.) By October
30, James Agate was writing in his diary
(published in *Ego 4*) of the anthology for the
forces he had been busy compiling called
Speak for England: 'Clemence Dane gave me
the title; it is the phrase shouted in the House
the other day when Arthur Greenwood got
up to speak on the declaration of the war.'
    However, writing up an account of the
session in his diary, Harold Nicolson (whose
usual habit was to make his record first
thing the following morning) wrote: 'Bob
Boothby cried out, "*You* speak for Britain".'
Boothby confirmed that he had said this
when shown the diary passage in 1964.
    The explanation would seem to be that
after Amery spoke, his cry was taken up not
only by Boothby but by others on the Tory
benches. From the Labour benches came
cries of 'What about Britain?' and 'Speak for
the working classes!' Interestingly, nobody
claims to have said the exact words as
popularly remembered. The intervention
went unrecorded in *Hansard*.

4 *This is what Cromwell said to the Long
Parliament when he thought it was no
longer fit to conduct the affairs of the
nation: 'You have sat too long here for
any good you have been doing. Depart,
I say, and let us have done with you. In
the name of God, go!'*

By May 1940 criticism was growing of the
British Government's handling of the war so
far. Norway and most of Scandinavia had
been lost to the Germans and yet a War
Cabinet had not yet been formed. It was
obvious that things were getting very bad
indeed. In a dramatic speech to the House of
Commons on 7 May, Amery said, 'Somehow or other we must get into the Government men who can match our enemies in
fighting spirit' and he quoted something that
Oliver Cromwell had said to John Hampden
'some three hundred years ago, when this
House found that its troops were being
beaten again and again by the dash and daring of the Cavaliers', namely, 'We cannot go
on being led as we are'.
    In his autobiography, Amery said, 'I

was not out for a dramatic finish, but for a practical purpose; to bring down the Government if I could.' And so he quoted Cromwell's words when dismissing the Rump of the Long Parliament in 1653. Chamberlain's Government did indeed go. Churchill became Prime Minister and formed a National Government three days later.

Amis, Kingsley
(later Sir Kingsley)
English novelist, poet and critic
(1922–   )

1 *Lucky Jim.*

Amis's comic novel (1953) about a hapless university lecturer, Jim Dixon, takes its title from a not terribly relevant American song by Frederick Bowers (1874–1961) and his vaudeville partner Charles Horwitz (though it is usually ascribed to Anon.). It tells of a man who has to wait for his childhood friend Jim to die before he can marry the girl they were once both after. Then, married to the woman and not enjoying it, he would rather he was dead like his friend: 'Oh, lucky Jim, how I envy him.'

2 *More means worse.*

Amis wrote about the expansion of higher education in an article in *Encounter* (July 1960), especially on 'the delusion that there are thousands of young people who are capable of benefiting from university training but have somehow failed to find their way there'. He added: 'I wish I could have a little tape-and-loudspeaker arrangement sewn into the binding of this magazine, to be triggered off by the light reflected from the reader's eyes on to this part of the page, and set to bawl out at several bels: MORE WILL MEAN WORSE.'
When *The Times* misquoted this as 'more means worse' on one occasion, Amis fired off a broadside (22 February 1983):

> I think the difference is substantial, but let that go for now. You show by your misquotation that you couldn't be bothered to look up the reference, thereby ignoring the context, any arguments or evidence put forward, etc.
>
> Having garbled my remark you say roundly that in the event I was wrong. Not altogether perhaps. Laziness and incuriosity about sources are familiar symptoms of academic decline.

3 *Outside every fat man there was an even fatter man trying to close in.*

See CONNOLLY 105:5.

4 *The Folk That Live On the Hill.*

It would be interesting to know on what linguistic grounds Kingsley Amis chose 'that' instead of 'who' in the title of his novel (1990). The song is called 'The Folks Who Live on the Hill' and was written by Jerome Kern and Oscar Hammerstein II for the 1937 US film *High, Wide and Handsome.*

Angell, Sir Norman
English pacifist (1872–1967)

5 *The Great Illusion.*

Angell's anti-war book was first published in 1909 with the title *Europe's Optical Illusion.* A year later it was republished as *The Great Illusion.* Angell was awarded the Nobel Peace Prize in 1933. Use of the phrase was further encouraged by its choice by Jean Renoir for his 1937 film *La Grande Illusion,* about French pilots captured by the Germans in the First World War.

Anka, Paul
American singer and songwriter (1941–   )

6 *And now the end is near*
And so I face the final curtain,
My friend, I'll say it clear,
I'll state my case of which I'm certain.
I've lived a life that's full, I've
*   travelled each and evr'y high-way*
And more, much more than this, I
*   did it my way.*

Lord George-Brown made an odd use of this song when he entitled his 1971 autobiography *In My Way,* but referring to 'My Way' he undoubtedly was. It is a song that has a peculiar hold over people. Anka's English lyrics (1969) were set to the music of a French song *Comme d'habitude* by Claude François and Jacques Revaux. A clear-eyed look at the lyrics reveals that they are at best not entirely literate, nor is their meaning clear. But that is the song's apparent strength — people can (and have) read into it whatever they like — above all, a feeling of triumphant individualism, that 'I' counts most of all. It gives them a feeling of self-justification, even if with no real basis.

Anonymous sayings

1 All publicity is good publicity.

An almost proverbial saying, which I first heard in the 1960s but which is probably as old as the public relations industry. Alternative forms include: 'There's no such thing as bad publicity', 'There's no such thing as over-exposure — only bad exposure', 'Don't read it — measure it' and 'I don't care what the papers say about me as long as they spell my name right'. The latter saying has been attributed to the American Tammany leader 'Big Tim' Sullivan.

CODP includes it in the form 'Any publicity is good publicity' but finds no example before 1974. However, in Dominic Behan's My Brother Brendan (1965), the Irish playwright is quoted as saying: 'There is no such thing as bad publicity except your own obituary.' And James Agate in Ego 7 (for 19 February 1944) quotes Arnold Bennett, 'All praise is good', and adds: 'I suppose the same could be said about publicity.'

2 And this too shall pass away.

Chuck Berry spoke the words of a 'song' called 'Pass Away' (1979), which told of a Persian king who had had carved the words 'Even this shall pass away'. George Harrison earlier called his first (mostly solo) record album 'All Things Must Pass' (1970). These musicians were by no means the first people to be drawn to this saying. As Abraham Lincoln explained in an address to the Wisconsin State Agricultural Society (1859): 'An Eastern monarch once charged his wise men to invent him a sentence to be ever in view, and which should be true and appropriate in all times and situations. They presented him with the words, "And this, too, shall pass away". How much it expresses! How chastening in the hour of pride! How consoling in the depths of affliction!'

But who was the oriental monarch? Benham (1948) says the phrase was an inscription on a ring — 'according to an oriental tale' — and the phrase was given by Solomon to a Sultan who 'desired that the words should be appropriate at all time'. In 1860 Nathaniel Hawthorne wrote in The Marble Faun of the 'greatest mortal consolation, which we derive from the transitoriness of all things — from the right of saying, in every conjuncture, "This, too, will pass away".'

3 And what they could not eat that night, The queen next morning fried.

Referring to a bag pudding, well-stuffed with plums, this tantalizing couplet comes from a nursery rhyme, 'When good King Arthur ruled this land,/He was a goodly king'. The Opies in The Oxford Dictionary of Nursery Rhymes (1951) find a version c 1799.

4 Any reform that does not result in the exact opposite of what it was intended to do must be considered a success.

Untraced. However, Peter F. Drucker (1909–), the American management consultant and author, has written: 'Look at governmental programs for the past fifty years. Every single one — except for warfare — achieved the exact opposite of its announced goal.' Compare also what Garrett Hardin (1915–), an American biologist, wrote in the February 1974 issue of Fortune: 'You can never do merely one thing. The law applies to any action that changes something in a complex system. The point is that an action taken to alleviate a problem will trigger several effects, some of which may offset or even negate the one intended.'

5 Attempt great things for God.

As a young man, c 1963, I can recall being exhorted to have 'Do great things' as an informal motto. Recently I noticed this formulation on a lectern in Westminster Abbey. I am not sure if it is supposed to be a text. In the Bible it is God who is frequently credited with having done the great things, but 2 Kings 5:13 has: 'My father, if the prophet had bid thee do some great thing, wouldest thou not have done it?'

6 Back to square one.

Meaning 'back to the beginning'. This is sometimes said to have gained currency in the 1930s onwards through its use by British radio football commentators. Radio Times used to print a map of the football field divided into numbered squares, to which commentators would refer thus: 'Cresswell's going to make it — FIVE. There it goes, slap into the middle of the goal — SEVEN. Cann's header there — EIGHT. The ball comes out to Britton. Britton manoeuvres. The centre goes right in — BACK TO EIGHT. Comes on to Marshall — SIX' (an extract from the BBC commentary on the 1933 Cup Final between Everton and Manchester City). The idea had largely been abandoned by 1940. Against this proposition is the fact that square 'one' was nowhere near the beginning. The game began at the centre spot, which was at the meeting point of squares 3, 4, 5 and 6.

In fact, Partridge/Catch Phrases prefers an earlier origin in the children's game of hopscotch or in the board game Snakes and Ladders. If a player was unlucky and his or her counter landed on the snake's head in square 97 or thereabouts, it had to make the long journey 'back to square one'.

1 Behind every great man stands a woman.

An unascribed saying that takes several forms and is probably most often encountered nowadays in parodied versions. Working backwards, here are some of the parodies:

'Behind every good man is a good woman – I mean an exhausted one' – the Duchess of York, speech, September 1987

'As usual there's a great woman behind every idiot' – John Lennon (quoted 1979)

'Behind every successful man you'll find a woman who has nothing to wear' – L. Grant Glickman (quoted 1977) or James Stewart (quoted 1979)

'We in the industry know that behind every successful screenwriter stands a woman. And behind her stands his wife' – Groucho Marx, quoted in 1977

'The road to success is filled with women pushing their husbands along' – Lord Thomas R. Dewar, quoted in Stevenson, The Home Book of Quotations (1967)

'And behind every man who is a failure there's a woman, too!' – John Ruge, cartoon caption, Playboy, March 1967

'Behind every successful man stands a surprised mother-in-law' – Hubert Humphrey, speech, 1964

An early example of the basic expression occurs in an interview with Lady Dorothy Macmillan, wife of the then just retired British Prime Minister (7 December 1963). In the Daily Sketch, Godfrey Winn concluded his piece with the (for him) typical sentiment (his capitals): 'NO MAN SUCCEEDS WITHOUT A GOOD WOMAN BEHIND HIM. WIFE OR MOTHER. IF IT IS BOTH, HE IS TWICE BLESSED INDEED.'

In Love All, a little known play by Dorothy L. Sayers, which opened at the Torch Theatre, Knightsbridge, London, on 9 April 1940 and closed before the end of the month, was this: 'Every great man has a woman behind him . . . And every great woman has some man or other in front of her, tripping her up.'

2 Believe only half of what you see and nothing that you hear.

I first heard this piece of advice from an Anglican clergyman (and former padre in the Western Desert) at confirmation class in 1958. Mencken finds a much earlier version in A Woman's Thoughts (1858) by Mrs (Dinah Mulock) Craik where it is already described as a 'cynical saying, and yet less bitter than at first appears'. As such, it builds upon the simpler 'Don't believe all you hear' which CODP finds in some form before 1300, perhaps even as a proverb of King Alfred the Great's.

The thought also appears in the song 'I Heard It Through the Grapevine' (by Norman Whitfield and Barrett Strong, c 1967), recorded notably by Marvin Gaye. One verse begins:

People say believe half of what you see, Son, and none of what you hear.

3 Bell, book and candle.

As in the title of John Van Druten's play (1950, filmed 1958) about a publisher who discovers his girlfriend is a witch, this refers to a solemn form of excommunication from the Roman Catholic Church. Bartlett (1980) says the ceremony has been current since the eighth century AD. There is a version dating from 1200 AD which goes: 'Do to the book [meaning, close it], quench the candle, ring the bell.' These actions symbolize the spiritual darkness the person is condemned to when denied further participation in the sacraments of the church.

Sir Thomas Malory in Le Morte d'Arthur (1485) has, 'I shall curse you with book and bell and candle'. Shakespeare has the modern configuration in King John (III.ii.22): 'Bell, book and candle shall not drive me back.'

4 The best/finest swordsman in all France.

A cliché of swashbuckling epics. 'Don't worry . . . my father was the best swordsman in France' is said to be spoken in the film Son of Monte Cristo (1940), though this is unverified. In 1984, a book by Keith

Miles on the subject of clichés in general was given the title *The Finest Swordsman in All France*. A relatively unselfconscious use occurs in Charles Dickens, *Barnaby Rudge*, Chap. 27 (1841): 'I have been tempted in these two short interviews, to draw upon that fellow, fifty times. Five men in six would have yielded to the impulse. By suppressing mine, I wound him deeper and more keenly than if I were the best swordsman in all Europe.' Completely straightforward is John Aubrey's use in his *Lives* (*c* 1697): 'Sir John Digby yielded to be the best swordsman of his time.'

1 *Better the chill blast of winter than the hot breath of a pursuing elephant.*

Said to be a 'Chinese saying' and included in *Livres Sans Nom*, five anonymous pamphlets (1929–33) by Geoffrey Madan (though it has not been found in the copies available to me). As with all such sayings (compare CONFUCIUS 105:2) authenticity is in doubt. In any case, might not Madan have invented it himself? The matter is discussed in *The Lyttelton Hart-Davis Letters*, Vol. 4 (1982).

2 *Box-office poison.*

This is said to be the verdict of the US Independent Motion Picture Theatre Proprietors on the actress Katharine Hepburn in 1938. The phrase is also said to have been used about her by a cinema-owner in a famous advertisement. However, in the same year, the *Independent Film Journal* also put Mae West, Greta Garbo, Joan Crawford, Marlene Dietrich and Fred Astaire in the same category.

3 *The boy who put his finger in the dike.*

A reference to the legendary Dutch boy who spotted a tiny hole in a canal dike, stuck his finger in it and stayed put all night, stopping a flood. The story is related in Chapter 18 of *Hans Brinker, or the Silver Skates* (1865) by the American author, Mary Mapes Dodge, who had never been to Holland. Her novel includes a recollection of this 'Hero of Haarlem', whose story, she suggests, had long been known to Dutch children. It is not clear whether she was making this up or not. What is clear, however, is that only as a result of the success of her book did various Dutch towns claim the boy as their own. A small statue was erected to him at Harlingen. But whatever the case, he

was never more than a legend. Sometimes, erroneously, he is given the name 'Hans Brinker' out of confusion with the hero of Dodge's book.

Hence, the figure of speech for someone who staves off disaster through a simple (albeit temporary) gesture. From *The Times* (9 October 1986): 'To try to stand in front of the markets like the Little Dutch Boy with his finger in the dike would have been an act of folly if the Government were not convinced that the dike was fundamentally sound'. (27 July 1989): ' "It was finger-in-the-dike stuff for us throughout the match," the Oxbridge coach, Tony Rodgers, said. "Ultimately the flood walls cracked".'

4 *By/my God, how the money rolls in.*

This is the last line of each verse in an anonymous song included in *Rugby Songs* (1967). It tells of the various fund-raising activities of a family. A typical verse:

My brother's a poor missionary,
He saves fallen women from sin,
He'll save you a blonde for a guinea,
My God how the money rolls in.

T.R. Ritchie in *The Singing Street* seems to favour 'By God' in the last line.

5 *Channel storms. Continent isolated.*

The original of this English newspaper headline remains untraced (if, indeed, it ever existed). In Maurice Bowra's *Memories 1898–1939* (1966) he recalled Ernst Kantorowicz, a refugee from Germany in the 1930s: 'He liked the insularity of England and was much pleased by the newspaper headline, "Channel storms. Continent isolated", just as he liked the imagery in, "Shepherd's Bush combed for dead girl's body".'

As an indicator of English isolationism, the phrase does indeed seem to have surfaced in the 1930s. John Gunther in his *Inside Europe* (1938 edition) had: 'Two or three winters ago a heavy storm completely blocked traffic across the Channel. "CONTINENT ISOLATED," the newspapers couldn't help saying.' The cartoonist Russell Brockbank drew a newspaper placard stating 'FOG IN CHANNEL — CONTINENT ISOLATED' (as shown in his book *Round the Bend with Brockbank*, published by Temple Press, 1948). By the 1960s and 1970s, and by the time of Britain's attempts to join the European Community, the headline was more often invoked as: 'FOG IN CHANNEL. EUROPE ISOLATED.'

1 Che sera sera.

In 1956 Doris Day had a hit with the song 'Whatever Will Be Will Be', the title being a translation of this foreign phrase which was also used in the choruses. She had sung it in the re-make of Alfred Hitchcock's *The Man Who Knew Too Much* in that year. Ten years later Geno Washington and the Ram Jam Band had a hit with a song entitled '*Que Sera Sera*'. So is it *che* or *que*? There is no such phrase as *che sera sera* in modern Spanish or Italian, though *che* is an Italian word and *sera* is a Spanish one. *Que sera? sera?* in Spanish translates as 'what will be? will be?' which is not quite right; *lo que sera, sera* makes sense but is not the wording of the song. However, in Christopher Marlowe's *Dr Faustus* (published 1604) Faustus's first soliloquy has:

> What doctrine call you this? Che sera, sera,
> What will be, shall be.

This is an old spelling of what would be, in modern Italian *che sara, sara*. In Faustus, however, it is probably Old French.

The *idea* behind the proverbial saying is simpler to trace. 'What must be, must be' can be found as far back as Chaucer's 'Knight's Tale' (*c* 1390): 'When a thyng is shapen, it shal be.' However, *che sera sera* is the form in which the Duke of Bedford's motto has always been written and so presumably that, too, is Old French or Old Italian.

2 *Cometh the hour, cometh the man.*

John 4:23 has 'But the hour cometh, and now is' and there is an English proverb 'Opportunity makes the man' (though originally, in the fourteenth century, it was 'makes the *thief*'), but when did the phrases come together? An American, William Yancey, said about Jefferson Davis, President-elect of the Confederacy in 1861: 'The man and the hour have met', which says the same thing in a different way.

Earlier, at the climax of Sir Walter Scott's novel *Guy Mannering*, Chap. 54 (1815), Meg Merrilies says, 'Because the Hour's come, and the Man'. In the first edition and in the *magnum opus* edition that Scott supervised in his last years the phrase is emphasized by putting it in italics.

Then, in 1818, Scott uses 'The hour's come, but not [sic] the man' as the fourth chapter heading in *The Heart of Midlothian*, adding in a footnote: 'There is a tradition, that while a little stream was swollen into a torrent by recent showers, the discontented voice of the Water Spirit [or Kelpie] was heard to pronounce these words. At the same moment a man, urged on by his fate, or, in Scottish language, *fey*, arrived at a gallop, and prepared to cross the water. No remonstrance from the by-standers was of power to stop him — he plunged into the stream, and perished.'

Both these examples appear to be hinting at some earlier core saying which is still untraced. It appears from a survey of ten British newspapers in recent years that the saying is especially a weapon (or cliché) in the sportswriter's armoury. From *Today* (22 June 1986): 'Beating England may not be winning the World Cup, but, for obvious reasons, it would come a pretty close second back in Buenos Aires. Cometh the hour, cometh the man? Destiny beckons. England beware.' From *The Times* (13 August 1991): ' "Graham [Gooch] is a very special guy," [Ted] Dexter said. "It has been a case of 'Cometh the hour, cometh the man.' I do not know anyone who would have taken the tough times in Australia harder than he did".' From the *Scotsman* (29 February 1992): 'In the maxim of "Cometh the hour, cometh the man," both the Scotland [Rugby Union] manager, Duncan Paterson, and forwards coach, Richie Dixon, indicated yesterday the need to look to the future.'

The use of the phrase in cricket seems especially well established. F.H. Loxley of Bristol recalled (1993): ' "Coometh the hour, coometh the man" was said by Cliff Gladwin, the Derbyshire fast bowler and England No. 10 as he went out to bat against South Africa on 20 December 1948. Seven runs were needed off the last over, and still one off the last ball which Gladwin padded away for the winning single.'

3 *Comfort the afflicted, and afflict the comfortable.*

This is a good example of a quotation formula which can be applied to more than one subject, to the extent that it is difficult to say what it was originally directed at. However, Mencken (1942) has 'Anon.' saying, 'The duty of a newspaper is to comfort the afflicted and afflict the comfortable', and newspapers seem likely to have been the original subject of the remark. In the film *Inherit the Wind* (1960), Gene Kelly gets to say to Fredric March: 'Mr Brady, it's the duty of a newspaper to comfort the afflicted and to flick the comfortable.'

To Michael Ramsey, the former Archbishop of Canterbury (1904–88), has been attributed this version: 'The duty of the church is to comfort the disturbed and to disturb the comfortable.' Clare Booth Luce introduced Eleanor Roosvelt at a 1950 dinner, saying: 'No woman has ever so comforted the distressed — or so distressed the comfortable.'

1 *The condemned man ate a hearty breakfast.*

The tradition seems to have been established in Britain (and/or the Old West) that a condemned man could have anything he desired for a last meal. Several such people took the opportunity to have something of a blowout. Nothing changes: in April 1992, when Robert Alton Harris, a double murderer, was executed at dawn in San Quentin prison, California, the authorities gave the media a description of his last meal — a huge bucket of Kentucky Fried Chicken, pizza and jellybeans.

As to the origin of the cliché, it presumably lies in ghoulish newspaper reports of the events surrounding executions in the days of capital punishment in Britain. There was a vast amount of popular literature concerning prominent criminals and public executions, especially in the late eighteenth and early nineteenth centuries, but so far citations date only from the twentieth and tend to be of a metaphorical nature.

Working backwards: in *No Chip on My Shoulder* (1957), Eric Maschwitz wrote: 'Far from closing for ever, *Balalaika* [was merely to be] withdrawn for a fortnight during which time a revolving stage was to be installed at Her Majesty's! It was almost ridiculously like an episode from fiction, the condemned man, in the midst of eating that famous "hearty breakfast", suddenly restored to life and liberty.' In the film *Kind Hearts and Coronets* (1949), Louis Mazzini, on the morning of his supposed execution, disavows his intention of eating 'the traditional hearty breakfast'. *The Prisoner Ate a Hearty Breakfast* was the title of a novel (1940) written by Jerome Ellison. In 1914, a book of short stories about the Royal Navy called *Naval Occasions and Some Traits of the Sailor* by 'Bartimeus', had: 'The Indiarubber Man opposite feigned breathless interest in his actions, and murmured something into his cup about condemned men partaking of hearty breakfasts.' The tone of this suggests it was, indeed, getting on for a cliché even then.

2 *Cowabunga!*

This cry was re-popularized by the Teenage Mutant Ninja Turtles phenomenon of the early 1990s, but had been around since the 1950s when, in the American cartoon series *The Howdy Doody Show*, it was used as an expression of anger — 'kowa-bunga' or 'Kawabonga' — by Chief Thunderthud. In the 1960s it transferred to *Gidget*, the American TV series about a surfer, as a cry of exhilaration when cresting a wave and was taken into surfing slang. In the 1970s the phrase graduated to TV's *Sesame Street*.

3 *Death is nature's way of telling you to slow down.*

A joke current in the US by 1960 (as in *Newsweek*, 25 April). It has been specifically attributed to Severn Darden (1937–), the American film character actor. It is capable of infinite variation: from *Punch* (3 January 1962): 'Some neo-Malthusians have been heard to suggest that the bomb is Nature's way . . . of checking . . . the overspawning of our species.' In 1978, the American cartoonist Garfield produced a bumper-sticker with the slogan: 'My car is God's way of telling you to slow down.'

4 *Der spring is sprung*
Der grass is riz
I wonder where dem boidies is?

Der little boids is on der wing,
Ain't dat absoid?
Der little wings is on der boid!

Entitled 'The Budding Bronx', this is described as by 'Anon (New York)' in Arnold Silcock's *Verse and Worse* (1952). Beyond that no source has been found.

5 *Dream on, baby, dream on.*

Meaning 'If you really believe that, then carry on kidding yourself', this expression crops up with some frequency. The country and western singer, Tammy Wynette, talked to the *Independent on Sunday* (24 November 1991) about an embarrassing encounter with an ex-husband who came up and asked her to autograph a photo for him: 'I thought, "Now what do I say here?" and then it hit me like a light and I wrote — "Dream on, baby, dream on!" . . . Sweet revenge at last.'

Does the phrase have a Black American blues origin, if not in fact a country and western one? As simply *Dream On*, it became the title of an 'American adult [TV] comedy series', featuring David Bowie and Tom Berenger, broadcast in the UK in 1991, while 'Dream On' has been the title of songs from Lynn Anderson (1990) right back to Herman's Hermits (1965). 'Dream On Baby' was recorded by Rosco Gordon in Memphis, Tennessee, in the 1950s, while 'Dream On, My Love, Dream On' was recorded by the Four Lads in 1955.

1 The eleventh commandment.

Mencken (1942) has that the so-called 'eleventh commandment' is 'mind your own business' as 'borrowed from Cervantes, *Don Quixote*, 1605'. Indeed, it is to be found there (in Pt I, Bk III, Chap. 8), although it is not described there as the 'eleventh commandment'. But Mencken also records, 'The Eleventh Commandment: Thou shalt not be found out — George Whyte-Melville, *Holmby House*, 1860', and this is certainly the more usual meaning. The *OED2* adds from the *Pall Mall Gazette* (10 September 1884): 'The new and great commandment that nothing succeeds like success'; and from *Paston Carew* (1886) by Mrs Lynn Lynton that the eleventh commandment was 'do not tell tales out of school'. Unverified is Charles Kingsley's 1850 observation that it is, 'Buy cheap, sell dear'.

It could be argued that the eleventh commandment *ought* to be what Christ suggests in John 13:34: 'A new commandment I give unto you, That ye love one another; as I have loved you, that ye also love one another.' Safire (1978) reports that 'Thou Shalt Not Speak Ill of Fellow Republicans' was the eleventh commandment advanced by Dr Gaylord E. Parkinson, California State Republican Chairman, in the run-up to the 1966 governorship elections. The 1981 re-make of the film *The Postman Always Rings Twice* was promoted with the slogan: 'If there was an 11th Commandment, they would have broken that too.'

2 English as she is spoke.

A way of referring to the language as it might be spoken by foreigners or the illiterate comes from an actual 'guide of the conversation in Portuguese and English' published in the nineteenth century. The guilty author, according to Mencken (1942), was 'P. Carolino'. According to the *PDQ* (1960) it was 'A.W. Tuer (1838–1900)'. According to *A Dictionary of Famous Quotations* (1973), it was 'Andrew White Tuer'.

In *Baldness Be My Friend* (1977) Richard Boston explored the facts. Originally, there was a French-Portuguese phrase-book, *O Novo Guia da Conversacão em frances e portuguez* by José da Fonseca, published in Paris in 1836. The text was in parallel columns. Then in 1865 a third column, carrying English translations, was added by one Pedro Carolino. His excellence as a translator can be shown by quoting from a section he cleverly but unwittingly called 'Idiotisms and Proverbs'. It included:

> In the country of blinds, the one-eyed
> men are kings.
> To do a wink to some body.
> The stone as roll not, heap up not
> foam.
> After the paunch comes the dance.
> To craunch the marmoset.
> To come back to their muttons.
> He sin in trouble water.

By 1883, the awfulness of this non-joke was known in London. Publishers Field and Tuer brought out a selection under the title *English as She is Spoke* (a phrase taken from the chapter on 'Familiar Dialogues'). The same year, Mark Twain introduced an edition of the complete work in the US.

3 An English summer — three fine days and a thunderstorm.

The observation has been attributed to King Henry VIII, but John Aiton's *Manual of Domestic Economy for Clergymen* (1842) has: 'Our [Scotch] summers are said to consist of 3 hot days and a thunder-storm', which would seem to suggest it is an old Scottish saying.

4 Et in Arcadia ego.

This inscription means either that, in death, the speaker is in Arcadia, or that he was formerly there. '*Et in Arcadia ego vixi*' [I lived] or '*Et in Arcadia fui pastor*' [I was a shepherd] are variants. Or, it is Death itself speaking: 'Even in Arcadia, I, Death, cannot be avoided.' Arcadia is the Greek name for a place of rural peace and calm taken from an actual area in the Peloponnese but used generally since classical times. '*Et in Arcadia ego*' is a phrase associated with tombs, skulls and Arcadian shepherds in classical paintings, though not before the seventeenth century. Most notably the phrase occurs in two paintings by the French artist Nicolas Poussin (1594–1665). Both of these depict shepherds reading the words carved on a tomb.

1 *Even your best friends won't tell you.*

A line that originated in the famous Listerine mouthwash advertisement headed 'Often a bridesmaid but never a bride', in the US in the 1920s. Originally, the line in the copy was *'and* even your *closest* friends won't tell you'. Partridge/*Catch Phrases* suggests that it became a catchphrase in the form 'your best friend(s) won't tell you (= "you stink!")'. In the film *Dangerous Moonlight* (UK, 1941), the Anton Walbrook character says to a man putting on hair oil (in New York), 'Even your best friend won't *smell* you'.

2 *Everyman, I will go with thee and be thy guide,*
In thy most need to go by thy side.

From the *Everyman* morality play of c 1509–91. These legendary lines are spoken by Knowledge and thus have been an appropriate choice as a slogan to promote the Everyman's Library series of book reprints of the classics. These have been published by J.M. Dent in Britain since the 1900s (and by E.P. Dutton in the US). Compare MILTON 242:4 and SIDNEY 311:2.

3 *The Father, the Son and the Pigeon.*

A French rhyme appeared in the introduction to *Some Limericks* (1928), privately printed by Norman Douglas (published 1969 as *The Norman Douglas Limerick Book*):

Il y avait un jeune homme de Dijon
Qui n'avait que peu de religion.
Il dit: 'Quant à moi,
Je déteste tous les trois,
Le Père, et le Fils, et le Pigeon.'

Which may be translated:

There was young man of Dijon
Who had only a little religion,
He said, 'As for me,
'I detest all the three,
'The Father, the Son and the Pigeon.'

To talk of the Holy Ghost in these terms seems to have been nothing new, even in the 1920s. Lord Berners describing his time at Eton in the 1890s in *A Distant Prospect* (1945) tells of a friend called Manston: 'At first I was inclined to be shocked by his irreverence – for instance, when he had said that the Trinity put him in mind of a music-hall turn – the Father, the Son and the Performing Pigeon.'

4 *From a grateful country/nation.*

A memorial phrase especially popular in the nineteenth century. At St Deiniol's, W.E. Gladstone's library in the village of Hawarden, Wales, where the British Prime Minister (1809–98) had his family home for almost fifty years, there is a plaque saying it was 'erected to his memory by a grateful nation'. W.M. Thackeray, writing in *The Virginians*, Chap. XXXV (1859), has: 'The late lamented O'Connell . . . over whom a grateful country has raised such a magnificent testimonial.' On the statue to General Havelock (1795–1857) in Trafalgar Square, London, is written: 'Soldiers! Your valour will not be forgotten by a grateful country.' The notable Alexander Column in the square outside the Winter Palace at St Petersburg was completed in 1834. On the base was the inscription (in Russian): 'To Alexander the First from a Grateful Russia.'
   Nowadays, the phrase is invariably used with irony. From the *Independent* (23 July 1992): 'There have been loads of Roy Orbisons and Neil Diamonds and Gene Pitneys, and, after Elvis, the man most often impersonated by a grateful nation . . . Cliff Richard.'

5 *— —, God bless 'im/'er.*

Originally, a toast to Royalty, this gradually turned into a more general, genial way of referring to such people and others. From George Eliot, *Felix Holt* (1866): 'You'll rally round the throne – and the King, God bless him, and the usual toasts.' From *Punch*, Vol. CXX (1902): 'The Queen God Bless 'Er.' Robert Lacey revived the custom in 1990 with a book entitled *The Queen Mother, God Bless Her*. The American cartoonist Helen Hokinson had one of her collections entitled *The Ladies, God Bless 'Em* (1950), which takes the toast out into a broader field.

6 *God Protect Me from My Friends.*

The title of a book (1956) by Gavin Maxwell about Salvatore Giuliano, the Sicilian bandit, derives from the proverbial expression: 'I can look after my enemies, but God protect me from my friends.' CODP traces this to 1477 in the forms 'God keep/save/ defend us from our friends' and says it is now often used in the abbreviated form, 'Save us from our friends'. It appears to be common to many languages. 'With friends like these/ with a Hungarian for a friend, who needs enemies?' are but two versions.

The diarist Chips Channon (21 February 1938) has: 'This evening a group of excited Communists even invaded the Lobby, demanding Anthony [Eden]'s reinstatement. God preserve us from our friends, they did him harm.' Morris (1977) finds a quotation from Maréchal Villars who, on leaving Louis XIV, said: 'Defend me from my friends; I can defend myself from my enemies.' In 1821, George Canning rhymed: 'Give me the avowed, the erect, the manly foe, / Bold I can meet — perhaps may turn his blow! / But of all plagues, Good Heaven, thy wrath can send, / Save, save, Oh, save me from the candid friend!' Charlotte Brontë also used the idea in a letter (untraced) in response to a patronizing review of one of her books.

1 The Gods do not deduct from man's allotted span the hours spent in fishing.

Described as a 'Babylonian proverb', this was apparently a favourite saying of President Hoover's.

2 The grass is always greener on the other side of the fence.

The ODP (1970) ignored the proverb in this form, preferring to cite a sixteenth-century translation of a Latin proverb, 'The corn in another man's ground seemeth ever more fertile than doth our own'. By 1956, the time of the Hugh and Margaret Williams play The Grass is Greener — 'on the other side of the hedge' — the modern form was well established. Wolfgang Mieder in Proverbium (1993) questions whether the two proverbs are in fact related but finds an earlier citation of the modern one: an American song with words by Raymond B. Egan and music by Richard A. Whiting entitled 'The Grass is Always Greener (In the Other Fellow's Yard)', published in 1924.

3 Hark the herald angels sing
Mrs Simpson's pinched our king.

Within days of the Abdication of King Edward VIII in December 1936 schoolchildren were singing this. A letter from Clement Attlee on 26 December included the information that his daughter Felicity had produced a 'ribald verse which was new to me' (quoted in Kenneth Harris, Attlee, 1982). Iona and Peter Opie in The Lore and Language of Schoolchildren (1959) commented on the rapidity with which the rhyme spread across the country. The con-

stitutional crisis did not become public until 25 November, the King abdicated on 10 December, 'yet at a school party in Swansea given before the end of term . . . when the tune played happened to be "Hark the Herald Angels Sing", a mistress found herself having to restrain her small children from singing this lyric, known to all of them, which cannot have been composed more than three weeks previously'.

4 Hear no evil, see no evil, speak no evil.

Bartlett (1980) describes this as a legend related to the Three Wise Monkeys carved over the door of the Sacred Stable, Nikko, Japan, in the seventeenth century. The three monkeys are represented having their paws over, respectively, their ears, eyes and mouth. 'Hear, see, keep silence' (often accompanied by a sketch of the Three Wise Monkeys) is the motto of the United Grand Lodge of Freemasons in the form Audi, Vide, Tace.
  The motto of Yorkshiremen is said to be:
  Hear all, see all, say nowt,
  Aight all, sup all, pay nowt,
  And if ever tha does owt for nowt
  Do it for thisen.
A Noel Gay song written in 1938 for Sandy Powell, the Yorkshire comedian, had the title 'Hear all, see all, say nowt'.

5 Heavens to Murgatroyd!

A cartoon lion called Snagglepuss, which came out of the Hannah-Barbera studios in the 1960s, was given to exclaiming 'Heavens to Murgatroyd!' He made his first appearance in The Yogi Bear Show, but his catchphrase was apparently not original, however. An American correspondent noted (1993): 'It was a favorite expression of a favorite uncle of mine in the 1940s, and my wife also remembers it from her growing-up years in the '40s.'
  Snagglepuss also used to say 'Exit stage left'.

6 Here lies a poor woman who always was tired,
For she lived in a place where help wasn't hired,
Her last words on earth were, 'Dear friends, I am going,
Where washing ain't done nor cooking nor sewing,
And everything there is exact to my wishes,

*For there they don't eat, there's no
    washing of dishes,
I'll be where loud anthems will
    always be ringing
(But having no voice, I'll be out of
    the singing).
Don't mourn for me now, don't
    grieve for me never,
For I'm going to do nothing for ever
    and ever'.*

Sometimes referred to as 'The Maid-of-all-
Works' Epitaph' or 'The Tired Woman's
Epitaph', this has two possible sources. As
'an epitaph for Catherine Alsopp, a Sheffield
washerwoman, who hanged herself, 7
August 1905', it was composed by herself
and included in E. Jameson, *1000 Curiosities of Britain* (1937). But a letter in *The
Spectator* (2 December 1922) from a correspondent at the British Museum asserted that
the inscription was once to be found in
a churchyard in Bushey, Hertfordshire. A
copy of the text was made before 1860,
but the actual stone had been destroyed by
1916. It was also discussed in *Notes and
Queries* for March 1889 and *Longman's
Magazine* for January 1884. Benham (1907)
states that it had been quoted 'before 1850'.

1 *Here's one I made/prepared earlier.*

Or 'This is one I prepared earlier . . .' This
curiously popular catchphrase in Britain
originated with 'live' TV cookery demonstrations in the 1950s in which it was important that the showing of the finished product
was not left to chance. But the phrase was
also borrowed by presenters of BBC TV's
children's programme *Blue Peter* (from 1963
onwards) who had to explain how to make
models of the Taj Mahal out of milk-bottle
tops, for example, but wouldn't actually be
seen doing so there and then.

2 *Here's to our next Merrie Meeting.*

As a catchphrase, this seemed at first to be
linked to Henry Hall's signature theme for
the BBC Dance Orchestra (which Hall took
over in March 1932):

    Here's to the next time and a merry
        meeting,
    Here's to the next time, we send you
        all our greeting,
    Set it to music, sing it in rhyme,
    Now, all together, Here's to the next
        time!

Then it was remembered that BBC Radio's
popular organist, Robin Richmond, was
for many years presenter of *The Organist
Entertains* and the phrase was his weekly
signing off. But the alliterative lure of 'merry
meetings' has been around a good deal
longer. King Richard III has 'Our stern
alarums chang'd to merry meetings' in the
famous opening speech to Shakespeare's
play. *Punch* for 27 July 1904 has in the
caption to a cartoon accompanying 'Oper-
atic Notes' 'TO OUR NEXT MERRY
MEETING!'

Even more significantly, the *Punch Almanack* for 1902 has a cartoon of two foxes
drinking in a club, celebrating the fact that
all the best hunting horses are away in the
Boer War. One fox is saying, 'To our next
merry meeting!' Does this indicate that this
was an established toast? Does it also suggest that the original 'meeting' referred to in
the phrase was the kind you have in
fox-hunting?

3 *Here's to pure scholarship. May it never
be of any use to anyone!*

A bravura toast, given at the centenary of a
college. John Julius Norwich commented
that his father, Duff Cooper (1890–1954),
used to quote this as a toast specifically to
higher mathematics.

4 *Here We Go Round the Mulberry Bush.*

The title of the novel (1965; film UK, 1967)
by Hunter Davies derives from the refrain
sung in the children's game (first recorded
in the mid-nineteenth century, though probably earlier) in which the participants
hold hands and dance in a ring. There are
numerous variations, using various fruits.

One theory of the rhyme's origin is that
a mulberry tree stood in the middle of the
exercise yard at Wakefield Prison in Yorkshire. The prisoners would have to go round
and round it on a 'cold and frosty morning'.
This may be, however, no more than a
coincidence.

5 *He who has the sea has the shore,
And the castle is his who has the
    plain;
But freedom dwells upon the
    mountain peaks.*

Untraced words quoted (1981) by a Colonel
Harcourt, Commanding Officer of the Sultan of Oman's Royal Guard. The connection between freedom and mountain top
also occurs in Joseph Rodman Drake's 'The

American Flag' (1819) which begins: 'When Freedom from her mountain height.'

1 *Hitler*
Has only got one ball!
Goering Has two, but very small!
Himmler
Has something similar,
But poor old Goebbels
Has no balls at all!

This was the title of an anonymous song (sung to the tune of 'Colonel Bogey') that was in existence by 1940. As with 'Not tonight Josephine' (250:2), the basis for this assertion about a political figure is obscure. The rumour had been widespread in Central Europe in the 1930s, and Martin Page in *Kiss Me Goodnight, Sergeant Major* (1973) writes of a Czech refugee who had referred in 1938 to the fact that Hitler had been wounded in the First World War, since when *'ihm fehlt einer'* [he lacks one]. Perhaps it was no more than a generalized slight against the Nazi leader's virility, which conveniently fitted the tune and also permitted a 'Goebbels/no balls' rhyme. There had earlier been a nineteenth-century American ballad about a trade union leader which began: 'Arthur Hall/Has only got one ball.'

2 *Hooray, Hooray, the first of May,*
Outdoor fucking begins today.

This 'Old Thurlestone saying' (whatever that may be — from the place in Devon?) was included in *Vice: An Anthology* (ed. Richard Davenport-Hines, 1993). But it was certainly current by the 1960s at least. In May *c* 1965, a version with 'outdoor sex' was published in the Oxford undergraduate magazine, *Isis*.

3 *If anything can go wrong, it will.*

Most commonly known as 'Murphy's Law', this saying dates back to the 1940s. *The Macquarie Dictionary* (1981) suggests that it was named after a character who always made mistakes in a series of educational cartoons published by the US Navy. *CODP* hints that it was invented by George Nichols, a project manager for Northrop, the Californian aviation firm, in 1949. He developed the idea from a remark by a colleague, Captain Edward A. Murphy Jr of the Wright Field-Aircraft Laboratory: 'If there is a wrong way to do something, then someone will do it.'

The most notable demonstration of Murphy's Law is that a piece of bread when dropped on the floor will always fall with its buttered side facing down (otherwise known as the Law of Universal Cussedness). This, however, pre-dates the promulgation of the Law. In 1867 A.D. Eichardson wrote in *Beyond Mississippi*: 'His bread never fell on the buttered side.' In 1884 James Payn composed the lines:

I never had a piece of toast
Particularly long and wide,
But fell upon the sanded floor
And always on the buttered side.

BDPF calls this an 'old north country proverb'. The corollary of this aspect of the Law is that bread always falls buttered side down *except when demonstrating the Law!*

Some have argued that the point of Captain Murphy's original observation was constructive rather than defeatist — it was a prescription for avoiding mistakes in the design of a valve for an aircraft's hydraulic system. If the valve could be fitted in more than one way, then sooner or later someone would fit it the wrong way. The idea was to design it so that the valve could be fitted only the right way.

4 *If the soup had been as warm as the wine, and the wine as old as the fish, and the fish as young as the maid, and the maid as willing as the hostess, it would have been a very good meal.*

Untraced restaurant criticism dating from the Austro-Hungarian Empire — at least, according to Clement Freud who quoted it on BBC Radio *Quote . . . Unquote* (1979).

5 *I know why the sun never sets on the British Empire: God wouldn't trust an Englishman in the dark.*

In Nancy McPhee, *The Book of Insults* (1978), this is ascribed to 'Duncan Spaeth' (is this John Duncan Spaeth, the US educator?) Clearly it plays upon NORTH 256:3. An Irish Republican placard held up during a visit to New York by Prince Charles in June 1981 had the slogan: 'The sun never sets on the British Empire because God doesn't trust the Brits in the dark.'

6 *In God we trust, all others pay cash.*

After the Washington summit between Mikhail Gorbachev and Ronald Reagan in December 1987, the US Secretary of State

George Schultz commented on a Russian slogan that Reagan had made much of: ' "Trust but verify" is really an ancient saying in the United States, but in a different guise. Remember the storekeeper who was a little leery of credit, and he had a sign in his store that said, "IN GOD WE TRUST — ALL OTHERS CASH"?' Referring to the verification procedures over arms reductions signed by the leaders in Washington, Shultz said, 'This is the cash'.

Mencken in 1942 was listing 'In God we trust; all others must pay cash' as an 'American saying'. 'In God we trust' has been the official national motto of the United States since 1956, when it superseded 'E Pluribus Unum', but had been known since 1864 when it was first put on a 2-cent bronze coin.

There is a similar joke in Britain, of the type printed on small cards and sold for display in pubs and shops. It made an appearance as a quote in the early 1940s in Flann O'Brien's column for the *Irish Times*: 'We have come to an arrangement with our bankers. They have agreed not to sell drink. We, on our part, have agreed not to cash cheques.'

A parallel saying to 'In God we trust etc.' is that attributed to the American striptease artiste, Gypsy Rose Lee (1914–70): 'God is love, but get it in writing.'

1 Is it kind? Is it true? Is it necessary?

In George Seaver's *Edward Wilson of the Antarctic* (1963), it is stated that Wilson's widow had this printed on her mantelshelf to remind herself to curb her sharp tongue. In the Dorothy L. Sayers novel *Gaudy Night* (1935) it is said (with the first two queries reversed) by that arch-quoter, Lord Peter Wimsey.

As such it bears a certain resemblance to part of the Four Way Test 'of the things we think, say or do' that Rotarians in the US devised in 1931: 'Is it the *truth*? Is it *fair*? Will it be *beneficial* to all concerned?' The most likely origin, however, is a poem called 'Three Gates' written in 1855 by Beth Day and said to be 'after the Arabian':

If you are tempted to reveal
A tale to you someone has told
About another, make it pass
Before you speak, three gates of gold.
These narrow gates: First, 'Is it true?'
Then, 'Is it needful?' In your mind
Give truthful answer. And the next
Is last and narrowest, 'Is it kind?'
And if to reach your lips at last

It passes through these gateways three,
Then you may tell the tale, nor fear
What the result of speech may be.

2 Is there a life before death?

This graffito was reported to me from Ballymurphy in Ireland, c 1971, and is confirmed by Seamus Heaney's poem 'Whatever You Say Say Nothing' from *North* (1975) which has:

Is there a life before death? That's
chalked up
In Ballymurphy . . .

But as if this underlines the saying's Irish origins too well, bear in mind that 'Is there life before death?' is the epigraph to Chapter 9 of Stephen Vizinczey's novel *In Praise of Older Women* (1966). There, it is credited to 'Anon. Hungarian'.

3 It's not the heat, it's the humidity.

One of S.J. Perelman's prose pieces had the punning title 'It's Not the Heat, It's the Cupidity'. What was the allusion there? Presumably the same as contained in the title of a revue put on by Combined Services Entertainment in the Far East (c 1947) and featuring the young actor Kenneth Williams. It was called 'It's Not So Much the Heat, It's the Humidity', though in his memoirs he simply calls it *Not So Much the Heat*. Whatever the form, was this is a common expression in the Second World War?

Ted Bell of Reading, who served with the RAF in the Middle East in 1945–7, confirmed (1992) that it was indeed a common expression then and thereabouts: 'What I heard (among *all* ranks; most of my time was in the Sergeants' Mess) was usually an *exaggerated* omission of the aspirate. The saying was often in the form of a piece of folklore recalling the long tradition of British service in those parts, notably in the period between the two World Wars. So the expression would be something like: "Hot? Very hot, but as they always say there, 'It's not the 'eat, it's the 'yoomidity'." You might have expected expletives to precede the abstract nouns, but most people appreciated that if used they spoilt the effect. I am pretty sure you would have to go back to the 1920s or beyond to approach the origins of the expression; it is clearly part of the very strong oral RAF and RFC tradition, and it is just possible that it might be traceable to an individual, whom I picture as a Warrant Officer 2nd class, with a mottled face, a bulbous nose and a bushy moustache.'

There is a case, however, for supporting an Anglo-American origin. In the first paragraph of P.G. Wodehouse's novel *Sam the Sudden* (1925), he describes the inhabitants of New York on a late August afternoon: '[one half] crawling about and asking those they met if this was hot enough for them, the other maintaining that what they minded was not so much the heat as the humidity.'

American use of the phrase may be further confirmed by Thomas Tryon's novel *The Other* which, though not published until 1971, is set in the New England of the mid-1930s. Several times it has characters saying, 'It ain't the heat, it's the humidity', in circumstances suggesting that it was a conversational cliché of the time and place.

In addition, Leonard Miall, who was the BBC's first peacetime correspondent in Washington D.C. after the Second World War, recalls the expression commonly being used in complaints about the climate of the US capital, and adds that around 1953, when McCarthyism was at its height, the saying was changed to, 'It's not so much the heat, it's the humiliation'.

1 *It's not the wild, ecstatic leap across that I deplore. It is the weary trudge home.*

From something called 'Double Beds versus Single Beds'. Quoted 1977. Untraced.

2 *It's worse than a crime, it's a blunder!*

There is no doubting that this was said about the execution of the Duc d'Enghien in 1804. Napoleon, suspecting the Duc of being involved in royalist conspiracies against him, had him found and executed, an act that hardened opinion against the French Emperor. But who said it? Comte Boulay de la Meurthe (1761–1840) was credited with the remark in C.-A. Sainte-Beuve's *Nouveaux Lundis* (1870), but among other names sometimes linked to it are Talleyrand, Joseph Fouché and Napoleon himself.

In French, the remark is usually rendered as: '*C'est pire qu'un crime; c'est une faute!*' Pearson has what he seems to think is the more correct translation: 'It is more than a crime; it is a political fault', from the *Memoirs of Fouché*.

3 *It takes seventy-two muscles to frown, but only thirteen to smile.*

A saying included in Celia Haddon, *The Yearbook of Comfort and Joy* (1991). 'This

reminder,' she says, 'came from a newsletter sent to traffic wardens.' But it is probably quite old and probably of American origin.

4 *I've seen the elephant, and I've heard the owl, and I've been to the other side of the mountain.*

'Seeing the elephant', according to John D. Unruh Jr, *The Plains Across: The Overland Emigrants and the Trans-Mississippi West, 1840–60* (1979), was a popular expression in the US, 'connoting, in the main, experiencing hardship and difficulty and somehow surviving'. The source of the longer version is untraced.

BDPF defines 'to see the elephant' as 'to see all there is to see'. Radford, *To Coin a Phrase* (1974), suggests that the original form, dating from the 1830s, was: ' "That's sufficient," as Tom Haynes said when he saw the elephant.' J.M. Dixon, *English Idioms* (c 1912), has the definition: 'To be acquainted with all the latest movements; to be knowing', which sharpens the idea somewhat. Partridge/*Slang* has, 'To see the world; gain worldly experience' and dates it to c 1840 in the US, 1860 in the UK.

Should there be any doubt as to why an elephant is chosen as the defining thing to see, the Lancashire squire, Nicholas Blundell, wrote in his diary for 6 March 1705: 'My wife rid behind me to Liverpool. She saw the elephant.'

5 *I was only obeying orders.*

The Charter of the International Military Tribunal at Nuremberg (1945–6) specifically excluded the traditional German defence of 'superior orders'. But the plea was, nevertheless, much advanced. This approach was summed up in the catchphrase 'I was only obeying orders', often used grotesquely in parody of such buckpassing. Rex Harrison says in the film *Night Train to Munich* (UK; as early as 1940): 'Captain Marsen was only obeying orders.' Kenneth Mars as a mad, Nazi-fixated playwright in *The Producers* (US, 1967) says, 'I only followed orders!'

Not that everyone seemed aware of the parodying. From the *New York Times* (6 July 1983): 'Herbert Bechtold, a German-born officer in the [US] counter-intelligence who became [the "handler" of Klaus Barbie, the Nazi war criminal] was asked if he questioned the morality of hiring a man like Barbie by the United States. "I am not in a position to pass judgement on that,"

Mr Bechtold replied, "I was just following orders".'

1 *I went to New Zealand but it was closed.*

This is a joke that gets rediscovered every so often but that tends to get ascribed on a fairly random basis. The Beatles found it in the 1960s; slightly before then, Anna Russell, the musical comedienne, said it on one of her records. It has also been attributed to Clement Freud. But William Franklyn, son of the Antipodean actor, Leo Franklyn, says that his father was saying it in the 1920s. Perhaps W.C. Fields began it all by saying 'I went to Philadelphia and found that it was closed' about the same time (if indeed he did).

2 *A Kestrel for a Knave.*

The novel with this title by Barry Hines (1968) — filmed simply as *Kes* (1969) — tells of a boy misfit who learns about life through training his kestrel hawk. The title comes from *The Boke of St Albans* (1486) and it is also in a Harleian manuscript: 'An Eagle for an Emperor, a Gyrfalcon for a King; a Peregrine for a Prince, a Saker for a Knight, a Merlin for a Lady; a Goshawk for a Yeoman, a Sparrowhawk for a Priest, a Musket for a Holy water Clerk, a Kestrel for a Knave.'

3 *The Killing Fields.*

Title of a film (UK 1984) concerning the mass-murders carried out by the Communist Khmer Rouge, under Pol Pot, in Cambodia between 1975 and 1978, when possibly three million people were killed. The mass graves were discovered in April 1979. In the film the phrase was seen to refer, literally, to paddy fields where prisoners were forced to work and where many of them were callously shot. The film was based on an article 'The Death and Life of Dith Pran' by Sydney Schanberg, published in the *New York Times* Magazine (20 January 1980), which tells of the journalist's quest for a reunion with his former assistant.

The article has the phrase towards the beginning: 'In July of 1975 — two months after Pran and I had been forced apart on April 20 — an American diplomat who had known Pran wrote me a consoling letter. The diplomat, who had served in Phnom Penh, knew the odds of anyone emerging safely from a country that was being transformed into a society of terror and purges and "killing fields".' So it appears that the coinage is due to the unnamed diplomat.

Compare the phrase 'killing *ground(s)*' which has entered the military vocabulary as a strategic term for an area into which you manouevre the enemy before finishing them off and which has been current since the Second World War. In a non-military sense, the phrase was used by Rudyard Kipling in his poem 'The Rhyme of the Three Sealers' (1893) about seal hunting.

4 *The king is dead — long live king!* [Le roi est mort, vive le roi!]

This declaration was first used in 1461 on the death of King Charles VII of France. Julia Pardoe in her *Life of Louis XIV* describes how that king's death (in 1715) was announced by the captain of the bodyguard from a window of the state apartment: 'Raising his truncheon above his head, he broke it in the centre, and throwing the pieces among the crowd exclaimed in a loud voice, "*Le Roi est mort!*" Then seizing another staff, he flourished it in the air as he shouted, "*Vive le Roi*".' The custom ended with the death of Louis XVIII (1824). The expression is now used allusively to denote a smooth transition of power of any sort.

5 Laborare est orare.

In full '*Orare est laborare, laborare est orare* [to pray is to work, to work is to pray]', this is the ancient motto of the Benedictine order. It has also been used by various families and institutions (the London Borough of Willesden, not least).

6 *Labour's Double Whammy.*

During the 1992 British general election, the Conservative Party introduced a poster showing a boxer wearing two enormous boxing gloves. One was labelled '1. More tax' and the other '2. Higher prices'. The overall slogan was 'LABOUR'S DOUBLE WHAMMY'. This caused a good deal of puzzlement in Britain, though the concept of the 'double whammy' had been well known in the US since the 1950s. One source suggested that it had come from the Dick Tracy comic strip in which it referred to a death-ray glare emitted by one of the characters. Another stated that cartoonist

Al Capp introduced the notion in his 'Li'l Abner' strip — the character Evil-Eye Fleegle boasted a 'double whammy . . . which I hopes I never hafta use'. In other words, a double whammy is a powerful blow.

1 Life's a bitch, and then you die.

This is a popular saying of untraced origin, though probably North American. A development of it, known both in the US and the UK, is 'Life's a bitch, *you marry a bitch*, and then you die'. Citations in print are not very plentiful. Working backwards: during the summer of 1991, the Body Shop chain in the UK was promoting sun-tan products with a window-display under the punning slogan 'Life's a beach — and then you fry'. A caption to an article in the London *Observer* (23 September 1990) about frozen food was the equally punning 'Life's a binge and then you diet'. In Caryl Churchill's play about the City, *Serious Money* (first performed March 1987), we find: 'I thought I'd be extremely rich. / You can't be certain what you'll get. / I've heard the young say Life's a bitch.' The earliest citation found so far comes from the *Sunday Times* of 21 December 1986: 'Life is a bitch, then you die. So says the pilot of a flying fuel tank who, last week took off to circumnavigate the globe with his girlfriend.'

Other suggested origins — Woody Allen's film *Love and Death* (1975) and the 1983 re-make of Jean-Luc Godard's *À Bout de Souffle* (in which the Jean-Paul Belmondo character originally died saying, '*La vie — c'est dégeulasse*' ['Life's a drag']) — have not proved fruitful sources.

'Life's a *beach*' seems to have taken on a life of its own as a slogan, especially in Australia, but probably developed from 'Life's a bitch', rather than the other way round.

Attention might be drawn to *An Essay on Woman* by 'Pego Borewell Esq.' which was published in about 1763 as a bawdy parody of Alexander Pope's *An Essay on Man*. It is thought to have been written by the politician John 'Friend of Liberty' Wilkes and one Thomas Potter, working in some form of collaboration. Interestingly, it starts like this:

Let us (since life can little more supply
Than just a few good fucks, and then
    we die)
Expatiate freely . . .

Something of the same spirit comes through here.

2 Little Jack Horner
Sat in the corner,
Eating a Christmas pie.
He put in his thumb,
And pulled out a plum,
And said, What a good boy am I?

A tradition has grown up that in the sixteenth century, at the time of the Dissolution of the Monasteries, the Abbot of Glastonbury sent his steward Jack Horner to London. In an attempt to appease King Henry VIII, Horner was bearing a Christmas pie containing the title deeds of twelve manors. But Horner 'put in his thumb' and pulled out the other kind of 'plum' — the deeds to the Manor of Mells in Somerset — and put them to his own use. A *Thomas Horner did* take up residence in Mells shortly after the Dissolution and his descendants lived there until late in the twentieth century.

[*Source:* Iona & Peter Opie, *The Oxford Dictionary of Nursery Rhymes*, 1951.]

3 The mail must get/go through.

A slogan of probable North American origin — as indicated by use of the word 'mail' rather than 'post'. Though 'Royal Mail' is still very much used in the UK, the older term 'post' predominates.

There is no citation of the precise slogan being used in Britain. The Longman *Chronicle of America* reports (as for 13 April 1860) the arrival in Sacramento, California, of the first Pony Express delivery — a satchel with 49 letters and three newspapers that had left St Joseph, Missouri, eleven days previously. 'The pace is an astounding improvement over the eight-week wagon convoys. But the brave riders, who vow "the mail must get through" despite all kinds of dangers ranging from hostile Indians on the prairie to storms in the mountains, may only be a temporary link [as the Iron Horse makes progress].'

The *Chronicle* does not provide a solid basis for invoking the slogan at this point but the connection with Pony Express seems very likely. It would be good to have an actual citation from the period. Raymond and Mary Settle in *The Story of the Pony Express* (1955) point out that the organization flourished only about 1860–1, soon being overtaken by telegraph and railroad, and add: 'A schedule, as exacting as that of a railroad timetable, was set up, and each rider was under rigid orders to keep it, day and night, fair weather or foul. Allowance was made for nothing, not even attack by Indians. Their motto was, "The mail must go through", and it did except in a very few, rare cases.'

1 Mairzy doats and dozy doats.

One of the most impenetrable graffiti jokes was, at least at first glance, the scribbled addition to a notice in Liverpool proclaiming: 'Mersey Docks and Harbour Board . . . and little lambs eat ivy.' This was recorded in 1944. The graffiti-writer had cleverly spotted that a Scouser (Liverpudlian) would pronounce Mersey, 'mairzy' and that the rhythm of 'Mersey Docks and Harbour Board' exactly matched the first line of a nonsense song popular in Britain and America at the time called 'Mairzy Doats and Dozy Doats (Mares Eat Oats and Does Eat Oats)'. It went:

I know a ditty nutty as a fruit cake
Goofy as a goon and silly as a loon . . .

　Mairzy doats and dozy doats
　And liddle lamzy divey.
　A kiddley divey too,
　Wouldn't you?

The song was 'written' by Milton Drake, Al Hoffman and Jerry Livingston but, as the Opies point out in their Oxford Dictionary of Nursery Rhymes, there is a 'catch' which, when said quickly, appears to be in Latin:

　In fir tar is,
　In oak none is,
　In mud eels are,
　In clay none are.
　Goat eat ivy
　Mare eat oats.

Say the Opies: 'The joke may be traced back 500 years to a medical manuscript in Henry VI's time.'

2 A man's gotta do what a man's gotta do.

A statement of obligation, as in film Westerns. Partridge/Catch Phrases dates popular use of this saying from c 1945, but its origin remains untraced, although an early example occurs in John Steinbeck's novel The Grapes of Wrath, Chap. 18 (1939): 'I know this — a man got to do what he got to do'. The film Shane (US, 1953), based on a novel by Jack Shaeffer, is sometimes said to contain the line, but does not (nor does the book). The John Wayne film Stagecoach (1939) does not include it either, as some sources state. By the 1970s, several songs had been recorded with the title.

3 Marriage is too important to be treated like a love affair.

Alluded to by Katharine Whitehorn in the Observer (1 March 1992). She obtained it from Gillian Tindall, but otherwise the quotation — if it is one — remains untraced.

4 May you live in interesting times.

Robert F. Kennedy, speaking in Cape Town, South Africa, on 7 June 1966, said: 'There is a Chinese curse which says, "May he live in interesting times". Like it or not, we live in interesting times . . .' This has since become a very popular observation, almost a cliché, though any Chinese source remains untraced.

5 A more efficient conduct of the war.

A phrase from the First World War. Its precise origin remains untraced. A.J.P. Taylor in his English History 1914–45 has: 'The Coalition government, which Asquith announced on 26 May 1915, claimed to demonstrate national unity and to promote a more efficient conduct of the war.' Writing of the following year (1916) in Clementine Churchill (1979), Mary Soames has 'more vigorous and efficient prosecution of the war'. Is it also sometimes given as 'more energetic' conduct?

6 A mugwump is a sort of bird that sits on a fence with his mug on one side and his wump on the other.

A mugquomp in the language of the Algonquin (American Indians) describes a great chief or person of high rank (and was so recorded by 1663). In 1884, however, the word was popularized and used to describe 'the little men attempting to be big chiefs' who felt unable to support James Blaine as the Republican candidate for the US Presidency and transferred their allegiance to the Democrat, Grover Cleveland. Hence, in American political parlance, a mugwump came to describe a 'bolter' or someone who held himself self-importantly aloof. More generally, it has been used to describe a fool.

　The definition of the mugwump as a bird derives from the Blue Earth (Minnesota) Post in the early 1930s.

7 My friend's friend is my enemy.

This expression was invoked, for example, at the time of the Suez crisis (1956). It might have been President Nasser of Egypt referring to the United States (the friend) and Israel (the friend's friend). There seem to be many precedents. Mencken lists a legal maxim, 'The companion of my companion is not my companion (*socii mei socius meus socius non est*)', but compare the French proverb, 'The enemy of my enemy is my friend', and the Flemish proverb, 'The friends of my friends are my friends'.

1 The Navy's here!

On the night of 16 February 1940, 299 British seamen were freed from captivity aboard the German ship *Altmark* as it lay in a Norwegian fjord. The destroyer *Cossack*, under the command of Captain Philip Vian, had managed to locate the German supply ship and a boarding party discovered that British prisoners were locked in its hold. As Vian described it, Lieutenant Bradwell Turner, the leader of the boarding party, called out: 'Any British down there?' 'Yes, we're all British,' came the reply. 'Come on up then,' he said, 'The Navy's here.'

The identity of the speaker is in doubt, however. Correspondence in the *Sunday Telegraph* (February/March 1980) revealed that Turner denied he had said it, that Leading Seaman James Harper was another candidate, and that Lieutenant Johnny Parker was the most likely person to have said it (and he had certainly claimed that he did).

The Times on 19 February 1940 gave a version from the lips of one of those who had been freed and who had actually heard the exchange: 'John Quigley of London said that the first they knew of their rescue was when they heard a shout of "Any Englishmen here?" They shouted "Yes" and immediately came the cheering words, "Well, the Navy is here." Quigley said — "We were all hoarse with cheering when we heard those words".'

2 Nice legs, shame about her face.

The title of a briefly popular song recorded by the Monks in 1979 gave rise to a format phrase which appeared, for example, in a take-off by BBC TV's *Not the Nine O'Clock News* team — 'Nice video, shame about the song' — and in a slogan for Hofmeister lager — 'Great lager, shame about the . . .' (both in 1982). At about the same time, Listerine ran an advertisement with the slogan 'Nice Face, Shame About the Breath'. Other examples include a headline to an *Independent* piece on the hundredth birthday of the 'The Red Flag': 'Good tune, shame about the words' (9 February 1989); a headline from the *Observer* (9 April 1989): 'Nice prints, shame about the books'. It is also used loosely: 'Victoria Wood is almost perfect. Lovely lady, pity about the voice' (*Cosmopolitan*, February 1987); and the headline to an *Observer* report on puny car horns in January 1989 was: 'NICE CAR, BUT WHAT A VOICE!'

3 The noise and the people!

Describing what it was like to be in battle, a certain Captain Strahan exclaimed, 'Oh, my dear fellow, the noise . . . and the people!' According to the *ODQ* (1979), quoting the *Hudson Review* (Winter, 1951), he said it after the Battle of Bastogne in 1944.

Various correspondents suggested it was earlier in the war than this, however. Roy T. Kendall wrote: 'I heard this phrase used, in a humorous manner, during the early part of 1942. It was related to me as having been said by a young Guards officer, newly returned from Dunkirk, who on being asked what it was like used the expression: the inference being, a blasé attitude to the dangers and a disdain of the common soldiery he was forced to mix with.'

Tony Bagnall Smith added that the Guards officer was still properly dressed and equipped when he said it, and that his reply was: 'My dear, the noise and the people — how they smelt!'

The *ODQ* (1992) appears to have come round to the earlier use regarding Dunkirk, in the form 'The noise, my dear! And the people!' It finds it already being quoted in Anthony Rhodes, *Sword of Bone*, Chap. 22 (1942).

A suggestion that it was said by the actor Ernest Thesiger in 1919, about his experiences in the First World War, may be discounted.

4 No one likes us — we don't care.

From the new lyrics sung by fans of Millwall football club to the tune of Rod Stewart's song 'Sailing'. Millwall fans are famous in London for their vocal and physical forcefulness. *No One Likes Us, We Don't Care*, was, consequently, the title given to a Channel 4 TV documentary about them in January 1990.

5 On Ilkla Moor Bah t'at.

The most famous — and impenetrable — of Yorkshire songs comes in two versions.

The older, said to have been written by Thomas Clark to the hymn tune 'Cranbrook' in 1805, was sung in a spirited way:

1 Wheear baht thee bahn when I been gone? [repeated three times]
Wheear baht?
On Ilkla Moor bah t'at [repeated twice]
Bah t'at, bah t'at.

2 Then thou wilt catch a cold and dee
In Lonnenfuit bah t'buit [repeated twice]
Bah t'buit, bah t'buit.

3 Then we shall cum and bury thee
In Saltruble Docks bah t'socks [repeated twice]
Bah t'socks, bah t'socks.

4 Then worms'll cum and eat up thee
On Ikla Moor bah t'at [etc.]

5 Then doocks'll cum and eat them worms
In Lonnenfuit bah t'buit [etc.]

6 Then we shall cum and eat them doocks
In Saltruble Docks bah t'socks [etc.]

7 Then we shall catch th'auld cold and dee
On Ilka Moor bah t'at [etc.]

(Salter Hebble Docks and Luddenden Foot are canal points on the Hebble and Calder rivers near Halifax.)

A later (and now more popular) version, is sung more dolefully. It has a second verse, beginning 'I've been a courting Mary Jane', and a final verse sung thus:

Then we shall all 'av 'etten thee
That's how we get our owen back
This is the moral of this tale
Doan't go a-courtin Mary Jane.

This version was reputedly composed on an outing to Ilkley Moor by the choir of Ebenezer Chapel, Halifax, in 1886. The meaning of the old saga is roughly this: 'You've been on Ilkley Moor without a hat, courting Mary Jane. You'll catch your death of cold, and we shall have to bury you. The worms will eat you up, and the ducks will eat up the worms. Then we shall eat the ducks, so we shall have eaten you.'

1 The only difference between men and boys is the price of their toys.

This modern proverbial expression has been credited both to Liberace and to Joyce Brothers in the US. In the UK, there is a difference: writer Derek Robinson talking in 1990 about the making of a TV version of his novel *Piece of Cake* said he noticed that everyone was fascinated by the Spitfire aircraft. All work would come to a stop when-

ever they were being used. A technician standing by remarked, 'You can tell the men from the boys by the size of their toys'.

2 Only the mediocre are always at their best.

A case of multiple attribution here. Among those credited with it have been Jean Giraudoux, Max Beerbohm and W. Somerset Maugham (the latter specifically referring to writers). Of these, the Beerbohm is said to appear in S.N. Behrman's *Conversations with Max* (1960) in the form: 'Only mediocrity can be trusted to be always at its best.' The Maugham appears in *Quotations for Speakers and Writers* (1969). The Giraudoux appears without source in Robert Byrne's *The 637 Best Things Anybody Ever Said* (1982).

3 The opera ain't/isn't over till the fat lady sings.

Relatively few modern proverbs have caught on in a big way but, of those that have, this one has produced sharp division over its origin. It is also used with surprising vagueness and lack of perception. If it is a warning 'not to count your chickens before they are hatched', it is too often simply employed to express a generalized view that 'it isn't over till it's over'.

So how did the saying come about? A report in the *Washington Post* (13 June 1978) had this version: 'One day three years ago [i.e. 1975], Ralph Carpenter, who was then Texas Tech's sports information director, declared to the press box contingent in Austin, "The rodeo ain't over till the bull riders ride." Stirred to that deep insight, San Antonio sports editor Dan Cook countered with, "The opera ain't over till the fat lady sings".'

Two days before this (i.e. 11 June 1978), the *Washington Post* had more precisely quoted Cook as coming up with his version *the previous April*, 'after the basketball playoff game between the San Antonio Spurs and the Washington Bullets, to illustrate that while the Spurs had won once, the series was not over yet. Bullets coach Dick Motta borrowed the phrase later during the Bullets' eventually successful championship drive, and it became widely known and was often mistakenly attributed to him.'

Another widely shared view is that the saying refers to Kate Smith, a handsomely proportioned American singer in the 1930s and 1940s. Her rendition of Irving Berlin's

'God Bless America' signified the end of events like the political party conventions and World Series baseball games. Hence, possibly, the alternative version: 'the *game's* not over till the fat lady sings'. On the other hand, it has been argued that American national anthems ('The Star-Spangled Banner' and 'America the Beautiful' are others) are usually sung at the *start* of baseball games, which would remove the point from the saying.

If the 'opera' version has very much meaning either, it derives from a hazy view of those sopranos with a 'different body image' who get to sing a big number before they die and thus bring the show to a close. But they do not do this invariably. In *Tosca*, for example, the heroine makes her final death plunge over the battlements without singing a big aria.

Whatever the case, allusive use of the proverb is widespread. The Fat Lady Sings is the name of an Irish (pop) band, formed *c* 1990. After winning the US presidential election in November 1992, Bill Clinton appeared at a victory party in Little Rock bearing a T-shirt with the slogan 'The Fat Lady Sang', which presumably meant no more than, 'It's over.' In July 1992 tennis champion Andre Agassi, describing the surprise climax of his Wimbledon final, said, 'I knew that it might just go to 30–30 with two more aces. I didn't hear the fat lady humming yet.' The American singers En Vogue had a song called 'It ain't over till the fat lady sings' about this time, and there were several books with approximate versions for their titles.

As is to be expected with a proverbial expression, the *idea* behind 'the fat lady' is nothing new. In Eric Maschwitz's memoir *No Chip on My Shoulder* (1957), he recalled Julian Wylie, 'The Pantomime King': 'He had a number of favourite adages about the Theatre, one of which I have always remembered as a warning against dramatic anti-climax: "Never forget," he used to say "that once the giant is dead, the pantomime is over!" ' Which is surely a corollary if there was one.

Proof that the 'opera' version is merely a derivative of some earlier American expression appears to be provided by *A Dictionary of American Proverbs* (1992), which lists both 'The game's not over until the last man strikes out' and 'Church is not out 'til they sing'. Bartlett (1992) finds in *Southern Words and Sayings* by F.R. and C.R. Smith, the expression 'Church ain't out till the fat lady sings'. As the Smiths' book was

published in 1976, this would seem to confirm that the 'opera' version of the proverb is only a derivative.

1 *Our Farnham which art in Hendon, Harrow be thy Name. Thy Kingston come. Thy Wimbledon, in Erith as it is in Heston.*
Give us this day our Leatherhead. And forgive us our Westminsters. As we forgive them that Westminster against us. And lead us not into Thames Ditton; But deliver us from Ealing: For thine is the Kingston, The Purley, and the Crawley, For Iver and Iver. Crouch End.

This 'Home Counties' version of the Lord's Prayer was printed in my book *Say No More!* (1987). Correspondence in the magazine *Oxford Today* (Hilary/Trinity Terms 1990) produced a number of variations and a date of composition somewhere in the 1930s, but no author. Peter Hay in *Business Anecdotes* (1988) includes a faintly similar parody written in 1930s America by a Ford motors worker before unionization. It begins:

Our Father, who art in Dearborn,
   Henry be thine name.
Let payday come. Thy will be done in
   Fordson as it is in Highland Park . . .

2 *A picture is worth a thousand words.*

This famous saying, which occurs, for example, in the song 'If' popularized by Bread in 1971, is sometimes said to be a Chinese proverb. Bartlett (1980) listed it as such in the form 'One picture is worth more than ten thousand words' and compared what Turgenev says in *Fathers and Sons*: 'A picture shows me at a glance what it takes dozens of pages of a book to expound.'

But *CODP* points out that it originated in an American paper *Printers' Ink* (8 December 1921) in the form 'One look is worth a thousand words'. It was later reprinted in the better known form in the same paper (10 March 1927) and there ascribed by its actual author, Frederick R. Barnard, to a Chinese source ('so that people would take it seriously', he told Burton Stevenson in 1948).

3 *A place within the meaning of the act.*

The *ODQ* (1979) merely stated that this was from 'the Betting Act', ignoring the fact that there was more than one such. In fact, the phrase comes from Section 2 of the 1853 Betting Act (which banned off-course betting on race horses).

1 *A politician is a person who approaches every subject with an open mouth.*

The short answer is that no one knows who originated this remark, but it should be approached with caution. Writing the foreword to *Kindly Sit Down* (1983), a compilation of after-dinner speech jokes, Margaret Thatcher put this: 'It was after all, the late Governor Adlai Stevenson who defined a politician as one who approached every question with an open mouth.' Unfortunately, one of the book contributor's, Roger Moate, ascribed it rather to Oscar Wilde (though this may be no more than another example of Churchillian Drift).

Leon A. Harris in *The Fine Art of Political Wit* (1966) plumps for Stevenson, though the remark has also been ascribed to Arthur Goldberg on diplomats.

2 Post coitum omne animal triste est *[Every creature is sad after sexual intercourse].*

A post-classical Latin proverb, according to *ODQ* (1979) on the grounds that it does not appear in classical texts. However, Laurence Sterne in *Tristram Shandy* (1662) ascribes it to Aristotle, presumably on the grounds that Aristotle did write: 'Why do young men, on first having sexual intercourse, afterwards hate those with whom they have just been associated?' The Roman author Pliny also wrote: 'Man alone experiences regret after first having intercourse.'

3 *A Postillion Struck by Lightning.*

The title of the first volume of Dirk Bogarde's autobiography (1977). Describing a holiday in early childhood (the 1920s presumably), he mentions an old phrase book (seemingly dated 1898), which contains lines like: 'This muslin is too thin, have you something thicker?'; 'My leg, arm, foot, elbow, nose, finger is broken'; and 'The postillion has been struck by lightning'. Which phrase book is this? Not *English as She is Spoke* (see 11:2), in which the 'postillion' line does not occur. A writer in *The Times* (30 July 1983) noted: ' "Look, the front postillion has been struck by lightning" . . . supposed to feature in a Scandinavian phrase book: but it may well be apocryphal.'

In the third volume of Bogarde's autobiography, *An Orderly Man* (1983), describing the writing of the first, he says: 'My sister-in-law, Cilla, on a wet camping holiday somewhere in northern France . . . once sent me a postcard on which she said . . . she had been forced to learn a little more French than the phrase "Help! My postillion has been struck by lightning!" I took the old phrase for the title of my book.'

A similarly untraced Russian/English phrasebook is said to have included: 'Don't bother to unsaddle the horses, lightning has struck the innkeeper.'

4 *A pound of tea at one and three*
And a pot of raspberry jam,
Two new-laid eggs, a dozen pegs,
And a pound of rashers of ham.

Eleanor Farjeon in her childhood autobiography *A Nursery in the Nineties* (1935) relates how she had to learn a 'rather silly poem' about a girl who tries to remember her shopping list and grows steadily more muddled. In those days children were expected to perform at parties. Farjeon had to recite 'A pound of tea', but soon got mixed up, gave up in despair and ran to her mother in tears.

In fact, the sex of the child is not apparent. The author of 'Going on an Errand', as it is usually called, has not been traced. The full text may be found in *This England's Book of Parlour Poetry* (1989).

5 *A priest is a man who is called Father by everyone except his own children who are obliged to call him Uncle.*

Rupert Hart-Davis says he came across this 'Italian saying' in 'a French novel, read in the train', but gives no further clue. From *The Lyttelton Hart-Davis Letters*, Vol. 1 (1978).

6 *Real pain for your sham friends, champagne for your real friends.*

An Edwardian toast that the painter Francis Bacon (1909–92) acquired from his father, according to Daniel Farson, *The Gilded Gutter Life of Francis Bacon* (1993).

7 *Rough seas make tough sailors.*

A search for a proverb to this effect in 1993 produced no result. However, *The Dictionary of American Proverbs* (1992) contains 'A good sailor likes a rough sea' (collected in

Ontario, Canada) and Benham (1948) has an Italian proverb, 'The good seaman is known in bad weather'.

1 Sarcasm is the lowest form of wit.

There is no doubt that this proverbial expression exists: 'Sarcasm is supposed to be the lowest form of wit. Never mind. It has its moments' — Greville Janner, *Janner's Complete Letterwriter* (1989). But it is hard to say where it came from. Thomas Carlyle remarked in *Sartor Resartus*, II.iv (1834) that, 'Sarcasm is the language of the devil'. The more usual observation is that 'Punning is the lowest form of wit', which probably derives from Dryden's comment on Ben Jonson's 'clenches' — 'The lowest and most grovelling kind of wit'. At some stage the comment on the one has been applied to the other.

The saying is definitely *not* Dr Johnson's definition of wit in his *Dictionary*.

2 Say it ain't so, Joe.

A small boy is reputed to have said this to the American baseball player 'Shoeless Joe' Jackson as he came out of a grand jury session in 1920 about corruption in the 1919 World Series. Jackson, of the Chicago White Sox, had been accused with others of deliberately losing the Series at the behest of gamblers. A journalist called Hugh Fullerton reported a boy asking, 'It ain't so, Joe. Is it?' and him replying, 'Yes, kid, I'm afraid it is'. Over the years, the words rearranged themselves into the more euphonious order. Ironically, Jackson denied that the exchange had ever taken place — using any set of words.

3 Say not in grief that he/she is no more But in thankfulness that he/she was.

These words, spoken at many a memorial or thanksgiving service, have been variously described as a Jewish prayer and/or from the Talmud. If so, the source remains untraced, except that the underlying thought is almost a commonplace. General George S. Patton said in a speech in 1945: 'It is foolish and wrong to mourn the men who died. Rather we should thank God that such men lived.' In 1992, *The Times* quoted the Queen Mother as having said of her husband King George VI's death in 1952: 'One must feel gratitude for what has been, rather than distress for what is lost.'

And, although it is not quite the same thing, that well-known quotation-scruncher, Margaret Thatcher, incorporated this in a VE-Day message to the Kremlin in May 1985: 'It is right that we should look back and pay tribute with pride and *thankfulness* for the heroism of those in both our countries who fought in a common cause, and with *grief* for the terrible sufferings involved.'

4 She Done Him Wrong.

When Mae West's play *Diamond Lil* was transferred to the screen in 1933, it was renamed *She Done Him Wrong*. The title must surely allude to the refrain from the famous anonymous American ballad 'Frankie and Johnny' (which Mencken dates *c* 1875). There are numerous versions (two hundred is one estimate) and it may be of Negro origin. 'Frankie and Johnnie were lovers' (or husband and wife) but he (Johnnie) went off with other women — 'He was her man, but he done her wrong.' So, to equal the score, Frankie shoots him and has to be punished for it (in some versions in the electric chair):

> Frankie walked up to the scaffold, as calm as a girl could be,
> She turned her eyes to Heaven and said 'Good Lord, I'm coming to Thee;
> He was my man, but I done him wrong'.

Bartlett (1980) draws a comparison with Shakespeare, *The Rape of Lucrece* (l.1462): 'Lucrece swears he did her wrong' and *King Lear* (I.ii.161): 'Some villain hath done me wrong.'

5 Somebody's Husband, Somebody's Son.

The title of Gordon Burn's (1984) book about the 'Yorkshire Ripper' murder investigation is taken from something said during the prolonged police hunt for the killer. George Oldfield, leading the police hunt, appeared on the Jimmy Young radio show on 9 February 1978 and 'urged the predominantly female audience to search their collective conscience and report any man of their acquaintance who they suspected of behaving oddly. Husband, father, brother, son — it shouldn't matter.' After another killing, a Yorkshire clergyman, the Revd Michael Walker told his congregation on Palm Sunday, 1979, 'He [the Ripper] needs help, he is somebody's child, husband or father.'

1 *Spake as he champed the unaccustomed food,*
This may be wholesome but it is not good.

'Anon. 1852' is the only hint given in *The Making of Verse: A Guide to English Metres* (1934) by Robert Swan and Frank Sidgwick, where this is given among examples of heroic couplets. In *The Dublin Review* (July 1937), J. Lewis May, while discussing 'Flashed from his bed the electric tidings came' (see AUSTIN 36:3), says: 'The name of the inventor of these immortal lines has not been handed down, but one may hazard a guess that they proceeded from the same source as those on another prince, also a subject for the Newdigate [prize poem at Oxford] — to wit, Nebuchadnezzar, "Who murmured — as he ate the unaccustomed food — /It may be wholesome, but it is not good".'

2 *[Texas is] the place where there are the most cows and the least milk and the most rivers and the least water in them, and where you can look the furthest and see the least.*

Mencken (1942) had this from an 'Author unidentified'. In 1993 it caused a discussion whether there had ever been anything said that was quotable and *complimentary* about Texas? Possibly coming into this category is the passage from John Gunther, *Inside U.S.A.* (1947): 'I like the story, doubtless antique, that I heard near San Antonio. A child asks a stranger where he comes from, whereupon his father rebukes him gently, "Never do that, son. If a man's from Texas, he'll tell you. If he's not, why embarrass him by asking".'
Then there is this from *LBJ: Images of a Vibrant Life* (published by Friends of the LBJ Library, 1973): 'The President [Lyndon Johnson] will rest in his beloved Hill Country [in Texas], where he has told us his father before him said he wanted to be — "Where folks know when you're sick and care when you die".'
In addition, there is this song (author untraced):

O beautiful, beautiful Texas,
Where the beautiful bluebonnets grow,
We're proud of our forefathers
Who died at the Alamo.
You can live in the plains or the mountains
Or down where the sea breezes blow,

But you'll still be in beautiful Texas —
The most beautiful State that I know.
(The bluebonnet is the state flower of Texas.)

3 *The things that will destroy us are . . .*
politics without principle;
pleasure without conscience;
wealth without work;
knowledge without character;
business without morality;
science without humanity; and
worship without sacrifice.

Probably American in origin, this was current in 1992 but the source remains untraced.

4 *The time is now.*

A slogan that has been used variously over the years. It was one of the promotional lines in the Ronald Reagan presidential campaign of 1980. In a speech at Wheeling, West Virginia, on 20 February 1950, Senator Joseph McCarthy, began his career as America's leading Red hunter by asking: 'Can there be anyone who fails to realize that the Communist world has said, "The time is now" — that this is the time for the show-down between a democratic Christian world and the Communist atheistic world?'

5 The Times *is a tribal noticeboard.*

It was said (in *The Times*, 21 January 1984) that a candidate for the editorship of the paper's Woman's Page in the 1960s described the newspaper thus. The then editor, Sir William Haley, was so tickled that he gave her the job, though he usually reacted against any suggestion that the paper was exclusive (and had opposed the advertising slogan 'Top People Take The Times', for example). According to Godfrey Smith in the *Sunday Times*, the successful candidate was Suzanne Puddefoot.

6 *TITANIC SINKS — HECKMOND-WIKE MAN ABOARD.*

A probably apocryphal headline from a Yorkshire newspaper in 1912. Even if it never actually appeared, it has become the paradigm of 'finding the local angle' in any story by the provincial press. (One headline that really did appear — in the *Weekly Dispatch* (London) — was 'MANY MILLIONAIRES MISSING.')

1 Today Germany, tomorrow the world!

The slogan for the National Socialist Press in Germany of the early 1930s, '*Heute Presse der Nationalsozialisten, Morgen Presse der Nation*' [Today the press of the Nazis, tomorrow the nation's press], reached its final form in '*Heute gehört uns Deutschland — morgen die ganze Welt*' [Today Germany belongs to us — tomorrow the whole world.] Although John Colville in *The Fringes of Power* states that by 3 September 1939, Hitler 'had already . . . proclaimed that "Today Germany is ours; tomorrow the whole world",' an example of Hitler actually saying it has yet to be found. However, in *Mein Kampf* (1925) he had said: 'If the German people, in their historic development, had possessed tribal unity like other nations, the German Reich today would be the master of the entire world.'

The phrase seems to have come from the chorus of a song in the Hitler Youth 'songbook':

Wir werden weiter marschieren
Wenn alles in Scherben fällt
Denn heute gehört uns Deutschland
Und morgen die ganze Welt.

Which may be roughly translated as:

We shall keep marching on
Even if everything breaks into fragments,
For today Germany belongs to us
And tomorrow the whole world.

Another version replaces the second line with '*Wenn Scheiße vom Himmel fällt*' [When shit from Heaven falls.] Sir David Hunt recalled hearing the song in 1933 or possibly 1934. By the outbreak of the Second World War, it was sufficiently well known, as John Osborne recalled in *A Better Class of Person* (1981), for an English school magazine to be declaring: 'Now soon it will be our turn to take a hand in the destinies of Empire. Today, scholars; tomorrow, the Empire.' In the 1941 British film *Forty-Ninth Parallel* Eric Portman as a German U-boat commander gets to say, 'Today, Europe . . . tomorrow the whole world!'

The construction is capable of innumerable variations. A New York graffito (reported in 1974) stated, 'Today Hollywood, tomorrow the world', and one from El Salvador (March 1982) ran: '*Ayer Nicaragua, hoy El Salvador, mañana Guatemala!* [Yesterday Nicaragua, today El Salvador, tomorrow Guatemala!]' the *Guardian* (6 July 1982) carried an advertisement with the unwieldy headline: 'Self-managing Socialism: Today, France — Tomorrow, the World?' A variation: from the black British MP Paul Boateng's victory speech in the Brent South constituency (June 1987): 'Brent South today — Soweto tomorrow!'

2 To save the town, it became necessary to destroy it.

An unnamed American major on the town of Ben Tre, Vietnam, during the Tet offensive, according to an AP dispatch published in the *New York Times* (8 February 1968). It is held up as a token of the futility of American activities in Vietnam.

3 We are the unwilling, led by the unqualified, doing the unnecessary for the ungrateful.

A slogan said to have been seen written on GI helmets in Vietnam. In the June 1980 issue of *Playboy* was a slightly different version from 'the Ninth Precinct': 'We the willing, led by the unknowing, are doing the impossible for the ungrateful. We have done so much for so long with so little, we are now qualified to do anything with nothing.' Somebody bitter about police salaries had amended the last line to read, 'To do anything for nothing'.

4 We have ways of making you talk.

The threat by an evil inquisitor to his victim appears to have come originally from 1930s Hollywood villains and was then handed on to Nazi characters from the 1940s onwards. In the film *Lives of a Bengal Lancer* (1935) Douglas Dumbrille, as the evil Mohammed Khan, said, 'We have ways of making *men* talk'. A typical 'Nazi' use can be found in the British film *Odette* (1950) when the eponymous French Resistance worker (Anna Neagle) is threatened with unmentioned nastiness by one of her captors. Says he: 'We have ways and means of making you talk.' Then, after a little stoking of the fire with a poker, he urges her on with: 'We have ways and means of making a woman talk.'

Later, used in caricature, the phrase saw further action in TV programmes like *Rowan and Martin's Laugh-In* (c 1968) when it was invariably pronounced with a German accent. Frank Muir presented a comedy series for London Weekend Television with the title *We Have Ways of Making You Laugh* (1968).

1 *The Welsh are the Italians in the rain.*

Quoted by the writer Elaine Morgan on BBC Radio *Quote . . . Unquote* (1983). An earlier version spoken, though probably not coined, by the journalist René Cutforth was: 'The Welsh are the Mediterraneans in the rain', which was quoted by Nancy Banks-Smith in the *Guardian* (17 October 1979).

2 *We who are about to die salute you.*

'*Morituri te salutant*' (literally, 'those who are . . .') were the words addressed to the Emperor by gladiators in ancient Rome on entering the arena. The practice seems to have first been mentioned in Suetonius, *Claudius*. In time, the phrase was extended to anyone facing difficulty, and then ironically so.

3 *What a wonderful bird the frog are!*
When he walk, he fly almost;
When he sing, he cry almost.
He ain't got no tail hardly, either.
He sit on what he ain't got almost.

A leading article in *The Times* on 20 May 1948 ascribed these lines to the pen of an African schoolgirl, causing one reader to write in and say he had always believed they had come from the mouth of a French Canadian. He also said he had an idea that he had first seen them in the *Manchester Guardian* 'about twenty years ago'.

The version that appears in Arnold Silcock's *Verse and Worse* (1952) is also ascribed to 'Anon (French Canadian)' and is fractionally different:

What a wonderful bird the frog are —
When he stand he sit almost;
When he hop, he fly almost.
He ain't got no sense hardly;
He ain't got no tail hardly either.
When he sit, he sit on what he ain't
got almost.

4 *When Pictures Look Alive With*
Movement Free
When Ships Like Fishes Swim
Beneath the Sea
When Men Outstripping Birds Can
Scan the Sky
Then Half the World Deep Trenched
in Blood Will Lie.

It has been said that this prophecy was 'carved on an Essex tombstone five hundred years ago'. It sounds more like a prediction by Mother Shipton, the sixteenth-century Yorkshire 'witch' or one of the nineteenth century fakers of her works. Described as 'A Prophecy . . . Anonymous, Written about AD 1400' it appears in *Junior Voices: The Fourth Book* (Penguin Education, 1970).

5 *When rape is inevitable, lie back and enjoy it.*

This is best described — as it is in Paul Scott's novel *The Jewel in the Crown* (1966) — as 'that old, disreputable saying'. Daphne Manners, upon whose 'rape' the story hinges, adds: 'I can't say, Auntie, that I lay back and enjoyed mine.' It is no more than a saying — a 'mock-Confucianism' is how Partridge/*Slang* describes it (giving a date *c* 1950) — and one is unlikely ever to learn when, or from whom, it first arose. A word of caution to anyone thinking of using it. An American broadcaster, Tex Antoine, said in 1975: 'With rape so predominant in the news lately, it is well to remember the words of Confucius: "If rape is inevitable, lie back and enjoy it".' ABC News suspended Antoine for this remark, then demoted him to working in the weather department and prohibited him from appearing on the air.

6 *Where Were You When the Lights Went Out?*

The title of a film (US 1968) inspired by the great New York blackout of 1965 when the electricity supply failed and, it was popularly believed, the birth-rate shot up nine months later. The phrase echoes an old music-hall song and/or the (American?) nonsense rhyme 'Where was Moses when the light went out?/Down in the cellar eating sauerkraut'. This last appears to have developed from the 'almost proverbial' riddle (as the Opies call it in *The Lore and Language of Schoolchildren*, 1959):

Q. Where was Moses when the light went out?
A. In the dark.

The Opies find this in *The Riddler's Oracle*, *c* 1821.

7 *Whiter than the whitewash on the wall.*

A song popular among British troops in France during the First World War was:

Oh, wash me in the water
That you washed the colonel's
daughter in
And I shall be whiter
Than the whitewash on the wall.

This would appear to be a parody of (or at least inspired by) one of the Sankey and Moody hymns, 'The Blood of the Lamb', which has the chorus:

Wash me in the Blood of the Lamb
And I shall be whiter than snow!
(Whiter than the snow!
(Whiter than the snow!)
Wash me in the Blood of the Lamb
And I shall be whiter than snow (the snow!)

1 *Willie, Willie, Harry, Stee,*
Harry, Dick, John, Harry Three.
One, Two, Three Neds, Richard Two.
Henries Four, Five, Six . . . then who?
Edward Four, Five, Dick the Bad.
Harries twain and Ned the Lad.
Mary, Bessie, James the Vain.
Charlie, Charlie, James Again.
William and Mary, Anna Gloria,
Four Georges, William and Victoria.

The mnemonic for remembering the order of the reigns of the Kings and Queens of England was probably in existence by 1900. A correspondent recalls learning it in 1933 with the additional couplet:

Edward Seventh next, and then
George the Fifth in 1910.

Further amendments were made in due course:

In '36 came Edward Eight
Who, in that year, did abdicate.

George Six followed. At his death
In '52, Elizabeth.

An American update for the reigns of Edward VIII and George VI was:

Eddie Eight went helter-skelter
Georgie reigned from a bomb-proof shelter.

Another version of the post-Victoria reigns is:

Edward Seven, George again
Edward Eight gave up his reign.

George Six, he of gentle mien
Elizabeth Two, God Save the Queen.

2 *With one bound Jack was free.*

Said now of anyone who escapes from a tricky situation or tight corner, the phrase underlines the preposterousness of the adventures in which such lines can be 'spoken' — in cartoon strips, subtitles to silent films, or from *Boy's Own Paper*-type serials of the early twentieth century in which the hero would frequently escape from seemingly impossible situations, most usually after he had been condemned to them in a 'cliff-hanger' situation. Possibly it all stems from a joke re-told in E.S. Turner, *Boys Will Be Boys* (1948): 'There is a delightful story, attributed to more than one publishing house, of the serial writer who disappears in the middle of a story. As he shows no sign of turning up, it is decided to carry on without him. Unfortunately he has left his hero bound to a stake, with lions circling him, and an avalanche about to fall for good measure (or some such situation). Relays of writers try to think of a way out, and give it up. Then at the eleventh hour the missing author returns. He takes the briefest look at the previous instalment and then, without a moment's hesitation, writes: "With one bound Jack was free".'

3 *With patience and saliva, the elephant screws the ant* [Con la patciencia et la saliva l'elephante la metio a la formiga].

A saying quoted by Valerie Bornstein in *Proverbium Yearbook of International Proverb Scholarship* (1991). The original language may have been Mexican Spanish or Catalan: it does not appear to be regular Spanish or Italian.

4 *With twenty-six soldiers of lead, I can conquer the world.*

The typographer F.W. Goudy (1865–1947) wrote in *The Type Speaks*, 'I am the leaden army that conquers the world — I am TYPE' — but he was probably re-working an old riddle. The *ODQ* (1979) finds in Hugh Rowley's *Puniana* (1867) the saying, 'With twenty-six lead soldiers [the characters of the alphabet set up for printing] I can conquer the world', and points to the (probably independently arrived at) French riddle: '*Je suis le capitaine de vingt-quatre soldats, et sans moi Paris serait pris,*' to which the answer is '*A.*' ('I am the captain of twenty-four [*sic*] soldiers and without me Paris would be taken' — remove the '*a*' from '*Paris*' and it becomes '*pris*' or 'taken'. But is the French alphabet at this time presumed to have only 24/25 letters?)

The phrase has been used as the title of a spiritual quest book, *Twenty-Six Lead Soldiers*, by Dan Wooding (1987): 'A top Fleet Street journalist and his search for the truth . . .' Wooding attributes the saying to 'Karl Marx or Benjamin Franklin'.

1 *Women's faults are many*
Men have only two:
Everything they say
And everything they do.

The observation regarding quotations or jokes that there is always an earlier example if only you can find it, is particularly true of graffiti. The rash of feminist graffiti of the 1970s (spreading in time to T-shirts, buttons, and so on) produced this popular verse. How ironic, therefore, that Mencken (1942) has this well-documented rhyme from the eighteenth century — and note the change of gender:

> We men have many faults:
> Poor women have but two —
> There's nothing good they say,
> There's nothing good they do.
>
> *Anon.*: 'On Women's Faults' (1727)

2 *Work hard, play hard, Xenophon was a Greek, use your toothbrush daily, hack no furniture.*

Said to have been embroidered on a cushion cover in the house of the publisher, Sir Rupert Hart-Davis. A number of correspondents recognized the phrases as coming from the 'copy books' that schoolchildren once used to practise their handwriting. These consisted of lines of printed copperplate writing interspersed with blank lines for the child to write on. One correspondent said she remembered these from her own schooldays *c* 1925 and said the books were still in print in 1948. Another noted, 'The phrases were quite random — chosen, I imagine, to fit the space available and/ or to give the child the opportunity of practising different combinations of letters . . . The compiler must have had quite a sense of humour to juxtapose such phrases — it certainly amused my husband (who was born in 1917) or he would hardly have remembered it from his early childhood.'

Anouilh, Jean
French playwright (1910–87)

3 *Ring Round the Moon.*

Christopher Fry's adaptation of Anouilh's play *L'Invitation au château* [The Invitation to the Castle/Château] was first performed in 1950 (following the Paris production of 1947). The English title alludes to the pro- verb 'Ring around the moon, brings a storm soon' (sometimes, '. . . rain comes soon'). This is a modern version of 'When round the moon there is a brugh [halo], the weather will be cold and rough' (*ODP* has it by 1631).

Archelaus
King of Macedonia (reigned 413–399BC)

4 *In silence.*

His reply when asked by a barber how he would like his hair cut. Quoted by W. & A. Durant in *The Story of Civilization* (1935–64) Possibly said, rather, by a successor, Philip II.

Archilochus
Greek poet (*fl.* seventh century BC)

5 *The fox knows many things — the hedgehog one* big *thing.*

A somewhat obscure opinion, but see how it is used by Isaiah Berlin in his book called *The Hedgehog and the Fox* (1953): 'There exists a great chasm between those, on one side, who relate everything to a single central vision . . . and, on the other side, those who pursue many ends, often unrelated and even contradictory . . . The first kind of intellectual and artistic personality belongs to the hedgehogs, the second to the foxes.'

Arendt, Hannah
German-born American philosopher (1906–75)

6 *It was as though in those last minutes he was summing up the lessons that this long course in human wickedness had taught us — the lesson of the fearsome, word-and-thought-defying banality of evil.*

The final phrase was Arendt's key observation when writing about the trial of Adolf Eichmann, the Nazi official who was executed as a war criminal by Israel in 1962. Her book *Eichmann in Jerusalem* (1963) was subtitled 'A Report on the Banality of Evil'. Her essay was controversial in arguing that Europe's Jews might have been complicit in their own destruction and that Eichmann was not an abnormal monster but a mechanical one, unable to pit a personal morality against the Nazi system.

Arens, Richard
American lawyer (1913–69)

1 *Are you now or have you ever been a member of a godless conspiracy controlled by a foreign power?*

Quoted in Peter Lewis, *The Fifties* (1978), this is Arens's version of the more usual question, 'Are you now or have you ever been a member of the Communist Party?', put to those appearing at hearings of the House of Representatives Committee on UnAmerican Activities (1947–c 1957), especially by J. Parnell Thomas. It was the stock phrase of McCarthyism, the pursuit and public ostracism of suspected US Communist sympathizers at the time of the war with Korea in the early 1950s. Senator Joseph McCarthy was the instigator of the 'witch hunts', which led to the blacklisting of people in various walks of life, notably the film business. *Are You Now Or Have You Ever Been?* was the title of a radio/stage play (1978) by Eric Bentley.

Arkell, Reginald
English poet (1882–1959)

2 *There is a lady, sweet and kind*
As any lady you will find.
I've known her nearly all my life;
She is, in fact, my present wife.

In daylight, she is kind to all,
But, as the evening shadows fall,
With jam-pot, salt and sugar-tongs
She starts to right her garden's wrongs.

An extract from Arkell's poem 'The Lady with the Lamp', which appeared in his *Green Fingers* (1934). 'There is a lady sweet and kind' is also the first line of a poem attributed to Thomas Ford (*d* 1648).

Arkwright, Sir John S.
English lawyer and poet (1872–1954)

3 *O valiant hearts, who to your glory came*
Through dust of conflict and through battle flame;
Tranquil you lie, your knightly virtue proved,
Your memory hallowed in the land you loved.

Proudly you gathered, rank on rank, to war,
As who had heard God's message from afar;
All you had hoped for, all you had, you gave
To save mankind — yourselves you scorned to save.

In the 1950s this moving hymn suffered a backlash and was dropped from Remembrance Day services by those who believed it was insufficiently critical of militarism. But how could it have been? From Arkwright's collection entitled 'The Supreme Sacrifice and Other Poems in Time of War' (1919).

The *OED2*'s earliest citation for the phrase 'supreme sacrifice' which, alas, became a cliché for death, is 1916.

Armstrong, Neil
American astronaut (1930–)

4 *That's one small step for a man, one giant leap for mankind.*

Armstrong claimed that this was what he actually said when stepping on to the moon's surface for the first time at 10.56 p.m. (EDT) on 20 July 1969. Six hundred million television viewers round the world watched, but what were his first words going to be? It seemed to him that every person he had met in the previous three months had asked him what he was going to say or had made suggestions. Among the hundreds of sayings he was offered were passages from Shakespeare and whole chapters from the Bible.

'I had thought about what I was going to say, largely because so many people had asked me to think about it,' Armstrong reflected afterwards in *First on the Moon* (1970). 'I thought about [it] a little bit on the way to the moon, and it wasn't really decided until after we got to the lunar surface. I guess I hadn't actually decided what I wanted to say until just before we went out.'

What the six hundred million *heard* was another matter. The indefinite article before 'man' was completely inaudible, thus ruining the nice contrast between 'a man' (one individual) and 'mankind' (all of us). However, this was how the line was first reported and, indeed, exactly how it sounds on recordings. There is no perceptible gap between 'for' and 'man'.

It is probably the most misheard remark

ever. *The Times* of 21 July had it as: 'That's one small step for man but [*sic*] one giant leap for mankind.' The *Observer* 'Sayings of the Week' column on the Sunday following the landing had: 'That's one small step for man, one giant leap for all [*sic*] mankind'. And reference books have continued the confusion ever since. Several follow the version — 'One small step for [. . .] man, one big step [*sic*] for mankind' — which appeared in the magazine *Nature* in 1974.

When he returned to earth, the astronaut spotted the near-tautology in a transcript of the mission and tried to put over a correct version. It was explained that the indefinite article 'a' had not been heard because of static on the radio link or because 'tape recorders are fallible'. But it is just as possible that Armstrong fluffed his mighty line. If the twentieth-century's most *audible* saying could result in such confusion, what hope is there for the rest?

Whatever the case, Armstrong launched an imperishable format. Here is but one example of it in use: 'SMALL STEP FOR NON-WHITE MANKIND' (*The Times*, 29 October 1983). The pronouncement has also been set to music. The Great Mormon Tabernacle Choir sing:

One small step for a man, one giant leap for mankind. It shows what a man can do, if he has the will.

And what's more, they get it right.

An unconfirmed recollection received is that a member of NASA said in an interview that the original author of the phrase was Wernher von Braun, the former German rocket scientist, who gave it to Armstrong as a suitably resonant line to say on landing. Armstrong, however, makes no mention of this in the work cited above.

1 *The Eagle has landed.*

The Apollo XI space mission that first put a man on the surface of the moon in July 1969 provided another phrase in addition to — and before — Armstrong's famous first words (above). As the lunar module touched down, he announced: 'Tranquillity Base here — the Eagle has landed.' Nobody at Mission Control had known that Armstrong would call it that, although the name was logical enough: the landing area was in the Sea of Tranquillity; 'Eagle' was the name of the craft (referring to the American national symbol).

Confusingly, the writer Jack Higgins later used the phrase *The Eagle Has Landed* as the title of a 1975 thriller about a German

kidnap attempt on Winston Churchill during the Second World War.

The *ODQ* (1992), basing itself on an inaccurate report in *The Times*, has the line delivered by Buzz Aldrin.

Armstrong, Sir Robert
(later Lord Armstrong)
English civil servant (1927–)

2 *Economical with the truth.*

On 18 November 1986 Armstrong, then the British Cabinet Secretary, was being cross-examined in the Supreme Court of New South Wales. The British Government was attempting to prevent publication in Australia of a book about MI5, the British secret service. Defence counsel Malcolm Turnbull asked Sir Robert about the contents of a letter he had written which had been intended to convey a misleading impression. 'What's a "misleading impression"?' inquired Turnbull. 'A sort of bent untruth?'

Sir Robert replied: 'It is perhaps being economical with the truth'. This explanation was greeted with derision not only in the court but in the world beyond, and it looked as if a new euphemism for lying had been coined. In fact, Sir Robert had prefaced his remark with: 'As one person said . . .' and, when the court apparently found cause for laughter in what he said, added: 'It is not very original, I'm afraid.'

Indeed not. Dr E.H.H. Green, writing to the *Guardian* on 4 February 1987, said he had found a note penned by Sir William Strang, later to become head of the Foreign Office, in February 1942. Describing the character of the exiled Czech President Beneš, Strang had written: 'Dr Beneš's methods are exasperating; he is a master of representation and . . . he is apt to be economical with the truth.'

The notion thus appears to have been a familiar one in the British Civil Service for a very long time — and not only there. Mark Twain said in *Pudd'nhead Wilson's New Calendar* (1897 version), 'Truth is the most valuable thing we have. Let us economize it.' And before him, Edmund Burke remarked, 'We practise an economy of truth that we may live to tell it the longer.'

In March 1988 Armstrong said in a TV interview that he had no regrets about having used the phrase. And he said again, it was not his own, indeed, but Edmund Burke's. The reference was to Burke's *Two*

Letters on Proposals for Peace (1796): 'Falsehood and delusion are allowed in no case whatsoever. But, as in the exercise of all the virtues, there is an economy of truth.'

Three other citations came to light about the same time: Rudyard Kipling in the short story 'Private Cooper' in *Traffics & Discoveries* (1904) had: 'Private Cooper thought for a moment of a faraway housemaid who might, if the local postman had not gone too far, be interested in his fate. On the other hand, he was, by temperament, economical of the truth.' Arnold Bennett in *These Twain*, Chap. 17 (1915) has: 'The boy was undoubtedly crafty; he could conceal subtle designs under a simple exterior; he was also undoubtedly secretive. The recent changes in his disposition had put Edwin and Hilda on their guard, and every time young George displayed cunning, or economized the truth, or lied, the fear visited them.' And Samuel Pepys apparently used the precise phrase in his evidence before the Brooke House Committee in its examination of the Navy Board in 1669–70 (Pepysian MSS. 2874, ff.388–90).

Arno, Peter
American cartoonist (1904–68)

1 *Well, back to the old drawing board.*

In the form 'back to the drawing board' this means 'we've got to start again from scratch' and is usually said after an earlier plan has ended in failure. It is just possible that this began life in the caption to Arno's cartoon which appeared in *The New Yorker* during the early 1940s (exact date unknown). An official, with a rolled-up engineering plan under his arm, is walking away from a recently crashed plane and saying this.

Arnold, Matthew
English poet and essayist (1822–88)

2 *A God, a God their severance ruled!*
And bade betwixt their shores to be
The unplumb'd, salt, estranging sea.

From Arnold's poem 'To Marguerite — Continued' (1852). The last sentence of *The French Lieutenant's Woman* (1969) by John Fowles (unattributed at that point, though it has been earlier) is: 'And out again, upon the unplumb'd, salt, estranging sea.'

Asquith, H.H.
(later 1st Earl of Oxford and Asquith)
British Liberal Prime Minister (1852–1928)

3 *You had better wait and see.*

To a persistent inquirer about the Parliament Act Procedure Bill, in the House of Commons, 4 April 1910. In fact, this was the fourth occasion on which Asquith had said 'Wait and see'. On 3 March he had replied to Lord Helmsey concerning the Government's intentions over the Budget and whether the House of Lords would be flooded with Liberal peers to ensure the passage of the Finance Bill: 'We had better wait and see.' So he was clearly deliberate in his use of the words. His intention was not to delay making an answer but to warn people off. Roy Jenkins commented in *Asquith* (1964): 'It was a use for which he was to pay dearly in the last years of his premiership when the phrase came to be erected by his enemies as a symbol of his alleged inactivity.'

In consequence, Asquith acquired the nickname 'Old Wait and See', and during the First World War French matches which failed to ignite were known either as 'Asquiths' or 'Wait and sees'.

4 *[Balliol men are distinguished from lesser souls by their] tranquil consciousness of effortless superiority.*

This is the version of Asquith's remark given by John Jones in his *Balliol College: A History 1263–1939*. Frances Bennion wrote to *Oxford Today* (Hilary Term 1992) to point out that the British Labour politician Denis Healey — an old member of the college — had misquoted this in his memoirs, *The Time of My Life* (1989), as, 'the conscious tranquillity of effortless superiority'. Which is not quite the same thing.

5 *Another Little Drink Wouldn't Do Us Any Harm.*

The boozer's jocular justification for another snort is, in fact, rather more than a catchphrase. It is alluded to in Edith Sitwell's bizarre lyrics for 'Scotch Rhapsody' in *Façade* (1922):

There is a hotel at Ostend
Cold as the wind, without an end,
Haunted by ghostly poor relations . . .

33

And 'Another little drink wouldn't do
us any harm,'
Pierces through the sabbatical calm.

The actual origin is in a song with the phrase as title, written by Clifford Grey to music by Nat D. Ayer, and sung by the comedian George Robey in *The Bing Boys Are Here* (1916). The song includes a reference to the well-known fact that Prime Minister Asquith was at times the worse for drink when on the Treasury Bench:

Mr Asquith says in a manner sweet
and calm:
And another little drink wouldn't do
us any harm.

Asquith, Margot
(later Countess of Oxford and
Asquith)

Wife of H.H. Asquith (1864–1945)

1 *My dear old friend King George V
always told me he would never have
died but for that vile doctor, Lord
Dawson of Penn.*

An observation by Lady Asquith, made several times in her old age, but especially to Lord David Cecil (and recorded first by Mark Bonham Carter in his introduction to *The Autobiography of Margot Asquith*, 1962 edition), turns out to be not so preposterous as might appear. On 20 January 1936, King George V lay dying at Sandringham. At 9.25 p.m., Lord Dawson of Penn, the King's doctor, issued a bulletin 'The King's life is moving peacefully towards its close' (see DAWSON 115:2). This was taken up by the BBC and repeated until the King died at 11.55 p.m.

In December 1986, Dawson's biographer suggested in *History Today* that the doctor had in fact hastened the King's departure with lethal injections of morphine and cocaine at the request of the Queen and the future Edward VIII. Dawson's notes reveal that the death was induced at 11 p.m. not only to ease the King's pain but to enable the news to make the morning papers, 'rather than the less appropriate evening journals'. *The Times* was advised that important news was coming and to hold back publication. So Dawson of Penn *might* have had a hand in the King's death, though quite how George V communicated his view of the matter to Margot Asquith is not known.

2 *The 't' is silent — as in 'Harlow'.*

Margot Asquith was noted for the sharp remarks she made about people but I am going to suggest that her most famous shaft was said by someone else in a notable demonstration of my two laws of quotation.

The story goes — and I first heard it *c* 1968 — that Margot Asquith went on a visit to the United States (*that* is not in dispute) where she met Jean Harlow. The film actress inquired whether the name of the Countess (which she was by this time, the 1930s) was pronounced 'Margo' or 'Margott'. ' "Margo",' replied the Countess, 'the "T" is silent — as in "Harlow".'

The story did not appear in print until T.S. Matthews's *Great Tom* in 1973. Then, in about 1983, a much more convincing version of its origin was given to me. Margot *Grahame* (1911–82) was an English actress who, after stage appearances in Johannesburg and London, went to Hollywood in 1934. Her comparatively brief career as a film star included appearances in *The Informer*, *The Buccaneer* and *The Three Musketeers* in the mid-1930s.

It was when she was being built up as a rival to the likes of Harlow (who died in 1937) that Grahame herself claimed the celebrated exchange had occurred. She added that it was not intended as a put-down. She did not realize what she had said until afterwards.

Grahame seems a convincing candidate for speaker of the famous line. When her star waned people attributed the remark to the other, better known and more quotable source.

3 *Kitchener is a great poster.*

A remark often attributed to Margot, but in *More Memories*, Chap. 6 (1933) she ascribed it to her daughter Elizabeth (1897–1945).

Astley, Sir Jacob
English soldier (1579–1652)

4 *O Lord! Thou knowest how busy I must
be this day: if I forget thee, do not Thou
forget me.*

Astley was a Royalist in the English Civil War and was hurt at the Battle of Edgehill (13 October 1642), the indecisive first engagement of the Civil War. His prayer before the battle was quoted in Sir Philip Warwick's *Memoirs* (1701). It was not said *by* Warwick, as given in Celia Haddon, *The Yearbook of Comfort and Joy* (1991).

Attlee, Clement
(later 1st Earl Attlee)
British Labour Prime Minister (1883–1967)

1 *You have no right whatever to speak on behalf of the Government. Foreign Affairs are in the capable hands of Ernest Bevin. His task is quite sufficiently difficult without the embarrassment of irresponsible statements of the kind which you are making . . . a period of silence on your part would be welcome.*

Quoted in *British Political Facts 1900–75.* From a letter to Harold Laski, Chairman of the Labour Party NEC (20 August 1945). Just after the Labour Government had come to power, Laski had been giving a constant flow of speeches and interviews, not always in accord with party policy. The put-down was typical of Attlee's clipped way and also reflected his own more reticent way with words.

Auden, W.H.
Anglo-American poet (1907–73)

2 *Look, Stranger!*

The use of Auden's phrase as the title of a BBC TV documentary series (1976) revealed an interesting state of affairs. Auden's famous poem has two versions of its first line: 'Look, stranger, at this island now' and '. . . on this island now'. 'At' is the original reading in the title poem of the collection *Look, Stranger!* published in the UK (1936). But the US title of the collection was *On This Island.* The text of the poem was changed to 'on' for the 1945 *Collected Poems*, published in the US. Just to complicate matters, the poem's title was changed variously to 'Seascape' and 'Seaside'.
   The reason for all this is that publishers Faber & Faber (in the person of T.S. Eliot) applied the title *Look, Stranger!* to the collection that Auden wanted called 'Poems 1936', when he was inaccessible in Iceland. He said the Faber title sounded 'like the work of a vegetarian lady novelist' and made sure that it was subsequently dropped.

3 *My face looks like a wedding-cake left out in the rain.*

No, it was not said *about* Auden (as stated, for example, in L. Levinson, *Bartlett's Unfamiliar Quotations*). The poet himself said to a reporter: 'Your cameraman might enjoy himself, because my face looks like a wedding-cake left out in the rain' (cited in Humphrey Carpenter, *W.H. Auden*, 1981). However, according to Noel Annan in *Maurice Bowra: a celebration* (1974), Bowra once referred to E.M. Forster's *work* as a wedding-cake left out in the rain.

4 *There is no such thing as the State*
And no one exists alone;
Hunger allows no choice
To the citizen or the police;
We must love one another or die.

Auden became embarrassed by the last line of his poem 'September 1, 1939' ('the most dishonest poem I have ever written') because it was 'a damned lie' — we must die in any case. When the editor of a 1955 anthology pleaded with Auden to include the entire text of the poem, Auden agreed provided that 'We must love one another *and* die' was substituted.

5 *In the prison of his days*
Teach the free man how to praise.

On the memorial slab to Auden in Poets' Corner, Westminster Abbey, is a quotation taken from his elegy on Yeats. The memorial was unveiled on 2 October 1974. Auden is actually buried at Kirchstetten, Austria.

Augier, Émile
French poet and playwright (1820–89)

6 La nostalgie de la boue [*Longing to be back in the mud*].

In the play *Le Mariage d'Olympe* (1855), Augier gave this as an explanation of what happens when you put a duck on a lake with swans. He will miss his own pond and eventually return to it. Taken up in many situations where there is a desire for degradation. At the very end of D.H. Lawrence's *Lady Chatterley's Lover* (1928), Sir Clifford says to Lady Connie: 'You're one of those half-insane, perverted women who must run after depravity, the *nostalgie de la boue*.'

Augustine of Hippo, Saint
North African Christian theologian
(354–430AD)

1 *A stiff prick hath no conscience.*

Quoted confidently by John Osborne in *Almost a Gentleman* (1991), this remark remains unverified, though it would not be surprising given Augustine's interesting activities prior to conversion (Compare 'Give me chastity and continency — but not yet!' from his *Confessions*, 397–8AD.)

Austen, Jane
English novelist (1775–1817)

2 *Pride and Prejudice.*

The title of her novel (written as *First Impressions*, 1797, published 1813) has been said to derive from the second chapter of Edward Gibbon's *The Decline and Fall of the Roman Empire* (published 1776). Writing of the enfranchisement of the slaves, Gibbon says: 'Without destroying the distinction of ranks a distant prospect of freedom and honours was presented, even to those whom pride and prejudice almost disdained to number among the human species.'
More to the point, the phrase occurs no fewer than three times, in bold print, towards the end of Fanny Burney's *Cecilia* (1787): '"The whole of this unfortunate business," said Dr Lyster, "has been the result of Pride and Prejudice . . . Yet this, however, remember; if to Pride and Prejudice you owe your miseries, so wonderfully is good and evil balanced, that to Pride and Prejudice you will also owe their termination".' This seems the most likely cue to Jane Austen. On the other hand, *OED2* provides six citations of the phrase 'pride and prejudice' before Burney, one of which has capital Ps.

Austin, Alfred
English Poet Laureate (1835–1913)

3 *Flash'd from his bed the electric tidings came,*
'He is not better, he is much the same.'

Lines often ascribed to Austin, as in A. & V. Palmer, *Quotations in History* (1976), and sometimes remembered as 'Across/along the electric wire the message came . . .' The couplet is often quoted as an example of bathos and of a Poet Laureate writing to order at his worst. As such, it needs some qualification, if not an actual apology to the poet's shade. D.B. Wyndham Lewis and Charles Lee in their noted selection of bad verse, *The Stuffed Owl* (1930), interestingly included a similar couplet, but ascribed it to a 'university poet unknown', and quite right, too. F.H. Gribble had included the slightly different version, 'Along the electric wire . . .' in his *Romance of the Cambridge Colleges* (1913).
What is not in dispute is that the lines were written to mark the Prince of Wales's illness in 1871. Unfortunately, to spoil a good story, it has to be pointed out that Austin never wrote them (though he *did* match them in awfulness on other occasions) and he did not become Poet Laureate until 1896, following in the illustrious footsteps of Tennyson. As J. Lewis May observed in *The Dublin Review* (July 1937), in an article about Austin as 'a neglected poet', the couplet was written 'when the then Prince of Wales (he who afterwards became King Edward VII) had recovered from the attack of typhoid fever which had caused the gravest anxiety throughout the country, [and] the subject set for the Newdigate Prize Poem at Oxford was "The Prince of Wales's illness"; whereupon some wag, with consequences of which he never dreamed, produced the following couplet, as a specimen of the sort of thing that might be sent in by competitors for the coveted guerdon . . . The name of the inventor of those immortal lines has not been handed down.'
The Editor of *The Author* (Spring 1993) questioned whether Austin had really attracted 'universal derision' (my phrase) because of his supposed authorship of the lines. To which I replied that, almost invariably, Austin was linked to them, with or without an 'attributed to' or other qualification, in such dictionaries of quotations as the *PDQ* (1960), the *Bloomsbury* (1987) and Robin Hyman's *Dictionary of Famous Quotations* (1962). Even the *ODQ* (1992) *mentions* Austin, although it places the couplet under 'Anonymous'.
As for Austin generally, Mrs Claude Bettington recalled in *All That I Have Met* (1929) that he had said to her in all seriousness one day, 'My child, have you ever noticed how many great men are called *Alfred* — Alfred the Great, Alfred Tennyson?' As a dutiful neice, she added, 'And *you*, Uncle Alf.' Mrs Bettington goes on: 'No one could fathom why he was made Poet Laureate, since his only claim to fame was his exquisite prose. I therefore asked a

neice of Lord Salisbury point blank, "Why on earth did your uncle give the laureateship to Uncle Alfred?" She answered, "Because it was absolutely the only honour Mr Austin would accept from the Government for his long years of service to the Conservative cause".'

Axelrod, George
American screenwriter (1922–   )

1 The Seven Year Itch.

His term for the urge to be unfaithful to a spouse after a certain period of matrimony. The *OED2* provides various examples of this phrase going back from the mid-twentieth to the mid-nineteenth century, but without the specific matrimonial context. For example, the 'seven year itch' describes a rash from poison ivy which was believed to recur every year for a seven-year period. Then one has to recall that since biblical days seven-year periods (of lean or fat) have had especial significance, and there has also been the army saying, 'Cheer up — the first seven years are the worst!'

But the specific matrimonial application was not popularized until used as the title of George Axelrod's play (1952) and then film (1955). 'Itch' had long been used for the sexual urge but, as Axelrod commented on BBC Radio *Quote . . . Unquote* (1979): 'There was a phrase which referred to a somewhat unpleasant disease but nobody had used it in a sexual [I think he meant 'matrimonial'] context before. I do believe I invented it in that sense.'

Oddly, there is no mention in reference books of 'itch' being used in connection with venereal diseases. Nonetheless, the following remark occurs in Robert Lewis Taylor, *W.C. Fields: His Follies and Fortunes* (published as early as 1950): 'Bill exchanged women every seven years, as some people get rid of the itch.'

B

Bacon, Francis
(1st Baron Verulam and Viscount St Albans)
English philosopher and statesman (1561–1626)

1 *If the mountain won't come to Mahomet, Mahomet must go to the mountain.*

What Bacon actually wrote in 'On Boldness', one of his *Essays* (1625) where the proverb made its first appearance, was: 'If the hill will not come to Mahomet, Mahomet will go to the hill.'

Bacon, Francis
Irish painter (1909–92)

2 *Three Screaming Popes.*

This is not the title of any painting by Bacon but of a musical work inspired by his three paintings of Popes which, in turn, were based on the Velásquez portrait 'Pope Innocent X'. The English composer Mark-Anthony Turnage (1960–), whose orchestral work with the title was first performed in 1989, says his initial idea was 'to write a piece which distorted a set of Spanish dances as Bacon had distorted and restated the Velásquez'. Bacon's paintings tend to be referred to drily along the lines of 'Study after Velásquez's Portrait of Pope Innocent X' (1953).

See also WERTENBAKER 350:4.

Baden-Powell, Sir Robert
(later 1st Baron Baden-Powell)
English soldier (1857–1941)

3 *Be prepared.*

The motto of the Boy Scout movement shares its initials with those of its founder (who was often referred to by its members as 'B-P'). The words first appeared in the handbook *Scouting for Boys* (1908) and mean that Scouts should always be 'in a state of readiness in mind and body' to do their duty. Winston Churchill wrote in *Great Contemporaries* (1937): 'It is difficult to exaggerate the moral and mental health which our nation had derived from this profound and simple conception. In those bygone days the motto Be Prepared had a special meaning for our country. Those who looked to the coming of a great war welcomed the awakening of British boyhood.'

With permission, the words were subsequently used as an advertising slogan for Pears' soap.

Bailey, Sydney D.
English writer (1916–)

4 *It has been said that this minister [the Lord Privy Seal] is neither a Lord, nor a privy, nor a seal.*

In his book *British Parliamentary Democracy* (3rd ed., 1971). The *ODMQ* (1991) curiously elevates Bailey to the status of originator for this joke when it is obvious that even he is not claiming it. The observation was already widely known, not least from its use on BBC TV's *The Frost Report* (1966–7).

Bairnsfather, Bruce
British cartoonist (1888–1959)

5 *Well, if you knows of a better 'ole, go to it.*

This comes from the caption to a cartoon published in *Fragments from France* (1915) depicting the gloomy soldier 'Old Bill', sitting on a shell crater in the mud on the

Somme during the First World War. The cartoon series was enormously popular. A musical (London, 1917; New York, 1918) and two films (UK, 1918; US, 1926), based on the strip, all had the title *The Better 'Ole.*

Baker, Howard
American Republican politician (1925–   )

1 *What did the President know, and when did he know it?*

At the US Senate Watergate Committee hearings during the summer of 1973, Baker, the vice-chairman — an earnest lawmaker from Tennessee — became famous when he framed this essential question about Richard Nixon. He repeated it several times and the answer led to Nixon's downfall.

Baldwin, James
American novelist (1924–87)

2 *The Fire Next Time.*

The title of Baldwin's novel (1963) is explained in the concluding sentence: 'If we do not now dare everything, the fulfilment of that prophecy, re-created from the Bible in song by a slave, is upon us: *God gave Noah the rainbow sign, No more water, the fire next time!*' As a warning of the use of fire in racial clashes it anticipated 'Burn, baby, burn!', the Black extremist slogan used following the August 1965 riots in the Watts district of Los Angeles, when entire blocks were burned down and thirty-four people killed.

Baldwin, Monica
English writer (c 1896–1975)

3 *I Leap Over the Wall.*

This book (1949) described 'a return to the world after twenty-eight years in a convent'. The author traced the title to a Baldwin family motto, *Per Deum Meum Transilio Murum* ('By the help of my God I leap over the wall'), which derived from the escape of an earlier Baldwin: 'Nearly 400 years ago, my ancestor Thomas Baldwin of Diddlesbury leaped to freedom from behind the walls of the Tower of London . . . His name with an inscription and the date "July 1585" can still be seen where he carved it on the wall of his cell in the Beauchamp Tower.' He added the motto to his arms and it was taken

up again by Stanley Baldwin when he took his Earldom. There may be an echo in it, too, of 2 Samuel 22:30, 'By my God have I leaped over a wall.'

Noël Coward in his published diary mentions having read Monica Baldwin's book and gives this critical comment: 'Very interesting, I must say. It has strengthened my decision not to become a nun.'

Baldwin, Stanley
(later 1st Earl Baldwin of Bewdley)
British Conservative Prime Minister (1867–1947)

4 *They are a lot of hard-faced men . . . who look as if they had done well out of the war.*

The members of the House of Commons who had been returned in the 1918 General Election were so described by a 'Conservative politician', according to John Maynard Keynes, the economist, in *The Economic Consequences of Peace* (1919). Baldwin is taken to be the one who said it. In his biography (1969) by Keith Middlemas and John Barnes, Baldwin is also quoted as having noted privately on 12 February 1918: 'We have started with the new House of Commons. They look much as usual — not so young as I had expected. The prevailing type is a rather successful-looking business kind which is not very attractive.'

The playwright Julian Mitchell, surveying the members of Mrs Thatcher's government in 1987 remarked that they looked like 'hard-faced men who had done well out of the peace'.

5 *Power without responsibility, the prerogative of the harlot.*

Attacking the press lords during a by-election campaign in London (18 March 1931), Baldwin said: 'The papers conducted by Lord Rothermere and Lord Beaverbrook are not newspapers in the ordinary acceptance of the term. They are engines of propaganda, for the constantly changing policies, desires, personal wishes, personal likes and dislikes of two men . . . What the proprietorship of these papers is aiming at is power, and power without responsibility — the prerogative of the harlot throughout the ages.'

Baldwin's cousin, Rudyard Kipling, had originated the remark many years previously. He had also already used them in argument with Beaverbrook. It is often mis-quoted: in Frank S. Pepper, *Handbook of 20th Century Quotations* (1984), it is given as 'the privilege of the harlot'. There are also those who would say that it is not actually the harlot who has the power without the responsibility — it is the harlot's customer. Harold Macmillan recalled that his father-in-law, the Duke of Devonshire, exclaimed at this point in Baldwin's speech: 'Good God, that's done it, he's lost us the tarts' vote.'

1 My lips are sealed.

In a debate in the House of Commons on the Abyssinia crisis (10 December 1935), what Baldwin actually said was: 'I shall be but a short time tonight. I have seldom spoken with greater regret, for my lips are not yet unsealed.' In the speech, he was playing for time with what, he admitted, was one of the stupidest things he had ever said. The car-toonist Low portrayed him for weeks after-wards with sticking plaster over his lips.

Meaning 'I am not giving anything away', and deriving originally perhaps, from the expression to seal up *another* person's lips or mouth, to prevent betrayal of a secret, the *OED2* has the expression by 1782.

2 I put before the whole House my own view with appalling frankness . . . sup-posing I had gone to the country and said . . . that we must rearm, does anybody think that this pacific demo-cracy would have rallied to that cry at that moment? I cannot think of any-thing that would have made the loss of the election from my point of view more certain.

Baldwin made an astonishing admission to the House of Commons on 12 November 1936. Winston Churchill had reproached him for failing to keep his pledge that parity should be maintained against air forces within striking distance of British soil. Why had this happened? Churchill commented on the reply in *The Second World War*, Vol. 1 (1948): 'This was indeed appalling frankness. It carried naked truth about his motives into indecency. That a prime minister should avow that he had not done his duty in regard to national safety because he was afraid of losing the election was an incident without parallel in our Parliamen-tary history.' G.M. Young wrote: 'Never I suppose in our history has a statesman used

a phrase so fatal to his own good name and at the same time, so wholly unnecessary, so incomprehensible.'

In *Baldwin* (1969), Keith Middlemas and John Barnes are at pains to assert that these judgements were made very much after the event and that the speech did not set off a horrified reaction at the time.

3 Once I leave, I leave. I am not going to speak to the man on the bridge, and I am not going to spit on the deck.

Statement to the Cabinet (28 May 1937) later released to the press, when Baldwin stepped down, flushed with success over his handling of the Abdication crisis. Earlier, on his inauguration as Rector of Edinburgh University in 1925, Baldwin had expressed a view of the limitations on the freedom of a former Prime Minister in similar terms: 'A sailor does not spit on the deck, thereby strengthening his control and saving un-necessary work for someone else; nor does he speak to the man at the wheel, thereby leaving him to devote his whole time to his task and increasing the probability of the ship arriving at or near her destination.' When Harold Wilson resigned as Prime Minister, he quoted Baldwin's 'Once I leave . . .' words in his own statement to the Cabinet (16 March 1976), also later released to the press.

Balfour, Arthur (later 1st Earl of Balfour)
British Conservative Prime Minister (1848–1930)

4 His Majesty's Government looks with favour upon the establishment in Pales-tine of a national home for the Jewish people.

Although Balfour had been Prime Minister (1902–5), he became Foreign Secretary in Lloyd George's wartime cabinet. Just before the British army in Palestine took Jerusalem in 1917, Balfour sought to curry favour with Jews in the United States and Central Europe by promising that Palestine should become a national home for the Jews and issued what has become known as the Balfour Declaration on 2 November 1917. This acted as a spur to Zionism and paved the way for the founding of the modern state of Israel in 1948. The declaration was con-tained in a letter addressed to the 2nd Lord Rothschild, a leader of British Jewry. The ambiguous rider was: 'Nothing shall be done which may prejudice the civil and religious rights of existing non-Jewish communities in Palestine.'

1 *Nothing matters very much and very few things matter at all.*

An attributed remark, unverified. Compare what Bishop Creighton (1843–1901) said when reassuring an anxious seeker after truth, that it was 'almost impossible to exaggerate the complete unimportance of everything' – quoted in *The Lyttelton Hart-Davis Letters* (for 2 May 1956).

Bankhead, Tallulah
American actress (1903–68)

2 *There's less in this than meets the eye.*

A frequently employed critical witticism derives its modern popularity from the use made of the words by Bankhead to Alexander Woollcott about the play *Aglavaine and Selysette* by Maurice Maeterlinck on 3 January 1922. However, in his journal, James Boswell attributed a version to Richard Burke, son of Edmund (1 May 1783): 'I suppose here *less* is meant than meets the ear.'

Barnum, P.T.
American showman (1810–91)

3 *There's a sucker born every minute.*

There is no evidence that Barnum ever used this exprssion – not least, it is said, because 'sucker' was not a common term in his day. He did, however, express the view that, 'The people like to be humbugged', which conveys the same idea. There was also a song of the period, 'There's a New Jay Born Every Day' (jay = gullible hick). By whatever route, Barnum took the attribution.

Barrie, Sir James
Scottish playwright (1860–1937)

4 Floreat Etona [*May Eton flourish*].

This is the motto of Eton College (founded 1440) in Berkshire. It is spoken by the villain 'Captain Hook' (presumably an Old Etonian), just before he is eaten by a crocodile in Barrie's play *Peter Pan* (1904). (In the novel version, *Peter Pan and Wendy*, 1911, he merely cries, 'Bad form'.) It was earlier used as the title of a painting (1882) by Elizabeth, Lady Butler depicting an attack on Laing's Neck (against the Boers in South Africa, 1881), after this eye-witness account: 'Poor Elwes fell among the 58th. He shouted to another Eton boy (adjutant of the 58th, whose horse had been shot) "Come along, Monck! Floreat Etona! we must be in the front rank!" and he was shot immediately.'

5 *Without Drums or Trumpets.*

There is a story told about Barrie's advice to a young writer who did not know what title to give his work. 'Are there any trumpets in it?' Barrie asked, and got the answer 'No'. 'Are there any drums in it?' he asked. 'No.' 'Then why not call it *Without Drums or Trumpets*?' Untraced. A similar story is told about the French playwright, Tristan Bernard (1866–1947) in Cornelia Otis Skinner's *Elegant Wits and Grand Horizontals* (1962). Somebody did take the advice: the English translation of Alec Le Vernoy's Second World War memoir was entitled *No Drums – No Trumpets* (1983).

Baruch, Bernard
American financier (1870–1965)

6 *Let us not be deceived – we are today in the midst of a cold war.*

The final phrase describes any tension between powers, short of all-out war, but specifically that between the Soviet Union and the West following the Second World War. In this latter sense it was popularized by Baruch, the American financier and Presidential adviser in a speech in South Carolina (16 April 1947). A year later he was able to note a worsening of the situation to the extent that he could tell the Senate War Investigating Committee: 'We are in the midst of a cold war which is getting warmer.'

The phrase was suggested to Baruch in June 1946 by his speechwriter Herbert Bayard Swope, former editor of the New York *World*, who had been using it privately since 1940. The columnist Walter Lippmann gave the term wide currency and is sometimes mistakenly credited with coining it. Swope clearly coined it; Baruch gave it currency.

Bateman, Edgar
English songwriter (*fl.* 1900)

1 *Oh it really is a wery pretty garden,*
  and Chingford to the eastward can
  be seen;
  Wiv a ladder and some glasses
  You could see to 'Ackney Marshes,
  If it wasn't for the 'ouses in between.

The Houses in Between was the title of a novel (1951) by Howard Spring who mentions in a foreword a music-hall song containing the words, 'You could see the Crystal Palace — if it wasn't for the houses in between'. Indeed, his title comes from a song (1894), popularized by Gus Elen (d 1940), which had lyrics by Bateman and music by George Le Brunn (1862–1905). The full lyrics given in *The Last Empires* (ed. Benny Green, 1986) do not include mention of the Crystal Palace, but no doubt extra verses were added over the years.

Baum, L. Frank
American author (1856–1919)

2 *The Wizard of Oz.*

Actually the title of Baum's children's classic is *The Wonderful Wizard of Oz.* It was shortened for the 1939 film and also for some later editions of the book. Baum wrote another thirteen books about Oz and twenty-six further titles were added after his death. Legend has it that Baum took the name 'Oz' from the label 'O–Z' on a filing cabinet. It has been observed how similar are Dorothy's adventures to those of *Alice in Wonderland* (1865). In each case, the heroine endures a succession of (mostly) unpleasant encounters and finally escapes back home — Dorothy to Kansas after a cyclone has blown her to Oz, Alice home after she has fallen down a rabbit hole.
  Note these other alterations between book and film:

3 *The road to the City of Emeralds is paved with yellow brick.*

That is what Baum put. He also wrote of 'the road of yellow brick'. The phrase 'Yellow Brick Road' only comes from the song 'Follow the Yellow Brick Road' in the film. The song 'Over the rainbow' (by E.Y. Harburg, with music by Harold Arlen) does not derive from anything in the book.

4 *Toto, I have a feeling we're not in Kansas any more.*

Again, this is a line from the film, not the book, but one that has achieved catchphrase status. Judy Garland as Dorothy says it on arrival in the Land of Oz, concluding, 'We must be over the rainbow'.

5 *The Wicked Witch of the West.*

This *was* the name of a character in *The Wonderful Wizard of Oz* (there was also one of the East; North and South were good witches). It produced a wonderfully alliterative way of describing women not liked. Allan Massie wrote of Margaret Thatcher: 'It would not convert those for whom she is She Who Must Be Obeyed and the Wicked Witch of the West rolled into one' (quoted in Michael Cockerell, *Live From Number 10,* 1989).

6 *Close your eyes and tap your heels together three times. And think to yourself, 'There's no place like home'.*

On how to get from the Land of Oz back to Kansas. Said at the end of the film by Glinda, the Witch of the South or the Good Witch. In the book she says: 'All you have to do is to knock the heels together three times and command the shoes to carry you wherever you wish to go.'

Bax, Sir Arnold
English composer (1883–1953)

7 *You should make a point of trying every experience once, excepting incest and folk-dancing.*

Often wrongly ascribed to Sir Thomas Beecham and others — also to Bax himself. In fact, it was said by 'a sympathetic Scotsman' and quoted by Bax in his book *Farewell, My Youth* (1943).

8 *You know you are getting old when the policemen start looking younger.*

Not said by Bax. What he said of *Arnold Bennett* in *Farewell, My Youth* (1943) was: '[He] once remarked that his earliest recognition of his own middle age came at a certain appalling moment when he realized for the first time that the policeman at the corner was a mere youth.'
  This realization has also been attributed to Sir Seymour Hicks (1871–1949), the

actor, in connection with old age (in C.R.D. Pulling, *They Were Singing*, 1952, for example). The source for this may be Hicks's own *Between Ourselves* (1930).

Beatty, Admiral Sir David (later 1st Earl Beatty)
English admiral (1871–1936)

1 *There seems to be something wrong with our bloody ships today, Chatfield.*

The Battle of Jutland on 31 May–1 June 1916 was not only the first naval engagement of the twentieth century but also the only major sea battle of the First World War. It was, on the face of it, an indecisive affair. The British grand fleet under its Commander-in-Chief, Sir John Jellicoe, failed to secure an outright victory. Admiral Beatty, commanding a battle cruiser squadron, saw one ship after another sunk by the Germans. At 4.26 on the afternoon of 31 May, the *Queen Mary* was sunk with the loss of 1,266 officers and men. This was what led Beatty to make the above comment to his Flag Captain, Ernle Chatfield. Sometimes the words 'and with our system' have been added to the remark, as also 'Turn two points to port' (i.e. nearer the enemy) and 'Steer two points nearer the enemy', but Chatfield denied that anything more was said (according to *ODQ*, 1953 and 1979).

Ultimately, the battle marked the end of any German claim to have naval control of the North Sea and, in that light, was a British victory, but Jutland was a disappointment at the time and has been chewed over ever since as a controversial episode in British naval history.

Beaverbrook, 1st Baron (Maxwell Aitken)
Canadian-born British politician and newspaper proprietor (1879–1964)

2 *I am the cat that walks alone.*

A favourite expression of his, alluding to 'The Cat That Walked By Himself' in *The Just-So Stories* (1902) by Rudyard Kipling. Discussed in A.J.P. Taylor, *Beaverbrook* (1966).

3 *Let me say that the credit belongs to the boys in the back-rooms. It isn't the man who sits in the limelight like me who should have the praise. It is not the men who sit in prominent places. It is the men in the back-rooms.*

As Minister of Aircraft Production, Beaverbrook paid tribute to the Ministry's research department in a broadcast on 19 March 1941. This version of the text has been taken direct from a recording and differs from that usually given (as for example in the *ODQ*, 1992).

In North America the phrase 'back-room boys' can be traced back to the 1870s at least, but Beaverbrook may be credited with the modern application to scientific and technical boffins. His inspiration for the phrase was quite obviously Marlene Dietrich singing his favourite song 'The Boys in the Back Room' in the film *Destry Rides Again* (1939). Written by Frank Loesser, this is more properly called 'See What the Boys in the Back Room Will Have'. According to A.J.P. Taylor, Beaverbrook believed that 'Dietrich singing the Boys in the Backroom is a greater work of art than the Mona Lisa'. Also in 1941, Edmund Wilson entitled a book, *The Boys in the Back Room: Notes on California Novelists*.

4 *Who's in charge of the clattering train?*

Beaverbrook was notorious for interfering with the running of his newspapers. His favourite inquiry as his mighty media machine rumbled on was: 'Who is in charge of the clattering train?' Ominously, this quotation was based on a remembering of the anonymous poem 'Death and His Brother Sleep', which includes the lines:

Who is in charge of the clattering train?
The axles creak, and the couplings strain . . .
For the pace is hot, and the points are near,
And Sleep hath deadened the driver's ear;
And signals flash through the night in vain.
Death is in charge of the clattering train!

It is possible that Beaverbrook borrowed the expression from Winston Churchill, who also quoted the poem in the first volume of his *The Second World War* (1948) saying: 'I had learnt them from a volume of Punch cartoons which I used to pore over when I was eight or nine years old at school in Brighton.' That would have been in 1882–3. In fact, the poem did not appear in *Punch* until 4 October 1890. It concerns a railway collision at Eastleigh. Due to fatigue, the driver and stoker had failed to keep a proper look-out.

A.J.P. Taylor states that Beaverbook's quotation was not quite accurate, but then proceeds to print an innacurate version himself, beginning 'Who is in charge of the *rattling* train . . .'

Beethoven, Ludwig van
German composer (1770–1827)

1 *England is a land without music.*

It seems he never said it. *Das Land ohne Musik* was, however, the title of a British-bashing book by Oscar A. Schmitz, published at the start of the First World War. The book had nothing to do with music but depicted England as a country 'without a soul'. The criticism has also been ascribed to Felix Mendelssohn, a frequent visitor to Britain, with even less reason.

Land Without Music was, coincidentally, the title of a film operetta (UK, 1936; US title *Forbidden Music*) about a Ruritanian ruler who bans music because her subjects are too busy singing to make money. Richard Tauber, Jimmy Durante and Diana Napier were in it.

[*Source:* letter from Arthur Jacobs in the *Independent* Magazine, 1 February 1992.]

Beeton, Mrs (Isabella)
English writer (1836–65)

2 *First catch your hare.*

In the proverbial sense this means, 'You can't begin to do something until you have acquired a necessary basic something (which may be difficult to acquire)'. *CODP* finds the equivalent thought *c* 1300 in Latin: 'It is commonly said that one must first catch the deer, and afterwards, when he has been caught, skin him.'

For a long time, the saying was taken to be a piece of practical, blunt good sense to be found in Mrs Beeton's *Book of Household Management* (1851), but it does not appear there. In Mrs Hannah Glasse's *The Art of Cookery made plain and easy* (1747), however, there is the practical advice, 'Take your hare when it is cased' (skinned).

It was known in the familar form by 1855 when it appeared in Thackeray's *The Rose and the Ring*. Similar proverbs include: 'Catch your bear before you sell its skin', 'Never spend your money before you have it' and 'Don't count your chickens before they are hatched.'

Begin, Menachem
Israeli Prime Minister (1913–92)

3 *BLOOD LIBEL. On the New Year (Rosh Hashana), a blood libel was levelled against the Jewish state, its government and the Israel Defense Forces . . .*

In September 1982, following allegations that Israeli forces in Lebanon had allowed massacres to take place in refugee camps, the Israeli government (headed by Begin) invoked the phrase 'blood libel' in a statement. Traditionally, it was the name given to accusations by medieval anti-Semites that Jews had crucified Christian children and drunk their blood at Passover.

Behan, Brendan
Irish playwright (1923–64)

4 *O, Death where is thy sting-a-ling-*
   a-ling,
O, grave, thy victoree?
The Bells of Hell go ting-a-ling-a-ling
For you but not for me.

Behan made notable use of this song in his play *The Hostage* (1958) but he was, in fact, merely adopting a song popular in the British Army in 1914–18. Even before that, though, it was sung — just like this — as a Sunday School chorus. It may have been in a Sankey and Moody hymnal, though it has not been traced. The basic element is from 1 Corinthians 15:55: 'O death, where is thy sting? O grave, where is thy victory?'

Bell, Daniel
American sociologist (1919–)

5 *Capitalism, it is said, is a system wherein man exploits man. And communism — is vice versa.*

From *The End of Ideology* (1960). Note the 'it is said'. Also sometimes described as a 'Polish proverb'.

Bell, H.E.
English university administrator (1925–)

6 *Parents are the very last people who ought to be allowed to have children.*

Ted Bell has an unusual problem — a remark has been fathered on him and he does not know whether he is entitled to claim paternity. In March 1977, as Senior Assistant Registrar in charge of undergraduate admissions at the University of Reading, he was speaking to a mixed group of people about the increasing complexity of the selection procedures and the variety of guidance available to prospective students. 'In this respect, being a parent of three children myself,' he noted (1992), 'I happened to say that in my view, "Parents are the very last people who ought to be allowed to have children". Reporters were present (I had invited them), the words appeared in the *Guardian*, and they were repeated in "Sayings of the Week" in the *Observer*. Later, in 1980, they appeared under my name in the second edition of *The Penguin Dictionary of Modern Quotations*.'

In truth, Bell was merely saying what oft had been thought but ne'er so pithily expressed. According to *The Treasury of Humorous Quotations* (1951), Bernard Shaw (inevitably) was credited with making the same point in rather more words: 'There may be some doubt as to who are the best people to have charge of children, but there can be no doubt that parents are the worst.' In fact, that was a misattribution. In Shaw's *Everybody's Political What's What?*, Chap. XIX (1944), he quotes *William Morris* ('great among the greatest Victorians as poet, craftsman, and practical man of business, and one of the few who remained uncorrupted by Victorian false prosperity to the end'). Speaking 'as a parent and as a Communist', Morris had said: 'The question of who are the best people to take charge of children is a very difficult one; but it is quite certain that the parents are the very worst.'

Bell, Mary Hayley
English novelist (1911–)

1 *Whistle Down the Wind.*

The title of this novel (1958; film UK, 1961) comes from an expression meaning either (1): to abandon or to cast off lightly (after the releasing of a hawk down wind, from the fist, by whistling), as in Shakespeare's *Othello* (III.iii.266): 'I'ld whistle her off, and let her down the wind'. This is what you do in falconry when you are turning a hawk loose. You send it into or against the wind when it is pursuing prey. Or (2): To talk or argue purposelessly. Noël Coward was quoted in *Panorama* Magazine (Spring 1952), as saying: 'I marched down to the

footlights and screamed: "I gave you my youth! Where is it now? Whistling down the wind! *où sont les neiges d'antan?*" . . . And I went madly on in French and Italian.' Or (3): Something to be avoided on board ship. The superstition is that whistling, because it sounds like the wind, can raise the wind, as if by magic – though this may more properly be 'whistle up the wind', as in 'to whistle for something'. (Whistling backstage at the theatre is also said to bring bad luck.)

Mary Hayley Bell said in 1980 that she had not been aware of the Shakespeare use until Len Deighton pointed it out to her. The relevance of the title to a story of children who believe that a murderer on the run is Jesus Christ may not be immediately apparent.

Bellamy, Francis
American clergyman and editor (1856–1931)

2 *I pledge allegiance to the flag of the United States of America and to the republic for which it stands, one nation under God, indivisible, with liberty and justice for all*

The Pledge of Allegiance to the Flag was put into its final form by Bellamy in 1892. A dispute as to who wrote it – he or James Upham – was decided in Bellamy's favour, eight years after his death, in 1939. Hence, the title of a 1979 film about the US legal system, *And Justice for All*.

The idea of 'justice for all' is, however, one that goes back to the Greeks. It also gave rise to MATHEW 239:1.

Belloc, Hilaire
French-born British poet and writer (1870–1953)

3 *When I am dead, I hope it may be said: 'His sins were scarlet, but his books were read'.*

Belloc wrote this jocular epitaph for himself in 'On his Books' (1923). He is actually buried in a family grave at the Church of Our Lady of Consolation, West Grinstead, Sussex, but, understandably, without this inscription. A few yards away, a plaque on the tower commemorates him, noting that he had been a member of the congregation for forty-eight years. The tower and spire were completed in 1964, 'in grateful recognition of his zealous and unwavering profession of our Holy Faith which he defended in his writings and noble verse'. Then follow his lines from 'The Ballade of Our Lady of Czestocjowa': 'This is the Faith that I have held and hold/and This is That in which I mean to die.'

Bellow, Saul
American novelist (1915–)

1 *All a writer has to do to get a woman is to say he's a writer. It's an aphrodisiac.*

Believed to have come from a BBC TV interview in the 1970s. Compare what Graham Greene said to *Radio Times* (10 September 1964): 'Fame is a powerful aphrodisiac.' Compare KISSINGER 205:9 and NAPOLEON 250:3.

Benchley, Robert
American humorist (1889–1945)

2 *I must get out of these wet clothes and into a dry martini.*

This was a line much enjoyed by Benchley and delivered by him to Ginger Rogers in the film *The Major and the Minor* (1942). It was in the form 'Why don't you get out of that wet coat and into a dry Martini?', according to Harry Haun's *The Movie Quote Book* (1980). Sometimes also attributed to Alexander Woollcott, the line may actually have originated with Benchley's press agent in the 1920s or with his friend Charles Butterworth. In any case, apparently, Mae West also adopted the line, as screenwriter, in *Every Day's a Holiday* (1937).

3 *See Hebrews 13:8.*

A capsule criticism of the play *Abie's Irish Rose* which ran so long (1922–7) that Benchley was incapable of saying anything new about it in the weekly edition of *Life* Magazine. The text he alluded to read: 'Jesus Christ the same yesterday, and today, and for ever.' (Between 1975 and 1990, when *A Chorus Line* was running on Broadway, the capsule criticism space for it in *The New Yorker*'s listings was given over to reprinting paragraphs from *War and Peace*.)

4 *And that, my dears, is how I came to marry your grandfather.*

Another brief, dismissive line — possibly also used in capsule criticism of *Abie's Irish*

Rose — and so quoted by Diana Rigg in *No Turn Unstoned* (1982). As though at the end of a long and rambling reminiscence by an old woman.

Benét, Stephen Vincent
American poet (1898–1943)

5 *I shall not rest quiet in Montparnasse.*
I shall not lie easy at Winchelsea.
You may bury my body in Sussex grass,
You may bury my tongue at Champmédy.
I shall not be there, I shall rise and pass.
Bury my heart at Wounded Knee.

In his poem 'American Names' (1927), Benét celebrates the 'sharp names that never get fat' of American places, extraordinary names such as 'Medicine Hat', and 'Lost Mule Flat'. He contrasts them with the names of other possible burial places in Europe — Montparnasse (where there is a famous cemetery) in Paris, Winchelsea (the 'ancient town' of Rye in Sussex and linked to Henry James), and Champmédy (the significance of which escapes me). *Bury My Heart At Wounded Knee* became the title of a book (1970) by Dee Brown, a historical survey of the West.

Benét, William Rose
American poet (1886–1950)

6 *I like to think of Shakespeare, not as when*
In our old London of the spacious time
He took all amorous hearts with honeyed rhyme . . .
[But] when, with brow composed and friendly tread,
He sought the little streets of Stratford town,
That knew his dreams and soon must hold him dead,
I like to think how Shakespeare pruned his rose,
And ate his pippin in his orchard close.

Written apparently by Stephen Vincent Benét's brother, this short poem was printed (anonymously) as an epilogue to E.K. Chambers, *Shakespeare: A Survey* (1925) and dated 1916. Some readers concluded that it must have been written by Chambers himself.

Bennett, Alan
English playwright and actor (1934–   )

1 *Snobbery with violence.*

In its obituary for Colin Watson, the detective story writer (21 January 1983), *The Times* mentioned his book *Snobbery with Violence* (1971) — a survey of the modern crime story — 'from which the phrase comes'. As usual, there is an earlier example of the phrase in use: in Alan Bennett's play *Forty Years On* (1969) a character talks of, 'Sapper, Buchan, Dornford Yates, practitioners in that school of Snobbery with Violence that runs like a thread of good-class tweed through twentieth-century literature'.

2 *Two of the nicest people if ever there was one.*

On the political thinkers, Sidney and Beatrice Webb. Alternatively, 'Two nice people if there was one'. This line does not appear in the published script of Bennett's play *Forty Years On* (1969), though spoken in the theatre. Having quoted the first version in my book *Quote . . . Unquote* (1978), I was interested to see it reappear in Kenneth Williams's anthology *Acid Drops* (1980) credited to *Arnold* Bennett.

3 *My claim to literary fame is that I used to deliver meat to a woman who became T.S. Eliot's mother-in-law.*

Quoted in the *Observer* (26 April 1992). Bennett's father was indeed a butcher and T.S. Eliot's second wife, Valerie Fletcher came from the same town in Yorkshire.

Bennett, Arnold
English novelist (1867–1931)

4 *Make love to every woman you meet.*

The Treasury of Humorous Quotations (Esar revised by Bentley, 1951) has this as though said by Bennett himself, in the form: 'Make love to every woman you meet; if you get five per cent on your outlay, it's a good investment.' In fact he was quoting someone else. In *The Journals*, his entry for 24 May 1904 includes this: 'Mrs Laye . . . told a good thing of a very old man on his dying bed giving advice to a youngster: "I've had a long life, and it's been a merry one. Take my advice. Make love to every pretty

woman you meet. And remember, if you get 5 per cent on your outlay it's a good return." '

Beresford, Lord Charles
English politician (1846–1919)

5 *VERY SORRY CAN'T COME. LIE FOLLOWS BY POST.*

Beresford is supposed to have telegraphed this message to the Prince of Wales (presumably the future Edward VII) after receiving a dinner invitation at short notice. It is reported by Ralph Nevill in *The World of Fashion 1837–1922* (1923). The same joke occurs in Marcel Proust, *Le Temps Retrouvé* (published in 1927 after his death in 1922), in the form: 'One of those telegrams of which M. de Guermantes has wittily fixed the formula: "Can't come, lie follows [*Impossible venir, mensonge suit*]." '

Berkeley, George
Irish philosopher and Anglican bishop (1685–1753)

6 *If a tree falls in a forest, and no one is there to hear it, it makes no sound.*

Which philosopher said this? Not Kant, apparently, though it was one of his preoccupations. Berkeley also seems a likely bet. In his writings on 'subjective idealism', he holds that there is no existence of matter independent of perception. But in his three best-known works, *Essays Towards a New Theory of Vision*, *A Treatise Concerning the Principles of Human Knowledge* and *Three Dialogues Between Hylas and Philonous*, the precise example does not occur. However in his *Dialogues* there is this: 'Can a real thing which is not *audible*, be like a *sound*?'

Bernard of Clairvaux, Saint
French theologian (1090–1153)

7 *Love me, love my dog.*

Meaning 'if you are inclined to take my side in matters generally, you must put up with one or two things you don't like at the same time', it comes from one of St Bernard's sermons: '*Qui me amat, amat et canem meum*' [Who loves me, also loves my dog]. A good illustration comes from an article by Valerie Bornstein in *Proverbium* (1991): 'I told my mother that she must love my father a lot because she tolerated his snoring! . . . She became aggravated with me and stated the proverb "*Aime moi, aime mon chien*". She told me that when you love someone, you accept all the things that go along with them, their virtues and faults.'

Alas, this was a different St Bernard from the one after whom the breed of Alpine dog is named. It was said (or quoted) by St Bernard of Clairvaux rather than St Bernard of Menthon (*d* 1008).

Berra, 'Yogi'
American baseball player and coach (1925–)

1 *The game isn't over till it's over.*

'Berraisms' like Goldwynisms have been put into his mouth more often than they have emerged from it unaided. Some of the more unlikely ones are: 'It's déjà vu all over again', 'We made too many wrong mistakes', 'Baseball is ninety per cent mental, the other half is physical' and 'Always go to other people's funerals, otherwise they won't go to yours'. Of those he has admitted to, 'Nobody ever goes there anymore, it's too crowded' has also been said by others before him; 'You can observe a lot by watching' is wisdom through tautology; as is, 'It ain't over till it's over' — his comment on a National League pennant race (1973) when he was managing the New York Mets.

Betjeman, Sir John
English Poet Laureate (1906–84)

2 *Ghastly Good Taste.*

The title of his book (1933), subtitled 'a depressing story of the Rise and Fall of English Architecture', neatly skewered an aspect of taste that is questionable — when taste is so tasteful it is tasteless. And how had this come about? Betjeman concludes: 'We have seen in this book how English architecture emerged from the religious unity of Christendom to the reasoned unity of an educated monarchic system, and then to the stranger order of an industrialised community. As soon as it became unsettled, towards the end of the nineteenth century, "architecture" *qua* architecture became self-conscious.' This probably applies equally to design in general.

Bevan, Aneurin
Welsh Labour politician (1897–1960)

3 *No amount of cajolery, and no attempts at ethical or social seduction, can eradicate from my heart a deep and burning hatred for the Tory Party that inflicted those experiences on me. So far as I am concerned they are lower than vermin.*

The fiery left-winger was on the eve of his most substantial achievement — launching the post-war Labour Government's National Health Service — when on 4 July 1948 he spoke at a rally in Belle Vue, Manchester. He contrasted Labour's social programme with the days of his youth between the wars when the Means Test reigned, when he had had to live on the earnings of his sister and when he had been told to emigrate. As abuse goes, it was traditional stuff. In Swift's *Gulliver's Travels* (1726), the king of Brobdingnag considers Gulliver's fellow countrymen to be 'the most pernicious race of little odious vermin that nature ever suffered to crawl upon the face of the earth'. But the Minister was not allowed to forget his remark. Harold Laski estimated that Bevan's use of the word 'vermin' had been worth two million votes lost to the Tories.

4 *We know what happens to people who stay in the middle of the road. They get run over.*

Quoted in the *Observer* (9 December 1953). But you can't keep a good line down. According to Kenneth Harris in his book *Thatcher* (1988), Mrs Thatcher once said to James Prior: 'Standing in the middle of the road is very dangerous, you get knocked down by traffic from both sides.' And a TV play called *A Very British Coup* (1988) had a fictional Prime Minister saying, 'I once tried the middle of the road . . . but I was knocked down by traffic in both directions.'

5 *A desiccated calculating machine.*

During a *Tribune* group meeting held on 29 September 1954 at the Labour Party Conference in Scarborough, Bevan countered Clement Attlee's plea for a non-emotional response to German rearmament by saying: 'I know that the right kind of leader for the Labour Party is a desiccated calculating machine who must not in any way permit himself to be swayed by indignation . . . He must speak in calm and objective accents and talk about a dying child in the same way as he would about the pieces inside an internal combustion engine.' This characterization came to be applied to Hugh Gaitskell who beat Bevan for the leadership of the Labour Party the following year. In 1959, however, Bevan told Robin Day in a TV interview: 'I never called him that. I was applying my words to a synthetic figure, but the press took it up and it's never possible to catch up a canard like that, as you know.' After the interview was over, he added: 'Of course I wasn't referring to Hugh Gaitskell. For one thing Hugh is not desiccated — he's highly emotional. And you could hardly call him a calculating machine — because he was three hundred millions out.' (Recounted in Michael Foot, *Aneurin Bevan*, Vol. 2, 1973).

1 *I am not going to spend any time whatsoever in attacking the Foreign Secretary. Quite honestly I am beginning to feel extremely sorry for him. If we complain about the tune, there is no reason to attack the monkey when the organ grinder is present.*

Wishing to address the Prime Minister (Harold Macmillan) rather than the Foreign Secretary (Selwyn Lloyd) in a post-Suez debate, House of Commons (16 May 1957). The saying has also been attributed to Winston Churchill during the Second World War — replying to a query from the British Ambassador as to whether he should raise a question with Mussolini or with Count Ciano, his Foreign Minister, but this is unverified.

2 *The commanding heights of the economy.*

Who originated this phrase? In a speech to the Labour Party Conference in November 1959, Bevan said: 'Yesterday, Barbara [Castle] quoted from a speech which I made some years ago, and she said that I believed that Socialism in the context of modern society meant the conquest of the commanding heights of the economy . . .' Hugh Gaitskell, the party leader, also quoted the same phrase, apparently, but no one has been able to find Bevan's original coinage, least of all his most recent biographer, John Campbell. Alan Watkins in a throwaway line in his

Observer column (28 September 1987) said 'the phrase was originally Lenin's'.

At the Labour Party Conference in October 1989, Neil Kinnock revived the phrase saying that education and training were 'the commanding heights of every modern economy'.

Bevin, Ernest
British Labour politician (1881–1951)

3 *Not while I'm alive, he ain't.*

On being told that another Labourite was 'his own worst enemy'. Reputedly levelled at Aneurin Bevan, Herbert Morrison, Emanuel Shinwell and others. Quoted in Michael Foot, *Aneurin Bevin*, Vol. 2 (1973), who footnoted: 'Perhaps once he had made it he recited it about all of them. Impossible to determine who was the original victim.' Douglas Jay in *Change and Fortune* (1980) added that it was 'Made, I have little doubt, though there is no conclusive proof about Bevan . . . I could never discover direct evidence for this oft-told story.'

4 *My policy is to be able to take a ticket at Victoria Station and go anywhere I damn well please.*

On his foreign affairs policy when Labour Foreign Secretary and so quoted in *The Spectator* (20 April 1951). Francis Williams in his biography of Bevin (1952) has a slightly different version — said to a diplomat about the most important objective of his foreign policy: 'Just to be able to go down to Victoria station and take a ticket to where the hell I like without a passport.'

Bible, The
Except where stated these quotations are in the form to be found in the Authorized Version or King James Bible (1611)

Old Testament
Genesis

5 *And the Lord God caused a deep sleep to fall upon Adam, and he slept: and he took one of his ribs, and closed up the flesh instead thereof; And the rib, which the Lord God had taken from man, made he a woman, and brought her unto the man. And Adam said, This is*

now bone of my bones, and flesh of my flesh: she shall be called Woman, because she was taken out of Man.

Genesis 2:21–3 stating that God made woman from one of Adam's ribs. Hence *Adam's Rib*, the title of a film (US, 1949) about husband and wife lawyers opposing each other in court (also of a 1923 Cecil B. de Mille marital film with biblical flashbacks) and *Spare Rib*, the title of a British feminist magazine (founded 1972) – a punning reference to the cuts of meat known as 'spare-ribs'.

1 *Esau selleth his birthright for a mess of potage.*

The expression 'to sell one's birthright for a mess of potage', meaning to sacrifice something for material comfort, has biblical origins but is not a quotation of a verse in the Bible. It appears as a chapter heading for Genesis 25 in one or two early translations of the Bible, though not in the Authorized Version.

The word 'mess' is used in its sense of 'a portion of liquid or pulpy food'. 'Potage' is thick soup (compare French *potage*).

2 *Behold, Esau my brother is a hairy man, and I am a smooth man.*

Genesis 27:11. This was the unlikely text preached upon by Alan Bennett's Anglican clergyman in the revue *Beyond the Fringe* (1961), which has become a model for how not to do it. One hopes it was intentional that the clergyman ascribes the text to 2 Kings 14:1. (He also misattributes RICE 280:5 to W.E. Henley.)

Exodus

3 *A land flowing with milk and honey.*

Referring to any idyllic, prosperous situation, the origin of the phrase is to be found in Exodus 3:8, where God says: 'And I am come to deliver them out of the hand of the Egyptians . . . unto a land flowing with milk and honey.'

4 *The fleshpots of Egypt.*

Now meaning 'any place of comparative luxury', the phrase was originally said by the Israelites (in Exodus 16:3): 'Would to God we had died by the hand of the Lord in the land of Egypt, when we sat by the flesh pots, and when we did eat bread to the full.'

Clementine Churchill wrote to Winston on 20 December 1910: 'I do so wish I was at Warter with you enjoying the Flesh Pots of Egypt! It sounds a delightful party . . .' (quoted in Mary Soames, *Clementine Churchill*, 1979).

1 Samuel

5 *God save the King.*

The third line of the English National Anthem (possibly written by Henry Carey or James Hogg or taken from an old Jacobite drinking song *c* 1725) occurs several times in the Bible – in 1 Samuel 10:24 (referring to Saul), also in 2 Samuel 16:16, 2 Kings 11:12 and 2 Chronicles 23:11.

6 *After whom is the king of Israel come out? after whom dost thou pursue? after a dead dog, after a flea.*

Yes, fleas are mentioned twice in the Bible, both in 1 Samuel – here, at 24:14, but also at 26:20.

2 Samuel

7 *The beauty of Israel is slain upon thy high places: how are the mighty fallen! Tell it not in Gath, publish it not in the streets of Askelon; lest the daughters of the Philistines rejoice.*

This is part of David's lamentation over the deaths of Saul and Jonathan, his son (2 Samuel 1:19–20). *Publish It Not . . .* was the title of a book (1975) by Christopher Mayhew and Michael Adams and subtitled 'the Middle East cover-up'.

8 *Saul and Jonathan were lovely and pleasant in their lives, and in their death they were not divided.*

Also taken from the lament of David for Saul and Jonathan (2 Samuel 1:23), the line 'in their death they were not divided' has often been used by epitaph writers, though not always with total appropriateness. They are the last words of George Eliot's novel *The Mill on the Floss* (1860), being the epitaph on the tomb of Tom and Maggie Tulliver, brother and sister, who have been drowned. Of course, the original couple, Jonathan and Saul, were of the same sex and died on the battlefield. When Joseph Severn, the friend of John Keats, died in 1879, his son Walter suggest that the text on the grave in the Protestant Cemetery, Rome, should be, 'In their death they were not divided'. He was told that this 'must seem highly inappropriate to anyone who recollects the original application of the phrase . . . [and] as more than sixty years elapsed between Keats's death and your father's.' On the memorial plaque to the British-born actors, Dame May Whitty (1865–1948) and Ben Webster (1864–1947), in St Paul's Church, Covent Garden, London, the full text is used ('They were lovely and pleasant'): they were husband and wife.

The film *They Were not Divided* (UK, 1950) was about British and American soldiers/friends who die during the advance on Berlin during the Second World War.

1 Kings

1 *A cloud no bigger than a man's hand.*

When something is described as such, it is not yet very threatening — as though a man could obliterate a cloud in the sky by holding up his hand in front of his face — and the context is usually of trouble ahead perceived while it is still apparently of little consequence. The phrase is from 1 Kings 18:44: 'Behold, there ariseth a little cloud out of the sea, like a man's hand.' In the New English Bible, the passage is rendered as, 'I see a cloud no bigger than a man's hand.'

The Revd Francis Kilvert, in his diary for 9 August 1871, has: 'Not a cloud was in the sky as big as a man's hand'. In a letter to Winston Churchill on 14 December 1952, Bob Boothby MP wrote of a dinner at Chartwell: 'It took me back to the old carefree days when I was your Parliamentary Private Secretary, and there seemed to be no cloud on the horizon; and on to the fateful days when the cloud was no bigger than a man's hand, and there was still time to save the sum of things.'

2 Kings

2 *Go up, thou bald head; go up, thou bald head.*

One of the more comical effusions in the whole Bible (2 Kings 2:23). It is how 'little children out of the city' mocked Elisha — the New English Bible has them saying, 'Get along with you, bald head, get along'. Comical, except that he 'cursed them in the name of the Lord', and two she bears came out a wood and mauled forty-two of them . . .

2 Chronicles

3 *They buried him among the kings because he had done good toward God and toward his house.*

This was the text placed on the tomb of the Unknown Soldier in Westminster Abbey in 1920, echoing 2 Chronicles 24:16: 'And they buried him in the city of David among the kings, because he had done good in Israel, both toward God, and toward his house.'

Job

4 *Man that is born of woman is of few days and full of trouble.*

Job 14:1 is correctly 'Man that is born of a woman'. Also Job 15:4 and 25:4.

5 *My bone cleaveth to my skin, and to my flesh, and I am escaped by the skin of my teeth.*

Job 19:20 is correctly 'escaped *with* the skin of my teeth'. To escape by the skin of one's teeth now means to do so by a very narrow margin indeed. *The Skin of Our Teeth* was the title of a play (1942) by Thornton Wilder.

6 *Thus far shalt thou go and no further.*

Job 38:11 has: 'Hitherto shalt thou come, but no further: and here shall thy proud waves be stayed?' Charles Stewart Parnell, the champion of Irish Home Rule, said at Cork in 1885: 'No man has a right to fix the boundary of the march of a nation; no man has a right to say to his country, Thus far shalt thou go and no further.' George Farquhar, the Irish-born playwright has this in *The Beaux' Stratagem* (1707): 'And thus far I am a captain, and no farther' (III.ii.).

Psalms

See also under BOOK OF COMMON PRAYER 66:3–66:6.

7 *Man of the world.*

This expression derives from Psalm 17:14: 'Deliver my soul from the wicked, which is thy sword: From men which are thy hand, O Lord, from men of the world, which have their portion in this life.' From 'irreligious, worldly', the term has come to mean (less pejoratively) 'one versed in the ways of the world' and has been used as a title of a novel by Henry Mackenzie (1773) and a comedy by Charles Macklin (1871).

1 *Moab is my washpot; over Edom will I cast out my shoe.*

One of the strangest sentences in the Bible. The New English Bible translation of Psalm 60:7 may make it clearer: (God speaks from his sanctuary) 'Gilead and Manasseh are mine; Ephraim is my helmet, Judah my sceptre; Moab is my wash-bowl, I fling my shoes at Edom; Philistia is the target of my anger.' In other words, God is talking about useful objects to throw, in his anger. (Moab was an ancient region of Jordan.)

2 *From sea to shining sea.*

This, in fact, is a line from the poem 'America the Beautiful' (1893) by Katharine Lee Bates:

America! America!
God shed his grace on thee
And crown thy good with brotherhood
From sea to shining sea!

(The words have also been set to music.) Perhaps they echo Psalm 72:8: 'He shall have dominion also from sea to sea.' The motto of the Dominion of Canada (adopted 1867) is, however a direct quote, albeit in Latin: '*A mari usque ad mare*' [From sea to sea].

3 *Kick the dust.*

No, the Bible does not have 'to kick the dust' for 'to die'. That usage is nicely illustrated by a passage from Thoreau's *Walden* (1854): 'I was present at the auction of a deacon's effects . . . after lying half a century in his garret and other dust holes . . . When a man dies he kicks the dust.' Nor does the Bible have 'kiss the dust'. The *OED2* mentions neither of these expressions, though it does find 'bite the dust' in 1856.

What Psalm 72:9 has is '*lick* the dust': 'They that dwell in the wilderness shall bow before him; and his enemies shall lick the dust' — though this is suggesting humiliation rather than death.

4 *They that go down to the sea in ships, that do business in great waters.*

Psalm 107:23. The Prayer Book version has, rather, 'occupy their business in the great waters'. The 'go down to the sea' here may have a bearing on MASEFIELD 238:4.

5 *If I take the wings of the morning, and dwell in the uttermost parts of the sea.*

This text on the tombstone of Charles A. Lindbergh (1902–74), the American aviator, on the island of Maui, Hawaii, is from Psalm 139:9, which concludes, 'Even there shall thy hand lead me, and thy right hand shall hold me.' Lindbergh made the first non-stop solo flight across the Atlantic in 1927.

Proverbs

6 *Inherit the wind.*

The title of a film (US, 1960) about the 1925 Scopes 'Monkey Trial' (concerning the teaching of evolution in schools) is explained *in* the film. It comes from Proverbs 11:29: 'He that troubleth his own house shall inherit the wind.' Not to be confused with *Reap the Wild Wind* (film US, 1942), which presumably alludes to Hosea 8:7: 'They have sown the wind, and they shall reap the whirlwind.'

7 *A soft answer turneth away wrath.*

Proverbs 15:1 continues: 'But grievous words stir up anger.'

8 *Pride goeth before a fall.*

This might seem to be a telescoped version of 'Pride goeth before destruction, and an haughty spirit before a fall' (16:18) but the proverb seems to have developed independently. *CODP* cites Alexander Barclay's *The Ship of Fools* (1509), 'First or last foul pride will have a fall', and Samuel Johnson wrote in a letter (2 August 1784), 'Pride must have a fall'. At some stage the biblical wording must have been grafted on to the original proverb.

One of Swift's clichés in *Polite Conversation* (1738) is, 'You were afraid that Pride should have a Fall'.

9 *From a far country.*

This was the title of a TV film (1981) of dramatized episodes from the early life of Pope John Paul II. The source seems to lie in the Old Testament where there are several examples of 'from a far land' and 'from a far country' (Deuteronomy 29:22, 2 Kings 20:14, Isaiah 39:3 and so on.) Most felicitously, there is 'good news from a far country' (Proverbs 25:25).

Compare *Crowned In a Far Country*, a

book (1986) by Princess Michael of Kent about people who had married into the British Royal Family. William Caxton in England's first printed book, *Dictes or Sayengis of the Philosophres* (1477), has: 'Socrates was a Greek born in a far country from here'. H.D. Thoreau, *On the Duty of Civil Disobedience* (1849) has: '[On going to prison] It was like travelling into a far country, such as I had never expected to behold, to lie there for one night.'

1 *Man proposes, God disposes.*

See THOMAS À KEMPIS 332:5.

Ecclesiastes

2 *The sun also rises.*

Famous as the title of an Ernest Hemingway novel about expatriates in Europe (1926; film US, 1957; also known as *Fiesta* in the UK), the source is Ecclesiastes 1:5: 'The sun also riseth, and the sun goeth down, and hasteth to his place where he arose'. It promoted the Hollywood joke, 'The son-in-law also rises', when Louis B. Mayer promoted his daughter's husband (David O. Selznick) *c* 1933. More recently, there has been a book about the Japanese economy called *The Sun Also Sets* by Bill Emmott (1990).

3 *There is nothing new under the sun.*

Ecclesiastes 1:9 is correctly 'There is no new thing under the sun'.

4 *A time to love and a time to die.*

The title of a film (US, 1958), from a novel by Erich Maria Remarque (*Zeit zu leben und zeit zu sterben*, 1954), is a blending of 'a time to love, and a time to hate' from Ecclesiastes 3:8 and 'a time to be born, and a time to die' (3:2).

5 *Evil under the sun.*

Used as the title of an Agatha Christie thriller about murder in a holiday hotel (1941; film UK, 1982), it is not explained in the text, though Hercule Poirot, the detective, remarks before any evil has been committed: 'The sun shines. The sea is blue . . . but there is evil everywhere under the sun.' Shortly afterwards, another character remarks: 'I was interested, M. Poirot, in something you said just now . . . It was almost a quotation from Ecclesiastes . . . "Yea, also the heart of the sons of men is full

of evil, and madness is in their heart while they live".' But Ecclesiastes (which finds everything 'under the sun') gets nearer than that: 'There is a sore evil which I have seen under the sun, namely, riches kept for the owners thereof to their hurt' (5:13) and: 'There is an evil which I have seen under the sun' (6:1, 10:1). Were it not for the clue about Ecclesiastes, one might be tempted to think that Christie had once more turned to an old English rhyme for one of her titles. In this one, the phrase appears exactly:

For every evil under the sun,
There is a remedy or there is none;
If there be one, try and find it;
If there be none, never mind it.

6 *The house of mirth.*

The title of an Edith Wharton novel (1905) about a failed social climber derives from Ecclesiastes 7:3–4: 'Sorrow is better than laughter: for by the sadness of the countenance is the heart made better. The heart of the wise is in the house of mourning; but the heart of fools is in the house of mirth.'

7 *A fly in the ointment.*

Meaning 'some small factor that spoils the general enjoyment of something', this expression would seem to derive from Ecclesiastes 10:1: 'Dead flies cause the ointment of the apothecary to send forth a stinking vapour.'

8 *Cast thy bread upon the waters: for thou shalt find it after many days.*

Ecclesiastes 11:1 is the origin of 'to cast one's bread upon the waters', meaning 'to reap as you shall sow'. Oddly expressed, presumably the idea is that if you sow seed or corn in a generous fashion now, you will reap the benefits in due course. The New English Bible translates this passage more straightforwardly as 'Send your grain across the seas, and in time you will get a return'.

Song of Solomon

9 *The flowers appear on the earth; the time of the singing of birds is come, and the voice of the turtle is heard in our land.*

2:12 is referring to spring. The turtle here is not the thing with a shell that ends up in soup, but the turtle dove, a more poetic image.

1 The little foxes.

The title of the play (1939; film US, 1941) by Lillian Hellman, comes from 2:15: 'Take us the foxes, the little foxes, that spoil the vines.' Hellman is writing about a family of schemers.

2 Until the day break, and the shadows flee away.

This text appears on the grave in Brookwood Military Cemetery, Surrey, of Flying Officer H.G. Holtrop, an RAF pilot who was killed on 10 June 1944, aged 33. His relatives chose a very popular gravestone text, which comes from the Song of Solomon 2:17 and (it is a love poem, after all) continues: 'Turn, my beloved, and be thou like a roe or a young hart upon the mountains of Bether.'

Isaiah

3 How long, O Lord, how long?

Now used in mock exasperation, this saying is an amplification of Isaiah 6:11. The prophet has a vision in which God tells him to do various things and he reports: 'Then said I, Lord how long?' The more familiar version occurs, for example, in schoolboy verse by G.K. Chesterton (c 1890): 'Not from the misery of the weak, the madness of the strong,/Goes upward from our lips the cry, "How long, oh Lord, how long?" '

4 The lion shall lie down with the lamb.

Only indirectly. This simplified version derives from Isaiah 17:6: 'The wolf also shall dwell with the lamb, and the leopard shall lie down with the kid; and the calf and the young lion and the fatling together.'

5 Watchman, what of the night?

Not a street cry. In Isaiah 21:11 the watchman replies, unhelpfully: 'The morning cometh, and also the night.' Used as the title of a Bernard Partridge cartoon in Punch (3 January 1900).

6 Let us eat, drink and be merry, for tomorrow we die.

This saying derives from Isaiah 22:13, which has the form: 'Let us eat and drink; for tomorrow we shall die.' BDPF calls it, however: 'A traditional saying of the Egyptians who, at their banquets, exhibited a skeleton to the guests to remind them of the brevity of life.' Ecclesiastes 8:15 has: 'A man hath no better thing under the sun, than to eat, and to drink, and to be merry', and Luke 12:19: 'Take thine ease, eat, drink and be merry.' Luke 15:23 has simply: 'Let us eat, and be merry.'

7 To make the desert bloom.

The modern state of Israel has made this injunction come true, but it 'dates from Bible times', according to Daniel J. Boorstin in The Image (1960). Adlai Stevenson also alluded to the phrase in a speech at Hartford, Connecticut (18 September 1952): 'Man has wrested from nature the power to make the world a desert or to make the deserts bloom.' The exact phrase does not appear in the Bible, though Isaiah 35:1 has: 'The desert shall rejoice, and blossom as the rose' and 51:3 has: 'For the Lord shall comfort Zion . . . and he will make . . . her desert like the garden of the Lord.' Cruden's Concordance (1737) points out: 'In the Bible this word [desert] means a deserted place, wilderness, not desert in the modern usage of the term.'

8 No peace for the wicked.

If quoting from Isaiah 48:22, this should be 'There is no peace, saith the Lord, unto the wicked' or from 57:21 'There is no peace, saith my God, to the wicked'.

Jeremiah

9 Can the leopard change his spots?

Jeremiah 13:23 should correctly be quoted as, 'Can the Ethiopian change his skin, or the leopard his spots?' (It continues: 'then may ye also do good, that are accustomed to do evil.')

Daniel

10 True, O king.

When someone makes an obvious remark, perhaps even a pompous one, other people will sometimes comment, 'True, O King!' The source for this expression is not absolutely certain but may well derive from the story of Nebuchadnezzar and the gentlemen who were cast into the burning fiery furnace. 'Did not we cast three men bound into the midst of fire?' Nebuchadnezzar asks (Daniel 3:24). 'They answered and said unto the king, True, O king.'

The nearest Shakespeare gets is the ironical ' "True?" O God!' in *Much Ado About Nothing* (IV.i.68), though he has any number of near misses like 'true, my liege', 'too true, my lord' and 'true, noble prince'.

Another version is 'True, O King! Live for ever'. In *The Diaries of Kenneth Williams* (1993) — the entry for 5 January 1971 — the comedian recounts being told on TV by an Irishman that he was a bore: 'I smiled acquiescence and said "How true, O King!" '

1 The writing is on the wall.

This way of expressing a hint, sign or portent, often doom-laden, derives — though not the precise phrase — from Daniel 5 when King Belshazzar is informed of the forthcoming destruction of the Babylonian Empire through the appearance of 'the handwriting on a wall' (as the Authorized Version's chapter heading has it): 'And this is the writing that was written, MENE MENE, TEKEL, UPHARSIN' [meaning 'God hath numbered thy kingdom, and finished it . . . Thou art weighed in the balances, and art found wanting . . . Thy kingdom is divided, and given to the Medes and Persians].'

This should not be confused with the passage from Edward Fitzgerald's translation of *The Rubáiyát of Omar Khayyám* (1859): 'The moving finger writes; and, having writ,/Moves on: nor all thy piety nor wit/Shall lure it back to cancel half a line,/Nor all thy tears wash out a word of it.'

The phrase became established in the nineteenth century. Lieutenant-General Sir Ian Hamilton, *A Staff Officer's Scrap Book during the Russo-Japanese War* (1907) has: 'I have today seen the most stupendous spectacle it is possible for the mortal brain to conceive — Asia advancing, Europe falling back, the wall of mist and the writing thereon.' In a BBC broadcast to Resistance workers in Europe (31 July 1941), 'Colonel Britton' (Douglas Ritchie) talked of the 'V for Victory' sign which was being chalked up in occupied countries: 'All over Europe the V sign is seen by the Germans and to the Germans and the Quislings it is indeed the writing on the wall.'

Micah

2 Nation shall speak peace unto nation.

The motto of the BBC (decided upon in 1927) echoes Micah 4:3: 'Nation shall not lift up a sword against nation'. In 1932, however, it was decided that the BBC's primary mission was to serve the home audience and not that overseas. Hence, '*Quaecunque*' [whatsoever] was introduced as an alternative reflecting the Latin inscription (composed by Dr Montague Rendall, an ex-headmaster of Winchester College) in the entrance hall of Broadcasting House, London, and based on Philippians 4:8: 'Whatsoever things are beautiful and honest and of good report . . .' '*Quaecunque*' was also taken as his own motto by Lord Reith, the BBC's first Director-General, who never liked the Corporation's 'peace' motto. In 1948 this same motto was reintroduced by the BBC.

Habbakuk

3 He who runs may read.

This expression is an alteration of Habbakuk 2:2, 'That he may run that readeth it', but is no more easily understandable. The New English Bible translates it as 'ready for a herald to carry it with speed' and provides the alternative 'so that a man may read it easily'. The OED2 has citations from 1672, 1784 and 1821, but possibly the most famous use is in John Keble's hymn 'Septuagesima' from *The Christian Year* (1827):

> There is a book, who runs may read,
> Which heavenly truth imparts,
> And all the lore its scholars need,
> Pure eyes and Christian hearts.

Given the obscurity, one of the most unlikely uses of the phrase has been an advertising slogan for *The Golden Book* in the 1920s (according to E.S. Turner in *The Shocking History of Advertising*, 1952).

Apocrypha (Old Testament)
2 Esdras

4 For the world has lost his youth, and the times begin to wax old.

2 Esdras 14:10 might just be the origin of the wistful expression 'When the world was young', a harking back not just to 'long ago' but also to a time more innocent than the present. Precisely as 'When the World Was Young', it was used as the title of a painting (1891) by Sir Edward John Poynter PRA, which shows three young girls in a classical setting, relaxing by a pool.

Ecclesiasticus

*1 Speak, you who are older, for it is
fitting that you should,
but with accurate knowledge, and
do not interrupt the music.*

A curious passage from 32:3. The meaning
is made clearer by the New English Bible
translation of the concluding words in this
section concerning 'Counsels upon social
behaviour': 'Where entertainment is provided, do not keep up a stream of talk; it is
the wrong time to show off your wisdom.'

2 Their name liveth for evermore.

This was the standard epitaph put over lists
of the war dead and composed after the First
World War by Rudyard Kipling. It is based
on 44:14: 'Their bodies are buried in peace;
but their name liveth for evermore.' Kipling
was invited by the Imperial War Graves
Commission to devise memorial texts for the
dead and admitted to 'naked cribs of the
Greek anthology'. He also used biblical
texts, as here.

New Testament
St Matthew

3 Salt of the earth.

Now meaning 'the best of mankind', this
expression comes from Christ's description
of his disciples in Matthew 5:13: 'Ye are the
salt of the earth: but if the salt have lost his
savour, wherewith shall it be salted?' Which
suggests, rather, that they should give the
world an interesting flavour, be a ginger
group, and not that they are simply jolly
good chaps. The New English Bible conveys
this meaning better as 'you are salt to the
world'.

4 Every jot and tittle.

Meaning 'the least item or detail', the words
come from Matthew 5:18: 'Till heaven and
earth pass, one jot or one tittle shall in no
wise pass from the law, till all be fulfilled.'
'Jot' is *iota*, the smallest Greek letter (compare 'not one iota') and 'tittle' is the dot over
the letter i (Latin *titulus*).

5 Do as you would be done by.

Matthew 7:12 (from Christ's Sermon on the
Mount) reads, properly, 'Therefore all
things whatsoever ye would that men should
do to you, do you even so to them: for this

is the law and the prophets.' Not 'Do as you
would be done by', or any of the other
derivatives. By the seventeenth century this
was known as 'The Golden Rule' or 'The
Golden Law'. (The 'rule of three' in
mathematics was, however, known as the
Golden Rule the century before that.)

6 The straight and narrow.

The idea of a straight and narrow path of
law-abiding behaviour or goodness — from
which it is easy to wander — is seemingly
misderived from Matthew 7:13-14, which
has, rather, 'strait is the gate, and narrow is
the way, which leadeth unto life, and few
there be that find it'.

7 By their fruits ye shall know them.

Meaning, you can judge people by the
results they produce, this has become almost
a format phrase. The original version occurs
in Matthew 7:20 in the part of the Sermon
on the Mount about being beware of false
prophets.

8 The birds of the air.

Matthew 8:20 has 'the foxes have holes, and
the birds of the air have nests'. A variant is
'fowl(s) of the air' (Genesis 1:26), though
much more commonly one finds 'fowls of
the heavens' in (mostly) the Old Testament.
Compare the 'fish(es) of the sea', which
occurs at least three times in the Old Testament (e.g. Genesis 1:26). 'All the beasts of
the forest' is biblical, too, (Psalm 104:20),
though more frequent is 'beasts of the field'
(e.g. Psalm 8:7).
   The phrase later made a notable appearance in the rhyme 'Who Killed Cock Robin?'
(first recorded in the eighteenth century):
'All the birds of the air/Fell a-sighing and a-
sobbing,/When they heard the bell toll/For
poor Cock Robin.'

*9 A prophet is without honour in his own
country.*

Meaning, you tend not to be appreciated
where you usually live or are known.
Matthew 13:57 has, precisely: 'A prophet is
not without honour, save in his own country, and in his own house.'

10 The blind leading the blind.

Meaning, the ignorant are incapable of
helping anybody similarly incapacitated.
Matthew 15:14 has: 'They be leaders of the

blind. And if the blind lead the blind, both shall fall into the ditch.' A form of words that demands parody. In 1958 Kenneth Tynan quoted people saying of *The New Yorker* that it was 'the bland leading the bland'.

See TYNAN 338:3.

1 A sign of the times.

In Matthew 16:3, Christ says: 'The sky is red and lowring. O ye hypocrites, ye can discern the face of the sky; but can ye not discern the signs of the times?' Hence, the expression used by everyone from Thomas Carlyle (as a book title — *Signs of the Times*, 1829) to the pop singer Prince (an album title — 'Sign o' the Times', 1987) to describe portents or general indications of current trends.

2 Get thee behind me, Satan.

Nowadays, an exclamation used in answer to the mildest call to temptation. It comes originally from Matthew 16:23, where Jesus Christ rebukes Peter with the phrase for something he has said.

3 It is easier for a camel to go through the eye of a needle than for a rich man to enter into the kingdom of God.

That is how Christ's words appear in Matthew 19:24 — also in Mark 10:25 and Luke 18:25, though the latter has 'through a needle's eye'. Note that the Koran contains a similar view and in Rabbinical writings there is the expression 'to make an *elephant* pass through the eye of a needle', which also appears in an Arab proverb. But why this camel/elephant confusion? Probably because the word for 'camel' in the older Germanic languages, including Old English, was almost like the modern word for 'elephant' (OE *olfend* 'camel'). In this biblical saying, however, it is possible that neither camel nor elephant was intended. The original Greek word should probably have been read as *kamilos* 'a rope', rather than *kamelos*, 'a camel'. The difficulty of threading a rope through the eye of a needle makes a much neater image.

4 At the eleventh hour.

Meaning 'at the last moment', the origin of this phrase lies in the parable of the labourers, of whom the last 'were hired at the eleventh hour' (Matthew 20:9). The

expression was used with a different resonance at the end of the First World War. The Armistice was signed at 5 a.m. on 11 November 1918 and came into force at 11 a.m. that day — 'at the eleventh hour of the eleventh day of the eleventh month'.

5 The poor are always with us.

That is the phrase as we would most likely say it now, but it is to be found in three different forms in three gospels: in Matthew 26:11 ('For ye have the poor always with you'), Mark 14:7 ('For ye have the poor with you always'), and John 12:8 ('For the poor always ye have with you'). Compare these allusions: *The Rich Are Always With Us* was the title of a film (US, 1932) and *The Rich Are With You Always*, the title of a novel (1976) by Malcolm Macdonald.

Mark

6 Their name is legion.

I.e. 'they are innumerable'. What the untamed 'man with an unclean spirit' speaking to Jesus in Mark 5:9 actually says is, 'My name is Legion: for we are many'. Jesus has said, 'Come out of the man, thou unclean spirit' and asked, 'What is thy name?' And this is the answer given. After Jesus expels the devils from the man, he puts them into a herd of swine which jump into the sea. The man is then referred to as 'him that was possessed with the devil, and had the legion'.

Luke

7 The halt and the blind.

From the parable of the great supper in Luke 14:21: 'Go out quickly into the streets and lanes of the city and bring in hither the poor, and the maimed, and the halt and the blind.' 'Halt' here means 'lame, crippled, limping'.

8 Abraham's bosom.

The place where the dead sleep contentedly takes its name from Luke 16:23: 'And it came to pass, that the beggar died, and was carried by the angels into Abraham's bosom.' This alludes to Abraham, the first of the Hebrew patriarchs.

John

9 Jesus wept.

John 11:35 is the shortest verse in the Bible (the shortest sentence would be 'Amen'). It occurs in the story of the raising of Lazarus. Jesus is moved by the plight of Mary and Martha, the sisters of Lazarus, who break down and weep when Lazarus is sick. When Jesus sees the dying man he, too, weeps.

Compare Victor Hugo's centenary oration on Voltaire (1878): 'Jesus wept; Voltaire smiled. Of that divine tear and of that human smile the sweetness of present civilization is composed.'

Like it or not, the phrase has also become an expletive to express exasperation. The most notable uttering was by Richard Dimbleby, the TV commentator, on 27 May 1965. In a broadcast in which everything went wrong during a Royal visit to West Germany, Dimbleby let slip this oath when he thought his words were not being broadcast.

A graffito from the 1970s, from the advertising agency which lost the Schweppes account, was: 'Jesus wepped.'

1 *Greater love hath no man than this . . .*

'that a man lay down his life for his friends' (John 15:13). In a memorable jibe at Harold Macmillan's 'night of the long knives' in 1962, Jeremy Thorpe told the House of Commons: 'Greater love hath no man than this, that he lay down his friends for his life.'

2 *A seamless robe.*

The title of a book, subtitled 'Broadcasting Philosophy and Practice' (1979) by Sir Charles Curran, a former Director-General of the BBC, was *The Seamless Robe*. The phrase was meant to describe 'the impossibility of separating out any one strand of the job from another . . . It was impossible to disentangle, in the whole pattern, one thread from another'. It derives from John 19:23: 'The soldiers, when they had crucified Jesus, took . . . his coat: now the coat was without seam, woven from the top throughout.'

3 *Now Barabbas was a robber.*

Now Barabbas . . . was the title of a film (UK, 1949) about prisoners, based on a play by William Douglas-Home, but also known as *Now Barabbas was a Robber*. Its origin is the passage in John 18:40 in which Pilate is asking the crowd whether Jesus should be the prisoner customarily released at Passover: 'Then cried they all again saying, Not this man, but Barabbas. Now Barabbas was a robber.'

See also BYRON 79:5.

Acts of the Apostles

4 *And he went on his way rejoicing.*

This expression used in allusion to Acts 8:39 should be treated with caution. It refers to a eunuch — a high official of the Queen of Ethiopia — who has been baptized by Philip.

Romans

5 *For the wages of sin is death; but the gift of God is eternal life through Jesus Christ our Lord.*

This is St Paul speaking in Romans 6:23. 'For sin pays a wage, and the wage is death', is the New English Bible's version. The strength of expression derives from the perfectly correct singular verb 'is', where the listener might be more comfortable with 'are'.

6 *Vengeance is mine, saith the Lord.*

No, he doesn't, nor does Paul the Apostle in his epistle to the Romans (12:19). Paul writes: 'Dearly beloved, avenge not yourselves, but rather give place unto wrath: for it is written, Vengeance is mine; I will repay, saith the Lord. Therefore if thine enemy hunger, feed him; if he thirst, give him drink: for in so doing thou shalt heap coals of fire on his head.'

Paul is quoting 'To me belongeth vengeance, and recompence', which occurs in Deuteronomy 32:35 and is also alluded to in Psalm 94:1 and Hebrews 10:30.

7 *The powers that be.*

Now used to describe any form of authority exercising social or political control, this phrase derives from Romans 13:1: 'Let every soul be subject unto the higher powers. For there is no power but of God: the powers that be are ordained of God.' The New English Bible has: 'the existing authorities are instituted by him.'

Galatians

8 *Be not deceived; God is not mocked: for whatsoever a man soweth, that shall he also reap.*

From Galatians 6:7. 'God is not mocked' is a favourite text of the super-religious when confronted with any form of blasphemy. The New English Bible chooses rather to say that, 'God is not to be fooled', which does not convey the same element of abusiveness towards the deity.

Philippians

1 *With Christ, which is far better.*

Quite a common text on gravestones, though it can seem rather ungenerous to those who survive. 'Better than what?' one is tempted to ask. The allusion is to St Paul's Epistle to the Philippians (1:23) in which Paul compares the folly of living with the wisdom of dying: 'For I am in a strait betwixt the two, having a desire to depart, and to be with Christ; which is far better.'

2 *The peace of God, which passeth all understanding, shall keep your hearts and minds through Christ Jesus.*

This 'grace' comes as Paul is signing off his letter (4:7), though the final verse (4:23) is: 'The grace of our Lord Jesus Christ be with you all.' Archdeacon Plume (1630–1704) recorded a remark of King James I's about the poet and cleric, John Donne: 'Dr Donne's verses are like the peace of God; they pass all understanding.'

See also LUTYENS 223:3.

1 Timothy

3 *A bishop then must be blameless, the husband of one wife . . . Not given to wine, no striker, not greedy of filthy lucre.*

3:2-3. The New English Bible translates 'no striker' as 'not a brawler'. Filthy lucre is 'money', though the original Greek suggests more 'dishonourable gain'. The phrase is also used by Paul, in the same context, in Titus 1:7 and 1:11, and in 1 Peter 5:2. The word 'lucre' also occurs in the Old Testament (1 Samuel 8:3).

4 *Money is the root of all evil.*

6:10 has, rather, 'the love of money is the root of all evil'.

Hebrews

5 *We have not here a lasting city.*

A request from a correspondent in Ireland wanting to know the 'author of [this] quota-

tion and the title of the book or poem, if any, in which it appeared' was instructive. At first glance it was not a very notable saying, but that has never stopped one from appealing to somebody, somewhere. The solution, however, was interesting, if only because it reminds us that there are more translations of the Bible than we may care to realize, and more ways of expressing the simplest thought than we might think possible.

It was soon spotted that it was probably a version of Hebrews 13:14, which goes (in the Authorized Version), 'For here have we no continuing city, but we seek one to come [i.e. heaven]'. The Revised Version says, 'For we have not here an abiding city'; the Good News Bible says, 'For there is no permanent city for us here on earth'; the Jerusalem Bible has, 'For there is no eternal city for us in this life'; the New English Bible, 'For we have no permanent home'; the New International Bible, kindly placed by my hotel bed, has, 'For here we do not have an enduring city, but we are looking for the city that is to come'.

Relaying this information back to the original questioner, I soon heard from him that he had now found *his* version in the Douai-Rheims Bible (1609): 'For we have not here a lasting city, but we seek one that is to come.' Next day I happened to be reading Chapter 3 of Churchill's *History of the English-Speaking Peoples* (Vol. 1) in which he quoted the verse, in the Authorized Version, of course. In T.S. Eliot's *Murder in the Cathedral* (1937) we find the line: 'Here is no continuing city, here is no abiding stay.'

Revelation

6 *Faithful unto death.*

2:10 − 'Be thou faithful unto death and I will give thee a crown of life' − became, in due course, the title of a painting by Sir Edward John Poynter PRA, showing a centurion staying at his sentry post during the eruption of Vesuvius which destroyed Pompeii in 79AD. In the background, citizens are panicking as molten lava falls upon them. The picture was inspired by the discovery of an actual skeleton of a soldier in full armour excavated at Pompeii in the late eighteenth or early nineteenth century. Many such remains were found of people 'frozen' in the positions they had held as they died. Bulwer-Lytton described what might have happened to the soldier in his *Last Days of Pompeii* (1834). Poynter painted the scene in 1865;

it now hangs in the Walker Art Gallery, Liverpool.

1 *And I looked, and behold a pale horse: and his name that sat on him was death.*

6:8 has given a phrase much used in titles: Katherine Anne Porter's novel *Pale Horse, Pale Rider* (1939), Agatha Christie's novel *Pale Horse* (1961), and Emeric Pressburger's film script *Behold a Pale Horse* (1964).

2 *The bottomless pit.*

A description of Hell from 20:1: 'And I saw an angel come down from heaven, having the key of the bottomless pit.' The phrase is quoted in Milton *Paradise Lost*, Bk. 6, l. 864 (1667):

> Headlong themselves they threw
> Down from the verge of Heaven, eternal wrath
> Burnt after them to the bottomless pit.

William Pitt the Younger, British Prime Minister (1783–1801, 1804–6) was nicknamed 'the Bottomless Pitt', on account of his thinness. A caricature attributed to James Gillray with this title shows Pitt as Chancellor of the Exchequer introducing his 1792 budget. His bottom is non-existent.

Apocrypha (New Testament)
Acts of St John

3 *The heavenly spheres make music for us. All things join in the dance.*

This is the unattributed text on the grave of Imogen Holst in the churchyard of St Peter and St Paul's, Aldeburgh, Suffolk. She was a musical educationalist, conductor, composer (especially of songs) and arranger of folk-songs. She collaborated with Benjamin Britten whose grave is but a few feet in front of hers. Her father, the composer Gustav Holst (1874-1934) unwittingly provided his daughter's epitaph. It comes from a text he prepared and translated himself from the Greek of the Apocryphal Acts of St John for his *Hymn of Jesus* (1917). The passage concerns Jesus, 'before he was taken by the lawless Jews', calling on his disciples to 'sing a hymn to the Father', at which they join hands in a ring and dance. Rosamund Strode of the Holst Foundation has commented: 'Since to Imogen dancing was every bit as important as music (and indeed she once hoped to be a dancer), the two lines seemed to us appropriate in every possible way.'

Vulgate

4 *Quo vadis? [Whither goest thou?]*

These words come from the Latin translation (the Vulgate) of John 13:36: 'Simon Peter said unto him, Lord, whither goest thou? Jesus answered him, Whither I go, thou canst not follow me now'; and from John 16:5 in which Christ comforts his disciples before the Crucifixion. The words also occur in Genesis 32:17 and in the Acts of St Peter among the New Testament Apocrypha in which, after the Crucifixion, Peter, fleeing Rome, encounters Christ on the Appian Way. He asks Him, '*Domine, quo vadis?*' ('Lord, whither goest thou?') and Christ replies, '*Venio Romam, iterum crucifigi*' ('I am coming to Rome to be crucified again'.)

Famously used as the title of a film (US, 1951, and of two previous Italian ones) and of an opera (1909) by Jean Nouguès, all of them based on a novel with the title (1896) by a Pole, Henryk Sienkiewicz.

See also: 'Cleanliness is next to Godliness' — WESLEY 351:1; 'God tempers the wind to the shorn lamb' — STERNE 320:2.

Bickerstaffe, Isaac
Irish playwright (*c* 1735–*c* 1812)

5 *I care for nobody, no, not I, And nobody cares for me.*

This should be 'I care for nobody, not I,/If no one cares for me', if one is quoting from Bickerstaffe's comic opera *Love in a Village* (1762). Is the misquoted version easier to sing?

Billings, Josh
(pseudonym of Henry Wheeler Shaw)
American humorist (1818–85)

6 *Love iz like the meazles.*

From the 'Affurisms' in *Josh Billings: His Sayings* (1865). He goes on: 'We kant have it bad but onst, and the later in life we have it the tuffer it goes with us.'

7 *'Vote early and vote often' is the Politishun's golden rule.*

From *Josh Billings' Wit and Humour* (1874), which seems merely to be recalling an adage. Indeed, earlier, William Porcher

Miles had said in a speech to the House of Representatives (31 March 1858): ' "Vote early and vote often", the advice openly displayed on the election banners in one of our northern cities.'

Safire (1978) ignores both these sources but mentions that historian James Morgan found 'in his 1926 book of biographies' that the original jokester was John Van Buren, a New York lawyer (d 1866), who was the son of President Martin Van Buren.

Binyon, Laurence
English poet (1869–1943)

1 *They shall grow not old, as we that are left grow old:*
Age shall not weary them, nor the years condemn.
At the going down of the sun and in the morning
We will remember them.

The poem 'For the Fallen' was first printed in *The Times*, 21 September 1914, and subsequently in Binyon's *The Four Years*. Spoken at numerous Armistice Day and Remembrance Day services since, the opening phrase is frequently rendered wrongly 'They shall *not grow old* . . .' — as, for example, on the war memorial at Staines, Middlesex.

Bird, John
English actor (1936–)

2 *That Was the Week That Was.*

This was the title of BBC TV's famous 'satire' series (1962–3), also used in the US. In *A Small Thing — Like an Earthquake* (1983), the producer, Ned Sherrin, credits the coinage to the actor John Bird who was originally going to take part in the programme. It was in conscious imitation of the 'That's Shell–That Was' advertisements of the early 1930s. Often abbreviated to 'TW3'.

Birt, John
English broadcasting executive (1944–)

3 *There is a bias in television journalism. It is not against any particular party or point of view — it is a bias against* understanding.

Birt, who later became Director-General of the BBC and famous for promoting a dry,

analytical approach to current affairs broadcasting, was working in the commercial sector when he coined the phrase 'bias against understanding'. In 1986, he told me: 'The problem of authorship that you raise is difficult. The phrase first appeared in the article in *The Times* of 28 February 1975. This article was written by me but was the result of a dialogue of years with Peter Jay. Subsequently we went on to write together a series of articles on the same subject. I don't think it would be wrong of me to claim authorship of the phrase; but it would only be just to acknowledge Peter's role.'

Bismarck, Otto von
Prusso-German statesman (1815–98)

4 *Blood and iron.*

When Bismarck addressed the Budget Commission of the Prussian House of Delegates on 30 September 1862, what he said was: 'It is desirable and it is necessary that the condition of affairs in Germany and of her constitutional relations should be improved; but this cannot be accomplished by speeches and resolutions of a majority, but only by iron and blood [*Eisen und Blut*].' On 28 January 1886, speaking to the Prussian House of Deputies, he did, however, use the words in the more familiar order: 'This policy cannot succeed through speeches and shooting-matches and songs; it can only be carried out through blood and iron [*Blut und Eisen*].'

The words may have achieved their more familiar order, at least to English ears, through their use by A.C. Swinburne in his poem 'A Word for the Country' (1884): 'Not with dreams, but with blood and with iron, shall a nation be moulded at last.' (Eric Partridge, while identifying this source correctly in *A Dictionary of Clichés*, 1966 edition, ascribes the authorship to Tennyson.) On the other hand, the Roman orator Quintillian (first century AD) used the exact phrase *sanguinem et ferrum*.

5 *When a lady says no, she means perhaps . . .*

In October 1982, Lord Denning, then a senior British jurist, was quoted as having commented on the difference between a diplomat and a lady, at a meeting of the Magistrates Association, in these words: 'When a diplomat says yes, he means perhaps. When he says perhaps, he means no. When he says no, he is not a diplomat. When a lady says no, she means perhaps. When she says perhaps, she means yes. But when she says yes, she is no lady.'

Whether Denning claimed it as his own is not recorded, but in Hans Severus Ziegler's *Heitere Muse: Anekdoten aus Kultur und Geschichte* (1974), the passage appears in a (possibly apocryphal) anecdote concerning Bismarck at a ball in St Petersburg. His partner, whom he had been flattering, told him, 'One can't believe a word you diplomats say' and provided the first half of the description as above. Then Bismarck replied with the second half.

Blackstone, Sir William
English jurist (1723–80)

1 *The king can do no wrong.*

Blackstone wrote in his *Commentaries on the Laws of England* (1765): 'That the king can do no wrong, is a necessary and fundamental principle of the English constitution.' That is the only citation in the ODQ (1992). Nevertheless, the concept was not original to Blackstone. John Selden's *Table-Talk* (1689) has, 'The King can do no wrong, that is no Process can be granted against him'; and one is told (unverified) that Judge Orlando Bridgeman said it in the the trial of the regicides after the restoration of the monarchy in 1660. But Bridgeman did go on to say that ministers *could* do wrong *in the king's name* and the fault should, therefore, be held against the ministers. In the same year, Cunelgus Bonde in his *Scutum regale; the royal buckler, or vox legis, a lecture to the traytors who most wickedly murthered Charles the I*, wrote: 'The King can do no wrong; Therefore cannot be a disseisor [dispossessor].'

Even earlier, John Milton in *Eikonoklastes* (1649) had written: 'As the King of England can doe no wrong, so neither can he doe right but . . . by his courts.' In other words, it was a venerable idea, even by the time Blackstone expressed it, as is attested by the legal maxim (of no known date) to the same effect, expressed in Latin: '*Rex non potest peccare.*'

Later, in 1822, giving judgement in the case of 'the goods of King George III, deceased', Mr Justice John Nicholl said: 'The king can do no wrong; he cannot constitutionally be supposed capable of injustice.' And, *mutatis mutandis*, Richard Nixon tried to assert the same principle on behalf of the American Presidency in his TV interviews with David Frost in May 1977:

'When the President does it, that means it is not illegal.'

Blake, Eubie
American jazz musician (1883–1983)

2 *If I'd known I was gonna live this long, I'd have taken better care of myself.*

The centenarian boogie-woogie pianist, ragtime composer and lyricist, was so quoted in the *Observer* (13 February 1983). Unfortunately, five days after marking his centennial, Blake died. Even so, his felicitous remark was not original. In *Radio Times* (17 February 1979), Benny Green quoted Adolph Zukor, founder of Paramount Pictures, as having said on the approach to his hundredth birthday: 'If I'd known how old I was going to be I'd have taken better care of myself'. Zukor died in 1976, having been born in 1873.

Blake, William
English poet and painter (1757–1827)

3 *And did those feet in ancient time?*
Walk upon England's mountains green?
And was the holy Lamb of God
On England's pleasant pastures seen?

And did the Countenance Divine
Shine forth upon our clouded hills?
And was Jerusalem builded here
Among these dark Satanic mills?

Blake's short preface to his poem *Milton* (1804–10) has come to be called 'Jerusalem' as a result of the immensely popular musical setting (1916) by Sir Hubert Parry which has become an alternative British National Anthem. It should not to be confused with Blake's other poem with the title *Jerusalem: The Emanation of the Giant Albion*. Because of the musical setting's magnificent hymn-like nature, it would not be surprising if most people believed the 'feet' were those of Jesus Christ, but this is not the case. Additionally, because of the poem's date, it might be assumed that the 'dark Satanic mills' had something to do with the Industrial Revolution.

In fact, as F.W. Bateson points out in *English Poetry* (1950), the poem would appear to be an 'anti-clerical paean of free love'. It originally came at the end of a prose preface, Bateson notes, in which Blake attacked the practice of drawing on 'Greek or Roman models'. The phrase 'in ancient time' alludes to the legend that Pythagoras derived his philosophical system from the British Druids. So, Blake is saying, it is foolish to rely on classical models when these originally derived from primitive Britain.

As for the significance of the name 'Jerusalem', Blake refers to this in a later Prophetic Book: 'Jerusalem is nam'd Liberty/ Among the sons of Albion'. Rather than indicating some Utopian ideal, 'Jerusalem' stands for something much more abstract — sexual liberty, Bateson thinks.

Another passage in *Milton* makes it clear that the 'dark Satanic mills' are nothing industrial but rather the altars of the churches on which the clergy of Blake's time were plying 'their deadly Druidic trade', in Bateson's phrase. It is no wonder that the meaning of the poem is so widely misunderstood when it can be perceived only through a thicket of footnotes.

1 *Chariots of Fire.*

This title was given to a film (UK, 1981) about the inner drives of two athletes (one a future missionary) in the 1924 Olympics. Appropriately for a film whose basic themes included Englishness, Christianity and Judaism, the title comes from Blake's *Milton*/'Jerusalem', which is sung in Parry's setting at the climax of the film:

> Bring me my bow of burning gold,
> Bring me my arrow of desire
> Bring me my spear! Oh, clouds unfold
> Bring me my chariot of fire.

Note the singular. 'Chariots of fire' in the plural occurs in 2 Kings 6:17: 'And the Lord opened the eyes of the young man; and he saw: and, behold, the mountain was full of horses and chariots of fire round about Elisha.'

2 *The Doors of Perception.*

Aldous Huxley gave this title to a book (1954) about his experiments with mescaline and LSD. Its source is Blake's *The Marriage of Heaven and Hell* (c 1790): 'If the doors of perception [i.e. the senses] were cleansed, every thing would appear to man as it is, infinite'. This view was seized upon by proponents of drug culture in the 1960s and from it was also derived the name of the US vocal/instrumental group the Doors.

3 *The eyes as windows of the soul.*

In *Zuleika Dobson* (1911) Max Beerbohm wrote: 'It needs no dictionary of quotations to remind me that the eyes are the windows of the soul.' Just in case it does, this is a reference to Blake's 'The Everlasting Gospel' (c 1818): 'This life's five windows of the soul/Distort the Heavens from pole to pole,/And leads you to believe a lie/When you see with, not thro', the eye'. Here, Blake seems to be saying that the five *senses* (or perhaps two eyes, two ears, and a nose?) are the windows of the soul. Compare ELIZABETH I 134:2.

4 *Heaven's Gate.*

Michael Cimino's 1980 film with this title is famous for having lost more money than any other film to date — about £34 million. In it, 'Heaven's Gate' is the name of a roller-skating rink used by settlers and immigrants in Wyoming in 1891. Conceivably, the name is meant to be taken as an ironic one for the rough situation many of the characters find themselves in as they arrive to start a new life.

The idea of a 'gate to heaven' goes back to the Bible. For example, Genesis 28:17 has: 'This is none other but the house of God, and this is the gate of heaven.' Psalm 78:23 has: 'He commanded the clouds from above, and opened the doors of heaven.' Shakespeare twice uses the phrase. In *Cymbeline* (II.iii.20) there is the song, 'Hark, hark, the lark at heaven's gate sings' and Sonnet 29 has 'Like to the lark at break of day arising/From sullen earth sings hymns at heaven's gate.'

Steven Bach in his book *Final Cut* (1985) about the making of the film cites two more possible sources. Blake in *Jerusalem* (1820) wrote:

> I give you the end of a golden string;
> Only wind it into a ball,
> It will lead you in at Heaven's gate,
> Built in Jerusalem's wall.

Browning uses the phrase and there is a poem by Wallace Stevens with the title 'The Worms at Heaven's Gate'.

Blanch, Lesley
English writer (1907–   )

5 *The Wilder Shores of Love.*

The title of a biographical study (1954) in which Blanch describes four nineteenth-century women 'who found fulfilment as women along wilder *Eastern* shores'. Describing Jane Digby, she writes: 'She was an Amazon. Her whole life was spent riding at breakneck speed towards the wilder shores of love.'

Blunt, Alfred
English Bishop (1879–1957)

1 *The benefit of the King's Coronation depends under God upon . . . the faith, prayer and self-dedication of the King himself . . . We hope that he is aware of this need. Some of us wish that he gave more positive signs of such awareness.*

Press comment on the relationship between King Edward VIII and Wallis Simpson finally burst through following these innocuous remarks made on 1 December 1936 by the Bishop of Bradford. Speaking at a diocesan conference, he was dealing with a suggestion that the forthcoming Coronation should be secularized and with criticism that the King was not a regular churchgoer. The *Yorkshire Post* linked the Bishop's words to rumours then in circulation. Dr Blunt claimed subsequently that his address had been written six weeks earlier, without knowledge of the rumours, and added: 'I studiously took care to say nothing of the King's private life, because I know nothing about it.'

Boesky, Ivan
American financier (1937–   )

2 *Greed is all right . . . Greed is healthy. You can be greedy and still feel good about yourself.*

Part of a commencement address when receiving an honorary degree at the University of California at Berkeley on 18 May 1986. Boesky also said, 'Seek wealth, it's good'. In December 1987 he was sentenced to three years imprisonment for insider dealing on the New York Stock Exchange. It was no coincidence that in the 1987 US film *Wall Street*, Oliver Stone gave Michael Douglas (playing Gordon Gekko) these words to say: 'Greed, for want of a better word, is good.' Bartlett (1992) has: 'Greed is good! Greed is right! Greed works! Greed will save the U.S.A.!'

Bogart, Humphrey
American film actor (1899–1957)

3 *Tennis, anyone?*

Wrongly said to have been Bogart's sole line in his first appearance in a stage play. A terrible wild-goose chase was launched by Jonah Ruddy and Jonathan Hill in their book *Bogey: The Man, The Actor, The Legend* (1965). Describing Bogart's early career as a stage actor (*c* 1921) they said: 'In those early Broadway days he didn't play menace parts. "I always made my entrance carrying a tennis racquet, baseball bat, or golf club. I was the athletic type, with hair slicked back and wrapped in a blazer. The only line I didn't say was, 'Give me the ball, coach, I'll take it through'. Yes, sir, I was Joe College or Joe Country Club all the time." It was hard to imagine him as the originator of that famous theatrical line – "Tennis anyone?" – but he was.'

It is clear from this extract that the authors were adding their own gloss to what Bogart had said. Bartlett (1968) joined in and said it was his 'sole line in his first play'. But Bogart had denied ever having said it (quoted in Goodman, *Bogey: The Good-Bad Boy*, 1965, and in an ABC TV film of 1974 using old film of him doing so.)

Alistair Cooke in *Six Men* (1977) is more cautious: 'It is said he appeared in an ascot and blue blazer and tossed off the invitation "Tennis, anyone?"' but adds that Bogart probably did not coin the phrase.

4 *Play it again, Sam.*

Of course, Humphrey Bogart never actually said this in the film *Casablanca* (1942), when talking to Sam, played by Dooley Wilson. Sam is the night club pianist and reluctant performer of the sentimental song 'As Time Goes By'. At one point Ingrid Bergman, as Ilsa, does have this exchange with him:

> *Ilsa:* Play it once, Sam, for old time's sake.
> *Sam:* I don't know what you mean, Miss Ilsa.
> *Ilsa:* Play it, Sam. Play, 'As Time Goes By.'

Later on Bogart, as Rick, also tries to get Sam to play it:

> *Rick:* You know what I want to hear.
> *Sam:* No, I don't.
> *Rick:* You played it for her, [and] you can play it for me.
> *Sam:* Well, I don't think I can remember it.
> *Rick:* If she can stand it, I can. Play it.

All one can say is that the saying was utterly well established by the time Woody Allen thus entitled his play *Play It Again Sam*

(1969, filmed 1972) about a film critic who is abandoned by his wife and obtains the help of Bogart's 'shade'. By listing it under Allen's name, Bartlett (1980 and 1992) might be thought to suggest that Allen coined the phrase. It would be interesting to know by which year it had really become established.

1 *Drop the gun, Louie.*

Alistair Cooke writing in *Six Men* (1977) remarked of Bogart: 'He gave currency to another phrase with which the small fry of the English-speaking world brought the neighbourhood sneak to heel: "Drop the gun, Looey!"' Quite how Bogart did this, Cooke does not reveal. We have Bogart's word for it: 'I never said, "Drop the gun, Louie"' (quoted in Ezra Goodman, *Bogey: The Good-Bad Guy*, 1965).

It is just another of those lines that people would like to have heard spoken but that never were. At the end of *Casablanca* (1942) what Bogart says to Claude Rains (playing Captain Louis Renault) is: 'Not so fast, Louis.' Ironically, it is *Renault* who says: 'Put that gun down.'

2 *If you want anything — just whistle.*

This is not a direct quotation (though often given as such) but is derived from lines in the film *To Have and Have Not* (1945). What Lauren Bacall says *to* Bogart (and not the other way round, as in *PDMQ*, 1980) is: 'You know you don't have to act with me, Steve. You don't have to say anything, and you don't have to do anything. Not a thing. Oh, maybe just whistle. You know how to whistle, don't you, Steve? You just put your lips together and blow.'

Bogart, John B.
American journalist (1845–1921)

3 *If a man bites a dog, that is news . . .*

As a definition of news, this has been variously ascribed. Chiefly, in the form, 'When a dog bites a man, that is not news, because it happens so often. But if a man bites a dog, that is news,' to John B. Bogart, city editor of the New York *Sun*, 1873–90. To Charles A. Dana, the editor of the same paper from 1868 to 1897, it has been ascribed in the form: 'If a dog bites a man, it's a story; if a man bites a dog, it's a good story.'

Bone, Sir David
Scottish novelist (1874–1959)

4 *It's 'Damn you, Jack — I'm all right!' with you chaps.*

From *The Brassbounder* (1910), one of Bone's many novels set on the sea and based on his own experiences (he rose to be Commodore of the Anchor Line). Partridge/ *Catch Phrases* suggests this saying (certainly not Bone's coinage) may have arisen *c* 1880 in the form 'Fuck you, Jack, I'm all right'. The bowdlerized versions 'typified concisely the implied and often explicit arrogance of many senior officers towards the ranks', in the navy, hence the use of 'Jack', the traditional name for a sailor since *c* 1700.

Book of Common Prayer, The
1662 version

5 *The quick and the dead.*

In the Apostles' Creed: 'From thence he [Christ] shall come to judge the quick and the dead', 'quick' meaning 'alive'.

To Lord Dewar (1864–1930), a British industrialist, is credited the joke that there are 'only two classes of pedestrians in these days of reckless motor traffic — the quick, and the dead'. George Robey ascribed it to Dewar in *Looking Back on Life* (1933). A *Times* leader in April that same year merely ventured: 'The saying that there are two sorts of pedestrians, the quick and the dead, is well matured.'

6 *The world, the flesh, and the devil.*

This expression with the words in the order given — as, for example, in a 1959 film title — comes from the Litany in the Book of Common Prayer: 'From fornication, and all other deadly sin; and from all the deceits of the world, the flesh and the devil, Good Lord, deliver us.' Again, in the Collect for the Eighteenth Sunday after Trinity, we find: 'Lord, we beseech thee, grant thy people grace to withstand the temptations of the world, the flesh, and the devil.'

The same combination also occurs in the Catechism, where the confirmee is asked what his Godfathers and Godmothers had promised for him at his baptism: 'First, that I should renounce the *devil* and all his works, the pomps and vanity of this wicked *world*, and all the sinful lusts of the *flesh*.'

In the sixteenth and seventeenth centuries, the words were also grouped together in a different order to denote 'our ghostly enemies' — as, for example, 'the devil, the world, and the flesh' (1530).

1 N or M.

In the Catechism the guide answer to the first question 'What is your name?' is not intended to indicate where a male or female Christian name should be inserted. 'N' is the first letter of the Latin *nomen* ('name') and 'M' is a contraction of 'NN' standing for the plural *nomina* ('names'). So it just means 'name or names'.

Agatha Christie used the title *N or M?* for a spy story published in 1941.

2 Till death us do part.

A frequently mistaken phrase from the Solemnization of Matrimony — i.e. *not* 'till death do us part'. Originally, the phrase was 'till death us depart' = 'separate completely'.

3 The iron has entered into his soul.

The Prayer Book version of Psalms 105:18 is: 'Whose feet they hurt in the stocks: the iron entered into his soul' (which is a mistranslation of the Hebrew). As a phrase meaning, 'he has become embittered, anguished', it was used notably by David Lloyd George about Sir John Simon (who split away from him in the Liberal Party): 'He has sat so long upon the fence that the iron has entered into his soul.' The English title of Jean-Paul Sartre's novel *La Mort dans L'âme* (1949) is *Iron in the Soul*.

4 All good things come to an end.

The proverbial expression meaning 'pleasure cannot go on for ever' would seem to be a corruption of the Prayer Book version of Psalm 119:96: 'I see that all things come to an end: but thy commandment is exceeding broad' (note the lack of 'good'). The original Bible text is: 'I have seen an end of all perfection: but thy commandment is exceeding broad.' But there are versions of the proverb going back to 1440, and as 'Everything has an end', the idea appears in Chaucer's *Troilus and Criseyde* (1385).

5 By the waters of Babylon we sat down and wept.

The metrical versions of the Psalms in the Prayer Book differ significantly in wording and verse numbering from the Psalms in the Bible. This is the Prayer Book version of Psalm 137:1, of which the original is: 'By the rivers of Babylon, there we sat down, yea, we wept, when we remembered Zion.'

The 'waters' version is the much preferred usage. Horace Walpole (in a letter, 12 June 1775) has: 'By the waters of Babylon we sit down and weep, when we think of thee, O America!'

6 O put not your trust in princes, nor in any child of man: for there is no help in them.

The Prayer Book version of Psalm 146:2 is different from the Bible's 146:3, which is: 'Put not your trust in princes, nor in the son of man, in whom there is no help.'

7 In which we serve.

The title of the Noël Coward naval film (UK, 1942) comes from the Prayer Book 'Forms of Prayer to Be Used at Sea': 'Be pleased to receive into thy Almighty and most gracious protection the persons of us thy servants, and the Fleet in which we serve.'

Booth, John Wilkes
American assassin (1838–65)

8 Sic semper tyrannis! The South is avenged.

Booth shot President Lincoln in his box the Ford Theatre, Washington D.C., on 14 April 1865. Then, falling from the box on to the stage, he addressed the audience with the Latin words meaning, 'Thus always to tyrants' (which is the motto of the State of Virginia). The rest of the cry may be apocryphal but was reported in the *New York Times* the following day.

'When Abraham Lincoln was murdered/ The one thing that interested Matthew Arnold/Was that the assassin shouted in Latin/As he leapt on the stage./This convinced Matthew/That there was still hope for America' — Christopher Morley (*d* 1957), *Points of View.*

Borges, Jorge Luis
Argentinian novelist (1899–1986)

9 The Falklands thing was a fight between two bald men over a comb.

The *ODMQ* (1991) and *ODQ* (1992) may have caused readers to think that it was

Borges who originated the remark about 'two bald men fighting over a comb'. Not so. Borges was quoted by *Time* Magazine on 14 February 1983 as having characterized the previous year's Falklands conflict between Britain and Argentina in these words. *Time* is unable to say for sure where it acquired this quotation, though it has had a good rummage among its yellowing files. It may have picked it up from the Spanish paper *La Nación* (28 June 1982), which was apparently quoting from an interview with Borges that had appeared in *Le Monde* the previous day.

But the basic expression about bald men fighting over combs had very definitely been around before 1983. Robert Nye wrote in *The Times* (18 June 1981): 'I think it was Christopher Logue who once characterized the drabness of the English Movement poets of the 1950s as being like the antics of two bald men fighting for possession of a comb.'

It occurs even earlier in *H.L. Mencken's Dictionary of Quotations* (1942) as 'Two baldheaded men are fighting over a comb' (listed as a 'Russian saying') and in Champion's *Racial Proverbs* (1938).

Bosquet, Pierre
French General (1810–61)

1 C'est magnifique — mais ce n'est pas la guerre *[It is magnificent, but it is not war]*.

This remark was made by Maréchal Bosquet (1810–61) about the Charge of the Light Brigade at the Battle of Balaclava (25 October 1854). It is the source of several witticisms: *Punch* during the First World War said of margarine: '*C'est magnifique, mais ce n'est pas le beurre*' [butter], and of the façade of Worcester College, Oxford, which has a splendid clock on it, Anon. said: '*C'est magnifique, mais ce n'est pas la gare*' [station].

Bourdillon, F.W.
English poet (1852–1921)

2 The Night Has a Thousand Eyes.

The story with this title (1945) by Cornell Woolrich (about a vaudeville entertainer who can predict the future) was adapted as a film (US, 1948), and gave rise to several songs. The phrase comes from the poem 'Light' by Francis William Bourdillon in *Among the Flowers* (1878). The phrase

'Night hath a thousand eyes' had occurred earlier, however, in the play *The Maydes Metamorphosis* (1600) by John Lyly.

Boyer, Charles
French film actor (1899–1978)

3 Come with me to the Casbah.

This is a line forever associated with the film *Algiers* (1938) and its star, Charles Boyer. He is supposed to have said it to Hedy Lamarr. Boyer impersonators used it and the film was laughed at because of it, but nowhere in is it said in the film. It was simply a Hollywood legend that grew up. Boyer himself denied he had ever said it and thought it had been invented by a press agent.

Braham, John
English singer and songwriter (1774–1856)

4 England, home and beauty.

'The Death of Nelson', from the opera *The Americans* (1811) by John Braham and S.J. Arnold, was one of the most popular songs of the nineteenth century. Here are the lyrics that suggest the phrase 'England, home and beauty', though the words do not appear exactly in that order:

'Twas in Trafalgar bay,
We saw the Frenchmen lay,
Each heart was bounding then,
We scorn'd the foreign yoke
For our ships were British Oak,
And hearts of Oak our men.

Our Nelson mark'd them on the wave,
Three cheers our gallant Seamen gave,
Nor thought of home or beauty (*rpt.*)
Along the line this signal ran,
'England expects that every man
This day will do his duty!' (*rpt.*)

Charles Dickens has Captain Cuttle quote, 'Though lost to sight, to memory dear, and England, Home, and Beauty!' in *Dombey and Son*, Chap. 48 (1844–6), though these words do not appear in the text consulted (there may be other versions).

Braham was not alone in perceiving the rhyming delights of 'duty' and 'beauty'. In Gilbert and Sullivan's *Trial by Jury* (1875), 'Time may do his duty' is rhymed with 'Winter hath a beauty', at which point, Ian Bradley in his annotated edition remarks: 'This is the first of no fewer than fifteen occasions, exclusive of repetitions, when the words "duty" and "beauty" are rhymed in the Savoy Operas . . . *HMS Pinafore* holds the record with four separate songs in which the words are rhymed.'

Home and Beauty (simply) was the title of a play (1919) by Somerset Maugham, concerning the complications surrounding a First World War 'widow' who remarries and whose original husband then turns up (in the US the play was known as *Too Many Husbands*).

Braine, John
English novelist (1922–86)

1 *Room at the Top.*

Braine merely re-popularized this phrase as the title of his immensely popular novel (1957). Much earlier, in reply to advice not to become a lawyer because it was an overcrowded profession, Daniel Webster (1782–1852) had replied, 'There is always room at the top'.

Brandeis, Louis D.
American jurist (1856–1941)

2 *Publicity is justly commended as a remedy for social and industrial diseases. Sunlight is said to be the best of disinfectants; electric light the most efficient policeman.*

Wise words from *Harper's Weekly* (20 December 1913). Compare the saying, 'Rain is the best policeman of all', heard from a senior police officer after London's Notting Hill Carnival had been rained off on the Late Summer Bank Holiday in August 1986. Meaning that the incidence of crime falls when the rain does (as it also does in very cold weather).

Brando, Marlon
American film actor (1924–)

3 *An actor's a guy who, if you ain't talking about him, ain't listening.*

Quoted in the *Observer* (January 1956). In fact, Brando appears to have been quoting George Glass (1910–84)

[*Source:* Bob Thomas, *Brando*, 1973.]

Branson, Richard
English entrepreneur (1950–)

4 *I believe in benevolent dictatorships, provided I am the dictator.*

His favourite remark. He was quoted as saying it in the *Observer* (25 November 1984) and again in the *Independent* (11 March 1989).

Brecht, Bertolt
German playwright (1898–1956)

5 *The alienation effect.*

Bertolt Brecht's name ('*Verfremdungseffekt*' in German) for his theory of drama, first promoted in 1937, in which the audience has to be reminded that the play it is watching is a play and not real. The effect is to distance the watchers from the players, to prevent too much emotional involvement and to reject the traditional make-believe element in theatre.

Bright, John
English Radical politician (1811–89)

6 *He is a self-made man and worships his creator.*

Mencken (1942) has, rather, Henry Clapp saying this (*c* 1858) about Horace Greeley, and dates Bright's use of the saying about Benjamin Disraeli ten years later, to *c* 1868.

7 *England is the mother of parliaments.*

That is what Bright said in a speech in Birmingham on 18 January 1865. Frequently misused, even at the highest levels. The phrase is *not* 'Westminster is the mother of parliaments'. Westminster is, rather, one of her children. Icelanders may well object that they have a prior claim to the title anyway.

Brittain, Ronald
English Regimental Sergeant-Major (*c* 1899–1981)

8 *You 'orrible little man.*

Reputed to have had the loudest voice in the British Army, Brittain received this accolade in his *Times* obituary (12 January 1981): 'With his stentorian voice and massive parade ground presence [he] came to epitomise the British Army sergeant. Though he himself denied ever using it, he was associated with the celebrated parade ground expression "You 'orrible little man" — in some quarters, indeed, was reputed to have coined it . . . His "wake up there!" to the somnolent after a command had in his opinion been inadequately executed was legendary — doubtless the ancestor of all the Wake Up Theres which have succeeded it.'

Britton, Colonel
(nom de guerre of Douglas Ritchie)
British propagandist (1905–67)

1 *The night is your friend. The V is your sign.*

During the Second World War the resistance movements in occupied Europe were encouraged from London by broadcasts over the BBC. In an English-language broadcast on 31 July 1941, 'Colonel Britton', as he was known, said: 'It's about the V — the sign of victory — that I want to talk to you now. All over Europe the V sign is seen by the Germans and to the Germans and the Quislings it is indeed the writing on the wall. It is the sign which tells them that one of the unknown soldiers has passed that way. And it's beginning to play on their nerves.

'They see it chalked on pavements, pencilled on posters, scratched on the mudguards of German cars. Flowers come up in the shape of a V; men salute each other with the V sign separating their fingers. The number five is a V and men working in the fields turn to the village clocks as the chimes sound the hour of five.'

In the same broadcast, the 'Colonel' also encouraged the use of the V in Morse code, three short taps and a heavy one: 'When you knock on a door, there's your knock. If you call a waiter in a restaurant, call him like this: "Eh, *garçon!*" [taps rhythm on wine glass] . . . Tell all your friends about it and teach them the V sound. If you and your friends are in a café and a German comes in, tap out the V sign all together.'

From these broadcasts emerged an evocative slogan: 'You wear no uniforms and your weapons differ from ours — but they are not less deadly. The fact that you wear no uniforms is your strength. The Nazi official and the German soldier don't know you. But they fear you . . . The night is your friend. The V is your sign.' (Cole Porter's song 'All Through the Night', 1934, had earlier contained the lines: 'The day is my enemy/The night is my friend.') Winston Churchill spoke of the V sign as a symbol of the 'the unconquerable will of the people of the occupied territories'. These kinds of broadcasts were also used for sending coded

messages to resistance workers in France: '*Le lapin a bu un apéritif*', '*Mademoiselle caresse le nez de son chien*', and '*Jacqueline sait le latin*' are examples of signals used to trigger sabotage operations or to warn of parachute drops.

Brooke, Rupert
English poet (1887–1915)

2 *These I have loved . . .*

A BBC radio record programme *These You Have Loved* has a history going back to 1938 when Doris Arnold introduced a selection of favourite middle-of-the-road music. The title was still being used forty years later. Originally it was chosen by way of allusion to the line 'These I have loved' in the poem 'The Great Lover' by Rupert Brooke. This is a 'list' poem in which Brooke mentions some of his favourite things' (rather as the song with that title did in the much later musical *The Sound of Music*). Brooke's 'loves' included 'white plates and cups' and 'the rough male kiss of blankets'.

3 *If I should die, think only this of me:
That there's some corner of a foreign field
That is for ever England.*

Published in 1914, Brooke's sonnet 'The Soldier' very soon made a perfect epitaph for the poet himself, who died of acute blood poisoning at Lemnos on 23 April 1915, and was buried in a foreign field. He was then a sub-lieutenant in the Royal Naval Division and was on his way by boat to fight in the Dardanelles. According to Edward Marsh's *Memoir*, at Brooke's burial a pencil inscription in Greek was put on a large white cross at the head of his grave, stating: 'Here lies the servant of God, Sub-Lieutenant in the English Navy, who died for the deliverance of Constantinople from the Turks.' Eventually (in 1983), a marble plaque bearing the whole poem was erected on the Greek island of Skyros where the poet is buried and may have replaced an earlier plaque bearing a quotation from the same poem.

Brooker, Gary
English musician and songwriter (1945–)

4 *A Whiter Shade of Pale.*

The song with this title written in 1967 by Brooker with Keith Reid — and performed by their group, Procul Harum — *appears* to contain several allusions. 'We skipped the light fandango' echoes the expression 'to trip the light fantastic', for 'to dance', which in turn echoes Milton's 'L'Allegro' ('Come, and trip it as ye go/On the light fantastic toe') or 'Comus' ('Come, knit hands, and beat the ground/In a light fantastic round'). 'As the miller told his tale' presumably refers to the 'Miller's Tale' in Chaucer's *Canterbury Tales*, and 'One of sixteen Vestal Virgins/ Were leaving for the coast' presumably refers to 'The Coast', i.e. the eastern/ western seaboards of the US.

The song as a whole — and especially the title — is a paradigm of the drug-influenced creativity of the 1960s.

Brooks, Thomas
English Puritan divine (1608–80)

1 *Heaven on Earth, or a Serious Discourse touching a well-grounded Assurance of Mens Everlasting Happiness.*

The phrase 'heaven on earth', meaning 'a perfect, very pleasant, ideal place or state of affairs' is not biblical. The title of this book (1654) is the only citation for the phrase in the *OED2*. From the *Guardian* (5 June 1986): 'The Prime Minister yesterday promised her party "a little bit of heaven on earth" produced by further tax cuts . . . Mrs Thatcher was in lyrical mood at the Conservative Women's Conference in London, talking of her vision of a society of satisfied consumers.' This was a slogan that did not catch on at all.

Brougham, Lord
Scottish jurist and politician (1778–1868)

2 *It adds a new terror to death.*

Pearson (1937) insists that what Brougham said in a 'speech on an ex-chancellor' was 'Death was now armed with a new terror', but he gives no source for the remark. What was being talked about? Biography, and in particular what Lord Campbell wrote in *Lives of the Lord Chancellors* (1845–7) without the consent of their heirs or executors. Lord Lyndhurst (three times Lord Chancellor, *d* 1863) said, 'Campbell has added another terror to death' (quoted 1924). On the other hand, the lawyer and

politician Sir Charles Wetherell (*d* 1846) is also quoted as having said of Lord Campbell: 'Then there is my noble and biographical friend who has added a new terror to death' — quoted in Lord St Leonards, *Mispresentation in Campbell's Lives of Lyndhurst and Brougham* (1869). So everyone seems to have been saying it.

Pearson adds that before all this, the expression had been used when bookseller Edmund Curll (1683-1747) used to churn out cheap lives of famous people as soon as they were dead. John Arbuthnot had called him, 'One of the new terrors of death' (in a letter to Swift, 13 January 1733).

Later came the remark attributed to Sir Herbert Beerbohm Tree (also by Pearson, in his biography of the actor, 1956) on the newly invented gramophone: 'Sir, I have tested your machine. It adds new terror to life and makes death a long-felt want.'

Brown, James
American singer/songwriter (1934–)

3 *Say It Loud, 'I'm Black and I'm Proud.'*

The title of Brown's hit song of 1968 had the force of a slogan. Curiously, it was soon adapted to 'Say it loud, we're gay and we're proud', a slogan of the Gay Liberation Front, *c* 1970.

Brown, Jerry
American Democratic politician (1938–)

4 *We carry in our hearts the true country and that cannot be stolen. We follow in the spirit of our ancestors and that cannot be broken.*

In a speech in October 1991, the former Governor of California announced his candidacy for the Democratic nomination for the Presidency (which he did not get — it went to Bill Clinton). Unusually for a politician, Brown had always been associated with rock music and musicians. On this occasion, he quoted from the song 'The Dead Heart' (1988), by the Australian rock group Midnight Oil, which has rather, 'We follow in the *steps* of our *ancestry* . . . '. Brown did not openly acknowledge the borrowing in his speech though an information sheet given to reporters did.

[*Source*: the *Guardian*, 26 October 1991.]

Brown, John Mason
American critic (1900–69)

1 *Some television programmes are so much chewing gum for the eyes.*

Interview, 28 July 1955. This was not his own remark — he was, in fact, quoting a young friend of his young son.

Brown, T(homas) E(dward)
English poet and schoolmaster (1830–97)

2 *A rich man's joke is always funny.*

From his poem 'The Doctor' (1887).

3 *A garden is a lovesome thing, God wot!*

Brown was the author of this curiously memorable line. It comes from 'My Garden' (1893), and seldom do any subsequent lines get quoted. But they are, in full:

Rose plot,
Fringed pool,
Fern'd grot —
The veriest school
Of peace; and yet the fool
Contends that God is not —
Not God! in gardens! when the eve
    is cool?
Nay, but I have a sign;
'Tis very sure God walks in mine.

It was included in *The Oxford Book of English Verse* (1900) and has quite frequently been parodied. *Yet More Comic and Curious Verse* (ed. J.M. Cohen, 1959) has 'My Garden with a stern look at T.E. Brown' by J.A. Lindon, which begins:

A garden is a lovesome thing? What rot!

'My Garden, New Style' by H.W. Hodges, appears in *Modern Humour* (ed. Pocock and Bozman, 1940) had, rather:

A garden is a loathsome thing — eh,
    what?
Blight, snail,
Pea-weevil,
Green-fly such a lot!
My hardest tool
Is powerless, yet the fool
Next door contends that slugs are not —
Not slugs! in gardens? when the eve is
    cool?
Nay, but I have some lime;
'Tis very sure they shall not walk in
    mine.

And Gerard Benson (included in *Imitations of Immortality*, ed. E.O. Parrott, 1986) had:

A garden is a loathsome thing, God
    wot!
. . . That geezer should be shot
What wrote that lot
Of Palgrave's Golden Tommy-rot . . .
I'd rather sun myself on Uncle's yacht.

Browne, Sir Thomas
English author and physician (1605–82)

4 *To join the great majority.*

I.e. 'to die'. If quoting Browne's Epistle Dedicatory to *Urn-Burial* (1658), the phrase is different: 'When the living might exceed, and to depart this world could not be properly said to go unto the greater number.' The *OED2* does not find use of 'to join/pass over to the majority', in this sense, before 1719 (Edward Young, *The Revenge*: 'Death joins us to the great majority'), though it does relate it to the Latin phrase *abiit ad plures*.

On his way out in 1884, the politician Lord Houghton quipped, 'Yes, I am going to join the Majority and you know I have always preferred Minorities.'
Compare NIXON 255:4.

Browning, Robert
English poet (1812–89)

5 *Never glad confident morning again.*

To be found very near the top of any list of over-used, mis-used quotations. It comes from Browning's poem 'The Lost Leader' (1845), in which Wordsworth was regretfully portrayed as a man who had lost his revolutionary zeal.

A correct — and devastating — use of the phrase came on 17 June 1963 when the British Government under Prime Minister Harold Macmillan had been rocked by the Profumo scandal. In the House of Commons, Tory MP Nigel Birch said to Macmillan:

I myself feel that the time will come very soon when my right hon. Friend ought to make way for a much younger colleague. I feel that that ought to happen. I certainly will not quote at him the savage words of Cromwell, but perhaps some of the words of Browning might be appropriate in his poem on 'The Lost Leader', in which he wrote:

. . . Let him never come back to us!
There would be doubt, hesitation
    and pain.

Forced praise on our part — the
glimmer of twilight,
Never glad confident morning
again!'

'Never glad confident morning again!' —
so I hope that the change will not be too
long delayed.

Birch was right. A few months later Macmillan was out of office; a year later, so was
the Government.

In November 1983, on the twentieth
anniversary of President Kennedy's assassination, Lord Harlech, former British
Ambassador in Washington, paid tribute
thus in the *Observer* Magazine: 'Since 1963
the world has seemed a bleaker place, and
for me and I suspect millions of my contemporaries he remains the lost leader —
"Never glad confident morning again".'
Harlech may have wanted to evoke a leader
who had been lost to the world, but surely
it was a mistake to quote a *criticism* of
one?

Also in November 1983, in the *Observer*,
Paul Johnson wrote an attack (which he
later appeared to regret) on Margaret
Thatcher: 'Her courage and sound instincts
made her formidable. But if her judgement
can no longer be trusted, what is left? A very
ordinary woman, occupying a position
where ordinary virtues are not enough. For
me, I fear it can never be "glad confident
morning again".'

Still at it in 1988 was Shirley Williams.
When part of the SDP united with the
Liberals, she used the words about David
Owen, the SDP's once and future leader.

1 *And did you once see Shelley plain?*

The first line of Browning's 'Memorabilia'
(1855) should be: 'Ah, did you once see
Shelley plain?'

Browning, Sir Frederick 'Boy'
English soldier (1896–1965)

2 *A Bridge Too Far.*

Such was the title of Cornelius Ryan's book
(1974; film UK/US, 1977) about the 1944
airborne landings in Holland. These were
designed to capture eleven bridges needed
for the Allied invasion of Germany — an
attempt that came to grief at Arnhem, with
the Allies suffering more casualties than
in the invasion of Normandy. On 10 September 1944, in advance of the action,

Lieutenant-General Browning protested to
Field-Marshal Montgomery, whose brain-
child the scheme was: 'But, sir, we may be
going a bridge too far' (quoted in R.E.
Urquhart, *Arnhem*, 1958).

The phrase is sometimes now used allu-
sively when warning of an unwise move.
For example: 'A BRIDGE TOO NEAR.
A public inquiry opened yesterday into
plans to re-span the Ironbridge Gorge in
Shropshire' (*The Times*, 20 June 1990);
'Ratners: A bid too far?' (*Observer*, 8 July
1990).

Brummell, Beau
English dandy (1778–1840)

3 *Who's your fat friend?*

The nicely alliterative phrase 'fat friend'
occurs as early as Shakespeare, *The Comedy
of Errors* (V.i.414): 'There is a fat friend at
your master's house.' But in the novel
Handley Cross (1843) by R.S. Surtees, there
is: 'When at length *our fat friend* got his
horse and his hounds . . . together again';
and in Anthony Trollope's *Castle Richmond*
(1860): 'Is it not possible that one should
have one more game of rounders? Quite
impossible, *my fat friend*.' More recently, in
1972, there was a West End play by Charles
Laurence called *My Fat Friend*. The play
was about a fat girl and her experiences
when she lost weight (it was originally going
to be called *The Fat Dress*).

As such, apart from the Shakespeare, one
suspects allusions to Brummell's famous
question to Lord Alvanley about the Prince
Regent. Brummell, almost a dandy by profession, had fallen out with the Prince of
Wales. He is said to have annoyed the Prince
by ridiculing his mistress and also by saying
once to his royal guest at dinner, 'Wales,
ring the bell, will you?' When they met in
London in July 1813, the Prince cut Brummell but greeted his companion. As the
Prince walked off, Brummell asked in ringing tones, 'Tell me, Alvanley, who is your fat
friend?'

4 *Yes, madam, I once ate a pea.*

Having taken it into his head not to eat
vegetables, Brummell was asked by a lady if
he had never eaten any in his life. This is
what he replied. Quoted in Daniel George,
A Book of Anecdotes (1958) and, much
earlier, in Charles Dickens, *Bleak House*,
Chap. 12 (1852–3).

Bryan, William Jennings
American Democratic politician (1860–1925)

1 *We will answer their demand for a gold standard by saying to them: You shall not press down upon the brow of labour this crown of thorns. You shall not crucify mankind upon a cross of gold.*

One of the most notable examples of American oratory, but little known in Britain, is Bryan's speech to the Democratic Convention on 8 July 1896. It contained an impassioned attack on supporters of the gold standard. Bryan had said virtually the same in a speech to the House of Representatives on 22 December 1894. He won the nomination and fought the Presidential election against William J. McKinley who supported the gold standard. Bryan lost. A 'cross of gold'-type speech is sometimes called for when a politician (such as Edward Kennedy in 1980) is required to sweep a Convention with his eloquence.

2 *No one ever made a million dollars honestly.*

He later modified the sum to two million dollars, once he himself had made one. Unverified.

Bulmer-Thomas, Ivor
(formerly Ivor Thomas)
English Labour, then Conservative, MP (1905–93)

3 *If ever he [Harold Wilson] went to school without any boots it was because he was too big for them.*

Thomas made this jibe in a speech at the Conservative Party Conference (12 October 1949) — a remark often wrongly ascribed to Harold Macmillan. It followed a press dispute involving Wilson the previous year (see WILSON 357:2).

Bulwer-Lytton, Edward
(1st Baron Lytton)
English novelist and politician (1803–73)

4 *The pen is mightier than the sword.*

According to a piece in the London *Standard* diary following the Gorbachev-Reagan summit in November 1987, Parker Pens broke new ground by placing an adver-

tisement in the *Moscow News* to draw attention to the fact that the treaty had been signed with one of its fountain pens. The advertisement's Russian slogan, translated directly, was, 'What is written with the pen will not be chopped up with an axe', which the *Standard* thought was the equivalent of 'The pen is mightier than the sword'.

Unfortunately, the *Standard* announced that 'The pen is . . . ' was the most famous maxim attributed to Cardinal Richelieu. But no. That was merely a line said by Richelieu in Edward Bulwer-Lytton's play *Richelieu*, II.ii (1839):

Beneath the rule of men entirely great,
The pen is mightier than the sword.

which is not quite the same as Richelieu himself having originated it. As for the idea, it was not, of course, Bulwer-Lytton's either. *CODP* finds several earlier attempts at expressing it, to which I would add this 'corollary' from Shakespeare's *Hamlet* (II.ii.344): 'Many wearing rapiers are afraid of goose-quills.' Cervantes, *Don Quixote* (Pt I, Bk IV, Chap. 10) has, in Motteux's translation: 'Let none presume to tell me that the pen is preferable to the sword.'

Bunyan, John
English writer and preacher (1628–88)

5 *The Man with the Muck-Rake.*

'In *Pilgrim's Progress*, the Man with the Muck-Rake is set forth as the example of him whose vision is fixed on carnal instead of on spiritual things. Yet he also typifies the man who in this life consistently refuses to see aught that is lofty, and fixes his eyes only on that which is vile and debasing.' So said President Theodore Roosevelt in a speech (14 April 1906). This led to the term 'muck-raker' being applied to investigative journalists who seek out scandals, especially about public figures.

Burgess, Anthony
English novelist and critic (1917–93)

6 *Who ever heard of a clockwork orange? . . . The attempt to impose upon man, a creature of growth and capable of sweetness, to ooze juicily at the last round the bearded lips of God, to attempt to impose, I say, laws and conditions appropriate to a mechanical creation, against this I raise my sword-pen.*

This passage from the novel *A Clockwork Orange* (1962, film UK, 1971) hints at the reason for the unusual title. The book describes an attempt to punish its criminal hero, Alex, by turning him into a 'mechanical man' through forms of therapy and brainwashing. But Burgess several times explained that he had taken the title from a cockney expression 'to be queer as a clockwork orange' (i.e. homosexual). This was not known to many but has been in use since the mid-1950s, according to Paul Beale in *Partridge/Slang*. As such, its relevance to the story, which has no overt homosexual element, is debatable.

1 *The End of the World News.*

The title of Burgess's novel (1982) derives from what BBC World Service newsreaders have sometimes said at the end of bulletins: 'That is the end of the world news' — leaving open the possibility that listeners had just been hearing the news of the end of the world.

Burghley, 1st Lord
(William Cecil)
English courtier and politician (1520–98)

2 *What! all this for a song?*

Burghley or Burleigh (the name is variously spelt) was Lord High Treasurer to Elizabeth I. He exclaimed this when told by the Queen to pay Edmund Spenser the sum of $100 for some poems. (Related by Thomas Birch in 'The Life of Mr Edmund Spenser' in an edition of *The Faerie Queene*, 1751.)

3 *Burghley's nod.*

Nothing to do with the actual Burghley. Within Sheridan's play *The Critic* (1779) is a mock-tragedy on the Spanish Armada. Burghley is represented as too preoccupied with affairs of state to be able to say anything, so he shakes his head and the character Puff explains what he means: 'Why by that shake of the head, he gave you to understand that even though they had more justice in their cause and wisdom in their measures — yet, if there was not a greater spirit shown on the part of the people — the country would at last fall a sacrifice to the hostile ambition of the Spanish monarchy . . .' 'The devil! — did he mean all that by shaking his head?' 'Every word of it — if he shook his head as I taught him.'

Hence, also, the expression, 'To be as significant as the shake of Lord Burghley's head.'

Burgon, John William
English poet and clergyman (1813–88)

4 *Match me such marvel, save in Eastern clime, —*
A rose-red city — 'half as old as Time'!

This famous couplet from Burgon's poem 'Petra' (1845) palpably contains a quotation. It comes from the epilogue to the poem *Italy* (1838) by Samuel Rogers: 'By many a temple half as old as time.'

Burke, Edmund
Irish-born statesman and philosopher (1729–97)

5 *Truth is stranger than fiction.*

Pearson (1937) points out that if quoting Burke's *On Conciliation with America* (1775), this should properly be 'Fiction lags after truth'. By the time of Byron's *Don Juan*, xiv.ci (1819–24), it was in the form: ' 'Tis strange, but true; for truth is always strange — /Stranger than fiction.' By the mid-nineteenth century, the version 'Fact is stranger than fiction' had also emerged.

6 *The age of chivalry is past.*

Should be 'The age of chivalry is gone', if alluding to Burke's *Reflections on the Revolution in France* (1790). The misquotation is probably caused by confusion with the proverb 'the age of miracles is past', which was current by 1602.

7 *The only thing necessary for the triumph of evil is for good men to do nothing.*

So Burke said, or at least is often quoted as having done. Bartlett (1968) cited it in a letter from Burke to William Smith (9 January 1795), but on checking found that it did not exist. In his book *On Language* (1980), William Safire described his unavailing attempts to find a proper source. In the House of Commons on 23 April 1770, Burke said 'When bad men combine, the good must associate; else they will fall one by one, an unpitied sacrifice in a contemptible struggle' — which seems to be heading somewhere in the right direction. But, for the moment, we have here another of those quotations which arrive apparently from nowhere, and gets quoted and re-quoted without justification. On the other hand, it is fair to assume that Burke would not have wished to disown it.

1 The Great Unwashed.

Meaning 'working-class people, the lower orders', this term is said (by Safire, 1978) to have been used originally by Burke (though untraced), and has also been attributed to Lord Brougham, perhaps echoing Shakespeare's reference to 'another lean unwash'd artificer' (*King John*, IV.ii.201). Lytton in *Paul Clifford* (1830) uses the full phrase. Thackeray has it in *Pendennis* (1848–50). Thomas Carlyle in his *History of the French Revolution* (1837) has: 'Man has set man against man, Washed against unwashed'.

Burnett, W.R.
American author (1899–1982)

2 The Asphalt Jungle.

This phrase was undoubtedly popularized by its use as the title of Burnett's novel (1949; film US, 1950) about an elderly criminal carrying out one last robbery. *OED2* finds it in 1920, however. It is one of several phrases that suggest that there are urban areas where the 'law of the jungle' may apply. Next came *The Blackboard Jungle*, a novel (1954; film US, 1955) by Evan Hunter, on the educational system. A little after, in 1969, came references to 'the concrete jungle'.

Burns, George
American comedian (1896–)

3 The secret of acting is sincerity — and if you can fake that, you've got it made.

Usually attributed to George Burns (as, for example, in Michael York, *Travelling Player*, 1991). Fred Metcalf in *The Penguin Dictionary of Modern Quotations* (1986) has Burns saying, rather: 'Acting is about honesty. If you can fake that, you've got it made.' However, Kingsley Amis in a devastating piece about Leo Rosten in his *Memoirs* (1991) has the humorist relating 'at some stage in the 1970s' how he had given a Commencement address including the line: 'Sincerity. If you can *fake that* . . . you'll have the world at your feet.' So perhaps the saying was circulating even before Burns received the credit. Or perhaps

Rosten took it from him? An advertisement in *Rolling Stone*, c 1982, offered a T-shirt with the slogan (anonymous): 'The secret of success is sincerity. Once you can fake that you've got it made.'

4 When the man shows up at the door to return the pictures, you've got to go.

Asked by William Safire of the *New York Times* about the origin of this saying, Burns explained: 'You see, I'm an old vaudeville actor — I'm going back 65 or 70 years — and in those days, your contract had a cancellation clause in it. If the manager didn't like your act, he was able to cancel you after your first show. All the actors carried their own pictures, so after the first show, if the manager knocked on your door and gave you back your pictures, you started packing.' Burns (then in his nineties) added: 'When the Guy knocks on my door with the pictures, I'm not going to answer.'

Burns, Robert
Scottish poet (1759–96)

5 Auld lang syne.

The song is traditionally massacred and half-remembered, if remembered at all, at farewell ceremonies and on New Year's Eve. It is not just inebriation that leads Sassenachs into gibbering incomprehensibility — there is widespread confusion as to what the words mean, how they should be pronounced and — indeed — what the correct words are.

In fact, Burns adapted 'Auld Lang Syne' from 'an old man's singing' in 1788. The title, first line and refrain had all appeared before as the work of other poets. Nevertheless, what Burns put together is now the accepted version. Here is the first verse and the chorus:

Should auld acquaintance be forgot,
And never brought to min[d]?
Should auld acquaintance be forgot,
And days of o' lang syne.

(*Chorus*)
For auld lang syne, my dear
For auld syne,
We'll take a cup o' kindness yet
For auld lang syne.

'For *the sake of* auld lang syne' should *not* be substituted at the end of verse and chorus. 'Auld lang syne' means, literally, 'old long since' i.e. 'long ago'. Hence, 'syne' should be pronounced with an 's' sound and not as 'zyne'.

1 *The Poetic Genius of my Country found me at the Plough and threw her inspring Mantle over me. She bade me sing the Loves, the Joys, the Rural Scenes and Rural Pleasures of my Native Soil, in my Native Tongue. I tuned my Wild, Artless Notes as She inspired.*

A large, seated statue of Burns with this text below it is to be found in Victoria Embankment Gardens, London (a city he never visited). The quotation comes from his address 'To the Noblemen and Gentlemen of the Caledonian Hunt' prefacing the 1787 'Edinburgh' edition of his poems. The Caledonian Hunt was an association of noblemen and country gentlemen who shared a keen interest in field sports, races, balls and social assemblies. The original text reads: 'The Poetic Genius of my Country found me, as the prophetic bard Elijah did Elisha — at the *plough* — and threw her inspiring mantle over me. She bade me sing the loves, the joys, the rural scenes and rural pleasures of my natal Soil, in my native tongue. I tuned my wild, artless notes, as she inspired. She whispered me to come to this ancient metropolis of Caledonia, and lay my Songs under your honoured protection. I now obey her dictates . . . I do not approach you, my Lords and Gentlemen, in the usual style of dedication, to thank you for past favours; that path is so hackneyed by prostituted Learning, that honest Rusticity is ashamed of it. Nor do I present this Address with the venal soul of a servile Author, looking for a continuation of those favours: I was bred to the Plough, and am independent . . .'

2 *O whistle, an' I'll come to you, my lad.*

From the poem (*c* 1788) by Burns. Compare 'Whistle and she'll come to you' from *Wit Without Money*, IV.iv. (1639) by Francis Beaumont and/or John Fletcher. *Oh, Whistle and I'll Come To You My Lad* became the title of a short story in *Ghost Stories of an Antiquary* (1904) by M.R. James, in which the wind is 'whistled up'.

3 *Scots, wha hae.*

This is not an exclamation ('Scots wu-hey!') but the title given to, and a phrase from the first line of, a battle-song. It is sometimes subtitled 'Robert Bruce's March to Bannockburn' or 'Robert Bruce's Address to his army, before the battle of Bannockburn', and was published in 1799:

Scots, wha hae [who have] wi' Wallace bled,
Scots, wham [whom] Bruce has aften led,
Welcome to your gory bed,
    Or to victorie.

A further comment, from James Murray (creator of the *OED*) in 1912: 'Even Burns thought that Scotch was defiled by "bad grammar" and tried to conform his Scotch to *English* grammar! Transforming e.g. the Scotch "*Scots 'at hae*" to *Scots wha hae* which no sober Scotch man in his senses ever naturally said.'

4 *John, don't let the awkward squad fire over me.*

Burns's dying words are said to have been these, presumably referring to his fear that literary opponents might metaphorically fire a volley of respect, as soldiers sometimes do, over a new grave. Reported in an 1834 biography. As for the phrase 'awkward squad' on its own, Sloppy in *Our Mutual Friend* (1864–5) is described by Charles Dickens as 'Full-Private Number One in the Awkward Squad of the rank and file of life'. Of military origin and used to denote a difficult, uncooperative person, the phrase originally referred to a squad which consisted of raw recruits and older hands who were put in it for punishment, but seems to have been used in other contexts for quite some time.

Burroughs, Edgar Rice
American author (1875–1950)

5 *Me Tarzan, you Jane.*

A box-office sensation of 1932 was the first sound Tarzan film, *Tarzan the Ape Man*. It spawned a long-running series and starred Johnny Weismuller, an ex-US swimming champion, as Tarzan and Maureen O'Sullivan as Jane. At one point the ape man whisks Jane away to his tree-top abode and indulges in some elementary conversation with her. Thumping his chest, he says, 'Tarzan!', pointing at her, he says, 'Jane!' So, in fact, he does not say the catchphrase commonly associated with him, though Weissmuller did use the words in an interview for *Photoplay Magazine* (June 1932).
    Interestingly, this great moment of movie dialogue appears to have been 'written' by the British playwright and actor Ivor Novello. In the original novel, *Tarzan of the Apes* (1914), by Edgar Rice Burroughs, the line does not occur (whatever it says in *PDMQ*, 1980), not least because, in the

jungle, Tarzan and Jane are able to communicate only by writing notes to each other.

Burroughs, William S.
American novelist (1914–)

1 *Heavy metal.*

The type of music known as Heavy Metal — very loud, amplified, clashing — was first described as such in 1968 when the group Steppenwolf used Burroughs's phrase 'heavy metal thunder' in their song 'Born To be Wild' (written by M. Bonfire). The Burroughs phrase remains untraced, though he did write in *Nova Express* (1964): 'At this point we got a real break in the form of a defector from The Nova Mob: Ukrainian Willy the Heavy Metal Kid.'
The use of the phrase 'heavy metal' in the sense of guns of large size and, figuratively, about human bodily or mental power dates back to the nineteenth century.

Burton, Sir Richard
English explorer and writer (1821–90)

2 *Prostitutes for pleasure, concubines for service, wives for breeding. . . A melon for ecstasy.*

When the late Pearl Binder (Lady Elwyn-Jones) appeared with octogenarian aplomb on BBC Radio *Quote. . . Unquote* in 1984, she chose as a favourite quotation what she claimed Burton had borrowed from Demosthenes: 'Prostitutes for pleasure, concubines for service, wives for breeding.' Alan Brien, who was in attendance, chimed in with, 'And a melon for ecstasy.'
What slightly off-colour, old joke did we have here? *A Melon for Ecstasy* was the title of a novel (1971) by John Fortune and John Wells, and presumably alluded to the same core remark. Apparently, the novelist John Masters ascribed to a 'Pathan tribesman', the saying 'A woman for duty, a boy for pleasure, a goat for ecstasy' and, apropos the main quotation, compare John Gay, 'The Toilette' (1716): 'A miss for pleasure, and a wife for breed.'

Bush, George
American Republican 41st President (1924–)

3 *The vision thing.*

As Bush debated with other potential Republican candidates for the Presidency,

he said: 'On vision — you have to have a vision. Mine is that education should be the No. 1 thing' (the *Washington Post*, 15 January 1988). But, shortly before this, he had coined the phrase 'vision thing', unintentionally characterizing his own lack of an overarching view of what he might do with the Presidency. His very use of the word 'thing' seemed to confirm his pragmatic, tongue-tied, earthbound stance.
In 1993 *The Vision Thing* became the title of a BBC TV play by Mark Lawson about a British Prime Minister who did have visions and was consequently eased out of office.

4 *My opponent won't rule out raising taxes, but I will. And the Congress will push me to raise taxes, and I'll say no, and they'll push again. And I'll say to them, read my lips, no new taxes.*

Although popularized by Bush in his speech accepting the Republican nomination at New Orleans on 18 August 1988, the expression 'read my lips' was not new. According to William Safire in an article in the *New York Times* Magazine (September 1988), the phrase is rooted in 1970s rock music (despite there being a song with the title copyrighted by Joe Greene in 1957). The British actor/singer Tim Curry used the phrase as the title of an album of songs in 1978. Curry said he took it from an Italian-American recording engineer who used it to mean, 'Listen and listen very hard, because I want you to hear what I've got to say'. Several lyricists in the 1980s used the phrase for song titles. A football coach with the Chicago Bears became nicknamed Mike 'Read My Lips' Ditka. There has been a thoroughbred race horse so named. Safire also cites a number of American politicians, also in the 1980s. In the film *Breathless* (1983), a scrap dealer says it to the Richard Gere character, encouraging him to believe that there is no money in the yard worth taking.
Needless to say, Bush did have to raise taxes in due course.

5 *I will keep America moving forward, always forward — for a better America, for an endless enduring dream and a thousand points of light.*

From the same acceptance speech, and used many times throughout the 1988 campaign, the words 'thousand points of light' were put on his lips by speechwriter Peggy Noonan. But what did they mean? The phrase was said to symbolize individual endeavour, voluntary charity efforts, across the country (later, in June 1989, President Bush announced details of his 'Points of Light Programme, costing $25 million, to encourage a voluntary crusade to fight poverty, drugs and homelessness). But Bush never seemed too sure what he was saying. On one occasion, he called it '1,000 points of life'. Herblock, the cartoonist, drew a drunk at a bar pledging his vote to Bush because he had promised '1,000 pints of Lite'.

Perhaps it was supposed to echo Shakespeare, *The Merchant of Venice* (V.i.90): 'How far that little candle throws his beams!/ So shines a good deed in a naughty world.' Light often comes in thousands: 'It was but for an instant that I seemed to struggle with a thousand mill-weirs and a thousand flashes of light' (Charles Dickens, *Great Expectations*, Chap. 54, 1860–1). In *Conducted Tour* (1981) Bernard Levin describes an English pantomime when parents were asked to take out matches and cigarette lighters — 'the vast shell of the Coliseum's auditorium was alive with a thousand tiny points of light'.

In her memoir *What I Saw at the Revolution* (1990), Peggy Noonan makes mention of several earlier uses of the phrase or parts of it. She does not, however, appear to have been aware of C.S. Lewis's *The Magician's Nephew* (1955): 'One moment there had been nothing but darkness, next moment a thousand points of light leaped out . . .', or of Thomas Wolfe's *The Web and the Rock* (1939): 'Instantly he could see the town below now, coiling in a thousand fumes of homely smoke, now winking into a thousand points of friendly light its glorious small design', though she had read it as a teenager. A speech made by a turn-of-the-century engineer was also found urging the electrification of Venice so that it would be filled with 'a thousand points of light'.

Oddly, Noonan does not draw attention to one possible point of inspiration. Having admitted earlier that she is a fan of Auden's poem 'September 1, 1939' ('We must love one another or die'), she overlooks the lines:

Defenceless under the night
Our world in stupor lies;
Yet, dotted everywhere,
Ironic points of light
Flash out wherever the Just
Exchange their messages . . .

1 *America is never wholly herself unless she is engaged in high moral purpose. We as a people have such a purpose today. It is to make kinder the face of the nation and gentler the face of the world.*

From Bush's Inaugural Address (20 January 1989). The 'kinder/gentler' theme had also appeared in the acceptance speech and during the campaign. Peggy Noonan suggests that Bush added the word 'gentler' to her 'I want a kinder nation' in the acceptance speech draft, but even so this was a familiar combination. In his 1932 autobiography, Clarence Darrow wrote: 'There may have lived somewhere a kindlier, gentler, more generous man than Eugene Debs, but I have not known him.' Charlie Chaplin in the film *The Great Dictator* (1940) urged: 'More than cleverness, we need kindness and gentleness.' In 1985 singer Roy Orbison said that Elvis Presley had 'made gentler and kinder souls of us all'.

Butler, Henry Montague
English academic (1833–1918)

2 *Would you, my dear young friends, like to be inside with the five wise virgins or outside, alone, and in the dark, with the five foolish ones?*

A favourite story, sometimes taken with a pinch of salt, coming in the category of Sermons We Would Like To Have Heard. Dr Butler who was Headmaster of Harrow then, from 1886, Master of Trinity College, Cambridge, was preaching a sermon in the college chapel when he posed this misguided rhetorical question. The source for this is Edward Marsh, *Ambrosia and Small Beer* (1964).

Butler, R.A.
(later Lord Butler)
English Conservative politician (1902–82)

3 *The best Prime Minister we have.*

In December 1955, passed over (not for the last time) for the Conservative Party leadership, Butler was confronted by a Press Association reporter just as he was about to board an aircraft at London Airport. Criticism was growing over the performance of Anthony Eden, the Prime Minister selected in preference to him. The reporter asked, 'Mr Butler, would you say that this is the best Prime Minister we have?' Butler's 'hurried assent' to this 'well-meant but meaningless proposition' was converted into the above statement. 'I do not think it did Anthony any good. It did not do me any good either.' In due course, Butler himself became known as 'the best Prime Minister we *never had*'.

1 *Politics is the art of the possible.*

Butler's memoirs entitled *The Art of the Possible* (1971) caused him to be credited with this view. However, in the preface to the paperback edition (1973) he pointed out that the thought appeared first to have been advanced in modern times by Bismarck in 1866–7 (in conversation with Meyer von Waldeck: '*Die Politik ist keine exakte Wissenschaft*'). Others who had touched on the idea included Cavour, Salvador de Madriaga, Pindar and Camus. To these might be added J.K. Galbraith's rebuttal: 'Politics is not the art of the possible. It consists in choosing between the disastrous and the unpalatable.'

2 *I think the Prime Minister has to be a butcher, and know the joints. That is perhaps where I have been not quite competent in knowing the ways that you cut up a carcass.*

Interviewed on BBC TV by Kenneth Harris (transcript in *The Listener*, 28 June 1966). Possibly alluding to Gladstone: 'The first essential for a Prime Minister is to be a good butcher.' In his 1977 TV interviews with David Frost, Richard Nixon said of his reluctance to sack his aides Ehrlichman and Haldeman during Watergate: 'I suppose you could sum it all up the way Gladstone summed it all up . . . I wasn't a good butcher.'

Butler, Samuel
English author (1835–1902)

3 *Make four people unhappy instead of two.*

In my very first quotation book I mistakenly attributed to Tennyson a view on the marriage of Thomas and Jane Carlyle. When it was suggested that the marriage had been a mistake — because with anyone but each other they might have been perfectly happy — I said that Tennyson had opined:

'I totally disagree with you. By any other arrangement *four* people would have been unhappy instead of *two*.'

This remark should have been credited to Butler. In a letter to a Miss Savage on 21 November 1884, he wrote: 'It was very good of God to let Carlyle and Mrs Carlyle marry one another and so make only two people miserable instead of four, besides being very amusing.' My inaccurate version was taken up by *The Faber Book of Anecdotes* (1985).

4 *Have you brought the cheque book, Alfred?*

Butler, though dying, was engaged in the purchase of the freehold of a house in Hampstead. To Alfred Emery Cathie, his clerk, 'servant and friend', he said, 'Have you brought the cheque book, Alfred?' Butler took off his spectacles and put them down on the table. 'I don't want them any more,' he said, his head fell back, and he died. 'Have you brought the cheque book, Alfred?' has subsequently become a family catchphrase in certain households.

[*Source*: Philip Henderson, *Samuel Butler: the Incarnate Bachelor*, 1953.]

Byron, Lord
English poet (1788–1824)

5 *Now Barabbas was a publisher.*

The story has it that when John Murray, Byron's publisher, sent the poet a copy of the Bible in return for a favour, Byron sent it back with the words 'Now Barabbas was a robber' (St John 18:40) altered to, 'Now Barabbas was a publisher . . .' This story was included in Kazlitt Arvine's *Cyclopedia of Anecdotes of Literature and the Fine Arts* published in Boston, Massachussetts, in 1851.

In 1981, the then head of the firm, John G. (Jock) Murray, told me that those involved were in fact the poet Coleridge and his publishers, Longmans. But when I asked for evidence in 1988, he could only say that, 'I have satisfied myself that it was not Byron'. The copy of Byron's Bible which exists has no such comment in it. He also drew my attention to the fact that in Byron's day publishers were more usually called booksellers. Mencken, on the other hand, gave Thomas Campbell (1777–1844) as the probable perpetrator, so did Benham, and so did Samuel Smiles in *A Publisher and his Friends: Memoir and Correspondence of the late John Murray*, Vol. 1, Chap. 14 (1891). Certainly, Campbell seems to have taken the required attitude. At a literary dinner he once toasted Napoleon with the words: 'We must not forget that he once shot a bookseller.'

1 *So, we'll go no more a-roving*
So far into the night.

The poem (written in 1817) should read 'so late into the night.'

2 *Those whom the Gods love die young.*

So said Byron in *Don Juan* (1819), adding that it was 'said of yore'. Indeed, Menander the Greek and Plautus said it in times BC. *Whom the Gods Love* was the title of a film (UK, 1936) about Mozart. Related to this saying is what Euripides and other classical authors put in the form: 'Whom the Gods wish to destroy, they first make mad.' Sophocles in *Antigone* (c 450BC) quotes as a proverb: 'Whom Jupiter would destroy, he first makes mad.' Cyril Connolly in *The Unquiet Grave* (1944) added: 'they first call promising.'

C

Caesar, Julius
Roman general and statesman (c 100–44BC)

1 *Caesar's wife must be above suspicion.*

It was Julius Caesar *himself* who said this of his wife Pompeia when he divorced her in 62BC. In North's translation of Plutarch's *Lives* — which is how the saying came into English in 1570 — Caesar is quoted thus: 'I will not, sayd he, that my wife be so much as suspected.'

Pompeia was Caesar's second wife. According to Suetonius, in 61BC she took part in the women-only rites of the Feast of the Great Goddess. But it was rumoured that a profligate called Publius Clodius attended wearing women's clothes and that he had committed adultery with Pompeia. Caesar divorced Pompeia and at the subsequent inquiry into the desecration was asked why he had done so. 'Caesar's wife must be above suspicion,' he replied. He later married Calphurnia.

An example of the phrase in use occurs in Lord Chesterfield's letters (published 1774): 'Your moral character must be not only pure, but, like Caesar's wife, unsuspected.' This should not to be confused with what a newly elected mayor (quoted by G.W.E. Russell in *Collections and Recollections*, 1898) once said. During his year of office he felt he should lay aside all his political prepossessions and be, like Caesar's wife, 'all things to all men'.

2 *Veni vidi vici.*

According to Suetonius, 'I came, I saw, I conquered' was an inscription displayed in Latin in Julius Caesar's Pontic triumph of 47BC. Plutarch states that it was written in a letter by Caesar, announcing the victory of Zela (in Asia Minor), which concluded the Pontic (Black Sea) campaign. In North's 1579 translation of Plutarch, it says: 'Julius Caesar fought a great battle with King Pharnaces and because he would advertise one of his friends of the suddenness of this victory, he only wrote three words unto Anicius at Rome: *Veni, Vidi, Vici*: to wit, I came, saw, and overcame. These three words ending all with like sound and letters in the Latin, have a certain short grace, more pleasant to the ear, than can well be expressed in any other tongue.'

Shakespeare alludes to Caesar's 'thrasonical brag' in four plays, including *Love's Labour's Lost* (IV.i.68) and *As You Like It* (V.ii.30).

3 *Et tu, Brute? [And you, Brutus?]*

Julius Caesar's supposed dying words to Brutus, one of his assassins in 44BC, were made famous through Shakespeare's use of the Latin in the form, '*Et tu, Brute?* — Then fall Caesar!'

The Latin words are not found in any classical source, but they do occur in English drama just before Shakespeare. *The True Tragedie of Richard Duke of Yorke* (printed in 1595) has 'Et tu, Brute, wilt thou stab Caesar too?'

The origin of the phrase lies probably in Suetonius's account of the assassination, in which Caesar is made to say in *Greek*, 'And thou, my son.' The 'son' has been taken literally — as, according to Suetonius, Caesar had had an intrigue with Brutus's mother and looked upon Brutus as his likely son.

Cagney, James
American actor (1899–1986)

4 *You dirty rat!*

Although impersonators of James Cagney always have him saying 'You dirty rat!' it

81

may be that he never said it like that himself. However, in Joan Wyndham's wartime diaries (*Love Lessons*, 1985) her entry for 1 October 1940 begins: 'Double bill at the Forum with Rupert. *Elizabeth and Essex*, and a gangster film where somebody actually *did* say "Stool on me would ya, ya doity rat!" ' What film could this have been? Note her surprise that the line was uttered at all.

The nearest Cagney seems to have got to uttering the phrase with which he is most associated was in the films *Blonde Crazy* (1931) (where he says, 'You dirty, double-crossing rat') and *Taxi* (1931) (where he says, 'Come out and take it, you dirty yellow-bellied rat, or I'll give to you through the door').

In a speech to an American Film Institute banquet on 13 March 1974, Cagney said: 'Frank Gorshin [a well-known impersonator] — oh, Frankie, just in passing: I never said [in any film] "Mmm, you dirty rat!" What I actually did say was "Judy! Judy! Judy!" ' (See GRANT 164:2.)

Caine, Michael
English actor (1933–)

1 Not many people know that.

It is rare for a personal catchphrase to catch on (as opposed to phrases in entertainment, films, advertising that are engineered to do so). But it has certainly been the case with the one that will always be associated with Caine. Peter Sellers started the whole thing off when he appeared on BBC TV's *Parkinson* show on 28 October 1972. The edition in question was subsequently released on disc ('Michael Parkinson Meets the Goons', BBC REC 259), thus enabling confirmation of what Sellers said: ' "Not many people know that" . . . this is my Michael Caine impression . . . You see Mike's always quoting from *The Guinness Book of Records*. At the drop of a hat he'll trot one out. "Did you know that it takes a man in a tweed suit five and a half seconds to fall from the top of Big Ben to the ground? Now there's not many people know that"!'

It was not until 1981–2 that the remark really caught on. Caine was given the line to say as an in-joke (in the character of an inebriated university lecturer) in the film *Educating Rita* (1983), and he put his name to a book of trivial facts for charity with the slight variant *Not a Lot of People Know That!* in 1984.

2 Been there, done that.

'Michael Caine was once asked if he had a motto: "Yeah — Been There, Done That. It'll certainly be on my tombstone. It'll just say, "Been There, Done That" ' — quoted in Elaine Gallagher *et al*, *Candidly Caine* (1990). This is what might be called a T-shirt motto and certainly not original to Caine. Ian Dury used the phrase 'been there' in the song 'Laughter' (*The Ian Dury Songbook*, 1979) to indicate that a seduction has been accomplished, but the motto isn't solely restricted to sex. It can cover all human activity. About 1989 there were T-shirts for jaded travellers with the words: 'Been there, done that, got the T-shirt.'

See also NAUGHTON 251:2.

Callaghan, James
(later Lord Callaghan)
British Labour Prime Minister (1912–)

3 We say that what Britain needs is a new Social Contract. That is what this document [Labour's Programme, 1972] is all about.

While it was in Opposition from 1970–4, the British Labour Party developed the idea of a social 'compact' between government and trades unions. In return for certain 'social' measures, like price subsidies, the unions would moderate their wage demands. This, in turn, meant that unpopular voluntary or statutory incomes policies could be abandoned. The use of the words 'social contract' differed from that of Rousseau, Hobbes and Locke in that they were thinking in terms of a compact between a government and a whole people, rather than with just one section of it.

Coinage of the term 'social contract', in this specific sense, has been credited to Dennis (later Lord) Lyons (*d* 1978), a public relations consultant who advised the Labour Party in five general elections. Callaghan used the phrase at the Labour Party Conference on 2 October 1972. Anthony Wedgwood Benn had used the term in a 1970 Fabian pamphlet, *The New Politics*. (Jean-Jacques Rousseau's *Du contrat social* was published in 1762.)

4 Bid ben, bid bont.

When Callaghan became Prime Minister in 1976, his first public engagement was a luncheon in Cardiff before opening a new bridge over the River Taff. He said that he was to be guided by the Welsh proverb '*Bid ben, bid bont*' — 'He who commands, must be a bridge'. 'I am to be a bridge between the Government and people, a bridge that links both together so that there is an easy understanding between us.' On 10 April 1976, *The Times* in its report of the speech managed to make a nonsense of the Welsh. Subsequently, in 1983, when George Thomas, former Speaker of the House of Commons, became Viscount Tonypandy, he took the words for his motto.

They come indirectly from The *Mabinogion*, the collection of ancient Welsh folk stories, in which the tale is told of a king, leading an invasion of Ireland, who came to a river without a bridge. ' "There is none," said he, "save that he who is chief, let him be a bridge. I will myself be a bridge." And then was that saying first uttered, and it is still used as a proverb. And then, after he had lain himself down across the river, hurdles were placed upon him, and his hosts passed through over him.' The Welsh form here is, apparently, '*A fo ben, bid bont*' — i.e. 'If he *be* a chief, let him be a bridge.'

1 A great debate.

In a speech at Ruskin College, Oxford, in October 1976, Callaghan, as Prime Minister, called for a 'national debate' on education policy, which also became known as a 'Great Debate'. Politicians like to apply the dignifying label 'great debate' to any period of discussion over policy. The rhyming phrase goes back to 1601, at least. 'The Conservative leaders now decided to bring a vote of no confidence against the Government [on its Defence Programme], and on February 15 [1951] the "Great Debate" as it was known in Tory circles was opened, by Churchill himself' (Martin Gilbert, *Never Despair*, 1988). From BBC TV, *Monty Python's Flying Circus* (4 January 1973): '*Stern music as the lights come on*. SUPERIMPOSED CAPTIONS: 'THE GREAT DEBATE' 'NUMBER 31' 'TV4 OR NOT TV4'.

2 Now, now, little lady, you don't want to believe all those things you read in the newspaper about crisis and upheavals, and the end of civilization as we know it. Dearie me, not at all.

This example of Callaghan's patronizing style when dealing, as Prime Minister, with the then Leader of the Opposition, Margaret

Thatcher, was quoted in all seriousness by *Newsweek*. It was, in fact, a parody written by John O'Sullivan that had appeared in the *Daily Telegraph* (10 June 1976).

3 A lie travels round the world while truth is putting on her boots.

In November 1976, as Prime Minister, Callaghan said in the House of Commons: 'A lie can be halfway round the world before the truth has got its boots on.' From time to time since, this has been credited to him as an original saying (as by the *PDMQ*, 1980 and the *ODMQ*, 1991). To Mark Twain has been attributed, 'A lie can travel half way round the world while the truth is putting on its shoes' — though this is probably no more than another example of the rule, 'When in doubt, say Mark Twain said it'.

A more certain user of the expression was C.H. Spurgeon (1834–92), the noted nineteenth-century Baptist preacher, though he even cited it as an 'old proverb' when saying: 'A lie will go round the world while truth is pulling its boots on' (*Gems from Spurgeon*, 1859). Benham (1948) suggests, however, that 'A lie travels round the world while Truth is putting on her boots' is 'probably [Spurgeon's] own' and ascribes it to his *John Ploughman's Almanack*.

The *Dictionary of American Proverbs* (1992) gives the variations: 'A lie can go around the world and back while the truth is lacing up its boots', 'A lie can travel round the world while the truth is tying up its shoestrings', 'A lie can go a mile before truth can put its boots on' and 'A lie will travel a mile while truth is putting on its boots'.

4 Stiff in opinions, always in the wrong;
Was everything by starts, and nothing long:
But, in the course of one revolving moon,
Was chemist, fiddler, statesman and buffoon.

Callaghan as the Rogue Quotationist, using a passage from Dryden's *Absalom and Achitophel* (1681) to attack Margaret Thatcher and the Conservative front bench in July 1978. Mrs Thatcher was at one time a chemist, but that is about the only link. Besides, Dryden was writing about a *man* — indeed, 'a man so various that he seemed to be/Not one, but all mankind's epitome' — in a work that dealt with the Exclusion

Crisis with various public figures given biblical names. 'Zimri', described here, was George Villiers, 2nd Duke of Buckingham (1628–87). He was a politician, Cabal member and close friend of Charles II. It has been urged that it is his personal qualities rather than his political ones that are described in these lines.

1 There I was waiting at the church . . .

As speculation mounted over an October general election in 1978, Callaghan teased the Labour Party Conference in September by saying, 'The commentators have fixed the month for me, they've chosen the date and the day, but I advise them, "Don't count your chickens before they're hatched." Remember what happened to Marie Lloyd. She fixed the day and the date, and then she told us what 'appened. As far as I remember it went like this: "There was I, waiting at the church . . . All at once, he sent me round a note. Here's the very note. This is what he wrote. Can't get away to marry you today. My wife won't let me".' Unfortunately, it wasn't Marie Lloyd's song. It was Vesta Victoria's. ('Waiting at the Church' had words by Fred W. Leigh, d 1924, and music by Henry W. Pether, d 1925).

In the end, Callaghan did not call an election until the following May, by which time the 'winter of discontent' had undermined his chances of re-election. Given his record on misquotations, perhaps this was appropriate punishment.

2 Crisis, what crisis?

Callaghan may be said to have been eased out of office by a phrase he did not (precisely) speak. Returning from a sunny summit meeting in Guadaloupe to Britain's 'winter of discontent' on 10 January 1979, he was asked by a journalist at a London airport press conference (and I have been back to the original tapes to verify this): 'What is your general approach and view of the mounting chaos in the country at the moment?' Callaghan replied: 'Well, that's a judgement that you are making. I promise you that if you look at it from the outside (and perhaps you are taking rather a parochial view), I don't think that other people in the world would share the view that there is mounting chaos.'

Next day, the Sun carried the headline: 'Crisis? What crisis?' Callaghan lost the May 1979 general election. The editor of the Sun was given a knighthood by the incoming Prime Minister.

Some people insist on recalling that Callaghan said something much more like 'Crisis? What crisis?' on the TV news. When told that these words do not survive on film, these people begin to talk about conspiracy theories. But the impression he created was a strong one. In The Diaries of Kenneth Williams (1993), the comedian noted in his entry for 10 January (the day of Callaghan's return and not of the Sun headline, which he would not have seen anyway): 'Saw the news. Callaghan arrived back from Guadeloupe saying, "There is no chaos" which is a euphemistic way of talking about the lorry drivers ruining all production and work in the entire country, but one admires his phlegm.'

Cambronne, Baron Pierre de
French General (1770–1842)

3 Merde!

At the Battle of Waterloo in 1815 the commander of Napoleon's Old or Imperial Guard is supposed to have declined a British request for him to surrender with the words, 'La garde meurt mais ne se rend jamais/pas [The Guards die but never/do not surrender].' However, it is quite likely that what he said, in fact, was, 'Merde! La garde meurt . . . [Shit! The Guards die . . .]'

The commander in question was Pierre Jacques Etienne, Count Cambronne. At a banquet in 1835 Cambronne specifically denied saying the more polite version. That may have been invented for him by Rougemont in a newspaper, L'Indépendent.

In consequence of all this, merde is sometimes known in France as le mot de Cambronne, a useful euphemism when needed. Unfortunately for Cambronne, the words he denied saying were put on his statue in Nantes, his hometown.

Campbell, Mrs Patrick
English actress (1865–1940)

4 It doesn't matter what you do, as long as you don't do it in the street and frighten the horses.

Although Ted Morgan's biography of Somerset Maugham (1980) actually attributes this to King Edward VII on the subject of the double standard of sexual morality, it is generally accepted as having been said by Mrs Pat. But what gave rise to the remark? Another version, as in Daphne Fielding's The Duchess of Jermyn Street (1964), is: 'It doesn't matter what you do *in the bedroom* as long as you don't do it in the street and frighten the horses.' Yet another (as in the ODQ, 1979) is, 'I don't mind where people *make love*, so long as they . . .'

Margot Peters, in her otherwise pains-takingly-footnoted biography *Mrs Pat* (1984), gives no reason for stating her belief that it was 'when told of a *homosexual affair* between actors' that the actress uttered: 'I don't care what people do, as long as they don't do it in the street and frighten the horses.'

One is reminded of the joke about the preacher who demanded that 'murder, rape and robbery be cleared from our streets . . . and brought back into our homes — where they really belong!' Alfred Hitchcock made a similar remark about television and murder in 1965.

Campbell, Thomas
Scottish poet (1777–1844)

1 *To live in hearts we leave behind*
Is not to die.

From Campbell's 'Hallowed Ground' (1825). This is probably the original of a sentiment frequently to be found on grave-stones. For example, RAF Aircraftsman 1st Class G.C.E. Hodges, who was killed in the Second World War on 18 September 1944, aged 42, and lies in Brookwood Military Cemetery, Surrey, has: 'TO LIVE IN THE HEARTS/OF THOSE WE LOVE/IS NOT TO DIE.' Another variation is: 'He lives for ever in the hearts of those who loved him.'

2 *What though my wingèd hours of*
bliss have been,
Like angel-visits, few and far between?

'Our semi-tautological phrase "few and far between" is a corrupt formulation by the nineteenth-century Scottish poet Thomas Campbell of an old folk saying to the effect that the visits of angels to our world are "brief and far between"' — the *Observer*, 26 June 1988. Campbell's reference in *The Pleasures of Hope*, II.378 (1799) was, in any case, an echo of what Robert Blair had written in *The Grave* (1743): 'Its Visits Like those of Angels' short, and far between.' William Hazlitt pointed that out.

The phrase 'few and far between' had existed before this in a different context. R. Verney wrote a letter *c* July 1668 saying 'Hedges are few and between' (*Memoirs of the Verney Family*, IV.iii.89).

See BYRON 79:5.

Canning, George
British Tory Prime Minister (1770–1827)

3 *I called the New World into existence, to redress the balance of the old.*

In a speech in the House of Commons on the affairs of Portugal (12 December 1826), Canning sought to justify his foreign policy in the face of French intervention to suppress Spanish liberal revolts. He said: 'If France occupied Spain, it was necessary . . . to avoid the consequences of the occupation . . . I sought materials for compensation in another hemisphere. Contemplating Spain as our ancestors had known her, I resolved that if France had Spain, it should not be Spain with the Indies.'

Canute
King of England, Norway and Denmark (*c* 995–1035)

4 *Know all inhabitants of earth, that vain and trivial is the power of kings nor is anyone worthy of the name of king save Him whose nod heaven and earth and sea obey under laws eternal.*

The name of Canute (or Knute or Cnut or Knut) is often evoked in a mistaken fashion. The tale is told of his having his throne carried down to the water's edge, his instructing the waves to go away from him and his failure thereat. The image is summoned up when one wants to portray pointless resis-tance to an idea, or the clinging to an untenable position. However, it is wrong to paint Canute as a fool. After all, the whole point of the story was that Canute carried out the demonstration in order to show his courtiers that there were limits to his power. The original anecdote, pointing the correct moral, first appears in Henry of Hunting-don's *Historia Anglorum*, a twelfth-century manuscript, from which the above quota-tion is taken.

Carlyle, Thomas
Scottish historian and philosopher (1795–1881)

5 *The soul politic.*

In contrast to the 'body politic' (the nation in its corporate character, the state), this phrase was used by Margaret Thatcher in speeches in the 1980s. But Carlyle had anticipated her in *Signs of the Times* (1829).

1 *The Seagreen Incorruptible.*

This was the nickname of Robespierre, the French revolutionary leader who established the Reign of Terror (1793–4) but was executed in it himself. The name comes from Carlyle's *History of the French Revolution*, II.iv.4 (1837): 'The most terrified man in Paris or France is . . . seagreen Robespierre . . . "A Republic?" said the Seagreen, with one of his dry husky unsportful laughs, "What is that?" O seagreen Incorruptible, thou shalt see!' There was no connection between Robespierre's greenness and his incorruptibility. He was green because of poor digestion, and he was incorruptible because he was a fanatic.

2 *Genius is an infinite capacity for taking pains.*

Carlyle did not quite say this in his life of *Frederick the Great* (1858–65) but, rather, 'Genius . . . which means transcendent capacity of taking trouble, first of all'. Disraeli, Samuel Butler and Leslie Stephen are among those credited with the idea or simply with using it. By 1870, Jane Ellice Hopkins in *Work Amongst Working Men* was saying, 'Gift, like genius, I often think only means an infinite capacity for taking pains'.

James Agate in *Ego 6* (1944) calls Carlyle's remark, 'The most misleading pronouncement ever made by a great man' and suggests that a better definition of genius would be: 'That quality in a man which enables him to do things that other people cannot do, and without taking pains.' Indeed, it can be argued that 'taking pains' has nothing to do with genius at all. Mental, spiritual and physical energy may have more to do with it. Compare EDISON 128:4.

3 *Silence is golden.*

This encouragement to silence is from a Swiss inscription written in German: '*Sprechen ist silbern, Schweigen ist golden*' and best known in Carlyle's English translation, 'Speech is silver(n), silence is golden' (*Fraser's Magazine*, June 1834). The original is sometimes given in the form, '*Reden ist Silber, Schweigen ist Gold*' ('Reden' = 'speech').

Carroll, Lewis
(Charles Lutwidge Dodgson)
English writer (1832–98)

4 *How doth the little crocodile*
Improve his shining tail,
And pour the waters of the Nile
On every golden scale!

A parody from *Alice's Adventures in Wonderland*, Chap. 2 (1865). The original, 'Against Idleness and Mischief' (1715) by Isaac Watts, goes:

How doth the little busy bee
    Improve each shining hour,
And gather honey all the day
    From every opening flower!

It appears that Johnny Mercer (1909–76) found the title-lyric of his song 'My Shining Hour' (first sung in the film *The Sky's the Limit*, 1943) in the same place.

5 *'You are old, father William,' the*
    young man said,
'And your hair has become very white;
And yet you incessantly stand on
    your head –
Do you think, at your age, it is right?'

Alice's recitation from Chapter 5 is a parody of a much more sober piece, 'The Old Man's Comforts and How He Gained Them' (1799) by Robert Southey:

'You are old, father William,' the young man cried,
'The few locks which are left you are grey;
You are a hale, father William, a hearty old man;
Now tell me the reason, I pray.'

6 *Why is a raven like a writing desk?*

In *Alice*, Chap. 7 (1865), the Hatter poses this riddle at the 'Mad Tea-Party', but Carroll stated positively that there was no answer. Nevertheless, various people have tried to supply one: 'a quill' — what a raven and a writing desk would have had in common in the last century (Christopher Brown of Portswood, Southampton); 'they both begin with the letter R' (Leo Harris); 'because it can produce a few notes, tho they are very flat; and it is never put with the wrong end in front' — these were Lewis Carroll's own possible solutions (1896 edition); 'because the notes for which they are noted are not noted for being musical notes'

(Sam Loyd); 'Edgar Allan Poe' — he wrote on both a raven and a writing desk (Sam Loyd); 'because bills and tales (tails) are among their characteristics; because they both stand on their legs; conceal their steels (steals); and ought to be made to shut up' (Sam Loyd); 'because it slopes with a flap' (A. Cyril Pearson); 'because there is a "B" in "both" ' (Dr E.V. Rieu). Some of these solutions are included in *The Annotated Alice*, ed. Martin Gardner, 1960.

1 *Twinkle twinkle little bat!*
How I wonder what you're at!
. . . Up above the world you fly,
Like a tea-tray in the sky.

The Hatter's song in *Alice*, Chap. 7 (1865) is a parody of Jane Taylor's poem 'The Star' (1806):

Twinkle, twinkle, little star.
How I wonder what you are!
Up above the world so high,
Like a diamond in the sky.

2 *Oh, 'tis love, 'tis love that makes the world go round.*

This is the proverb the Duchess speaks in *Alice*, Chap. 9 (1865). W.S. Gilbert in *Iolanthe* (1882) has a song made up of proverbial sayings and includes:

In for a penny, in for a pound —
It's love that makes the world go round.

Ian Bradley in his *Annotated Gilbert and Sullivan* (Vol. 1) notes how a previous commentator wondered if this had to do with the old saying: 'It's drink that makes the world go round', and also finds it in *Our Mutual Friend* by Charles Dickens [published in the same year as *Alice*]. But earlier than these was a French song (published 1851, but recorded as early as 1700):

C'est l'amour, l'amour
Qui fait le monde/À la ronde.

There is an English song, 'Love Makes the World Go Round' by Noel Gay, but that was not written until c 1936.

3 *Change Lobsters and Dance.*

This is the English title of the autobiography (1974) of the film actress Lilli Palmer, originally called *Dicke Lilli, gutes Kind*. It alludes to the 'Lobster Quadrille' passage in *Alice*, Chap. 10 (1865), perhaps because Palmer quite frequently changed marriage partners. The precise words do not appear

in *Alice*, though the instruction 'change lobsters' does.

4 *'The time has come,' the Walrus said,*
'To talk of many things:
Of shoes — and ships — and
sealing-wax —
Of cabbages and kings.'

The phrase 'cabbages and kings' was taken by the American writer O. Henry for the title of his first collection of short stories published in 1904, and there was a book entitled *Of Kennedys and Kings: Making Sense of the Sixties* by Harris Wofford (1980). It has been the title of more than one TV series, including the ITV version (1979–82) of the radio quiz *Quote . . . Unquote*. It derives from Chapter 4 — the 'Walrus and the Carpenter' episode — of *Through the Looking Glass and What Alice Found There* (1872).

However, the conjunction of 'cabbages' and 'kings' pre-dates Carroll. In Hesketh Pearson's *Smith of Smiths*, a biography of the Revd Sydney Smith (1771–1845), he quotes Smith as saying about a certain Mrs George Groce: 'She had innumerable hobbies, among them horticulture and democracy, defined by Sydney as "the most approved methods of growing cabbages and destroying kings".'

5 *Anglo-Saxon Attitudes.*

The title of Angus Wilson's novel (1956) about a historian investigating a possible archaeological forgery originates in Chapter 7 of *Through the Looking Glass*. Alice observes the Messenger, 'skipping up and down, and wriggling like an eel, as he came along'. When she expresses surprise, the King explains: 'He's an Anglo-Saxon Messenger — and those are Anglo-Saxon attitudes'. Harry Morgan Ayres in *Carroll's Alice* suggests that the author may have been spoofing the Anglo-Saxon scholarship of his day.

Carter, Jimmy
American Democratic 39th President (1924–   )

6 *Why not the best?*

Carter's official slogan, used as the title of a campaign book and song, as he ran for the Presidency in 1976, originated with an interview he had had with Admiral Hyman Rickover when applying to join the nuclear submarine programme in 1948. 'Did you do your best [at Naval Academy]?' Rickover asked him. 'No, sir, I didn't *always* do my best,' replied Carter. Rickover stared at him for a moment and then asked: 'Why not?'

1 *Jimmy who?*

The question was posed when Carter came from nowhere (or at least the Governorship of Georgia) to challenge Gerald Ford, successfully, for the US Presidency in 1976. It acquired almost the force of a slogan.

2 *Hawae the lads!*

On a visit to the north-east of England in 1977, President Carter (no doubt put up to it by the British Prime Minister, James Callaghan) used the traditional Geordie greeting when addressing a crowd. It means something like 'Come on, lads!' — a cry of encouragement — and also appears in the forms 'Haway' (or 'Howay') and 'Away' (or 'A-wee'). According to Frank Graham, *New Geordie Dictionary* (1979), it is a corruption of 'hadaway' as in 'hadaway wi'ye', which means the opposite, 'begone!'

'Cassandra'
(William Connor)
English journalist (1909–67)

3 *As I was saying when I was interrupted, it is a powerful hard thing to please all the people all the time.*

In September 1946, 'Cassandra' resumed his column in the *Daily Mirror* after the Second World War with quite a common form of words. In June of that same year, announcer Leslie Mitchell is also reported to have begun BBC TV's resumed transmissions with: 'As I was saying before I was so rudely interrupted.' The phrase sounds as if it might have originated in music-hall routines of the 'I don't wish to know that, kindly leave the stage' type. Compare A.A. Milne, *Winnie-the-Pooh* (1926): ' "AS — I — WAS — SAYING," said Eeyore loudly and sternly, "as I was saying when I was interrupted by various Loud Sounds, I feel that — ".' Fary Luis de León, the Spanish poet and religious writer, is believed to have resumed a lecture at Salamanca University in 1577 with, '*Dicebamus hesterno die . . .* [We were saying yesterday].' He had been in prison for five years.

Castle, Ted
(later Lord Castle)
English journalist (1907–79)

4 *In Place of Strife.*

This was Castle's suggested title for an ill-fated Labour Government White Paper on industrial relations legislation put forward by his wife, Barbara Castle, Secretary of State for Employment, on 17 January 1969. It was clearly modelled on *In Place of Fear*, the title of a book about disarmament (1952) by Aneurin Bevan.

Castling, Harry
British songwriter (*fl.* 1904–30)

5 *Let's all go down the Strand — have a banana!*

From the song, 'Let's All Go Down the Strand' (1904), written with C.W. Murphy. The words 'Have a banana' were interpolated by audiences. Although not part of the original lyrics, they were included in later versions.

Cato the Elder
Roman statesman and orator (234–149BC)

6 Delenda est Carthago *[Carthage must be destroyed].*

Cato punctuated or ended his speeches to the Roman Senate with this slogan for eight years, c 157BC, realizing the threat that the other state posed. It worked — Carthage was destroyed (in 146BC) and Rome reigned supreme, though Cato had not lived to see the effect of his challenge. He did have the decency to precede the slogan with the words '*ceterum censeo* [in my opinion]'.

Cavell, Edith
English nurse (1865–1915)

7 *Patriotism is not enough.*

Bartlett (1992) is not alone in describing these, inaccurately, as her 'Last words [12 October 1915], before her execution by the Germans'. Cavell was a British Red Cross nurse who, without question, broke the rules of war by using her job to help Allied prisoners escape from German-occupied territory. She was condemned by a German court-martial for 'conducting soldiers to the enemy' and shot. Her 'message to the world' was: 'This I would say, standing as I do in view of God and Eternity: I realize that patriotism is not enough; I must have no hatred and bitterness towards anyone.' These were not in the form of 'last words' spoken before the firing squad but were said the previous day (11 October 1915) to an English chaplain, the Revd Stirling Gahan, who visited her in prison.

Challoner, Richard
English bishop (1691–1781)

1 *[Sanctity] does not so much depend upon doing extraordinary actions, as upon doing our ordinary actions extraordinarily well.*

In a letter to the *Independent* Magazine (22 May 1993), David Pocock of Lewes, East Sussex, pointed out that when, in an earlier issue, Stephen Bayley had written concerning Peter Boizot (founder of the Pizza Express restaurant chain in Britain), 'Doing ordinary things extraordinarily well is a true mark of genius', he had unwittingly misascribed Challoner's remark.

Chamberlain, Neville
British Conservative Prime Minister (1869–1940)

2 *My good friends, this is the second time in our history that there has come back from Germany to Downing Street peace with honour. I believe it is peace for our time. Go home and get a nice quiet sleep.*

On his return from signing the Munich agreement with Hitler in September 1938, Chamberlain spoke from a window at 10 Downing Street — 'Not of design but for the purpose of dispersing the huge multitude below' (according to his biographer Keith Feiling). Two days before, when someone had suggested the Disraeli phrase 'peace with honour', Chamberlain had impatiently rejected it. Now, according to John Colville, *Footprints in Time* (1976), Chamberlain used the phrase at the urging of his wife.

Chamberlain's own phrase 'peace for our time' is often misquoted as 'peace in our time' — as by Noël Coward in the title of his 1947 play set in an England after the Germans have conquered. Perhaps Coward, and others, were influenced by the phrase from the Book of Common Prayer, 'Give Peace in our time, O Lord'.

Chandler, Raymond
American novelist (1888–1959)

3 *She gave me a smile I could feel in my hip pocket.*

From *Farewell, My Lovely* (1940) — in which Chandler also wrote, 'It was a blonde. A blonde to make a bishop kick a hole in a stained glass window.' But what does this line mean? A winning smile, presumably — but is the reference to the hip pocket meant to suggest something about money (where the wallet might be kept) or even about guns?

4 *Down these mean streets a man must go who is not himself mean; who is neither tarnished nor afraid.*

Chandler wrote this of the heroic qualities a detective should have in 'The Simple Art of Murder' (in the *Atlantic Monthly*, December 1944, reprinted in *Pearls Are a Nuisance*, 1950). However, the phrase 'mean streets' was not original. In 1894, Arthur Morrison had written *Tales of Mean Streets* about impoverished life in the East End of London. The usage was well established by 1922 when the *Weekly Dispatch* was using the phrase casually: 'For him there is glamor even in the mean streets of dockland.'

Charles (The Prince of Wales)
Heir apparent to the British throne (1948–)

5 *A kind of vast municipal fire station . . . I would understand better this type of high-tech approach if you demolished the whole of Trafalgar Square, but what is proposed is like a monstrous carbuncle on the face of a much-loved and elegant friend.*

On 30 May 1984 Prince Charles described a proposed design for a new wing of the National Gallery in London during a speech to the Royal Institute of British Architects. It had an effect: the design was scrapped and replaced by another one. In the same speech he called a planned Mies van der Rohe office building in London a 'glass stump', and opening a factory in May 1987 he likened the new building to a 'Victorian prison'.

The Prince's ventures into architectural criticism have not gone unnoticed, and the image of a 'monstrous carbuncle' ('a red spot or pimple on the nose or face caused by habits of intemperance' – OED2) has become part of the critical vocabulary. A report in the *Independent* (1 March 1988) about plans for a new lifeboat station dominating the harbour at Lyme Regis concluded by quoting a local objector: 'They've called this building a design of the age. What we've got here is a Prince Charles Carbuncle, and we don't like carbuncles down on Lyme harbourside.' The Prince's step-mother-in-law, the Countess Spencer, had earlier written in a book called *The Spencers on Spas* (1983) of how 'monstrous carbuncles of concrete have erupted in Gentle Georgian squares.' Long before, in 1821, William Cobbett had characterized the whole of London as 'the Great Wen of all' – a 'wen' being a lump or protuberance on the body, a wart (see also 103:2).

Chayefsky, Paddy
American playwright (1923–81)

1 Altered States.

Chayefsky's novel with this title (1978) was filmed (US, 1980) but his screen credit was in the form 'Sidney Aaron' because he had disowned the script. The novel/film was a sci-fi thriller about genetic experimentation or, as one of the film guides puts it, about a 'psychophysiologist who hallucinates himself back into primitive states of human evolution, in which guise he emerges to kill'.
Could the phrase have anything to do with what Dr Albert Hofmann observed of his discovery, the psychedelic drug LSD? He noted in his diary for 1943: 'An intense stimulation of the imagination and an altered state of awareness of the world.'

2 I'm as mad as hell and I'm not going to take this any more.

From *New Society* (25 November 1982): 'Some years ago the irascible Howard Jarvis, author of California's Proposition 13 (the one that pegged taxes), coined the immortal political slogan: I'm mad as Hell and I'm Not Taking Any More.' Well, no, he didn't. Chayefsky wrote the film *Network* (1976) in which Peter Finch played a TV pundit-cum-evangelist who exhorted his viewers to get mad: 'I want you to get up right now and go to the window, open it and stick your head out and yell: "I'm as mad as hell,

and I'm not going to take this any more!"'
In 1978, Howard Jarvis (1902–86), the California social activist, merely adopted the slogan and came to be associated with it. As a result, fifty-seven per cent voted to reduce their property taxes. Jarvis entitled a book *I'm Mad as Hell* but duly credited Chayevsky with the coinage. He added: 'For me, the words "I'm mad as hell" are more than a national saying, more than the title of this book; they express exactly how I feel and exactly how I felt about the . . . countless other victims of exorbitant taxes.'

Cher
American singer and actress
(1946–)

3 Stripped, washed and brought to my tent.

Cher spent a certain amount of time in March 1988 denying, apropos some toy-boy lover, that she had ever ordered him, metaphorically speaking, to be stripped, washed and brought to her tent. The allusion here was not terrifically precise. Presumably, the suggestion was that she had behaved as, say, an Arab prince might to an underling (either male or female).

Chesterfield, 4th Earl of
English politician and writer (1694–1773)

4 The pleasure is momentary, the position ridiculous, the expense damnable.

Chesterfield's alleged remark on sex is well known but has not been found in any of his works, not even in the letters of advice (1774) to his natural son for which he is best remembered. It may be that the original utterance was in French – by Voltaire, perhaps, or La Rochefoucauld – in the form '*Le plaisir est court et la position ridicule*'. It appears increasingly likely that the authorship has been imposed on Chesterfield as someone who had a reputation for handing out views like this. In fact, it doesn't quite sound like him.
The earliest source found to date is an unsigned piece in the journal *Nature*, Vol. 227 (22 August 1970). It begins: 'Lord Chesterfield once remarked of sexual intercourse "the pleasure is momentary, the position ridiculous, and the expense damnable".' Another example of an anonymous saying ascribed to a convenient author?

Chesterton, G.K.
English writer (1874–1936)

1 Am in Market Harborough. Where ought I to be?

This is often misquoted as 'Am in Wolverhampton' or several other places. Chesterton was noted for being disorganized and according to one biographer, Maisie Ward, in *Return to Chesterton* (1944), a hundred different places have been substituted for 'Market Harborough'. Chesterton's wife, Frances, on this occasion cabled the answer 'Home' — because, as she exclaimed, it was easier to get him home and start him off again. Yes, Market Harborough was the original and is confirmed by Chesterton's own *Autobiography* (1936).

2 The sallowest bimetallist in that part of Cheshire.

A curious description from Chesterton's novel *The Napoleon of Notting Hill* (1904). In Chapter 3, Dr Polycarp is described as, 'an unusually sallow bimetallist. "There," people of wide experience would say, "There goes the sallowest bimetallist in Cheshire".'

3 The Man Who Was Thursday.

The Man Who Was Thursday: a Nightmare was the title of a short novel (1908) by Chesterton. It was a fantasy with an anarchist background. The seven members of the Central Anarchist Council are named after the days of the week. Hence, all the many later newspaper headlines of 'The Man Who Was —' variety.

4 The prime truth of woman, the universal mother . . . that if a thing is worth doing, it is worth doing badly.

From 'Folly and Female Education', in *What's Wrong with the World* (1910). Obviously, a cynical variation of the proverbial 'If a job [*or* thing] is worth doing, it's worth doing well' — which *CODP* finds Lord Chesterfield using by 1746.

The father of someone I know always used to say: 'If a thing's worth doing, it's worth doing *well enough*.'

5 Talk about the pews and steeples
And the cash that goes therewith!
But the souls of Christian peoples . . .
Chuck it, Smith!

In his 'Antichrist, or the Reunion of Christendom' (1912), Chesterton satirized the pontificating of F.E. Smith (later 1st Earl of Birkenhead) on the Welsh Disestablishment Bill. Hence, the popularizing, though not coinage, of the phrase 'Chuck it — —!' meaning, 'abandon that line of reasoning, that posturing'. Partridge/*Slang* guesses that it is of twentieth-century origin.

A more recent example from the BBC's *World at One* radio programme in May 1983 during the run-up to a general election: Labour politician Roy Hattersley complained that he was being questioned only on the ten per cent of the Labour Party manifesto with which he disagreed. Robin Day, the interviewer, replied: 'Chuck it, Hattersley!'

6 I think I will not kill myself today.

In fact, the line is 'I think I will not hang myself today' from 'A Ballade of Suicide' (1915). This short poem is about a suicide who finds reasons for putting off the deed.

7 Termino nobis donet in patria.

The Latin text on Chesterton's grave in the Roman Catholic cemetery at Beaconsfield, Buckinghamshire, is taken from the final stanza of the Matins hymn for the Feast of Corpus Christi. The entire office was written by St Thomas Aquinas, and Chesterton was said to have known large parts of it by heart. As Father Ian Brady, editor of *The Chesterton Review*, has pointed out (1992), the words would also have been familiar to Chesterton because they formed part of the hymn sung at the once-popular short devotional service of Benediction — a hymn that began with the words, 'O *salutaris hostia*', and concluded with this prayer to the Holy Trinity:

> *Uni trinoque Domino*
> *sit sempiterna gloria,*
> *qui vitam sine termino*
> *nobis donet in patria.*

['Everlasting glory be to the Lord, Three in One, who gives us life without end in heaven.'] In Maisie Ward's *Return to Chesterton* (1944), there is a letter from one of Chesterton's Beaconsfield friends in which Chesterton is quoted as saying that he regarded the phrase '*in patria*' as a perfect definition of heaven. 'Our native land,' he said, 'it tells you everything.' Fr Brady adds that perhaps the fact that Chesterton died on the Sunday within the Octave of Corpus Christi also influenced the choice of these words for his monument. The words were also an especial favourite of Chesterton's friend and colleague, Hilaire Belloc. It is said that Belloc was unable to hear the closing lines of the hymn without being moved to tears.

Christie, Agatha
(later Dame Agatha)
English detective novelist (1890–1976)

1 *I believe that a well-known anecdote exists to the effect that a young writer, determined to make the commencement of his story forcible and original enough to catch the attention of the most blasé of editors, penned the first sentence: ' "Hell!" said the Duchess'.*

These are the opening lines of Christie's *The Murder on the Links* (1923). Later, *Hell! Said the Duchess* was the title of 'A Bed-time Story' (1934) by Michael Arlen. Partridge/ *Catch Phrases* dates the longer phrase, 'Hell! said the Duchess when she caught her teats in the mangle', to *c* 1895 and says it was frequently used in the First World War. Compare the suggested newspaper headline containing all the ingredients necessary to capture a reader's attention (sex, royalty, religion, etc.): 'Teen-age Dog-loving Doctor-priest in Sex-change Mercy-Dash to Palace' (a joke current by 1959 and quoted in *The Lyttelton Hart-Davis Letters*, Vol. 4, 1959). Hence, *PDMQ* (1980)'s attribution of 'Teenage sex-change priest in mercy dash to Palace' to Magnus Linklater in the BBC Radio programme *Between the Lines* (18 September 1976) is misleading.

2 *An archaeologist is the best husband any woman can have; the older she gets, the more interested he is in her.*

Attributed, for example, in Laurence J. Peter, *Quotations for Our Time* (1977). Christie was married to the archaeologist, Sir Max Mallowan, and so it seemed quite feasible when she was quoted as saying this in a news report, 8 March 1954, also quoted in the *Observer* on 2 January 1955. However, according to G.C. Ramsey, *Agatha Christie: Mistress of Mystery* (1967), she vehemently denied having said it, insisting that it would have been a very silly remark for anyone to make, and neither complimentary nor amusing.

Frank S. Pepper in his *Handbook of 20th*

Century Quotations (1984) placed the remark in Christie's *Murder in Mesopotamia* (1936), but it is not be found in that book.

Churchill, Winston
(later Sir Winston)
British Conservative Prime Minister (1874–1965)

3 *A terminological inexactitude.*

In 1906, the status of Chinese workers in South Africa was mentioned in the King's speech to Parliament as 'slavery'. An Opposition amendment of 22 February of the same year was tabled regretting, 'That Your Majesty's ministers should have brought the reputation of this country into contempt by describing the employment of Chinese indentured labour as slavery'. Churchill, as Under-Secretary at the Colonial Office, replied by quoting what he had said in the previous election campaign:

> The conditions of the Transvaal ordinance under which Chinese Labour is now being carried on do not, in my opinion, constitute a state of slavery. A labour contract into which men enter voluntarily for a limited and for a brief period, under which they are paid wages which they consider adequate, under which they are not bought or sold and from which they can obtain relief on payment of seventeen pounds ten shillings, but it cannot in the opinion of His Majesty's Government be classified as slavery in the extreme acceptance of the word without some risk of terminological inexactitude.

This phrase has been taken, almost invariably, as a humorously long-winded way of indicating a 'lie', but the context shows that this is not the meaning. One of the first to misunderstand it, however, was Joseph Chamberlain (1836–1914). Of 'terminological inexactitude' he said: 'Eleven syllables, many of them of Latin or Greek derivation, when one good English word, a Saxon word of a single syllable, would do!'

4 *I once went to bed with a man to see what it was like.*

According to Ted Morgan, *Somerset Maugham* (1980), this was Churchill's reply when asked by Maugham if he had ever had any homosexual affairs. Maugham asked him who the man was. Churchill replied,

'Ivor Novello'. 'And what was it like?' 'Musical.' The source for this story was Alan Searle, one of Maugham's acolytes. Churchill's daughter, Mary Soames, questioned it when it was included in my *Dictionary of Twentieth Century Quotations* (Fontana, 1987), and it is surely of dubious veracity.

1 One is a majority.

Any number of British parliamentarians have used this expression to lessen the importance of achieving only a small majority in an election or parliamentary vote. It is fair to assume that a proportion of them attributed the phrase to Churchill (as Margaret Thatcher did in April 1988). The *Observer* Magazine had ' "One vote is enough" — Churchill' in a compendium of election sayings on 5 April 1992. Possibly Churchill *did* say it, but if he did, he was quoting or alluding. It was Benjamin Disraeli who wrote, 'As for our majority . . . one is enough' in Chapter 64 of his novel *Endymion* (1880).

Compare, from the US, 'One with the law is a majority' in Calvin Coolidge's Speech of Acceptance, 27 July 1920, and 'One man with courage makes a majority', often ascribed to Andrew Jackson. Also, Wendell Phillips in a speech at Brooklyn on 1 November 1859 said: 'One, on God's side, is a majority.'

2 Blood, sweat and tears.

In his classic speech to the House of Commons on 13 May 1940 upon becoming Prime Minister, Churchill said: 'I would say to the House, as I said to those who have joined this Government: I have nothing to offer but blood, toil, tears and sweat' — note the order of the words. There is an echo in this of earlier speeches and writings. The combination makes an early appearance in John Donne's line from *An Anatomy of the World* (1611): ''Tis in vain to do so or mollify it with thy tears or sweat or blood.' Byron follows with 'blood, sweat and tear-wrung millions' in 1823. Theodore Roosevelt spoke in an 1897 speech of 'the blood and sweat and tears, the labour and the anguish, through which, in the days that have gone, our forefathers moved to triumph'. This more usual order of the words was later enshrined in the name of the 1970s American band. Churchill seemed to avoid this configuration, however. In 1931, he had already written of the Tsarist armies: 'Their sweat, their tears, their blood bedewed the endless plain.'

Possibly the closest forerunner of Churchill's 'backs to the wall' exhortation was Giuseppe Garibaldi's impromptu speech to his followers on 2 July 1849 before Rome fell to French troops. The speech was not taken down at the time, so this version is made up of various accounts. Seated upon a horse in the Piazza of St Peter's, he declared: 'Fortune, who betrays us today, will smile on us tomorrow. I am going out from Rome. Let those who wish to continue the war against the stranger, come with me. I offer neither pay, nor quarters, nor provisions; I offer hunger, thirst, forced marches, battles and death [*fame, sete, marcie forzate, battaglie e morte*]. Let him who loves his country with his heart, and not merely his lips, follow me.' As precedents go, this is obviously quite a close one, and it is probable that Churchill had read G.M. Trevelyan's series of books about Garibaldi, published at the turn of the century, in which the lines occur. Having launched such a famous phrase, Churchill referred to it five more times during the course of the war.

Right from the start, people seem to have had difficulty in getting the order of the words right. The natural inclination is to put 'blood', 'sweat' and 'tears' together. Joan Wyndham in *Love Lessons — A Wartime Diary* (1985) concludes her entry for 13 May 1940 with: 'Later we listened to a very stirring speech by Churchill about "blood, toil, sweat and tears".' There is a slight suspicion that this diary may have been 'improved' somewhat in the editing, but not, obviously, to the point of imposing accuracy. Boller & George's *They Never Said It* (1989), dedicated to exposing quotation errors, has Churchill saying, 'blood *and* toil, tears and sweat'.

3 You ask, what is our aim? I can answer in one word: victory, victory at all costs, victory in spite of all terror, victory, however long and hard the road may be.

From the same 13 May 1940 speech. Compare Clemenceau's speech to the Chamber of Deputies in France (8 March 1918): 'My home policy? I wage war. My foreign policy? I wage war. Always, everywhere, I wage war.'

4 Let us go forward together.

A political cliché, chiefly made so by Churchill. 'I can only say to you let us go forward together and put these grave matters to the proof' (the conclusion of a speech on Ulster, 14 March 1914); 'Let us go forward together in all parts of the Empire, in all parts of the Island' (speaking on the war, 27 January 1940); and 'I say, "Come then, let us go forward together with our united strength"' (in his 'blood, sweat and tears' speech, 13 May 1940).

1 *We shall fight on the beaches, we shall fight on the landing grounds, we shall fight in the fields and in the streets, we shall fight in the hills; we shall never surrender.*

At the end of May 1940 some 338,000 Allied troops were evacuated from the Dunkirk area of northern France — a formidable achievement celebrated as a victory although it was a retreat. In a speech to the House of Commons on 4 June, Churchill tried to check the euphoria. He ended thus, however, on a note of hope.

2 *If we can stand up to [Hitler], all Europe may be free and the life of the world may move forward into broad, sunlit uplands.*

From a speech in the House of Commons (18 June 1940). In Churchill's long speaking career there was one thematic device he frequently resorted to for his perorations. It appears in many forms but may be summarized as the 'broad, sunlit uplands' approach. In his collected speeches there are some thirteen occasions when he made use of this construction. 'The level plain . . . a land of peace and plenty . . . the sunshine of a more gentle and a more generous age' (1906); 'I earnestly trust . . . that by your efforts our country may emerge from this period of darkness and peril once more in the sunlight of a peaceful time' (at the end of a speech on 19 September 1915 when Churchill's own position was precarious following the failure of the Gallipoli campaign); in his 'finest hour' speech, Churchill hoped that, 'the life of the world may move forward into broad, sunlit uplands' (1940); 'it is an uphill road we have to tread, but if we reject the cramping, narrowing path of socialist restrictions, we shall surely find a way — and a wise and tolerant government — to those broad uplands where plenty, peace and justice reign' (1951, prior to the general election).

3 *What General Weygand called the Battle of France is over. I expect that the Battle of Britain is about to begin.*

The urge to give names to battles — even before they are fought and won — is well exemplified by Winston Churchill's coinage of 18 June 1940. The 'Battle of Britain' duly became the name by which the decisive overthrowing of German invasion plans by 'the Few' is known. The order of the day, read aloud to every pilot on 10 July, contained the words: 'The Battle of Britain is about to begin. Members of the Royal Air Force, the fate of generations is in your hands.' Another Churchill coinage — 'The Battle of Egypt' (speech, 10 November 1942) — caught on less well.

4 *Let us therefore brace ourselves to our duties, and so bear ourselves that, if the British Empire and its Commonwealth last for a thousand years, men will say, This was their finest hour.*

This is Churchill's version of what he said at the conclusion of his 18 June 1940 speech. *Hansard*'s version differs in one or two details — for example, 'duty' for 'duties', 'lasts' for 'last'. He repeated the speech over the radio, as was his custom during the war (though not invariably), later in the day.

5 *Set Europe ablaze.*

This ringing call was one of the last Churchillisms to become publicly known. E.H. Cookridge wrote in *Inside S.O.E.* (1966): 'The Special Operations Executive was born on 19 July 1940' on the basis of a memo from Winston Churchill ' "to coordinate all action by way of subversion and sabotage against the enemy overseas". Or, as the Prime Minister later put it "to set Europe ablaze".' The title of the first chapter of Cookridge's book is 'Set Europe Ablaze'.

6 *Never in the field of human conflict was so much owed by so many to so few.*

Churchill's classic tribute to the fighter pilots of the Royal Air Force on 20 August 1940 was made well before the Battle of Britain had reached its peak. There is a clear echo of Shakespeare's lines 'We few, we happy few, we band of brothers' in *Henry V.* Benham (1948) quotes Sir John Moore (1761–1809) after the fall of Calpi (where Nelson lost an eye): 'Never was so much work done by so few men.'

Another pre-echo may be found in Vol. 2 of Churchill's own *A History of the English-Speaking Peoples* (1956, but largely written pre-war). In describing a Scottish incursion in 1640 during the run-up to the English Civil War, he writes: 'All the Scots cannon fired and all the English army fled. A contemporary wrote that "Never so many ran from so few with less ado". The English soldiers explained volubly that their flight was not due to fear of the Scots, but to their own discontents.'

Earlier outings of the phraseology in Churchill's own speeches include: 'Never before were there so many people in England and never before have they had so much to eat' (Oldham by-election, 1899); and 'Nowhere else in the world could so enormous a mass of water be held up by so little masonry' (of a Nile dam, 1908).

The bookish phrase 'in the field of human conflict' tended to be dropped when Churchill's speech was quoted. It is interesting that Harold Nicolson, noting the speech in his diary, slightly misquoted this passage: '[Winston] says, in referring to the RAF, "never in the history of human conflict *has* so much been owed by so many to so few".' The immediate impact of Churchill's phrase was unquestionable, however, and is evidenced by a letter to him of 10 September from Lady Violet Bonham Carter (from the Churchill papers, quoted by Martin Gilbert in Vol. 6 of the official biography): 'Your sentence about the Air-war — "Never in the history [*sic*] of human conflict has [*sic*] so much been owed by so many to so few" — will live as long as words are spoken and remembered. Nothing so simple, so majestic & so true has been said in so great a moment of human history. You have beaten your old enemies "the Classics" into a cocked hat! Even my Father [H.H. Asquith] would have admitted that. How he would have loved it!'

By 22 September, Churchill's daughter, Mary, was uttering a *bon mot* in his hearing about the collapse of the France through weak leadership: 'Never before has so much been betrayed for so many by so few' (recorded by John Colville, *The Fringes of Power*, Vol. 1, 1985).

1 *For while the tired waves, vainly breaking,*
Seem here no painful inch to gain,
Far back, through creeks and inlets making,
Comes silent, flooding in, the main.
And not by eastern windows only,

When daylight comes, comes in the light,
In front, the sun climbs slow, how slowly,
But, westward, look, the land is bright.

In a radio broadcast on 3 May 1941, hinting at future American involvement in the war, Churchill responded to the quotation (see 284:6) sent to him by President Roosevelt by quoting from 'Say Not the Struggle Nought Availeth' by Arthur Hugh Clough (1819–61). 'I have,' he said by way of introduction, 'some other lines which are less well known but which seem apt and appropriate to our fortunes tonight, and I believe they will be so judged wherever the English language is spoken or the flag of freedom flies.' He quoted them in the form shown here.

2 *This is not the end. It is not even the beginning of the end. But it is, perhaps, the end of the beginning.*

In a speech at the Mansion House on 10 November 1942, Winston Churchill spoke of the Battle of Egypt in these terms. The formula seems to have a particular appeal to people, judging by the number of times it has been recalled. One occasion that comes to mind is when Ian Smith, the Rhodesian leader, broadcast a speech containing — or so it seemed at the time — a commitment to majority rule, after Dr Henry Kissinger's shuttle diplomacy in the autumn of 1976.

Note that Talleyrand went only half-way when he said, 'It is the beginning of the end [*Voilà le commencement de la fin*]' either after Napoleon's defeat at Borodino (1812) or during the Hundred Days (20 March–28 June 1815).

In *F.E. Smith, First Earl of Birkenhead* (1983) John Campbell observes that Churchill was sitting next to F.E. when Smith addressed an all-party meeting in London on 11 September 1914. The Battle of the Marne, he said, was not the beginning of the end, 'it is only the end of the beginning'. And, Campbell suggests, Churchill 'remembered and tucked [it] away for use again twenty-seven years later'.

3 *The Cross of Lorraine is the heaviest cross I have had to bear.*

In France the Resistance movement had a symbol — the Cross of Lorraine — and when Charles de Gaulle was told that Churchill had made this remark in reference to him, he commented: 'If we consider that the other crosses Churchill had to bear were the Germany army, submarine warfare, the bombing of Britain and the threat of annihilation, then when he says that the heaviest of all these was de Gaulle, it is quite a tribute to a man alone, without an army, without a country, and with only a few followers' (Romain Gary, *Life* Magazine, December 1958). According to Colonel Gilbert Rémy, *Ten Years with De Gaulle* (1971), the film producer Alexander Korda asked Churchill in 1948, 'Winston, did you really say that of all the crosses you ever had to bear, the heaviest was the Cross of Lorraine?' and Churchill replied, 'No, I didn't say it; but I'm sorry I didn't, because it was quite witty . . . and so true!'

1 *He is like a female llama surprised in her bath.*

Churchill denied that he had ever said this about Charles de Gaulle, according to Lord Moran, *The Struggle for Survival* (1966).

2 *The soft underbelly of Europe.*

The phrase 'soft underbelly', for a vulnerable part, appears to have originated with Churchill. Speaking in the House of Commons on 11 November 1942, he said: 'We make this wide encircling movement in the Mediterranean . . . having for its object the exposure of the under-belly of the Axis, especially Italy, to heavy attack.' In *The Second World War* (Vol. 4), he describes a meeting with Stalin before this, in August 1942, at which he had outlined the same plan: 'To illustrate my point I had meanwhile drawn a picture of a crocodile, and explained to Stalin with the help of this picture how it was our intention to attack the soft belly of the crocodile as we attacked his hard snout.'

Somewhere, subsequently, the 'soft' and the 'underbelly' must have joined together to produce the phrase in the form in which it is now used.

3 *[On a long-winded memorandum by Anthony Eden] As far as I can see, you have used every cliché except 'God is love' and 'Please adjust your dress before leaving'.*

This is quoted in Maurice Edelman, *The Mirror: A Political History* (1966) together with Churchill's comment: 'This offensive story is wholly devoid of foundation.' In 1941, Churchill took the unusual course of

writing to Cecil King of the *Daily Mirror* about the matter. The columnist 'Cassandra' had used the story, though labelling it apocryphal and saying he had taken it from *Life* Magazine. *Reader's Digest* in August 1943 certainly carried this version by Allan A. Michie: 'Asked once to look over a draft of one of Anthony Eden's vague speeches on the post-war world, he sent it back to the Foreign Minister with this curt note: "I have read your speech and find that you have used every cliché known to the English language except 'Please adjust your dress before leaving'." '

4 *In war, resolution; in defeat, defiance; in victory, magnanimity; in peace, goodwill.*

Churchill's memoirs of the Second World War were published in six volumes between 1948 and 1954. He took as the motto of the work some words that had occurred to him just after the First World War, as Eddie Marsh, at one time his Private Secretary, recalled: 'He produced one day a lapidary epigram on the spirit proper to a great nation in war and peace . . . (I wish the tones in which he spoke this could have been "recorded" — the first phrase a rattle of musketry, the second "grating harsh thunder", the third a ray of the sun through storm-clouds; the last, pure benediction).'

In 1941, Churchill said the words had been devised (and rejected) as an inscription for a French war memorial, in the form: 'In war fury, in defeat defiance . . .' Perhaps he had been inspired by one of the Latin quotations he knew — '*parcere subiectis et debellare* [spare the conquered and subdue the proud]' — Virgil, *Aeneid*, vi:854.

5 *The special relationship.*

A term used to describe affiliations between countries (the earliest *OED2* citation is for one between Britain and Galicia in 1929), but particularly referring to that supposed to exist between Britain and the US on the basis of historical ties and a common language. The notion was principally promoted by Churchill in his attempts to draw the US into the 1939–45 war, though whether he used the phrase prior to 1941 is not clear. In the House of Commons on 7 November 1945, Churchill said: 'We should not abandon our special relationship with the United States and Canada about the atomic bomb.' In his 1946 'Iron Curtain' speech at Fulton, Missouri, he asked: 'Would a special relationship between the United States and the British Commonwealth be inconsistent with our over-riding loyalties to the World Organization [the UN]?'

1 No socialist Government conducting the entire life and industry of the country could afford to allow free, sharp, or violently worded expressions of public discontent. They would have to fall back on some form of Gestapo.

In a party political radio broadcast on 4 June 1945 in the run-up to the general election that he lost, Churchill attempted to reinforce his view of a socialist future with a misjudged reference to the Gestapo. Evidently his wife had begged him to leave out the passage, but, in what was a significant miscalculation and a possible token of waning powers, Churchill went ahead and was duly much criticized by his political opponents, though he did also receive some support.

2 A blessing in disguise.

Meaning 'a misfortune which turns out to be beneficial', this phrase has been in existence since the early eighteenth century. A perfect example is provided by the noted exchange between Churchill and his wife Clementine. She attempted to console him after his defeat in the 1945 general election by saying, 'It may well be a blessing in disguise'. To which he replied: 'At the moment, it seems quite effectively disguised.' Despite this comment, Churchill seems to have come round to something like his wife's point of view. On 5 September 1945 he wrote to her from an Italian holiday: 'This is the first time for very many years that I have been completely out of the world . . . Others having to face the hideous problems of the aftermath . . . It may all indeed be "a blessing in disguise".'

The anecdote about Churchill's wife was told by ex-President Nixon in his Memoirs (1978). Before that, as though related by Churchill himself, it appeared in The Wit of Sir Winston (1965) and, indeed, it is given in his own words in The Second World War, Vol. 6 (1954).

3 Saving is a very fine thing especially when your parents have done it for you.

Unverified. Quoted in Fred Metcalf, The Penguin Dictionary of Humorous Quotations (1986).

4 From Stettin in the Baltic to Trieste in the Adriatic, an iron curtain has descended across the Continent.

This famous reference to an imaginary division between the Eastern and Western blocs in Europe, caused by the hard-line tactics of the Soviet Union after the Second World War, came in a speech at Fulton, Missouri (5 March 1946). Churchill had already used the phrase 'iron curtain' in telegrams to President Truman and in the House of Commons.

Before him there were any number of uses, all alluding to the iron 'safety' curtains introduced in theatres as a fire precaution in the eighteenth century. In the specific Soviet context, Ethel Snowden was using the phrase as early as 1920 in her book Through Bolshevik Russia. Describing her arrival in Petrograd with a Labour Party delegation, she said: 'We were behind the "iron curtain" at last!' Joseph Goebbels, Hitler's propaganda chief, wrote in an article for the weekly Das Reich (dated 23 February 1945): 'Should the German people lay down their arms, the agreements between Roosevelt, Churchill and Stalin would allow the Soviets to occupy all Eastern and South-Eastern Europe together with the major part of the Reich. An iron curtain would at once descend on this territory.' These remarks were reprinted in British newspapers at the time.

5 The sinews of peace.

Churchill's speech at Fulton was entitled 'The Sinews of Peace'. This was an allusion to the phrase 'nervi belli pecunia' from Cicero's Philippics where the 'sinews of war' meant 'money'. The 'sinews of peace' recommended by Churchill in dealing with the Soviet Union amounted to recourse to the newly formed United Nations Organization.

6 An empty taxi arrived at 10 Downing Street, and when the door was opened Attlee got out.

Succeeded by the Labour leader, Clement Attlee, after the 1945 general election, Churchill was obliged to oppose the man who had been his deputy in the wartime coalition. So this was another joke that went the rounds about the time. When John Colville told Churchill it was being attributed to him, he commented gravely, 'after an awful pause': 'Mr Attlee is an honourable and gallant gentleman, and a faithful colleague who served his country well at the time of her greatest need. I should be obliged if you would make it clear whenever an occasion arises that I never would make such a remark about him, and that I strongly disapprove of anybody who does.' This denial was reported in Kenneth Harris, *Attlee* (1982).

1 A sheep in sheep's clothing.

Churchill is supposed to have described Clement Attlee thus — as in Willans & Roetter, *The Wit of Winston Churchill* (1954). According to *Safire's Political Dictionary* (1980), however, Churchill told Sir Denis Brogan that he had said it not about Attlee but about Ramsay MacDonald, with rather more point. If so, it would appear that he was quoting a joke made by the humorous columnist 'Beachcomber' c 1936. Aneurin Bevan alluded to this same source c 1937 — 'Beachcomber once described Mr Ramsay MacDonald as . . . It applies to many of the front-bench men with whom the Parliamentary Labour Party is cursed' (quoted in Michael Foot, *Aneurin Bevan*, Vol. 1, 1962).

Sir Edmund Gosse is supposed to have said the same of T. Sturge Moore, the 'woolly-bearded poet', c 1906 — and was quoted as such by Ferris Greenslet in *Under the Bridge* (1943).

2 There, but for the grace of God goes God.

Churchill did not deny having made this remark about the Labour politician, Sir Stafford Cripps. It was quoted in Willans & Roetter, *The Wit of Winston Churchill* (1954) but had already been noted by Geoffrey Madan who died in July 1947 (see his *Notebooks*, published in 1981).

In so speaking, Churchill was adapting a remark made by John Bradford (who died in 1555) on seeing criminals going to their execution: 'There, but for the grace of God, goes John Bradford.' This is normally now rendered proverbially as 'There, but for the grace of God, go I.'

3 I would kick him up the arse, Alfred.

A report in *The Times* Diary (29 March 1983) recalled a speech at the Royal Academy in 1949 when the president was Sir Alfred Munnings. One of his guests was Churchill, who had just been admitted to the Academy, and Munnings supposedly ruffled the politician's feathers by saying in his speech: 'Seated on my left is the greatest Englishman of all time. I said to him just now: "What would you do if you saw Picasso walking ahead of you down Piccadilly?" — and he replied: "I would kick him up the arse, Alfred".'

Alas, the BBC recording of the event fails to confirm that Munnings ever said this. Not a born speaker, to put it mildly, what he said was, 'Once he said to me, "Alfred, if you met Picasso coming down the street, would you join with me in kicking his something-something?" I said, "Yes, sir, I would!"'

The Times report also suggested that, 'as the laughter died, Munnings yelled at the top of his voice: "Blunt, Blunt [i.e. Sir Anthony Blunt, the art connoisseur later unmasked as a traitor] — you're the one who says he prefers Picasso to Sir Joshua Reynolds!"' If he did yell it he was very quiet about it, because the barb is not audible on the recording.

4 The trees do not grow up to the sky.

Is this an actual proverb or a made up one? And what does it mean? John Colville quotes Churchill as saying it on 6 January 1953 in a situation where he is recommending a 'wait and see' policy. The full version seems to be, 'The trees are tall but they do not reach to the sky'. In other words, 'trees may be tall, but they're not that tall' or, metaphorically, 'no person is that important, however grand they may appear'. Later in the same year, on 9 November, in his speech to the Lord Mayor's Banquet, Churchill said: 'Another old saying comes back to my mind which I have often found helpful or at least comforting. I think it was Goethe who said, "The trees do not grow up to the sky". I do not know whether he would have said that if he had lived through this frightful twentieth century where so much we feared was going to happen did actually happen. All the same it is a thought which should find its place in young as well as old brains.'

Goethe? So perhaps it isn't Russian after all. Nevertheless, it sounds just like what that great utterer of obscure proverbial sayings, Nikita Khrushchev, might have come up with: 'If you start throwing hedgehogs under me, I shall throw two porcupines under you'; 'If you cannot catch a bird of paradise, better take a wet hen'; 'Those who wait for the Soviet Union to abandon communism must wait until a shrimp learns to whistle'; and so on. But people do manufacture Russian folk proverbs. Anon. devised one for Khruschev himself: 'Great oafs from little ikons grow.' Either Dr Walter Heydecker or Lyndon Irving sent this one into a *New Statesman* competition: 'Even a short leg reaches the ground.'

1 *The portrait is a remarkable example of modern art. It certainly combines force and candour. These are qualities which no active member of either house can do without or should fear to meet.*

On his eightieth birthday (30 November 1954), both Houses of Parliament presented Churchill with a portrait painted by Graham Sutherland. He did not like it but accepted the portrait with a gracefully double-edged compliment. Lady Churchill's dislike of the portrait took a more practical form: she had it destroyed.

2 *I look as if I was having a difficult stool.*

Remark on the same portrait, quoted in Ted Morgan, *Somerset Maugham* (1980) but earlier in *The Lyttelton Hart-Davis Letters* (for 20 November 1955). Other versions of this criticism are: 'How do they paint one today? Sitting on a lavatory!' (said to Charles Doughty, secretary of the committee which organized the tribute), and 'Here sits an old man on his stool, pressing and pressing.'

3 *Not a pillar of the church but a buttress.*

When Churchill was reproached for not going to church he replied that he was not a pillar of the church but a buttress — he supported it from the outside. (Recalled by Montague Browne in a speech to the International Churchill Society, London, 25 September 1985.)
Note, however, that it was said of John Scott, Lord Eldon (1751–1838): 'He may be one of its [the Church's] buttresses, but certainly not one of its pillars, for he is never found within it.' (H. Twiss, *Public and Private Life of Eldon*, 1844). The ODQ (1992) adds that this remark was latter attributed to Lord Melbourne.

4 *I am ready to meet my Maker. Whether my Maker is ready for the ordeal of meeting me is another matter.*

These have been reproduced as Churchill's 'last words', but they were not. They were said on his seventy-fifth birthday. In *Clementine* (1979), Mary Soames reported that her father's last comprehensible words before he died were, 'I'm so bored with it all'.

Ciano, Count Galeazzo
Italian politician (1903–44)

5 *As always, victory finds a hundred fathers, but defeat is an orphan.*

Mussolini's foreign minister (and son-in-law) made this diary entry on 9 September 1942 (translation published 1946). President Kennedy quoted the 'old saying' following the Bay of Pigs disaster in April 1961.

Cibber, Colley
English playwright (1671–1757)

6 *Off with his head — so much for Buckingham.*

In his 1700 edition of Shakespeare's *Richard III*, Colley Cibber extended III.iv.75 thus, by four words. It proved a popular and lasting emendation. In 'Private Theatres' (1835), one of the *Sketches by Boz*, Charles Dickens describes the roles on offer to amateur actors who at that time could *pay* to take certain roles in plays: 'For instance, the Duke of Glo'ster is well worth two pounds . . . including the "off with his head!" — which is sure to bring down the applause, and it is very easy to do — "Orf with his ed" (very quick and loud; — then slow and sneeringly) — "So much for Bu-u-u-uckingham!" Lay the emphasis on the "uck;" get yourself gradually into a corner, and work with your right hand, while you're saying it, as if you were feeling your way, and it's sure to do.'
The extra phrase was also included in Laurence Olivier's film of Shakespeare's play (1955).

Clare, John
English poet (1793–1864)

7 *Fields were the essence of the song*
& fields & woods are still as mine
Real teachers that are all divine
So if my song be weak or tame
Tis I not they who bear the blame.

The first line of this quotation from Clare's 'Progress of Rhyme' is on his memorial tablet set in Poets' Corner, Westminster Abbey. The 'Northamptonshire Peasant

Poet' is also remembered on a Gothic memorial in Helpston where he was born and where he is buried in the churchyard of St Botolph. He died in an asylum for the insane.

Clark, Kenneth
(later Lord Clark)
English art historian (1903–83)

1 *Another Part of the Wood.*

The title of the first volume of Clark's autobiography (1974) is taken from the stage direction to Act III, Scene ii of Shakespeare, *A Midsummer Night's Dream*: 'Another Part of the Wood.' Scene locations such as this were mostly not of Shakespeare's own devising but were added by later editors. Clark said he wished also to allude to the opening of Dante's *Inferno*: 'I found myself in a dark wood where the straight way was lost.' Lillian Hellman had earlier entitled one of her plays, *Another Part of the Forest* (1946).

Clarke, Arthur C.
English writer (1917–   )

2 *Open the pod-bay doors, Hal!*

In the script that he wrote with Stanley Kubrick for the film *2001: A Space Odyssey* (UK, 1968), this is what the stranded astronaut, Dave Bowman (Keir Dullea), says to the errant computer. Not 'Open the pod door, Hal' as in *PDMQ* (1980).

Clarke, Roy
British writer (1930–   )

3 *The Last of the Summer Wine.*

The title of this long-running BBC TV comedy series (1974–   ) — about a trio of elderly school friends in a Yorkshire village finding themselves elderly and unemployed — is not a quotation, according to its writer. In *Radio Times* (February 1983), Clarke described it as: 'Merely a provisional title which seemed to suit the age group and location. I expected it to be changed but no one ever thought of anything better.' The phrase 'summer wine', on its own, had already been used in a song 'If I Thought You'd Ever Change Your Mind' by John Cameron, which was recorded in 1969 by Kathe Green ('. . . feed you winter fruits and summer wine . . .')

'Last of the wine' had also been used earlier to describe things of which there is only a finite amount or of which the best is gone. From a programme note by composer Nicholas Maw for *The Rising of the Moon*, Glyndebourne Festival Opera, 1970: 'In a recent television interview, Noël Coward was asked if he thought it still possible to write comedy for the stage. Did his own generation not have the "last of the wine"?' In the 1950s, Robert Bolt wrote a radio play with the title *The Last of the Wine* and Mary Renault, a novel (1956).

Cleaver, Eldridge
American political activist (1935–   )

4 *If you're not part of the solution, you're part of the problem.*

CODP's earliest citation for this (anonymous) modern proverb is in Malcolm Bradbury's novel *The History Man* (1975). But there is little doubt that Cleaver said it in a 1968 speech in San Francisco. It may even be included in his *Soul on Ice* (1968). One form of Cleaver's remark is: 'What we're saying today is that you're either part of the solution or you're part of the problem.' Another: 'There is no more neutrality in the world. You either have to be part of the solution, or you're going to be part of the problem.'

Compare: 'If you're not part of the steamroller, you're part of the road' — attributed to Michael Eisner, Chairman of Walt Disney, in 1993.

Clemenceau, Georges
French Prime Minister (1841–1929)

5 *If you don't vote Socialist/Communist before you are twenty, you have no heart — if you do vote Socialist/Communist after you are twenty, you have no head.*

The saying to this effect may derive from what Bennett A. Cerf attributed to Georges Clemenceau in *Try and Stop Me* (1944). It is supposedly what Clemenceau replied when told that his son had just joined the Communist party: 'My son is twenty-two years old. If he had not become a Communist at twenty-two I would have disowned him. If he is still a Communist at thirty, I will do it then.'

Another suggested source is Dean Inge, the 'Gloomy Dean' of St Paul's (d 1954). And then there is the remark, attributed loosely to Benjamin Disraeli, in Laurence J. Peter's *Quotations for Our Time* (1977): 'A man who is not a Liberal at sixteen has no heart; a man who is not a Conservative at sixty has no head.'

Pass the Port Again (1980) has this version, ascribed to Maurice Maeterlinck: 'If a man is not a Socialist at twenty he has no heart. If he is a Socialist at thirty, he has no brain.'

Putting it another way, Will Durant, the American teacher, philosopher and historian (1885–1982), said, 'There is nothing in Socialism that a little age or a little money will not cure.' The American poet, Robert Frost, wrote in 'Precaution' (1936): 'I never dared be radical when young/For fear it would make me conservative when old.'

Compare what George Bernard Shaw said in a lecture at the University of Hong Kong in February 1933: 'Steep yourself in revolutionary books. Go up to your neck in Communism, because if you are not a red revolutionist at 20, you will be at 50 a most impossible fossil. If you are a red revolutionist at 20, you have some chance of being up-to-date at 40.'

1 J'accuse.

The Dreyfus Affair in France arose in 1894 when Captain Alfred Dreyfus, who had Jewish origins, was dismissed from the army on trumped-up charges of treason. Condemned to life imprisonment on Devil's Island, he was not reinstated until 1906. In the meantime, the case had divided France. The writer Émile Zola (1840–1902) came to the defence of Dreyfus with two open letters addressed to the President of the French Republic and printed in the paper *L'Aurore*. The first, under the banner headline, '*J'accuse*' ('I accuse'), was published on 13 January 1898 — each paragraph began with the words; the second, more moderate in tone, on 22 January.

It is a small point, perhaps, but Clemenceau, who played a prominent part in the campaign with Zola, claimed in a letter (19 June 1902) that: 'It was I who gave the title "*J'accuse*" to Zola's letter.' He also said that he had written most of the second letter.

[*Source*: D.R. Watson, *Clemenceau*, 1974.]

2 War is too serious a business to be left to the generals [La guerre, c'est une chose trop grave pour la confier à des militaires].

In France Parliament had suspended its sittings at the outbreak of the First World War and the conduct of the war had been entrusted to the goverment and to Joffre and the General Staff. By 1915, however, opinion was changing. It may have been about this time that Clemenceau, who became French Prime Minister again in 1917, uttered this, his most famous remark. The notion has also been attributed to Talleyrand (Briand quoted him as such to Lloyd George during the war) and, indeed, Clemenceau may have said it himself much earlier (in 1886 even). Subsequently, the saying's format has been applied to many other professions. De Gaulle followed with: 'Politics is too important to be left to the politicians' (quoted in 1961 by Clement Attlee, to whom de Gaulle had written it 'after the war'), and on 18 October 1968, Tony Benn, the Labour Minister of Technology, said 'Broadcasting really is too important to be left to the broadcasters'. In 1990, Helmut Sihler, president of a West German chemical company, said, 'The environment is too important to be left to the environmentalists'.

3 America is the only nation in history which miraculously has gone directly from barbarism to degeneration without the usual interval of civilization.

So ascribed to Clemenceau by Hans Bendix in *The Saturday Review of Literature* (1 December 1945). No more substantial attribution appears to exist.

4 Oh, to be seventy again!

Said to have been exclaimed on his eightieth birthday (i.e. in 1921) when walking down the Champs-Élysées with a friend and a pretty girl passed them (quoted by James Agate, *Ego 3*, 1938). The same remark is ascribed to Oliver Wendell Holmes Jr (1841–1935), the American jurist, on reaching his eighty-seventh year (by Fadiman & van Doren in *The American Treasury*, 1955). Bernard de Fontenelle (1657–1757), the French writer and philosopher, is said in great old age to have attempted with difficulty to pick up a young lady's fan, murmuring, 'Ah, if I were only eighty again!'

(Pedrazzini & Gris, *Autant en apportent les mots*, 1969).

Cleveland, Grover
American Democratic 22nd and
24th President (1837–1908)

1 *We love him for the enemies he has made.*

A curious campaign slogan for Cleveland was derived from a speech made by Governor Edward Stuyvesant Bragg, seconding Cleveland's Presidential nomination (9 July 1884). He won the first of his two separate Presidential terms.

Clinton, Bill (William J.)
American Democratic 42nd President
(1946–)

2 *When I was in England [as a Rhodes Scholar], I experimented with marijuana a time or two, and I didn't like it, and I didn't inhale and I never tried it again.*

From a report in the *Washington Post* (31 March 1992). During his campaign for the Presidency, Clinton had to fend off criticisms that not only had he been to Oxford (anathema to the incumbent President, George Bush), but also had not fought in Vietnam and was generally associated with 1960s habits. While seeking the Democratic nomination, Clinton appeared on TV with a rival candidate, Jerry Brown. The two men were asked if they had ever violated state, federal or international laws. Under 'pinpoint questioning that closed all avenues of escape', according to the *Post*, he finally confessed to the above banality.

3 *After the winter comes the spring.*

It was unfair of the *Independent* Magazine (13 February 1993) to suggest that President Clinton had strayed into *Being There* territory during his Inaugural speech (20 January 1993). What Chauncey Gardiner, the platitudinous sage played by Peter Sellers in the 1980 film, said was: 'After the winter comes the spring.' Clinton said, rather, in his opening paragraph: 'This ceremony is held in the depth of winter. But, by the words we speak and the faces we show the world, we force the spring.' That is not at all

the same thing, though it may have been ill-advised of the new President to foster such a comparison.

Clough, Arthur Hugh
English poet (1819–61)

4 *Thou shalt not kill; but need'st not strive*
Officiously to keep alive.

Clough's 'The Latest Decalogue' (1862) was an *ironical* version of the Ten Commandments — so this line was not serious advice to doctors (in which sense it has sometimes been quoted, however).

5 *Bring on the champagne and damn*
*   the expense,*
I've seen it observed by a person of
*   sense*
The labouring classes would not last
*   a day*
If fellows like us didn't eat, drink and
*   pay!*
How pleasant it is to have money,
*   heigh ho!*
How pleasant it is to have money.

On BBC Radio *Quote . . . Unquote* (in 1980), Wynford Vaughan-Thomas's recited this verse and attributed it to Clough. It appears to have been Vaughan-Thomas's own version of the poem 'Dipsychus', which includes somewhat different lines, including:

> As I sat at the café, I said to myself,
> They may talk as they please about
>   what they call pelf,
> They may sneer as they like about
>   eating and drinking,
> But help it I cannot, I cannot help
>   thinking,
> How pleasant it is to have money,
>   heigh ho!
> How pleasant it is to have money.

The poem was found in Clough's papers after his death and not published till then, which may perhaps explain why there are rather free versions of it in circulation. Clough's 'The Latest Decalogue' (see above) and his well-known 'Say not the struggle nought availeth' were also only published posthumously.

See also CHURCHILL 95:1.

Cobb, Irvin S.
American humorist and writer (1876–1944)

1 *Nothing trivial, I trust?*

When Cobb was a reporter on the New York *World*, he had to work under Charles E. Chapin, whom he found to be a difficult boss. Arriving at the office one day, Cobb was told that Chapin was off sick. Cobb made this inquiry. Recounted in Ralph L. Marquard, *Jokes and Anecdotes* (1977), this may possibly be the origin of the oft-told tale.

Cobbett, William
English radical writer (1762–1835)

2 *But what is to be the fate of the great wen of all? The monster, called . . . 'the metropolis of empire'?*

In *Rural Rides: The Kentish Journal* in Cobbett's *Weekly Political Register* (5 January 1822), Cobbett asked this of London. A 'wen' is a lump or protuberance on a body; a wart. Compare CHARLES 89:5.

Cockburn, Claud
English journalist (1904–81)

3 *Small earthquake in Chile. Not many dead.*

In his book *In Time of Trouble* (1956) (included in *I Claud . . .*, 1967), Cockburn claimed to have won a competition for dullness among sub-editors on *The Times* with this headline in the late 1920s: 'It had to be a genuine headline, that is to say one which was actually in the next morning's newspaper. I won it only once.' At Cockburn's death it was said, however, that an exhaustive search had failed to find this particular headline in the paper. It may just have been a smoking-room story. However, the idea lives on: it became (perhaps inevitably) the title of a book (1972) by Alastair Horne about the Allende affair (in Chile). The journalist Michael Green called a volume of memoirs *Nobody Hurt in Small Earthquake* (1990), and the cartoonist Nicholas Garland called his 'Journal of a year in Fleet Street' *Not Many Dead* (1990).

Cohn, Irving
American songwriter (1898–1961)

4 *Yes, we have no bananas,*
We have no bananas today.

From the song 'Yes, We Have No Bananas' (1923), to music by Frank Silver (1892–1960). According to Ian Whitcomb in *After the Ball* (1972), the title line came from a cartoon strip by Tad Dorgan and not, as the composers were wont to claim, from a Greek fruit-store owner on Long Island. Alternatively, it was a saying picked up by US troops in the Philippines from a Greek pedlar. In Britain, Elders & Fyffes, the banana importers, embraced the song and distributed 10,000 hands of bananas to music-sellers with the slogan: 'Yes! we have no bananas! On sale here.'

Coke, Desmond
English writer and schoolmaster (1879–1931)

5 *All rowed fast, but none so fast as stroke.*

In *Sandford of Merton*, Chap. 12 (1903), Coke wrote: 'His blade struck the water a full second before any other: the lad had started well. Nor did he flag as the race wore on: as the others tired, he seemed to grow more fresh, until at length, as the boats began to near the winning-post, his oar was dipping into the water nearly twice as often as any other.' This is deemed to be the original of the modern proverbial saying.
The 'misquotation' is sometimes thought to have been a deliberate distortion of something written earlier than Coke, by Ouida, 'designed to demonstrate the lady's ignorance of rowing, or indeed of any male activity' — Peter Farrer in *Oxford Today* (Hilary Term 1992).

Coleman, David
English broadcaster (1926–)

6 *Juantorena opens wide his legs and shows his class.*

Since the late 1970s *Private Eye* Magazine has had a column with the title 'Colemanballs' devoted chiefly to the inanities of TV and radio sports commentators. The title was derived from the name of BBC TV's principal sports commentator at the time. Coleman was generally supposed to have committed any number of solecisms, tautologies and what-have-you in the cause of keeping his tongue wagging. Hearers who report his sayings have often been inaccurate. It is believed, however, that he did say, among other things, 'This man could be a black horse', 'There is only one winner in this race' and — of the footballer Asa Hartford who had a hole in the heart operation — 'He is a whole-hearted player'.

To be fair, however, the boob that started it all has been revealed as being perpetrated by another. At the 1976 Montreal Olympics, it was said of the athlete Alberto Juantorena, competing in the 400 metres heats, that he 'opens wide his legs and shows his class'. It was not Coleman who said this but Ron Pickering (1930–91).

Coleridge, Samuel Taylor
English poet and writer (1772–1834)

1 *Water, water, everywhere,*
And not a drop to drink.

That is how everyone remembers it, but what Coleridge wrote in his poem 'The Ancient Mariner' (1798) was:

> Water, water everywhere,
> And all the boards did shrink;
> Water, water, everywhere
> *Nor any* drop to drink.

2 *On awaking he . . . instantly and eagerly wrote down the lines that are here preserved. At this moment he was unfortunately called out by a person on business from Porlock.*

From Coleridge's introductory note to 'Kubla Khan' (1816) describing how he, the poet, was interrupted in writing out the two or three hundred lines that had come to him in his sleep, when staying in Somerset. The incident happened in 1797 after Coleridge had taken opium and fallen asleep. Hence, the expression 'person from Porlock' to describe any kind of distraction, but especially from literary or other creative work.

3 *And from this chasm, with ceaseless turmoil seething,*
As if this earth in fast thick pants were breathing,
A mighty fountain momently was forced.

The 'fast thick pants' from 'Kubla Khan' (1816) have occasioned much schoolboy laughter over the years. C.S. Lewis evidently posed the question whether the pants were 'woollen or fur?'

4 *That willing suspension of disbelief for the moment, which constitutes poetic faith.*

Coleridge's phrase 'willing suspension of disbelief' for what is an essential part of much artistic experience, not just in poetry, comes from Chapter XIV of his *Biographia Literaria* (1817). It has been called 'one of the most famous phrases ever coined' and describes the state of receptiveness and credulity required by the reader or 'receiver' of a work of literature, as well as the acceptance of dramatic and poetic conventions. In the original context, Coleridge was writing of two possible subjects for poetry: 'In this idea originated the plan of the Lyrical Ballads; in which it was agreed, that my endeavours should be directed to persons and characters supernatural, or at least romantic; yet so as to transfer from our inward nature a human interest and a semblance of truth sufficient to procure from these shadows of imagination that willing suspension of disbelief for the moment, which constitutes poetic faith.'

Colson, Charles
American Watergate conspirator (1931–)

5 *I would walk over my grandmother if necessary [to get something done].*

This was a view applied to Colson rather than anything he ever actually said himself, but he subsequently muddied the water by appearing to endorse the sentiment. An article in the *Wall Street Journal* in 1971 had portrayed Colson, a special counsel of President Nixon, as someone who, in the words of another Washington official, would be prepared to walk over his grandmother if he had to. In 1972, when Nixon sought re-election as US President, Colson misguidedly sent a memo to campaign staff which stated: 'I am totally unconcerned about anything other than getting the job done . . . Just so you understand me, let me point out that the statement . . . "I would walk over my grandmother if necessary" is absolutely accurate.' This was leaked to the *Washington Post*.

Subsequently convicted for offences connected with Watergate and then emerging as a born-again Christian, Colson tried unavailingly to point out that he had never really said it. In his book *Born Again* (1977) he wrote: 'My mother failed to see the humour in the whole affair, convinced that

I was disparaging the memory of my father's mother . . . Even though both of my grandmothers had been dead for more than twenty-five years (I was very fond of both).' Such are the penalties for tangling with figures of speech.

In an earlier age — the 1880s — the editor of the *Pall Mall Gazette*, W.T. Stead, famous for his exposé of the child prostitution racket, said: 'I would not take libel proceedings if it were stated that I had killed my grandmother and eaten her.' Another even earlier image often invoked was of 'selling one's own grandmother'.

Conable, Barber B., Jr
American Republican politician and banker (1922–)

1 *I guess we have found the smoking pistol, haven't we?*

The term 'smoking pistol/gun' was popularized during the Watergate affair. Conable said this of a tape of President Nixon's conversation with H.R. Haldeman, his chief of staff, on 23 June 1972, which contained a discussion of how the FBI's investigation of the Watergate burglary could be 'limited'. The phrase simply means 'incriminating evidence', as though a person found holding a smoking gun could be assumed to have committed an offence with it — as in Conan Doyle's Sherlock Holmes story 'The "Gloria Scott" ' (1894): 'Then we rushed on into the captain's cabin . . . and there he lay . . . while the chaplain stood, with a smoking pistol in his hand'.

Confucius
Chinese philosopher (551–479BC)

2 *There is no spectacle more agreeable than to observe an old friend fall from a roof-top.*

Sometimes it is a 'neighbour': 'Even a virtuous and high-minded man may experience a little pleasure when he sees his neighbour falling from a roof.' The earliest citation to hand dates only from 1970, and one suspects that, like so many other Confucian sayings, it has nothing whatever to do with the Chinese philosopher who, nevertheless, undoubtedly did exist and did say a number of wise things (some through his followers). Even when not prefaced by 'Confucius, he say . . .' there is a tendency — particularly

in the US — to ascribe any wry saying to him.

With regard to this one, similar thoughts have occurred to others: 'Philosophy may teach us to bear with equanimity the misfortunes of our neighbours' — Oscar Wilde, *The English Renaissance of Art* (1882); 'I am convinced that we have a degree of delight, and that no small one, in the real misfortunes and pains of others' — Edmund Burke, *On the Sublime and Beautiful* (1756); and, especially, 'In the misfortune of our best friends, we find something that is not displeasing to us [*Dans l'adversité de nos meilleurs amis, nous trouvons toujours quelque chose qui ne nous deplaît pas*]' — Duc de La Rochefoucauld (1665).

Congreve, William
English playwright (1670–1729)

3 *Hell hath no fury like a woman scorned.*

The fury of a disappointed woman had been characterized along these lines before Congreve, but insofar as he coined this proverbial expression, it should be noted that in his *The Mourning Bride* (1697) the text is: 'Heav'n has no Rage like Love to Hatred turn'd,/Nor Hell a Fury, like a Woman scorn'd.'

4 *Music has charms to soothe a savage breast.*

From the same play. Not 'hath charms' and not 'savage beast'.

Connolly, Cyril
English writer and critic (1903–74)

5 *Imprisoned in every fat man a thin one is wildly signalling to be let out.*

Connolly wrote this in *The Unquiet Grave* (1944) but, five years before, George Orwell had written in *Coming Up for Air*: 'I'm fat, but I'm thin inside. Has it ever struck you that there's a thin man inside every fat man, just as they say there's a statue inside every block of stone?' Great minds think alike. The coincidence was pointed out in a letter to *Encounter* in September 1975.

Not to be outdone, Kingsley Amis twisted the idea round in *One Fat Englishman* (1963): 'Outside every fat man there was an even fatter man trying to close in.' And Timothy Leary was quoted in 1979 as having said: 'Inside every fat Englishman is a thin Hindu trying to get out.'

1 She looked like Lady Chatterley above the waist and the gamekeeper below.

In his *Customs and Characters* (1982), Peter Quennell described the poet Vita Sackville-West's celebrated affair with Virginia Woolf. The former's appearance, he wrote, was 'strange almost beyond the reach of adjectives . . . she resembled a puissant blend of both sexes — Lady Chatterley and her lover rolled into one, I recollect a contemporary humorist observing . . . her legs, which reminded Mrs Woolf of stalwart tree trunks, were encased in a gamekeeper's breeches and top-boots laced up to the knee.'

Quennell may have been alluding to the rather more pointed remark that Vita Sackville-West looked 'like Lady Chatterley above the waist and the gamekeeper below'. In fact, by 'contemporary humorist' he probably meant Cyril Connolly, who went with him on a joint visit to Sackville-West at Sissinghurst in 1936. Certainly, that is the form in which Connolly's remark is more usually remembered.

Conran, Shirley
English journalist and novelist
(1932–   )

2 Life is too short to stuff a mushroom.

The epigraph to her home hints volume, *Superwoman* (1975), is in the tradition of such remarks. Richard Porson (1759–1808), Regius Professor of Greek at Cambridge, is quoted by Thomas Love Peacock in *Gryll Grange* (1861) as having said, 'Life is too short to learn German'.

Coolidge, Calvin
American Republican 30th President
(1872–1933)

3 He was against it.

Coolidge went to church alone one Sunday because his wife was unable to accompany him. She asked on his return what the sermon was about. 'Sin,' he replied. 'But what did he say about it?' Coolidge said 'He was against it.' This story made an early appearance in John Hiram McKee, *Coolidge Wit and Wisdom* (1933). Mrs Coolidge said it was just the sort of thing he would have said. Coolidge himself said it would be funnier if it were true.

4 You lose.

A story about Coolidge's taciturnity was told by his wife: a woman sat down to him at a dinner party and said, 'You must talk to me, Mr Coolidge. I made a bet with someone that I could get more than two words out of you.' Coolidge replied: 'You lose.' This made an early appearance in Gamaliel Bradford, *The Quick and the Dead* (1931).

5 I do not choose to run.

That is not quite what Coolidge said, and, in any case, he didn't actually *say* it. Having been President since 1923, his words to newsmen on 2 August 1927 were 'I do not choose to run for President in 1928'. And rather than speak, 'Silent Cal' handed slips of paper with these words on them to waiting journalists. For some reason, the unusual wording of the announcement caught people's fancy and the phrase was remembered. In 1928, there was a silly song recorded in New York about a recalcitrant wristwatch. It was performed by Six Jumping Jacks with Tom Stacks (vocal) and was called 'I Do Not Choose To Run'.

6 After all, the chief business of the American people is business.

Speech to the American Society of Newspaper Editors (17 January 1925). *ODQ* (1979) simply had, 'The business of America is business'.

Cornford, Frances
English poet (1886–1960)

7 O why do you walk through the fields in gloves,
Missing so much and so much?
O fat white woman whom nobody loves.

Lines from Cornford's short poem 'To a Fat Lady Seen from a Train' (1910), which the *Oxford Companion to English Literature* describes as 'curiously memorable though undistinguished'. Part of the fascination must lie in the fact that we must all have wondered at some time about the people we have glimpsed from trains. It was Cornford's assumptions about the fat white woman, however, that caused G.K. Chesterton to provide the other side of the story. His 'The Fat White Woman Speaks' was published in *New Poems* (1932):

Why do you flash through the flowery
  meads,
Fat-headed poet that nobody reads;
And how do you know such a frightful
  lot
About people in gloves as such?

'Beachcomber' (J.B. Morton) also wrote a
riposte, 'The Fat Lady Seen from a Train
Replies to the Scornful Poet'.

Cornford, Francis
English academic (1874–1943)

1 *Nothing should ever be done for the
first time.*

From his *Microcosmographia Academica*
(1908). The precise wording is: 'Every
public action, which is not customary, either
is wrong, or, if it is right, is a dangerous
precedent. It follows that nothing should
ever be done for the first time.' Francis Cornford, who was married to Frances *above*,
was Professor of Ancient Philosophy at
Cambridge.

Cory, William
English poet and schoolmaster (1823–92)

2 *At school you are engaged not so much
in acquiring knowledge as in making
mental efforts under criticism.*

Cory, who was born William Johnson, was
an assistant master of some distinction at
Eton College but left under a cloud and
changed his name to Cory. His view of
education continues: 'A certain amount of
knowledge you can indeed with average
faculties acquire so as to retain; nor need
you regret the hours you spent on much that
is forgotten, for the shadow of lost knowledge at least protects you from many illu-
sions. But you go to a great school not so
much for knowledge as for arts and habits;
for the habit of attention, for the art of
expression, for the art of assuming at a
moment's notice a new intellectual position,
for the art of entering quickly into another
person's thoughts, for the habit of submit-
ting to censure and refutation, for the art of
indicating assent or dissent in graduated
terms, for the habit of regarding minute
points of accuracy, for the art of working
out what is possible in a given time, for taste,
for discrimination, for mental courage, and
for mental soberness.' The passage, which
may be from Cory's 'Notes on Education', is

quoted in *The Lyttelton Hart-Davis Letters*,
Vol. 2 (1979).

3 *Jolly boating weather,
And a hay-harvest breeze,
Blade on the feather,
Shade off the trees.
Swing, swing together,
With your bodies between your
  knees.*

Cory wrote the 'Eton Boating Song' in 1863
and it was published two years later in *The
Eton Scrap Book*, a school magazine. The
phrase *Blade on the Feather* was taken as the
title of a TV play (1980) by Dennis Potter,
whose main character was an Old Etonian
author and spy. 'On the feather' is a rowing
term for when the oar's blade is returned
horizontally at the end of a stroke, and out
of the water.

4 *He is one of those who like the palm
without the dust.*

In the 1860s Cory wrote this of one of his
pupils, the future Prime Minister, Lord
Rosebery, then aged fifteen. The comment
was published in Johnson's *Letters and Journals* in 1897 and came to haunt Rosebery.
As Robert Rhodes James notes in *Rosebery*
(1963), it has been seized upon by countless
persons as the key to the aristocratic politician's complex personality. The allusion is
to Horace, the Roman author, who talked
of 'the happy state of getting the victor's
palm without the dust of racing'. Con-
versely, '*Palma non sine pulvere* [no palm
without labour]' is a motto of the Earls of
Liverpool, among others.

Coué, Émile
French psychologist (1857–1926)

5 *Every day and in every way I am getting
better and better* [Tous les jours, à tous
(les) points de vue, je vais de mieux en
mieux].

(Sometimes rendered 'every day in every
way' . . . or 'day by day in every way . . .').
Coué was the originator of a system of
'Self-Mastery Through Conscious Auto-
Suggestion', which had a brief vogue in the
1920s. His patients had to repeat the words
over and over and they became a popular
catchphrase of the time, though physical
improvement did not necessarily follow.
Couéism died with its inventor, though
there have been attempted revivals. John

Lennon alludes to the slogan in his song 'Beautiful Boy' (1980).

Coward, Noël
(later Sir Noël)
English entertainer and writer (1899–1973)

1 *Just know your lines and don't bump into the furniture.*

This advice to actors was attributed to Spencer Tracy by Bartlett (1980) but to Coward in the 1992 edition. Alfred Lunt has also been credited with the line. In *Time* Magazine (16 June 1986), it was reported that President Reagan had offered a few hints on appearing before the cameras to a White House breakfast for Senators: 'Don't bump into the furniture,' he said, 'and in the kissing scenes, keep your mouth closed.' Coward seems to be the originator, but a source is lacking.

2 *Poor Little Rich Girl.*

The title of the Coward song from *Charlot's Revue* (1926) is not original. The phrase had been used as the title of a Mary Pickford film of 1917 (which was re-made in 1936).

3 *Strange how potent cheap music is.*

The archetypal Coward line occurs in his play *Private Lives* (1930). Some texts of the play (as quoted by Bartlett and the *ODQ*, for example) employ 'extraordinary', but 'strange' is what Gertrude Lawrence says on the record she made with Coward of the relevant scene in 1930. The line may be popular for two reasons. Coward's voice can be heard quite clearly in it and there is an in-joke — he, as playwright, is referring to one of his own compositions ('Someday I'll Find You'), which is being played at that moment.

4 *The Stately Homes of England*
How beautiful they stand,
To prove the upper classes
Have still the upper hand.

Although this is one of Coward's best-known songs (from the show *Operette*, 1938), it is based on the ballad 'The Homes of England' (1827) by Mrs Felicia Dorothea Hemans:

> The stately homes of England,
> How beautiful they stand!
> Amidst their tall, ancestral trees,
> O'er all the pleasant land.

5 *It made me feel that Albert had married beneath his station.*

Coward's alleged comment on an inadequate portrayal of Queen Victoria was quoted in *The Wit of Noël Coward* (ed. Dick Richards, 1968). However, James Agate has this in *Ego 6* (for 17 August 1943): 'At a luncheon party to-day I heard two women discussing historical films. One said, "My dear, they have a certain social value. Until I saw Anna Neagle and Anton Walbrook in the film about Queen Victoria [*Sixty Glorious Years*, 1938] I had no idea that the Prince Consort married beneath him!" ' This may be no more than Agate purposely obscuring a source which was known to him, if indeed Coward was the originator. Coward makes no comment on the film in his published diaries.

6 *Chase me, Charlie.*

The title of a song from Coward's *Ace of Clubs* (1950) was not original. It had also been the title of a popular song current in 1900.

7 *Dear boy.*

If the many people who have tried to imitate Coward's clipped delivery over the years are to be believed, the words he uttered most often in his career were 'Dear boy'. His friend Cole Lesley claimed, however, in *The Life of Noël Coward* (1978) that, 'He rarely used this endearment, though I expect it is now too late for me to be believed.' William Fairchild who wrote dialogue for the part of Coward in the film *Star* was informed by the Master, after he had checked the script: 'Too many Dear Boys, dear boy.'

8 *Count your profits and count your sheep*
Life is flying above your heads
Just turn over and try to sleep.
Lie in the dark and let them go
Theirs is a world you'll never know
Lie in the dark and listen.

W.F. Deedes wrote in the *Daily Telegraph* (28 September 1992): 'My advice to General Sir Michael Gray, Colonel Commandant of the Parachute Regiment, if he wants to make them wince at Broadcasting House [about a BBC TV play], is to send them a copy of Noël Coward's verse written during the last war with its cruel jibe at "Soft, hysterical little actors . . ." which caused offence at the time to a certain galerie. But on no account, General, tell them I suggested it.'

Challenged by one of his readers (who had been unable to find it in Coward's lyrics) to give chapter and verse, Deedes said he couldn't. It was eventually traced to Coward's *Collected Verse* (as opposed to his lyrics, that is). 'Lie in the Dark and Listen' is an unusual, critical poem about those remaining at home in wartime (including the actors 'safe in your warm, civilian beds') while bomber crews fly overhead, off on another mission. On being told the news, Deedes gave, 'A thousand thanks. Failure to trace that line was seriously interfering with my sleep. Interesting verses; not quite Coward's style.'

1 *She could eat an apple through a tennis racquet.*

Coward often recycled witticisms from his own conversation in his plays, but this firm example of borrowing from another appears in *Come Into the Garden, Maud* (1966). Earlier, a note in his diary for 10 December 1954 recorded: 'Lunched and dined with Darryl Zannuck who, David Niven wickedly said, is the only man who can eat an apple through a tennis racquet!'

2 *When Eve said to Adam 'Stop calling me madam'*
The world became far more exciting;
And turned to confusion the modern delusion
That sex is a question of lighting.

From Coward's introduction on the album 'Marlene Dietrich at the Café de Paris' (a recording of her London cabaret performance, 1954). Misquoted as 'sex is a question of *liking*' in the *Observer* (24 March 1992).

Cowley, Abraham
English poet and essayist (1618–67)

3 *I never had any other Desire so Strong and so like to Covetousness, as that one which I have had always, that I might be Master at last of a small House and large Garden, with very moderate Conveniences joined to them, and there dedicate the Remainder of my Life to the Culture of them, and study of nature.*

From the introduction to Cowley's poem *The Garden* (1664), dedicated to John Evelyn, the diarist. 'Conveniences' here has the meaning 'material arrangements conducive to ease of action or saving of trouble' rather than the modern one.

Cowper, William
English poet (1731–1800)

4 *The cup that cheers.*

Meaning 'tea' (usually), in preference to alcohol. In 'The Winter Evening' from Cowper's *The Task* (1785), the container is actually in the plural:

Now stir the fire, and close the shutters fast,
Let fall the curtains, wheel the sofa round,
And, while the bubbling and loud-hissing urn
Throws up a steamy column, and the cups,
That cheer but not inebriate, wait on each,
So let us welcome peaceful ev'ning in.

Eric Partridge lists 'cups that cheer but not inebriate' in his *Dictionary of Clichés* (1940), and notes that Bishop Berkeley had earlier said of tar water (in *Siris*, 1744), that it had a nature 'so mild and benign and proportioned to the human constitution, as to warm without heating, to cheer but not inebriate'.

5 *I am monarch of all I survey,*
My right there is none to dispute;
From the centre all round to the sea
I am lord of the fowl and the brute.

The first line is nowadays used as a light-hearted proprietorial boast. The words are from Cowper's 'Verses Supposed to be Written by Alexander Selkirk' (the original of 'Robinson Crusoe), c 1779. Kenneth Tynan, writing about Noël Coward (in *Panorama*, 1952) said: 'He is, if I may test the trope, monocle of all he surveys'.

Craik, Mrs
(Dinah Maria Mulock)
English novelist (1826–87)

6 *Each in his place is fulfilling his day, and passing away, just as that Sun is passing. Only we know not whither he passes; while whither we go we know,*

and the Way we know, the same yesterday, today and for ever.

Words to be found on the marble tablet to Mrs Craik (born Dinah Mulock) in Tewkesbury Abbey. The quotation comes from the final chapter of the most celebrated of her novels, *John Halifax, Gentleman* (1857), which is set in and around Tewkesbury. Shortly before Halifax dies, the narrator tells how new tenants of the old family house are going to turn it into an inn. Halifax says, 'What a shame! I wish I could prevent it. And yet, perhaps not . . . Ought we not rather to recognize and submit to the universal law of change? how each in his place is fulfilling his day, and passing away.'

Cromwell, Oliver
English soldier and parliamentarian
(1599–1658)

1 *Put your trust in God, my boys, and keep your powder dry.*

Thus Cromwell during his Irish campaign in 1649. There is some doubt whether he really said it at all, as it was ascribed to him only about a century after his death by a certain Valentine Blacker in an Orange ballad. The part about keeping one's powder dry is no more than sensible advice from the days when gunpowder had to be kept dry if it was to be used at all. The overall idiomatic injunction means, 'remain calm and prepared for immediate action', 'be prudent, practical, on the alert'.

2 *Warts and all.*

According to Horace Walpole's *Anecdotes of Painting in England*, Vol. 3 (1763), what Cromwell said to the portrait painter, Sir Peter Lely, was: 'I desire you would use all your skill to paint my picture truly like me, and not flatter me at all; but remark all these roughnesses, pimples, *warts, and everything* as you see me; otherwise I will never pay a farthing for it.' It is now thought more likely that Cromwell made the remark to Samuel Cooper, the miniaturist, whom Lely copied.

3 *I beseech you, in the bowels of Christ, think it possible you may be mistaken.*

From his Letter to the General Assembly of the Kirk of Scotland (3 August 1650). However strange it may sound to modern ears, the bowels were once thought to be the seat of tender and sympathetic emotions — kindness, mercy, pity, compassion and feeling. Hence, to refer to Christ's bowels was to heighten the imagery. John Wycliffe wrote in 1382: 'I covet you all in the bowels of Christ . . .' Bowels, in this sense, are often evoked in the Bible, mostly in the Old Testament — again, often with puzzling effect on modern sensibilities: 'My beloved put in his hand by the hole of the door, and my bowels were moved for him' (Song of Solomon 5:4).

Cronkite, Walter
American broadcaster (1916–   )

4 *And that's the way it is.*

Cronkite was the anchor of CBS TV's *Evening News* for nineteen years, for most of which he had used these words as his sign-off line. On the final occasion, before his retirement, he said: 'And that's the way it is, Friday March 6, 1981. Goodnight.'

Crossman, Richard
English Labour politician (1907–74)

5 *Already I realize the tremendous effort it requires not to be taken over by the Civil Service. My Minister's room is like a padded cell, and in certain ways I am like a person who is suddenly certified a lunatic and put safely into this great vast room, cut off from real life . . . Of course, they don't behave quite like nurses because the Civil Service is profoundly deferential — 'Yes, Minister! No, Minister! If you wish it, Minister! Yes, minister.*

Yes Minister was the title of a BBC TV comedy series (1980–5) about the relationship between British government ministers and the Civil Service. It has been said (for example, in *The Listener* (c 1985) that the title came from the above description by Richard Crossman, a minister in Labour governments of the 1960s and 1970s, of his first day in office as a Cabinet Minister, in October 1964 (taken from *The Diaries of a Cabinet Minister*, Vol. 1, 1975). Antony Jay (co-author with Jonathan Lynn) of the TV series said in 1993: 'I think the Crossman attribution is probably fair. We didn't have it consciously in mind when we thought up the title, but the *Diaries* were one of our set texts and I feel that it was an echo of it that was running through our minds when we gave the series that title, though the original idea predated Crossman.'

Crowther, Leslie
English entertainer (1933–   )

1 *Come on down!*

The *ODMQ* (1991) credits Crowther with this catchphrase as host of the ITV game show *The Price is Right* (1984–8). But the phrase was already established when the show was imported from the US. In the American version (from 1956), the host (Bill Cullen was the first) would appear to summon contestants from the studio audience by saying '[name], come on down!'

Crumb, Robert
American cartoonist (1943–   )

2 *Keep on truckin'.*

This expression, meaning that you've got to 'persevere' or 'keep on keeping on', was described in Bartlett (1980) as the 'slogan of a cartoon character' created by Robert Crumb. Crumb drew semi-pornographic cartoons for a number of underground periodicals like *Snatch* in the 1960s and 1970s. He also created Fritz the Cat, later the subject of a full-length cartoon film. There were a number of records produced with the title in this period, and there was certainly a vogue for the phrase. But it was not original to Crumb. There was a song called simply 'Truckin'' in 1935 (words by Ted Koehler and music by Rube Bloom), and the *OED2* finds that 'the truck' or 'trucking' was a jerky dance which emerged from Harlem in the summer of 1934. Partridge/*Catch Phrases* plumps for a suggestion that the phrase, while of Negro dance origin, came out of the great American dance marathons of the 1930s, though one of Partridge's contributors hotly disputes this.

Stuart Berg Flexner discussing 'hoboes, tramps and bums' on the American railroad in *Listening to America* (1982) probably gets nearest to the source. He defines 'trucking it' thus: 'Riding or clinging to the *trucking* hardware between the wheels. This may have contributed to the jitterbug's use of trucking (also meaning to leave or move on in the 1930s) and to the 1960 students' phrase *keep on trucking*, keep moving, keep trying, keep "doing one's (own) thing" with good cheer.'

Curran, John Philpot
Irish judge (1750–1817)

3 *The price of liberty is eternal vigilance.*

Speaking on the right of election of the Lord Mayor of Dublin (10 July 1790), what Curran said precisely was: 'The condition upon which God hath given liberty to man is eternal vigilance; which condition if he break, servitude is at once the consequence of his crime, and the punishment of his guilt.' Not said by Thomas Jefferson, as is popularly supposed.

Curzon, George
(later 1st Marquess Curzon)
English Conservative politician (1859–1925)

4 *This omnibus business is not what it is reported to be. I hailed one at the bottom of Whitehall and told the man to take me to Carlton House Terrace. But the fellow flatly refused.*

On his first trip by bus. This is among the 'Curzonia' included in *The Oxford Book of Political Anecdotes* (1986), though it is not quite clear what the original source was. In fact, it is doubtful whether Curzon, the 'most superior person', *ever* went anywhere by bus. This may be yet another example of an old story being fixed on an obviously suitable subject. As always, the origin of the tale could lie in *Punch*. On 10 April 1901, there was a cartoon by Everard Hopkins with this caption:

> A GIRLISH IGNORANCE
> *Lady Hildegarde, who is studying the habits of the democracy, determines to travel by Omnibus. Lady Hildegarde.*
> 'CONDUCTOR, TELL THE DRIVER TO GO TO NO. 104, BERKELEY SQUARE, AND THEN HOME!'

5 *Ladies never move.*

A correspondent suggested, *en passant*, that it was Lord Curzon who originated the saying, 'She should lie back and enjoy it.' I puzzled over this for a number of years, unsure in what circumstances he might have said it and how it could ever be verified. Then I came across what he really said (and perhaps my correspondent may be forgiven for his confusion). According to *The Oxford Book of Political Anecdotes* (1986), Curzon, when instructing his second wife on the subject of love-making, said, 'Ladies never move'. No precise source is given, however. The book of *New Statesmen* competition winners called *Salome Dear, Not With a Porcupine* (1982 — edited by Arthur Marshall) prefers, 'A lady does not move' (and proceeds to provide the circumstances in which it might first have been said).

Note, however, that a completely different source for the story is given by Rupert Hart-Davis in *The Lyttelton Hart-Davis Letters* (for 19 August 1956). When researching Cora, Lady Strafford, a thrice-married American, he discovered that: 'Before one of her marriages (perhaps the second — to Lord Strafford) she thought it would be a good thing to get a little sex-instruction, so she went over to Paris and took a few lessons from a leading cocotte. On her wedding night she was beginning to turn precept into practice when her bridegroom sternly quelled her by saying: "Cora, *ladies don't move!*"' Alas, he does not give a source for this version either.

Cust, Harry
English poet (1861–1917)

1 *High heart, high speech, high deeds.*

Wording on the tomb of 'Henry Iohn Cokayne Cust' in Belton Church, Leicestershire, which also bears a Greek inscription and the Latin motto *OMNI DITIOR AESTIMATIONE* ('richly endowed beyond all estimation'). Harry Cust was heir to the childless 3rd Earl Brownlow but predeceased him, without leaving any legitimate children of his own. He was an MP, edited the *Pall Mall Gazette* and wrote poetry. The words 'High heart, high speech, high deeds 'mid honouring eyes' occur in his poem '*Non Nobis*', which is in the *Oxford Book of English Verse*.

D

Daily Express

British London-based newspaper, founded 1900

1 *Britain will not be involved in a European war this year, or next year either.*

A front-page headline (30 September 1938). Contrary to popular myth this was the only time the paper predicted as much in a headline though, occasionally, the view that 'There will be no European war' appeared in leading articles. While the statement turned out to be true up to the comma, Lord Beaverbrook, the paper's proprietor, unfortunately insisted on the 'or next year either'. He said: 'We must nail our colours *high* to the mast.' Something like the phrase 'Britain will not be involved in a European war' appeared eight times in the *Express* between September 1938 and August 1939 (A.J.P. Taylor, *Beaverbrook*, 1966).

A copy of the paper bearing the message '*Daily Express* holds canvass of its reporters in Europe. And ten out twelve say NO WAR THIS YEAR' was later shown with ironic effect in Noël Coward's film *In Which We Serve* (1942). It was seen bobbing up and down amid the wreckage of a British destroyer that had been torpedoed by the Germans. As a result, Beaverbrook launched a campaign to try to suppress the film.

Daily Mirror

British London-based newspaper, founded 1903

2 *'The price of petrol has been increased by one penny'* — *Official.*

This was the caption to a cartoon by Philip Zec, published on 6 March 1942. It showed a torpedoed sailor adrift on a raft. The caption was suggested by 'Cassandra' (William Connor). Together they led to the paper almost being suppressed by the Government.

3 *'Here you are — don't lose it again.'*

The caption to a cartoon by Philip Zec, published on 8 May 1945 (Victory in Europe Day). The cartoon showed a wounded soldier bearing the slogan 'Victory and peace in Europe.'

4 *Whose finger on the trigger?*

'WHOSE FINGER?' was the actual front-page headline on 25 October 1951 — general election day — and the culmination of a campaign to ensure that the Labour Government was re-elected and the Conservatives under Winston Churchill not allowed back. Earlier, the paper had asked, 'Whose finger do you want on the trigger when the world situation is so delicate?' The choice was between Churchill and Clement Attlee. Churchill's response (in a speech, 6 October 1951) was: 'I am sure we do not want any fingers upon any trigger. Least of all do we want a fumbling finger . . . But I must tell you that in any case it will not be a British finger that will pull the trigger of a Third World War. It may be a Russian finger or an American finger, or a United Nations Organization finger, but it cannot be a British finger . . . the control and decision and the timing of that terrible event would not rest with us. Our influence in the world is not what it was in bygone days.' As it happens, the *Mirror* was unable to stir the electorate and the Conservatives came back to power under Churchill. The Prime Minister then issued a writ for libel against the newspaper because he took the view that the slogan implied that he was a war-monger. The case was settled out of court.

See also MACMILLAN 230:1.

Daladier, Édouard
French politician (1884–1970)

1 C'est une drôle de guerre [It's a phoney war].

At first, when war was declared in September 1939, nothing happened. Chamberlain talked of a 'Twilight War' and on 22 December Daladier, the French Prime Minister, used this expression (spelt 'phony' in the US). On 19 January 1940, the *News Chronicle* had a headline: 'This is Not a Phoney War: Paris Envoy.' And Paul Reynaud employed the phrase in a radio speech on 3 April 1940: ' "It must be finished", that is the constant theme heard since the beginning. And that means that there will not be any "phoney peace" after a war which is by no means a "phoney war" ' – he used the phrases in English despite speaking French.

Daly, Daniel
American soldier (fl. 1918)

2 *Come on you sons of bitches! Do you want to live for ever?*

According to Flexner (1976), Marine Sergeant Daly is remembered for having shouted this during the Battle of Belleau Wood in June 1918 (during the First World War). Mencken (1942) has it from 'an American sergeant . . . addressing soldiers reluctant to make a charge', in the form: 'What's the matter with you guys? Do you want to live forever?' Otherwise this saying remains untraced.

Whatever the case, Daly was not the first military man to use this form of encouragement. Frederick the Great (1712–86) demanded of hesitating guards at Kolin (18 June 1757), '*Ihr Racker/Hunde, wollt ihr ewig leben?* [Rascals/Dogs, would you live for ever?]' (or '*immer leben?*') Mencken concludes that the cry is 'probably ancient', anyway.

Daniels, Paul
English entertainer (1938–)

3 *You're going to like this . . . not a lot . . . but you'll like it.*

ODMQ (1991) has this as Daniels's catchphrase in his conjuring act 'especially on television from 1981 onwards'. However, in a letter to me (19 March 1979), Daniels stated that he found his catchphrase early

on in his career. He was being heckled by someone who didn't like his act. 'A pity,' he said, 'because I like your suit. Not a lot, but I like it.' The phrase was well established on TV by 1979.

Dante Alighieri
Italian poet (1265–1321)

4 *Abandon hope all ye who enter here!*

This is a popular translation of the words written over the entrance to Hell in Dante's *Divina Commedia* (c 1320). However, 'All hope abandon, ye who enter here!' would be a more accurate translation of the Italian '*lasciate ogni speranza voi ch'entrate!*'

Daugherty, Harry
American Republican supporter (1860–1941)

5 *[A group of senators]) bleary eyed for lack of sleep [will have to] sit down about two o'clock in the morning around a table in a smoke-filled room in some hotel and decide the nomination.*

As quoted by Safire (1978) – actually from the *New York Times* (21 February 1920) – Daugherty's prediction concerning the 'smoke-filled room' refers to the choosing of the Republican Party's Presidential candidate in Chicago the following June, if – as in fact happened – the Convention failed to make up its mind. Daugherty, the eventual winner Warren Harding's chief supporter, denied that had he ever used the phrase 'smoke-filled'. ODMQ (1991) cites a news report dated 12 June from Kirke Simpson of the Associated Press: '[Warren] Harding of Ohio was chosen by a group of men in a smoke-filled room early today as Republican candidate for President.' But this is clearly alluding to an already established phrase.

Suite 408–409–410 (previously rooms 804–5) of the Blackstone Hotel in Chicago became the 'smoke-filled room' that, whoever coined it, gave us a vivid phrase evoking cigar-smoking political bosses coming to a decision after much horse-trading.

Davies, Sir John
English poet (1569–1626)

6 *What mean the mermaids when they dance and sing*
But certain death unto the mariner?

From Stanza 101 of Davies's poem 'Orchestra' (1594). An early reference to the legendary capacity of mermaids to lure mariners to their deaths. They are generally shown singing alone, mirror in hand, combing their hair 'With a comb of pearl/On a throne', as Tennyson later put it. At Zennor in Cornwall 'for several centuries' there has been told the story of a mermaid's singing that so beguiled a church chorister and the squire's son, Matthew Trewhella, that he went off with her and was never seen again. It is said that their voices are still heard on calm nights.

In 'The Love Song of J. Alfred Prufrock' (1917), T.S. Eliot has him say: 'I have heard the mermaids singing, each to each./I do not think that they will sing to me.'

Davis, Bette
American film actress (1908–89)

1 *Yes, I killed him. And I'm glad, I tell you. Glad, glad, glad!*

In the 1940 film version of W. Somerset Maugham's *The Letter*, Davis plays a woman who has killed a man in what seems to have been self-defence. According to Leslie Halliwell in his *Filmgoer's Book of Quotes* (1978), she utters the memorable line — 'Yes, I killed him. And I'm glad, I tell you. Glad, glad, glad!' — but I have never encountered this in any actual showing of the film. Might the line have been used on posters rather than in the film itself? Or could it be that Halliwell imagined hearing it? After all, he notes in his book, 'They even used the line as catch-phrase on the posters'. The line does not appear in Maugham's play. It is, however, in 'I Love a Film Cliché', a list song (1974) by Dick Vosburgh and Peter Lomax from the show *A Day in Hollywood, A Night in the Ukraine* (1980).

Dawson of Penn, Lord
English physician (1864–1945)

2 *The King's life is moving peacefully towards its close.*

On Monday, 20 January 1936, King George V lay dying at Sandringham (not Buckingham Palace, as stated in *ODQ*, 1992). At 9.25 p.m. Lord Dawson of Penn, the King's doctor, issued this bulletin which he had drafted on a menu-card. It was taken up by the BBC. All wireless programmes were cancelled and every quarter of an hour the announcer, Stuart Hibberd, repeated the

medical bulletin until the King died at 11.55 p.m. and the announcement was made at 12.15 a.m. On the 21st, James Agate entered in his diary (*Ego 2*, 1936) that he 'heard afterwards that the Queen drafted this [bulletin]'.

It seems to be a difficult statement to get right. Harold Nicolson, the King's official biographer (1952), has 'to its close' rather than 'towards'. Chips Channon in his diary (entry for 20 January 1936) has: 'The life of the King is moving slowly to its close.' George Lyttelton wrote to James Agate to point out what he perceived to be an error in the passage already quoted from *Ego 2* (1936): 'Page 321. "The King's life is moving peacefully *to* (not 'towards') its close." I could swear to this. Surely the beauty of the sentence would be severely damaged by *ds* coming before "its" ' (*Ego 6*, 1944).

But no. The above version, preceded by the words, 'This is London. The following bulletin was issued at 9.25 . . .' has been checked against the BBC Sound Archives recording. Indeed, in *Ego 7* (for 23 May 1944), Agate authenticated the wording similarly. He told Lyttelton: 'In Noël Coward's film *This Happy Breed*, which I saw tonight, a lower middle-class family listens to the wireless on that January evening. You can distinctly hear Stuart Hibberd say, "The King's life is moving peacefully towards its close." The thing is obviously a record. *Now* what have you to say for yourself?' Lyttelton was reasonably contrite — but persuaded Hibberd to check with his diary just the same. Compare ASQUITH 34:1.

Day-Lewis, Cecil
Anglo-Irish poet and critic (1904–72)

3 *The eye of the wind.*

When Peter Scott, the artist and naturalist, came to write his autobiography (published 1961), he set his heart on calling it *The Eye of the Wind*, but nowhere could he find a poem or passage of suitable prose containing the words. Eventually, in desperation, he asked Cecil Day-Lewis (C. Day Lewis) to write a poem from which he could quote them.

The *OED2* has citations for the exact phrase going back to 1725 and for 'the wind's eye' to 1562. 'In the wind's eye' means 'in the direction of the wind'; 'into the wind's eye' means 'to windward'.

Deakin, Ralph
English journalist (1888–1952)

1 *Nothing is news until it has appeared in the columns of* The Times.

In *I, Claud* (1967) Claud Cockburn described the 'Foreign and Imperial News Editor' of the London *Times*: 'Mr Deakin was believed to be the originator of the statement that nothing was news until it had appeared in the columns of *The Times*, and at that period he gave — from his shining shoes to the beautifully brushed bowler on the rack behind him — an impression of mental and physical discretion and complacency which could have been offensive had it not been, in its childish way, touching.'

The equivalent complacency, not to say pomposity, in the BBC was enshrined in the remark, 'The BBC does not have scoops' — thought to have been the philosophy of Tahu Hole (1908–85), an austere New Zealander who was Editor of BBC News from 1948 to 1958.

Decatur, Stephen
American naval officer (1779–1820)

2 *My country, right or wrong!*

Correctly, Decatur's toast at a public dinner in Norfolk, Virginia, in April 1816 was: 'Our country! in her intercourse with foreign nations, may she always be in the right; but our country, right or wrong!' This is sometimes referred to as 'Decatur's Toast'.

Compare: '"My country right or wrong" is a thing that no patriot would think of saying, except in a desperate case. It is like saying, "My mother, drunk or sober"' — so wrote G.K. Chesterton in *The Defendant* (1901).

De Coubertin, Baron Pierre
French founder of the modern Olympics Games (1863–1937)

3 *The most important thing in the Olympic Games is not winning but taking part, just as the most important thing in life is not the triumph but the struggle. The essential thing in life is not conquering but fighting well.*

Speaking on the 24 July 1908 at a banquet for officials of the Olympic Games which were being held that year in London, de Coubertin spoke in French: '*L'imporant*

dans cest olympiades, c'est moins d'y gagner que d'y prendre part . . . L'important dans la vie ce n'est point le triomphe mais le combat.' A few days previously, his view had been anticipated by the Bishop of Pennsylvania preaching in St Paul's Cathedral. He said: 'The important thing is not so much to have been victorious as to have taken part.'

De Coubertin repeated his words on many occasions and they later appeared on the electronic scoreboards during the opening ceremony of the Olympics (even if they were ignored by many of the participants). Thus was born a modern proverb. Compare RICE 280:5.

De Gaulle, Charles
French general and President (1890–1970)

4 *France has lost a battle, but France has not lost the war!* [La France a perdu une bataille! Mais la France n'a pas perdu la guerre!]

This memorable line appeared in a proclamation dated 18 June 1940 and circulated later in the month, but it was not spoken in de Gaulle's famous broadcast appeal of that date, from London, to Frenchmen betrayed by Pétain's armistice with the Germans. Earlier, on 19 May 1940, Winston Churchill, in his first broadcast to the British people as Prime Minister, had said: 'Our task is not only to win the battle — but to win the war' (meaning the battle *for* Britain).

5 *Now she is like the others* [Maintenant, elle est comme les autres].

Jean Lacouture in his biography (1965) of de Gaulle recorded the remark the future French President made at the graveside of his mentally handicapped daughter, Anne, who died shortly before her twentieth birthday in 1948. Yvonne de Gaulle had written to a friend when Anne was born: 'Charles and I would give everything, everything, health, fortune, promotion, career, if only Anne were a little girl like the others.' Hence, the particular nature of the later, poignant remark.

6 *How can you govern a country which produces 246 different kinds of cheese?*

There are many versions of de Gaulle's aphorisms. This is probably an accurate summing up of his view of the French people, although the number of cheeses varies.

246 is Ernest Mignon's version in *Les Mots du Général* (1962). The *ODQ* (1979) has 265 — the circumstance given for this version is the 1951 election when de Gaulle's political party, though the largest, still did not have an overall majority.

Compare the older view of De la Reyniere (*d* 1838): '*On connoit en France 685 manières differentes d'accommoder les oeufs* [in France, there are 685 different ways of using eggs]'.

1 Je vous ai compris . . . Vive l'Algérie française! *[I have understood you . . . Long live French Algeria!]*

De Gaulle became President in 1958 amid the turmoil created by resistance from French colonialists to the idea of Algerian independence. He eventually led his country in quite the opposite direction to the one expected of him, but from the beginning he spoke with a forked tongue. On 4 June he flew to Algiers and told a rally 'I have understood you' — which could have meant anything — at the same time as '*Vive l'Algérie française!*' — which could have been taken to imply that he supported the continuation of colonial rule.

2 *I can see her in about ten years from now on the yacht of a Greek petrol millionaire.*

An attributed remark about Jackie Kennedy after de Gaulle had attended President Kennedy's funeral. In *Fallen Oaks* (1972), André Malraux recalls de Gaulle having said, rather, 'She is a star, and will end up on the yacht of some oil baron'. In 1968 she married Aristotle Onassis, the Greek shipping tycoon. When later reminded of his prediction, de Gaulle told Malraux: 'Did I say that? Well, well . . . Fundamentally I would rather have believed that she would marry Sartre. Or you!'

3 *Reform, yes, bed-shitting, no* [La réforme, oui; la chienlit, non.]

In private de Gaulle had a colourful way of describing his political opponents — for example, he would call them *pisse-vinaigres* ('vinegar pissers') and 'eunuchs of the Fourth Republic' or '*politichiens*'. Returning from a visit to Romania at the time of the May 1968 student uprising in France, he asked the Minister of Education: 'What about your students — still the *chienlit?*' Quite what this meant was much debated at the time.

The polite dictionary definition is 'carnival masquerade' or 'ridiculous disguise' but if spelt 'chie-en-lit' it can mean 'bed-shitting' which seems more appropriate in the context. A day or two later, on 19 May, de Gaulle used the expression again at a Cabinet meeting while giving his view of the students' demands, as above. It was his Prime Minister, Georges Pompidou, who passed this remark on to the press. One of the many banners appearing in the streets at the time responded with a cartoon of the President and the charge '*La chienlit c'est lui!*' This was outside the Renault factory at Billancourt where workers were staging a sit-in.

4 *Where there is mystery, there is power.*

Or 'Where there is no mystery there is no power.' This unverified statement was made by de Gaulle to André Malraux in the context of a discussion about the importance of a politicians not exposing themselves too frequently on television.

Compare what Walter Bagehot said in 1867 about royalty: 'Above all this our royalty is to be reverenced, and if you begin to poke about it you cannot reverence it. When there is a Select Committee on the Queen, the charm of royalty will be gone. In its mystery is its life. We must not let daylight in upon magic.'

5 *Old age is a shipwreck* [La vieillesse est un naufrage].

De Gaulle was referring particularly to Pétain when he made this observation in *Les Mémoires de Guerre* (1954). Compare other attributed sayings: J.M. Synge: 'Old age is a poor, untidy thing'; and Winston Churchill's reference to 'the surly advance of decrepitude'.

Delane, John Thaddeus
English newspaper editor (1817–79)

6 *The first duty of the Press is to obtain the earliest and most correct intelligence of the events of the time, and instantly, by disclosing them to make them the common property of the nation.*

From *The Times* of 6 February 1852. Attributed to Delane (the paper's influential editor for thirty-six years) but in fact written by Robert Lowe and Henry Reeve. The correction was given by Harold Evans in a lecture on 4 March 1974.

Delderfield, R.F.
English novelist (1912–72)

1 *God is an Englishman.*

The title of Delderfield's novel (published in 1970) might derive from a saying attributed (but untraced) to George Bernard Shaw: 'The ordinary Britisher imagines that God is an Englishman.' But, however expressed, the arrogant assumption is almost traditional. Harold Nicolson recorded in his diary for 3 June 1942 that three years before, R.S. Hudson, the Minister of Agriculture, was being told by the Yugoslav minister in London of the dangers facing Britain. 'Yes,' replied Hudson, 'you are probably correct and these things may well happen. But you forget that God is English.'

James Morris in *Farewell the Trumpets* has a Dublin balladeer at the time of the 1916 Easter Rising singing: 'God is not an Englishman and truth will tell in time.' In a June 1977 edition of BBC Radio *Quote . . . Unquote*, Anna Ford (a clergyman's daughter) mentioned the (apocryphal?) priest who prayed: 'Dear God, as you will undoubtedly have read in the leader column of *The Times* this morning . . .' R.A. Austen-Leigh's *Eton Guide* (1964) points out that on the south wall of Lower Chapel an inscription begins, 'You who in the chapel worship God, an Etonian like yourselves . . .'. Somerset Maugham once quoted Augustus Hare (*d* 1834) on why he omitted all passages glorifying God when he read aloud to his household from the Prayer Book. Hare's reply was, 'God is a gentleman and no gentleman cares to be praised to his face.'

In July 1987, on *Quote . . . Unquote*, the actor Brian Glover drew attention to the adage: 'God was a Yorkshireman.'

By way of contrast, there is apparently a Greek saying — presumably of reassurance — which states: 'Never mind, God isn't an Albanian.'

2 *To Serve Them All My Days.*

The title of Delderfield's 1972 novel sounds as if it *ought* to be a quotation, but contains no more than echoes of several religious lines: 'And to serve him truly all the days of my life' from the Catechism in the Book of Common Prayer; 'To serve thee all my happy days', from the hymn 'Gentle Jesus, meek and mild' in the Methodist Hymnal; the Devon carol, 'We'll bring him hearts that love him / To serve him all our days'; and, the Sunday school hymn: 'I must like a

Christian / Shun all evil ways, / Keep the faith of Jesus, / And serve him all my days.'

Dempsey, Jack
American heavyweight boxer (1895–1983)

3 *Honey, I just forgot to duck.*

Dempsey said this to his wife, on losing his World Heavyweight title to Gene Tunney during a fight in Philadelphia on 23 September 1926. In his *Autobiography* (1977), he recalled: 'Once I got to the hotel, Estelle [his wife] managed to reach me by telephone, saying she'd be with me by morning and that she'd heard the news. I could hardly hear her because of the people crowding the phone. "What happened, Ginsberg? (That was her pet name for me.) "Honey, I just forgot to duck."' The line was recalled by ex-sports commentator Ronald Reagan when explaining to *his* wife what had happened during an assassination attempt in 1981.

Dent, Alan
British critic (1905–78)

4 *This is the tragedy of a man who could not make up his mind.*

From the introduction to Dent's adaptation of Shakespeare's *Hamlet* for filming in 1948. Laurence Olivier spoke the words but did not write them, as is suggested by the *ODQ* (1992). Dent's capsule comment was criticized on the grounds that *Hamlet* is not so much about a man who could not make up his mind as about one who could not bring himself to take necessary action.

Desani, G.V.
Indian-born novelist (1909–   )

5 *Geography is everywhere.*

In the days when humorous graffiti were all the rage, I was sent a photograph of a curious daub on a brick wall in the middle of a field in Bedworth, Warwickshire. It proclaimed: 'GEOGRAPHY IS EVERYWHERE — G.V. DESANI.' The identity of the given author of this profound thought puzzled me, but latterly I have learned that Desani actually exists. His novel *All About H. Hatterr* was published to acclaim in 1948. Until his retirement he was a visiting professor at the University of Austin, Texas. The last line of *Hatterr* is the (seemingly very

Indian), 'Carry on, boys, and continue like hell!'

Diaghilev, Serge
Russian ballet impresario (1872–1929)

1 *Etonne-moi! [Astonish me!].*

He said this to Jean Cocteau, the French writer and designer, in Paris in 1912. Cocteau had complained to Diaghilev that he was not getting enough encouragement and the Russian exhorted him with the words, 'Astound me! I'll wait for you to astound me.'

In Cocteau's *Journals* (published 1956), he comments: 'I was at the absurd age when one thinks oneself a poet, and I sensed in Diaghilev a polite resistance.' When Cocteau received the command he felt it was one he could, and should, obey. In due course, he may be said to have done so.

Dickens, Charles
English novelist (1812–70)

Barnaby Rudge (1841)

2 *He was not only a spectre at their licentious feasts; a something in the midst of their revelry and riot that chilled and haunted them; but out of doors he was the same.*

This sentence from Chapter 16 is the earliest citation found to date of the expression 'spectre at the feast'. Meaning 'some ghost from the past that comes to unsettle some person or persons in the present', this phrase has been curiously neglected by reference works. Is the allusion simply to Banquo's ghost in Shakespeare's *Macbeth* (III.iv), or does it take in the Commendatore in Mozart's *Don Giovanni* and the writing on the wall at Belshazzar's Feast in the Book of Daniel (see THE BIBLE 55:1)?

A modern example from the *Independent* (3 June 1993): ' "There was just one nomination for spectre at the feast," said one of the contributors to . . . BBC1's chocolate box recollection of Coronation Day. He had the Duke of Windsor in mind (who didn't turn up in the end, to everyone's relief), but the casual remark brought home to you the fact that a fateful presence did make it into the abbey that day.'

But why '*spectre* at the feast' rather than 'ghost' or 'apparition' — because it is more euphonious?

The Cricket on the Hearth (1846)

3 *The Cricket on the Hearth.*

As for the title of the Christmas book for 1846, the cricket, so described, influences the main character to overcome a misunderstanding. Dickens probably took the idea from a ballad in what is known to be one of his favourite works — Goldsmith's *The Vicar of Wakefield* (1766):

The cricket chirrups on the hearth,
The crackling faggot flies.

Earlier, in Milton's 'Il Penseroso' (1632), there had been:

Far from all resort of mirth,
Save the cricket on the hearth.

David Copperfield (1850)

4 *Accidents will happen in the best-regulated families.*

This proverbial expression is best remembered in the form delivered by Mr Micawber in Chapter 28: ' "Copperfield," said Mr. Micawber, "accidents will occur in the best-regulated families; and in families not regulated by . . . the influence of Woman, in the lofty character of Wife, they must be expected with confidence, and must be borne with philosophy".' However, the saying is not original to Dickens. Sir Walter Scott wrote in Chapter 49 of *Peveril of the Peak* (1823): 'Nay, my lady, . . . such things will befall in the best regulated families.'

The *CODP* finds 'P. Atall' writing in *Hermit in America* (1819), 'Accidents will happen in the best regulated families' and, even earlier, George Colman in *Deuce is in Him* (1763) has the more basic, 'Accidents will happen'.

Dombey and Son (1846–8)

5 *Said Mr Morfin, 'I have whistled, hummed tunes, gone accurately through the whole of Beethoven's Sonata in B, to let him know that I was within hearing, but he never heeded me.'*

From Chapter 53. Unfortunately, there is no Sonata in B by Beethoven — though there is a Piano Sonata in B flat major.

6 *What are the wild waves saying?*

Nowhere in the novel does Dickens use these precise words, though the book is fairly awash with the idea of a 'dark and unknown sea that rolls round all the world' (Chapter 1, end). At the end of Chapter 8, in Brighton, young Paul Dombey says to his sister, Florence, 'I want to know what it says . . . The sea, Floy, what is it that it keeps on saying?' Then, a line or two later: 'Very often afterwards, in the midst of their talk, he would break off, to try to understand what it was that the waves were always saying; and would rise up in his couch to look towards that invisible region, far away.' The title of Chapter 16 is 'What the Waves were always saying'.

What we have here is the title line of a Victorian song with words by J.E. Carpenter (1813–85) and music by Stephen Glover (1813–70):

> What are the wild waves saying,
>   Sister, the whole day long:
> That ever amid our playing,
>   I hear but their low, lone song?
> Not by the seaside only,
>   There it sounds wild and free;
> But at night when 'tis dark and
>   lonely,
>   In dreams it is still with me.

The song is a duet between the characters Paul and Florence Dombey and based on an incident in the novel *Dombey and Son*.

Compare this: an advertisement for Igranic wireless coils, dating from the early 1920s, which plays upon the idea of radio waves and asks, 'What are the wild waves saying?'

Great Expectations (1860–1)

1 *I had cherished a profound conviction that her bringing me up by hand gave her no right to bring me up by jerks.*

In Chapter 8 there occurs a passage of delight to grubby schoolboys. It is included in Edward Gathorne-Hardy, *A New Garden of Bloomers* (1967).

2 *What larks, Pip!*

In *The Kenneth Williams Diaries* (1993) (entry for 30 August 1970), the actor writes: 'Tom played the piano and all the girls danced with us & I stuck me bum out and oh! what larks Pip!' Ned Sherrin dedicates his *Theatrical Anecdotes* (1991), 'For Judi [Dench] and Michael [Williams]: "What larks!"' Both these refer to the characteristic phrase of Joe Gargery, the blacksmith, who

looks after his brother-in-law and apprentice, Pip, in the boy's youth. Chapter 13 has him saying 'calc'lated to lead to larks' and Chapter 57, 'And when you're well enough to go out for a ride — what larks!' The recent use of the phrase probably has more to do with the 1946 film of the book in which Bernard Miles played Joe. As he sees Pip off on a stage coach, he says, 'One day I'll come to see you in London and then, what larks, eh?' and similarly, after Pip's breakdown, 'You'll soon be well enough to go out again, and then — what larks!' Even here, the name Pip is not actually included in the phrase.

Martin Chuzzlewit (1843–4)

3 *When she sang, he sat like one entranced. She touched his organ, and from that bright epoch, even it, the old companion of his happiest hours, incapable as he had thought of elevation, began a new and deified existence.*

A passage that one feels Dickens might have felt the need to improve, if he were writing today. It occurs in Chapter 24 and is included in Edward Gathorne-Hardy, *An Adult's Garden of Bloomers* (1966).

Nicholas Nickleby (1838–9)

4 *The Infant Phenomenon.*

This was the stage billing of Ninetta Crummles (who has been ten years old for at least five years). The term also appears earlier in *Pickwick Papers*, Chap. 26 (1836–7) when Sam Weller says to Master Bardwell: 'Tell her I want to speak to her, will you, my hinfant fernomenon?' This suggests that the phrase was in general use before this novel came to be written or was something Dickens had picked up from an actual case. In 1837 the eight-year-old Jean Davenport was merely billed as 'the most celebrated juvenile actress of the day'. George Parker Bidder (*b* 1806), who possessed extraordinary arithmetical abilities, had been exhibited round the country as a child, billed as 'the calculating phenomenon'.

5 *All gas and gaiters.*

The title of a BBC TV comedy series about the clergy (1966–70), was taken from Chapter 49: 'All is gas and gaiters' — gaiters (leg coverings below the knee) being traditionally associated with bishops.

The Old Curiosity Shop (1840–1)

1 Does Little Nell die?

A query not from the book but *about* its most famous character, Nell Trent, the child heroine. She attempts to look after her inadequate grandfather and to protect him from various threats, but her strength gives out. According to one account, 'Does Little Nell die?' was the cry of 6,000 book-loving Americans who hurried to the docks in New York to ask this question of sailors arriving from England. Another version is that it was longshoremen demanding 'How is Little Nell?' or 'Is Little Nell dead?' As the novel was serialized, they were waiting for the arrival of the final instalment of the magazine to find out what had happened to the heroine. Little Nell's death came to typify the heights of Victorian sentimental fiction. Oscar Wilde later commented: 'One must have a heart of stone to read the death of Little Nell without laughing.'

Oliver Twist (1837)

2 The law is an ass.

Pedantic it may be, but strictly speaking, if one is quoting Dickens, what Mr Bumble says in Chapter 51, is: 'If the law supposes that . . . the law is a ass — a idiot.' He is dismayed that the law holds him responsible for his wife's actions.

Our Mutual Friend (1864–5)

3 Our Mutual Friend.

The title refers to the novel's hero, John Harmon, who feigns death and whose identity is one of the mysteries of the plot. This is a rare example of Dickens using an established phrase for a title (he usually chooses the invented name of a character). 'Our mutual friend' was an expression established by the seventeenth century, but Dickens undoubtedly further encouraged its use. Some have objected that 'mutual friend' is a solecism, arguing that it is impossible for the reciprocity of friendship to be shared with a third party. Even before Dickens took it for a title, a correspondent was writing to the journal *Notes and Queries* in 1849 and asking: 'Is it too late to make an effective stand against the solecistic expression "mutual friend"?' The *Oxford Dictionary for Writers and Editors* (1981) points out that it is an expression used also by Edmund Burke, George Eliot and others, but 'the alternative "common" can be ambiguous'.

4 A fair day's wages for a fair day's work is ever my partner's motto.

T. Attwood in a speech in the House of Commons (14 June 1839) said: 'They only ask for a fair day's wages for a fair day's work', which is probably the first time the slogan was uttered. This is no more than picked up by Charles Dickens in *Our Mutual Friend* (Bk. I, Chap. 13). In any case, Benjamin Disraeli had used the slogan earlier in his novel *Sybil* (1845).

A Tale of Two Cities (1859)

5 It is a far, far better thing that I do than I have ever done; it is a far, far better rest that I go to, than I have ever known.

These words, appearing at the end of *A Tale of Two Cities*, are sometimes said to be Sydney Carton's last words as he ascends the scaffold to be guillotined. But he does not actually speak them. They are prefaced with: 'If he had given any utterance to his [last thoughts], and they were prophetic, they would have been these . . .' One editor refers to this as, 'A complicated excursus into the pluperfect subjunctive.' In dramatizations, however, Carton has actually *said* the lines — as did Sir John Martin-Harvey in the play, *The Only Way* (1898) by F. Wills.

Disney, Walt
American cartoon film-maker (1901–66)

6 All the world owes me a living.

This expression is used as the epigraph of Graham Greene's novel *England Made Me* (1935), viz.:

'All the world owes me a living.'
Walt Disney
(*The Grasshopper and the Ants*)

Did Disney really claim credit for the phrase? The cartoon in question — one of the first 'Silly Symphonies' — was released in 1934. It is based on the Aesop fable 'Of the ant and the grasshopper' (as it is called in Caxton's first English translation, 1484), which tells of a grasshopper asking an ant for corn to eat in winter. The ant asks, 'What have you done all the summer past?' and the grasshopper can only answer, 'I have sung'. The moral is that you should provide yourself in the summer with what you need in winter. Disney turns the grasshopper into a fiddler and gives him a song to sing (written by Larry Morey to music by Leigh Harline):

Oh! the world owes me a living
Deedle, diedle, doedle, diedledum.
Oh! the world owes me a living
Deedle, diedle, doedle, diedleum, etc.

This develops in time to:

Oh, the world owes us a living . . .
You should soil your Sunday pants
Like those other foolish ants,
So let's play and sing and dances . . .

And then, when the error of his ways has been pointed out to him, the grasshopper sings:

I owe the world a living . . .
I've been a fool the whole year
   long.
Now I'm singing a different song,
You were right and I was wrong.

This song became quite well known and presumably helped John Llewellyn Rhys choose *The World Owes Me a Living* for his 1939 novel about a redundant RFC hero who tries to make a living with a flying circus (filmed 1944). It is a little odd rendered in this form, because on the whole it is not something a person would say about himself. More usually, another would say, pejoratively, 'The trouble with you is, you think the world owes you a living.' The phrase was used before Disney. In W.G. Sumner's *Earth Hunger* (1896), he had written: 'The men who start out with the notion that the world owes them a living generally find that the world pays its debt in the penitentiary or the poorhouse.' Sumner was an American economist but the phrase may not have originated in the US.

1 *I come from a land, from a faraway place where the caravan camels roam.*
Where they cut off your ear if they don't like your face. It's barbaric, but — hey it's home.

From the opening song 'Arabian Nights' in the Walt Disney cartoon film of *Aladdin* (1993) — produced long after Disney's death, of course. When the film opened in Britain, in order not to offend Arab sensibilities, the lyrics had become: 'Where it's flat and immense and the heat is intense/It's barbaric but hey it's home.' The original lyric was written by Howard Ashman (music by Alan Menken), the amendment by Peter Schneider.

Disraeli, Benjamin
(1st Earl of Beaconsfield)
British Conservative Prime Minister
(1804–81)

2 *I will sit down now, but the time will come when you will hear me.*

When Disraeli gave his maiden speech in the House of Commons (7 December 1837), he wanted to take the House by storm. His subject was the validity of certain Irish elections, but he was greeted with hisses, catcalls and hoots of laughter. The above was his concluding sentence.

3 *The Church of England is the Tory Party at prayer.*

This description of the Church of England is often attributed to Disraeli. However, Robert Blake, the historian and author of *Disraeli* (1966) told the *Observer* (14 April 1985) that he could not say who had said it first and that a correspondence in *The Times* some years before had failed to find an answer. According to Robert Stewart's *Penguin Dictionary of Political Quotations* (1984), Agnes Maude Royden, the social reformer and preacher, said in an address at the City Temple, London (1917): 'The Church should no longer be satisfied to represent only the Conservative Party at prayer' — but this sounds rather as though it is alluding to an already established saying.

4 *A dark horse.*

Figuratively, the phrase refers to a runner about whom everyone is 'in the dark' until he comes from nowhere and wins the race — of whatever kind. Possibly the phrase originated in Disraeli's novel *The Young Duke: A Moral Tale Though Gay* (1831) in which 'a dark horse, which had never been thought of . . . rushed past the grandstand in sweeping triumph'. It is used especially in political contexts.

5 *Never complain, never explain.*

Stanley Baldwin said to Harold Nicolson (21 July 1943): 'You will find in politics that you are much exposed to the attribution of false motive. Never complain and never explain.' Earlier, Admiral Lord Fisher had written in a letter to *The Times* (5 September

1919): 'Never contradict. Never explain. Never apologize. (Those are the secrets of a happy life!)'. According to an article in the *Oxford Chronicle* (7 October 1893), a favourite piece of advice given to young men by Benjamin Jowett, who became Master of Balliol College, Oxford, in 1870, was, 'Never regret, never explain, never apologize.' Each must, however, have been referring back to, or at least echoing, Disraeli who was quoted as having said 'Never complain and never explain' (specifically about attacks in Parliament) in John Morley's *Life of Gladstone* (1903).

1 *Jews are only the Arabs on horseback.*

A correspondent asked whether this was any more than the 'Anonymous saying' that the *PDMQ* (1980) said it was? Yes, it is. 'The Arabs are only Jews upon horseback' is from Disraeli's novel *Tancred*, Bk iv, Chap. iii (1847).

2 *You have it, madam.*

In a letter to Queen Victoria (24 November 1875), Disraeli announced something of a coup: he had successfully bought Britain shares in the Suez Canal Company.

3 *There are lies, damn lies — and statistics.*

Although often attributed to Mark Twain — because it appears in his *Autobiography* (1924) — this should more properly be ascribed to Disraeli, as indeed Twain took trouble to do. On the other hand, the remark remains untraced among Disraeli's writings and sayings.

4 *Many thanks; I shall lose no time in reading it.*

Acknowledgement to an author who had sent him an unsolicited manuscript. Quoted by Wilfrid Meynell in *The Man Disraeli* (1927).

5 *Sir, you are intoxicated by the exuberance of your own verbosity.*

In *Scouse Mouse* (1984), George Melly describes how this was ascribed to Dr Johnson by a headmaster called W.W. Twyne. A common mistake. Disraeli said it of Gladstone in *The Times* (29 July 1878)

in the form: 'A sophistical rhetorician, inebriated with the exuberance of his own verbosity.'

6 *When a man fell into his anecdotage it was a sign for him to retire from the world.*

From Disraeli's novel *Lothair* (1870). Earlier, however, his father, Isaac Disraeli, had noted in his *Curiosities of Literature* (1839): 'Among my earliest literary friends, two distinguished themselves by their anecdotical literature: James Petit Andrews, by his "Anecdotes, Ancient and Modern", and William Seward, by his "Anecdotes of Distinguished Persons". These volumes were favourably received, and to such a degree, that a wit of that day, and who is still a wit as well as poet, considered that we were far gone in our "Anecdotage".' (The word 'anecdotage' in a less critical sense had been used by De Quincey in 1823 simply to describe anecdotes collectively.)

7 *She would only ask me to take a message to Albert.*

These are not Disraeli's last words. During his final illness, it was suggested that he might like to receive a visit from Queen Victoria. 'No, it is better not,' he replied, 'She would only ask me to take a message to Albert.' This is a perfectly genuine quotation and is confirmed by Robert Blake in his life, *Disraeli* (1966). The last authenticated words Disraeli uttered were: 'I had rather live but I am not afraid to die.'

Donne, John
English poet and divine (1572–1631)

8 *Go, and catch a falling star*
Get with child a mandrake root,
Tell me, where all past years are.
Or who cleft the Devil's foot.

Since at least 1563 a 'falling star' has been another name for a meteor or shooting star. John Donne's 'Song' has a somewhat different message. Here it is clearly just one of four impossible tasks. Compare 'Hitch your wagon to a star' — R.W. Emerson, *Society and Solitude* (1870).

'Catch a falling star' was also the title of a 1958 song, popularized by Perry Como:

Catch a falling star
And put it in your pocket,
Never let it fade away.

1 *For whom the bell tolls.*

The title of the novel (1940; film US, 1943) by Ernest Hemingway, set in the Spanish Civil War, originates in John Donne's *Meditation XVII*, which begins: 'No man is an Island, entire of it self . . . And therefore never send to know for whom the bell tolls; It tolls for thee.' Hemingway's approach to the matter of choosing the title is described in a letter to Maxwell Perkins (21 April 1940; included in *Ernest Hemingway Selected Letters 1917–1961*, ed. Carlos Baker, 1981): 'I think it has the magic that a title has to have. Maybe it isn't too easy to say. But maybe the book will make it easy. Anyway I have had thirty some titles and they were all possible but this is the first one that has made the bell toll for me. Or do you suppose that people think only of tolls as long distance charges and of Bell as the Bell of the telephone system? If so it is out. The Tolling of the Bell. No. That's not right.'

2 *His death diminishes us all.*

A possible source for this modern funerary cliché is Donne's *Devotions*, XVII (1624): 'Any man's death diminishes me, because I am involved in Mankind: and therefore never send to know for whom the bell tolls; It tolls for thee.'
   'Sir William's death diminishes us all' was how André Previn commented on the death of William Walton in March 1983. 'One must not be too hard on Mr Previn,' commented the *Guardian*. 'Music is his chosen medium, not words.'

Dowson, Ernest
English poet (1867–1900)

3 *Days of Wine and Roses.*

This was the title of a film (US, 1962) about an alcoholic (though the phrase is often used to evoke romance). It is taken from Dowson's poem '*Vitae Summa Brevis*' (1896): 'They are not long, the days of wine and roses.'

4 *Always True To You In My Fashion.*

The song by Cole Porter from *Kiss Me Kate* (1948) echoes, consciously or unconsciously, the line 'I have been faithful to thee, Cynara! in my fashion' from Dowson's '*Non Sum Qualis Eram*' (1896).

5 *Non Sum Qualis Eram [I am not what I was].*

The title of a poem (1896), also known as 'Cynara', by Dowson, from which come the titles 'Always True to You in My Fashion', *Days of Wine and Roses* and *Gone With the Wind*. 'Cynara' is a woman to whom the poet professes faithfulness even when consorting with others.

Doyle, Sir Arthur Conan
Scottish-born writer (1859–1930)

6 *Elementary my dear Watson!*

The Sherlock Holmes phrase appears nowhere in Conan Doyle's writings, though the great detective does exclaim 'Elementary' to Dr Watson in 'The Crooked Man' in *The Memoirs of Sherlock Holmes* (1894). Conan Doyle brought out his last Holmes book in 1927. His son Adrian (in collaboration with John Dickson Carr) was one of those who used the phrase in follow-up stories — as have adapters of the stories in film and broadcast versions. In the 1929 film *The Return of Sherlock Holmes* — the first with sound — the final lines of dialogue are:

Watson: Amazing, Holmes!
Holmes: Elementary, my dear Watson, elementary.

Drake, Sir Francis
English sailor and explorer (*c* 1540–96)

7 *There must be a beginning of any great matter, but the continuing unto the end until it be thoroughly finished yields the true glory.*

The title of a documentary film *The True Glory* (UK/US, 1945) about the end of the Second World War was taken from the dispatch from Sir Francis Drake to Sir Francis Walsingham before the Battle of Cadiz (1587). In a speech on 15 August 1945 about the surrender of Japan, Winston Churchill said: 'This is the true glory, and long will it gleam upon our forward path.' It was also a favourite phrase of Margaret Thatcher. She paraphrased it in a speech (21 May 1980) and alluded to the rest of Drake's dispatch in an address to the 1922 Committee of backbench MPs (19 July 1984): 'After reminding them of their success in the recent Euro-elections, and pointing out that few people during last year's general election could have foreseen a 19-week pit strike, she declared that it was not the beginning of the struggle that mattered. It was the continuation of the fight until it was truly concluded' (report, *Guardian*, 20 July).

1 *The singeing of the King of Spain's beard.*

Drake's own phrase for his impish attack on the Spanish fleet and stores at Cadiz in 1587, which delayed the sailing of the Armada until the following year. Reported in Francis Bacon, *Considerations touching a War with Spain* (1629).

2 *There is plenty of time to win this game, and to thrash the Spaniards too.*

An example of world-class insouciance. Possibly apocryphal, but this is what everyone would like to believe was said by Drake as he played bowls on Plymouth Hoe when the Armada was sighted. So attributed in *DNB* (1917). His game of bowls was first mentioned in a prefix to the 1736 edition of Sir Walter's *History of the World*. The saying, sometimes rendered as 'There is time to finish the game and beat the Spaniards afterwards', is 'the work of a later embroiderer', according to another source.

Drury, Allen
American novelist (1918–)

3 *Advise and Consent.*

The title of Allen Drury's novel (1959; film US, 1962) about Washington politics is taken from Senate Rule 38: 'The final question on every nomination shall be, "Will the Senate advise and consent to this nomination?" ' In the US Constitution (Art. II, Sect. 2), dealing with the Senate's powers as a check on the President's appointive and treaty-making powers, the phrase is rather 'Advice and consent'. Originally, George Washington as President went in person to the Senate Chamber (22 August 1789) to receive 'advice and consent' about treaty provisions with the Creek Indians. Vice-President Adams used the words, 'Do you advise and consent?' Subsequent administrations have sent written requests.

Dryden, John
English poet and playwright (1631–1700)

4 *Everything by starts and nothing long.*

See CALLAGHAN 83:4.

Dubček, Alexander
Czechoslovak politician (1921–92)

5 *Give socialism back its human face.*

Slogan used frequently in 1968 – sometimes 'Socialism [or Communism] with a human face' – when a brief flowering of independence in Czechoslovakia gave rise to the 'Prague Spring'. The phrase was first suggested to Dubček, Communist Party First Secretary, by Radovan Richta in a private conversation (according to Robert Stewart, *Penguin Dictionary of Political Quotations*, 1984). A party group in the Ministry of Foreign Affairs referred to Czech foreign policy acquiring 'its own defined face' (Rudé právo, 14 March 1968). The slogan was later applied to domestic affairs.

The experiment was quashed when the Soviet Union invaded the country in August 1968. Dubček was later removed from power.

Du Bellay, Joachim
French poet (1522–60)

6 Heureux qui comme Ulysse a fait un beau voyage *[Happy he who, like Ulysses, has made a great journey].*

From *Les Regrets*, Sonnet 31 (1558). Used as an inscription on the headstone of the grave of Sir Henry Channon (1897–1958), the American-born socialite and Conservative MP, who achieved posthumous fame through the publication of his diaries. He is buried at Kelvedon in Essex. Robert Rhodes James, editor of *Chips: The Diaries of Sir Henry Channon* (1967), refers to 'the words [from a sonnet] of Du Bellay which had been his special favourite'. The translation continues: 'Or like that man [Jason] who won the Fleece and then came home, full of experience and good sense, to live the rest of his time among his family.'

Much depends on the translation. Another: 'Happy the man who's journeyed much, like Ulysses./Or like the traveller who won the Golden Fleece,/And has returned at last, experienced and wise,/To end his days among his family in peace.'

George Seferis (1900-71), 'On a Line of Foreign Verse', develops the idea: 'Fortunate he who's made the voyage of Odysseus./Fortunate if on setting out he's felt the rigging/Of a love strong in his body, spreading there like/veins, where the blood throbs . . . / . . . To see once more the smoke/Ascending from his warm hearth and the dog grown/Old waiting by the door.'

Dulles, John Foster
American politician (1888-1959)

1 *Agonizing reappraisal.*

A political term for the process of reconsideration, possibly before a decision is made to make a U-turn. The modern use stems from a speech that Dulles, as US Secretary of State, made to the National Press Club, Washington, in December 1953: 'When I was in Paris last week, I said that . . . the United States would have to undertake an agonizing reappraisal of basic foreign policy in relation to Europe.'

Dumas, Alexandre
(Dumas Père)
French novelist (1802-70)

2 *All for one and one for all* [Tous pour un, un pour tous].

The motto of the Three Musketeers made famous in the novel *Les Trois Mousquetaires* (1844-5). Earlier, Shakespeare in his poem, *The Rape of Lucrece*, lines 141-4 (1594) had written:

The aim of all is but to nurse the life
With honour, wealth and ease, in waning age;
And in this aim there is much thwarting strife
That *one for all, or all for one* we gage [= pledge].

More prosaically, 'Each for all and all for each' has been used in Britain as a slogan of the Co-operative Wholesale Society.

Durant, Will
American writer (1885-1981)

3 *There is nothing in Socialism that a little age or a little money will not cure.*

Unverified. Compare CLEMENCEAU 100:5.

Durocher, Leo
American baseball coach (1906-91)

4 *Nice guys finish last.*

In his autobiography with the title *Nice Guys Finish Last* (1975), Durocher recalled that what he had said to reporters concerning the New York Giants in July 1946, was: 'All nice guys. They'll finish last. Nice guys. Finish last.' However, Frank Graham of the New York *Journal-American* had written down something slightly different: 'Why, they're the nicest guys in the world! And where are they? In seventh place!' Hence, the title of Ralph Keyes's book on misquotations *Nice Guys Finish Seventh* (1992).

Dylan, Bob
American singer and songwriter (1941–)

5 *All Along the Watchtower.*

A 1968 Dylan song begins: 'All along the watchtower, princes kept the view.' This is probably after Isaiah 21:5, prophesying the fall of Babylon: 'Prepare the table, watch in the watchtower, eat, drink: arise ye princes, and anoint the shield.' (*The Watchtower*, magazine of Jehovah's Witnesses, presumably takes its name from the same source.)

Dyson, Will
Australian-born cartoonist (1883-1938)

6 *Curious! I seem to hear a child weeping!*

This caption to a cartoon in the *Daily Herald* appeared at the conclusion of the Versailles Peace Conference in 1919. The picture showed the 'Big Four' — President Wilson, Clemenceau, Orlando of Italy and Lloyd George — leaving the conference hall and hearing a child — signifying the next generation — bewailing the breakdown of their peace efforts. The headline is 'Peace and Future Cannon Fodder'; the caption has 'The Tiger' (Clemenceau) speaking; and the child is prophetically labelled '1940 Class'. If the biographical details of Dyson are correct as above, then he did not live to see his prophetic observation come true.

E

Eastwood, Clint
American film actor (1930–   )

1 Go ahead, make my day!

This popular laconicism was originally spoken by Eastwood as a cop, himself brandishing a .44 Magnum, to a gunman he is holding at bay in *Sudden Impact* (1983). At the end of the film he says (to another villain, similarly armed), 'Come on, make my day'. In neither case does he add 'punk', as is sometimes supposed. (From the *Independent*, 14 July 1993: 'When Clint Eastwood said "Go ahead, punk, make my day" . . .') This may come from confusion with *Dirty Harry* (1971) in which Eastwood holds a .44 Magnum to the temple of a criminal and says 'Well, do ya [feel lucky], punk?')

In March 1985, President Ronald Reagan told the American Business Conference: 'I have my veto pen drawn and ready for any tax increase that Congress might even think of sending up. And I have only one thing to say to the tax increasers. Go ahead — make my day.' The phrase may have been eased into Reagan's speech by having appeared in a parody of the New York *Post* put together by editors, many of them anti-Reagan, in the autumn of 1984. Reagan was shown starting a nuclear war by throwing down this dare to the Kremlin (information from *Time Magazine*, 25 March 1985).

Ebb, Fred
American songwriter (1932–   )

2 Money makes the world go around.

A modern proverbial phrase, this derives, apparently, from the song, 'Money, Money' in the musical *Cabaret* (1966; filmed 1972), with lyrics by Ebb and music by John Kander. As with 'Tomorrow Belongs To Me' (below), we may have to thank the writers of *Cabaret* for either creating an instant 'saying' or, in this instance, for introducing to the English language something that has long been known in others. 'Money makes the world go around' is clearly built on the well-established proverb 'Tis love, that makes the world go round' (see 87:2), but it is not recorded in either the *ODP* or the *CODP*. The nearest these get is, 'Money makes the mare to go'.

'Money makes the world go around' appears in the English language key to the 'Flemish Proverbs' picture by David Teniers the Younger (1610–90), at Belvoir Castle. The painting shows an obviously wealthy man holding a globe. The key may, however, be modern. How odd that it should, apparently, have taken a song in a 1960s musical to get the expression into English.

3 Tomorrow Belongs to Me.

Has this ever been used as a political slogan, either as 'Tomorrow belongs to me' or 'to us'? Harold Wilson in his final broadcast before the 1964 General Election said, 'If the past belongs to the Tories, the future belongs to us — all of us'. At a Young Conservative rally before the 1983 General Election, Margaret Thatcher asked: 'Could Labour have organized a rally like this? In the old days perhaps, but not now. For they are the Party of Yesterday. Tomorrow is ours.' What one can say is that, in *Cabaret*, Ebb wrote a convincing pastiche of a Hitler Youth song:

> The babe in his cradle is closing his
> eyes, the blossom embraces the bee,
> But soon says a whisper, 'Arise, arise',
> Tomorrow belongs to me.
> O Fatherland, Fatherland, show us the
> sign your children have waited to see,
> The morning will come when the
> world is mine,
> Tomorrow belongs to me.

So much so that the song was denounced as a real Nazi anthem. Ebb told the *Independent* (30 November 1993): 'The accusations against "Tomorrow Belongs to Me" made me very angry . . . "I knew that song as a child," one man had the audacity to tell me. A rabbinical person wrote me saying he had absolute proof it was a Nazi song.'

The *idea*, rather, seems likely to have been current in Nazi Germany. A popular song, '*Jawohl, mein Herr*', featured in the 1943 episode of the German film chronicle *Heimat* (1984), included the line, 'For from today, the world belongs to us'.

The nearest the slogan appears to have been actually used by any (admittedly right-wing) youth organization is referred to in this report from the *Guardian* (30 October 1987): 'Contra leader Adolfo Calero . . . was entertained to dinner on Wednesday by Oxford University's Freedom Society, a clutch of hoorays . . . A coach-load of diners . . . got "hog-whimpering" drunk . . . and songs like "Tomorrow Belongs To Us" and "Miner, Cross that Picket Line" were sung on the return coach trip.'

The same paper, reporting a meeting addressed by the SDP leader, Dr David Owen, on 1 February 1988 noted: 'Down, sit down, he eventually gestured; his eyes saying Up, stay up. It reminded you of nothing so much as a Conservative Party conference in one of its most Tomorrow-belongs-to-us moods.' In each of these last two examples, it is the song from the musical that is being evoked rather than any Nazi original.

Eco, Umberto
Italian novelist (1932–)

1 *The Name of the Rose* [Il Nomme della Rosa].

Title of novel (1981). But what does it mean? Eco's own *Reflections on The Name of the Rose* (1985) explains how the title derives from the Latin hexameter with which the book ends: '*Stat rosa pristina nomine, nomina nuda tenemus.*' This comes from a satirical poem *De contemptu mundi* by the twelfth-century monk, Bernard of Cluny. Broadly speaking, the title has to do with the passing of things. The dying rose is merely another symbol of this — and only its name remains. Eco, incidentally, states in *Reflections*: 'A title must muddle the reader's ideas, not regiment them.'

Eden, Sir Anthony
(later 1st Earl of Avon)
British Conservative Prime Minister (1897–1977)

2 *A property-owning democracy.*

See SKELTON 312:2.

3 *We are in an armed conflict; that is the phrase I have used. There has been no declaration of war.*

Speaking in the House of Commons (1 November 1956) about Britain's response to the Egyptian take-over of the Suez Canal, Eden seemed curiously punctilious about his words. Possibly he was obsessed by the thought of becoming a war-monger when, as he said in a TV and radio broadcast two days later: 'All my life I have been a man of peace, working for peace, striving for peace, and negotiating for peace. I have been a League of Nations man and a United Nations man. And I am still the same man, with the same convictions, and the same devotion to peace. I could not be other even if I wished, but I am utterly convinced that the action we have taken is right.'

Edison, Thomas Alva
American inventor (1847–1931)

4 *Genius is one per cent inspiration and ninety-nine per cent perspiration.*

Quoted in *Life/Harper's Monthly* Magazine (September 1932), having originally been said by him *c* 1903. Earlier, the French naturalist, the Comte de Buffon (1707–88), was quoted in 1803 as having said, 'Genius is only a greater aptitude for patience.' Compare CARLYLE 86:2.

Edmonds, J.M.
English poet and academic (1875–1958)

5 *Went the day well?*
We died and never knew.
But, well or ill,
Freedom, we died for you.

An anonymous epigraph appears on screen at the start of the 1942 British film *Went the Day Well?* (re-titled *48 Hours* in the US). At the time the film was released, some thought it was a version of a Greek epitaph. Based on a story by Graham Greene entitled *The Lieutenant Died Last*, the film tells of a typical English village managing to repel

Nazi invaders. The epigraph thus presumably refers to the villagers who die defending 'Bramley End'. Penelope Houston in her 1992 British Film Institute monograph on the film describes it as a quotation from an anonymous poem that appeared in an anthology of tributes to people killed in the war to which Michael Balcon, head of Ealing Studios, contributed a memoir of the dead director Pen Tennyson.

But it is not an anonymous poem. *The Times* (London) for 6 February 1918 printed 'Four Epitaphs', of which this was one:

> *On Some who died early in the Day of Battle*
> Went the day well? we died and never knew;
> But well or ill, England we died for you.

Edmonds was the poet. He also composed the following even more famous epitaph about the same time:

1 *When you go home*
Tell them of us and say
For your tomorrow
We gave our today.

Such is the text on the 2nd British Division's memorial at Kohima War Cemetery, Assam (now Nagaland), India (and on many other war graves round the world), though no credit ever finds its way to Edmonds. He wrote:

> When you go home, tell them of us and say,
> 'For your to-morrow these gave their to-day.'

This version first appeared in *The Times Literary Supplement* on 4 July 1918 and had been written by Edmonds as one of a series of suggested epitaphs, this one 'For a British graveyard in France'. However, by the Second World War, it was frequently stated that 'the words are a translation from the Greek'. Many people still appear to think that it is an allusion to the Greek poet Simonides. The second line should not read 'tomorrows', as in *ODMQ* (1991) and *ODQ* (1992).

The BBC received a somewhat crusty letter from Edmonds (by this time a Fellow of Jesus College, Cambridge), dated 23 July 1953, in which he said, 'I thought the Greek origin of my epitaph used — and altered — at Kohima had been denied in print often enough; but here it is again. It is no translation, nor is it true to say it was suggested by one of the beautiful couplets which you will find in *Lyrica Graeca* (Loeb Classical

Library), though I *was* at work on that book in 1917 when my Twelve War Epitaphs were first printed in *The Times* and its *Literary Supplement* . . . The epitaph, of course, should be used only abroad. Used in England its "home" may be just round the corner — which makes the whole thing laughable.'

Edward III
English Sovereign (1312–77)

2 Honi Soit Qui Mal Y Pense [*Evil be to him who evil thinks*].

The motto of the Order of the Garter, founded by Edward *c* 1348, is traditionally said to have been uttered by him as he adjusted the Countess of Salisbury's garter when it fell down. The tale was current by the reign of Henry VIII and was included in Polydore Vergil's *Anglicae Historiae* (1534–55).

Accordingly, the version given by Sellar and Yeatman in their comic history *1066 and All That* (1930) is not so wide of the mark: 'Edward III had very good manners. One day at a royal dance he noticed some men-about-court mocking a lady whose garter had come off, whereupon to put her at her ease he stopped the dance and made the memorable epitaph: "*Honi soie qui mal y pense*" ("Honey, your silk stocking's hanging down").'

Edward VII
British Sovereign (1841–1910)

3 We are all socialists nowadays.

Edward is said to have said this, when Prince of Wales, in a speech at the Mansion House, London, on 5 November 1895 — though no record exists of him making any such speech on that day. His biographer, Sir Philip Magnus, makes no mention of him doing so either. The ODQ dropped the entry after pointing out in the Corrigenda to the 1941 edition that the saying should more correctly be ascribed to Sir William Harcourt (1827–1904). Harcourt is quoted as saying it in *Fabian Essays* (1889, edited by Bernard Shaw) (i.e. six years before the supposed 1895 speech). Harcourt was Lord Rosebery's (Liberal) Chancellor of the Exchequer and an impassioned enemy of the House of Lords. He introduced estate duty tax in his Budget of 1894.

Whoever said it first, the foundation was

laid for a much later remark by Jeremy Thorpe, the Liberal politician, in a speech in the House of Commons on 6 March 1974. After a general election which resulted in no party having a clear majority — a Liberal coalition with the Conservatives had been mooted but rejected — he observed, 'Looking around the House, one realizes that we are all minorities now'.

Edward VIII
(later Duke of Windsor)
British Sovereign (1894–1972)

1 *The young business and professional men of this country must get together round the table, adopt methods that have proved sound in the past, adapt them to the changing needs of the times and, whenever possible, improve them.*

In a speech, as Prince of Wales, at the British Industries Fair in Birmingham, 1927. Hence the name 'round table' — although it may have some echoes of Arthurian knights working together — and the motto of the National Association of Round Tables of Great Britain and Ireland (in the form 'Adopt, adapt, improve'). The Round Table movement is a social and charitable organization for young professional and business men under the age of forty (after which age Rotary takes over).

2 *Something must be done.*

In November 1936 the King went to South Wales to tour the depressed areas and moved the public with his expressions of concern. At the Bessemer steel works at Dowlais, where 9,000 men had been made unemployed, hundreds sang an old Welsh hymn. Afterwards the King was heard to say to an official: 'These works brought all these people here. Something must be done to find them work' [or 'get them at work again']. Occasionally quoted as 'something ought to be done' and followed the next day by the promise, 'You may be sure that all I can do for you, I will', the King's words were taken as an indication of his concern for ordinary people and of his impatience with established authority.

Although his distress at what he saw in South Wales was no doubt genuine, the King's assurances might look less hollow if we did not now know that by then he had already informed his family and the Prime Minister of his decision to abdicate.

3 *I have found it impossible to carry the heavy burden of responsibility and to discharge my duties as King as I would wish to do without the help and support of the woman I love.*

Edward abdicated on 11 December 1936. That evening, before he left the country, 'His Royal Highness Prince Edward', as he was introduced, took the opportunity of broadcasting a message to his former subjects. Nothing in Edward's short reign became him like the leaving of it. He later commented (in *A King's Story*, 1951): 'It has become part of the Abdication legend that the broadcast was actually written by Mr Churchill. The truth is that, as he had often done before with other speeches, he generously applied the final brush strokes.' Such phrases as 'bred in the consitutional tradition by my father' and 'one matchless blessing . . . a happy home with his wife and children' are the two most obvious of those strokes. They were applied to a basic text drawn up by Edward's lawyer, Walter Monckton. The BBC's chief, Sir John Reith, who introduced the broadcast from Windsor Castle, noted that he had 'never [seen] so many alterations in a script'.

The moving speech could be heard by all his subjects over the wireless, a unique event. However relieved people may subsequently have been that Edward's reign was not prolonged, for the moment they were touched, if not reduced to tears, by the courageous tones in which the broadcast was delivered and by the protestations of love and duty it included.

4 *England . . . the waste . . . the waste.*

These, if truly the Duke of Windsor's dying words, might seem to be appropriate, insofar as their meaning can be guessed at. Their provenance is, however, not recorded. A biographer of the Duchess of Windsor suggests rather that what the ex-King said on his deathbed in Paris was 'Darling' and 'Mama, mama, mama, mama'. On the other hand, Bryan & Murphy, *The Windsor Story* (1979) state that there were *no* last words.

Ehrlichman, John D.
American Presidential aide (1925–   )

5 *It'll play in Peoria.*

About 1968, during the Nixon election campaign, Ehrlichman is credited with devising this yardstick for judging whether policies would appeal to voters in 'Middle America'. He later told Safire (1978): 'Onomatopoeia was the only reason for Peoria, I suppose. And it . . . exemplified a place, far removed from the media centres on the coasts where the national verdict is cast.' Peoria is in Illinois.

1 *I think we ought to let him hang there. Let him twist slowly, slowly in the wind.*

Richard Nixon's henchmen may have acted wrongly and, for much of the time, spoken sleazily. Occasionally, however, they minted political phrases that have lingered on. Ehrlichman, Nixon's Assistant for Domestic Affairs until he was forced to resign over Watergate in 1973, came up with one saying that caught people's imagination. In a telephone conversation with John Dean (Counsel to the President) on 7–8 March 1973 he was speaking about Patrick Gray (Acting Director of the FBI). Gray's nomination to take over the FBI post had been withdrawn by Nixon during Judiciary Committee hearings – though Gray had not been told of this. Ehrlichman suggested he be left in ignorance of this – and in suspense.

From the *Guardian* (28 January 1989): 'The foreign press observed with admiration the way President Bush stressed in words that he was not ditching the beleaguered Mikhail Gorbachev by playing his China card, while making it clear he was doing exactly that, and leaving the Soviet leader to twist a little longer in the wind.'

Ehrmann, Max
American writer (?–1945)

2 *Go placidly amid the noise and haste . . .*

There can have been few bedroom walls during the great poster-hanging craze of the late 1960s which did not bear a copy of a text called 'Desiderata' ('things desired'), reputedly found in Old St Paul's Church, Baltimore, and dating from 1692. It continues: 'and remember what peace there may be in silence. As far as possible without surrender be on good terms with all persons. Speak your truth quietly and clearly; and listen to others, even the dull and ignorant; they too have their story. Avoid loud and aggressive persons, they are vexations to the spirit.'

Les Crane spoke the words on a hit record in 1972. However, 'Desiderata' had nothing to do with Old St Paul's. That was a fanciful idea incorporated in the first US edition of the poster. Nor did 1692 come into it. The words were written by Max Ehrmann in 1927 and copyright was renewed in 1954 by Bertha K. Ehrmann. In 1983, the poster was still on sale as 'from 1692' but carrying the correct copyright lines.

Einstein, Albert
German-born physicist (1879–1955)

3 *God does not play dice with the universe.*

What he actually wrote to Max Born (on 4 December 1926) (in German) was simply: 'At any rate, I am convinced that *He* does not play dice.' This was his way of objecting to quantum mechanics, in which physical events can only be known in terms of probabilities. What he was saying was, there is no uncertainty in the material world.

Eisenhower, Dwight D.
American general and Republican 34th President (1890–1969)

4 *I like Ike.*

These words began appearing on buttons in 1947 as Eisenhower began to be spoken of as a possible Presidential nominee (initially as a Democrat). By 1950, Irving Berlin was including one of his least memorable songs, 'They Like Ike', in *Call Me Madam*, and 15,000 people at a rally in Madison Square Gardens were urging Eisenhower to return from a military posting in Paris and run as a Republican in 1952, with the chant 'We like Ike'. It worked. The three sharp monosyllables and the effectiveness of the repeated 'i' sound made it an enduring slogan throughout the 1950s.

5 *I shall go to Korea and try to end the war.*

During the Presidential election campaign, Eisenhower made this promise in a speech on 24 October 1952. Between his election and inauguration, he did make a three-day visit to Korea but it had no discernible effect on the negotiations towards a truce.

6 *You have a row of dominoes set up. You knock over the first one and what will happen to the last one is that it will go over very quickly.*

The old metaphor of falling over 'like a stack of dominoes' was first used in the context of Communist take-overs by the American political commentator, Joseph Alsop. Then President Eisenhower said at a press conference (7 April 1954): 'You have broader considerations that might follow what you might call the "falling domino" principle. You have a row of dominoes set up. You knock over the first one, and what will happen to the last one is that it will go over very quickly.' In South-East Asia, the theory was proved true to an extent in the 1970s. When South Vietnam collapsed, Cambodia then fell to the Khmer Rouge and Laos was taken over by the Communist-led Pathet Lao. In 1989 when one eastern European country after another renounced Communism, there was talk of a 'reverse domino theory'.

1 *In the councils of government, we must guard against the acquisition of unwarranted influence, whether sought or unsought, by the military-industrial complex. The potential for the disastrous rise of misplaced power exists and will persist.*

Eisenhower's Presidency was characterized by dull speech-making and convoluted extempore remarks. The only phrase for which he is remembered, if at all, occurred in his farewell address on 17 January 1961. The political scientist Malcolm Moos helped formulate the passage. Harry Truman, never able to say anything good about his successor, commented: 'Yes, I believe he did say something like that. I think somebody must have written it for him, and I'm not sure he understood what he was saying. But it's true.'

Eliot, George
(Mary Ann Evans)
English novelist (1819–80)

2 *Any coward can fight a battle when he's sure of winning; but give me the man who has pluck to fight when he's sure of losing. That's my way, sir; and there are many victories worse than defeat.*

From *Janet's Repentance*, Chap. 6 (1857). Sometimes remembered as: 'Give me the man, Sir, who fights when he is sure of losing. He's my kind of man, Sir, and there's many a victory worse than a defeat.'

3 *Of those immortal dead who live again in minds made better by their presence.*

The quotation on Eliot's grave in Highgate Cemetery, London, is from one of her poems, 'Oh May I Join the Choir Invisible', which was sung by the graveside at her funeral.

4 *The first condition of human goodness is something to love; the second something to reverence.*

The novelist is also commemorated in Poets' Corner, Westminster Abbey, with this quotation from *Scenes of Clerical Life*, Chap. 10 (1857). 'It is a quotation of which we are particularly fond,' said the Secretary of the George Eliot Fellowship, which was responsible for the worldwide appeal for funds to place the memorial stone in 1980, 'and it describes, we feel, George Eliot's own philosophy.'

5 *The happiest women, like the happiest nations, have no history.*

Eliot adapted the proverbial expression to her own ends in *The Mill on the Floss*, Bk 6, Chap. 3 (1860). In the form, 'Happy the people whose annals are blank in history-books!', the saying was ascribed to Montesquieu by Thomas Carlyle in his *History of Frederick the Great* (1858–65). In *The French Revolution – A History* (1838), Carlyle had earlier written: 'A paradoxical philosopher, carrying to the uttermost length that aphorism of Montequieu's, "Happy the people whose annals are tiresome," has said, "Happy the people whose annals are vacant".' Theodore Roosevelt said in a speech (10 April 1899): 'It is a base untruth to say that happy is the nation that has no history. Thrice happy is the nation that has a glorious history. Far better it is to dare mighty things, to win glorious triumphs, even though checkered by failure, than to take rank with those spirits who neither enjoy much nor suffer much because they live in the grey twilight that knows neither victory nor defeat.' The earliest form of the proverb found by CODP is in Benjamin Franklin, *Poor Richard's Almanack* (1740): 'Happy that Nation, — fortunate that age, whose history is not diverting.'

Eliot, T.S.

American-born English poet, playwright and critic (1888–1965)

1 *Shall I part my hair behind? Do I*
   dare to eat a peach?
   I shall wear white flannel trousers,
   and walk upon the beach.
   I have heard the mermaids singing,
   each to each.

A passage from 'The Love Song of J. Alfred Prufrock' (1917) has inspired two film titles: *I've Heard the Mermaids Singing*, a Canadian film (1987) about a gauche girl who develops a crush on her (female) boss, and — even more allusively — *Eat the Peach* (Ireland, 1986).

2 *April is the cruellest month, breeding*
   Lilacs out of the dead land.

The first five words of *The Waste Land* (1922) are frequently misquoted, often with 'August' being substituted, possibly out of confusion with *August is a Wicked Month*, the title of a novel (1965) by Edna O'Brien. Or, rather, the observation is much abused allusively: 'After the highs and lows of Christmas and the winter holidays, February always seems to me the cruellest month' (*Daily Telegraph*, 15 February 1992); 'Sometimes March can be the cruellest month' (*Northern Echo*, 18 February 1992); 'August used to be the cruellest month' (*The Times*, 25 August 1992); 'June is the cruellest month in politics' (*The Times*, 5 June 1993); 'August has always been the cruellest month' (*The Times*, 25 August 1993).

3 *O O O O that Shakespeherian Rag.*

In *The Waste Land*, Eliot provided notes to explain the numerous allusions. However, he neglected to mention that lines 128–30:

   O O O O that Shakespeherian Rag
   It's so elegant
   So intelligent

had been taken from a popular song 'That Shakespearian Rag' published in 1912 by the Edward Marks Music Corp. (in the US) and written by Gene Buck, Herman Ruby and David Stamper. The chorus goes: 'That Shakespearian Rag, most intelligent, very elegant.' This was pointed out by Ian Whitcomb in *After the Ball* (1972).

4 *When lovely woman stoops to folly.*

From the *Observer* Magazine (28 November 1993): 'For some reason, T.S. Eliot's line "When lovely woman stoops to folly" comes to mind.' Yes, but as he acknowledged in the extensive notes to *The Waste Land*, it is a reference to the song in Goldsmith's *The Vicar of Wakefield* (1766):

   When lovely woman stoops to folly
   And finds too late that men betray,
   What charm can soothe her
      melancholy,
   What art can wash her guilt away?

Kate Hardcastle in Goldsmith's play *She Stoops to Conquer* (1773) also 'stoops' but not to folly, as the Epilogue points out:

   Well, having stooped to conquer with
      success,
   And gained a husband without aid
      from dress,
   Still as a Barmaid, I could wish it too,
   As I have conquered him to conquer you.

Mary Demetriadis once reworked the couplet for a *New Statesman* competition:

   When lovely woman stoops to folly
   The evening can be awfully jolly.

5 *I will show you fear in a handful of dust.*

From 'The Burial of the Dead' in *The Waste Land*. As acknowledged, *A Handful of Dust*, the novel (1934) by Evelyn Waugh, takes its title from this. Compare 'the heat of life in the handful of dust' in Joseph Conrad's novel *Youth* (1902). Earlier, a 'handful of earth' was a symbol of mortality.

6 *The common pursuit.*

This became the title of a book of essays by the critic F.R. Leavis (1952), quoting Eliot's essay 'The Function of Criticism' (1923) — the critic, 'must compose his differences with as many of his fellows as possible in the common pursuit of true judgement'. In turn, it became the title of a play (1984) by Simon Gray about a group of Cambridge undergraduates and graduates who produce a literary magazine called *The Common Pursuit*.

7 *In my beginning is my end . . .*
   In my end is my beginning.

From 'East Coker' in *Four Quartets* (1940). As to the second of these phrases, compare *'En ma fin git mon commencement'* — a motto reputedly embroidered with an emblem of her mother by Mary, Queen of Scots (d 1587).

Elizabeth I
English Sovereign (1533–1603)

1 The heart and stomach of a king.

What Elizabeth is supposed to have said in a speech to her army of 20,000 gathered at Tilbury during the approach of the Spanish Armada in 1588 is: 'My loving people, we have been persuaded by some that are careful for our safety to take heed how we commit ourselves to armed multitudes, for fear of treachery. But I assure you I do not desire to live to distrust my faithful and loving people. Let tyrants fear. I have always so behaved myself that, under God, I have placed my chiefest strength and safeguard in the loyal hearts and goodwill of my subjects; and therefore I am come amongst you, as you see, resolved, in the midst and heat of the battle, to live or die amongst you all, to lay down for my God, and for my kingdom, and for my people, my honour and my blood, even in the dust.

'I know I have the body of a weak and feeble woman, but I have the heart and stomach of a king, and of a king of England too; and think foul scorn that Parma or Spain, or any prince of Europe, should dare to invade the borders of my realm; to which, rather than any dishonour shall grow by me, I myself will take up arms, I myself will be your general, judge, and rewarder of every one of your virtues in the field. I know already for your forwardness you have deserved rewards and crowns; and we do assure you, in the word of a prince, they shall be duly paid you.'

In an article published in History Today (May 1988) Felix Barker contended that the Queen might never have used these words because of the absence of any contemporary accounts of her doing so. The sole source is an undated letter to the Duke of Buckingham (not published until 1691) from Leonel Sharp, a chaplain who was at Tilbury but who had a reputation for being 'obsequious and ingratiating' (according to the DNB). The only recorded contemporary account of the speech is by a poet called James Aske, but it contains none of the above phrases. Why did no one else quote the good bits at the time, Felix Barker wondered, if they had in fact been used? For reasons of delicacy presumably; when Flora Robson came to give the speech in the film Fire Over England (1937), she found herself saying, 'But I have the heart and valour of a king' rather than the traditional 'heart and stomach'.

2 I would not open windows into men's souls.

Elizabeth is often cited as saying this, when in fact the phrase is most likely Francis Bacon's rationalization of her religious intolerance. In drafting a letter for her, he was attempting to say that the Queen, while not liking to do so, was forced into it by the people she had to deal with.

Sir Christopher Hatton (1540–91), Elizabeth's Lord Chancellor, is said to have commented, similarly: 'The queen did fish for men's souls, and had so sweet a bait that no one could escape her network.'

[Source: letter from Professor William Lamont, University of Sussex, in the Observer, 13 November 1988.]

Elizabeth II
British Sovereign (1926–   )

3 My husband and I.

George VI had quite naturally spoken the words 'The Queen and I' but something in his daughter's drawling delivery turned her version into a joke. It first appeared during her second Christmas broadcast (made from New Zealand) in 1953 — 'My husband and I left London a month ago' — and still survived in 1962: 'My husband and I are greatly looking forward to visiting New Zealand and Australia in the New Year.' By 1967 the phrase had become 'Prince Philip and I'. At a Silver Wedding banquet in 1972, the Queen allowed herself a little joke: 'I think on this occasion I may be forgiven for saying "My husband and I".' Compare the title of the Rodgers and Hammerstein musical The King and I (1951).

4 1992 is not a year I shall look back on with undiluted pleasure. In the words of one of my more sympathetic correspondents, it has turned out to be an Annus Horribilis.

Speaking at a lunch in the City of London on 24 November 1992 to mark her fortieth year on the British throne, the Queen deftly reflected her current mood: she had a cold, part of Windsor Castle had been burned down four days previously, and the marriages of three of her children had collapsed or were collapsing. She states that she had the phrase from a correspondent, but it seems more likely that it was inserted by her private secretary and speechwriter, Sir Robert Fellowes. The more usual phrase is, of course, modern (as opposed to classical) Latin's *annus mirabilis* ['wonderful year']. The Queen had quoted Latin before: speaking (19 May 1982) to pupils of Winchester College on its 600th anniversary she attempted the words of Apollo to Ascanius, son of Aeneas, before battle, as reported by Virgil: '*Macte nova virtute, puer, sic itur ad astra* [Go to it with fresh courage, young man; this is the way to the stars].'

Ellington, Duke
American bandleader, pianist and composer (1899–1974)

1 *There'll be some changes made.*

In the early 1990s Alistair Cooke asserted in three different *Letter from America* broadcasts on BBC Radio, that: ' "There'll be some changes made", *as Duke Ellington used to say.*' In fact, Ellington never recorded the song with that title (written by Overstreet and Higgins in 1929). Most likely Cooke was confusing it with the Mercer Ellington / Ted Person's 1939 composition 'Things Ain't What They Used To Be'.

Ellis, A.E.
English novelist (*fl.* 1958)

2 *The Rack.*

Ellis's novel (published in 1958) is about the ordeal of a man in a sanitorium. The last page explains where the title comes from: 'He picked up [Benjamin] Haydon's *Journal* and turned to the entry which the latter had made just before killing himself: "22nd. God forgive me. Amen. Finis of B.R. HAYDON. 'Stretch me no more on this rough world' — Lear." Something was grotesquely wrong. He opened his Shakespeare. ". . . O, let him pass! he hates him / That would upon the rack of this tough world / Stretch him out longer." "The rack," he murmured. "Haydon forgot the rack".' Kent, at the very end of *King Lear* (V.iii.313) does speak of 'this tough world' rather than Haydon's 'rough world'.

Emerson, Ralph Waldo
American poet and essayist (1803–82)

3 *All the world loves a lover.*

A little remarked proverb. In an essay on 'Love', Emerson has, precisely, 'All mankind *love* a lover'. In 1958 there was a popular song by Richard Adler and Robert Allen, 'Everybody Loves a Lover'. Compare the proverb, 'Everybody loves a Lord', which *CODP* finds by 1869.

4 *I hate quotations.*

The *ODQ* (1979) had Emerson writing this in his journal for May 1849. Even toilers in the quotation vineyard feel like echoing this thought from time to time when they hear yet another person about to launch into some over-familiar line with, 'As the poet has it . . .' or 'As George Bernard Shaw once said . . .'
  Oddly enough, and ironically, what the *ODQ* had (the entry was dropped from the 1992 edition) is a *misquotation*. What Emerson actually wrote was: '*Immortality*. I notice that as soon as writers broach this question they begin to quote. I hate quotation. Tell me what you know.' (*Journals and Miscellaneous Notebooks*, Vol. XI.)
  So it is 'quotation' not 'quotations'. There is a difference.

5 *Next to the originator of a good sentence is the first quoter of it.*

From 'Quotation and Originality' in *Letters and Social Aims* (1876). Not 'misquoter of it', as at the beginning of the present book.

6 *If a man write a better book, preach a better sermon, or make a better mouse-trap than his neighbour, tho' he build his house in the woods, the world will make a beaten path to his door.*

Sarah Yule claimed (in 1889) that she had heard Emerson say this in a lecture. Elbert Hubbard also claimed authorship. Either way, this is a remark alluded to whenever people talk of 'beating a path to someone's door' or a 'better mousetrap'. In his journal for February 1855, Emerson had certainly entertained the notion: 'If a man . . . can make better chairs or knives . . . than anybody else, you will find a broad hard-beaten road to his house, though it be in the woods.'

7 *Do your own thing.*

The 1960s expression meaning, 'establish your own identity' / 'follow your star', is said to have been anticipated by Emerson (e.g. in *Time* Magazine, 10 May 1982). The passage from his 'Essay on Self Reliance' actually states: 'If you maintain a dead church, contribute to a dead Bible-society, vote with a great party either for the government or against it . . . under all these screens, I have difficulty to detect the precise man you are . . . But do your [. . .] thing, and I shall know you.'

1 *Glittering generalities! They are blazing ubiquities.*

An attributed remark, referring to Rufus Choate's criticism of the Declaration of Independence (in Choate's letter to the Maine Whig Central Committee, 9 August 1856) as being full of 'glittering generalities'.

Englebrecht, H.C.
American author (*fl.* 1934)

2 *Merchants of Death.*

This was the title of book (1934), written jointly with F.C. Hanighan, about munitions makers who stood to profit from war. Later, the term was applied to dealers in drugs, tobacco and guns.

Erwin, Dudley
Australian politician (1917–   )

3 *It is shapely, it wiggles, and it's name is Ainslie Gotto.*

When asked the reason for his dismissal as Australian Air Minister in 1969, Erwin accused Ms Gotto, the secretary of Prime Minister John Gorton, of exerting undue influence. He said she ruled Gorton with 'ruthless authority'. Twelve years later, Ms Gotto — no longer involved in Australian

politics — commented: 'That was another life . . . I never wiggled, I was never aware of wielding power, and the rest was nonsense — the folklore of reporting.'

Ewer, W.N.
English journalist (1885–1976)

4 *How odd*
Of God
To choose
The Jews.

A frequently misattributed rhyme — perhaps because it was composed in an informal setting and not published originally in written form — is the one composed by the foreign correspondent, W.N. Ewer. In a letter to the *Observer* (13 March 1983), Alan Wykes, Honorary Secretary of the Savage Club in London, described the rhyme's origins: 'In the Savage Club, one of the guests was trying to make his mark with the Jewish pianist Benno Moiseiwitsch, who was not a man to be trifled with. "Is there," asked this Hooray Henry, "Any anti-Semitism in the club?" To this Benno snarled back: "Only amongst the Jews." Trilby Ewer, on the fringe of this conversation, thereupon coined the quatrain, which has since passed into history.'

There has been more than one corollary or rejoinder. This, published in 1924, was by Cecil Browne:

But not so odd
As those who choose
A Jewish God
Yet spurn the Jews.

Another, quoted in the early 1960s, went:

Who said he did?
Moses. But he's a yid.

F

Fairlie, Henry
English journalist (1924–90)

1 *I have several times suggested that what I call the 'Establishment' in this country is today more powerful than ever before. By the 'Establishment' I do not mean only the centres of official power — though they are certainly part of it — but rather the whole matrix of official and social relations within which power is exercised . . . the 'Establishment' can be seen at work in the activities of, not only the Prime Minister, the Archbishop of Canterbury and the Earl Marshal, but of such lesser mortals as the Chairman of the Arts Council, the Director-General of the BBC, and even the editor of* The Times Literary Supplement, *not to mention dignitaries like Lady Violet Bonham Carter.*

As a nickname for a conservative, partly hereditary, secretive, self-perpetuating ruling class, the term 'Establishment' was brought to prominence by Fairlie in a series of articles for *The Spectator* in 1955. On 23 September, he wrote the above. Hugh Thomas, editing a book on the phenomenon and called *The Establishment* (1959), stated: 'The word was, however, in use among the thoughtful at least a year previously; I recall myself employing it while passing the Royal Academy in a taxi in company with Mr Paul Johnson of *The New Statesman* in August 1954.' An earlier example of the phrase's use among the 'thoughtful' has, indeed, come to light in A.J.P. Taylor's *Essays in English History*. In one on William Cobbett (originally a review in *The New Statesman*, in 1953) he wrote: 'Trotsky tells how, when he first visited England, Lenin took him round London and, pointing out the sights, exclaimed: "That's *their* Westminster Abbey! That's *their* Houses of Parliament!" Lenin was making a class, not a national emphasis. By "them" he meant not the English, but the governing classes, the Establishment so clearly defined and so complacently secure.' *OED2* has other citations of the phrase in its modern sense going back to 1923, to which might be added one in George Eliot's *Daniel Deronda*, Bk 2, Chap. 12 (1876).

Farley, James
American Democratic politician (1888–1976)

2 *As Maine goes, so goes Vermont.*

In the 1936 US Presidential election, Farley was Franklin D. Roosevelt's campaign manager. On 4 November, Farley predicted that Roosevelt would carry all but two states — Maine and Vermont. The above is how he put it in a statement to the press, alluding to an earlier political maxim: 'As Maine goes, so goes the nation' (which Bartlett dates *c* 1888).

Farquhar, George
Irish playwright (1678–1707)

3 *As the saying is.*

Boniface, the landlord, in Farquhar's play *The Beaux' Stratagem* (1707) has a curious verbal mannerism. After almost every phrase, he adds, 'As the saying is . . .'. This was a well-established phrase even then. In 1548, Hugh Latimer in *The Sermon on the Ploughers* had: 'And I fear me this land is not yet ripe to be ploughed. For as the saying is: it lacketh weathering.'

Nowadays, we are more inclined to use, 'as the saying goes'.

Faulkner, William
American novelist (1897–1962)

1 The long hot summer.

This bright phrase rapidly turned into a journalist's cliché following the 1967 riots in the black ghettos of eighteen US cities, notably Detroit and Newark. In June of that year the Revd Dr Martin Luther King Jr warned: 'Everyone is worrying about the long hot summer with its threat of riots. We had a long cold winter when little was done about the conditions that create riots.'

The coinage follows the film title *The Long Hot Summer* (1958) and that of the spin-off TV series (1965–6). The film was based on 'The Hamlet', a story by Faulkner, published in 1928, which contained the chapter heading 'The Long Summer' (*sic*). So it is not correct to say that Faulkner 'coined' the longer phrase. Bartlett (both 1980 and 1992) suggests that there was a film with the longer title in 1928. Some mistake surely?

2 The Sound and the Fury.

Title of a novel (1929) — presumably based on Shakespeare, *Macbeth* (V.v.16): 'A tale/Told by an idiot, full of sound and fury,/Signifying nothing'.

Fawkes, Guy
English conspirator (1570–1606)

3 Desperate diseases require desperate remedies.

Commonly ascribed to Fawkes on 6 November 1605 (following his arrest on the day after he had attempted to blow up the Houses of Parliament), 'A desperate disease requires a dangerous remedy' (*DNB* wording) was apparently said by him to King James I, one of his intended victims. The King asked if he did not regret his proposed attack on the Royal Family. Fawkes replied that one of his objects was to blow the Royal Family back to Scotland. He was subsequently tried and put to death.

What he said, however, appears to have been a version of an established proverbial saying. In the form, 'Strong disease requireth a strong medicine', *ODP* traces it to 1539. In *Romeo and Juliet* (IV.i.68) (*c* 1595), Shakespeare has 'I do spy a kind of hope,/ Which craves as desperate an execution/ As

that which we would prevent' — and alludes to the saying on two other occasions.

Fellini, Federico
Italian film director and writer (1920–93)

4 La Dolce Vita [The Sweet Life].

The title of Federico Fellini's 1960 Italian film passed into the English language as a phrase suggesting a high-society life of luxury, pleasure, and self-indulgence — a precursor of the Swinging Sixties. Meaning simply 'the sweet life', it is not clear how much of a set phrase it was in Italian before it was taken up by everybody else. Compare the long-established Italian phrase *dolce far niente* [sweet idleness].

Field, Eric
English advertising practitioner (*fl.* 1914)

5 Your King and Country need you.

Field Marshal Lord Kitchener was appointed Secretary of State for War on 6 August 1914, two days after the outbreak of the First World War. He set to work immediately, intent on raising the 'New Armies' required to supplement the small standing army of the day, which would not be adequate for a major conflict. In fact, advertising for recruits had started the year before, and the *month* before, Field of the Caxton Advertising Agency had received a call from a Colonel Strachey who 'swore me to secrecy, told me that war was imminent and that the moment it broke out we should have to start at once'. That night, Field wrote an advertisement with this slogan and only the royal coat of arms as illustration. The day after war was declared — 5 August — it appeared prominently in the *Daily Mail* and other papers.

The alliterative linking of 'king' and 'country' was traditional. Francis Bacon (1625) wrote: 'Be so true to thyselfe, as thou be not false to others; specially to thy King, and Country.' In 1913, J.M. Barrie included in his play *Quality Street*: 'If . . . death or glory was the call, you would take the shilling, ma'am . . . For King and Country.'

6 Your Country Needs You!

This version of Field's slogan, accompanied by the famous drawing of Kitchener with staring eyes and pointing finger, was taken up by the Parliamentary Recruiting Committee for poster use (issued 14 September 1914). The slogan and Alfred Leete's drawing were widely imitated abroad. In the US, James Montgomery Flagg's poster of a pointing Uncle Sam bore the legend 'I want *you* for the US Army'. The British slogan also became a catchphrase used when telling a man he had been selected for a dangerous or disgusting task.

Fields, W.C.
American comedian (1879–1946)

1 *Any man who hates children and dogs can't be all bad.*

Or 'Anybody who hates dogs and babies can't be all bad'. Often ascribed to the comedian, it was, in fact, said *about* Fields by Leo Rosten (1908–   ) at a Masquer's Club dinner (16 February 1939).

2 *Elusive spondulicks.*

A phrase used by Fields in the film *The Bank Dick* (1940). 'Spondulicks' or 'spondoolicks' or 'spondulacks' was an Americanism, current by the 1850s, for money, cash. Partridge/*Slang* convincingly suggests that the origin lies in the Greek word '*spondulikos*', from the noun '*spondulos*' — a species of shell used as money in prehistory and early history.

3 *On the whole I'd rather be in Philadelphia.*

What the comedian actually submitted as a suggested epitaph to *Vanity Fair* Magazine in 1925 was: 'Here lies W.C. Fields. I would rather be living in Philadelphia.' This does not appear on his actual gravestone (which bears his name and dates only). The saying may have evolved from an older expression 'Sooner dead than in Philadelphia'.

One of the quips trotted out by President Reagan when he was lying in hospital, wounded by a would-be assassin's bullet, in March 1981 was, 'All in all, I'd rather be in Philadelphia'. The following week, the London *Times* noted that historians of humour are unclear where Fields got the quip from: 'Some believe it was made originally by . . . George Washington who became disatisfied with New York after he was chosen President in 1789. As a result of this chance remark, which he may have made to Alexander Hamilton, the capital was moved to Philadelphia.

'A chronically restless man, Washington later made a joke that has survived less well: "Come to think of it, I'd rather be on the Potomac," he told Aaron Burr. It was then that the present-day capital was built and named after him.'

4 *Never give a sucker an even break.*

This saying has been attributed to various people but has largely become associated with Fields. He is believed to have ad-libbed it in the musical *Poppy* (1923) and certainly spoke it in the film version (1936). The words are not uttered, however, in the film called *Never Give a Sucker an Even Break* (1941). Bartlett (1992) attributes the saying to Edward Francis Albee (1857–1930).

5 *It ain't a fit night out for man or beast.*

From a film called *The Fatal Glass of Beer* (1933). In a letter from Fields, dated 8 February 1944, quoted in *W.C. Fields by Himself* (1974), he states that the catchphrase was first used by him in a sketch in Earl Carroll's *Vanities* and then as the title of a picture he made for Mack Sennett. He concluded: 'I do not claim to be the originator of this line as it was probably used long before I was born in some old melodrama.'

Fillmore, Millard
American 13th President (1800–74)

6 *Peace at any price.*

'Peace at any price; peace and union' was the slogan of the American (Know-Nothing) Party in the 1856 US Presidential election. The party supported ex-President Fillmore and the slogan meant that it was willing to accept slavery for blacks in order to avoid a civil war. Fillmore lost to James Buchanan.

It has been suggested that the phrase had been coined earlier (in 1820 or 1848) by Alphonse de Lamartine, the French foreign affairs minister in his *Méditations Poétiques* in the form '*La paix à tout prix*'. However, the Earl of Clarendon quoted an 'unreasonable calumny' concerning Lord Falkland in his *History of the Rebellion* (written in 1647): 'That he was so enamoured on peace, that he would have been glad the king should have bought it at any price.' When Neville Chamberlain signed his pact with Hitler in 1938, many praised him for trying to obtain 'peace at any price.'

Fisher, Lord (Jacky)
English admiral (1841–1920)

1 *[Some day the Empire will go down because it is] Buggins's turn.*

From a letter (dated 8 January 1917), reprinted in his *Memories* (1919). He also used the expression in a letter in 1901, though he may not have originated it. The phrase gives the reason for a job appointment having been made — because it is somebody's turn to receive it rather than because the person is especially well qualified to do so. The name Buggins is used because it sounds suitably dull and humdrum. ('Joseph Buggins, Esq. J.P. for the borough' appears in one of G.W.E. Russell's *Collections and Recollections*, 1898. Trollope gave the name to a civil servant in *Framley Parsonage*, 1861. The similar sounding 'Muggins', self-applied to a foolish person, goes back to 1855, at least.)

But what do people with the name Buggins think of it? In February 1986, a Mr Geoffrey Buggins was reported to be threatening legal action over a cartoon that had appeared in the London *Standard*. It showed the husband of Margaret Thatcher looking through the New Year's Honours List and asking, 'What did Buggins do to get an MBE?' She replies: 'He thought up all those excuses for not giving one to Bob Geldof' (the pop-star and fund-raiser who only later received an Honorary KBE). The real-life Mr Buggins (who had been awarded an MBE for services to export in 1969), said from his home near Lisbon, Portugal: 'I am taking this action because I want to protect the name of Buggins and also on behalf of the Muddles, Winterbottoms and the Sillitoes of this world.' The editor of the *Standard* said: 'We had no idea there was a Mr Buggins who had the MBE. I feel sorry for his predicament, but if we are to delete Buggins's turn from the English language perhaps he could suggest an alternative.'

Fitzgerald, Edward
English poet (1809–93)

2 *A Jug of Wine, a Loaf of Bread — and Thou.*

Burnam (1980) makes the point that in Fitz-Gerald's somewhat free translation of Omar Khayyám's *Rubáiyát*, the 'thou' could refer to either sex. In Victorian times, the assumption was female, but a literal translation would make it clear that the person being addressed was, in fact, a 'comely youth'.

3 *Ah, take the cash in hand and waive the rest;*
Oh, the brave music of a distant *drum!*

A quotation scornfully applied by Aneurin Bevan to those who 'wanted to escape from awkward present conflicts altogether' and quoted by Michael Foot in his biography of Bevan. It is from the 1859 *Rubáiyát* (st. 12). Fitzgerald revised his poem so many times that it is difficult to pin him down. 'Nor heed the rumble of a distant drum!' is the 1879 version.

4 *Lost to a world in which I crave no part,*
I sit alone and commune with my heart,
Pleased with my little corner of the earth,
Glad that I came — not sorry to depart.

From the translation of *Omar Khayyám* by Richard Le Gallienne (1866–1947) — i.e. not Fitzgerald's in which the lines do not appear. Compare Psalm 4:4: 'Commune with your own heart upon your bed, and be still'. It is one of the quotations displayed on plaques in the gardens of the Villa Cimbrone, Ravello, Italy.

5 *Ah, moon of my delight that knows no wane*
The moon of heaven is rising once again.
How oft hereafter rising shall one look
Through this same garden after us in vain.

Based on Stanza 74 of the *first edition* of Fitzgerald's *Rubáiyát*. On a plaque in the garden of the Villa Cimbrone, Ravello, Italy.

Fitzgerald, F. Scott
American novelist (1896–1940)

6 *Then wear the gold hat, if that will move her;*
If you can bounce high, bounce for her too,
Till she cry 'Lover, gold-hatted, high-bouncing lover,
I must have you!'

As the epigraph to *The Great Gatsby* (1925), this is attributed to one 'Thomas Park D'Invilliers'. He remains untraced, so one wonders whether perhaps it was Fitzgerald in disguise? He did, after all, write poetry himself, some of which has been published.

See also HEMINGWAY 175:6.

Fitzpatrick, James A.
American film-maker (1902–   )

1 *And so we say farewell . . .*

The travelogues made by Fitzpatrick were a supporting feature of cinema programmes from 1925 onwards. With the advent of sound, the commentaries to 'Fitzpatrick Traveltalks' became noted for their closing words:

> And it's from this paradise of the Canadian Rockies that we reluctantly say farewell to Beautiful Banff . . .
>
> And as the midnight sun lingers on the skyline of the city, we most reluctantly say farewell to Stockholm, Venice of the North . . .
>
> With its picturesque impressions indelibly fixed in our memory, it is time to conclude our visit and reluctantly say farewell to Hong Kong, the hub of the Orient . . .

Frank Muir and Denis Norden's notable parody of the genre — 'Bal-ham — Gateway to the South' — first written for radio *c* 1948 and later performed on record by Peter Sellers (1958) accordingly contained the words, 'And so we say farewell to the historic borough . . .'.

Fleming, Ian
English novelist and journalist (1908–64)

2 *A martini shaken not stirred.*

This example of would-be sophistication became a running-joke in the immensely popular James Bond films of the 1960s and 1970s. However, the idea stems from the very first book in the series, *Casino Royale* (1953), in which Bond orders a cocktail of his own devising. It consists of one dry Martini 'in a deep champagne goblet', three measures of Gordon's gin, one of vodka — 'made with grain instead of potatoes' — and half a measure of Kina Lillet. 'Shake it very well until it's ice-cold.' Bond justifies this fussiness a page or two later: 'I take a ridiculous pleasure in what I eat and drink.

It comes partly from being a bachelor, but mostly from a habit of taking a lot of trouble over details. It's very pernickety and old-maidish really, but when I'm working I generally have to eat all my meals alone and it makes them more interesting when one takes trouble.'

This characteristic was aped by the writers of the first Bond story to be filmed — *Dr No* (1962). A West Indian servant brings Bond a vodka and Martini and says: 'Martini like you said, sir, and not stirred.' Dr No also mentions the fad, though the words are not spoken by Bond himself. In the third film, *Goldfinger* (1964), Bond (played by Sean Connery) does get to say 'a Martini, shaken not stirred' — he needs a drink after just escaping a laser death-ray — and there are references to it in *You Only Live Twice* (1967) and *On Her Majesty's Secret Service* (1969), among others.

The phrase was taken up in all the numerous parodies of the Bond phenomenon on film, TV and radio, though — curiously enough — it may be a piece of absolute nonsense. According to one expert, shaking a dry Martini 'turns it from something crystal-clear into a dreary frosted drink. It should be stirred quickly with ice in a jug.'

The *ODMQ* (1991) claimed to have discovered the source for this remark actually in one of Fleming's novels — *Dr No* (1958) ('Bond said . . . Martini — with a slice of lemon peel. Shaken and not stirred, please'), and this was taken up by Bartlett (1992). But it appears in the novels earlier than that: 'The waiter brought the Martinis, shaken and not stirred, as Bond had stipulated' (*Diamonds are Forever*, 1956).

See also KAEL 197:1.

Fletcher, John
English playwright (1579–1625)

3 *Nothing can cover his high fame but Heaven;*
No pyramids set off his memories,
But the eternal substance of his greatness.

This is the epitaph on the grave of Sir Thomas Beecham (1879–1961), the orchestral conductor. He was originally buried in Brookwood Cemetery, near Woking, but was re-interred at the parish cemetery of Limpsfield, Surrey, in April 1991. The inscription is taken from John Fletcher's play *The False One* (*c* 1620). Beecham arranged music for several productions of

Fletcher's plays and gave the Oxford Romanes Lecture on the playwright in 1956.

Fo, Dario
Italian playwright (1926–)

1 *Can't Pay Won't Pay.*

This is the English title (1981) of the play *Non Si Paga! Non Si Paga!* (1974), as translated by Lino Pertile in 1978. In 1990, it was adopted as a slogan by those objecting to the British Government's Community Charge or 'poll tax' and by other similar protest groups.

Foot, Michael
British Labour politician (1913–)

2 *Guilty Men.*

The title of a tract 'which may rank as literature' (A.J.P. Taylor), written by Foot with Frank Owen and Peter Howard under the collective pseudonym 'Cato', has passed into the language. Published in July 1940, it taunted the appeasers who had brought about the situation where Britain had had to go to war with Germany. The preface contains this anecdote: 'On a spring day in 1793 a crowd of angry men burst their way through the doors of the assembly room where the French Convention was in session. A discomforted figure addressed them from the rostrum. "What do the people desire?" he asked. "The Convention has only their welfare at heart." The leader of the angry crowd replied, "The people haven't come here to be given a lot of phrases. They demand a dozen guilty men." '
The phrase 'We *name* the guilty men' subsequently became a cliché of popular 'investigative' journalism. The 'guilty men' taunt was once much used in the 1945 General Election by the Labour Party (and was referred to in a speech by Winston Churchill in the House of Commons, 7 May 1947).

3 *Is it always his desire to give his imitation of a semi-house-trained polecat?*

Quite a good example of political abuse to show that the art is not dead. This was Foot, when leader of Britain's Labour Party, talking about Norman Tebbit, the prickly Conservative Party Chairman. Foot said it at an eve-of-poll rally in Ebbw Vale in 1983. He noted that he had said it first in the House of Commons 'a few years ago' — indeed, on 2 March 1978. Foot lost the general election overwhelmingly. Tebbit continued to bite people in the leg for a few years more.

Ford, Gerald
American Republican 38th President (1913–)

4 *There is no Soviet domination of Eastern Europe and there never will be under a Ford administration.*

In a TV debate with Jimmy Carter, the Democratic challenger for the Presidency (6 October 1976), Ford could be said to have scuppered his chances of a further term as President with this view. Pressed to elaborate, he said, 'I don't believe . . . Romanians consider themselves dominated by the Soviet Union. I don't believe that the Poles consider themselves dominated by the Soviet Union. Each of those countries is independent, autonomous . . . And the United States does not concede that those countries are under the domination of the Soviet Union.' After a couple of further clarifying statements, he finally admitted: 'I was perhaps not as precise as I should have been.'

Ford, Henry
American industrialist (1863–1947)

5 *GREAT WAR ENDS CHRISTMAS DAY. FORD TO STOP IT.*

Initially, it was thought that the First World War would not last very long. Having started in August 1914, it would be 'over by Christmas'. The fact that this promise was not fulfilled did not prevent Ford from saying, as he tried to stop the war a year later: 'We're going to try to get the boys out of the trenches before Christmas. I've chartered a ship, and some of us are going to Europe.' He was not referring to American boys because the United States had not joined the war at this stage. The *New York Tribune* encapsulated it all in the above headline. Of almost every war since, it has been said that it would be 'over by Christmas'.

6 *History is bunk.*

In the course of a libel action against the *Chicago Tribune*, which came to court in the spring of 1919 — an editorial had described Ford as an 'anarchist' and an 'ignorant idealist' — the motor magnate found himself as much on trial as the defendant. Cross-examined for no fewer than eight days, Ford was continually tripped up by his ignorance. He could not say when the United States came into being. He suggested 1812 before 1776. He was asked about a statement reported by Charles N. Wheeler in an interview with Ford on 25 May 1916: 'History is more or less bunk. It's tradition.' Ford explained: 'I did not say it was bunk. It was bunk to me . . . but I did not need it very bad.' The *Tribune* was found guilty of libel — and fined six cents.

1 Any colour as long as it's black.

To convey that there is no choice, this expresssion originated with Ford who is supposed to have said it about the Model T Ford, which came out in 1909. Hill and Nevins in *Ford: Expansion and Challenge* (1957) have him saying: 'People can have it any colour — so long as it's black.' However, in 1925, the company had to bow to the inevitable and offer a choice of colours.

Forrest, Nathan B.
American general (1821–77)

2 Firstest with the mostest.

To describe anything as 'the mostest' might seem exclusively American. However, *OED2* finds English dialect use in the 1880s and Partridge/*Slang* recognizes its use as a jocular superlative without restricting it to the US. As such, it is a consciously ungrammatical way of expressing extreme degree. Whether this was consciously the case with the Confederate general, Nathan B. Forrest, is very much in doubt. He could hardly read or write but he managed to say that the way to win battles was to be 'Firstest with the mostest', or that you needed to 'Git thar fustest with the mostest'. Bartlett (1992) gives this last as the usual rendering of the more formally reported words: 'Get there first with the most men'. In Irving Berlin's musical *Call Me Madam* (1950) there is a song with the title 'The Hostess with the Mostes' on the Ball'. One assumes that Berlin's use, like any evocation of 'the mostest' nowadays, refers back to Forrest's remark.

Forster, E.M.
English novelist (1879–1970)

3 A Passage to India.

He acknowledged that the title of his novel (1924) was derived from the title of a poem 'Passage to India' (1871) in Walt Whitman's *Leaves of Grass*.

4 Marriage is a heaven/paradise below.

Attending a Methodist wedding in 1966, I recall hearing the minister say that 'Marriage is a paradise below'. An interesting way of looking at it. In Chapter 3 of *Where Angels Fear to Tread* (1905), Forster has: 'He was passionately in love with her; therefore she could do exactly as she liked. "It mayn't be heaven below," she thought, "but it's better than Charles".' A fairly general nineteenth-century view of matters, I suppose. But in Neville Coghill's translation (1951) of Chaucer's 'The Merchant's Tale', he puts: 'For wedlock is so easy and so clean/It is a very paradise on earth.' In Chaucer's original, the second line is: 'That in this world it is a paradys.'

5 Only connect! That was the whole of her sermon. Only connect the prose and the passion, and both will be exalted, and human love will be seen at its height.

This is the epigraph to *Howard's End* (1910). Goronwy Rees wrote in *A Chapter of Accidents* (1972): 'It could be said that those two words, so misleading in their ambiguity, had more influence in shaping the emotional attitudes of the English governing class between the two world wars than any other single phrase in the English language.' The words also occur in the body of Forster's book: 'Only connect! That was the whole of her sermon. Only connect the prose and the passion, and both will be exalted, and human love will be seen at its height. Live in fragments no longer. Only connect, and the beast and the monk, robbed of the isolation that is life to either, will die.' Forster's message was that barriers of all kinds must be dismantled if the harmony lacking in modern life is to be discovered.

6 I hate causes, and if I had to choose between betraying my country and betraying my friend, I hope I should have the guts to betray my country.

In *Two Cheers for Democracy* ('What I Believe') (1938). This was quoted by the traitor Anthony Blunt when trying to persuade friends not to the tell the British authorities what they knew about the 1951 defectors, Burgess and Maclean. Goronwy

Rees (as above) replied to Blunt: 'Forster's antithesis was a false one. One's country [is] not some abstract conception which it might be relatively easy to sacrifice for the sake of an individual; it [is] itself made up of a dense network of individual and social relationships in which loyalty to one particular person formed only a single strand.' Blunt, Burgess and Maclean were part of the between-the-wars generation at Cambridge influenced by Forster's thinking.

Foster, Sir George
Canadian politician (1847–1931)

1 *In these somewhat troublesome days when the great Mother Empire stands splendidly isolated in Europe.*

A speech in the Canadian House of Commons (16 January 1896) was the occasion for the coining of the phrase 'splendid isolation', which was the headline in the London *Times* over its subsequent account. Foster was MP for North Toronto. 'A flattering Canadian conception of Britain's lonely magnificence' — Jan Morris in *Farewell the Trumpets* (1978). The 1st Lord Goschen picked up the phrase in a speech at Lewes (26 February 1896): 'We have stood here alone in what is called isolation — our splendid isolation, as one of our colonial friends was good enough to call it'.

Fox, Charles James
British politician (1749–1806)

2 *No Greek: as much Latin as you like; never French in any circumstances: no English poet unless he has completed his century.*

Fox's advice for using quotations in House of Commons speeches. Quoted in *Geoffrey Madan's Notebooks* (ed. Gere & Sparrow, 1981).

Francis of Assisi, Saint
Italian monk (*c* 1181–1226)

3 *Where there is hatred let me sow love . . .*

On first becoming Prime Minister, Margaret Thatcher stood in Downing Street on 4 May 1979 and said: 'I would just like to remember some words of St Francis of Assisi which I think are really just particularly apt at the moment — "Where there is discord, may

we bring harmony; where there is error may we bring truth; were there is doubt, may we bring faith; and where there is despair, may we bring hope."'

According to Sir Ronald Millar, one of her speechwriters, it was he who at four o'clock on Mrs Thatcher's first morning as Prime Minister gave her the words to read out, 'ignoring the advice of harder-nosed associates who thought the sentiments too trite even for that emotional occasion' (*Sunday Times*, 23 November 1980). It was inevitable that the quotation would in time be held against her.

Bartlett (1980) has a fuller version and a different translation, saying no more than that the words are 'attributed' to St Francis. In 1988, this was the version entitled 'Prayer for Peace' that was available (unattributed) in Britain on prayer cards. There was even a version on a tea-towel on sale at York Minster. At the Basilica of St Francis at Assisi, it was, of course, available in any number of languages:

> Lord, make me an instrument of your peace.
> Where there is hatred, let me sow love.
> Where there is injury, pardon.
> Where there is doubt, faith.
> Where there is despair, hope.
> Where there is darkness, light.
> Where there is sadness, joy.
>
> O Divine Master, grant that I may not so much seek
> To be consoled as to console,
> To be understood as to understand,
> To be loved as to love.
>
> For it is in giving that we receive,
> It is in pardoning that we are pardoned,
> It is in dying that we are born to eternal life.

Actually, there is some doubt as to whether St Francis had anything to do with the prayer at all. The Rt Revd Dr J.R.H. Moorman (1905–89), a former Bishop of Ripon, wrote to the *Church Times* stating that the prayer was written in France in 1912 (according to the *Observer*, 7 September 1986).

Francis II
Austrian Emperor (1768–1835)

4 *But is he a patriot for me?*

A distinguished servant of the Austrian Empire was being recommended to Francis II as a sterling patriot, so the last Holy Roman Emperor asked this. A. & V. Palmer,

Quotations in History (1976) mistakenly ascribe this to 'Francis I' but add: 'Remark on being told of the patriotic qualities of a candidate for high office, *c* 1821)'. Hence the title of John Osborne's play *A Patriot for Me* (1965).

Franklin, Benjamin
American politician and scientist (1706–90)

1 Snug as a bug in a rug.

In the July 1816 edition of the *New Monthly Magazine*, among the curious epitaphs printed from Waddington in Yorkshire (now in Lancashire) was one, 'In memory of WILLIAM RICHARD PHELPS, late Boatswain of H.M.S. Invincible. He accompanied Lord Anson in his cruise round the world, and died April 21, 1789'. It reads:

When I was like you,
For years not a few,
On the ocean I toil'd,
On the line I have broil'd
In Greenland I've shiver'd,
Now from hardship deliver'd,
Capsiz'd by old death,
I surrender'd my breath.
And now I lie snug
As a bug in a rug.

The best-known use of that final phrase is to be found seventeen years before in a *letter* from Franklin to Miss Georgiana Shipley (26 September 1772) on the death of her pet squirrel:

Here Skugg lies snug
As a bug in a rug.

However, lest it be thought that, by its inclusion in dictionaries of quotations, Franklin originated the phrase, let it be noted that there are earlier uses. In an anonymous work *Stratford Jubilee* (commemorating David Garrick's Shakespeare festival in 1769) we find:

If she [a rich widow] has the mopus's [money]
I'll have her, as snug as a bug in a rug.

Probably, however, it was an established expression even by that date, if only because in 1706 Edward Ward in *The Wooden World Dissected* had the similar 'He sits as snug a Bee in a Box' and in Thomas Heywood's play *A Woman Killed with Kindness* (1603) there is 'Let us sleep as snug as pigs in pease-straw.'
Wolfgang Mieder in *Proverbs Are Never Out of Season* (1993) has provided a useful corrective to the view that Franklin was a great coiner of proverbs. In fact, of the 1,044 proverbs in *Poor Richard's Almanack* (1740), only 5 per cent can be said to have been coined by Franklin himself.

2 Never pick a quarrel with someone who buys their ink in barrels.

Or, 'Never disagree with anyone who buys ink by the barrel' — i.e. with a journalist or professional arguer. This was attributed to Franklin by the *Observer* (27 July 1992) but remains unverified.

3 *The body*
of Benjamin Franklin, printer,
(Like the cover of an old book,
Its contents worn out,
And stript of its lettering and gilding)
Lies here, food for worms!
Yet the work itself shall not be lost,
For it will, as he believed, appear once more
In a new
And more beautiful edition,
Corrected and amended
By its Author!

An epitaph suggested for himself and written *c* 1728. Benham (1948) compares the Revd Joseph Capen (nineteenth century), 'Lines on Mr John Foster': 'Yet at the resurrection we shall see / A fair edition, and of matchless worth, / Free from erratas, new in heaven set forth.' Benham also suggests that the idea was borrowed from the Revd Benjamin Woodbridge, chaplain to Charles II, who wrote these 'Lines of John Cotton' (1652): 'O what a monument of glorious worth, / When in a new edition he comes forth, / Without erratas, may we think he'll be / In leaves and covers of eternity!'
In fact, Franklin lies with his wife under a simple inscription in Christ Church, Philadelphia: 'Benjamin and Deborah Franklin 1790.'

Fraser, Malcolm
Australian Liberal Prime Minister (1930–)

4 Life is not meant to be easy.

Fraser was Prime Minister of Australia 1975–83. The phrase was very much associated with him and was used as the title of a biography by John Edwards in 1977. Douglas Aiton asked Fraser in an interview for the London *Times* (16 March 1981) if he had ever actually said it. Fraser replied, 'I said something very like it. It's from *Back to Methuselah* by Bernard Shaw . . . A friend I was visiting in hospital asked me why I didn't give up politics and return to the good life [on his sheep farm]. I said life wasn't meant to be like that. That would be too easy. So that's what it grew from. I wouldn't mind a cent for every time it's been quoted or misquoted. It's the best thing I ever said.' Presumably, Shaw would have agreed.

The derivation from Shaw was probably an afterthought, however. (Shaw's line in the play is, 'Life is not meant to be easy, my child; but take courage: it can be delightful.') In a Deakin lecture on 20 July 1971, which seems to have been his first public use of the phrase, Fraser made no mention of Shaw. Referring rather to Arnold Toynbee's analysis of history, Fraser said: 'It involves a conclusion about the past that life has not been easy for people or for nations, and an assumption for the future that that condition will not alter. There is within me some part of the metaphysic, and thus I would add that life is not meant to be easy.'

It is not, of course, a startlingly original view. In A.C. Benson's essays *The Leaves of the Tree* (1912), he quotes Brooke Foss Westcott, Bishop of Durham, as saying: 'The only people with whom I have no sympathy . . . are those who say that things are easy. Life is not easy, nor was it meant to be.'

Freeman, Samuel
American jurist (fl. 1862–90)

1 *Never walk when you can ride, never sit when you can lie down.*

Freeman apparently served in the US Supreme Court from 1862 to 1890. Claire Rayner, the British 'agony aunt', has a longer version according to the Sister Tutor who trained her as a nurse back in the 1950s: 'Nurse, never stand when you can sit, never sit when you can lie down, and never lie if there's any chance they might find you out.' Compare GEORGE V 154:5.

Freud, Sigmund
Austrian psychiatrist (1856–1939)

2 *Two Jews were conversing about bathing. 'I take a bath once a year,' said one, 'whether I need one or not.'*

Having been told a joke concerning Elizabeth I — that she would take a bath once a month 'whether she need it or no' — the search was on to find the origin. But it turned out to be a case of an old line becoming attached to a famous person. Certainly, the story has been told of people other than the Virgin Queen. Indeed, it is quoted as an anti-Semitic joke by Freud in *Jokes and their Relation to the Unconscious* (1905). He adds, helpfully, 'It is clear that this boastful assurance of his cleanliness only betrays his sense of uncleanliness'.

3 *The great question that has never been answered and which I have not yet been able to answer, despite my thirty years of research into the feminine soul, is 'What does a woman want?'*

From a letter to Marie Bonaparte, quoted in Ernest Jones, *Sigmund Freud: Life and Work* (1955). The question became a rallying cry in the resurgence of feminism from the 1970s onwards. *What Do Women Want?* was the title of a book by Luise Eichenbaum and Susie Orbach (1983).

4 *Sometimes a cigar is just a cigar.*

This utterance remains untraced, but Ralph Keyes in *Nice Guys Finish Seventh* (1992) rather misses its point. Freud had nominated cigars as phallic symbols in dreams symbolism but — as perhaps he never said — they were not *always* to be regarded as such. Sometimes, a cigar was just a cigar.

Friedman, Milton
American economist (1912–   )

5 *There is no such thing as a free lunch.*

In the US the concept of the 'free lunch' dates back to at least 1840, according to Flexner (1976). It might have amounted to no more than thirst-arousing snacks like pretzels in saloon bars, but even so it was not strictly speaking 'free' because you had to buy a beer to obtain it. Quite at what point the saying 'There ain't no such thing as a free lunch' — meaning 'there's always a catch' or 'don't expect something for nothing' — arose is hard to say. The *ODMQ* (1991) found this in *The Moon is a Harsh Mistress*, a science fiction novel (1966) by Robert A. Heinlein:

'Oh, "tanstaafl". Means "There ain't no such thing as a free lunch." And isn't,' I added, pointing to a FREE LUNCH sign across room, 'or these drinks would cost half as much. Was reminding her that anything free costs twice as much in the long run or turns out worthless.'

But it was wrong of the *ODMQ* to proffer this as if it were the original coinage when the observation that free lunches have hidden costs was already well established. In the epilogue to his *America* (1973) Alistair Cooke ascribes to 'an Italian immigrant, when asked to say what forty years of American life had taught him' — 'There is no free lunch'.

Milton Friedman gave the saying new life in the 1970s, using it in articles, lectures and as the title of a book (1975) to support his monetarist theories. But he did not coin the phrase either, even if it came to be much associated with him.

Frohman, Charles
American theatrical producer
(1860–1915)

1 *Why fear death? It is the most beautiful adventure of life.*

These were the last words of Charles Frohman, producer of plays in Britain and America, before going down with the *Lusitania* in 1915. The words were reported by survivors and quoted in I.F. Marcosson and D. Frohman, *Charles Frohman* (1916). Undoubtedly Frohman was alluding to the line 'To die will be an awfully big adventure' in J.M. Barrie's play *Peter Pan* (1904) which Frohman had produced.

2 *For it is not right that in a house the muses haunt mourning should dwell. Such things befit us not.*

These are the words on the fountain monument to Frohman near the church (but outside the churchyard) of All Saints, Marlow, Buckinghamshire. Frohman used to spend weekends at Marlow and, indeed, expressed a wish to die and to be buried there. The monument shows a nude marble maiden, and the inscription runs round the base. J. Camp in *Portrait of Buckinghamshire* (1972) comments: 'His memorial is a graceful tribute to the female form, and a reminder of the pleasure his stage presentations gave to so many on both sides of the Atlantic in late Victorian and Edwardian days.' The inscription is a bit of an oddity but does not appear to be a quotation.

Frost, Sir David
English broadcaster (1939–   )

3 *Hello, good evening, and welcome.*

A greeting well known on both sides of the Atlantic derives from the period when Frost was commuting back and forth to host TV chat shows in London and New York, and in particular from ITV's *The Frost Programme* (1966). It may have been contrived to say three things where only one is needed, but it became an essential part of the Frost impersonator's kit (not to mention the Frost self-impersonator's kit). He was still saying it in 1983 when, with a small alteration, it became 'Hello, good *morning* and welcome!' at the debut of TV-am, the breakfast-TV station. The original phrase was used as the title of a BBC TV 'Wednesday Play' about a TV interrogator (16 October 1968), so was obviously well established by then.

The *ODMQ* (1991) wrongly ascribes *The Frost Programme* to BBC Television, whereas it was an Associated Rediffusion production.

4 *Seriously, though, he's doing a grand job!*

After a satirical attack in BBC TV's *That Was The Week That Was* (1962–3), Frost would proffer this pretend conciliation. It was taken up by clergymen and others, but Ned Sherrin, the show's producer, claims that the phrase was used on the programme no more than half a dozen times in all.

5 *The chemistry thing is really important . . . chemistry — sexual or otherwise — that is important.*

In the period prior to the start of TV-am, the British breakfast television station, in 1983, Frost talked about hoped-for new approaches to on-screen presentation. He either invented the phrase 'sexual chemistry', or merely endorsed it when it was suggested to him by a reporter, to describe what it was important for Frost and his colleagues to have. 'Personal chemistry' to describe the attraction between two people had long been remarked where it existed in other walks of life. G.B. Shaw in *You Never Can Tell* (1898) had: 'Not love: we know better than that. Let's call it chemistry . . . Well, you're attracting me irresistibly — chemically.'

Frost, Robert
American poet (1874–1963)

1 *Good fences make good neighbours.*

This proverbial thought is best known because of the poem 'Mending Wall' in Frost's *North of Boston* (1914), which includes the lines:

My apple trees will never get across
And eat the cones under his pines, I
tell him.
He only says, Good fences make good
neighbours.

The thought is an old one, as Burnham (1975) notes. E. Rogers (1640), in a letter quoted in the Winthrop Papers, wrote: 'A good fence helpeth to keepe peace between neighbours; but let us take heed that we make not a high stone wall, to keep us from meeting.' However, as Frost's poem makes clear, this is not the poet's point of view. It is the neighbour ('an old-stone savage armed') who says the line. Frost is pointing out that good fences do not necessarily make good neighbours at all: 'Before I built a wall I'd ask to know/What I was walling in or walling out.'

2 *I have promises to keep.*

Frost suffered misquotation at the hands of President Kennedy (who much admired his work, however, and had him read a poem at the 1961 Inauguration). As a rousing, uplifting end to speeches, Kennedy would frequently quote Frost's poem 'Stopping by Woods on a Snowy Evening' (1923):

The woods are lovely, dark and deep.
But I have promises to keep,
And miles to go before I sleep,
And miles to go before I sleep.

However, until Jacqueline Kennedy pointed it out to her husband, he would frequently combine the poem with another (by Emerson) and say: 'I'll hitch my wagon to a star/But I have promises to keep.' Or he would work in the venue of his speech, as in 'Iowa is lovely, dark and deep.'

[*Source:* Theodore C. Sorensen, *Kennedy*, 1965.]

3 *'Home is the place where, when you have to go there,
They have to take you in.'*

From his poem 'The Death of a Hired Man' (1914). Note the quotation marks. Compare THATCHER 332:4.

4 *Summoning artists to participate
In the august occasions of the state
Seems something artists ought to celebrate.*

At the Inaguration of President Kennedy in January 1961, Frost attempted to read a specially commissioned poem, but couldn't see to read it, so he stopped after three lines and recited another poem 'The Gift Outright' from memory. Perhaps as well, as the commissioned poem had such lines as 'A golden age of poetry and power/Of which this noonday's the beginning hour'.

5 *The land was ours before we were the land's.
She was our land more than a hundred years
Before we were her people . . .*

From 'The Gift Outright', spoken from memory by Frost at President Kennedy's inauguration (20 January 1961).

6 *Fire and Ice.*

Title of a short poem (1923) by Frost: 'Some say the world will end in fire,/Some say in ice.' Here fire = desire, ice = hate, either of which is strong enough to kill. The word combination has appealed to many over the ages. A.E. Housman in *A Shropshire Lad* (1896) had: 'And fire and ice within me fight/Beneath the suffocating night.' Dante's *Inferno* has: 'Into the eternal darkness, into fire and into ice.' Psalm 148:7 in the Book of Common Prayer has 'fire and hail'. Latterly, it has been used to refer to the death of the planet Earth by atomic warfare or a new ice age. The ice skaters Jayne Torville and Christopher Dean had a routine with the title in the late 1980s.

7 *Two roads diverged in a wood, and I —
I took the one less travelled by,
And that has made all the difference.*

From his poem 'The Road Not Taken' (1916). *The Road Less Travelled* was taken as the title of a popular work on psychotherapy by M. Scott Peck.

Fuchida, Mitsuo
Japanese pilot (1902–   )

8 *Tora-tora-tora.*

Fuchida was the leader of the Japanese attack on the US Pacific Fleet at Pearl

Harbor (7 December 1941). On confirming that the fleet was indeed being taken by surprise at dawn, he uttered this codeword to signal that the rest of the Japanese plan could be put into operation. 'Tora' means 'tiger'.

Fukuyama, Francis
American State Department official (1953–)

1 *What we may be witnessing is not the end of the Cold War but the end of history as such; that is, the end point of man's ideological evolution and the universalization of Western liberal democracy.*

The 'end of history' was a concept promoted by Fukuyama in the summer 1989 edition of the American journal *National Interest* to describe western democracy's perceived triumph over Communism in eastern Europe.

Fulbright, J. William
American politician (1905–)

2 *The Arrogance of Power.*

The title of a book (1967) questioning the basis of US foreign policy, particularly in Vietnam and the Dominican Republic. In the previous year, Fulbright — the Democratic chairman of the Senate Foreign Relations Committee — had given lectures establishing his theme: 'A psychologicial need that nations seem to have . . . to prove that they are bigger, better or stronger than other nations.'

3 *A policy that can be accurately, though perhaps not prudently, defined as one of 'peaceful co-existence'.*

From a speech in the Senate (27 March 1964), but the phrase had long been current. In 1920 Lenin had spoken of 'peaceful cohabitation with the peoples, with the workers and peasants of all nations'. In the 1950s and 1960s, the possibilty of fair competition between eastern and western ideologies was also much mooted, though whether the Soviets and the Americans meant quite the same thing by the phrase is doubtful.

4 *We must dare to think 'unthinkable' thoughts. We must learn to explore all the options and possibilities that confront us in a complex and rapidly changing world. We must learn to welcome and not to fear the voices of dissent. We must dare to think about 'unthinkable' things because when things become unthinkable, thinking stops and action becomes mindless.*

Speech in the Senate (27 March 1964). Earlier, Herman Kahn had written a book with the title *Thinking the Unthinkable* (1962). Fulbright had in mind collaboration with the Soviets on various schemes.

Fuller, Sam
American film writer and director (1912–)

5 *The film is like a battleground . . . love . . . hate . . . action . . . violence . . . death . . . In one word: emotions.*

This is a maxim spoken by Fuller in a cameo appearance in Jean-Luc Godard's film *Pierrot le Fou* (1966). It has been wrongly attributed to Nicholas Ray.

Fuller, Thomas
English preacher and historian (1608–61)

6 *Here lies Fuller's Earth.*

A punning epitaph suggested for himself by the author of *The History of the Worthies of England*. T. Webb in *A New Select Collection of Epitaphs* (1775) mentions it. Fuller was buried in the church of which he had been rector, at Cranford, West London, but it no longer survives. His actual epitaph was a sober Latin text.

Fuller, Thomas
English writer and physician (1654–1734)

7 *Be you never so high the law is above you.*

From his book *Gnomologia* (1732). During a landmark ruling in the British High Court in January 1977, Lord Denning quoted Fuller's words 'to every subject of this land, however powerful' in the matter of the 'South African mail boycott case'. He ruled that the Attorney-General, Sam Silkin, could not suspend or dispense with the execution of the law.

Funk, Walther
German Nazi minister (1890–1960)

1 Kristallnacht *[Night of Broken Glass]*.

A euphemistic but still chilling phrase attributed to Funk, Hitler's Minister of Economics, to describe the Nazi pogrom against Jews in Germany on the night of 9–10 November 1938. The cause of the pogrom was retaliation for the murder of a German diplomat by a Jew in Paris. Nazi hooligans were let loose on the streets during a night of terror in which 7,500 shops were looted, 101 synagogues were destroyed by fire and 76 demolished. In Nuremberg the synagogues were actually set on fire by the Fire Brigade.

G

Gabor, Zsa Zsa
Hungarian-born film actress (1919–)

1 *Of course, darling, return the ring —
but keep the diamonds.*

The source of this remark was sought
as a quiz question in the *Sunday Express*
Magazine (14 February 1988), but the
answer was never revealed. When subsequently the question was posed through
Godfrey Smith's column in the *Sunday
Times* in 1992, there was a 'blizzard' of
readers' letters all pointing to Gabor as the
source. She had said it on 'a TV chat show',
apparently. Could the blizzard of readers
have been thinking, rather, of Gabor's well-
attested line, 'I never hated a man enough to
give him his diamonds back'? And, surely,
the above words need to be said by a *man*?

Gaitskell, Hugh
British Labour politician (1906–63)

2 *There are some of us . . . who will fight
and fight and fight again to save the
party we love.*

When Austrian armies threatened France,
Danton exhorted his fellow countrymen to:
'Dare! and dare! and dare again!' Gaitskell,
leader of the British Labour Party, used a
similar construction memorably at the Party
Conference on 3 October 1960. When,
against the wishes of the Party leadership,
the conference looked like taking what
Gaitskell called the 'suicidal path' of uni-
lateral disarmament 'which will leave our
country defenceless and alone', he was faced
with making the most important speech of
his life — for his leadership was at stake.
Many delegates who were free to do so
changed their votes, but the Party executive
was still defeated. Nevertheless, Gaitskell

reduced his opponents to a paper victory,
and the phrase is often recalled in tribute to
a great personal achievement.

3 *It does mean, if this is the idea, the end
of Britain as an independent European
state . . . it means the end of a thousand
years of history.*

In a speech to the Labour Party Conference
(3 October 1962), Gaitskell advanced this
view of a proposal that Britain should join
the European Economic Community. It
is always dangerous these days to use the
phrase 'thousand years'. Adolf Hitler,
speaking at the Reichstag (26 April 1942)
said: 'This war . . . is one of those elemental
conflicts which usher in a new millenium
and which shake the world once in a thousand years.' Speaking on European unity (14
February 1948), Winston Churchill said:
'We are asking the nations of Europe
between whom rivers of blood have flowed,
to forget the feuds of a thousand years.' Ian
Smith, the Rhodesian Prime Minister, said
in a broadcast (20 March 1976): 'Let me
say again, I don't believe in black majority
rule ever in Rhodesia. Not in a thousand
years.' Best avoided — depending on the
company you wish to keep, of course.

Galbraith, John Kenneth
American economist (1908–)

4 *The Affluent Society.*

Galbraith's book (1958) with this title was
about the effect of high living standards on
economic theories that had been created
to deal with scarcity and poverty. The
resulting 'private affluence and public squalor' stemmed from an imbalance between
private and public sector output. For
example, there might be more cars and TV
sets but not enough police to prevent them

from being stolen. The Revd Dr Martin Luther King Jr, in a 1963 letter from gaol, used the phrase thus: 'When you see the vast majority of your twenty million Negro brothers smouldering in an airtight cage of poverty in the midst of an affluent society . . . then you will understand why we find it difficult to wait.' The notion was not new to the mid-twentieth century, however. Tacitus, in his *Annals* (*c* AD115) noted that 'many, amid great affluence, are utterly miserable', and Cato the Younger (95–46BC), when denouncing the contemporary state of Rome said: '*Habemus publice egestatem, privatim opulentiam* [public want, private wealth].'

The punning tag of 'effluent society', a commonplace by the 1980s, had appeared in Stan Gooch's poem 'Never So Good' in 1964.

1 *The Great Wall, I've been told, is the only man-made structure on earth that is visible from the moon. For the life of me I cannot see why anyone would go to the moon to look at it, when, with almost the same difficulty, it can be viewed in China.*

From an article in the *Sunday Times* Magazine (23 October 1977) — a prime example of Galbraith's laconic style. At the time, China had not opened itself up to tourism. The idea of 'the Wall of China' being 'the only work of man visible from the moon' was current by August 1939 when it was mentioned in the *Fortnightly Review*.

Galileo Galilei
Italian astronomer and physicist
(1564–1642)

2 Eppur si muove *[But it does move].*

Muttered comment after his recantation of the theory that the earth moves around the sun, in 1632. First reported in an Italian history book (1757), the remark is most unlikely ever to have passed Galileo's lips.

Garbo, Greta
Swedish-born film actress (1905–90)

3 *I want to be alone.*

Garbo claimed (in *Life* Magazine, 24 January 1955) that 'I only said, "I want to be

let alone"' — i.e. she wanted privacy rather than solitude. Oddly, as Alexander Walker observed in *Sex in the Movies* (1968): 'Nowhere in anything she said, either in the lengthy interviews she gave in her Hollywood days when she was perfectly approachable, or in the statements on-the-run from the publicity-shy fugitive she later became, has it been possible to find the famous phrase, "I want to be alone". What one can find, in abundance, later on, is "Why don't you let me alone?" and even "I want to be left alone", but neither is redolent of any more exotic order of being than a harassed celebrity. Yet the world prefers to believe the mythical and much more mysterious catchphrase utterance.'

What complicates the issue is that Garbo herself *did* employ the line several times on the screen. For example, in the 1929 silent film *The Single Standard* she gives the brush-off to a stranger and the subtitle declares: 'I am walking alone because I want to be alone.' And, as the ageing ballerina who loses her nerve and flees back to her suite in *Grand Hotel* (1932), she actually *speaks* it. Walker calls this 'an excellent example of art borrowing its effects from a myth that was reality for millions of people'.

The phrase was obviously well established by 1932 when the impressionist Florence Desmond spoke it on record in her sketch 'The Hollywood Party'. In 1935 Groucho Marx uttered it in *A Night at the Opera*. Garbo herself said, 'Go to bed, little father. We want to be alone,' in *Ninotchka* (1939). So it is not surprising that the myth has taken such a firm hold, and particularly since Garbo became a virtual recluse for the second half of her life.

4 *I think I go home.*

At one time, 'I tink I go home', spoken in a would-be Swedish accent, was as much part of the impressionist's view of Garbo as 'I want to be alone'. A caricatured Garbo was shown hugging Mickey Mouse in a cartoon film in the 1930s. She said, 'Ah tahnk ah kees you now' and 'Ah tink ah go home.' One version of how the line came to be spoken is told by Norman Zierold in *Moguls* (1969): 'After such films as *The Torrent* and *Flesh and the Devil*, Garbo decided to exploit her box-office power and asked Louis B. Mayer for a raise — from three hundred and fifty to five thousand dollars a week. Mayer offered her twenty-five hundred. "I tank I go home," said Garbo. She went back to her hotel and stayed there for a full seven months until Mayer finally gave way.'

Alexander Walker in *Garbo* (1980) recalls, rather, what Sven-Hugo Borg, the actress's interpreter, said of the time in 1926 when Mauritz Stiller, who had come with her from Sweden, was fired from directing *The Temptress*: 'She was tired, terrified and lost . . . as she returned to my side after a trying scene, she sank down beside me and said so low it was almost a whisper, "Borg, I think I shall go home now. It isn't worth it, is it?"'

Walker comments: 'That catchphrase, shortened into "I think I go home", soon passed into the repertoire of a legion of Garbo-imitators and helped publicize her strong-willed temperament.'

García Lorca, Frederico
Spanish poet (1899–1936)

1 *Bullfight critics row on row*
Crowd the vast arena full
But only one man's there who knows
And he's the man who fights the bull.

RQ (1989) reports that President Kennedy was fond of quoting these lines and attributing them thus, but adds that they are believed not to be by Lorca. The true source remains untraced.

Gardner, Ava
American actress (1922–90)

2 *On the Beach is a story about the end of the world, and Melbourne sure is the right place to film it.*

This remark was attributed to Gardner in 1959. As revealed, however, by *The Dictionary of Australian Quotations* (1984), it was in fact an invention of a Melbourne journalist, Neil Jillett. The manufacture was recounted in the *Age* (Melbourne) of 14 January 1982.

Garfield, James A.
American Republican 20th President (1831–81)

3 *From Log Cabin to White House.*

This was the title of a biography (1881) of President Garfield by the Revd William Thayer. Earlier Presidents, such as Henry Harrison and Abraham Lincoln, had used their log-cabin origins as a prop in their campaigns. Subsequently most Presidential aspirants have sought a humble 'log cabin' substitute to help them on their way.

Garner, John Nance
American Democratic Vice-President (1868–1967)

4 *[The Vice-Presidency] isn't worth a pitcher of warm piss.*

Usually bowdlerized to 'warm spit', as apparently it was by the first journalist who reported it and (invariably) by Alastair Cooke. Garner was Vice-President (1933–41) during F.D. Roosevelt's first two terms. Furthermore, Garner said, in 1963, that the job 'didn't amount to a hill of beans'.

Theo Lippman Jr in the *San Francisco Chronicle* (25 December 1992) provided this further Garner story: he was walking down the halls of the Capitol one day when the circus was in Washington. A fellow came up to him and introduced himself. 'I am the head clown in the circus,' he said. Very solemnly, Garner replied, 'And I am the Vice-President of the United States. You'd better stick around here a while. You might pick up some new ideas.'

Gay, John
English poet and playwright (1685–1732)

5 *Life is a jest, and all things show it;*
I thought so once; and now I know it.

The couplet forms part of the inscription on the pedestal of Gay's monument in Westminster Abbey. The lines were written by Gay himself, author of the hugely successful *The Beggar's Opera*.

6 *It made Gay rich and Rich gay.*

A popular view of *The Beggar's Opera*, first performed in London in 1728. It was written by Gay and produced by John Rich, the manager of Covent Garden.

Geddes, Sir Eric
British Conservative politician (1875–1937)

7 *The Germans, if this Government is returned, are going to pay every penny; they are going to be squeezed as a lemon is squeezed — until the pips squeak. My only doubt is not whether we can squeeze hard enough, but whether there is enough juice.*

Calls for reparations or 'indemnities' at the end of the First World War were fierce. Geddes, who had lately been First Lord of the Admiralty, said this in an electioneering speech at the Beaconsfield Club, Cambridge, on 10 December 1918. The previous night at the Guildhall, Cambridge, he had said the same thing in a slightly different way as part of what was obviously a stump speech: 'I have personally no doubt we will get everything out of her that you can squeeze out of a lemon and a bit more . . . I will squeeze her until you can hear the pips squeak . . . I would strip Germany as she has stripped Belgium.'

The slang term 'pip-squeak' for an insignificant, little person was current before this (by 1910). In the First World War it was also the name given to a high velocity German shell which made the noise in flight. Presumably Geddes constructed his idiom out of these earlier elements.

See also HEALEY 173:6.

Geldof, Bob
Irish musician and songwriter
(1954–   )

1 *Most people get into bands for three very simple rock and roll reasons: to get laid, to get fame, and to get rich.*

In his autobiography *Is That It?* (1986), Geldof commented on the differences between his own band, the Boom Town Rats, and other punk outfits. One was that the Rats did not mind success: 'This was not what punk bands were supposed to do. They were certainly not supposed to delight in it. I continually annoyed the purists by saying in interviews, as I had done ever since the early days in Dublin, that what I wanted out of pop music was to get rich, get famous and get laid.' The above is an example from *Melody Maker* (27 August 1977).

2 *I don't like Mondays.*

The title of a hit song written and performed by Geldof and the Boom Town Rats (1979) derives from the excuse given by Brenda Spencer, a San Diego schoolgirl, for opening fire and killing an elementary school principal and a custodian, and wounding nine others in January 1979. A journalist rang her up and asked her why she was doing it and she replied, 'Something to do. I don't like Mondays.'

3 *Do they know it's Christmas?*

Title of a song written by Bob Geldof and Midge Ure in 1984. Performed by Band Aid — an ad hoc group of pop singers and musicians — it became the UK Christmas No. 1 record in 1984 and again in 1989. In 1984, by drawing attention to those suffering in the Ethiopian civil war and famine, it laid the foundations of the Band Aid concert in July 1985.

George V
British Sovereign (1865–1936)

4 *Wake up England!*

In a speech at the Guildhall, London, on 5 December 1901 — four days before he was created Prince of Wales — the then Duke of York, on returning from an Empire tour, warned against taking the Empire for granted: 'To the distinguished representatives of the commercial interests of the Empire . . . I venture to allude to the impression which seemed generally to prevail among our brethren overseas, that the old country must wake up if she intends to maintain her old position of pre-eminence in her Colonial trade against foreign competitors.' This statement was encapsulated by the popular press in the phrase 'Wake up, England!' which George did not precisely say himself. *Punch* was still using the phrase the following year (Vol. 123).

5 *Never miss an opportunity to relieve yourself; never miss a chance to sit down and rest your feet.*

In *A King's Story* (1951), George's son and heir (who became the Duke of Windsor) wrote: 'Perhaps one of the only positive pieces of advice that I was ever given was that supplied by an old courtier who observed: "Only two rules really count. Never miss an opportunity to relieve yourself; never miss a chance to sit down and rest your feet".' The 'old courtier' may well in fact have been George V himself, to whom this advice has also been attributed directly. A correspondent who wished to remain anonymous told me in 1981 that a naval officer of her acquaintance who was about to accompany Prince George, Duke of Kent, on a cruise, was asked by George V to make sure that the Prince was properly dressed before going ashore. He also advised: 'Always take an opportunity to relieve yourselves.' Another correspondent suggested, rather, that King Edward VII was the first to say this when he was Prince of Wales.

On the other hand, more than a century earlier, the 1st Duke of Wellington had said: 'Always make water when you can.'

1 *My father was frightened of his mother, I was frightened of my father, and I'm damned well going to make sure that my children are frightened of me.*

Quoted by Randolph Churchill in *Lord Derby: King of Lancashire* (1960). Doubt has been cast on the likelihood of George V saying this.

2 *Bugger Bognor!*

What the King said in reply to a suggestion that his favourite watering place be dubbed Bognor Regis, c 1929. They are not his dying words, as often supposed. For example, Auberon Waugh in his *Private Eye* diary entry dated 9 August 1975 stated: 'Shortly before the King died, a sycophantic courtier said he was looking so much better he should soon be well enough for another visit to Bognor, to which the old brute replied "Bugger Bognor" and expired.'

The dating is given by Kenneth Rose in his biography *George V* (1983) where it is linked to the King's recuperative visit to Bognor after his serious illness in the winter of 1928–9: 'A happier version of the legend rests on the authority of Sir Owen Morshead, the King's librarian. As the time of the King's departure from Bognor drew near, a deputation of leading citizens came to ask that their salubrious town should henceforth be known as Bognor Regis.

'They were received by Stamfordham, the King's private secretary, who, having heard their petition, invited them to wait while he consulted the King in another room. The sovereign responded with the celebrated obscenity, which Stamfordham deftly translated for the benefit of the delegation. His Majesty, they were told, would be graciously pleased to grant their request.'

3 *No more coals to Newcastle, no more Hoares to Paris.*

A rare example of a royal joke comes from the period just before George V's death. In December 1935, it was revealed that Sir Samuel Hoare, the Foreign Secretary, had come to an arrangement with M. Laval, his French counterpart, whereby Abyssinia

was virtually to be consigned to the Italians behind the League of Nations' back. The Hoare-Laval Pact had been concluded in Paris when Sir Samuel was passing through on his way to a holiday in Switzerland. In the furore that followed he had to resign. The King may have been repeating a remark that was current anyway and it is surely unlikely that he made it direct to Hoare himself, despite Lord Avon's recollection of what the King told him (in *Facing the Dictators*, 1962).

4 *How is the Empire?*

This is the leading contender for the King's *actual* last, dying words. But, oddly enough, there are several others. On Monday 20 January 1936, a few members of the Privy Council gathered in the King's bedroom at Sandringham to witness the signing of a proclamation constituting a Council of State. The King was so weak it took a long time. To the Privy Councillors he murmured: 'Gentlemen, I am sorry for keeping you waiting like this — I am unable to concentrate.' These are sometimes referred to as his last words.

The King died just before midnight. The next day, Stanley Baldwin, the Prime Minister, broadcast a tribute which included a different version of the deathbed words: 'There is one thing I can tell you without any impropriety, for though much, and most indeed, of what passes near the end is sacred . . . I think I may tell you this. The King was having brief intervals of consciousness, and each time he became conscious it was some kind enquiry or kind observation of someone, some words of gratitude for kindness shown. But he did say to his Secretary [Lord Wigram] when he sent for him, "How is the Empire?" — an unusual phrase in that form. And the Secretary said: "All is well, sir, with the Empire," and the King gave him a smile and relapsed once more into unconsciousness.'

Other accounts make it clear that the wonderfully imperial inquiry arose *before* the Privy Council meeting. One of them suggests that only the word 'Empire' was audible and the rest of the inquiry merely assumed by the King's Secretary. Lord Dawson, the King's physician, reported in his diary yet another version of the last words: 'God damn you.' Could this possibly relate to Margot Asquith's celebrated dictum? (ASQUITH 34:1).

See also DAWSON 115:2.

George, David Lloyd
(later 1st Earl Lloyd George of Dwyfor)
British Liberal Prime Minister
(1863–1945)

1 *This is the leal and trusty mastiff which is to watch over our interests, but which runs away at the first snarl of the trade unions? A mastiff? It is the right hon. Gentleman's Poodle. It fetches and carries for him. It barks for him. It bites anybody that he sets it on to.*

Lloyd George spoke in the House of Commons on 26 June 1907 in the controversy over the power of the upper House. He questioned the House of Lords' role as a 'watchdog' of the constitution and suggested that A.J. Balfour, the Conservative leader, was using the party's majority in the upper chamber to block legislation by the Liberal government (in which Lloyd George was president of the Board of Trade). As such it is encapsulated in the phrase 'Mr Balfour's poodle'.

2 *Sporting terms are pretty well understood wherever English is spoken . . . Well, then. The British soldier is a good sportsman . . . Germany elected to make this a finish fight with England . . . The fight must be to a finish — to a knock out.*

As Secretary of State for War, Lloyd George gave an interview to Roy W. Harris, President of the United Press of America. It was printed in *The Times* (29 September 1915). Lloyd George was asked to 'give the United Press, in the simplest possible language, the British attitude toward the recent peace talk'. Hence, the particular form of the above remarks. In his memoirs, Lloyd George entitled one chapter 'The Knock-out Blow' — which is how this notion was popularly expressed.

3 *What is our task? To make Britain a fit country for heroes to live in.*

This is precisely what Lloyd George said in a speech at Wolverhampton on 24 November 1918. It turned into the better known slogan 'A land fit for heroes' or, occasionally, 'A country fit for heroes.' By 1921, with wages falling in all industries, the sentiment was frequently recalled and mocked.

4 *Lloyd George knew my father.*

Even before Lloyd George's death in 1945, Welsh people away from home liked to claim some affinity with the Great Man. In time, this inclination was encapsulated in the singing of the words 'Lloyd George knew my father, my father knew Lloyd George' to the strains of 'Onward Christian Soldiers', which they neatly fit. In Welsh legal and Liberal circles the credit for this happy coinage has been given to Tommy Rhys Roberts QC (1910–75), whose father did indeed know Lloyd George. Arthur Rhys Roberts was a Newport solicitor who set up a London practice with Lloyd George in 1897. The partnership continued for many years, although on two occasions Lloyd George's political activities caused them to lose practically all their clients.
The junior Rhys Roberts was a gourmet, a wine-bibber and of enormous girth. Martin Thomas QC, a prominent Welsh liberal of the next generation, recalled: 'It was, and is a tradition of the Welsh circuit that there should be, following the after-dinner speeches, a full-blooded sing-song. For as long as anyone can remember, Rhys Roberts's set-piece was to sing the phrase to the tune of "Onward Christian Soldiers" — it is widely believed that he started the practice . . . By the 'fifties it had certainly entered the repertoire of Welsh Rugby Clubs. In the 'sixties, it became customary for Welsh Liberals to hold a Noson Lawen, or sing-song, on the Friday night of the Liberal Assemblies. It became thoroughly adopted in the party. I recall it as being strikingly daring and new in the late 'sixties for Young Liberals to sing the so-called second verse, "Lloyd George knew my mother". William Douglas-Home's play *Lloyd George Knew My Father* was produced in London in 1972. One of the leading Welsh Silks recalls persuading Rhys Roberts to see it with him.'
From Robert Robinson, *Landscape with Dead Dons* (1956): 'He had displayed a massive indifference to the rollicking scientists who would strike up *Lloyd George Knew My Father* in a spirit of abandoned wickedness.'

5 *Ninepence for fourpence.*

A political slogan dating from 1908–9 when the Welfare State was being established in Britain. The phrase indicated how people stood to benefit from their contributions to the new National Health Insurance scheme.

Associated with Lloyd George and said by A.J.P. Taylor (in *Essays in English History*) to have been snapped up from an audience interruption and turned into a slogan by him.

Gibbon, Edward
English historian (1737–94)

1 *Such was the public consternation when the barbarians were hourly expected at the gates of Rome.*

Nowadays, the phrase 'barbarians at the gates' is commonly used to describe a situation when the end of civilization is alleged to be at hand. In 1990 it was used as the title of a book about goings-on in Wall Street (subtitled 'The Fall of RJR Nabisco', by Bryan Burrough), suggesting that unregulated behaviour had broken out. It is just one of those ideas which seems always to have been there, but there is a good example (as above) in Book 1 of Gibbon's *Decline and Fall of the Roman Empire* (1776–88). Is there a variation, 'The Goths are in the citadel/capitol'?

2 *Twenty-two acknowledged concubines, and a library of sixty-two thousand volumes, attested the variety of his inclinations, and from the productions which he left behind him, it appears that the former as well as the latter were designed for use rather than ostentation.*

An example of Gibbon's stony-faced sense of humour, on the Emperor Gordian, from Chapter VII of *The Decline and Fall of the Roman Empire* (1776–88). In a footnote, Gibbon adds: 'By each of his concubines, the younger Gordian left three or four children. His literary productions were by no means contemptible.'

3 *After a powerful struggle, I yielded to my fate. I sighed as a lover, I obeyed as a son.*

From *Memoirs of My Life* (1796). As a young man, Gibbon fell for Mlle Suzanne Curchod (later the wife of Jacques Necker, the French statesman) at Lausanne, Switzerland, in 1757. But he did not get married to her because of his father's objections.

Gilbert, Sir Humphrey
English navigator (1537–83)

4 *We are as near to heaven by sea as by land!*

Quoted in Richard Hakluyt, *Third and Last Volume of the Voyages . . . of the English Nation* (1600). Gilbert's ship sank on his return from Newfoundland where he had founded an English colony at St John's. He said this to put heart into his men as their ship *Squirrel* foundered. Compare what Friar Elstow is reported to have said when threatened with drowning by Henry VIII: 'With thanks to God we know the way to heaven, to be as ready by water as by land, and therefore we care not which way we go' (recounted by John Stow, *The Annals of England*, but not until 1615).

Gilbert, (Sir) W.S.
English writer and lyricist (1836–1911)

5 *Funny without being vulgar.*

A Quaker singer, David Bispham, noted in his *Recollections* (1920) that he had heard Gilbert say something like this to Sir Henry Beerbohm Tree about his Hamlet. On the stage of the Haymarket Theatre, London, after the first performance, Gilbert said: 'My dear fellow, I never saw anything so funny in my life, and yet it was not in the least vulgar.'
At the time, the line quickly went round in its abbreviated form, and apparently Tree put up a brave show of not being offended. He wrote to Gilbert on 25 March 1893:

> By the bye, my wife told me that you were under the impression that I might have been offended at some witticism of yours about my Hamlet. Let me assure you it was not so. On the contrary, it was I believe *I* who circulated the story. There could be no harm, as I knew you had not seen me act the part, and moreover, while I am a great admirer of your wit, I have also too high an opinion of my work to be hurt by it.

Hesketh Pearson in his 1956 biography of Tree seems to think this letter shows the actor claiming not only to have circulated the story against himself but to have *invented* it. On the other hand, Pearson in his biography of Gilbert and Sullivan does report that Bernard Shaw told him that Gilbert complained shortly before his death

(1911) of the way ill-natured witticisms had been fathered on him and instanced the description of Tree. There seems little doubt, though, that he did say it.

Shaw himself had used the phrase in a review of pantomime in *London Music* on 23 January 1897: 'Pray understand that I do not want the pantomime artists to be "funny without being vulgar". That is the mere snobbery of criticism. Every comedian should have vulgarity at his fingers' ends.'

J.B. Booth in *Old Pink 'Un Days* (1924) recalled an exchange in a London theatre after Pavlova's successes when a a large lady from Oldham or Wigan was attempting to pass herself off as a Russian dancer. 'What do you think of her?' asked one. Came the reply, 'Funny without being Volga.'

1 *When I am lying awake at night, and the pale moonlight streams through the latticed casement, strange fancies crowd upon my poor mad brain, and I sometimes think that if we could hit upon some word for you to use whenever I am about to relapse — some word that teems with hidden meaning — like 'Basingstoke' — it might recall me to my saner self.*

So says the character Mad Margaret in Gilbert and Sullivan's *Ruddigore* (1887). The mention of the place still raises a laugh, being one of those English names which, from sound alone, is irresistibly funny. Others would include Chipping Sodbury, Godalming, Scunthorpe, Wigan and Surbiton. More recently Neasden has joined the select band. However, it has been suggested that the modest Hampshire town had another claim upon the laughter of the original *Ruddigore* audience. Possibly the Conservative Party had recently held its annual conference there? Ian Bradley in his *Annotated Gilbert and Sullivan: 2* (1984) makes no mention of this theory and dismisses a suggestion that it was because Basingstoke had a well-known mental hospital, on the grounds that this had not been built in 1887. He relays another theory that Gilbert's father had featured the town in his novel *The Doctor of Beauvoir*, and that his father and sister lived in Salisbury, which would have necessitated his passing through Basingstoke when paying visits.

A magazine called *Figaro* reporting on rehearsals for *Ruddigore* in December 1886 made mention of a character called Mad Margaret 'with that blessed word Barnstaple' — which suggests that Basingstoke was not Gilbert's first choice.

Basingstoke had already rated a mention in Shakespeare (*Henry IV, Part 2*, II.i.169), but with rather less comic result.

2 *Youth must have its fling.*

Meaning 'let the young enjoy themselves while they can', this proverbial saying appears in Gilbert's lyrics for *The Pirates of Penzance* (1879):

I pray you, pardon me, ex-Pirate King,
Peers will be peers, and youth must
   have its fling

and *The Mikado* (1885): 'But youth, of course, must have its fling'. Gilbert greatly enjoyed proverbs and, indeed, wrote two songs completely made up of them. In this instance, he appears to have created a more memorable version of the older proverbs 'Youth will have his course' (known from the sixteenth century) and 'Youth will be served' (though this latter did not appear until the early nineteenth century). In *The Water Babies* (1863), Charles Kingsley has:

When all the world is young lad
And all the trees are green:
. . . Young blood must have its
   course, lad
And every dog his day.

John Ray's *Compleat Collection of English Proverbs* (1670) has 'Youth will have its swing' (as a version of 'youth will have its course'), which means much the same as 'fling'.

3 *Now Bach is decomposing.*

In the archaeology of humour one is never really going to know who first cracked a joke. Nevertheless, as it can be dated, why not allow Gilbert to claim credit for originating a famous exchange? On a visit to the United States with Arthur Sullivan in 1879–80, Gilbert was told by a matron at a dinner party, 'Your friend Mr Sullivan's music is really too delightful. It reminds me so much of dear Baytch [Bach]. Do tell me: what is Baytch doing just now? Is he still composing?'

'Well, no, madam,' Gilbert returned, 'just now, as a matter of fact, dear Baytch is by way of decomposing.' This, at any rate, is how the joke appears in *Gilbert and Sullivan* by Hesketh Pearson (1947).

1 *Are you old enough to marry, do you think?*
Won't you wait till you are eighty in the shade?

No more than a catchphrase used to express extreme temperature. However, one notes that it is alluded to comically with regard to age rather than temperature in Gilbert and Sullivan's *The Mikado* (1885). Ko-Ko asks Katisha the above. There is also a song 'Charming Weather' in Lionel Monckton's *The Arcadians* (1908) with the lines:

> Very, very warm for May
> Eighty in the shade they say,
> Just fancy!

2 *His foe was folly & his weapon wit.*

This is inscribed on Gilbert's memorial on the Victoria Embankment, London, and the line was provided in 1915 by Anthony Hope (Sir Anthony Hope Hawkins, author of *The Prisoner of Zenda*), who recalled: 'Whilst on the committee of the Authors' Society I had something to do with the memorial. The words on the memorial are mine, except that I put them first into prose — "Folly was his foe, and wit his weapon", — then somebody (I forget who) pointed out that transposed they would make a line, and this was adopted.'

See also GRAHAME 164:1.

Ginsberg, Allen
American poet and novelist (1926–)

3 *I saw the best minds of my generation destroyed by madness, starving hysterical naked,*
dragging themselves through the negro streets at dawn looking for an angry fix,
angelheaded hipsters burning for the ancient heavenly connection to the starry dynamo in the machinery of the night.

From *Howl* (1956), a Jeremiad which has been described as the opening salvo of the Beat Generation. Ginsberg denounces the mechanistic dehumanization of a society whose God is Moloch, demanding human sacrifice.

4 *Liverpool is at the present moment the centre of the consciousness of the human universe.*

Attributed remark *c* 1964, when the Beatles were at their most famous. Quoted in *The Liverpool Scene* (ed. Edward Lucie-Smith, 1967).

Glasgow, Ellen
American novelist (1874–1945)

5 *In This Our Life.*

This is the puzzling title of a 1942 American film based on Glasgow's novel about a neurotic girl who, according to one plot summary, 'steals her sister's husband, leaves him in the lurch, dominates her hapless family and is killed while on the run from the police'. Glasgow's novel gives no clue as to the relevance of the title, and does not even have a quotation as an epigraph, but the 'this our life' formula goes back to the sixteenth century at least. Within one scene, Shakespeare's *As You Like It* (II.i) has 'And this our life' and 'Yea, and of this our life'. Even earlier, the Preface to Thomas Cranmer's Book of Common Prayer (1549) employs the phrase 'in this our time'. So perhaps it was from some religious source? The Revd Francis Kilvert, the diarist, used the expression 'in that her young life' on 26 March 1872.
   The exact phrase occurs in George Meredith's poem Modern Love (1862):

> Ah, what a dusty answer gets the soul
> When hot for certainties in this our
> life!

It also occurs earlier in Thomas Carlyle's *Sartor Resartus* (1831): 'To me, in this our life . . . which is an internecine warfare with the Time-spirit, other warfare seems questionable.' And exactly also in Thomas Heywood's poem 'The Hierarchy of the Blessed Angels' (1635). All this would seem to indicate that it was just an old phrase rather than a quotation when used as the title of Glasgow's novel.

Godard, Jean-Luc
French film director (1930–)

6 *Movies should have a beginning, a middle and an end, but not necessarily in that order.*

ODQ (1992) has this being said to Georges Franju and quoted in *Time* (14 September

1981), but 'Every film should have a beginning, a middle and an end — but not necessarily in that order' was quoted in Len Deighton, *Close Up* (1972).

Godley, A.D.
English classicist (1856–1925)

1 *What is this that roareth thus?*
Can it be a motor bus?

There are many versions of Godley's macaronic which beginneth thus. The *ODQ* (1992), which prints only part of it, gives the source as a letter the English classicist sent to C.R.L. Fletcher on 10 January 1914, reprinted in *Reliquiae* (1926). The magazine *Oxford Today* (Michaelmas Term 1992) took the trouble to find a complete, definitive version. :

> What is this that roareth thus?
> Can it be a Motor Bus?
> Yes, the smell and hideous hum
> Indicat Motorem Bum!
> Implet in the Corn and High
> Terror me Motoris Bi:
> Bo Motori clamitabo
> Ne Motore caedar a Bo —
> Dative be or Ablative
> So thou only let us live:
> Whither shall thy victims flee?
> Spare us, spare us, Motor Be!
> Thus I sang; and still anigh
> Came in hordes Motores Bi,
> Et complebat omne forum
> Copia Motorum Borum.
> How shall wretches live like us
> Cincti Bis Motoribus?
> Domine, defende nos
> Contra hos Motores Bos!

The references to the Corn and High locate the poet in Oxford, where he taught most of his life. Motor buses were first introduced to Oxford in 1913, so Godley would seem to have developed a rapid dislike of them.

Goebbels, Joseph
German Nazi leader (1897–1945)

2 *We can do without butter, but, despite all our love of peace, not without arms. One cannot shoot with butter, but with guns.*

From a translation of his speech, given in Berlin (17 January 1936). When a nation is under pressure to choose between material comforts and some kind of war effort, the choice has to be made between 'guns *and* butter'. Some will urge 'guns *before* butter'. Later that same year, Hermann Goering said in a broadcast, 'Guns will make us powerful; butter will only make us fat', so he may also be credited with the 'guns or butter' slogan.

But there is a third candidate. Airey Neave in his book *Nuremberg* (1978) stated of Rudolf Hess: 'It was he who urged the German people to make sacrifices and coined the phrase: "Guns before butter".'

Goering, Hermann
German Nazi leader (1893–1946)

3 *When I hear the word Culture, I reach for my pistol.*

Although Goering is often linked with this remark, it comes, in fact, from a play by an unsuccessful Nazi playwright, Hanns Johst (1890–1978), who was president of the Reich Chamber of Literature, a group of authors, translators and publishers which excluded those who refused to toe the party line. In 1933, he wrote *Schlageter*, a play about a martyr of the French occupation of the Ruhr after the First World War. A storm-trooper's line '*Wenn ich Kultur höre . . . entsichere ich meinen Browning*' is more accurately translated as 'When I hear the word "culture", I release the safety catch of' — or 'I cock' — 'my Browning' (automatic rifle).

Goethe, Johann Wolfgang von
German poet, novelist and playwright (1749–1832)

4 *Then indecision brings its own delays,*
And days are lost lamenting o'er lost days.
Are you in earnest? Seize this very minute;
What you can do, or dream you can, begin it;
Boldness has genius, power and magic in it.

Translation from *Faust* (1808). The last sentence is especially popular in motivational writings. It is spoken by the Manager in the 'Prelude at the Theatre' in John Anster's translation (1835).

Goldoni, Carlo
Italian playwright (1707–93)

1 The Servant of Two Masters.

English title of the Goldoni's play *Il Servitore Di Due Padroni*. The presumed origin is 'No man can serve two masters' (Matthew 6:24 and Luke 16:13). Compare: 'He who serves two masters has to lie to one of them' — Portuguese proverb; 'It is better to obey the laws of one master than to seek to please several' — Catherine the Great; 'Not bound to swear allegiance to any master, wherever the wind takes me I travel as a visitor' — Horace.

Goldsmith, Sir James
British businessman (1933–   )

2 If you pay peanuts, you get monkeys.

This remark — in connection with the pay given to journalists on his short-lived news magazine *Now!* (*c* 1980) — is not original. The modern proverb was in use by 1966.

Goldsmith, Oliver
Irish-born playwright and writer (1730–74)

3 The Citizen of the World.

This was the title of a collection of letters by Goldsmith purporting to be those of Lien Chi Altangi, a philosophic Chinaman living in London and commenting on English life and characters. They were first published as 'Chinese Letters' in the *Public Ledger* (1760–1), and then again under the above title in 1762. Earlier, *OED2* finds the phrase in Caxton (1474); and 'If a man be gracious and courteous to strangers, it shows he is a citizen of the world' in Francis Bacon's 'Goodness, and Goodness of Nature' (1625). Even earlier, 'I am citizen, not of Athens or Greece, but of the world' is ascribed to Socrates. Cicero has '*civem totius mundi*', meaning 'one who is cosmopolitan, at home anywhere'. James Boswell, not unexpectedly, in his *Journal of a Tour to the Hebrides* (1786) reflects: 'I am, I flatter myself, completely a citizen of the world . . . In my travels through Holland, Germany, Switzerland, Italy, Corsica, France, I never felt myself from home; and I sincerely love "every kindred and tongue and people and nation".'

4 Ill fares the land, to hast'ning ills a prey, Where wealth accumulates, and men decay.

From *The Deserted Village* (1770), Goldsmith's view of the depopulation of villages caused by mercantilism and the drift to the cities. In many cases, the 'bold peasantry, their country's pride' had been forced into emigration. Later, a film by Bill Bryden about people leaving the island of St Kilda, off the west coast of Scotland, had the title *Ill Fares the Land* (1982).

5 At church, with meek and unaffected grace, His looks adorn'd the venerable place; Truth from his lips prevailed with double sway, And fools, who came to scoff, remained to pray.

From *The Deserted Village* also. The origin of the expression 'fools who come to scoff and remain to pray', meaning people who undergo some kind of conversion or change of heart. (From Clive James, *The Crystal Bucket*, 1981: 'I came to mock *Dallas* but stayed to pray.')

6 As for murmurs, mother, we grumble a little now and then, to be sure. But there's no love lost between us.

Tony Lumpkin says this to his mother, Mrs Hardcastle, in *She Stoops to Conquer*, IV.i (1773). The editor of the New Mermaids edition (1979) states that Goldsmith coined the phrase 'No love lost', but this is true neither of the literal sense nor of the current ironic, opposite one. The *OED2* finds uses of the phrase in both senses over a century before Goldsmith's play.

Goldwater, Barry M.
American Republican politician (1909–   )

7 I would remind you that extremism in the defence of liberty is no vice. And let me remind you also that moderation in the pursuit of justice is no virtue.

Accepting his party's nomination for the Presidency, San Francisco Convention (16 July 1964), Goldwater's extremist tag-line did him no good in the subsequent election. Lyndon Johnson beat him with a landslide and rejoined: 'Extremism in pursuit of the Presidency is an unpardonable vice.

Moderation in the affairs of the nation is the highest virtue' (Speech, New York, 31 October 1964).

Perhaps Goldwater would have done better to quote Thomas Paine's *The Rights of Man* (1792), directly: 'A thing moderately good is not so good as it ought to be. Moderation in temper is always a virtue; but moderation in principle is always a vice.' To give him his due, Goldwater disclaimed any originality, saying the idea could be found in Cicero and in Greek authors.

Goldwyn, Sam
Polish-born American film producer (1882–1974)

1 *The reason so many people showed up at his funeral was because they wanted to make sure he was dead.*

Goldwyn's remark on Louis B. Mayer's funeral (quoted in Bosley Crowther, *Hollywood Rajah*, 1960) is probably apocryphal, if only because the funeral was in fact sparsely attended.

2 *An oral [or verbal] contract isn't worth the paper it's written on.*

Samuel Goldwyn Jr (interviewed by Michael Freedland in *TV Times*, 13 November 1982) has commented on the 'twenty-eight' genuine sayings attributed to his father and included this as one. Carol Easton in *The Search for Sam Goldwyn* (1976) claims that what he actually said about fellow mogul Joseph L. Mankiewicz was: 'His verbal contract is worth more than the paper it's written on.'

3 *In two words — impossible!*

Sam Goldwyn Jr was doubtful about this one. According to Alva Johnston, quoted in Norman Zierold, *The Moguls* (1969), this joke appeared in a humour magazine late in 1925, and was subsequently imposed upon Goldwyn.

4 *Bloody and thirsty.*

The story is told that when James Thurber was arguing with Goldwyn over the amount of violence that had crept in to a film treatment of his story *The Secret Life of Walter Mitty*, eventually released in 1947, Goldwyn said, 'I'm sorry you felt it was too bloody and thirsty'. Thurber, with commendable presence of mind, replied, 'Not only did I think so, I was horror and struck.' For some reason, Boller & George, *They Never Said It* (1989), doubt whether this exchange took place, because 'Goldwyn secretaries would have weeded out the solecism'. But who says it was a written exchange? Arthur Marx in *Goldwyn: A Biography of the Man Behind the Myth* (1976), apparently.

5 *Include me out.*

This apparently arose when Goldwyn and Jack L. Warner were in disagreement over a labour dispute. Busby Berkeley, who had made his first musical for Goldwyn, was discovered moonlighting for Warner Brothers. Goldwyn said to Warner: 'How can we sit together and deal with this industry if you're going to do things like this to me? If this is the way you do it, gentlemen, include me out!'

Scott Berg, working on the official biography, told the *Sunday Times* (3 May 1981) that he claimed the ability to tell which Goldwynisms are genuine and suggested this one *may* be, as Goldwyn himself might appear to have acknowledged when speaking at Balliol College, Oxford, on 1 March 1945: 'For years I have been known for saying "Include me out" but today I am giving it up for ever.' On the other hand, Boller & George, *They Never Said It* (1989), report Goldwyn as having denied saying it and claiming rather to have said to members of the Motion Picture Producers and Distributors of America: 'Gentlemen, I'm withdrawing from the association.'

Gordon, Adam Lindsay
Australian poet (1833–70)

6 *I've had my share of pastime, and I've*
    done my share of toil,
And life is short.
. . . And none will weep when I go
    forth,
Or smile when I return.

The first line and a half are from 'The Sick Stockrider' (written 1869). The remaining two lines remain untraced and are not from this poem.

Grade, Lew
(later Lord Grade)
Russian-born British media tycoon (1906–   )

7 *It would have been cheaper to lower the Atlantic.*

Grade produced a famously expensive and unsuccessful film called *Raise the Titanic* (1980). He is supposed to have commented, ruefully, the above. Alas, on TV-am's *Frost on Sunday* (23 November 1987), Grade denied having said it. All he had actually managed was, 'I didn't raise the Titanic high enough'.

Graham, D.M.
British former undergraduate
(1911–)

1 *That this House will in no circumstances fight for its King and Country.*

Hitler came to power in January 1933. On 9 February, the Oxford Union Debating Society carried this motion by 275 votes to 153. Graham was the Librarian that term and worded the motion. It has been suggested that this pacifist rather than disloyal motion, although adopted by an unrepresentative group of young people, encouraged Hitler to believe that his programme of conquests would go unchallenged by the British. There appears to be no evidence that Hitler ever referred to the Oxford Union debate, though Goebbels and his propaganda ministry certainly knew of it. As a result, Churchill wrote in *The Second World War* (1948): 'In Germany, in Russia, in Italy, in Japan, the idea of a decadent, degenerate Britain took deep root and swayed many calculations.' Erich von Richthofen confirmed this view in the *Daily Telegraph* (4 May 1965): 'I am an ex-officer of the old Wehrmacht and served on what you would call the German General Staff at the time of the Oxford resolution. I can assure you, from personal knowledge, that no other factor influenced Hitler more and decided him on his course than that "refusal to fight for King and Country", coming from what was assumed to be the intellectual élite of your country.'

Sir John Colville, Churchill's Private Secretary during the war, recalled in a letter to *The Times* (12 February 1983): 'At Tubingen University in July 1933, I was contemptuously informed by a group of Nazi students that my contemporaries and I would never fight; and the Oxford debate was quoted in evidence.'

On the other hand, Sir Hugh Greene, Berlin correspondent of the *Daily Telegraph* (1934–9) commented in 1983: 'Obviously one did not have the opportunity of discussing the matter with Hitler personally, but one did talk from time to time with high Nazi officials and members of the German armed forces. I am sure that the subject was never mentioned. Why should Hitler concern himself with Oxford undergraduates when he could base his thinking on the attitude of British ministers?'

Mussolini is known, however, to have referred to the debate several times.

Graham, Philip L.
American newspaper publisher
(1915–63)

2 *News [or journalism] is the first [rough] draft of history.*

From the *Washington Post* (24 November 1985): 'The summit coverage was textbook stuff of the "journalism-as-first-draft-of-history" variety'. And on 28 February 1988: 'A daily newspaper such as the *Post* is, as someone once put it, the first rough draft of history.' From the *Washington Post* (10 July 1988): 'The newspaper, *Post* executives have often reminded us, is merely a "first rough draft of history".' From the editor of Britain's ITN in *The Times* (21 December 1990): 'Journalism is the first draft of history.' From *The Times* (27 April 1991): 'When foreign governments want to know what matters are weighing on the minds of the US establishment, they have always turned to the *New York Times*, the sober "grey lady" which has been recording America's first draft of history for the past 140 years.' From the *Washington Post* (29 September 1991): 'Daily journalism is "the first rough draft of history", in the phrase of former *Washington Post* publisher, Philip Graham.'

The phrase has also been attributed to Ben Bradlee (*b* 1921), an editor of the *Washington Post*.

Grahame, Kenneth
Scottish-born writer (1859–1932)

3 *The Piper at the Gates of Dawn.*

The first album recorded by Pink Floyd in 1967 took its title — in somewhat '60s style — from the title of Chapter 7 of Kenneth Grahame's *The Wind in the Willows* (1908). 'The Piper at the Gates of Dawn' describes a lyrical, not to say mystical, experience that Mole and Ratty have when they hear the god Pan piping at dawn.

1

TO
THE BEAUTIFUL MEMORY
OF KENNETH GRAHAME
HUSBAND OF ELSPETH
AND
FATHER OF ALASTAIR
WHO PASSED THE RIVER
ON THE 6TH OF JULY 1932
LEAVING
CHILDHOOD & LITERATURE
THROUGH HIM
THE MORE BLEST
FOR ALL TIME.

Grahame's epitaph in St Cross churchyard, Oxford, was composed by Anthony Hope (author of *The Prisoner of Zenda*), who was Grahame's cousin. (*See also* GILBERT 159:2.) The use of the phrase 'passing the river' for death is absolutely appropriate for an author who wrote so enchantingly of the river bank and 'messing about in boats'. It may also be taken to allude to the classical use of crossing the rivers of Styx, Acheron, Lethe and so on, as a symbol of death, but chiefly to the Christian use. In John Bunyan's *The Pilgrim's Progress* (1678) Christian passes through the River of Death (which has no Bridge) and quotes Isaiah 43:2, 'When thou passest through the waters, I will be with thee, and through the Rivers, they shall not overflow thee.'

Grant, Cary
English-born film actor (1904–86)

2 *Judy . . . Judy . . . Judy!*

Impersonators always put this line in Grant's mouth (as alluded to by CAGNEY 81:4), but Grant always denied that he had ever said it and had a check made of all his films (in which, presumably, if he was referring to Judy Garland in character, he wouldn't have been calling her by her actual name, anyway). According to Richard Keyes, *Nice Guys Finish Seventh* (1992), Grant once said: 'I vaguely recall that at a party someone introduced Judy by saying, "Judy, Judy, Judy," and it caught on, attributed to me.'

There may be another explanation. Impersonators usually seek a key phrase which, through simple repetition, readily gives them the subject's voice. It is possible that one of these impersonators found that saying 'Judy' helped summon up Grant's distinctive tones, and it went on from there.

Besides, many an impersonator, rather than ape his subject, simply impersonates fellow impersonators.

Graves, John Woodcock
British huntsman and songwriter (1795–1886)

3 *Yes, I ken John Peel, and Ruby too,*
Ranter and Ringwood, Bellman and True,
From a find to a check, from a check to a view,
From a view to a death in the morning.

A View to a Kill was the title of a James Bond film (UK, 1985). The original title of the short story by Ian Fleming (published in 1960 in *For Your Eyes Only*) was 'From a View To a Kill'. As such it is very close to the title of Anthony Powell's 1933 novel *From a View to a Death*, which is a direct quotation from the song 'D'ye ken John Peel', written in 1832 by Graves.

In foxhunting terminology, a 'check' is a loss of scent, a 'view (halloo)' is the huntsman's shout when a fox breaks cover, and a 'kill' or a 'death' is what it says.

This verse from Graves's song also provided the title of a film (UK, 1988) based on a novel by Desmond Lowden, *Bellman and True*. Although Bellman and True are mentioned in the list of hounds, the book and film are about a 'bellman' in the criminal sense: a man who disables with alarm systems so that robberies can take place.

Graves, Robert
English poet (1895–1985)

4 *Far away is close at hand in images of elsewhere.*

In the late 1970s this very noticeable graffiti text, painted in large letters, stood by the side of the track outside Paddington railway station in London. It became quite famous and puzzled many people. No one is ever likely to know who wrote it. ('Peter Simple' in the *Daily Telegraph* attributed it to 'the Master of Paddington'.) Whoever it was may have had in mind the opening lines of the 'Song of Contrariety' (1923) by Graves (in *Collected Poems*, 1975):

Far away is close at hand
Close joined is far away,
Love shall come at your command
Yet will not stay.

Gray, Thomas
English poet (1716–71)

1 *Far From the Madding Crowd.*

The title of Thomas Hardy's novel (1874; film UK, 1967) comes from Thomas Gray's 'Elegy Written in a Country Church-Yard' (1751):

> Far from the madding crowd's ignoble strife
> Their sober wishes never learn'd to stray.

'Madding' here means 'frenzied, mad' — not 'maddening'.

Grayson, Victor
British Labour politician (1881–1920)

2 *Never explain: your friends don't need it and your enemies won't believe it.*

So attributed (in 1977) to the MP who simply disappeared without trace, but this may be no more than a posthumously imposed, reworking of the line from the American writer and editor, Elbert Hubbard (1856–1915). *The Note Book of Elbert Hubbard* (1927) has: 'Never Explain — your Friends do not need it and your Enemies will not believe you anyway.'

Greeley, Horace
American editor and politician (1811–72)

3 *Go West, young man!*

An early example of a misattribution that refuses to be corrected. Its originator was John Babsone Lane Soule, who first wrote it in the Terre Haute, Indiana, *Express* in 1851 when, indeed, the thing to do in the United States was to head westwards, where gold and much else lay promised. However, Horace Greeley repeated it in his New York newspaper, the *Tribune*, and, being rather more famous, a candidate for the Presidency, and all, it stuck with him. Greeley reprinted Soule's article to show where he had taken it from, but to no avail.

The original sentence was, 'Go west, young man, and grow up with the country'.

To 'go west' meaning 'to die' is a completely separate coinage, I believe. It dates back to the sixteenth century and alludes to the setting of the sun.

4 *The moment a newspaperman tires of his own campaign is the moment the public begins to notice it.*

Attributed to Greeley by the British journalist and editor, Harold Evans, in the *Independent on Sunday* (29 December 1991). A version has also been encountered in connection with Richard Nixon's view of a politician getting over his policies: 'When you get tired of saying it, that's when they're just beginning to listen.'

Green, Hannah
(Joanne Greenberg)
American novelist (1932–   )

5 *I Never Promised You A Rose Garden.*

Coined as the title of a best-selling (American) novel (1964; film US, 1977), this expression presumably means: 'It wasn't going to be roses, roses all the way between us — or a bed of roses — but maybe what we have is still acceptable.' A song 'Rose Garden' by Joe South had the line in 1968 and was a hit for Lyn Anderson in 1971. Fernando Collor de Mello, the then President of Brazil, said in a TV address (reported 26 June 1990) to his shaken countrymen: 'I never promised you a rose garden . . . following the example of developed countries, we are also cutting state spending.'

Greene, Hugh Carleton
(later Sir Hugh Greene)
English broadcasting executive (1910–87)

6 *Although . . . the BBC does try to attain the highest standards of impartiality, there are some respects in which it is not neutral, unbiased or impartial. That is, where there are clashes for and against the basic moral values — truthfulness, justice, freedom, compassion, tolerance. Nor do I believe that we should be impartial about certain things like racialism, or extreme forms of political belief.*

From an address entitled 'The Conscience of the Programme Director' given to the International Catholic Association for Radio and Television in Rome (9 February 1965). At that time, Greene was Director-General of the BBC. Elsewhere it was confirmed that the BBC was also not impartial about crime. It was against it.

Gregory, Lady (Augusta)
Irish writer (1852–)

1 *The Rising of the Moon.*

The title of a one-act play (1907) by Lady Gregory has also been shared by a film (Ireland, 1957) and by an opera (Glyndebourne, 1970) with libretto by Beverley Cross and music by Nicholas Maw. All these works (with Irish themes) borrow the title of an Irish patriotic song. The phrase came to be synonymous with the rising of the Irish themselves.

Grellet, Stephen
French missionary (1773–1855)

2 *I shall not pass this way again.*

Born Etienne de Grellet du Mabillier, in France, he eventually settled in the US. Now sometimes referred to as a Quaker 'saint', he is supposed to have said, 'I expect to pass through this world but once; any good thing therefore that I can do now, or any kindness that I can show to any fellow-creature, let me do it now; let me not defer or neglect it, for I shall not pass this way again.' However, this passage is not to be found in any of his writings and has been attributed to others. Benham (1907) exhaustively explores the alternatives and mentions William C. Gannett in *Blessed be Drudgery* (1897) as having: 'The old Quaker was right . . .' (and then quoting as above).

Grey, Sir Edward
(later Viscount Grey of Fallodon)
British Liberal politician (1862–1933)

3 *The lamps are going out all over Europe; we shall not see them lit again in our lifetime.*

Grey was Foreign Secretary at the outbreak of the 1914–18 war and with this statement tolled the knell for the era that was about to pass. In *Twenty-five Years* (1925), he recounted: 'A friend came to see me on one of the evenings of the last week — he thinks it was on Monday August 3. We were standing at a window of my room in the Foreign Office. It was getting dusk, and the lamps were being lit in the space below on which we were looking. My friend recalls that I remarked on this with the words . . .'

Griffith-Jones, Mervyn
British lawyer (1909–79)

4 *Is it a book that you would even wish your wife or your servants to read?*

When Penguin Books Ltd was tried at the Old Bailey in October 1960 for publishing an unexpurgated edition of D.H. Lawrence's novel *Lady Chatterley's Lover* (1928), the jury and the public at large were entertained by the social attitudes revealed by Griffith-Jones, the senior prosecuting counsel, especially by the question posed in his opening address on the first day of the trial.

Gerald Gardiner, in his closing speech for the defence, commented: 'I cannot help thinking that this was, consciously or unconsciously, an echo from an observation which had fallen from the Bench in an earlier case: "It would never do to let members of the working class read this." I do not want to upset the Prosecution by suggesting that there are a certain number of people nowadays who as a matter of fact don't *have* servants. But of course that whole attitude is one which Penguin Books was formed to fight against.'

The publishers were found not guilty of having published an obscene book, and from the trial is usually dated the permissive revolution in British sexual habits (if not in social attitudes).

Guinan, Texas
American nightclub hostess (1884–1933)

5 *Fifty million Frenchmen can't be wrong.*

A good deal of confusion surrounds this phrase. As a slightly grudging expression it appears to have originated with American servicemen during the First World War, justifying support for their French allies. The precise number of millions was variable. Partridge/*Catch Phrases* suggests that it was the last line of a First World War song 'extolling the supreme virtue of copulation, though in veiled terms'. Partridge may, however, have been referring to a song with the title (by Rose, Raskin & Fisher), which was not recorded by Sophie Tucker until 15 April 1927. Cole Porter's musical *Fifty Million Frenchmen* opened in New York on 27 November 1929. An unrelated US film with this three-word title was released in 1931.

Where the confusion has crept in is that Guinan was refused entry into France with her girls in 1931 and said: 'It goes to show that fifty million Frenchmen *can* be wrong.' She returned to America and renamed her show *Too Hot for Paris*. Perversely, the *ODQ* (1979, 1992) has her saying 'Fifty million Frenchmen *can't* be wrong' in the *New York World-Telegram* on 21 March 1931, and seems to be arguing that she originated the phrase as she had been using it 'six or seven years earlier'.

Bernard Shaw also held out against the phrase. He insisted: 'Fifty million Frenchmen can't be right.'

Gunn, Thom
English-born poet (1929–)

1 *He turns revolt into style.*

From Gunn's poem 'Elvis Presley' (1957). Used as the title of a book about the pop arts in Britain (1970) by George Melly.

H

Haggard, Sir Henry Rider
English writer (1856–1925)

1 *She who must be obeyed.*

The original 'she' in Haggard's novel *She* (1887) was the all-powerful Ayesha, 'who from century to century sat alone, clothed with unchanging loveliness, waiting till her lost love is born again'. But also, 'she was obeyed throughout the length and breadth of the land, and to question her command was certain death'.

From the second of these two quotations we get the use of the phrase by barrister Horace Rumpole regarding his formidable wife in the 'Rumpole of the Bailey' stories by John Mortimer (in TV plays from 1978 and novelizations therefrom). Hence, too, one of the many nicknames applied to Margaret Thatcher — 'She-Who-Must-Be-Obeyed'.

Haig, Alexander
American general and Republican politician (1924–   )

2 *As of now, I am in control [here] at the White House.*

After the assassination attempt on President Reagan in March 1981, Secretary of State Haig made this claim while the President was in an operating theatre and the Vice-President was flying back to the White House. The *New York Times* reported that Haig's 'voice was trembling and his face perspiring'. In fact, he had made the claim without authority, and it was open to question whether he was entitled to make the assumption. *The Times* (1 April 1981) presciently noted, 'The phrase may come back to haunt him.'

In his memoirs (*Caveat: Realism, Reagan & Foreign Policy*, 1984) Haig admitted that he had been wrong to say that 'constitutionally . . . you have the President, the

Vice-President and the Secretary of State in that order'. He should have said 'traditionally', as the Secretary of Defense was third in line, at least on defence matters. It is only fair to point out that Haig also added to his statement the words, 'pending return of the Vice-President'.

But his physical aspect counted against him — 'My appearance became a celebrated media happening. It is now far too late to correct the impressions made' — and he never ran for President as at one time seemed probable.

3 *I'll have to caveat my response, senator, and I'll caveat that.*

When Haig was being examined at his confirmation hearings in the Senate for the Secretaryship, he came out with this curious use of noun as verb, presumably meaning, 'I'll say that with this warning'. (Perhaps that is why he called his memoirs *Caveat*?) Subsequently, his way with the language became known as 'Haigspeak', 'Haigese' and 'Haigravation'. Multisyllabic jargon and verbal distortions flowed from his mouth. An aide asked him for a pay increase. Haig replied: 'Because of the fluctuational predisposition of your position's productive capacity as juxtaposed to government standards, it would be momentarily injudicious to advocate an increment.' The perplexed aide replied, 'I don't get it'. Haig said, 'That's right' (*The Times*, 29 January 1983).

Haig, Sir Douglas
(later 1st Earl Haig)
British soldier (1861–1928)

4 *A very weak-minded fellow, I'm afraid, and, like the feather pillow, bears the marks of the last person who has sat on him!*

Haig's famous phrase was contained in a letter written to his wife on 14 January 1918. He was talking about the 17th Earl of Derby, generally considered an uninspiring choice as Secretary for War (1916–18). Lloyd George, as Prime Minister, took over Derby's responsibilities the following March. Haig's private papers were made public in an edition edited by Robert Blake in 1952.

1 *With our backs to the wall, and believing in the justice of our cause, each one of us must fight on to the end.*

The expression 'backs to the wall', meaning 'up against it', dates back to at least 1535, but it was memorably used when the Germans launched their last great offensive of the First World War. On 12 April 1918 Haig, as British Commander-in-Chief on the Western Front, issued an order for his troops to stand firm: 'Every position must be held to the last man: there must be no retirement.' A.J.P. Taylor in his *English History 1914–45* (1966) commented: 'In England this sentence was ranked with Nelson's last message. At the front, the prospect of staff officers fighting with their backs to the walls of their luxurious chateaux had less effect.'

Halberstam, David
American journalist (1934–)

2 *The Best and the Brightest.*

In Halberstam's book with this title (1972) the phrase applies to the young men from business, industry and the academic world whom John F. Kennedy brought into government in the early 1960s but who were ultimately responsible for the quagmire of American involvement in the Vietnam War. The alliterative combination is almost traditional: 'Political writers, who will not suffer the best and brightest of characters . . . to take a single right step for the honour or interest of the nation' (*Letters of Junius*, 1769); 'Best and brightest, come away!' (Shelley, 'To Jane: The Invitation', 1822; originally the letter poem 'The Pine Forest of the Cascine Near Pisa'); 'Brightest and best of the sons of the morning' (the hymn by Bishop Heber, 1827); 'The best, the brightest, the cleverest of them all!' (Trollope, *Dr Thorne*, Chap. 25, 1858).

Haldeman, H.R.
American government official (1926–93)

3 *Once the toothpaste is out of the tube, it is awfully hard to get it back in.*

Remark to John Dean on the Watergate affair (8 April 1973) and reported in *Hearings . . . Watergate and Related Activities* (Vol. 4, 1973). The remark has been wrongly attributed to his colleague, John D. Ehrlichman, and to President Nixon, but it is probably not an original expression in any case.

Halm, Friedrich
(Baron von Münch-Bellinghausen)
German playwright (1806–71)

4 *Two minds with but a single thought, Two hearts that beat as one.*

What Pearson (1937) says Halm wrote near the end of Act II of *Der Sohn der Wildnis* is, 'Two *souls* with but a single thought . . .' (as in Maria Lovell's translation of the play as *Ingomar the Barbarian*, 1854). The original German is, indeed, '*Zwei Seelen und ein Gedanke*'. But the 'two minds' version is the one that entered the English language. Partridge/*Catch Phrases* draws attention to the similar phrase 'Great minds think alike' — which may have influenced the English form. Kenneth Horne contributed an article entitled 'TMWNAST' to *Radio Times Annual* (1954): 'The title of this article is how Murdoch and I would write it in our script if it were a catchphrase . . . It is quite true that when Murdoch and I get together to write our epic stuff we are two minds with not a single thought.'

Hamilton, Richard
English painter (1922–)

5 *Just What Is It That Makes To-Day's Home So Different, So Appealing?*

Dating from 1956, this is the title of what is held to be the first British 'pop art' painting. Hamilton produced a small collage of magazine photographs of, for example, a Charles Atlas muscleman carrying a baseball bat (with 'POP' written on it), a female nude, and various 'modern' artefacts like a TV set and a tape-recorder. A painting on the wall comes from a comic book called *Young Romance*, and out of the window there is a winking neon cinema sign advertising an Al

Jolson film. (The first recorded use of the word 'Pop' in art is in Eduardo Paolozzi's picture 'I Was a Rich Man's Plaything' (*c* 1947) which is a modest collage of advertisements and the cover of *Intimate Confessions*. A pistol, pointed at a pin-up, is going 'Pop!') Possibly Hamilton also found his title in a magazine or an advertisement? Whatever the case, it lingers. From the heading to an article in the *Sunday Times* (16 January 1994): 'Just what is it that makes today's Catholicism so different, so appealing, to aristocratic Anglicans? Cristina Odone, the editor of the *Catholic Herald*, explains.'

Hampton, Christopher
English playwright (1946–)

1 *Asking a working writer what he thinks about critics is like asking a lamp-post how it feels about dogs.*

For some reason this is frequently misascribed to John Osborne (e.g. in Metcalf, *The Penguin Dictionary of Modern Humorous Quotations*, 1986). Hampton's view was quoted originally in the *Sunday Times Magazine* of 16 October 1977. This misattribution may have come about because Osborne is the more famously combative of the two playwrights.

Hanff, Minnie Maud
American advertising copywriter (1880–1942)

2 *Vigor, Vim, Pefect Trim;*
Force made him, Sunny Jim.

From a jingle for Force breakfast cereal (1903). The name, character and appearance of 'Sunny Jim' were invented by two young American women — Miss Hanff and a Miss Ficken — and the name has passed into the language. One might say, 'Ah, there you are . . . I've been looking for you, Sunny Jim', even if the person weren't called Jim. Lady Cynthia Asquith writing in her diary (13 July 1918) says: 'I like McKenna [a politician]. He is such a "Sunny Jim" and ripples on so easily.' So it is a name applied to a cheerful person, but it can also be used in a slightly patronizing way. Thus it was applied to James Callaghan, when British Prime Minister, who was nothing if not patronizing in return with his air of a bank manager who knew best (an *Observer*

headline of 18 March 1979 stated, 'Sunny Jim tires of wheeler-dealing').

The Force Food Company was founded in 1901. A London office was established the following year. In the US, the product has now disappeared from sale but in 1970, the A.C. Fincken Company relaunched it in the UK.

3 *High o'er the fence leaps Sunny Jim,*
Force is the food that raises him.

Hanff wrote numerous little rhymes to promote the cereal. This is from the same promotion (1920).

Hanrahan, Brian
English journalist (1949–)

4 *I'm not allowed to say how many planes [Harrier jets from HMS Hermes] joined the raid, but I counted them all out and I counted them all back.*

In a report broadcast by BBC Television on 1 May 1982. Hanrahan was attempting to convey the success of a British attack on Port Stanley airport during the Falklands War. As Alasdair Milne commented in *DG: The Memoirs of a British Broadcaster* (1988), it was, 'An elegant way of telling the truth without compromising the exigencies of military censorship.'

Harben, Joan
English actress (1909–53)

5 *It's being so cheerful as keeps me going.*

Harben would utter this catchphrase in the character of 'Mona Lott', a gloomy laundrywoman with a dreary, flat voice, in *ITMA*, the BBC's immensely popular radio comedy show (1939–49). When told to 'keep her pecker up' by the star of the show, Tommy Handley, she would reply, 'I always do, sir, it's being so cheerful as keeps me going'. Her family was always running into bad luck, so she had plenty upon which to exercise her cheerfulness. Scripts for the show were by Ted Kavanagh and Handley himself. The catchphrase had earlier appeared in a *Punch* cartoon during the First World War (27 September 1916): 'Wot a life. No rest, no beer, no nuffin. It's only us keeping so cheerful as pulls us through.'

Harding, Warren G.
American Republican 29th President
(1865–1923)

1 *America's present need is not heroics but
healing, not nostrums but normalcy.*

The slogans 'Back to Normalcy' and 'Return
to Normalcy with Harding' were both based
on a word extracted from a speech Harding
made in Boston, Massachusetts, on 14 May
1920: 'America's present need is not heroics
but healing, not nostrums but normalcy, not
revolution but restoration, not agitation but
adjustment, not surgery but serenity, not the
dramatic but the dispassionate, not experiment but equipoise, not submergence in
internationality but sustainment in triumphant nationality.' Out of such an
alliterative bog stuck the word 'normalcy', a
perfectly good Americanism, though it has
been suggested that Harding was actually
mispronouncing the word 'normality'. He
himself claimed that 'normalcy' was what he
had meant to say, having come across it in
a dictionary.

Hardy, Oliver
American film comedian (1892–1957)

2 *Well, here's another nice mess you've
gotten me into.*

Hardy's exasperated cry to his partner Stan
Laurel (1890–1965) after some piece of
ineptitude was spoken in several of their
films. Oddly, both *ODMQ* (1991) and
ODQ (1992) place the saying under Laurel's
name while acknowledging that it was
always said *to* him. It is one of the few film
catchphrases to register because there was a
sufficient number of Laurel and Hardy
features for audiences to become familiar
with it. Latterly, it has often been remembered as 'another fine mess', possibly on
account of one of the duo's thirty-minute
features (released in 1930) being entitled
Another Fine Mess. The *Independent* (21
January 1994) carried a letter from Darren
George of Sheffield — clearly a Laurel and
Hardy scholar — which stated that 'nice
mess' was what was 'invariably' spoken and
that in *Another Fine Mess* 'the duo inexpli-
cably misquote themselves'.

Hare, David
English playwright (1947–   )

3 *Paris by Night.*

The title of David Hare's film (1988) is
derived from a promotional tag for tourism
in the French capital, in use since at least the
1950s. A London West End revue had the
somewhat nudging phrase for its title in
1955. In 1943 there had been a US film *Paris
After Dark*. From the 1930s onwards there
was also a cheap perfume, available from
Woolworth and manufactured by Bourjois
(*sic*), called 'Evening in Paris', which also
traded on the city's reputation for sophisticated pleasures.

4 *Racing Demon.*

The title of a play (1990) about the Church
of England came from the name of a
'patience' card game played by several
players, each with his own pack of cards.

5 *Murmuring Judges.*

The title of a play (1991) about the British
criminal justice system came from an old
legal expression meaning to speak ill of the
judiciary. So, to 'murmur' a judge is to
complain or grumble against his actions. In
Scottish law it is still an offence to do so.

Hargreaves, William
English songwriter (1846–1919)

6 *I'm Burlington Bertie
I rise at ten thirty and saunter along
    like a toff,
I walk down the Strand with my
    gloves on my hand,
Then I walk down again with them off.*

From the song, 'Burlington Bertie from
Bow' (1915), and not to be confused with
the earlier 'Burlington Bertie' (1900) by
Harry B. Norris. That song, performed by
Vesta Tilley, is about a 'swell' gentleman.
Hargreaves was writing about a more down-
at-heel character (for his wife Ella Shields,
the male impersonator, to perform). It is a
kind of parody but is probably better known
now than the original.

Harlow, Jean
American film actress (1911–37)

7 *Would you be shocked if I put on something more comfortable?*

'Do you mind if I put on something more
comfortable?' and 'Excuse me while I slip
into something more comfortable' are just

two of the misquotations of this famous line. What Jean Harlow as Helen actually says to Ben Lyon as Monte in *Hell's Angels* (1930) is, of course, by way of a proposition and she duly exchanges her fur wrap for a dressing gown.

Harris, Joel Chandler
American writer (1848–1908)

1 *Lying low, like Brer Rabbit, and saying nuffin.*

In Kenneth Harris's biography of Clement Attlee (1982), he says at one point that the former British Prime Minister was, 'lying low, like Brer Rabbit, and saying nuffin'. This is a fairly common conflation of what Harris actually wrote in 'The Wonderful Tar-Baby Story' from *Uncle Remus and His Legends of the Old Plantation* (1881): 'Tar-baby ain't sayin' nuthin', en Brer Fox, he lay low.'

In fact, the phrase 'en Brer Fox, he lay low' is a phrase repeated rhythmically throughout the piece, as Frank Muir has noted, 'like a line in a Blues song'.

Harris, John
English author (1916–   )

2 *The Sea Shall Not Have Them.*

This was the title of a novel (filmed UK, 1954) about air-sea rescue operations during the Second World War. But was it ever the actual motto of an air-sea rescue unit? Apparently so. In Harris's original book (1953), there is a note explaining it as 'the motto of Air-Sea Rescue High-Speed Launch Flotillas.' In other words, this was indeed the motto of Coastal Command's A.S.R. Service.

Harrison, Tony
English poet (1937–   )

3 *Yan Tan Tethera.*

A modern opera (1986) by Sir Harrison Birtwistle with text by Harrison is about a shepherd who moves down from the north of England to Wiltshire and enters into rivalry with a local shepherd. The title refers to an old shepherd's spell 'Yan, tan, tethera, 1-2-3, Sweet Trinity, Keep us. And our sheep'. The method of counting Yan = 1, T(y)an = 2, Tethera = 3, Methera = 4, Pimp = 5 and so on is one used, for

example, by old-time Yorkshire shepherds and farmers. James Agate in *Ego 3* (1938) calls them 'Cymric numerals still used by shepherds in counting sheep' and gives this version of 1–20: 'Yan tan tethera pethera pimp, sethera lethera hovera bovera dik, yan-a-dik tan-a-dik tethera-dik pethera-dik bumfit, yan-a-bumfit tan-a-bumfit tethera-bumfit pethera-bumfit figgit.'

Haskins, Minnie Louise
English teacher and writer (1875–1957)

4 *And I said to the man who stood at the Gate of the Year, 'Give me a light that I may tread safely into the unknown'. And he replied, 'Go out into the darkness, and put your hand into the Hand of God. That shall be to you better than light, and safer than a known way.'*

If one were to look for an equivalent British example of President Reagan's quoting of J.G. Magee's 'High Flight' poem at the time of the Challenger disaster in 1986 (231:1) — that is to say, an outstanding choice of quotation in a head of state's speech — the most obvious, and possibly only, candidate would be found in King George VI's Christmas radio broadcast of 1939.

George VI, hampered by a severe speech impediment, was scarcely a man noted for what he said. Yet when he quoted an obscure poet that year, he captured the public imagination as few other Royals had done (and certainly not since). He concluded his message by quoting (anonymously) words written by Haskins, a retired lecturer at the London School of Economics, who had written them as the introduction to a poem called *The Desert* in 1908.

One can imagine how the nation collectively responded to the King's difficult delivery of the words, especially given that this was the first Christmas of the war. The King added: 'May that Almighty Hand guide and uphold us all.'

Haskins did not hear the broadcast herself but was soon inundated with writing offers. Her reprinted poem sold 43,000 copies, she was ushered into *Who's Who* and merited an obituary in *The Times* — all testimony to the power of being quoted by the right person at the right time. One assumes that the King's speech was written for him by a member of the Royal Household. According to the King's official biographer, John Wheeler-Bennett, the poem had merely been 'sent to him shortly before the text of his broadcast was completed'.

Hawker, R.S.
English clergyman (1803–75)

1 *And shall Trelawny die?*
Here's twenty thousand Cornish men
Will know the reason why.

The refrain from Hawker's 'Song of the Western Men' (1845) refers to Bishop Sir Jonathan Trelawny of Bristol. In 1688 Trelawny was sent to the Tower by King James II with six other bishops on charges of seditious libel. They were acquitted. Hawker obtained the whole refrain from an old Cornish ballad, traditional since 1688.

Hawkesworth, John
English TV playwright (1920–   )

2 *By the Sword Divided.*

Hawkesworth gave this title to a BBC TV historical drama series (1983–5) set in the English Civil War. He commented (1991): 'When I first wrote down the idea for a story about the Civil War I called it 'The Laceys of Arnescote' . . . [but] I decided the title didn't convey the sort of Hentyish swashbuckling style that we were aiming at, so I thought again. The title "By the Sword Divided" came to me as I was walking along a beach in Wales.'
   The phrase sounds like a quotation but apparently is not. In dealing with the Civil War period, Macaulay in his *History of England*, Chaps. 1–2 (1848) had earlier written: 'Thirteen years followed during which England was . . . really governed by the sword'; 'the whole nation was sick of government by the sword'; 'anomalies and abuses . . . which had been destroyed by the sword'.

Hayward, Abraham
English essayist (1801–84)

3 *He writes too often and too fast . . . If he persists much longer in this course, it requires no gift of prophecy to foretell his fate — he has risen like a rocket, and he will come down like a stick.*

So Hayward wrote of Charles Dickens when reviewing *Pickwick Papers* for *The Quarterly Review* (October 1838). Not entirely original. Tom Paine had said of Edmund

Burke in 1792, 'As he rose like the rocket, he fell like the stick.'

Hazlitt, William
English essayist (1778–1830)

4 *The Spirit of the Age.*

Hazlitt's book of essays (1825) was devoted to examinations of the work and characters of contemporary writers. The phrase had been used by Shelley in a letter of 1820: 'It is the spirit of the age, and we are all infected with it.' Later, the *Pall Mall Gazette* was stating (6 August 1891): 'The Spirit of the Age is against those who put party or programme before human needs.' In 1975 the title *Spirit of the Age* was given to a BBC TV series on the history of architecture, with Alec Clifton-Taylor.

Healey, Denis
(later Lord Healey)
English Labour politician (1917–   )

5 *Savaged by a dead sheep.*

What is the true source of the most famous parliamentary jibe of recent years? In a speech to the House of Commons on 14 June 1978, Healey, as Chancellor of the Exchequer, on being attacked by Sir Geoffrey Howe in a debate over his Budget proposals, said: 'That part of his speech was rather like being savaged by a dead sheep.'
   In 1987 Alan Watkins of the *Observer* suggested that Sir Roy Welensky, of Central African Federation fame, had earlier likened an attack by Iain Macleod to being *bitten* by a sheep. We had to wait until 1989 and the publication of Healey's memoirs to be told that, 'the phrase came to me while I was actually on my feet; it was an adaptation of Churchill's remark that an attack by Attlee was "like being savaged by a pet lamb". Such banter can often enliven a dull afternoon.'
   The Churchill version remains untraced, but he was noted for his Attlee jokes (and busily denied that he had ever said most of them, see CHURCHILL 98:1). In 1990, the victim of Healey's phrase, Geoffrey Howe, also claimed that it wasn't original. 'It came from a play', he said sheepishly.

6 *I warn you that there are going to be howls of anguish from the 80,000 people who are rich enough to pay over 75 per cent on the last slice of their income.*

This is what Healey said to the Labour Party Conference on 1 October 1973 (when Shadow Chancellor), explaining that Labour's programme would cost money and the only way to raise it was through taxation. He promised increased income tax and a wealth tax if the party won the next election. Not 'howls of anger', as quoted in the *Sunday Telegraph* (October 1980). In his autobiography *The Time of My Life* (1989), Healey said the phrase 'make the rich howl with anguish' still 'hangs round my neck like Wilson's phrase "the pound in your pocket", and Heath's election promise to cut prices "at a stroke". I never said either that I would "squeeze the rich until the pips squeak", though I did quote Tony Crosland using this phrase of Lloyd George's in reference to property speculators, not to the the rich in general.' Phrase of Lloyd George's? Surely, he meant GEDDES 153:7.

Healy, Tim
Irish politician (1855–1931)

1 *He is not a man to go tiger-shooting with.*

This jibe was reputedly fired at the somewhat weak and vacillating Lord Rosebery by Healy, the Irish Nationalist leader who sat in the Westminster Parliament (1880–1918). It is quoted by Robert Rhodes James in *Rosebery* (1963). If not the first use of this slur, it is the most famous. In 1961, Lord Montgomery was quoted as saying: '[Chairman] Mao has a very fine strong face. He's the sort of man I'd go in the jungle with.' In 1970, I was told of a university appointments secretary who would add his own comments on the bottom of application forms he was forwarding to employers on behalf of students. On one he wrote: 'This chap would be splendid to shoot tigers with.'

Heath, Edward
(later Sir Edward)

British Conservative Prime Minister (1916–   )

2 *The full-hearted consent of the Parliament and people of the new member countries.*

On 5 May 1970, a month and a half before he became Prime Minister, Heath addressed the Franco-British Chamber of Commerce in Paris. Looking ahead to the forthcoming enlargement of the EEC through British,

Irish and other membership, he said that this would not be in the interests of the Community, 'except with the full-hearted consent . . .' The statement, penned by Douglas Hurd, then a Heath aide, was seized upon subsequently by those seeking a referendum on EEC entry.

3 *This would, at a stroke, reduce the rise in prices, increase productivity and reduce unemployment.*

A press release (No. G.E.228), from Conservative Central Office, dated 16 June 1970, was concerned with tax cuts and a freeze on prices by nationalized industries. The words, though never actually spoken by Heath, came to haunt him, when he became Prime Minister two days later.

4 *It is the unpleasant and unacceptable face of capitalism, but one should not suggest that the whole of British industry consists of practices of this kind.*

In 1973 it was revealed that a former Tory Cabinet minister, Duncan Sandys, had been paid £30,000 in compensation for giving up his £50,000 a year consultancy with the Lonrho company. The money was to be paid, quite legally, into an account in the Cayman Islands to avoid British tax. This kind of activity did not seem appropriate when the government was promoting a counterinflation policy. Replying to a question from Jo Grimond MP in the House of Commons on 15 May, Heath, as Prime Minister, created a format phrase that has since been used to describe the 'unacceptable face of' almost anything. In the text from which he spoke (said to have been prepared by his then aide, Douglas Hurd), it apparently had 'facet'.

Heath, Robert
English poet (*fl.* 1650)

5 *Things of so small concern or moment, who*
Would stuff his Diary with, or care to know?
As what he wore, thought, laugh'd at, where he walked,
When farted, where he pissed, with whom he talked.

From *Clarastella*, 'Satyr 1' (1650). Not a very encouraging view of diary keeping.

Heber, Reginald
English bishop (1783–1826)

1 *What though the spicy breeze*
Blow soft o'er Ceylon's isle;
Though every prospect pleases,
And only man is vile.

This was what Heber originally wrote in the hymn 'From Greenland's icy mountains' (1821), leading up to the lines about 'the heathen in his blindness' bowing down 'to wood and stone'. In 1827, however, he changed 'Ceylon's' to 'Java's'. Sir Peter Kemp, writing to the *Independent* Magazine (15 May 1993), said that he had been told there were two reasons for this change: Java, with its accent on the first syllable, goes better with the tune that is usually used. Secondly, 'the Colonial Office of the day objected to Bishop Heber's traducing of a part of the Empire and insisted on the change'. Heber became Bishop of Calcutta in 1823.

Heller, Joseph
American novelist (1923–)

2 *Catch–22.*

The title of Heller's novel (1961; film US, 1970) about a group of US fliers in the Second World War has become a widely used catchphrase. 'It was a Catch–22 situation,' people will say, as if resorting to a quasi-proverbial expression like 'Heads you win, tails I lose' or 'Damned if you do, damned if you don't'. What Heller did was to affix a name to the popular view that 'there's always a catch', some underlying law that defeats people by its brutal, ubiquitous logic. Ooddly, Heller had originally numbered it 18. In the book, the idea is explored several times. Captain Yossarian, a US Air Force bombardier, does not wish to fly any more missions. He goes to see the group's MO, Doc Daneeka, about getting grounded on the grounds that he is crazy:

> *Daneeka:* There's a rule saying I have to ground anyone who's crazy.
> *Yossarian:* Then why can't you ground me? I'm crazy.
> *Daneeka:* Anyone who wants to get out of combat duty isn't really crazy.

This is the catch — 'Catch–22'.

Helmsley, Leona
American hotelier (*c* 1920–)

3 *We don't pay taxes. Only the little people pay taxes.*

In August 1989 Helmsley, New York's self-styled 'hotel queen', was found guilty of evading more than $1 million in taxes. During the trial her housekeeper, Elizabeth Baum, recounted how Helmsley had made this unfortunate observation (quoted in the *New York Times*, 13 December 1989). Helmsley received a four-year jail term and a $7 million fine for tax fraud.

Hemingway, Ernest
American novelist (1899–1961)

4 *The Sun Also Rises.*

Title of novel (1926).

See THE BIBLE 53:2.

5 *Grace under pressure.*

In an interview with *The New Yorker* (30 November 1929), Hemingway gave this as a definition of 'guts'. It was based on the Latin *'fortiter in re, suaviter in modo'* and was later invoked by John F. Kennedy at the start of his book *Profiles in Courage* (1956).

6 *The very rich are different from you and me./Yes, they have more money.*

In Burnam (1980) the facts are neatly established about a famous exchange said to have occurred between Hemingway and F. Scott Fitzgerald. In his short story 'The Rich Boy' (1926) Fitzgerald had written: 'Let me tell you about the very rich. They are different from you and me.' Twelve years later in *his* short story 'The Snows of Kilimanjaro' (1938) Hemingway had the narrator remember 'poor Scott Fitzgerald', his awe of the rich and that 'someone' had said, 'Yes, they have money'.

When Fitzgerald read the story, he protested to Hemingway who dropped Fitzgerald's name from further printings. In any case, the put-down 'Yes, they have more money' had not been administered to Fitzgerald but to Hemingway himself. In 1936, Hemingway said at a lunch with the critic Mary Colum: 'I am getting to know the rich.' She replied: 'The only difference between the rich and other people is that the rich have more money.'

Also discussed in *Scott and Ernest* (1978) by Mathew J. Bruccoli.

1 *A Moveable Feast.*

The title of a book (1964) by Hemingway. The epigraph explains: 'If you are lucky enough to have lived in Paris as a young man, then wherever you go for the rest of your life, it stays with you, for Paris is a moveable feast.'

In the ecclesiastical world, a moveable feast is one that does not fall on a fixed date but, like Easter, occurs according to certain rules.

2 *Did the earth move for you?*

Jokily addressed to one's partner after sexual intercourse, this appears to have originated as 'Did thee feel the earth move?' in Hemingway's *For Whom the Bell Tolls* (1940). It is not spoken in the 1943 film version, however.

Headline from the *Sport* (22 February 1989): 'SPORT SEXCLUSIVE ON A BONK THAT WILL MAKE THE EARTH MOVE.'

Hendrix, Jimmy
American rock musician (1942–70)

3 *Once you're dead, you're made for life.*

This attributed remark was certainly prescient in Hendrix's own case. His success was enhanced following his early death in September 1970. Within six weeks he had a No. 1 hit in the UK with 'Voodoo Experience'. The pattern of a surge of interest — indeed, *increased* popularity — after death has been accorded to any number of pop stars who have died relatively young. Elvis Presley in 1977 and John Lennon in 1980 benefited similarly. A graffito (reported in *Time* Magazine, 8 April 1985) following Presley's death commented: 'Good career move.'

Henri IV (Henri of Navarre)
French King (1553–1610)

4 *Paris is well worth a mass* [Paris vaut bien une messe].

Said either by Henri or his minister Sully (in conversation with him), though no real evidence exists. Henri had led the Protestant forces in the Third Huguenot War (1569–72) as King of Navarre, but in 1589 he

marched on Catholic-held Paris and became King of France. In 1593 he renounced Protestantism and converted to Catholicism, hence this cynical if pragmatic remark, which was first recorded in 1622.

In 1681 Hardouin de Péréfixe commented in *Histoire de Henry le Grand*: 'The Politiques . . . said to him that of all canons, the Canon of the Mass was the best to reduce the towns of his kingdom.'

5 *I will make sure that there will be no labourer in my kingdom without the means of having a chicken in his pot.*

A remark recorded by a contemporary lawyer, Pierre de l'Estoile. Péréfixe (1681) reported the French form as: '*Je veux qu'il n'y ait si pauvre paysan en mon royaume qu'il n'ait tous les dimanches sa poule au pot.*' 'A chicken in every pot' accordingly became one of the earliest political slogans. In 1928, running for the US Presidency, Herbert Hoover did say, 'The slogan of progress is changing from the "full dinner pail" to the full garage' and by 1932 this was sometimes interpreted as 'a chicken in every pot and two cars in every garage'. In 1960 John F. Kennedy misquoted Hoover as having uttered the slogan 'Two chickens for every pot' in 1928.

6 Toujours perdrix [*Always partridge*].

(Or, in Latin, *semper perdrix*.) An expression meaning 'too much of a good thing' comes from a tale told about Henri IV. The King was reproved by his confessor for his marital infidelities, so he ordered the priest to be fed on nothing but partridge. When the priest complained that it was 'always partridge', the King replied it was the same if you had only one mistress.

Henry II
English Sovereign (1133–89)

7 *Will no man rid me of this turbulent priest?*

Henry II's rhetorical question regarding Thomas à Beckett — which was unfortunately acted upon by the Archbishop's murderers in 1170 — is ascribed to 'oral tradition' by *ODQ* (1979) in the form: 'Will no one revenge me of the injuries I have sustained from one turbulent priest?' The King, who was in Normandy, had received reports that the Archbishop was ready 'to tear the crown from' his head. 'What a pack of fools and cowards I have nourished in my house,' he cried, according to another version, 'that not one of them will avenge me of this turbulent priest!' Yet another version has, 'of this upstart clerk'.

An example of the phrase used allusively in conversation was played on tape at the conspiracy-to-murder trial involving Jeremy Thorpe MP in 1979. In one tape, Andrew Newton speaking of the alleged plot said: 'They feel a Thomas à Beckett was done, you know, with Thorpe sort of raving that would nobody rid me of this man.'

Henry IV
English Sovereign (1367–1413)

1 *I should not die but in Jerusalem.*

The last words of Henry IV, according to Raphael Holinshed's *The Chronicles of England, Scotland and Ireland* (1587), are supposed to have been: 'Lauds be given to the Father of heaven, for now I know that I shall die here in this chamber, according to the prophecy of me declared, that I should depart this life in Jerusalem.' He had just been told that he was lying in the Jersualem Chamber of Westminster Abbey. He had been preparing for an expedition to the Holy Land and was visiting the Abbey on the eve of his departure when taken ill.

Shakespeare in *Henry IV, Part 2* takes this situation almost word for word from the chronicle (IV.v.232):

> *King:*
> Doth any name particular belong
> Unto the lodging where I first did swoon?
> *Warwick:*
> 'Tis called Jerusalem, my noble lord.
> *King:*
> Laud be to God! Even there my life must end.
> It hath been prophesied to me, many years,
> I should not die but in Jerusalem,   ·
> Which vainly I suppos'd the Holy Land.
> But bear me to that chamber; there I'll lie;
> In that Jerusalem shall Harry die.

After the dissolution of the Abbey, the Jerusalem Chamber became the meeting place of the Dean and Chapter. Its name derives from mention of Jerusalem in inscriptions round the fireplace or from the original tapestry hangings.

Henry VIII
English Sovereign (1491–1547)

2 *The things I've done for England.*

In Sir Alexander Korda's film *The Private Life of Henry VIII* (1933), Charles Laughton as the King is just about to get into bed with one of his many wives when, alluding to her ugliness, he sighs: 'The things I've done for England.' The screenplay was written by Lajos Biro and Arthur Wimperis. There is no historical precedent.

The phrase caught on, to be used ironically when confronted with any unpleasant task. In 1979, Prince Charles on a visit to Hong Kong sampled curried snake meat and, with a polite nod towards his ancestor, exclaimed: 'Boy, the things I do for England.'

Henry, Patrick
American statesman (1736–99)

3 *I know not what course others may take; but as for me, give me liberty or give me death!*

Henry was the foremost opponent of British rule and the leading orator of American independence. His speech in the Virginia Convention (23 March 1775) helped carry the vote for independence. He became Governor of the new state and was four times re-elected.

Henry, Philip
English clergyman (1631–96)

4 *All This and Heaven Too.*

The title of a novel (1939; film US, 1940) by Rachel Field. As acknowledged in the book, Matthew Henry, the nonconformist divine and Bible commentator (*d* 1714), attributed the saying to his minister father in his *Life of Mr Philip Henry* (1698). Compare the title *All This and World War II* (film US, 1976).

Heraclitus
Greek philosopher (*c* 540–*c* 480BC)

5 *The past and present*
Are as one —
Accordant and discordant
Youth and age
And death and birth —
For out of one came all
From all comes one.

Dame Edith Sitwell (1887–1964), the poet and writer, is buried in St Mary's churchyard extension, Weedon Lois, Northamptonshire, under a headstone designed by Henry Moore. It bears her own version of words from Heraclitus, which she had quoted in the concluding lines of her poem 'The Wind of Early Spring'.

Herodotus
Greek historian (c 485–425BC)

1 *Neither rain nor snow nor heat of day nor gloom of night stays these couriers from the swift completion of their appointed rounds.*

These words are inscribed on the stone face of the New York City Post Office. The text is adapted from the *Histories* of Herodotus. He is describing how King Cyrus the Great of Persia set up what is thought to have been the first organized system of mounted messengers (in the sixth-century BC). But the New York inscription has given rise to the comment, 'Well, what is it then?'

Herrick, Robert
English poet and clergyman
(1591–1674)

2 *Be she showing in her dress,*
Like a civil wilderness;
That the curious may detect
Order in a sweet neglect.

Herrick twice refers to types of 'disorder in the dress' in his poetry. The above comes from 'What Kind of Mistress He Would Have'. In 'Delight in Disorder' (also published in *Hesperides*, 1647), he writes:

A sweet disorder in the dress
Kindles in clothes a wantonness . . .

And he concludes that such distractions bewitch him more than 'when Art/Is too precise in every part'.

Hewart, Gordon
(later Viscount Hewart)
British jurist (1870–1943)

3 *Justice should not only be done, but should manifestly and undoubtedly be seen to be done.*

The origin of this noted legal observation is contained in a ruling by Hewart (King's Bench Reports, 1924). A man named McCarthy in Hastings had been accused of dangerous driving. There had been an accident in which people were injured. He was convicted, but it was later discovered that a partner in the firm of solicitors who had demanded damages against him was also clerk to the Hastings justices. As Robert Jackson noted (*The Chief*, 1959), no one believed that the clerk had acted improperly during the case but the circumstances warranted an application by McCarthy's solicitor for the conviction to be quashed in a Divisional Court. Hewart ruled in his favour in the case of Rex *v.* Sussex Justices (9 November 1923).

When a fellow-judge joked that the word 'seen' was a misprint for 'seem', Hewart made it clear that justice must always be 'seen' to be done in view of the defendant and of the world.

4 *If it's only wind, I'll call it . . .*

F.E. Smith, 1st Earl of Birkenhead, taunted Hewart, when Lord Chief Justice, about the size of his stomach. 'What's it to be − a boy or a girl?' Replied Hewart: 'If it's a boy I'll call him John. If it's a girl I'll call her Mary. But if, as I suspect, it's only wind, I'll call it F.E. Smith.'

I printed that anecdote in my book *Quote . . . Unquote* (1978). The story had come to me the previous year from a *Quote . . . Unquote* listener who said it had been told to her brother 'by a stranger in a bus queue in Harrogate in 1923'. Smith died in 1930, Hewart in 1943.

According to Humphrey McQueen in *Social Sketches of Australia* (1978), the Antipodean version has Sir George Houstoun Reid (1845–1918) replying, in answer to the question, apropos his stomach, 'What are you going to call it, George?': 'If it's a boy, I'll call it after myself. If it's a girl, I'll call it Victoria after our Queen. But if, as I strongly suspect, it's nothing but piss and wind, I'll call it after you.'

According to *Pass the Port Again* (1981 ed.) the exchange occurred between Lord Haldane and Winston Churchill, as also in John Parker, *Father of the House* (1982), in which the exchange is specifically located at the Oxford Union in 1926. *The Faber Book of Anecdotes* (1985) records the US version: President Taft (*d* 1930) making the retort to Senator Chauncey Depew (*d* 1929).

Hill, Charles
(later Lord Hill)
British doctor, politician and broadcaster
(1904–89)

1 *Black-coated workers.*

Referring to prunes as laxatives, this term
was popularized by Hill as the 'Radio Doctor' from 1941 onwards in an early morning
BBC programme *The Kitchen Front*. He
noted in his autobiography *Both Sides of the
Hill* (1964): 'I remember calling on the Principal Medical Officer of the Board of Education . . . At the end of the interview this shy
and solemn man diffidently suggested that
the prune was a black-coated worker and
that this phrase might be useful to me. It
was.' Earlier, Chips Channon (8 April 1937)
had used the phrase in a literal sense concerning the clerical and professional class
when he wrote: 'The subject was "Widows
and Orphans" the Old Age Pensions Bill,
a measure which affects Southend and its
black-coated workers'.

[*Source*: Chips: *The Diaries of Sir Henry Channon*, ed. Robert Rhodes James, 1967.]

Hill, Patty Smith
American teacher (1868–1946)

2 *Happy Birthday to You.*

Originally entitled 'Good Morning to All'
and published in *Song Stories for Children*
(1893), Hill's well-known song with this
title was eventually copyrighted in 1935.
The music was written by her sister, Mildred
J. Hill (1859–1916). What we have here is
the 'most frequently sung phrase in English',
according to *The Guinness Book of Records*
(which also lists 'For He's a Jolly Good
Fellow' and 'Auld Lang Syne' as the top
songs of all time). 'Happy Birthday to You'
was the first line of the second stanza of the
original song. It has had a chequered legal
history because of the widespread belief that
it is in the public domain and, therefore, out
of copyright. It is not.

Hill, Rowland
English preacher (1744–1833)

3 *Why must the devil have all the best
tunes?*

According to E.W. Broome's biography of
Hill, what he said was: 'I do not see any good
reason why the devil should have all the

good tunes.' He was referring to Charles
Wesley's defence of the practice of setting
hymns to the music of popular songs. The
phrase is now used generally to rebut the
necessity for the virtuous and worthy to be
dull and dreary. This Revd Hill is not to be
confused with Sir Rowland Hill, originator
of the English penny postage system.

A perhaps better known – but later –
use of the phrase concerns William Booth
(1829–1912), the founder of the Salvation Army. It was his practice to use established tunes to accompany religious lyrics.
In this way, more than eighty music-hall
songs acquired religious lyrics, 'Champagne
Charlie is My Name', for example, becoming, 'Bless His Name He Sets Me Free'.
When Booth was challenged on the suit-
ablity of such a process, he was doubtful at
first, but then exclaimed, 'Why should the
Devil have all the best tunes!'

Hillary, Edmund
(later Sir Edmund)
New Zealand mountaineer (1919–   )

4 *Well, we knocked the bastard off!*

The first two climbers to reach the summit
of the world's highest mountain, Mount
Everest, in the Himalayas, were Hillary and
his Sherpa guide, Tenzing Norgay. They
were members of the British-led expedition
in 1953. In his autobiography *Nothing Venture, Nothing Win* (1975), Hillary described
what happened when they came down from
the summit on 29 May: 'George [Lowe] met
us with a mug of soup just above camp, and
seeing his stalwart frame and cheerful face
reminded me how fond of him I was. My
comment was not specially prepared for
public consumption but for George . . . He
nodded with pleasure . . . "Thought you
must have!"' Among the frequent mis-
renderings of the remark is, 'We done the
bugger!' – as in *PDMQ* (1980). That version has also been wrongly ascribed to
Tenzing Norday (who did not even speak
English).

Hillebrand, Fred
American songwriter (1893–1963)

5 *Home, James, and don't spare the
horses!*

A catchphrase used jocularly, as if talking
to your driver, telling someone to get a

move on. From the title of a song (1934) by Hillebrand and recorded by Elsie Carlisle in that year and by Hillebrand himself in 1935. The component 'Home, James!' had existed long before — in the works of Thackeray, for example.

Hillingdon, Lady (Alice)
Wife of 2nd Baron Hillingdon
(1857–1940)

1 *Close your eyes and think of England.*

The source that Partridge/*Catch Phrases* (1977) gives for this saying — in the sense of advice to women when confronted with the inevitability of sexual intercourse, or jocularly about doing almost anything unpalatable — is the *Journal* (1912) of Lady Hillingdon: 'I am happy now that Charles calls on my bedchamber less frequently than of old. As it is, I now endure but two calls a week and when I hear his steps outside my door I lie down on my bed, close my eyes, open my legs and think of England.'

There *was* a Lady Hillingdon who married the 2nd Baron in 1886. He was Conservative MP for West Kent (1885–92) and, according to *Who's Who* owned 'about 4,500 acres' when he died (in 1919). A portrait of Lady Hillingdon was painted by Sir Frank Dicksee PRA in 1904. A rose was also named after her.

But where her journals are, if they ever indeed existed, is unknown. Jonathan Gathorne-Hardy also quotes the 'journal' in *The Rise and Fall of the British Nanny* (1972), but just to complicate matters, he refers to her as Lady 'Hillingham', though *ODMQ* (1991) and *ODQ* (1992) in picking up this reference do not appear to have noticed.

Salome Dear, Not With a Porcupine (ed. Arthur Marshall, 1982) has it instead that the newly wedded Mrs Stanley Baldwin is supposed to have declared: 'I shut my eyes tight and thought of the Empire.' We may discount Bob Chieger's assumption in *Was It Good for You, Too?* (1983) that 'Close your eyes and think of England' was advice given to Queen Victoria on her wedding night. In 1977 there was a play by John Chapman and Anthony Marriott at the Apollo Theatre, London, with the title *Shut Your Eyes and Think of England*.

Sometimes the phrase occurs in the form 'lie back and think of England' but this is a conflation with 'she should lie back and enjoy it'.

Hills, Denis
English teacher and writer (1913–)

2 *[On President Idi Amin of Uganda] A village tyrant . . . a black Nero.*

Hills was sentenced to death for treason on account of these words in his book *The White Pumpkin* (1975) but was pardoned and freed after the intervention of the Queen and the Foreign Secretary. The 'village tyrant' taunt was not new. In his biography *Aneurin Bevan*, Vol. 2 (1975), Michael Foot describes the setting up of the National Health Service in the late 1940s and quotes Dr Roland Cockshut, one of the leading spokesmen on the BMA Council, as saying: 'We might have been going to meet Adolf Hitler . . . [but] he is no village tyrant, but a big man on a big errand.'

Hilton, James
English novelist (1900–54)

3 *Random Harvest.*

The novel (1941; filmed US, 1942) takes its title, as Hilton acknowledges, from an error in German wartime propaganda when it was claimed an attack had been launched on the British town of 'Random'. This was on the basis of a British communiqué that had stated that 'bombs were dropped at random'.

Hippocrates
Greek physician (c 460–357BC)

4 *Life is short, the art long.*

Usually quoted in the Latin form, *Ars longa vita brevis*. From his *Aphorisms*. Having read CONNOLLY 106:1, you may appreciate the saying 'Ars Longa, Vita Sackville-West', which was used as a chapter heading in my *Quote . . . Unquote* (1978).

Hitchcock, Raymond
American comedian (c 1870–1929)

5 *All dressed up and nowhere to go.*

The phrase comes from a song popularized by Hitchcock in *The Beauty Shop* (New York, 1914) and *Mr Manhattan* (London, 1915):

> When you're all dressed up and no
>   place to go,
> Life seems dreary, weary and slow.

My heart has ached as well as bled
For the tears I've shed,
When I've had no place to go
Unless I went back to bed . . .

The words gained further emphasis when they were used by newspaper editor William Allen White to describe the Progressive Party following Theodore Roosevelt's decision to retire from the Presidential competition in 1916. He said it was: 'All dressed up with nowhere to go.'

The *OED2* has this phrase starting life in a song by 'G. Whiting' (1912), 'When You're All Dressed Up and Have No Place to Go', but Lowe's *Directory of Popular Music* ascribes it to Silvio Hein and Benjamin Burt.

Cole Porter wrote a parody in 1914 concluding with the words '. . . and don't know Huerto Go'.

Hitler, Adolf

German Nazi leader (1889–1945)

1 *It was no secret that this time the revolution would have to be bloody . . . When we spoke of it, we called it 'The Night of the Long Knives* [Die Nacht der Langen Messer]'.

During the weekend of 29 June to 2 July 1934, there occurred in Nazi Germany the Night of the Long Knives, a phrase that has passed into common use for any kind of surprise purge in which no actual blood is spilt. On the original occasion, Hitler, aided by Himmler's black-shirted SS, liquidated the leadership of the brown-shirted SA. The SA, undisciplined storm-troopers, had helped Hitler gain power but were now getting in the way of his dealings with the German army. Some eighty-three were murdered on the pretext that they were plotting another revolution. Hitler's explanation (above) to the Reichstag on 13 July does not make it clear whether he himself coined the phrase. Indeed, it seems that he may have been alluding to an early Nazi marching song.

2 Nacht und Nebel [*Night and Fog*].

Nacht und Nebel was the name of a 1941 decree issued over Hitler's signature. It described a simple process: anyone suspected of a crime against occupying German forces was to disappear into 'night and fog'. Such people were thrown into the concentration camp system, in most cases never to be heard of again. Alain Resnais, the French film director, made a cinema short about a

concentration camp and called it *Nuit et Brouillard* (1955). Possibly, too, there is an echo in the title of Woody Allen's film *Shadows and Fog* (1992).

The phrase comes from Wagner's opera *Das Rheingold* (1869) — '*Nacht und Nebel niemand gleich*' is the spell that Alberich puts on the magic Tarnhelm, which renders him invisible and omnipresent. It means approximately, 'In night and fog no one is seen' or 'Night and fog is the same as being no one, a non-person' or 'Night and fog make you no one instantly'.

3 *The Final Solution* [Endlösung] *of the Jewish Problem.*

A euphemistic term given by Nazi officials from the summer of 1941 onwards to Hitler's plan to exterminate the Jews of Europe. Gerald Reitlinger in *The Final Solution* (1953) says that the choice of phrase was probably, though not certainly, Hitler's own. Before then it had been used in a non-specific way to cover other possibilities, such as emigration. It is estimated that up to six million Jews.

4 *Is Paris burning* [Brennt Paris]?

Following the D-Day landings on the northern coast of France, the next target was the liberation of Paris. The Allied forces managed to reach the French capital ahead of German Panzer divisions who would have tried to destroy the city. When Hitler put the above inquiry to Jodl at Oberkommando der Wehrmacht at Rastenberg (25 August 1944) — after Paris had been recaptured by the Allies — he received no reply. Later, the phrase was used as the title of a film (US, 1965).

5 *A last appeal to reason.*

On Friday, 19 July 1940 Adolf Hitler made a speech to the Reichstag. Following, as it did, the Fall of France and the May Blitz on London, it somewhat surprisingly appeared to contain an offer of peace to the British (though Hitler tried to draw a distinction between ordinary British folk and their warmongering leaders, principally Winston Churchill).

The speech and the peace proposal, although reported prominently in *The Times* next morning, were largely ignored, and the Germans were much annoyed by the British rejection of the peace offer that followed, notably from Lord Halifax, the Foreign Secretary, within the next few days. In an attempt to appeal to the British people, literally over the heads of the leadership, copies of the speech were dropped on England by the Luftwaffe in a leaflet-raid on the night of 1–2 August. The Imperial War Museum displays an actual copy of the tabloid newspaper-sized leaflet dropped over Somerset a little later, on 11 August. It is headed 'A LAST APPEAL TO REASON/BY/ADOLF HITLER/Speech before the Reichstag 19th July 1940', and makes very tedious reading.

A correspondent writes: 'I saw a copy myself at the time and tried to read it. Nearly half was taken up, I remember, by long lists of appointments, transfers and promotions in the German armed forces and civil administration . . . Needless to say, public opinion generally regarded the leaflet as beneath contempt. I remember hearing about an item on the subject in a cinema newsreel, which ended by showing a pair of hands cutting up the leaflet into small rectangles, threading a string through the corners, and hanging the bundle on a hook on a tiled wall. Very explicit for those prudish days: the audience, I was told, roared approval.'

1 *War is the father of all things.*

To add to his many other atrocities, Hitler was apparently a misquoter. In *The War Path: Hitler's Germany 1933–9* (1978), David Irving says that Hitler's favourite quotation was the above, which he attributed to Karl von Clausewitz. But, according to Mr Irving, it was in fact uttered by Heracles. Unverified.

In a speech at Chemnitz (2 April 1938), Hitler himself said: 'Man has become great through struggle . . . Struggle is the father of all things.'

Hobart, Alice Tisdale
American novelist (1882–1967)

2 *Oil for the Lamps of China.*

Hobart's novel with this title (1933; film US, 1935) was an exposé of American oil companies and their habit of sending bright young men to the Far East and dropping them when they were used up. The phrase is an old expression, used when winning anything or receiving a windfall. Other similar expressions include 'corn in Egypt' and 'little fishes are sweet'.

Hobbes, Thomas
English philosopher (1588–1679)

3 *Nasty, brutish and short.*

This description of life was given by Thomas Hobbes in *Leviathan, or the Matter, Form, and Power of a Commonwealth, Ecclesiastical and Civil*, Chap. 13 (1651). In this treatise of political philosophy, Hobbes sees man not as a social being but as a selfish creature. The state of nature in which he resides is one in which there are: 'No arts; no letters; no society; and which is worst of all, continual fear and danger of violent death; and the life of man, solitary, poor, nasty, brutish, and short.'

The last portion of this bleak view has fallen victim to over-quoting, as Philip Howard, Literary Editor of *The Times* noted on 15 August 1984. He warned of the danger that: 'We become so fond of hackneyed quotation that we trot it out, without thinking, at every opportunity.' He gave, as his example, 'the one about the life of man being "solitary, poor, nasty, brutish, and short," just to let everybody know that I am an intellectual sort of chap who reads Hobbes in the bath'.

Curiously, later that year, on 1 November, when *The Times* had a first leader on the assassination of Mrs Indira Gandhi, it began by observing that world figures know all too sickeningly well 'the continual fear and danger of violent death' that Thomas Hobbes identified as a condition of man. It went on to say: 'With that awful daily awareness, now goes for some a reminder of his definition of life as nasty, brutish and short.'

Holland, Henry Scott
English Anglican clergyman (1847–1918)

4 *Death is nothing at all . . . I have only slipped away into the next room.*

Hardly a day passes without newspaper reports of memorial services noting that 'so-and-so read from the works of Canon Henry Scott Holland'. The passage in question is the one beginning, 'Death is nothing at all', and judging by its popularity, the words have a message capable of comforting many who are bereaved.

But how did the reading enter into common use and where does it come from? It can be found printed, for example, in a booklet *Prayers Before & After Bereave-*

ment (Mayhew McCrimmon Ltd, 1985) and in a small, illustrated hardback (Souvenir Press, 1987), but in both cases these are abbreviated texts and taken out of context. For the real answer, we must go back to the author himself. One suggestion was that Holland had put the words in a letter, which he directed to be read after his own death and at his own funeral.

Holland was editor of the magazines *Commonwealth* and *Miracles*, he was a Canon of St Paul's Cathedral, noted for his sermons (some of which were published), and he became Regius Professor of Divinity at Oxford. He has a memorial tablet in St Paul's crypt (erected by his sisters) but it makes no reference to 'Death is . . .' — understandably, as the popularity of the words is of only recent origin. According to the *Dictionary of National Biography*, Holland was buried at Cuddesdon Church, Oxfordshire, but his grave has not been located, if it is there.

The popular passage comes from a sermon on death entitled 'The King of Terrors'. Holland delivered it in St Paul's Cathedral on 15 May 1910, at which time the body of King Edward VII was lying in state at Westminster. The context is important:

I suppose all of us hover between two ways of regarding death, which appear to be in hopeless contradiction with each other. First, there is the familiar and instinctive recoil from it as embodying the supreme and irrevocable disaster . . .

But, then, there is another aspect altogether which death can wear for us. It is that which first comes to us, perhaps, as we look down upon the quiet face, so cold and white, of one who has been very near and dear to us. There it lies in possession of its own secret. It knows it all. So we seem to feel. And what the face says in its sweet silence to us as a last message from one whom we loved is: 'Death is nothing at all. It does not count. I have only slipped away into the next room. Nothing has happened. Everything remains exactly as it was. I am I, and you are you, and the old life that we lived so fondly together is untouched, unchanged. Whatever we were to each other, that we are still. Call me by the old familiar name. Speak of me in the easy way which you always used. Put no difference into your tone. Wear no forced air of solemnity or sorrow. Laugh as we always laughed at the little jokes that we enjoyed together. Play, smile, think of

me, pray for me. Let my name be ever the household word that it always was. Let it be spoken without an effort, without the ghost of a shadow upon it. Life means all that it ever meant. It is the same as it ever was. There is absolute and unbroken continuity. What is this death but a negligible accident? Why should I be out of mind because I am out of sight? I am but waiting for you, for an interval, somewhere very near, just around the corner. All is well. Nothing is hurt; nothing is lost. One brief moment and all will be as it was before. How we shall laugh at the trouble of parting when we meet again!'

So the face speaks. Surely while we speak there is a smile flitting over it; a smile as of gentle fun at the trick played us by seeming death . . .

The sermon was published posthumously in a collection entitled *Facts of the Faith* (1919).

There is a basic similarity of thought contained in a sermon by an earlier Dean of St Paul's, with whose works one assumes Holland must have been familiar, John Donne. Preaching about death (as he did so often), on Easter Day 1627, Donne said in St Paul's (the earlier building): 'Though death have divided us . . . yet we do live together already, in a Holy Communion of Saints . . . If the dead, and we, be not upon one floore, nor under one story, yet we are under one roofe. We think not a friend lost, because he is gone into another roome, nor because he is gone into another Land; And into another world, no man is gone; for that Heaven, which God created, and this world, is all one world.'

Homer

Greek poet (*fl.* eighth century BC)

1 Yield to the Night.

Title of a film (UK, 1956) — the actress Diana Dors's finest hour as a condemned murderess — based on a novel by Joan Henry. But where does the phrase come from and what does it mean? One translation of a passage from *The Iliad* (Bk VII) is: 'But night is already at hand; it is well to yield to the night.' Alas, another is: 'The light is failing. We should do well to take the hint.' Either way, in the original Greek, Maurice Baring used to say that it was the most beautiful line in Homer.

Hood, Thomas
English poet (1799–1845)

1 *There is a silence where hath been*
  no sound,
  There is a silence where no sound
  may be,
  In the cold grave — under the deep,
  deep sea.

From Hood's sonnet, 'Silence'. These were
the last words heard in the film *The Piano*
(1993) by the New Zealand writer and
director, Jane Campion. They are 'spoken'
by the dumb heroine who has just consigned
her piano to the bottom of the sea and who
has also come near to death herself by being
dragged down with it.

Hoover, Herbert
American Republican 31st President
(1874–1964)

2 *We are challenged with a peacetime*
  choice between the American system of
  rugged individualism and a European
  philosophy of diametrically opposed
  doctrines — doctrines of paternalism
  and state socialism.

So said Hoover, running for the Presidency,
in a speech in New York on 22 October
1928. Six years later he commented: 'While
I can make no claim for having introduced
the term "rugged individualism", I should
have been proud to have invented it. It
has been used by American leaders for
over half a century in eulogy of those God-
fearing men and women of honesty whose
stamina and character and fearless assertion
of rights led them to make their own way in
life.'

3 *The grass will grow in the streets of a*
  hundred cities, a thousand towns.

From a speech (31 October 1932) on proposals 'to reduce the protective tariff to a
competitive tariff for revenue'. The image
had earlier been used by William Jennings
Bryan in his 'Cross of Gold' speech (73:1):
'Burn down your cities and leave our farms,
and your cities will spring up again as if by
magic; but destroy our farms and the grass
will grow in the streets of every city in the
country.'

Horace
Roman poet (65–8BC)

4 Pro patria mori.

This epitaph, frequently put on the graves
of those killed on active service, is also a
family motto. The full phrase is '*dulce et
decorum est pro patria mori* [it is sweet and
honourable to die for one's country]' (*Odes*,
III.ii.13). The poet Wilfred Owen (1893–
1918) used the saying with an ironic sense in
his 1917 poem 'Dulce et Decorum Est'.

5 *Even Homer nods.*

Meaning 'even the greatest, best and wisest
of us can't be perfect all the time, and can
make mistakes'. Current by the eighteenth
century at least is the form: 'Let Homer,
who sometimes nods, sleep soundly upon
your shelf for three or four years' (letter
of Lord Chesterfield to Lord Huntingdon,
31 August 1749). Mencken has 'Even
Homer sometimes nods' as an English proverb derived from Horace, *De Arte Poetica*
(*c* 8BC): 'I am indignant when worthy
Homer nods' — and familiar since the
seventeenth century. Longinus (*c* 213–
273AD) evidently added: 'They say that
Homer sometimes nods. Perhaps he does —
but then he dreams as Zeus might dream.'

Housman, A.E.
English poet (1859–1936)

6 *I had a visit not long ago from Clarence*
  Darrow, the great American barrister
  for defending murderers. He had only
  a few days in England but he could
  not return home without seeing me,
  because he had so often used my poems
  to rescue his clients from the electric
  chair. Loeb and Leopold owe their
  life sentence partly to me; and he gave
  me a copy of his speech, in which,
  sure enough, two of my pieces are
  misquoted.

From a letter to Basil Housman (dated 29
December 1927), included in *The Letters of
A.E. Housman* (1971).

7 *That is indeed very good. I shall have to*
  repeat that on the Golden Floor.

So Housman said to his doctor who told him
a risqué story to cheer him up before he died

(quoted in the *Daily Telegraph*, 21 February 1984). 'Golden floor' is an expression for heaven, possibly derived from 'threshing floor', as in various Old Testament verses. Current by 1813 (Shelley, 'Queen Mab'), the phrase also occurs in the Harvest Festival hymn 'Come ye thankful people, come'.

Howe, Sir Geoffrey
(later Lord Howe)
British Conservative politician (1926–)

1 *I have more than one pair of trousers.*

In November 1982, when Howe was Chancellor of the Exchequer, he was travelling by rail on an overnight sleeper and had his trousers stolen. He merely commented, 'I have more than one pair of trousers', and it was left to an anonymous colleague — probably a fellow member of the Cabinet — to say, 'I am thrilled about the loss of your trousers . . . because it revealed your human face'. This would seem to be quite a reliable quote, as it was repeated by Lady Howe in a magazine interview two years later.

Howitt, Mary
English writer (1799–1888)

2 *'Will you walk into my parlour?'*
Said the spider to the fly.

Should be 'said a spider to a fly', if quoting Howitt's 'The Spider and the Fly' (1834). There have been several musical settings of this poem, but even in the Rolling Stones song called 'The Spider and the Fly' (written by Nanker and Phelge, recorded 1971) the lyric states correctly: 'Don't say Hi! like a spider to a fly' and 'I said my, my, my, like a spider to a fly,/Jump right ahead in my web.'
The verse was parodied by Lewis Carroll in *Alice's Adventures in Wonderland* (1965) as: ' "Will you walk a little faster?" said a whiting to a snail.'

Hume, David
Scottish philosopher (1711–76)

3 *It is much more likely that human testimony should err, than that the laws of nature should be violated.*

In *My Early Life*, Chap. 9 (1930), Winston Churchill says, 'Close reasoning can conduct one to the precise conclusion that miracles are impossible: that . . .', and then quotes the above passage without attribution. Many readers assume that it must be from Hume but have been unable to find the exact words in that man's works. The Revd Dr L.M. Brown of Edinburgh offered this instead, from Thomas Paine's *The Age of Reason* (1793): 'If we are to suppose a miracle to be something so entirely out of course of what is called nature, that she must go out of that course to accomplish it, and we see an account of such a miracle by the person who said he saw it, it raises a question in the mind very easily decided; which is, is it more probable that nature should go out of her course, or that a man should tell a lie? We have never seen, in our time, nature go out of her course . . . it is therefore at least millions to one that the reporter of a miracle tells a lie.'
Dr Brown commented: 'It is perhaps not impertinent to remark that this argument, though deserving serious consideration, is not so unanswerable as Thomas Paine seems to imagine.' Churchill's quotation may simply be his own paraphrase of Paine or Hume.

Humphrey, Hubert
American Democratic Vice-President (1911–78)

4 *It was once said that the moral test of government is how that government treats those who are in the dawn of life, the children; those who are in the twilight of life, the elderly; and those who are in the shadows of life, the sick, the needy and the handicapped.*

From his speech at the dedication of the Hubert H. Humphrey building (1 November 1977), but the source of the 'once said' remains untraced.

Hussein, Saddam
Iraqi President (1937–)

5 *The great, the jewel and the mother of battles has begun.*

Said at the start of the Gulf War (6 January 1991, quoted in the *Independent*, 19 January 1991). Although, as a result, 'the mother of – –' became a catchphrase format in the West, Hussein was simply using the commonplace Arabic 'mother of' construction.

Hutchins, Robert M.
American educator (1899–1977)

1 *Whenever I feel like exercise, I lie down until the feeling passes.*

Untraced, but apparently said by the former University of Chicago President rather than all the other candidates (Wilde, Twain, W.C. Fields and so on). Ascribed by J.P. McEvoy in *Young Man Looking Backwards* (1938). However, Hutchin's biographer, Harry S. Ashmore, ascribes it to McEvoy and says that it was merely one of many sayings Hutchins collected to use when appropriate. In the film *Mr Smith Goes to Washington* (US, 1939), Thomas Mitchell speaks the line: 'Every time I think of exercising, I have to lie down till the feeling leaves me.'

Hutchinson, A.S.M.
British novelist (1879–1971)

2 *Once aboard the lugger and the girl is mine.*

In 1908 Hutchinson called a novel *Once Aboard the Lugger — the History of George and Mary*, but he was merely alluding to an established 'male catchphrase either joyously or derisively jocular', as Partridge/ *Catch Phrases* notes. It may have come originally from a late Victorian melodrama — either *My Jack and Dorothy* by Ben Landeck (*c* 1890) or from a passage in *The Gypsy Farmer* by John Benn Johnstone (*d* 1891): 'I want you to assist me in forcing her on board the lugger; once there, I'll frighten her into marriage.'

The phrase also occurred later in the music-hall song 'On the Good Ship Yacki-Hicki-Doo-La', written and composed by Billy Merson in 1918. Benham (1948) has a different version, as often. According to him 'Once aboard the lugger and all is well' was said to have been an actor's gag in *Black Eyed Susan*, a nautical melodrama (*c* 1830).

Huxley, Aldous
English novelist (1894–1963)

3 *The Gioconda Smile.*

The title of a Huxley short story (included in *Mortal Coils*, 1922, and dramatized, 1948). It refers to Leonardo da Vinci's portrait of a young woman, known as 'Mona Lisa' (*c* 1503), now in the Louvre, Paris, which has a curious, enigmatic, unsmiling smile, almost a smirk. '*La Gioconda*' and '*La Joconde*', the titles by which the painting is also known, may either be translated as 'the jocund lady', as might be expected, or refer to the sitter's actual surname. She may have been the wife of Francesco del Giocondo (whose name does, however, derive from 'jocund').

The smile was already being mentioned by 1550 in Giorgio Vasari's life of the painter. Vasari probably made up the story that Leonardo employed 'singers and musicians or jesters' to keep the sitter 'full of merriment'. Any number of nineteenth-century writers were fascinated by the smile, some seeing it as disturbing and almost evil. More recently, Lawrence Durrell commented: 'She has the smile of a woman who has just dined off her husband', and Cole Porter included 'You're the smile/On the Mona Lisa' in his list song 'You're the Top!' (1934). Ponchielli's opera *La Gioconda* (1876), after Victor Hugo's drama, and a D'Annunzio play (1898) are not connected with da Vinci's portrait (except that they feature jocund girls).

4 *I looked down by chance, and went on passionately staring by choice, at my own crossed legs. Those folds in the trousers — what a labyrinth of endlessly significant complexity! And the texture of the grey flannel — how rich, how deeply, mysteriously sumptuous!*

Huxley's famous piece describing a discovery he made using mescaline occurs in *The Doors of Perception* (1954) and caused people much amusement when quoted in the druggy 1960s.

I

Ibarruri, Dolores
('La Pasionaria')
Spanish Communist leader (1895–1989)

1 *Fascism will not pass, the executioners of October will not pass.*

From a translation of a radio speech given in Madrid (18 July 1936). As '*No pasarán* [They shall not pass]' it became a Republican slogan in the Spanish Civil War (1936–9). Compare PÉTAIN 264:2.

2 *It is better to die on your feet than to live on your knees.*

Said in a radio speech from Paris calling on the women of Spain to help defend the Republic (3 September 1936). According to her autobiography (1966), she had used these words earlier, on 18 July, when broadcasting in Spain (see above). Emiliano Zapata (c 1877–1919), the Mexican guerilla leader, had used the expression before her in 1910: 'Men of the South! It is better to die on your feet than to live on your knees! [. . . *mejor morir a pie que vivir en rodillas*]'. Franklin D. Roosevelt picked up the expression in his message accepting an honorary degree from Oxford University (19 June 1941): 'We, too, are born to freedom, and believing in freedom, are willing to fight to maintain freedom. We, and all others who believe as we do, would rather die on our feet than live on our knees.'

Ibsen, Henrik
Norwegian playwright (1828–1906)

3 *You should never have your best trousers on when you go out to fight for freedom and truth.*

From Ibsen's play *An Enemy of the People* (1882). Mieder & Co. in *A Dictionary of American Proverbs* (1992) have it, anonymously, as a proverb: 'Never wear your best trousers when you go out to fight for freedom.'

Inge, William
English clergyman and theologian (1860–1954)

4 *From a pillar of the church to a column in the* Evening Standard.

Sometimes this saying is rendered as 'a lot of pillars of society end up as columns in the *News of the World*', but it seems that the original is what Dean Inge said — having 'ceased to be a pillar of the Church, [he was] now two columns of the *Evening Standard*', quoted in Alfred Noyes, *Two Worlds for Memory* (1953).

Ingham, Sir Bernard
English civil servant (1932–)

5 *Kill the Messenger.*

Ingham was Chief Press Secretary to the Prime Minister, Margaret Thatcher, from 1979 to 1990. The somewhat surprising title of his memoirs (1990) was an apparent allusion to what reputedly happened to messengers bringing bad news in classical times. Ingham's implication would seem to be that press officers get blamed for their master's — or in this case mistress's — doings, just as the media are often blamed for the news which they report rather than initiate. As early as Sophocles, *Antigone* (l.277), a sentinel was saying to Creon: 'None love the messenger who brings bad news.' Compare the maltreatment of messengers in several Shakespeare plays: in *Antony and Cleopatra* (II.v.85), Cleopatra threatens a messenger with a knife and the messenger says, 'It is never good to bring bad news'.

J

Jackson, 'Stonewall'
American general (1824–63)

1 *Let us cross over the river, and rest under [the shade of] the trees.*

Jackson's dying words are said to have been to this effect. The Confederate general in the American Civil War had been shot in error by his own troops in May 1863. *Across the River and Into the Trees* was the title of a novel (1950) by Ernest Hemingway. Accordingly, E.B. White's noted parody of Hemingway's style (collected 1954) was called 'Across the Street and Into the Grill'. Often used allusively: 'Then we began to notice, as we lazily cropped the grass that it was greener across the river at Shepperton Studios than at Pinewood. It was time for The Archers and their followers to move across the river and into the trees' — Michael Powell, *Million-Dollar Movie* (1992).

Jacobs, Joe
American boxing manager (1896–1940)

2 *We wuz robbed!*

Believing that his client, Max Schmeling, had been cheated of a heavyweight title by Jack Sharkey (21 June 1932), Jacobs shouted this protest into a microphone.

3 *I should have stood in bed.*

Jacobs left his sick-bed to attend the baseball World Series in October 1935. Having bet on the losers, he opined accordingly. Quoted in John Lardner, *Strong Cigars and Lovely Women* (1951). Leo Rosten in *Hooray for Yiddish* (1983) puts his own gloss on: 'The most celebrated instance of this usage was when Mike [*sic*] Jacobs, the fight promoter, observing the small line at his

ticket window, moaned, "I should of stood in bed!" *Stood* is a calque for the Yiddish *geshtanen*, which can mean both "stood" and "remained". Mr Jacobs' use of "of" simply followed the speech pattern of his childhood.'

James I
(James VI of Scotland)
English/Scottish Sovereign (1566–1625)

4 *Have I three kingdoms and thou must needs fly into my eye?*

To a fly, quoted in John Selden *Table Talk* (1689). Compare Laurence Sterne, *Tristram Shandy*, Bk 2, Chap. 12 (1759–67): ' "I'll not hurt thee," says my uncle Toby, rising from his chair, and going across the room with the fly in his hand . . . lifting up the sash, and opening his hand as he spoke . . . "go, poor devil, get thee gone, why should I hurt thee? — This world surely is wide enough to hold both thee and me".'

James, Henry
American novelist (1843–1916)

5 *All human life is there.*

In James's 'Madonna of the Future' (1879) there occurs the line: 'Cats and monkeys, monkeys and cats — all human life is there.' What is the connection, if any, with the *News of the World*, which used the line to promote itself *c* 1958–9? In 1981 Maurice Smelt, the advertising copywriter, explained: ' "All human life is there" was my idea, but I don't, of course, pretend that they were my words. I simply lifted them from *The Oxford Dictionary of Quotations*. I didn't bother to tell the client that they were from Henry James, suspecting that, after the "Henry James–WHO HE?" stage, he would come up with tiresome arguments about being too high-hat for his readership. I did check whether we were clear on copyright, which we were by a year or two . . . I do recall its use as baseline in a tiny little campaign trailing a series that earned the *News of the World* a much-publicized but toothless rebuke from the Press Council. The headline of that campaign was: " 'I've been a naughty girl', says Diana Dors". The meiosis worked, as the *News of the World* knew it would. They ran an extra million copies of the first issue of the series.'

1 *So here it is at last, the distinguished thing.*

After suffering a stroke (2 December 1915), James reported that he had heard a voice saying this (as recounted in Edith Wharton, *A Backward Glance*, 1934). These are not his dying words, however. He did not die until 28 February. His last recorded words, said to Alice James, were, 'Tell the boys to follow, to be faithful, to take me seriously' (H. Montgomery Hyde, *Henry James at Home*, 1969).

Jefferson, Thomas
American polymath and 3rd President (1743–1826)

2 *We hold these truths to be self-evident; that all men are created equal; that they are endowed by their creator with certain unalienable rights; that among these are life, liberty, and the pursuit of happiness.*

From the Declaration of Independence (4 July 1776), which Jefferson drafted. Note, not 'inalienable'. George Mason had already drafted the Virginia Declaration of Rights (1774), that 'all men are by nature equally free and independent and have certain inherent rights'.

3 *You retire from the great theatre of action with the blessings of your fellow citizens.*

From the President of Congress's remarks at the resignation of George Washington as commander-in-chief (23 December 1783), probably penned by Jefferson. Compare Horace Walpole: 'That splendid theatre of pitiful passion', said when he was quitting the House of Commons, which he did by way of protest at the small-mindedness of the men at the top (and recalled in *Memoirs of the Reign of King George III*, 1845).

4 *Avoid all foreign entanglements.*

Not quite what Jefferson said in his first inaugural address (4 March 1801) — rather, 'Peace, commerce, and honest friendship with all nations, entangling alliances with none . . .' — but a cornerstone of American foreign policy for generations.

5 *The price of liberty is eternal vigilance.*

See CURRAN 111:3.

6 *Peace is our passion.*

In a letter to Sir John Sinclair (30 June 1803). Compare 'Peace is our profession', the slogan of America's Strategic Air Command (by 1962).

7 *Government is best which governs least.*

Quoted in Fawn M. Brodie, *Thomas Jefferson: An Intimate History* (1974), but otherwise untraced.

8 *No one more sincerely wishes the spread of information among mankind than I do, and none has greater confidence in its effect upwards, supporting free and good government.*

Quoted in 1810 and reported in *The President Speaks* (1984) but otherwise untraced.

9
> HERE WAS BURIED
> THOMAS JEFFERSON
> AUTHOR OF THE
> DECLARATION
> OF
> AMERICAN INDEPENDENCE,
> OF THE
> STATUTE OF VIRGINIA
> FOR RELIGIOUS FREEDOM,
> AND FATHER OF THE
> UNIVERSITY OF VIRGINIA.
>
> BORN APRIL 2 1743 O.S.
> DIED JULY 4 1826

Jefferson devised his own epitaph, 'because by these, as testimonials I have lived, I wish most to be remembered'. He omitted that he had been US President for two terms. His birthdate would be April 13, following calendar revision; his draft, of course, left the date of death to be inserted. The epitaph is now to be found inscribed on an obelisk over Jefferson's grave in the family cemetery near his house, Monticello, Virginia, though this stone is a replacement for the original and dates from 1883.

Jenkin, Patrick
(later Lord Jenkin)
British Conservative politician (1926–   )

1 *People can clean their teeth in the dark.*

Advice to members of the public as Energy Minister, during Britain's 'Three-Day Week' energy crisis in 1974 (caused by a coal miners' strike). Interviewed on BBC Radio 1 *Newsbeat* on 15 January, Jenkin appealed to householders to save energy and reduce the consumption of electricity: 'You don't even [need to] do your teeth with the light on. You can do it in the dark.' He was photographed using his electric razor by candlelight.

Jenkins, Roy
(later Lord Jenkins)
Welsh-born Labour, then Social Democrat, then Liberal Democrat politician (1920–   )

2 *Breaking the mould [of British politics].*

'The politics of the left and centre of this country are frozen in an out-of-date mould which is bad for the political and economic health of Britain and increasingly inhibiting for those who live within the mould. Can it be broken?' So said Jenkins in a speech at a House of Commons Press Gallery lunch on 8 June 1980. The following year, when the Social Democratic Party was established, there was much talk of 'breaking the mould of British politics' — i.e. doing away with the traditional two-party system.

This was by no means a new way of describing political change and abolishing an old form of government in a way that prevented its being reconstituted. Indeed, Jenkins had quoted Andrew Marvell's 'Horatian Ode Upon Cromwell's Return from Ireland' (1650): 'And cast the kingdoms old,/Into another mould' in his book *What Matters Now*, as early as 1972.

A.J.P. Taylor in his *English History 1914–1945* (1965), had written: 'Lloyd George needed a new crisis to break the mould of political and economic habit.' The image evoked, as in the days of the Luddites,

was of breaking the mould from which iron machinery is cast so completely that the machinery has to be re-cast from scratch.

Jerome, Jerome K.
English writer (1859–1927)

3 *I like work: it fascinates me. I can sit and look at it for hours.*

From his masterwork *Three Men In a Boat* (1889). Jerome also wrote *Idle Thoughts of an Idle Fellow* (1886). How appropriate, then, that the inscription on his grave in St Mary's churchyard, Ewelme, Oxfordshire, is: 'For we are labourers together with God' (1 Corinthians 3:9).

Jessel, George
American entertainer (1898–1981)

4 *Same old story: you give 'em what they want and they'll fill the theatre.*

On the large number of mourners at film producer Harry Cohn's funeral (in 1958). Quoted in Lillian Hellman, *Scoundrel Time* (1976) and also attributed to Red Skelton. An unattributed version appears in Oscar Levant, *The Unimportance of Being Oscar* (1968).

Joad, C.E.M.
English philosopher (1891–1953)

5 *It all depends what you mean by . . .*

The Brains Trust was a discussion programme first broadcast by the BBC in 1941, taking its title from President Roosevelt's name for his circle of advisers (in America, more usually '*brain* trust'). Joad was a regular participant, who became a national figure and was often called 'Professor', though he was not entitled to be. His discussion technique was to jump in first and leave the other speakers with little else to say. Alternatively, he would try to undermine arguments by using the phrase for which he became famous. When the chairman once read out a question from a listener, Mr W.E. Jack of Keynsham — 'Are thoughts things or about things?' — Joad inevitably began his answer with, 'It all depends what you mean by a "thing".'

His broadcasting career ended rather abruptly when he was found travelling by rail using a ticket that was not valid. The BBC banished him.

Joffre, Joseph Jacques Césaire
French general (1852–1931)

1 *Troops that can advance no farther must, at any price, hold on to the ground they have conquered and die on the spot rather than give way.*

Joffre, as French Commander-in-Chief, issued his order for the start of the (first) Battle of the Marne on 5 September 1914. In his memoirs (1932), he recalled that his staff was installed in an ancient convent of the Order of Cordeliers, 'and my own office was in what had formerly been a monk's cell. It was from here that I directed the Battle of the Marne and it was in this room that, at half past seven next morning, I signed the following order addressed to the troops . . .'. The text was apparently written by General Maurice Gustave Gamelin (1872–1958). Together, the French and British managed to push the Germans back along the 200-mile front of the Marne river, preventing the enemy from reaching Paris as it had threatened to do.

John of the Cross, Saint
Spanish mystic and poet (1542–91)

2 *Dark night of the soul.*

Denoting mental and spiritual suffering prior to some big step, the phrase 'La Noche oscura del alma' was used as the title of a work in Spanish by St John of the Cross. This was a treatise based on his poem 'Songs of the Soul Which Rejoices at Having Reached Union with God by the Road of Spiritual Negation' (c 1578). In *The Crack-Up* (1936), F. Scott Fitzgerald wrote: 'In a real dark night of the soul it is always three o'clock in the morning, day after day.' Douglas Adams wrote *The Long Dark Teatime of the Soul* (1988).

John, Augustus
Welsh artist (1878–1961)

3 *We have become, Nina, the sort of people our parents warned us about.*

This was noted down about the time Michael Holroyd's two-volume biography of John appeared (1974–5), but it is not in that book. Holroyd confirms it *was*

addressed to Nina Hamnett, something of a figure in London Bohemia, but says that he encountered it only *after* he had written his biography. He first used it in 1981 in his entry on John in *Makers of Modern Culture*. It was broadcast in BBC Radio *Quote . . . Unquote* in January 1977.

When it appeared in the second *Quote . . . Unquote* book, Bernard Davis wrote in 1981 from Turkish Cyprus, saying: 'An acquaintance of mine, York-Lodge, a close friend of Claud Cockburn and Evelyn Waugh, was continually saying, "We are the sort of people our parents warned us against", and claiming it as his own. This was about 1924.'

It was probably a common expression dating from between the wars, if not before. The saying was reported as graffiti from New York City in the early 1970s ('We are the people our parents warned us about') and a placard carried at a demonstration by homosexuals in New York in 1970 asserted, 'We're the people our parents warned us against'. In 1968, Nicholas Von Hoffman brought out a book on hippies with the title *We Are the People Our Parents Warned Us Against*.

Johnson, Arte
American entertainer (1934–)

4 *Very interesting . . . but stupid!*

Although I used this as the title of a 'book of catchphrases from the world of entertainment' (1980), because it seemed to describe the contents, it was not strictly speaking the fixed form of a catchphrase. For no accountable reason, Johnson used to appear on the TV series *Rowan and Martin's Laugh-In* as a bespectacled German soldier wearing a helmet. He would sometimes peer through a potted plant and comment on the proceedings with the thickly-accented words, 'Verrrry interesting . . . but it stinks!' or 'but stupid!' or whatever.

An enormous hit on US television from its inception in 1967, *Laugh-In* lasted until 1973 and was briefly revived, without Rowan and Martin and with little success, in 1977. The original was a brightly coloured, fast-moving series of sketches and gags, with a wide range of stock characters, linked together by the relaxed charm of Dan Rowan (1922–87) and Dick Martin (b 1923).

In *ODMQ* (1991) this catchphrase is ascribed to Rowan and Martin themselves.

Johnson, Burges
American writer (1877–1963)

1 *I wish poor Bella's knees were made*
to bend,
I truly am as sorry as can be.
I hope that You won't mind, and that
You'll send
The blessings that each dolly asks of
Thee.
And, Lord, I pray that You will just
pretend
This is my dollies' talking 'stead of me.

From Johnson's 'Hear My Dollies' Prayer', which appeared on a picture postcard (1909) showing a little girl praying at her bedside, flanked by her dolls, all kneeling except 'Poor Bella' whose knees have not been 'made to bend'. Remembered nostalgically by many.

Johnson, Hiram
American all-party Senator (1866–1945)

2 *The first casualty when war comes is*
truth.

In a speech to the US Senate, *c* 1917 but untraced. Curiously, his namesake Samuel said much the same thing less pithily in *The Idler* (11 November 1758) : 'Among the calamities of war, may be justly numbered the diminution of the love of truth, by the falsehoods which interest dictates and credulity encourages.'

Johnson, Lyndon B.
American Democratic 36th President (1908–73)

3 *The Great Society.*

Richard N. Goodwin suggested the name for Johnson's policy platform in the US. After tentative use in over a dozen speeches, the phrase was first elevated to capital letters in a speech at the University of Michigan at Ann Arbor in May 1964: 'In your time, we have the opportunity to move not only toward the rich society and the powerful society but upward to the Great Society.' According to Hugh Sidey, *A Very Personal Presidency* (1986), Goodwin stumbled on the phrase one midnight in early March 1964 when working as a part-time speechwriter. Even when Goodwin was taken on full time, Johnson was reluctant to admit that he had a hand in the President's speeches.

4 *We Americans know, although others*
appear to forget, the risks of spreading
conflict. We still seek no wider war.

In a broadcast address on 4 August 1964. 'No wider war', 'No more war' and 'Never again', although recurring slogans, were probably not much heard before the twentieth century. At the UN in 1965 Pope Paul VI quoted President Kennedy 'four years ago' to the effect that 'mankind must put an end to war, or war will put an end to mankind . . . No more war, never again war.' (He said this in Italian.)

Earlier, the phrase was used by Winston Churchill at the end of a letter to Lord Beaverbrook in 1928 (quoted in Martin Gilbert's biography of Churchill, Vol. 5.) A.J.P. Taylor in his *English History 1914–45* suggests that the slogan was 'irresistible' at the end of the First World War. David Lloyd George had said in a newspaper interview (*The Times*, 29 September 1916): ' "Never again" has become our battle cry.' Churchill in his *The Second World War* (Vol. 1) said of the French: 'with one passionate spasm [they cried] never again.'

In *Goodbye to Berlin* (1939), Christopher Isherwood describes a Nazi book burning. The books are from a 'small liberal pacifist publisher'. One of the Nazis holds up a book called '*Nie Wieder Krieg* [Never again war]' as though it were 'a nasty kind of reptile'. 'No More War!' a fat, well-dressed woman laughs scornfully and savagely. 'What an idea!'

Later, in the mid-1960s, 'Never again' became the slogan of the militant Jewish Defence League in reference to the Holocaust. A stone monument erected near the birthplace of Adolf Hitler at Braunau, Austria, in 1989 (the centenary of his birth) bore the lines 'For Peace, Freedom and Democracy — Never Again Fascism [*Nie wieder Faschismus*] — Millions of Dead are a warning'.

5 *For the world which seems to lie out*
before us like a land of dreams.

In the summer of 1965 the poet Robert Lowell had outraged Johnson by refusing to attend a Festival of the Arts at the White House, in protest at America's involvement in the Vietnam War. A few weeks later, in an address to a gathering of students, Johnson said: 'Robert Lowell, the poet, doesn't like everything around here. But I like one of his lines where he wrote . . .'

Unfortunately for Johnson, the above was not a line of Lowell's but from Matthew Arnold's 'Dover Beach'. Lowell had used the line as an epigraph to his book *The Mills of the Kavanaughs*. Also, Arnold did not write 'lie out', simply 'lie'. Stand up the speechwriter who landed the President in this soup.

1 *That Gerald Ford. He can't fart and chew gum at the same time.*

Quoted in J.K. Galbraith, *A Life in Our Times* (1981). This is the correct version of the oft-misquoted: 'He couldn't walk and chew gum at the same time.'

2 *It is true that a house divided against itself is a house that cannot stand. There is a division in the American house now and believing this as I do, I have concluded that I should not permit the Presidency to become involved in the partisan divisions that are developing in this political year. Accordingly, I shall not seek, and I will not accept, the nomination of my party for another term as your President.*

Unable to cope with the Vietnam War, Johnson surprised everyone by announcing in a TV address on 31 March 1968 his intention not to stand again as President. Even an hour before the broadcast he did not know whether he would use the extra portion about his retirement. Apart from the biblical reference to a 'house divided' (St Mark 3:25, which perhaps had come to Johnson by way of a Lincoln speech in 1858 on the circumstances that had led to the American Civil War), there is also an echo of General Sherman's words to the Republican Convention in 1884 (see 310:3).

Johnson, Dr Samuel
English writer and lexicographer (1709–84)

3 *The Common Reader.*

The title of the two volumes of Virginia Woolf's collected essays, published in 1925 and 1932, comes from Dr Johnson's life of Gray in *The Lives of the English Poets* (1779–81). Praising the 'Elegy', he writes: 'In the character of his Elegy I rejoice to concur with the common reader . . . The churchyard abounds with images which find a mirror in every mind, and with sentiments to which every bosom returns an echo.'

4 *No, you smell, I stink.*

An exchange is reported thus: someone said to Dr Johnson, 'You smell!' Replied the sage and lexicographer, 'No, *you* smell, *I* stink'. Michael Grosvenor Myer commented (1992): 'Surely merely a folktale about a pedant insisting on precise application of words, attributed to Dr Johnson because, as a lexicographer, he would be thought fastidious about usage. Compare the somewhat similar tale of Webster (another famous lexicographer) discovered by his wife as he embraced one of the maidservants: "Why, Noah, I am surprised!" "No, dear, you are astonished; it is I who am surprised".'

5 *An exotick and irrational entertainment.*

This is not Dr Johnson's definition of 'opera' in his *Dictionary* (1755), as is often supposed. The remark occurs rather in his piece on John Hughes in *The Lives of the English Poets* (1779–81). He is referring in particular to *Italian* opera 'which has been always combated, and always has prevailed.' Johnson was self-admittedly unmusical but had no objection to *English* opera.

In Kenneth Clark's *Civilisation* (1969, and in the TV original), he says: 'Opera, next to Gothic architecture, is one of the strangest inventions of western man. It could not have been foreseen by any logical process. Dr Johnson's much quoted definition, which as far as I can make out he never wrote, "an extravagant and irrational entertainment", is perfectly correct; and at first it seems surprising that it should have been brought to perfection in the age of reason.' Clark is quite right that Johnson did not call it an 'extravagant and irrational entertainment' but how interesting that he did not go so far as to check and find out what Johnson *did* say.

In his *Dictionary* Johnson does not in fact define the word 'opera' himself, but merely quotes Dryden: 'An *opera* is a poetical tale or fiction, represented by vocal and intrumental musick, adorned with scenes, machines and dancing.'

6 *When a man is tired of London, he is tired of life; for there is in London all that life can afford.*

Recorded in Boswell's *Life* (on 20 September 1777). One of the worst examples of 'quote abuse' I have ever come across was something attributed to Robert Moses by Barbara Rowes in *The Book of Quotes* (1979): 'Every true New Yorker believes with all his heart that when a New Yorker is tired of New York, he is tired of life.'

1 *I would rather praise it than read it.*

Johnson said this about William Congreve's novel *Incognita* (1691) in his life of Congreve in *The Lives of the Poets*. Congreve went on to become better known, of course, as a playwright.

2 *Pastern: the knee of a horse.*

Largely working alone on his great *Dictionary* (1755), Johnson committed one or two errors. In the first edition he gave the wrong definition of the word 'pastern', which is, in a horse, rather the equivalent of the ankle in humans. It was corrected in later editions but when a woman asked how he had come to make this mistake, he splendidly forebore to give an elaborate defence and said, 'Ignorance, Madam, pure ignorance' (as reported in Boswell's *Life*, for 1755).

3 *What is obvious is not always known, what is known is not always present. Sudden fits of inadvertency will surprise vigilance; slight avocations will seduce attention, and casual eclipses of the mind will darken learning.*

From the Preface to the *Dictionary* (1755) — a magnificent disclaimer for any errors.

4 *Snakes in Iceland.*

'There are no snakes to be met with throughout the whole island' — those words are the entire contents of Chapter 72 of *The Natural History of Iceland* by a Dane called Horrebow (1758). As a joke, Johnson used to boast of being able to repeat the whole chapter (Boswell's *Life*, 13 April 1778) and then do so. Sometimes *Ireland* rather than Iceland is mistakenly put into the joke, presumably out of confusion with the fact that St Patrick traditionally did drive all the snakes of that country by ringing a bell.

5 OLIVARII GOLDSMITH, Poetae, Physici, Historici, qui nullum fere scribendi genus non tetigit, nullum quod tetigit non ornavit *[Of Oliver Gold-*

smith, A Poet, Natural Philosopher, and Historian, who left no species of writing untouched by his pen, and touched none that he did not adorn].

Goldsmith's epitaph in Poets' Corner, Westminster Abbey, was written by Johnson, but not without dissent among Goldsmith's other friends and admirers. As James Boswell records in his *Life of Johnson* (16 May 1776), the 'Epitaph gave occasion to a *Remonstrance* to the MONARCH OF LITERATURE'. Various emendations were suggested to Johnson's draft and presented to him in the form of a round robin. Sir Joshua Reynolds took it to Johnson 'who received it with much good humour, and desired Sir Joshua to tell the gentlemen, that he would alter the Epitaph in any manner they pleased, as to the sense of it; but *he would never consent to disgrace the walls of Westminster Abbey with an English inscription.*' Johnson argued further that, 'the language of the country of which a learned man was a native, is not the language fit for his epitaph, which should be in an ancient and permanent language. Consider, Sir; how you should feel, were you to find at Rotterdam an epitaph upon Erasmus *in Dutch*!' And so it remained in Latin, despite the protest from Goldsmith's friends. The above is an extract only.

6 *At this man's table I enjoyed many cheerful and instructive hours . . . with David Garrick, whom I hoped to have gratified with this character of our common friend; but what are the hopes of man! I am disappointed by that stroke of death, which has eclipsed the gaiety of nations, and impoverished the public stock of harmless pleasure.*

Johnson was Garrick's great friend (and one-time schoolteacher in Lichfield) and they continued to see each other when Garrick had become the foremost actor of the age. The 'epitaph' appears in the life of Edmund Smith, one of Johnson's *Lives of the English Poets* (published in 1779, the year of the actor's death). Eva Maria, Garrick's widow, had the words engraved below his memorial bust in the south transept of Lichfield Cathedral. John Wilkes had his doubts about the tribute and made an 'attack' on the phrase about eclipsing the gaiety of nations. Boswell relayed this to Johnson, who replied: 'I could not have said more nor less, for 'tis truth; "eclipsed", not "extinguished", and his death did eclipse; 'twas like a storm.'

'But why *nations*?' Boswell continued. 'Did his gaiety extend farther than his own nation?' Johnson deftly tossed in the Scots ('if we allow the Scotch to be a nation, and to have gaiety') but Boswell pressed on, 'Is not *harmless pleasure* very tame?' To which Johnson replied: 'Nay, Sir, harmless pleasure is the highest praise. Pleasure is a word of dubious import; pleasure is in general dangerous, and pernicious to virtue; to be able therefore to furnish pleasure that is harmless, pleasure pure and unalloyed, is as great a power as men can possess.' Boswell's initial account of this exchange appears in his journal for 24 April 1779 and appears in substantially the same form in his *Life of Johnson*.

When Charles Dickens died in 1870, Thomas Carlyle wrote: 'It is an event world-wide, a *unique* of talents suddenly extinct, and has "eclipsed" (we too may say) "the gaiety of nations".'

1 *Like a woman's preaching . . .*

A saying of Johnson's often invoked to describe something about which there is little complimentary to be said comes from Boswell's *Life* (1791): 'Sir, a woman's preaching is like a dog's walking on his hinder legs. It is not done well; but you are surprised to find it done at all' (remark, 31 July 1763).

2 *Sir, there is no settling the point of precedency between a louse and a flea.*

This was Johnson's reply when asked to decide which of two poets — Derrick and Smart — was the better. Recounted in Boswell's *Life*, in 1783.

Jolson, Al
American entertainer (1888–1950)

3 *You ain't heard nothin' yet!*

It seems that when Jolson exclaimed this in the first full-length talking picture *The Jazz Singer* (1927), he was not just ad-libbing — as is usually supposed — but was promoting the title of one of his songs. He had recorded 'You Ain't Heard Nothing Yet', written by Gus Kahn and Buddy de Sylva, in 1919. In addition, Martin Abramson in *The Real Story of Al Jolson* (1950) suggests that Jolson had also uttered the slogan in San Francisco as long before as 1906. Inter-

rupted by noise from a building site across the road from a café in which he was performing, Jolson had shouted, 'You think that's noise — you ain't heard nuttin' yet!'

Listening to the film soundtrack makes it clear that Jolson did not add 'folks' at the end of his mighty line, as Bartlett (1992), the *PDMQ* (1980) and the *ODQ* (1979) all say he did.

Jonson, Ben
English playwright and poet (1572–1637)

4 *O Rare Ben Johnson.*

Jonson's epitaph in Westminster Abbey was composed in the year he died. According to Abbey tradition (recounted in the *Official Guide*, 1988 revision), Jonson died in poverty and was buried upright to save space. So he was, in the north aisle of the nave, with a small square stone over him. The stone, with the inscription spelt as above, was set upright in the north aisle wall in 1821 to save the inscription from being worn away, and it may still be found there. (There is also a wall plaque 'O RARE BEN IOHNSON', erected before 1728, in Poets' Corner.)

Another tradition, according to John Aubrey, had it that the original epitaph was 'done at the charge of Jack Young, afterwards knighted, who, walking here when the grave was covering, gave the fellow eighteen pence to cut it'. The inscription has also been ascribed to the playwright, Sir William D'Avenant (1608–68) who succeeded Jonson as unofficial Poet Laureate. His own gravestone set in the floor of Poets' Corner reads, 'O RARE S. WILLIAM DAVENANT' (or 'O rare Sir Will. Davenant' as Aubrey has it, 'in imitation of that on Ben Johnson'). Either way, the spelling is not at fault — 'Jonson' is merely an alternative that has become accepted. An attempt has been made to suggest that what the epitaphist meant to say was '*Orare Ben Jonson*' — 'pray for Ben Jonson' — but this is questionable Latin.

Jordan, Louis
American singer, musician and songwriter (1908–75)

5 *Is You Is Or Is You Ain't My Baby?*

The title of a song (1943) written by Jordan with Billy Austin. It suffered a revival in *c* 1990 when commercials for a British credit card included the jingle, 'Does you does or does you don't take Access?'

Joseph II
Holy Roman Emperor (1741–90)

1 Too many notes.

Joseph's comments were directed at Mozart's opera *Die Entführung aus dem Serail* [The Escape from the Seraglio], first performed in 1782. Unwilling to concede, Mozart replied that it had 'just as many as are necessary'. Franz Xaver Niemetschek's biography of the composer (1798) provides the context: 'The monarch, who at heart was charmed by this deeply stirring music, said to Mozart nevertheless: "Too beautiful for our ears and an extraordinary number of notes, dear Mozart." "Just as many, Your Majesty, as are necessary," he replied with that noble dignity and frankness which so often go with great genius.'

James Agate, *Ego 6* (1942) has the opera as *Le Nozze di Figaro* and Mozart's reply as: 'Not one too many, your Majesty.'

Joyce, William
Irish-American propagandist (1906–46)

2 Germany calling, Germany calling.

Joyce broadcast Nazi propaganda from Hamburg during the Second World War, was found guilty of treason (on the technicality that he held a British passport at the beginning of the war) and was hanged in 1946. He had a threatening, sneering, lower middle class delivery, which made his call-sign sound more like 'Jarmany calling'. Although Joyce was treated mostly as a joke in wartime Britain, he is credited with giving rise to some unsettling rumours. No one seemed to have heard the particular broadcast in question, but it got about that he had said the clock on Darlington Town Hall was two minutes slow, and so it was supposed to be. His nickname of 'Lord Haw-Haw' was inappropriate as he did not sound the slightest bit aristocratic. *That* soubriquet

had been applied by Jonah Barrington, the *Daily Express* radio correspondent, to Joyce's predecessor who *did* speak with a cultured accent but lasted only a few weeks from September 1939. This original was Norman Baillie-Stewart. He is said to have sounded like Claud Hulbert or one of the Western Brothers. An imaginary drawing appeared in the *Daily Express* of a Bertie Woosterish character with a monocle and receding chin. Baillie-Stewart said that he understood there was a popular English song called 'We're Going to Hang Out the Washing on the Siegfried Line' which ended 'If the Siegfried Line's still there'. 'Curiously enoff,' he said, 'the Siegfried Line is still they-ah.'

Jung, Carl
Swiss psychologist (1875–1961)

3 Liverpool is the pool of life.

Returning to my home town in 1982, I was intrigued to find a sign in Mathew Street — sacred site of the erstwhile Cavern Cub — saying: 'Liverpool is the pool of life./C.J. JUNG 1927'. An agreeable compliment, but is there any record of the Swiss psychologist ever having set foot in the fair city? None. His *Memories, Dreams, Reflections* (1963) make clear that he was simply describing a dream he had had. He saw a round pool, and in the middle of it a small island. While everything round about was obscured by rain, fog, smoke and dimly lit darkness, the little island blazed with sunlight. 'I had had a vision of unearthly beauty,' Jung says, 'and that was why I was able to live at all. Liverpool is the "pool of life". The "liver", according to an old view, is the seat of life — that which "makes to live".'

Unfortunately, even here, Jung is basing his supposition on fanciful etymology, presumably just hearing the name 'Liverpool', and never having been there. The derivation of the place name is 'pool with clotted water', rather more to the point than 'pool of life'. By 1987 the sign had been taken down.

K

Kael, Pauline
American film critic (1919–)

1 *Kiss Kiss Bang Bang.*

Title of a book (1968) of collected criticism. She says the words came from an Italian poster — 'perhaps the briefest statement imaginable on the basic appeal of movies'. Usually, they are taken to refer to the James Bond movies.

Indeed, Bond's creator Ian Fleming described his books in a letter (*c* 1955) to Raymond Chandler as 'straight pillow fantasies of the bang-bang, kiss-kiss variety'.

John Barry, composer of music for most of the Bond films, named one of his themes 'Mr Kiss Kiss Bang Bang' in *Thunderball* (1965).

Kearney, Denis
Irish-born American labour leader (1847–1907)

2 *Horny-handed sons of toil.*

Kearney used this expression describing labourers who bear the marks of their work in a speech at San Francisco (*c* 1878). He was leading a 'workingman's protest movement against unemployment, unjust taxes, unfair banking laws, and mainly against Chinese labourers' (Flexner, 1982).

Earlier, the American poet J.R. Lowell had written in 'A Glance Behind the Curtain' (1843): 'And blessèd are the horny hands of toil.'

The 3rd Marquess Salisbury, the British Conservative Prime Minister, had also used the phrase earlier in *The Quarterly Review* (October 1873).

Keating, Paul
Australian Labour Prime Minister (1944–)

3 *I learned about self-respect and self-regard for Australia, not about some cultural cringe to a country [Britain] which decided not to defend the Malaysian peninsula, not to worry about Singapore, and not to give us our troops back to keep ourselves free from Japanese domination. This was a country that you people [the Opposition] wedded yourselves to. Even as they walked out on you and joined the Common Market, you were looking for your MBEs and your knighthoods. You take Australia right back down the time tunnel to the cultural cringe where you've always come from.*

From a speech made in Parliament at Canberra (27 February 1992). The phrase 'cultural cringe', referring to the belief that one's own country's culture is inferior to that of others, was not coined by Keating, although it is certainly well-established in Australia.

Arthur Angell Phillips wrote in 1950: 'Above our writers — and other artists — looms the intimidating mass of Anglo-Saxon culture. Such a situation almost inevitably produces the characteristic Australian Cultural Cringe — appearing either as the Cringe Direct, or as the Cringe Inverted, in the attitude of the Blatant Blatherskite, the God's-own-country and I'm-a-better-man-than-you-are Australian bore.'

Keats, John
English poet (1795–1821)

1 *Or like stout Cortez when with eagle eyes*
He star'd at the Pacific — and all his men
Look'd at each other with a wild surmise —
Silent, upon a peak in Darien.

There are two minor errors of fact in Keats's poem 'On First Looking Into Chapman's Homer' (1817). It was, in fact, Balboa, a companion of Cortez, who became the first European to set eyes on the Pacific Ocean at Darien on the Isthmus of Panama in 1513. Nor was he silent: he exclaimed, '*Hombre!*', an expression of surprise, the equivalent of the modern 'Man, look at that!'

2   *For lo!*
He cannot see the heavens, nor the flow
Of rivers, nor hill-flowers running wild
In pink and purple chequer, nor, up-pil'd,
The cloudy rack slow journeying in the west,
Like herded elephants.

A clever stroke to compare 'up-pil'd' clouds to 'herded elephants', as Keats did in *Endymion*, Bk II, l. 289 (1818). Of course, it was quite likely that Keats had seen an individual elephant but one wonders how he had any idea of what a *herd* would look like? But then, he was a poet.

3 *My ear is open like a greedy shark,*
To catch the tunings of a voice divine.

Another surprising animal image, this time from Keats's 'Imitation of Spenser' (1817). In the novel *Gaudy Night* (1935) by Dorothy L. Sayers, Lord Peter Wimsey quotes the shark remark and describes it as 'the crashing conclusion of a sonnet by Keats'.

4 *Loads every rift with ore.*

This phrase comes from Keats's letter to Shelley (August 1820): 'You I am sure will forgive me for sincerely remarking that you might curb your magnanimity and be more of an artist, and "load every rift" of your subject with ore.' The quotation marks are taken to indicate a reference to Edmund Spenser's *The Faerie Queene*, Bk 2, Canto 7,

St. 28 (1596): 'And with rich metal loaded every rift.'

5 *And other spirits there are standing apart*
Upon the forehead of the age to come:
These, these will give the world another heart,
And other pulses. Hear ye not the hum
Of mighty workings?

Michael Foot's account of his unsuccessful leadership of the British Labour Party during the 1983 General Election was entitled *Another Heart and Other Pulses* (1984). The title comes from Keats's sonnet 'Addressed to the Same' (i.e. Benjamin Robert Haydon) (1817).

6 *Here lies One*
Whose Name was writ in Water.

Keats's own choice of epitaph on his anonymous grave in the English cemetery, Rome. A few days before he died, Keats said that on his gravestone there should be no mention of his name or country. As he lay dying, listening to the fountain outside on the Spanish Steps in Rome, it is said he kept being reminded of the lines from Beaumont and Fletcher's play *Philaster*: 'All your better deeds/Shall be in water writ, but this in marble.' Robert Gittings in his biography of Keats (1968) comments: 'The quotations that may have suggested this phrase are many; but the gentle sound of the fountain, which had been his companion for so many nights as he lay in the narrow room above the square, may have seemed the right symbol for his end.'
    One of the possible sources? Shakespeare, in *Henry VIII* (IV.ii.45) has: 'Men's evil manners live in brass; their virtues/We write in water.'

Kelly, Ned
Australian outlaw (1855–80)

7 *Such is life.*

Kelly was the son of a transported Irish convict and himself became a horse thief. He was hanged in Melbourne and his last words were, 'Ah well, I suppose it has come to this! . . . Such is life!' (quoted in Frank Clune, *The Kelly Hunters*, 1958). That last phrase Partridge/*Slang* calls a 'world-old, worldwide truism' and Partridge/*Catch Phrases* adds 'world-weary'. W.J. Temple wrote in his diary (7 April 1796) 'This interruption is very teasing; but such is Life'. From Charles Dickens, *Martin Chuzzlewit*, Chap. 29 (1846): ' "Sairey," says Mrs Harris, "sech is life. Vich likeways is the hend of all things!" ' The British pop singer and political clown Lord David Sutch felicitously entitled his autobiography *Sutch Is Life* (1992).

Kelly, Walt
American cartoonist (1913–73)

1 *We have met the enemy and he is us.*

Kelly's syndicated comic strip featured an opossum called Pogo. This phrase was used in a 1970 Pogo cartoon used on the 1971 Earth Day poster. Kelly had taken some time to get round to this formulation. In his introduction to *The Pogo Papers* (1953) he wrote: 'Resolve then, that on this very ground, with small flags waving and tinny blasts on tiny trumpets, we shall meet the enemy, and not only may he be ours, he may be us.'

Kennedy, John F.
American Democratic 35th President (1917–63)

2 *We stand today on the edge of a New Frontier . . . But the New Frontier of which I speak is not a set of promises — it is a set of challenges. It sums up not what I intend to offer the American people, but what I intend to ask of them.*

Accepting the Democratic nomination in Los Angeles (15 July 1960). Theodore C. Sorensen in his book *Kennedy* (1965), suggests that Kennedy had a hand in coining the slogan for the forthcoming administraton: 'I know of no outsider who suggested the expression, although the theme of the Frontier was contained in more than one draft.' In 1964 Harold Wilson said in a speech in Birmingham: 'We want the youth of Britain to storm the new frontiers of knowledge.' The last sentence of Kennedy's speech above is a clear pre-echo of a theme in his Inaugural speech.

3 *Let the word go forth from this time and place, to friend and foe alike, that the torch has been passed to a new generation of Americans, born in this century,* tempered by war, disciplined by a hard and bitter peace, proud of our ancient heritage, and unwilling to witness or permit the slow undoing of those human rights to which this nation has always been committed, and to which we are committed today at home and around the world.

Let every nation know, whether it wishes us well or ill, that we shall pay any price, bear any burden, meet any hardship, support any friend, oppose any foe to assure the survival and the success of liberty.

From his Inaugural address, Washington D.C. (20 January 1961). As preparation, Kennedy told Sorensen to read all the previous Inaugural speeches and suggestions were solicited from the likes of Adlai Stevenson, J.K. Galbraith and Billy Graham. Kennedy laid down basic rules: the speech was to be as short as possible, to deal almost exclusively with foreign affairs, to leave out the first person singular and to emulate Lincoln's Gettysburg address by using one-syllable words wherever possible.

The sentence beginning 'Let every nation . . .' was later inscribed on the Kennedy memorial at Runnymede, near London.

4 *To those old allies whose cultural and spiritual origins we share, we pledge the loyalty of faithful friends. United, there is little we cannot do in a host of co-operative ventures.*

Sorensen says 'no Kennedy speech underwent so many drafts . . . Kenneth Galbraith suggested "co-operative ventures" with our allies in place of "joint ventures", which sounded like a mining partnership.'

5 *To our sister republics south of our border, we offer a special pledge: to convert our good words into good deeds, in a new alliance for progress, to assist free men and free governments in casting off the chains of poverty.*

The 'Alliance for Progress', used as the name of Kennedy's Latin American policy, had first been mentioned by him in October 1960. Speechwriter Richard Goodwin said he took it from the title of a Spanish American magazine, *Alianzo*. *Alianza para Progreso* was officially launched in March 1961.

1 *To those nations who would make themselves our adversary, we offer not a pledge but a request: that both sides begin anew the quest for peace, before the dark powers of destruction unleashed by science engulf all humanity in planned or accidental self-destruction.*

Walter Lippmann suggested that references to the Communist bloc be changed from 'enemy' to 'adversary'.

2 *Let us never negotiate out of fear, but let us never fear to negotiate.*

The contrapuntal form of words became a hallmark of Kennedy speech-making.

3 *All this will not be finished in the first one hundred days. Nor will it be finished in the first one thousand days, nor in the life of this Administration, nor even perhaps in our lifetime on this planet. But let us begin.*

The phrase 'hundred days' is used to refer to a period of intense political action (often immediately upon coming to power). The allusion is to the period during which Napoleon ruled between his escape from Elba and his defeat at the Battle of Waterloo in 1815. During the 1964 general election, Harold Wilson (see WILSON 358:1) said Britain would need a 'programme of a hundred days of dynamic action' such as President Kennedy had promised in 1961. In fact, Kennedy specifically ruled out a hundred days, saying that even 'a thousand days' would be too short (hence the title of Arthur M. Schlesinger's memoir, *A Thousand Days*, 1965, referring also to the 1,056 days of Kennedy's Presidency).

4 *And so, my fellow Americans, ask not what your country can do for you; ask what you can do for your country.*

Kennedy's speech employed a number of phrases that had been used by the President (and others) before. The 'Ask not . . .' idea, for example, had been used by him three times during the election campaign. In a TV address during September 1960, Kennedy had said, 'We do not campaign stressing what our country is going to do for us as a people. We stress what we can for the country, all of us.' In his memoir *A Thousand Days* (1965), Arthur M. Schlesinger, a

Kennedy aide, traced the president's interest in the 'Ask not' theme back to a notebook he had kept in 1945 which included the Rousseau quotation, 'As soon as any man says of the affairs of state, What does it matter to me?, the state may be given up as lost.'

Other antecedents that have been cited include Kahlil Gibran, writing in Arabic after the First World War: 'Are you a politician asking what your country can do for you or a zealous one asking what you can do for your country? If you are the first, then you are a parasite; if the second, then you are an oasis in the desert.' Warren G. Harding said at the Republican National Convention in Chicago (1916): 'We must have a citizenship less concerned about what the government can do for it and more anxious about what it can do for the nation.' The Mayor of Haverhill, Massachusetts, said at the funeral of John Greenleaf Whittier (1892): 'Here may we be reminded that man is most honoured, not by that which a city may do for him, but by that which he has done for the city.' Oliver Wendell Holmes's Memorial Day Address 1884 contained the words: 'It is now the moment when by common consent we pause to become conscious of our national life and to rejoice in it, to recall what our country has done for each of us, and to ask ourselves what we can do for our country in return.'

In Britain, meanwhile, in October 1893, the Hon. St John Broderick MP told an audience in the Tennant Hall, Leeds: 'Clergymen do well to preach the neglected doctrine that the first duty of a citizen is to consider what he can do for the state and not what the state will do for him.'

It was Kennedy's inverted use of 'Ask not', however, that made what was obviously not a new concept eminently memorable.

5 *My fellow citizens of the world, ask not what America will do for you, but what together we can do for the freedom of man.*

Dean Rusk suggested that the other peoples of the world be challenged to ask 'what together we can do for freedom' instead of 'what you can do for freedom'.

6 *He mobilized the English language and sent it into battle.*

At a ceremony granting honorary US citizenship to Sir Winston Churchill on 9 April 1963 (at which Churchill was not present),

Kennedy used this phrase, but it was not his own. In a broadcast to mark Churchill's eightieth birthday in 1954, Edward R. Murrow had said: 'He mobilized the English language and sent it into battle to steady his fellow countrymen and hearten those Europeans upon whom the long dark night of tyranny had descended.' The borrowing was not surprising, as the veteran broadcaster had been drafted to help with Kennedy's speeches.

1 *All free men, wherever they may live, are citizens of Berlin, and, therefore, as a free man, I take pride in the words* Ich bin ein Berliner.

On 26 June 1963 Kennedy proclaimed a stirring slogan outside the City Hall in the then newly divided city of West Berlin. Ben Bradlee noted in *Conversations with Kennedy* (1975) that the President had to spend 'the better part of an hour' with Frederick Vreeland and his wife before he could manage to pronounce this and the other German phrases he used. It detracts only slightly to know that the President need only have said, '*Ich bin Berliner*' to convey the meaning 'I am a Berliner'. It could be argued that the '*ein*' adds drama because he is saying not 'I was born and bred in Berlin' or 'I live in Berlin', but 'I am one of you'. But by saying what he did, he drew attention to the fact that in Germany '*ein Berliner*' is a doughnut.

2 *Yesterday, a shaft of light cut into the darkness.*

From a speech on 26 July 1963. For the first time an agreement had been reached on bringing the forces of nuclear destruction under international control. A nuclear Test Ban Treaty had been initialled by the US, USSR and UK.

3 *According to the ancient Chinese proverb, 'A journey of a thousand miles must begin with a single step'.*

From the same speech. The Chinese origin is unverified. The proverb appears, however, in Stevenson, *Home Book of Proverbs* (1948).

Kennedy, Joseph P.
American politician and businessman (1888–1969)

4 *When the going gets tough, the tough get going.*

On the election of John F. Kennedy as US President in 1961, attention was focused on several axioms said to come from the Boston-Irish political world and more precisely from Joseph P. Kennedy, his father. At this distance, it would be impossible to say for sure whether this wealthy, ambitious businessman/ambassador/politician originated the expressions, but he certainly instilled them in his sons. This one is quoted in J.H. Cutler, *Honey Fitz* (1962).

5 *Don't get mad, get even.*

Quoted in Ben Bradlee, *Conversations with Kennedy* (1975) and attributed to 'the Boston-Irish political jungle'. *Don't Get Mad Get Even* became the title of a book (1983), 'a manual for retaliation' by Alan Abel.

6 *If you want to make money, go where the money is.*

Quoted in Arthur M. Schlesinger, *Robert Kennedy and His Times* (1979).

7 *Kennedys don't cry.*

Quoted in *ibid.* A family rendering of his 'We don't want any crying in this house'. Other similar sayings included: 'Only winners come to dinner' and 'We don't want any losers around here. In this family we want winners. Don't come in second or third — that doesn't count — but win' (sometimes shortened to 'Kennedys always come first').

Kenyatta, Jomo
Kenyan President (*c* 1889–1978)

8 *Originally, the Africans had the land and the English had the Bible. Then the missionaries came to Africa and got the Africans to close their eyes and fold their hands and pray. And when they opened their eyes, the English had the land and the Africans had the Bible.*

This saying was attributed to Kenyatta on BBC Radio *Quote ... Unquote* (13 October 1984), but later in the *Observer*, 'Sayings of the Week' (16 December 1984) had Desmond Tutu, Bishop of Johannesburg, saying it. A version relating to the American Indians had earlier been said by Chief Dan George (*d* 1982): 'When the white man came we had the land and they had the Bibles; now they have the land and we have the Bibles' — *Bloomsbury Diction-ary of Quotations* (1987).

Keppel, Alice
(Mrs George Keppel)
English mistress of King Edward VII
(1869–1947)

1 *Things were done better in my day.*

This remark was made on the day of King Edward VIII's abdication, according to Janet Flanner writing in the magazine *Travel & Leisure* and quoted by Bryan & Murphy, *The Windsor Story* (1979). Flanner (1892–1978) was Paris correspondent for *The New Yorker* (1925–75). What Keppel meant to convey was, 'The King didn't have to abdi-cate in order to carry on. He married pro-perly and then took whoever he fancied as mistresses.' The remark has also been attri-buted to Miss Maxine Elliott, the Edwar-dian actress and another former mistress of Edward VII's, in the form, 'We did it better in my day'. According to Andrew Barrow, *Gossip* (1978), Elliott said it to Winston Churchill at a dinner with the Duke and Duchess of Windsor near Cannes on 7 January 1938.

Compare a similar lament: from Laurence Sterne, *A Sentimental Journey* (1768): 'They order, said I, this matter better in France', which, by 1818, had become in Lady Morgan's *Autobiography* (not published until 1859): 'So you see, my dear Olivia, they manage these things better in France.'

In a letter to former President Eisenhower (20 July 1965), Harold Macmillan moaned: 'Naturally, people consult me, but they never take my advice, so I give it without much sense of responsibility. Yes, indeed, we managed things much better in our time.'

Kerouac, Jack
American novelist (1922–69)

2 *The Beat Generation.*

The *Guardian* for 4 April 1988 announced in an obituary: 'Although a novelist, poet and lecturer at many universities, John Clellon Holmes was chiefly known for giv-ing the Beat Generation its name. The phrase first appeared in his 1952 novel *Go*.' The headline to the piece (by William J. Weatherby) was, 'The naming of a genera-tion'. This came as news to those who had believed until then that it was Kerouac who was not only the presiding genius of that phenomenon of the 1950s but had given the name to it. Indeed, in the book *The Origins of the Beat Generation* and in *Playboy* (June 1959), Kerouac admitted to borrowing the phrase from a broken-down drug addict called Herbert Huncke.

Turning to Randy Nelson's *The Almanac of American Letters* (1981), we discover a description of the moment of coinage. He reports Kerouac as saying: 'John Clellon Holmes . . . and I were sitting around trying to think up the meaning of the Lost Genera-tion and the subsequent existentialism and I said, "You know, this is really a beat genera-tion": and he leapt up and said, "That's it, that's right".' Holmes actually attributed the phrase directly to Kerouac in the *New York Times* Magazine of 16 November 1952.

When these versions were put to Weatherby in 1988, he replied: 'I based my comment on what Holmes told me close to the end of his life. It's possible his memory was shadowed by then or he had over-simplified the past, but the majority view seems to be he fathered the phrase or at least it emerged in a conversation in which he was involved. I don't believe Kerouac himself thought it up or even cared much for it.'

Keynes, John Maynard
(later Lord Keynes)
British economist (1883–1946)

3 *[On David Lloyd George] When he's alone in a room, there's nobody there.*

So quoted by Baroness Asquith in *As I Remember*, BBC TV, on 30 April 1967. However, James Agate in *Ego 5* (for 30 September 1941): 'Sat next to Lady Oxford, who was in great form . . . "Lloyd George? There is no Lloyd George. There is a marvellous brain; but if you were to shut him in a room and look through the keyhole there would be nobody there".' It is strange that Baroness Asquith who was familiar with most of her step-mother's witticisms should have chosen to attribute this one to Keynes.

Khruschev, Nikita
Soviet Communist Party leader (1894–1971)

4 *We say this not only for the socialist states who are more akin to us. We base ourselves on the idea that we must peacefully co-exist. About the capitalist states, it doesn't depend on you whether*

or not we exist. If you don't like us, don't accept our invitations, and don't ask us to come and see you. Whether you like it or not, history is on our side. We will bury you. [Applause from colleagues. Laughter from Mr Gomulka.]

Said to western diplomats at a Moscow reception for the Polish leader Wladislaw Gomulka at the Polish Embassy in Moscow on 18 November 1956. The last two sentences were not reported at the time by either *Pravda* or the *New York Times* but they were by *The Times* of London (on 19 November 1956), perhaps because the previous night at a Kremlin reception the British Ambassador, Sir William Hayter, had walked out when Khruschev described Britain, France and Israel as 'fascists' and 'bandits' (over the Suez affair).

'We will bury you' can also be translated as 'We will be present at your funeral', i.e. outlive you, and Khruschev made several attempts in later years to make plain that he meant 'outstrip' or 'beat' in the economic sense, rather than anything more threateningly literal. The remark may have been exaggerated by western commentators.

Kierkegaard, Sören

Danish philosopher and religious thinker (1813–55)

1 *The lowest depth to which people can sink before God is defined by the word 'journalist'. If I were a father and had a daughter who was seduced I should not despair over her; I would hope for her salvation. But if I had a son who became a journalist and continued to be one for five years, I would give him up.*

Untraced but being quoted by 1980.

2 *Life must be lived forwards, but it can only be understood backwards.*

Quoted as an epigraph by John Mortimer in his novel *Paradise Postponed* (1986) and used as a promotional line for George Melly's volume of autobiography called *Scouse Mouse* (1984), this obscure thought can be found in Kierkegaard's *Journals and Papers*, Vol. 1 (1843): 'Philosophy is perfectly right in saying that life must be understood backward. But then one forgets the other clause — that it must be lived forward.'

King, Revd Dr Martin Luther, Jr

American Civil Rights leader (1929–68)

3 *I have a dream that one day this nation will rise up and live out the true meaning of its creed — 'We hold these truths to be self-evident that all men are created equal'. I have a dream . . .*

The largest protest rally in US history took place on 28 August 1963, when nearly 250,000 people joined the March on Washington. The Civil Rights demonstration reached its climax near the Lincoln Memorial with a sixteen-minute speech by King in which he applied the repetitions and rhythms of a revivalist preacher to a clear challenge on the lack of Negro progress since the Emancipation Proclamation of exactly one hundred years before. King used his familiar technique of delivering almost ritualistic invocations of the Bible and American lore in a sob-laden voice. He summoned up themes and phrases from his own speeches dating back to 1956. In Detroit, as recently as the 23 June, he had used the 'I have a dream' motif — 'I have a dream this evening that one day we will recognize the words of Jefferson that all men are created equal . . .'

4 *Free at last, free at last, thank God Almighty, we are free at last!*

His peroration (in both the Washington and Detroit speeches) came, as he acknowledged, from an old negro spiritual. On his grave in South View Cemetery, Atlanta, Georgia, is carved a slightly altered version of these words: 'thank God Almighty, I'm free at last.'

5 *I've been to the mountain top . . . I've looked over, and I've seen the promised land. I may not get there with you, but I want you to know tonight that we as a people will get to the promised land. So, I'm happy tonight. I'm not worried about anything. I'm not fearing any man. Mine eyes have seen the glory of the coming of the Lord.*

On the night before he was assassinated, King said this in a speech at Memphis (3 April 1968). Did he have a premonition? The original 'promised land' (not called as such in the Bible, but referring to Canaan, western Palestine, and by association,

203

Heaven) was promised to the descendants of Abraham, Isaac and Jacob. In Numbers 14:39–40: 'Moses told these sayings unto all the children of Israel . . . And they rose up early in the morning and gat them up into the top of the mountain, saying, Lo, we be here, and will go up unto the place which the Lord hath promised.'

King, Philip
English playwright (1904–79)

1 *Sergeant, arrest several of these vicars!*

Tom Stoppard once claimed this as the funniest line anywhere in English farce. Alas, King's *See How They Run* (first performed in 1944) does not have quite that line in it. For reasons it would be exhausting to go into, the stage gets filled with various people who are, or are dressed up as, vicars, and the order is given: 'Sergeant, arrest most of these people.'

Kinnock, Neil
Welsh Labour politician (1942–)

2 *If Margaret Thatcher is re-elected as Prime Minister, I warn you . . . that you will have poverty . . . that you will be cold . . . If Margaret Thatcher wins — I warn you not to be ordinary. I warn you not to be young. I warn you not to fall ill. I warn you not to get old.*

Speech, Bridgend (7 June 1983), during a general election campaign. In fact, virtually the whole speech was a list of 'I warn you's'. Labour lost the election and Kinnock became the party's leader four months later. There is a mild, ironical, echo — almost certainly unconscious — of a passage from Bernard Shaw's bibliographical appendix to *The Intelligent Woman's Guide to Socialism and Capitalism* (1928) in which Shaw recalls a point he had made in the various prefaces to his plays: 'I . . . made it quite clear that . . . under Socialism you would not be allowed to be poor. You would be forcibly fed, clothed, lodged, taught, and employed whether you liked it or not . . . Also you would not be allowed to have half a crown an hour when other women had only two shillings, or to be content with two shillings when they had half a crown. As far as I know I was the first Socialist writer to whom it occurred to state this explicitly as a necessary postulate of permanent civilization; but as nothing that is true is ever new I daresay it had been said again and again before I was born.'

3 *Why am I the first Kinnock in a thousand generations to be able to get to university? Why is Glenys [his wife] the first woman in her family in a thousand generations to be able to get to university? Was it because all our predecessors were 'thick'? . . . Of course not. It was because there was no platform upon which they could stand . . . no method by which the communities could translate their desires for those individuals into provision for those individuals.*

From a speech delivered at Llandudno (15 May 1987), and also used in a Party Political Broadcast (21 May). Later in that year it was famously plagiarized by US Senator Joe Biden, who was shaping up to run for the Democratic ticket in the 1988 Presidential election. At other times, Biden had credited Kinnock with the words but not on 23 August when he said: 'Why is it that Joe Biden is the first in his family ever to go to university? . . . Is it because our fathers and mothers were not so bright? . . . It's because they didn't have a platform upon which to stand.' His rivals pounced, the speeches were reproduced side by side, and Biden, who had little chance of winning any primaries, was soon out of the race.

Kipling, Rudyard
English poet and novelist (1865–1936)

4 *A woman is only a woman, but a good Cigar is a Smoke.*

This view, which would now be seen as an outrageous example of male chauvinism, is expressed in Rudyard Kipling's poem 'The Betrothed' (1886). Lest Kipling, as usual, take more blame than he should for what one of his characters says, it is worth pointing out that the man in question (the poem is in the first person) is choosing between his cigars and his betrothed, a woman called Maggie. The situation arose in an actual breach of promise case, *c* 1885, in which the woman had said to the man: 'You must choose between me and your cigar.'
The poem ends:
Light me another Cuba — I hold to
my first-sworn vows.
If Maggie will have no rival, I'll have
no Maggie for Spouse!

1 *But that's another story . . .*

A catchphrase popular around 1900 derives from Kipling, though not exclusively. He used it in *Plain Tales from the Hills* (1888), but earlier it had appeared in Laurence Sterne's *Tristram Shandy* (1760), intended to prevent one of the many digressions with which that novel is full.

2 *The Man Who Would Be King.*

Title of a story (1888; film US, 1975) by Kipling about two adventurers in India in the 1880s who find themselves accepted as kings by a remote tribe. Compare *The Man Born To Be King* — Jesus Christ — in the title of a verse drama for radio (1942) by Dorothy L. Sayers; and 'the lad that's born to be king' in 'The Skye Boat Song' (1908) by Sir Harold Edwin Boulton.

3 *We know that the tail must wag the dog, for the horse is drawn by the cart;*
But the Devil whoops, as he whooped of old:
'It's clever, but is it Art?'

From 'The Conundrum of the Workshops' (1892). Possibly the origin of the 'But is it Art?' question.

4 *Lest we forget.*

From Kipling's poem 'Recessional' (1897), written as a Jubilee Day warning that while empires pass away, God lives on. Kipling himself may have agreed to the adoption of 'Lest we forget' as an epitaph during the of his work for the Imperial War Graves Commission after the First World War. Another use to which the phrase was put: it was the title of the Fritz Lang film *Hangmen Also Die* (US, 1943) when it was re-issued.

5 *Nursed the pinion that impelled the steel.*

In the story headed 'An Unsavoury Interlude' (1899) in Kipling's *Stalky & Co.*, Little Hartopp quotes about King that he 'nursed the pinion that impelled the steel' but does not explain the allusion. It is from Byron, *English Bards & Scotch Reviewers*, l.846 (1809).

6 *Sussex by the sea.*

From a poem called 'Sussex' written in 1902 by Kipling (who lived there). But the phrase also occurs in a song with this title (words and music by W. Ward-Higgs, *d* 1936):

> We plough and sow and reap and mow,
> And useful men are we . . .
> You may tell them all that we stand or fall
> For Sussex by the sea.

That song was not published until 1908, so it looks as though Kipling got there first. (Incidentally, the English county has since been cut in two. It is still by the sea, however.)

7 *If you can keep your head when all about you*
Are losing theirs and blaming it on you . . .
If you can meet with triumph and disaster
And treat those two impostors just the same . . .

The poem 'If — —' from *Rewards and Fairies* (1910) is one of the most plundered and parodied poems in the language: the second two lines above are inscribed over the doorway to the Centre Court at Wimbledon: 'As someone pointed out recently, if you can keep your head when all about you are losing theirs, it's just possible you haven't grasped the situation' — Jean Kerr, *Please Don't Eat the Daisies* (1958); also, 'If you can keep your girl when all about you/Are losing theirs and blaming it on you . . .' — an anonymous verse, source untraced, of the kind that says it is written 'with apologies to Rudyard Kipling Esq.'.

8 *The snow lies thick on Valley Forge,*
The ice on the Delaware,
But the poor dead soldiers of King George
They neither know nor care.

Lines which come, a touch surprisingly, from Kipling. 'The American Rebellion (1776)' is one of his 'Songs written for C.R.L. Fletcher's "A History of England"' (1911).

Kissinger, Henry
American Republican politician (1923–)

9 *Power is the ultimate aphrodisiac.*

An unverified remark, diagnosing his success as a 'swinger'. Also, in the form 'power is the great aphrodisiac', this was quoted in the *New York Times* (19 January 1971).

Compare BELLOW 46:1 and NAPOLEON 250:3.

1 *We are [all] the President's men and we must behave accordingly.*

All the President's Men was the title given by Carl Bernstein and Bob Woodward to their first book on Watergate (1974; film US, 1976). It might seem to allude to the lines from the nursery rhyme 'Humpty Dumpty' (first recorded in 1803):

All the king's horses
And all the king's men,
Couldn't put Humpty together again.

But there was also a Robert Penn Warren novel (and film US, 1949) based on the life of southern demagogue Huey 'Kingfish' Long and called *All the King's Men*. More directly, the Watergate book may have taken its title from a saying of Kissinger's at the time of the 1970 Cambodia invasion: 'We are all the President's men and we must behave accordingly' (quoted in Kalb and Kalb, *Kissinger*, 1974).

Kitchen, Fred
British entertainer (1872–1950)

2 *Meredith, we're in!*

The catchphrase originated as a shout of triumph in a music-hall sketch called 'The Bailiff' (or 'Moses and Son') performed by Kitchen, the leading comedian with Fred Karno's company. The sketch was first seen about 1907, and the phrase was used each time a bailiff and his assistant looked like gaining entrance to a house. Kitchen is reputed to have had it put on his gravestone, though its whereabouts is unknown.

Knox, Ronald
English priest and writer (1888–1957)

3 *As no less than three of [these poems] wear the aspect of a positively last appearance [i.e. a promise not to write more], they have been called in the words of so many eminent preachers 'ninthlies and lastlies'.*

Knox's *Juxta Salices* (1910) includes a group of poems he had written when still at Eton and is prefaced with the above. The expression 'ninthlies and lastlies' — or at least the

idea behind it — is, as he indicates, not original. The *OED2* has Thomas B. Aldrich writing in *Prudence Palfrey* (1874–85) of: 'The poor old parson's interminable ninthlies and finallies,' and there is a 'fifthly and lastly' dated 1681. Benjamin Franklin, in 1745, concluded his *Reasons for Preferring an Elderly Mistress* with: 'Eighth and lastly. They are so grateful!!' Ultimately, the origin for all this must be the kind of legal nonsense-talk parodied by Shakespeare's Dogberry in *Much Ado About Nothing* (*c* 1598): 'Marry, sir, they have committed false report; moreover, they have spoken untruths; secondarily, they are slanders; *sixthly and lastly*, they have belied a lady; thirdly, they have verified unjust things; and to conclude, they are lying knaves.'

See also REAGAN 276:4.

Koch, Ed
American politician (1924–)

4 *How'm I doin'?*

Koch was Mayor of New York City in 1977–89. He helped balance the city's books after a period of bankruptcy by drastically cutting services. His catchphrase during this period was 'How'm I doing?', which he called out to people as he ranged around New York. 'You're doing fine, Ed', they were supposed to shout back. A 1979 cartoon in *The New Yorker* showed a woman answering the phone and saying to her husband: 'It's Ed Koch. He wants to know how he's doin'.' A booklet of Koch's wit and wisdom took the phrase as its title. An old song with the same title was disinterred in due course. Unfortunately for him, Koch's achievements did not carry him forward to the State Governorship as he had hoped. Voters concluded that he wasn't doin' very well at all.

Koestler, Arthur
Hungarian-born writer (1905–83)

5 *Darkness at Noon.*

Koestler's novel (1940) about the imprisonment, trial and execution of a Communist who has betrayed the Party, was originally going to be called *The Vicious Circle*. Though originally written in German and translated for Koestler, the book's title appears always to have been rendered in

English (Koestler was dealing with a London publisher). As such, it echoes Milton's *Samson Agonistes* (1671): 'O dark, dark, dark, amid the blaze of noon.' *Darkness at Noon, or the Great Solar Eclipse of the 16th June 1806* was the title of an anonymous booklet published in Boston, Massachusetts (1806).

Kundera, Milan
Czech novelist (1929–   )

1 *The Unbearable Lightness of Being.*

The English title of Kundera's novel (1984; film US, 1987). In Czech it is *Nesnesitelná lehkost bytí* (which means, more literally, 'the unbearable easiness/facility of being').

L

Lamb, Charles
English writer (1775–1834)

1 *Mary, where are all the naughty people buried?*

As a boy in the 1780s, Lamb is credited with having remarked this to his sister, on observing the fulsome epitaphs in a churchyard (quoted in Leonard Russell, *English Wits*, 1940). William Wordsworth, in the second of his essays on epitaphs (posibly written about 1812), recalls the story (old even in his day, I imagine) of the person who, tired of reading so many fulsome epitaphs on 'faithful wives, tender husbands, dutiful children and good men of all classes', exclaimed, 'Where are all the bad people buried?' Perhaps he was referring to Lamb? Whoever first made the comment, Wordsworth argues that there is a lot to be said for having, 'in an unkind world, one enclosure where the voice of Detraction is not heard . . . and there is no jarring tone in the peaceful concert of amity and gratitude'.

Lamont, Norman
English Conservative politician (1942–)

2 *The turn of the tide is sometimes difficult to discern. What we are seeing is the return of that vital ingredient — confidence. The green shoots of economic spring are appearing once again.*

Lamont used this horticultural metaphor in a speech to the Conservative Party Conference at Blackpool on 9 October 1991. As Chancellor of the Exchequer he was earnestly endeavouring to convince his audience that Britain was coming out of a recession. It had not obviously done so before he was relieved of his responsibilities in 1993. In the *Independent* (30 November 1993), Lamont reflected: 'My wife tried to talk me out of that phrase, but only because I used it in October, the wrong season for green shoots.'

Compare this use: in a letter to a lover (6 May 1962), the poet Philip Larkin wrote: 'Spring comes with your birthday, and I love to think of you as somehow linked with the tender green shoots I see on all the trees and bushes . . . I wish I could be with you and we could plunge into bed.'

Lang, Julia
British broadcaster (1921–)

3 *Are you sitting comfortably? Then I'll/we'll begin.*

This way of beginning a story on *Listen With Mother*, BBC radio's daily spot for small children, was used from the programme's inception in January 1950. Lang, the original presenter, recalled in 1982: 'The first day it came out inadvertently. I just said it. The next day I didn't. Then there was a flood of letters from children saying, "I couldn't listen because I wasn't ready".' It remained a more or less essential part of the proceedings until the programme was threatened with closure in 1982.

In *The Times* obituary of Frieda Fordham, an analytical psychologist (18 January 1988), it was stated that *she* had actually coined the phrase when advising the BBC's producers.

Laski, Harold
English political scientist (1893–1950)

1 *In that state of resentful coma that they dignified by the name of research.*

In one of his letters to Oliver Wendell Holmes Jr (dated 10 October 1922, published 1953), Laski recounted how he had recently spoken at a Conference on Workers' Education at Oxford: 'I made an epigram in my address which pleased me. A trade-unionist attacked Oxford for being slow to respond to the workers' demand for education. I said that I was amazed at the speed of the response in dons who spent most of their days in . . .' Laski was so pleased with his epigram that he used it soon afterwards in *three* other letters to Holmes without any apparent awareness that he was repeating himself.
    In *The Lyttelton Hart-Davis Letters* (for 27 October 1955), it is suggested that 'Laski produced it — mendaciously — as his own in a letter to Judge Holmes'. If the remark was not his own, the originator remains untraced.
    In *Geoffrey Madan's Notebooks* (ed. Gere & Sparrow, 1981 — but Madan died in 1947) there is the uncredited quotation: ' "Research" is a mere excuse for idleness.'

Law, Andrew Bonar
British Conservative Prime Minister (1858–1923)

2 *I must follow them; I am their leader.*

Quoted in Edward Raymond, *Mr Balfour* (1920).

See LEDRU-ROLLIN 210:4.

Lawrence, D.H.
English novelist and poet (1885–1930)

3 Homo sum! *the Adventurer.*

The quotation on Lawrence's memorial (1985) in Poets' Corner, Westminster Abbey, comes from his essay 'Climbing down Pisgah', which was published posthumously. At a ceremony in the Abbey to mark Lawrence's birthday in September 1987, Professor James T. Boulton gave an address in which he explained his choice of this epitaph. He quoted Lawrence as saying, 'Man is nothing . . . unless he adventures. Either into the unknown of the world, of his environment. Or into the unknown of

himself.' Boulton added: 'The very essence of man and human life, in Lawrence's view, is bound up with the act of knowing and the nature of knowledge . . . That commitment to adventure, in Lawrence's view, is what should motivate all human beings.'

Lawrence, T.E.
English soldier and writer (1888–1935)

4 *I loved you, so I drew these tides of men into my hands and wrote my will across the sky in stars*
to earn you freedom, the seven pillared worthy house, that your eyes might be shining for me when we came.

This verse, which forms the epigraph to *The Seven Pillars of Wisdom* (1926), is dedicated 'To S.A.' This has been taken to refer to Selim Ahmed, an Arab friend who died in 1918. The innocent suggestion that 'S.A.' stands for 'Saudi Arabia' is thus a little wide of the mark.
    The 'seven pillared worthy house' derives from Proverbs 9:1: 'Wisdom hath builded her house, she hath hewn out her seven pillars.'

5 *All men dream: but not equally. Those who dream by night in the dusty recesses of their minds wake in the day to find that it was vanity; but the dreamers of the day are dangerous men, for they may act their dream with open eyes, to make it possible. This I did.*

An elusive quotation from *ibid.* It is included in the 'Introductory Chapter', originally 'Chapter 1' and suppressed from the first edition.

Lazarus, Emma
American poet (1849–87)

6 *Give me your tired, your poor,*
Your huddled masses yearning to breathe free,
The wretched refuse of your teeming shore,
Send these, the homeless, tempest-tossed, to me:
I lift my lamp beside the golden door.

'The New Colossus' (1883), inscribed on the Statue of Liberty, New York. Although Lazarus was not an immigrant herself —

she was born in New York — she championed oppressed Jewry.

Lear, Edward
English poet and artist (1812–88)

1 *On the coast of Coromandel*
Where the early pumpkins blow,
In the middle of the woods,
Lived the Yonghy-Bonghy-Bó.

From 'The Courtship of the Yonghy-Bonghy-Bó' (1871). This poem was itself parodied in the 1930s by an untraced author who wrote: 'On the coast of Coromandel/Danced we to the tunes of Handel' (Lear went on, rather: 'Two old chairs, and half a candle; — 'One old jug without a handle, — /These were all his worldly goods.'
   The alliterative phrase 'on the coast of Coromandel' has long been around (not surprising when one considers that Coromandel is mostly coast and nothing else). The Coast was the scene of the Franco-British struggle for supremacy in India in the eighteenth century. The *OED2* has citations from 1697, 'On the coast of Coromandel . . . they call them catamarans' and from 1817, 'The united fleet appeared on the coast of Coromandel', and several others. The phrase had also been used earlier by Macaulay in his essay 'Frederick the Great' (1842).

2 *Below the high Cathedral stairs,*
Lie the remains of Agnes Pears.
Her name was Wiggs; it was not Pears.
But Pears was put to rhyme with stairs.

This is but one form of the 'forced rhyme' epitaph. It occurs in Lear's diary (entry for 20 April 1887). With 'Susan Pares' replacing 'Agnes Pears', the rhyme was first published without date in *Queery Leary Nonsense* (1911), edited from manuscripts by Lady Constance Strachey. The most usual form ends: 'Her name was Smith; it was not Jones;/But Jones was put to rhyme with Stones.'

Le Corbusier
(Charles Edouard Jeanneret)
French architect (1887–1965)

3 *A house is a machine for living in* [La maison est une machine à habiter].

Some feel that Le Corbusier's description of the purpose of a house is a rather chilling

one. The phrase first appeared in *Vers une Architecture*, 1923, but in the context of his expanded explanation, it is not so bleak. He wrote in *Almanach de l'Architecture* (1925): 'The house has [three] aims. First it's a machine for living in, that is, a machine destined to serve as a useful aid for rapidity and precision in our work, a tireless and thoughtful machine to satisfy the needs of the body: comfort. But it is, secondly, a place intended for meditation and thirdly a place whose beauty exists and brings to the soul that calm which is indispensable.'
   Compare from Leo Tolstoy, *War and Peace*, Bk 10, Chap. 29 (1865–9): '*Notre corps est une machine à vivre* [Our body is a machine for living].'

Ledru-Rollin, Alexandre Auguste
French politician (1807–74)

4 *I must follow them for I am their leader.*

Ledru-Rollin became Minister of the Interior in the provisional government during the 1848 Paris revolution. He was looking from his window one day as a mob passed by and he said: '*Eh, je suis leur chef, il fallait bien les suivre* [Ah well, I'm their leader, I really ought to follow them].' It is said that 'he gave offence by his arbitrary conduct' (of which this would seem to be a prime example) and had to resign.
   The remark was being quoted by 1857 and is now a frequently invoked form of political abuse. Winston Churchill is supposed to have said of Clement Attlee: 'We all understand his position. "I am their leader, I must follow them".'

See also LAW 209:2.

Lee, Robert E.
American general (1807–70)

5 *I determined to avoid the useless sacrifice of those whose past services have endeared them to their countrymen.*

Lee put this in 'General Order No. 9', a written address dated 10 April 1865, at the conclusion of the American Civil War. He was explaining to the Confederate troops he was leading why he had surrendered to General Grant at Appomattox Court House, Virginia, the previous day. The army of North Virginia had been compelled to yield to overwhelming numbers and Lee also said, 'It is our duty to live. What will become of the women and children of the South if we are not here to protect them?'

In March 1976 the British Labour politician Roy Jenkins was quoted as saying, 'I am determined to avoid the useless sacrifice' when, not making progress in his bid for the party leadership, he withdrew from the race. In his memoirs, *A Life at the Centre* (1991), Jenkins states: 'I quoted (or more probably misquoted) Lee's message' and then goes on to quote a substantial passage from Lee's order, though pointedly omitting the actual 'useless sacrifice' phrase.

Lejeune, C.A.
English film critic (1897–1973)

1 *Me no Leica.*

A small joke, but a good one. There was a vogue for dismissive one-line criticisms of plays and films, especially in the 1930s, '40s and '50s, when suitable opportunities presented themselves. It was either when Christopher Isherwood's Berlin stories were turned first into a play, *I am a Camera* (1951), or subsequently into a film (1955), that one critic summed up his/her reaction with the words 'Me no Leica'. This has been variously attributed to Caroline Lejeune, George Jean Nathan, Walter Kerr and Kenneth Tynan. It is a comment on the transitory nature of much criticism that one cannot say for sure who did originate the joke.

John Van Druten based his play on the stories of Christopher Isherwood. In 'A Berlin Diary' (included in *Goodbye to Berlin*, 1939) Isherwood had written: 'I am a camera with its shutter open, quite passive, recording, not thinking.' Later, the play became the basis of the musical *Cabaret*.

Another short review of Lejeune's is said to have been of the film *My Son My Son* (US, 1940). She put: 'My Son My Son, my sainted aunt!'

Lenin (Vladimir Ilyich Ulyanov)
Russian revolutionary (1870–1924)

2 *Give us the child for eight years and it will be a Bolshevik forever.*

Lenin *may* have said this to the Commissars of Education in Moscow in 1923, but the earliest source is tainted — it is *100 Things You Should Know About Communism* published by the Committee on Un-American Activities in 1951.

Compare, however, 'Give us a child until it is seven and it is ours for life', a saying usually attributed to the Jesuits, founded in 1534 by St Ignatius Loyala, but possibly wished on them by their opponents. Another version is: 'Give us the child, and we will give you the man.' *Lean's Collecteana*, Vol. 3 (1903) has, as a 'Jesuit maxim', 'Give me a child for the first seven years, and you may do what you like with him afterwards'.

Muriel Spark in her novel *The Prime of Miss Jean Brodie* (1962) has her heroine, a teacher, say: 'Give me a girl at an impressionable age and she is mine for life.'

3 *One Step Forward Two Steps Back* [Shag vpered dva shaga nazad].

In 1904, Lenin wrote a book about 'the crisis within our party' under this title. Note that in *Conducted Tour* (1981), Bernard Levin refers to Lenin's 'pamphlet' under the title *Four Steps Forward, Three Steps Back*. Vilmos Voigt pointed out in *Proverbium Yearbook of International Proverb Scholarship* (1984) that just after the publication of his work, Lenin referred to the 'current German form, *Ein Schritt vorwärts, zwei Schritte zurück* [one step forwards, two steps back]', and Voigt wondered what precisely the source of Lenin's phrase was and in which language.

4 *Those who make revolutions by halves are digging their own graves.*

Sometimes attributed to Lenin, this had been said earlier by the French revolutionary Saint-Just to the National Convention in 1794, in the form: '*Ceux qui font des révolutions à moitié n'ont fait que se creuser un tombeau.*' George Büchner quoted it, too, in *Dantons Tod* (1835) but ascribed it to Robespierre: '*Wer eine Revolution zur Hälfte vollendet, gräbt sich selbst sein Grab.*'

5 *Communism is Soviet power plus the electrification of the whole country.*

From Lenin's Report to the 8th Congress (1920). Could this have been alluded to in *The Electrification of the Soviet Union*, the title of an opera with libretto by Craig Raine and music by Nigel Osborne, first presented at Glyndbourne in 1986? The opera is based on a novella by Boris Pasternak called *The Last Summer*, but the only hint in the published text is two quotations: 'and the neat man/To their east who ordered Gorki to be electrified' (W.H. Auden) and 'Next, he introduced electricity to Ethiopia, first in the palaces and then in other buildings'.

Lennon, John
English singer and songwriter (1940–80)

1 Being for the Benefit of Mr Kite.

The title of a track on The Beatles' *Sgt Pepper* album (1967) comes from a standard nineteenth-century phrase used in advertising 'testimonial' performances. Compare the title of Chapter 48 of *Nicholas Nickleby* (1838–9) by Charles Dickens: 'Being for the benefit of Mr Vincent Crummles, and Positively his last Appearance on this Stage.' As for the lyrics, largely written by John Lennon, though credited jointly to him and Paul McCartney, they derive almost word for word, as Lennon acknowledged, from the wording of a Victorian circus poster he bought in an antique shop. Or that was the story, until Derek Taylor revealed in *It Was Twenty Years Ago Today* (1987) that the poster was 'liberated' from a café during the filming of promotional clips for the 'Penny Lane/Strawberry Fields Forever' record. Headed 'Pablo Fanque's Circus Royal' in the Town Meadows, Rochdale, the poster announces:

> Grandest Night of the Season!
> And Positively the
> Last Night But Three!
> Being for the Benefit of Mr. Kite,
> (late of Wells's Circus) and
> Mr. J. Henderson,
> the Celebrated Somerset Thrower!
> Wire Dancer, Vaulter, Rider, &c.

On Tuesday Evening, February 14th, 1843. ('Somerset' is an old word for somersault.)

2 A Day in the Life.

The memorable track from the 1967 Beatles album *Sgt Pepper* presumably took its name from that type of magazine article and film documentary which strives to depict twenty-four hours in the life of a particular person or organization. In 1959, Richard Cawston produced a TV documentary which took this form, with the title *This is the BBC*. In 1962, the English title of a novel (film UK, 1971) by Alexander Solzhenitsyn was *One Day in the Life of Ivan Denisovich*. Lennon and McCartney's use of the phrase for the description of incidents in the life of a drug-taker may have had something to do with the subsequent *Sunday Times* Magazine

feature 'A Life in the Day' (running since the 1960s) and the play *A Day in the Death of Joe Egg* by Peter Nichols (1967; film UK, 1971).

3 *I heard the news today oh boy*
four thousand holes in Blackburn,
Lancashire
and though the holes were rather small
they had to count them all
now they know how many holes it takes
to fill the Albert Hall.

These odd lines come from the Lennon and McCartney lyrics for 'A Day In the Life' on the Beatles' *Sgt Pepper* album (1967). The inspiration for them — nothing to do with drug needlemarks or anything like that — can be traced directly to the *Daily Mail* of 17 January 1967. Lennon had the newspaper propped up on his piano as he composed. The original brief story, topping the 'Far & Near' column stated: 'There are 4000 holes in the road in Blackburn, Lancashire, or one twenty-sixth of a hole per person, according to a council survey. If Blackburn is typical there are two million holes in Britain's roads and 300,000 in London.'

4 It's been a hard day's night.

The title of the Beatles' first feature film (UK, 1964) was apparently chosen towards the end of filming when Ringo Starr used the phrase to describe a 'heavy' night out (according to Ray Coleman, *John Lennon*, 1984). What, in fact, Ringo must have done was to use the title of the Lennon and McCartney song (presumably already written if it was towards the end of filming) in a conversational way. Indeed, Hunter Davies in *The Beatles* (1968) noted: 'Ringo Starr came out with the phrase, though John had used it earlier in a poem.' It certainly sounds like a Lennonism and may have had some limited general use subsequently as a catchphrase meaning that the speaker has had 'a very tiring time'.

5 Christianity will go. It will vanish and shrink. I needn't argue about that. I'm right and I'll be proved right. We're more popular than Jesus now.

An observation from Lennon's interview with Maureen Cleave of the London *Evening Standard* (4 March 1966) lay dormant for several months, but when the Beatles paid a visit to the USA it was reprinted and caused an outcry. The Beatles were burned in effigy and their records banned by radio stations in Bible-belt states. Lennon subsequently withdrew the remark: 'I just said what I said — and I was wrong' (press conference, Chicago, 11 August 1966).

An interesting pre-echo occurs in a remark by Zelda Fitzgerald, recorded in Ernest Hemingway's *A Moveable Feast* (1964): 'Ernest, don't you think Al Jolson is greater than Jesus?'

1 *Life is what happens to you while you're busy making other plans.*

In the lyrics of Lennon's song 'Beautiful Boy' (included on his 'Double Fantasy' album, 1980), this is one of two quotations (the other is the slogan 'Every day in every day I'm getting better and better', *see also* COUÉ 107:5). So it is wrong to credit Lennon with either line, as has been done.

In Barbara Rowe's *The Book of Quotes* (1979), she ascribes the 'Life is . . .' saying to Betty Talmadge, divorced wife of Senator Herman Talmadge, in the form 'Life is what happens to you when you're making other plans.' Dr Laurence Peter in *Quotations for Our Time* (1977) gives the line to 'Thomas La Mance', who remains untraced.

Leonard, Elmore
American novelist (1925–)

2 *Erotic is when you do something sensitive and imaginative with a feather. Kinky is when you use the whole chicken.*

Attributed to Leonard by William Rushton in 1987. However, in a BBC TV *Moving Pictures* profile of Roman Polanski (reviewed in the *Guardian*, 25 November 1991), Peter Coyote ascribed the remark to Polanski in the form: 'Eroticism is using a feather, while pornography is using the whole chicken.'

Leoncavallo, Ruggiero
Italian composer and librettist (1858–1919)

3 *On with the motley!*

Partridge/*Catch Phrases* suggests that this is what one says to start a party or trip to the theatre. It may also mean 'on with the show, in spite of what has happened'. Either way, the allusion is to the Clown's cry — '*vesti la giubba*' — in Leoncavallo's opera

I Pagliacci (1892). The Clown has to 'carry on with the show' despite having a broken heart. So it might be said jokingly nowadays by anyone who is having to proceed with something in spite of difficulties. Laurence Olivier used the phrase in something like its original context when describing a sudden dash home from Ceylon during a crisis in his marriage to Vivien Leigh: 'I got myself on to a plane . . . and was in Paris on the Saturday afternoon. I went straight on home the next day as I had music sessions for *The Beggar's Opera* from the Monday; and so, on with the motley' (*Confessions of an Actor*, 1982).

'*Giubba*' in Italian, means simply 'jacket' (in the sense of costume), and 'the motley' is the old English word for an actor or clown's clothes, originally the many-coloured coat worn by a jester or fool (as mentioned several times in Shakespeare's *As You Like It*). The popularity of the phrase in English probably dates from Enrico Caruso's 1902 recording of the aria, which became the first gramophone record eventually to sell a million copies.

See also RABELAIS 274:2.

Lermontov, Mikhail
Russian novelist and poet (1814–41)

4 *Land of the unwashed, goodbye!*
Land of the masters, land of knaves!
You, in neat blue uniforms!
You who live like cringing slaves!
In my exile I may find
Peace beneath Caucasian skies, —
Far from slanderers and tsars,
Far from ever-spying eyes.

From a Lermontov poem written *c* 1840, expressing his exasperation with Mother Russia. It was quoted by Nicholas Daniloff, an American journalist accused of spying, on his release from imprisonment in the Soviet Union (October 1986).

Lerner, Alan Jay
American songwriter and playwright (1918–86)

5 *My Fair Lady.*

It was understandable when Lerner and the composer Frederick Loewe wished to make a musical out of Shaw's *Pygmalion* that they should seek a new title. After all, not even in Shaw's Preface (only in his Afterword) does he allude to the relevance of the Greek legend to his story of a Covent Garden flower-girl who gets raised up and taught to 'speak proper' just like a Mayfair lady.

Lerner and Loewe turned, it seems, to the refrain of a nursery rhyme (first recorded in the eighteenth century):

London Bridge is broken down,
    Broken down, broken down,
London Bridge is broken down,
    My fair lady.

It has also been suggested that they were drawn to the title because 'my fair lady' is how a cockney flower-seller would pronounce the phrase 'Mayfair lady'.

1 *Camelot . . .*
Where once it never rained till after
    sundown
By eight a.m. the morning fog had
    flown
Don't let it be forgot
That once there was a spot
For one brief shining moment that
    was known
As Camelot . . .

From the title song of Lerner and Loewe's musical *Camelot*, first produced on Broadway in December 1960 just before President Kennedy took office. Hence, the name 'Camelot' came to be applied to the romantic concept of his Presidency. As Lerner wrote in *The Street Where I Live* (1978): when Jackie Kennedy quoted the lines in an interview with *Life* Magazine after her husband's assassination in 1963: '*Camelot* had suddenly become the symbol of those thousand days when people the world over saw a bright new light of hope shining from the White House . . . For myself, I have never been able to see a performance of *Camelot* again.'

In 1983, on the twentieth anniversary of President Kennedy's death, William Manchester wrote a memorial volume with the title *One Brief Shining Moment*.

Lester, Alfred
English comedian (1872–1925)

2 *Always merry and bright.*

Lester — who was always lugubrious — was especially associated with this phrase. He played 'Peter Doody', a jockey in the Lionel Monckton/Howard Talbot/Arthur Wimperis musical comedy *The Arcadians* (1909). He had it as his motto in a song, 'My Motter'. *Punch* quoted the phrase on 26

October 1910. Somerset Maugham in a letter to a friend (1915) wrote: 'I am back on a fortnight's leave, very merry and bright, but frantically busy — I wish it were all over.' An edition of *The Magnet* from 1920 carries an advertisement for a comic called *Merry and Bright*. P.G. Wodehouse used the phrase in *The Indiscretions of Archie* (1921).

Larry Grayson suggested (1981) that it was later used as the billing for Billy Danvers, the red-nosed music-hall comedian (*d* 1964). However, there may have been confusion with Danvers's undoubted bill-matter 'Cheeky, Cheery and Chubby' (*c* 1918).

Lever, William Hesketh
(1st Viscount Leverhulme)
English soap-maker and philanthropist
(1851–1925)

3 *Half the money I spend on advertising is wasted, and the trouble is I don't know which half.*

Quoted by David Ogilvy in *Confessions of an Advertising Man* (1963), this observation has also been fathered on John Wannamaker and, indeed, on Ogilvy himself. Leverhulme remains the most likely originator — he made his fortune through the manufacture of soap from vegetable oils instead of from tallow. Ogilvy had Lever Brothers as a client and could presumably have picked up the remark that way. However, Wannamaker, who more or less invented the modern department store in the US, was active by the 1860s and so possibly could have said it first.

Ley, Robert
German Nazi official (*d* 1945)

4 *Strength through joy* [Kraft durch Freude].

A German Labour Front slogan was coined *c* 1933 by Robert Ley, the head of this Nazi organization which provided regimented leisure.

Liberace
(Wladziu Valentino Liberace)
American pianist and entertainer (1919–87)

5 *I cried all the way to the bank.*

The flamboyant pianist discussed criticism of his shows in an autobiography (1973): 'I think the people around me are more apt to become elated about good reviews (or depressed by bad ones) than I am. If they're good I just tell them, "Don't let success go to your head." When the reviews are bad I tell my staff that they can join me as I cry all the way to the bank.' Liberace gave currency to this saying long before 1973, however, and he may not have invented it.

Richard Keyes, in *Nice Guys Finish Seventh* (1992), suggests that the accepted version is now 'I *laughed* all the way to the bank', which is questionable. Whatever the form, it became a catchphrase meaning that the speaker is in a position to ignore criticism.

It has been suggested that Liberace's use of the phrase dates back to his 1959 libel action in London against the *Daily Mirror* whose columnist 'Cassandra' (William Connor) had described him as 'fruit-flavoured'. This was taken to imply that he was homosexual. Liberace won the case and £8,000. However, as early as 1954, Liberace was apparently being quoted as saying: 'What you said hurt me very much. I cried all the way to the bank.'

Lincoln, Abraham
16th American President (1809–65)

1 *If you once forfeit the confidence of your fellow citizens, you can never regain their respect and esteem. You may fool all the people some of the time; you can even fool some of the people all the time; but you can't fool all of the people all the time.*

There is so much Lincolniana — and so much that can't be verified — but this has the authentic ring about it, although it has also been ascribed to Phineas T. Barnum. The saying first appeared in Alexander K. McLure, *Lincoln's Yarns and Stories* (1904).

2 *People who like this sort of thing will find this the sort of thing they like.*

What has been called 'the world's best book review' (by Hilary Corke in *The Listener* (28 April 1955) can only loosely be traced back to Lincoln. G.W.E. Russell had it in his *Collections and Recollections* (1898). Bartlett has steadily ignored it in recent years.

As recounted by S.N. Behrman in *Conversations with Max* (1960), Max Beerbohm once mischievously invented a classical

Greek source for the remark, and passed it off in a letter to the press under Rose Macaulay's signature. This was no more than mischief. In his novel *Zuleika Dobson* (1911), Beerbohm commented of the heroine when she is at a college concert at which the Duke of Dorset is playing: 'She was one of the people who say, "I don't know anything about music really, but I know what I like".'

3 *In giving freedom to the slave, we assure freedom to the free — honorable alike in what we give and what we preserve. We shall nobly save or meanly lose the last, best hope of earth.*

Referring to the act of giving freedom to the slaves, the phrase 'last, best hope of earth' comes from Abraham Lincoln's Second Annual Message to Congress (1 December 1862). It is not 'on earth', but has been endlessly quoted and alluded to by later Presidents and politicians. One example: in President Kennedy's inaugural speech (1961), the United Nations was 'our last best hope'.

4 *Four score and seven years ago our fathers brought forth on this continent a new nation, conceived in Liberty, and dedicated to the proposition that all men are created equal . . . The world will little note, nor long remember what we say here, but it can never forget what they did here. It is for us, the living, rather to be dedicated here to the unfinished work which they who fought here have thus far so nobly advanced. It is rather for us to be here dedicated to the great task remaining before us, that from these honoured dead we take increased devotion to that cause for which they gave the last full measure of devotion; that we here highly resolve that these dead shall not have died in vain, that this nation, under God, shall have a new birth of freedom . . .*

The Federal victory at the Battle of Gettysburg in the American Civil War foreshadowed the ultimate defeat of the Confederacy. But what immortalized the battle was Lincoln's address, as President, at the dedication of the battlefield cemetery at Gettysburg on 19 November 1863. Lincoln's prophecy that the world would 'little note or long remember' what he said seemed likely to be true, judging by initial reaction to the speech. One American paper spoke of the President's 'silly remarks'. *The Times* of London (as did many American papers) ignored the speech in its report of the ceremony. Later *The Times* was to say: 'Anything more dull and commonplace it wouldn't be easy to reproduce.' The *Chicago Tribune* wrote, however, that the words would, 'Live among the annals of man'. There is a legend that Lincoln jotted down the Gettysburg Address on the back of an envelope on a train going to the battlefield, but the structure of the words is so tight that this seems unlikely and Burnam (1980) suggests that there were some five drafts of the speech. Also, the Associated Press was apparently given an advance copy.

1 *Government of the people, by the people, for the people.*

Thirty-three years before Lincoln delivered the Gettysburg Address, which included this famous line, Daniel Webster had spoken of 'The people's government, made for the people, made by the people, and answerable to the people' (Second Speech on Foote's Resolution, 26 January 1830).

According to Bartlett (1992), Theodore Parker, a clergyman, had used various versions of this credo in anti-slavery speeches during the 1850s. Lincoln's law partner William H. Herndon gave him a copy of Parker's speeches. Before composing Gettysburg, Lincoln marked the words 'democracy is direct self-government, over all the people, by all of the people, for all of the people' in a Parker sermon dating from 1858.

2 *God must have loved the common people; he made so many of them.*

There is no evidence that Lincoln said this. James Morgan in a book called *Our Presidents* (1928) was the first to put it in his mouth.

3 *He ain't heavy, he's my brother.*

King George VI concluded his 1942 Christmas radio broadcast by reflecting on the European allies and the benefits of mutual cooperation, saying: 'A former President of the United States of America used to tell of a boy who was carrying an even smaller child up a hill. Asked whether the heavy

burden was not too much for him, the boy answered: "It's not a burden, it's my brother!" So let us welcome the future in a spirit of brotherhood, and thus make a world in which, please God, all may dwell together in justice and peace.'

Benham (1948) suggests that the American President must have been Lincoln — though it has not been possible to trace a source for the story. In fact, the King's allusion seems rather to have been a dignification of an advertising slogan and a charity's motto. As an advertising headline, 'He ain't heavy . . . he's my brother' the expression may have been used first by Jack Cornelius of the BBD&O agency in a 1936 American advertisement for the 'Community Chest' campaign ('35 appeals in 1'). But it is difficult to tell what relationship this has, if any, with the similar slogan used to promote the Nebraska orphanage and poor boys' home known as 'Boys Town'.

In the early 1920s, the Revd Edward J. Flanagan — Spencer Tracy played him in the film *Boys' Town* (1938) — admitted to this home a boy named Howard Loomis who could not walk without the aid of crutches. The larger boys often took turns carrying him about on their backs. One day, Father Flanagan is said to have seen a boy carrying Loomis and asked whether this wasn't a heavy load. The reply: 'He ain't heavy, Father . . . he's m'brother.' In 1943, a 'two brothers' logo (similar to, though not the same as, the drawing used in the Community Chest campaign) was copyrighted for Boys Town's exclusive use. Today, the logo and the motto (in the 'Father/ m'brother' form) are registered service marks of Father Flanagan's Boys' Home (Boys Town).

My feeling is that the saying probably *does* predate the Father Flanagan story, though whether it goes back to Lincoln is anybody's guess. More recent applications have included the song with the title, written by Bob Russell and Bobby Scott, and popularized by the Hollies in 1969. Perhaps the brief Lennon and McCartney song 'Carry that Weight' (September 1969) alludes similarly? — 'Boy — you're gonna carry that weight,/Carry that weight a long time.'

4 *You cannot bring about prosperity by discouraging thrift. You cannot strengthen the weak by weakening the strong. You cannot help small men up by tearing big men down. You cannot help the wage earner by pulling down the wage*

payer. You cannot further the brother-hood of man by encouraging class hatred. You cannot help the poor by destroying the rich. You cannot esta-blish sound security on borrowed money. You cannot keep out of trouble by spending more than you earn. You cannot build character and courage by taking away man's initiative and inde-pendence. You cannot help men per-manently by doing for them what they could and should do for themselves.

That Lincoln never said all or any of this is a fact that few people seem obliged to accept, especially if they are proponents of free enterprise. The playwright Ronald Millar described in the *Sunday Times* (23 November 1980) what had happened when he wrote his first speech for Margaret That-cher as Prime Minister: 'I dashed off a piece including the quote from Abraham Lincoln, "Don't make the rich poorer, make the poor richer." I gave her the first draft and she immediately delved into her handbag for a piece of yellowing paper on which was writ-ten the very same Lincoln quotation. "I take it everywhere with me," she said. And from then on I've worked for her whenever she's asked me.'

Ex-President Ronald Reagan attributed the line, 'You cannot strengthen the weak by weakening the strong' to Lincoln in an address to the Republican Covention in August 1992. When it was pointed out that this had in fact been uttered by 'a Revd William Boetker of Pennsylvania', a spokes-woman for Mr Reagan 'said it was not really his fault; he had found the line, attributed to Lincoln, in a handbook of quotes' (*Indepen-dent*, 20 August 1992). On the other hand, if he had referred to the Congressional Research Service's authoritative *Respect-fully Quoted*, he would have found that President Calvin Coolidge had said, 'Don't expect to build up the weak by pulling down the strong' in a speech to Massachusetts State Senate on 7 January 1914.

The misattribution of all or part of the 'Ten Points' was most likely first made by a member of the US Congress, but the list has been widely distributed since the 1940s. In *Harper's* Magazine (May 1950), Albert A. Woldman claimed that the quotation came rather from *The Industrial Decalogue*, a pamphlet published in 1911 by one William Boetcker (sometimes described as the Revd William J.H. Boetcker).

1 *I have always plucked a thistle and planted a flower where I thought a flower would grow.*

Untraced, but attributed to Lincoln in 1993.

2 *Now he belongs to the ages.*

This was said *about* Lincoln — on his death, 15 April 1865 — by Edwin McMasters Stanton.

Lindner, R.M.
American psychologist (1914–56)

3 *Rebel Without a Cause.*

According to *ODQ* and *ODMQ*, with the subtitle 'The hypnoanalysis of a criminal psychopath', this was the title of a book published in 1944, though Lindner was not the 'novelist' that *ODQ* calls him. The phrase became famous later when used as the title of an otherwise unrelated film (1955), for which the screenplay credit was given to Stewart Stern 'from an original story by the director, Nicholas Ray'. *The Motion Picture Guide* (1990) gives the pro-venance of the script, however, as 'based on an adaptation by Irving Shulman of a story line by Ray inspired from the story *The Blind Run* by Dr Robert M. Lindner.' The film's study of adolescent misbehaviour had little to do with what one would now think of as psychopathic but it helped popularize the phrase 'rebel without a cause' to describe a certain type of alienated youth of the period. It was the film that projected its star, James Dean, to status as chief 1950s rebel, a position confirmed when he met his premature end soon after.

Livingstone, David
Scottish missionary and explorer (1813–73)

4 *All I can add in my solitude is, may heaven's rich blessing come down on everyone, American, English, or Turk — who will help heal this open sore of the world.*

These words are inscribed on Livingstone's grave in Westminster Abbey. The quotation referring to the slave trade is taken from the last words he had addressed to the *New York Herald*.

Llewellyn, Richard
Welsh novelist (1907–83)

1 *None But the Lonely Heart.*

The title of this novel (1943; film US, 1944) is apparently an original coinage. But compare, 'None But the Weary Heart', the English title often given to a song by Tchaikovsky (Op. 6, No. 6). The lyrics of this song have been translated into English as, 'None but the weary heart can understand how I have suffered and how I am tormented'. It originated as 'Mignon's Song' in the novel *Wilhelm Meister* by Goethe — '*Nur wer die Sehnsucht kennt* [Only those who know what longing is]' — which was translated into Russian by Mey.

Lloyd, Marie
English music-hall entertainer (1870–1922)

2 *She sits among the cabbages and peas.*

In 1929, Leslie Sarony, the British entertainer (1897–1985), wrote a song called 'Mucking About the Garden' using the *nom de plume* 'Q. Cumber' or 'Q. Kumber'. Unfortunately, I have been unable to find the sheet music (published by Lawrence Wright) to see if it really does contain the immortal lines, 'She sits among the cabbages and peas/Watching her onions grow', as has been suggested. The only recording I have heard of the song, by George Buck, does not have the couplet. I suspect that the recording by Sarony himself with Tommy Handley and Jack Payne (on Columbia 5555), which I have not heard, does not have it either.

What I can't work out is whether this is the same song as that apparently made famous by Marie Lloyd. According to the story, when forbidden by a watch committee (local guardians of morals) to sing 'He/she sits among the cabbages and peas,' she substituted, 'He/she sits among the cabbages and leeks.'

Lloyd's song, if different, has not been found either, so this remains a puzzle.

Logue, Christopher
English poet (1926–)

3 *Come to the edge.*
We might fall.
Come to the edge.
It's too high!
COME TO THE EDGE!

And they came,
and he pushed,
and they flew.

From Logue's *New Numbers* (1969). In a profile of Tom Stoppard (*The New Yorker*, 19 December 1977), Kenneth Tynan described the playwright addressing a class of drama students in Santa Barbara: 'What is the real dialogue that goes on between the artist and his audience? [Stoppard asks at the end]. By way of reply, he holds the microphone close to his mouth and speaks eight lines by the English poet Christopher Logue . . . A surge of applause. In imagination, these young people are all flying.'

Curiously, the lines have also been attributed to Guillaume Apollinaire (1880–1918).

Lombardi, Vince
American football coach (1913–70)

4 *Winning isn't everything. It's the only thing.*

Various versions of this oft-repeated statement exist. Lombardi, coach and general manager of the Green Bay Packers team from 1959 onwards, claimed *not* to have said it in this form but, rather, 'Winning is not everything — but making the effort to win is' (interview 1962). The first version of Lombardi's remarks to appear in print was in the form, 'Winning is not the most important thing, it's everything'. One Bill Veeck is reported to have said something similar. Henry 'Red' Sanders, a football coach at Vanderbilt University, *does* seem to have said it, however, c 1948, and was so quoted in *Sports Illustrated* (26 December 1955). John Wayne, playing a football coach, delivered the line in the 1953 film *Trouble Along the Way.*

Compare 'Winning in politics isn't everything; it's the only thing' — a slogan for the infamous 'Committee to Re-Elect the President' (Nixon) in 1972.

Long, Huey
American politician (1893–1935)

5 *Everyman a king but no man wears a crown.*

The Louisiana Governor (and demagogue) found this slogan for his Share-the-Wealth platform — which he espoused from 1928 until his assassination — in William

Jennings Bryan's 'Cross of Gold' speech (1896) — see BRYAN 73:1. He suggested that only 10 per cent of the American people owned 70 per cent of the wealth. As Safire (1978) points out, the full slogan used 'everyman' as one word.

Longfellow, Henry Wadsworth
American poet (1807–82)

1 *The shades of night were falling fast,*
As through an Alpine village passed
A youth, who bore, 'mid snow and ice,
A banner with the strange device,
Excelsior!

The poem 'Excelsior' (1842), of which this is the first verse, became a favourite recitation of the parlour poetry school and was also set to music more than once. It gave rise to a delightful parody 'The Shades of Night', which was written, apparently, by A.E. Housman:

> The shades of night were falling fast
> And the rain was falling faster
> When through an Alpine village passed
> An Alpine village pastor.

2 *Fold their tents like the Arabs.*

At the conclusion of his case for the defence in the Jeremy Thorpe trial (1979), Mr George Carman QC said to the Old Bailey jury: 'I end by saying in the words of the Bible: "Let this prosecution fold up its tent and quietly creep away".'
His client should not have got off after that. The words are not from the Bible, but from Longfellow's 'The Day is Done':

> And the night shall be filled with music
> And the cares that infest the day
> Shall fold their tents, like the Arabs,
> And as silently steal away.

3 *Into each life some rain must fall,*
But too much is falling in mine.

The song 'Into Each Life A Little Rain Must Fall' (as it is sometimes worded, but which also contains 'some rain' in the lyrics) was written by Allan Roberts and Doris Fisher (1944). They based the title line, however, on Longfellow's poem 'The Rainy Day' (1842):

> Thy fate is the common fate of all,
> Into each life some rain must fall,
> Some days must be dark and dreary.

4 *The lady with a/the lamp.*

So was dubbed Florence Nightingale (1820–1910), philanthropist and nursing pioneer, in commemoration of her services to soldiers at Scutari during the Crimean War (1854–6). She inspected hospital wards at night, carrying a lamp — a Turkish lantern consisting of a candle inside a collapsible shade. The phrase (with 'a' lamp) appears to have been coined by Longfellow in his poem *Santa Filomena* (1858 — i.e. very shortly after the events described):

> Lo! in that hour of misery
> A lady with a lamp I see
>   Pass through the glimmering gloom,
>   And flit from room to room.
> And slow, as in a dream of bliss
> The speechless sufferer turns to kiss
>   Her shadow, as it falls
>   Upon the darkening walls.

On her death, Moore Smith & Co. of Moorgate, London, published a ballad with the title 'The Lady with the Lamp', which begins:

> The Lady with the Lamp —
> Let this her title be
> Remembered through the ages
> That will dawn and flee.
>
> Straight to an Empire's heart
> Her noble way she trod.
> She lives, she lives for ever
> Now she rests, she rests with God.

The film biography (1951), with Anna Neagle as Miss Nightingale, was called *The Lady with a Lamp* and was based on a play by Reginald Berkeley.

5 *The mills of God grind slowly yet they grind exceeding small.*

The meaning of this saying is that the ways in which reforms are brought about, crime is punished, and so on, are often slow, but the end result may be perfectly achieved. The saying comes from Longfellow's translation of Friedrich von Logau, a German seventeenth-century poet.

6 *And when she was good*
She was very, very good,
But when she was bad she was
* horrid.*

From Longfellow's short poem 'There Was a Little Girl' ('who had a little curl/Right in the middle of her forehead'), said to have been composed and sung to his second daughter when she was a babe in arms. Thus was born a much-invoked description.

1 *The heights by great men reached*
  and kept
  Were not attained by sudden flight,
  But they, while their companions slept,
  Were toiling upward in the night.

Inspirational lines that must have adorned
many a motivational speech-day or commencement speech. They come from Longfellow's 'The Ladder of St Augustine'
(1858).

2 *Underneath the spreading chestnut*
  tree
  The village smithy stands;
  The smith a mighty man is he
  With large and sinewy hands
  And the muscles of his brawny arms
  Are strong as iron bands.

Some sort of prize should surely be awarded
to Longfellow for providing in 'The Village
Blacksmith' (1842) one of the most parodied
and plundered of verses. He started with the
above. In the nineteenth century there were
musical settings by several composers but
that by W.H. Weiss (1820–67) was the most
popular (in 1854). There was then a lull
until a song was written called 'The Chestnut Tree' in 1938. This was a joint effort by
Jimmy Kennedy, Tommie Connor and
Hamilton Kennedy:

  Underneath the Spreading Chestnut Tree
  I loved her and she loved me.
  There she used to sit upon my knee
  'Neath the Spreading Chestnut Tree.
  There beneath the boughs we used to
    meet,
  All her kisses were so sweet.
  All the little birds went tweet tweet tweet
  'Neath the Spreading Chestnut Tree.

The actual blacksmith only manages to
make an appearance in this song by exclaiming 'Chest . . . nuts!' which gave rise to
interesting gestures by performers. Instructions as to how to do these were given on the
sheet music for this 'novelty singing dance
sensation'.

During the build-up to the Second World
War, between the Munich Agreement and
the end of 1939, there then arose a play-
ground rhyme in Britain which went:

  Under the spreading chestnut tree,
  Neville Chamberlain said to me:
  'If you want to get your gas mask free,
  Join the blinking A.R.P.'

In fact — as Norman Longmate points out
in *How We Lived Then* — this was not true.

You were given a free gas mask anyway, but
the A.R.P. (Air Raid Precautions) people
were given more sophisticated ones.

In George Orwell's novel *1984* (1948),
there is another variation:

  Under the spreading chestnut tree
  I sold you and you sold me:
  There lie they, and here lie we
  Under the spreading chestnut tree.

Arnold Silcock's *Verse and Worse* (1952)
includes this anonymous parody:

  Under a spreading gooseberry bush the
    village burglar lies,
  The burglar is a hairy man with
    whiskers round his eyes
  And the muscles of his brawny arms
    keep off the little flies.
  He goes on Sunday to the church to
    hear the Parson shout
  He puts a penny in the plate and takes
    a pound note out
  And drops a conscience-stricken tear in
    case he is found out.

The latest word I have on the subject is from
American graffiti, collected by 1980:

  Beneath the spreading chestnut tree
  The village idiot sat —
  Amusing himself
  By abusing himself
  And catching it all in his hat.

Longworth, Alice Roosevelt
American political hostess (1884–1980)

3 *If you haven't got anything nice to say*
  about anyone, come and sit by me.

Embroidered on a cushion at Longworth's
Washington D.C. home. The daughter of
Theodore Roosevelt, she had a reputation
for barbed wit, but many of her 'sayings'
were not entirely original.

4 *[Calvin Coolidge] looked as if he had*
  been weaned on a pickle.

She admitted hearing this 'at my dentist's
office. The last patient had said it to him and
I just seized on it. I didn't originate it — but
didn't it describe him exactly?' (*New York
Times*, 25 February 1980). The ODQ
(1992) has it as an 'anonymous remark'
quoted in Longworth's *Crowded Hours*
(1933).

5 *[Thomas E. Dewey] looks like the*
  bridegroom on the wedding cake.

A description that helped destroy Dewey
when he stood against President Truman in

1948 came from one Grace Hodgson Flandrau. Longworth admitted: 'I thought it frightfully funny and quoted it to everyone. Then it began to be attributed to me.' Sometimes just 'the man on the wedding cake', Dewey did indeed have a wooden appearance, and a black moustache.

1 *[Franklin Roosevelt is] one part mush and two parts Eleanor.*

Or, 'one-third sap, two-thirds Eleanor'. Longworth denied saying any such thing.

Lorca
(see García Lorca)

Lorenz, Edward
American meteorologist (1917–)

2 *Predictability: Does the Flap of a Butterfly's Wings in Brazil Set Off a Tornado in Texas?*

Title of a paper on predicability in weather forecasting delivered to the American Association for the Advancement of Science, Washington D.C., on 29 December 1979. Apparently, Lorenz originally used the image of a seagull's wing flapping. What is now called 'The Butterfly Effect' — how small acts lead to large — appeals to chaos theorists. J. Gleick gives another example in *Chaos: Making a New Theory* (1988), also from weather forecasting: 'The notion that a butterfly stirring the air today in Peking can transform storm systems next month in New York.'

Louis XIV
French King (1638–1715)

3 *Has God forgotten then what I have done for him?* [Dieu, a-t-il donc oublié ce que j'ai fait pour lui?]

Alleged remark after the Battle of Malplaquet (1709). An allied army under Marlborough defeated the French in the last pitched battle of the War of the Spanish Succession.

4 *L'état c'est moi [I am the state].*

An alleged remark to parliament on 13 April 1655, but there is no contemporary evidence for it.

Louis XVI
French King (1754–93)

5 Rien *[Nothing].*

His complete diary entry made at Versailles on the evening of 14 July 1789 — the day of the storming of the Bastille. In fact, he wrote '*Rien*' on most of the days that July and put only one-line entries most of the time, anyway.

6 *Frenchmen, I die innocent: it is from the scaffold and near appearing before God that I tell you so. I pardon my enemies: I desire that France . . .*

Louis's last words before execution (21 January 1973) are given here as reported by Thomas Carlyle in his *The French Revolution — A History*, III.ii.8 (1837). The remainder of the last sentence was drowned out by the sound of drumming, but others have it that he went on: 'Pray God that my blood fall not on France!' or 'I hope that my blood may cement the happiness of the French people'.

Louis, Joe
American boxer (1914–81)

7 *He can run, but he can't hide.*

Before a World Heavyweight Championship fight with the quick-moving Billy Conn (whom he beat by a knock-out on 19 June 1946), Louis was reported as saying this of him in the *New York Herald Tribune* (9 June 1946).
In the wake of the hijacking of a TWA airliner to Beirut in the summer of 1985, President Reagan issued a number of warnings to international terrorists. In October, he said that America had 'sent a message to terrorists everywhere. The message: "You can run, but you can't hide".' Coming from a former sports commentator, the allusion was clear, but one suspects that the saying possibly pre-dates Louis in any case.

Lovell, James
American astronaut (1928–)

8 *OK, Houston we have had a problem here . . . Houston, we have a problem.*

The Apollo 13 space mission took off at 13.13 Houston time on 11 April 1970. Two days into the mission — i.e. on the 13th —

and 200,000 miles from Earth, an oxygen tank exploded, seriously endangering the crew. Lovell, the commander, noted the happenening with notable understatement. It is hard to decipher precisely what he said. *The Times* (15 April) had, 'Hey, we've got a problem.' Asked to repeat this, Lovell said: 'Houston, we've had a problem. We've had a main bus interval' (indicating a fault in the electrical system). Emergency procedures allowed the crew to make a safe return to earth. The words have also been ascribed to another crew member, John L. Swigert Jr (as in *Time* Magazine, 10 January 1983). A TV movie in 1974 was entitled *Houston, We've Got a Problem.*

Low, David
British cartoonist (1891–1963)

1 *Very well, alone.*

A caption to his cartoon in the London *Evening Standard* (18 June 1940) reflected the mood of the British nation following the Fall of France. The cartoon showed a British soldier confronting a hostile sea and a sky full of bombers.

Lowell, J.R.
American poet (1819–91)

2 *Onwards and upwards.*

Possibly the first appearnce of this uplifting call occurs in Lowell's *The Present Crisis* (1844): 'They must upward still, and onward, who would keep abreast of truth.' But it was an idea that appealed to many others. The first lines of the nineteenth-century hymn 'Onward! Upward!' (words by F.J. Crosby, music by Ira D. Sankey), are:

Onward! upward! Christian soldier.
Turn not back nor sheath thy sword;
Let its blade be sharp for conquest
In the battle for the Lord.

Sankey also set the words of Albert Midlane in 'Onward, Upward, Homeward!', of which the refrain is:

Onward to the glory!
Upward to the prize!
Homeward to the mansions
Far above the skies!

Or could the words be from a motto? The Davies-Colley family of Newfold, Cheshire, have them as such in the form 'Upwards and Onwards'. Now it has become a light-hearted catchphrase. 'Nicholas Craig' in *I,*

An Actor (1988) asks of young actors: 'Will you be able to learn the language of the profession and say things like "onwards and upwards", "Oh well, we survive" and "Never stops, love, he *never stops*".'

Lowell, Robert
American poet (1917–77)

3 *If we see light at the end of the tunnel, It's the light of the oncoming train.*

From 'Since 1939' (1977). The idea was probably not original. The *ODQ* (1992) has Paul Dickson citing 'Rowe's Rule: the odds are five to six that the light at the end of the tunnel is the headlight of an oncoming train' (*The Washingtonian*, November 1978). On BBC Radio *Quote . . . Unquote* (1980), John Lahr said it had been a favourite remark of his father — the actor, Bert Lahr (d 1967).

Lucas, George
American film director and writer (1944–)

4 *May the Force be with you.*

A delicious piece of hokum from the film *Star Wars* (scripted by Lucas, 1977) was this benediction and valediction. At one point, Alec Guinness explains what it means: 'The Force is what gives the Jedi its power. It's an energy field created by all living things. It surrounds us, it penetrates us, it binds the galaxy together.'

The phrase turned up in Cornwall a short while after the film was released in Britain — as a police force recruiting slogan. Later, President Reagan, promoting his 'Star Wars' weapon system, said: 'It isn't about fear, it's about hope, and in that struggle, if you'll pardon my stealing a film line, "The force is with us".'

Compare 'The Lord be with you' from, for example, Morning Prayer in the Anglican Book of Common Prayer.

Luce, Clare Boothe
American writer and ambassador (1903–87)

5 *Stuffed Shirts.*

There seems to be an urge among obituary writers to credit the recently deceased with the coining of phrases, even when the facts do not really support it. Patrick Brogan writing of Mrs Luce in the *Independent* (12 October 1987) stated: 'She wrote a series of articles poking fun at the rich and pompous, coining for them the descriptive phrase "stuffed shirts", a title she used for her first book.' That book was published in 1933, but the OED2 has an example of the phrase dating from 1913 (when Luce was a mere ten), which makes it clear that by then it was already current US usage for pompous people. So though she may have repopularized the phrase she certainly did not coin it.

See also PARKER 261:1 and RABELAIS 274:1.

Ludendorff, Erich
German general (1865–1937)

1 [On British troops in the First World War] Lions led by donkeys.

Field Marshal von Falkenhayn in his memoirs records the following exchange — Ludendorff: 'The English fight like lions' — Hoffman: 'True. But don't we know that they are lions led by donkeys?' If so, the real credit for this phrase should go to General Max Hoffman (1869–1927), who succeeded Ludendorff as chief of the German general staff in 1916. Alan Clark in a book called The Donkeys (1961) quotes a slightly different version of the exchange as its epigraph:
> Ludendorff: The English soldiers fight like lions.
> Hoffman: True. But don't we know that they are lions led by donkeys.

Clark gives the Falkenhayn source — but the exchange remains untraced. One wonders if Clark might have invented it himself?

Lumley, Joanna
English actress (1946–)

2 I had no wish to tiptoe into old age alone.

Explaining the reason for her re-marriage. So quoted in the Observer 'Sayings of the Week' column on 23 November 1986. On 4 January 1987, the Observer stated that Ms Lumley claimed she had never actually made the remark to the Daily Mail journalist who had attributed it to her in an interview (and in a headline) the previous November. In fact, it transpired that the journalist had not even put the remark in her copy — it was added in the editing stage.

Lutyens, Sir Edwin
English architect (1869–1944)

3 The piece of cod passeth all understanding.

When Lutyens's son, Robert, was attempting to write a book about his father, they met for lunch at the Garrick Club in London so that Sir Edwin could make known his views on the project and its author. When the matter was broached, however, Sir Edwin, embarrassed, merely exclaimed, 'Oh, my!' Then, as the fish was served, he looked at his son over the two pairs of spectacles he was wearing and made the above comment. Recounted in Robert Lutyens, Sir Edwin Lutyens (1942). Compare 59:2.

4 The answer is in the plural and they bounce.

Said to have been the response given by Lutyens to a Royal Commission (quoted without source in PDMQ, 1980). However, according to Robert Jackson, The Chief (1959), when Gordon (later Lord) Hewart was in the House of Commons, he was answering questions on behalf of David Lloyd George. For some time, one afternoon, he had given answers in the customary brief parliamentary manner — 'The answer is in the affirmative' or 'the answer is in the negative'. After one such noncommittal reply, several members arose to bait Hewart with a series of rapid supplementary questions. He waited until they had all finished and then replied: 'The answer is in the plural!'

Lyte, H.F.
English clergyman and hymn writer (1793–1847)

5 Change and decay in all around I see;
O Thou, who changest not, abide with me.

Probably written in 1847, the hymn 'Abide With Me' may have been inspired by Luke 24:29: 'Abide with us: for it is toward evening, and the day is far spent.'

M

MacArthur, Douglas
American general (1880–1964)

1 I shall return.

MacArthur was forced by the Japanese to pull out of the Philippines and left Corregidor on 11 March 1942. On 20 March he made his commitment to return when he arrived by train at Adelaide. He had journeyed southwards across Australia and was just about to set off eastwards for Melbourne. So, although he had talked in these terms before leaving the Philippines, his main statement was delivered not there but on Australian soil. At the station, a crowd awaited him and he had scrawled a few words on the back of an envelope: 'The President of the United States ordered me to break through the Japanese lines and proceed from Corregidor to Australia for the purpose, as I understand it, of organizing the American offensive against Japan, a primary object of which is the relief of the Philippines. I came through and I shall return.'

MacArthur had intended his first words to have the most impact — as a way of getting the war in the Pacific a higher priority — but it was his last three words that caught on. The Office of War Information tried to get him to amend them to 'We shall return', foreseeing that there would be objections to a slogan which seemed to imply that he was all-important and that his men mattered little. MacArthur refused. In fact, the phrase had first been suggested to a MacArthur aide in the form 'We shall return' by a Filipino journalist, Carlos Romulo. 'America has let us down and won't be trusted,' Romulo had said. 'But the people still have confidence in MacArthur. If he says he is coming back, he will be believed.' The suggestion was passed to MacArthur who adopted it — but adapted it.

MacArthur later commented: ' "I shall return" seemed a promise of magic to the Filipinos. It lit a flame that became a symbol which focused the nation's indomitable will and at whose shrine it finally attained victory and, once again, found freedom. It was scraped in the sands of the beaches, it was daubed on the walls of the barrios, it was stamped on the mail, it was whispered in the cloisters of the church. It became the battle cry of a great underground swell that no Japanese bayonet could still.'

As William Manchester wrote in *American Caesar* (1978): 'That it had this great an impact is doubtful . . . but unquestionably it appealed to an unsophisticated oriental people. Throughout the war American submarines provided Filipino guerillas with cartons of buttons, gum, playing cards, and matchboxes bearing the message.'

On 20 October 1944, MacArthur did return. Landing at Leyte, he said to a background of still continuing gunfire: 'People of the Philippines, I have returned . . . By the grace of Almighty God, our forces stand again upon Philippine soil.'

2 The world has turned over many times since I took the oath on the Plain at West Point, and the hopes and dreams have long since vanished. But I still remember the refrain of one of the most popular barrack ballads of that day, which proclaimed, most proudly, that old soldiers never die. They just fade away. And like the old soldier of that ballad, I now close my military career and just fade away — an old soldier who tried to do his duty as God gave him the light to see that duty. Goodbye.

In 1951, President Truman sacked MacArthur from his command of UN forces in

Korea for repeatedly criticizing the administration's policy of non-confrontation with China. Even so, Truman had to allow MacArthur a hero's return home and a chance to address Congress (on 19 April). In fact, the ballad quoted by MacArthur and which he dated as 'turn of the century' was a British Army song of the First World War. It is a parody of the gospel hymn 'Kind Words Can Never Die'. J. Foley copyrighted a version of the parody in 1920. The more usual form of the words is, 'Old soldiers never die — they simply fade away.'

Macaulay, Thomas
(1st Baron Macaulay)
English writer and politician (1800–59)

1 *The gallery in which the reporters sit has become the fourth estate of the realm.*

In 1828, Macaulay wrote this of the Press representatives in the House of Commons — i.e. 'fourth estate' after the Lords Spiritual, the Lords Temporal, and the Commons — but a number of others have also been credited with the coinage. Edmund Burke, for example, is said to have pointed at the press gallery and remarked: 'And yonder sits the fourth estate, more important than them all.'

The phrase was originally used to describe various forces outside Parliament — such as the Army (as by Falkland in 1638) or the Mob (as by Fielding in 1752). When William Hazlitt used it in 'Table Talk' in 1821, he meant not the press in general but just William Cobbett. Two years later, Lord Brougham is said to have used the phrase in the House of Commons to describe the press in general. So when Macaulay used it in *The Edinburgh Review* in 1828, it was obviously an established expression. Then Carlyle used it several times — in his article on Boswell's *Life of Johnson* in 1832, in his History of the *The French Revolution* in 1837 and in his lectures 'On Heroes, Hero-Worship, & the Heroic in History' in 1841. But he attributed the phrase to Burke (who died in 1797). It has been suggested that the BBC (or the broadcast media in general) now constitute a *fifth* estate, as also, at one time, did the trades unions.

2 *As every schoolboy knows.*

Robert Burton wrote 'Every schoolboy hath the famous testament of Grunius Corocotta Porcellus at his fingers' ends' in *The Ana-*

tomy of Melancholy (1621) and Bishop Jeremy Taylor used the expression 'every schoolboy knows it' in 1654. In the next century, Jonathan Swift had 'to tell what everybody schoolboy knows'. But the most noted user of this rather patronizing phrase was Macaulay who would say things like, 'Every schoolboy knows who imprisoned Montezuma, and who strangled Atahualpa' (essay on 'Lord Clive', January 1840).

3 *Lars Porsena of Clusium*
By the nine gods he swore.

From Macaulay's poem 'Horatius' in *Lays of Ancient Rome* (1842). Hence, *Lars Porsena, or the Future of Swearing and Improper Language*, the title of a short study (1920) by Robert Graves.

McAuliffe, Anthony C.
American general (1898–1975)

4 *Nuts!*

In December 1944 the Germans launched a counteroffensive in what came to be known as the Battle of the Bulge. 'Old Crock' McAuliffe was acting commander of the American 101st Airborne Division and was ordered to defend the strategic town of Bastogne in the Ardennes forest. This was important because Bastogne stood at a Belgian crossroads through which the advancing armies had to pass. When the Americans had been surrounded like 'the hole in a doughnut' for seven days, the Germans said they would accept a surrender. On 23 December, McAuliffe replied: 'Nuts!'

The Germans first of all interpreted this one word reply as meaning 'crazy' and took time to appreciate what they were being told. Encouraged by McAuliffe's spirit, his men managed to hold the line and thus defeat the last major enemy offensive of the war.

McAuliffe recounted the episode in a BBC broadcast on 3 January 1945: 'When we got [the surrender demand] we thought it was the funniest thing we ever heard. I just laughed and said, "Nuts", but the German major who brought it wanted a formal answer; so I decided well, I'd just say "Nuts", so I had it written out: "QUOTE, TO THE GERMAN COMMANDER: NUTS. SIGNED, THE AMERICAN COMMANDER UNQUOTE".'

When Agence France Presse sought a way of translating this it resorted to, '*Vous n'êtes* que de vieilles noix [You are only old fogeys]' — although 'noix' in French slang also carries the same testicular meaning as 'nuts' in English. When McAuliffe's obituary came to be written, the *New York Times* observed: 'Unofficial versions strongly suggest that the actual language used by the feisty American general was considerably stronger and more profane than the comparatively mild "Nuts", but the official version will have to stand.'

McCormick, Peter Dodds
Scottish-born Australian songwriter
(1834–1916)

1 *Australia's sons, let us rejoice,*
For we are young and free,
We've golden soil and wealth for toil,
Our home is girt by sea;
Our land abounds in nature's gifts
Of beauty rich and rare;
In hist'ry's page, let ev'ry stage
Advance Australia Fair,
In joyful strains then let us sing
Advance Australia fair.

The song 'Advance Australia Fair' was first performed in Sydney in 1878, but the alliterative phrase 'Advance Australia' had existed much earlier when Michael Massey Robinson wrote in the *Sydney Gazette* (1 February 1826): ' "ADVANCE THEN, AUSTRALIA",/Be this thy proud gala/ . . . And thy watch-word be "FREEDOM FOR EVER!" '

'Advance Australia' became the motto of the Commonwealth of Australia when the states united in 1901. In the 1970s and 1980s, as republicanism grew, it acquired the force of a slogan and was used in various campaigns to promote national pride (sometimes as 'Let's Advance Australia'). In 1984, 'Advance Australia Fair' superseded 'God Save the Queen' as the national anthem. The first line became 'Australians all let us rejoice . . .'. McCormick's second verse was mostly ignored:

When gallant Cook from Albion sailed
To trace wide oceans o'er,
True British courage bore him on
Till he landed on our shore.
Then here he raised Old England's flag,
The standard of the brave.
With all her faults we love her still
Britannia rules the wave.
In joyful strains then let us sing,
Advance Australia Fair.

McGill, Donald
English comic postcard artist
(1875–1962)

2 *I've lost my little Willie!*

McGill drew his first comic postcard in 1905 and, judging by the style and appearance of one of his most famous cards, it probably dates from within the next ten to fifteen years. The card shows a fat man with an enormous stomach (or 'corporation') which prevents him from seeing the small boy seated at his feet. The caption is the double-entendre: 'Can't see my little Willy.' The postcard is signed prominently by the artist.

'I've lost my little Willie!' (which rather obscures the joke) was used as the title of a 'celebration of comic postcards' (1976) by Benny Green. This book title may have been taken from the caption to a re-drawing of the idea by another cartoonist.

3 *'Do you like Kipling?'*
'I don't know, you naughty boy,
I've never kippled.'

This caption to one of McGill's postcards — undated, but possibly from the 1930s — might just be the origin of a little joke. However, J.K. Stephen (1859–92) had already seen the possibilities in the name in his poem 'To R.K.' which ends:

When the Rudyards cease from kipling
And the Haggards ride no more.

Machiavelli, Niccolò
Florentine statesman and philosopher
(1469–1527)

4 *There is nothing more difficult to take in hand, nor perilous to conduct, or more uncertain in its success, than the introduction of a new order of things, because the innovator has for enemies all those who have done well under the old conditions, and lukewarm defenders in those who may do well under the new.*

Marmaduke Hussey, a beleaguered Chairman of the BBC, admitted in an interview with the *Independent on Sunday* (16 December 1991) that he clung to this quotation which was 'provided by an ally he turned to for advice'. It is taken from *The Prince* (1532).

Mackintosh, Sir James
Scottish historian and philosopher
(1765–1832)

1 *The commons, faithful to their system, remained in a wise and masterly inactivity.*

In *Vindiciae Gallicae* (1791). Mackintosh was writing about the 'third estate' at the first session of the Estates General summoned in France in 1789.
   Alan Watkins in the *Observer* (19 February 1989) ascribed the phrase to the 3rd Marquess of Salisbury (the British Prime Minister), when writing of 'Mr Nigel Lawson's display of masterly inactivity'.
   Benham (1948) compares Horace — '*strenua nos exercet inertia* [strenuous inertia urges us on]'.

McCrae, John
Canadian poet (1872–1918)

2 *In Flanders fields the poppies blow
Between the crosses, row on row,
That mark our place; and in the sky
The larks, still bravely singing, fly
Scarce heard amid the guns below.*

From 'In Flanders Fields', written after the second Battle of Ypres and sent anonymously to *Punch* where it was published on 8 December 1915. McCrae was a Canadian academic turned volunteer medical officer. He himself died of wounds in a Normandy hospital in May 1918. His poem was the inspiration for the Poppy Day appeals which became an annual event from 1921, raising money for ex-servicemen. These appeals have been described as the best marketing idea in the history of charities.

3 *If ye break faith with us who die
We shall not sleep, though poppies
    grow
On Flanders fields.*

McCrae's own reputed last words ('Tell them this: If ye break faith with us who die we shall not sleep') are taken from the last lines of the same poem.

McKinney, Joyce
American former beauty queen (1950–   )

4 *I loved Kirk so much, I would have skied down Mount Everest in the nude with a carnation up my nose.*

A former Miss Wyoming, McKinney was charged in an English court with kidnapping Kirk Anderson, a Mormon missionary and her ex-lover. She allegedly abducted Mr Anderson to a remote country cottage where he was chained to a bed and forced to make love to her. In Epsom Magistrates' Court (6 December 1977) McKinney told a stunned jury of her feelings in the matter.

Macleish, Archibald
American poet (1892–1982)

5 *To see the earth as it truly is, small and blue and beautiful in that eternal silence where it floats, is to see ourselves as riders on the earth together, brothers on that bright loveliness in the eternal cold — brothers who know they are truly brothers.*

Written for the *New York Times* (25 December 1968) after an Apollo space mission returned with a photograph that showed the earth as seen from beyond the moon. Macleish revised the wording to provide an epigraph for his *Riders on the Earth* (1978): 'To see the earth as we now see it, small and blue and beautiful in that eternal silence where it floats, is to see ourselves as riders on the earth together; brothers on that bright loveliness in the unending night — brothers who *see* now they are truly brothers.'

Macleod, Norman
Scottish divine (1812–72)

6 *Courage brother! do not stumble,
    Though thy path be dark as night;
There's a star to guide the humble;
    Trust in God, and do the Right.*

From 'Trust in God'. This *may* just possibly be the source of the expression 'Trust in God, and do the right', which has been much used subsequently as a gravestone inscription. For example, it appears on the grave of Douglas, 1st Earl Haig (1861–1928), in the ruins of Dryburgh Abbey, Berwickshire (Borders). Haig was Commander-in-Chief of British forces in France and Flanders for most of the First World War. The headstone, at Haig's request, is identical to those in the cemeteries of France. A notice near the grave suggests that the wording of the epitaph was that used on many graves of First World War dead of lower rank. ('For

God and the right' is another form of this motto-like idea.)

McMahon, Ed
American broadcaster (1923–   )

1 *Here's Johnny!*

Said with a drawn-out, rising inflection on the first word, this was McMahon's introduction to Johnny Carson on NBC-TV's *Tonight* show in the US (from 1961 until the early 1990s). In full, what McMahon (a former circus clown) said was: [*Drum roll*] 'And now . . . heeeeere's Johnny!' It was emulated during Simon Dee's brief reign as a chat-show host in Britain during the 1960s. The studio audience joined in the rising inflection of the announcer's 'It's Siiiiiimon Dee!' Jack Nicholson, playing a psychopath, chopped through a door with an axe and cried 'Here's Johnny!' in the film *The Shining* (1981).

Macmahon, Comte Maurice de
French general (1808–93)

2 *Here I am, and here I stay* [J'y suis et j'y reste].

Said at the taking of the Malakoff fortress during the Crimean War (8 September 1855). In his home at the Château de Sully is an engraving of Macmahon standing on the parapet of a Russian gun position at Sebastopol, which has just been captured after heavy opposition. An English sailor, approaching the general to warn him that the position is mined, receives the reply: '*Libre à vous porter où vous voulez, quant à moi, j'y suis et j'y reste* [Up to you to go where you like, as for me, here I am and here I stay].'

Macmillan, Harold
(later 1st Earl of Stockton)
English Conservative Prime Minister (1894–1986)

3 *The Middle Way.*

A book (1938) with this title by Macmillan set out the arguments for a middle course in politics, that is to say one occupying 'the middle ground' between extremes. Not unexpectedly, the phrase had been used before — indeed, it dates back to the thirteenth century. John Adams, the 2nd US President, said in a letter (23 March 1776),

'I agree with you that in politics the middle way is none at all'. Winston Churchill ended an election address on 11 November 1922 by saying: 'What we require now is not a period of turmoil, but a period of stability and recuperation. Let us stand together and tread a sober middle way.' The 'Middle Way' is also believed to be a tenet of Buddhism.

4 *Delicately poised between the cliché and the indiscretion.*

At the time of the 1981 royal wedding between Prince Charles and Lady Diana Spencer, Robert Runcie, the then Archbishop of Canterbury, was quoted in *The Times* (14 July) as having said of the discussions he had had with the couple prior to marrying them: 'My advice was delicately poised between the cliché and the indiscretion.' He appears to have been echoing Macmillan who was quoted in *Newsweek* (30 April 1956) as having said that his life as Foreign Secretary was 'forever poised between a cliché and an indiscretion'. This appears to have been extracted from a speech he had made in the House of Commons on 27 July 1955: 'A Foreign Secretary — and this applies also to a prospective Foreign Secretary — is always faced with this cruel dilemma. Nothing he can say can do very much good, and almost anything he may say may do a great deal of harm. Anything he says that is not obvious is dangerous; whatever is not trite is risky. He is forever poised between the cliché and the indiscretion.'

5 *There ain't gonna be no war.*

As Foreign Secretary to Prime Minister Eden, Macmillan attended a four-power summit conference at Geneva where the chief topic for discussion was German reunification. Nothing much was achieved but the 'Geneva spirit' was optimistic and on his return to London he breezily told a press conference on 24 July 1955, 'There ain't gonna be no war'. Why this conscious Americanism?

One, rather good, suggestion was that he was alluding to Mark Twain's *Tom Sawyer Abroad*, Chap. 1 (1894): 'There's plenty of boys that will come hankering . . . when you've got an apple . . . but when they've got one . . . they . . . say thank you 'most to death, but there ain't agoing to be no core.' This situation may also have appeared as a *Punch* cartoon, *c* 1908.

But Macmillan's phrase is, without doubt, a direct quote from the *c* 1910 music-hall song, which was sung in a raucous cockney accent by a certain Mr Pélissier (1879–1913) in a show called 'Pélissier's Follies' during the reign of Edward VII:

There ain't going to be no waar
So long as we've a king like Good King Edward.
'E won't 'ave it, 'cos 'e 'ates that sort of fing.
Muvvers, don't worry,
Not wiv a king like Good King Edward.
Peace wiv honour is 'is motter [*snort*] — Gawd save the King!

Sir David Hunt confirmed to me (1988) that it was the Pélissier song that Macmillan had in mind. In fact, he (Hunt) had sung it to him on one occasion. Although Macmillan was born the year *Tom Sawyer Abroad* was published, it is to the song of his youth rather than the novel that he was referring. And yet why did he say 'gonna'? Emulating cockney pronunciation, maybe, but some time before December 1941 an American called Frankl did write a song called, precisely, 'There Ain't Gonna Be No War', which had a brief vogue:

Rock-a-bye, my baby
There ain't gonna be no war over here
We ain't goin' to need no ride of Paul Revere.
We're going to have peace and quiet
And if they start a riot
We'll just sit back and keep score.
The only place you'll go marching to
Will be the corner grocery store.
So rock-a-bye, my baby
There ain't gonna be no war.

1 *I thought the best thing to do was to settle up these little local difficulties, and then turn to the wider vision of the Commonwealth.*

'Little local difficulties' is now a phrase used to demonstrate a dismissive lack of concern. In 1958, as Prime Minister, Harold Macmillan made a characteristically airy reference to the fact that his entire Treasury team, including the Chancellor of the Exchequer, had resigned over a disagreement about budget estimates. In a statement at London airport before leaving for a tour of the Commonwealth on 7 January, Macmillan said: 'I thought the best thing to do was to settle up these little local difficulties, and then turn to the wider vision of the Commonwealth.'

2 *Jaw-jaw is better than war-war.*

On 30 January 1958 in Canberra, Australia, Macmillan consciously echoed a saying of Winston Churchill's — 'To jaw-jaw is always better than to war-war' — which Churchill had uttered at a White House luncheon in Washington D.C. on 26 June 1954.

3 *You've never had it so good.*

A phrase that will forever be linked with Macmillan's name was first used by him in a speech at Bedford on 20 July 1957. He took pains to use the phrase not boastfully but as a warning: 'Let's be frank about it. Most of our people have never had it so good. Go around the country, go to the industrial towns, go to the farms, and you'll see a state of prosperity such as we have never had in my lifetime — nor indeed ever in the history of this country. What is beginning to worry some of us is "Is it too good to be true?" or perhaps I should say "Is it too good to last?" For amidst all this prosperity, there is one problem that has troubled us, in one way or another, ever since the war. It is the problem of rising prices. Our constant concern is: Can prices be steadied while at the same time we maintain full employment in an expanding economy? Can we control inflation?'

Macmillan is said to have appropriated the phrase from Lord Robens (a former Labour minister who had rejected socialism and who had used the phrase in conversation with the Prime Minister not long before). However, as 'You Never Had It So Good', it had been a slogan used by the Democrats in the 1952 US Presidential election. As early as 1946, *American Speech* (XXI.243) was commenting on the phrase: 'This is a sardonic response to complaints about the Army; it is probably supposed to represent the attitude of a peculiarly offensive type of officer.'

In his memoirs, Macmillan commented: 'For some reason it was not until several years later that this phrase was taken out of its context and turned into a serious charge against me, of being too materialistic and showing too little of a spiritual approach to life . . . curiously enough these are the inevitable hazards to which all politicians are prone.'

Given the way the phrase came to dog him, it would have been surprising if it had ever been used as an official Tory party slogan. It was rejected — in so many words — for the 1959 general election by the Conservatives' publicity group, partly because it 'violated a basic advertising axiom that statements should be positive, not negative'. There was, however, an official poster that came very close with, 'You're Having It Good, Have It Better'.

1 Enough is enough.

A basic expression of exasperation, this phrase is often employed in political personality clashes — though usually without result. 'What matters is that Mr Macmillan has let Mr [Selwyn] Lloyd know that at the Foreign Office, in these troubled times, enough is enough' (*The Times*, 1 June 1959). Having fed the story to *The Times*, Macmillan was prevented by the fuss it caused from firing Lloyd and the Foreign Secretary remained in place for a further year. On 10 May 1968, the *Daily Mirror* carried a front-page headline: 'Enough is Enough', referring to the Labour Government of Harold Wilson. It was over an article by Cecil H. King, Chairman of the International Publishing Corporation, but it led to his fall from power, however, and not the Government's.

2 Exporting is fun.

A Macmillan slogan that misfired, though in this instance he never actually 'said' it. The phrase was included in a 1960 address to businessmen, but when Macmillan came to the passage he left out what was later considered to be a rather patronizing remark. The press, however, printed what was in the advance text of the speech as though he had actually said it. Compare the earlier Labour slogan, 'We must export — or die', which arose out of a severe balance of payments problem under the Labour Government in 1945–6.

3 The most striking of all the impressions I have formed since I left London a month ago is of the strength of this African national consciousness. In different places it may take different forms, but it is happening everywhere. The wind of change is blowing through this continent. Whether we like it or not, this growth of national consciousness is a political fact.

Speaking to both houses of the South African parliament on 3 February 1960, Macmillan gave his hosts a message they cannot have wanted to hear. The phrase 'wind of change' — though not, of course, original — was contributed to the speech-writing team by the diplomat (later Sir) David Hunt. The *OED2* acknowledges that the use of the phrase 'wind(s) of change' increased markedly after this speech. When Macmillan sought a title for one of his volumes of memoirs he plumped for the more common, plural usage — *Winds of Change*.

In a similar windy metaphor, Stanley Baldwin had said in 1934: 'There is a wind of nationalism and freedom round the world, and blowing as strongly in Asia as elsewhere.' President George Bush made 'a new breeze is blowing' the theme of his Inauguration speech on 20 January 1989.

4 She didn't say yes, she didn't no . . .

The song 'She Didn't Say Yes' by Jerome Kern and Otto Harbach from the musical *The Cat and the Fiddle* (1931) was memorably quoted by Macmillan when Prime Minister in October 1962. Speaking to the Conservative Party Conference at Llandudno he referred to the Labour Party's attitude to the government's attempts (from July 1961) to open negotiations for Britain's entry to the European Common Market: 'What did the socialists do? . . . They solemnly asked Parliament not to approve or disapprove, but to "take note" of our decision. Perhaps some of the older ones among you [oh, wonderful Macmillanism!] will remember that popular song —

> She didn't say yes, she didn't say no,
> She didn't say stay, she didn't say go.
> She wanted to climb, but dreaded to fall,
> She bided her time and clung to the wall.'

Private Eye perhaps inspired by a recent American record which had taken President Kennedy's Inaugural speech and added a music track — put out a record of Macmillan 'singing' the song to a tinny 1960s backing. Very droll it was, too, and now sadly evocative of a bygone era.

5 [The sale of assets is common with individuals and the state when they run into financial difficulties . . .] First of all the Georgian silver goes, and then all that nice furniture that used to be in the saloon. Then the Canalettos go.

Summarized as 'selling off the family silver', meaning 'to dispose of valuable assets which, once gone, cannot be retrieved', this allusion was memorably used in a speech to the Tory Reform Group by Macmillan, by then Earl of Stockton, on 8 November 1985. He was questioning the government's policy of privatizing profitable nationalized industries.

Magee, John Gillespie
American/British airforce pilot and poet (1922–41)

1 *Oh! I have slipped the surly bonds of earth,*
And danced the skies on laughter-silvered wings;
The high untrespassed sanctity of space,
Put out my hand, and touched the face of God.

From 'High Flight', a sonnet written by Magee, a pilot with the Royal Canadian Air Force in the Second World War. He came to Britain, flew in a Spitfire squadron, and was killed at the age of nineteen on 11 December 1941 during a training flight from the airfield near Scopwick, Lincolnshire (where the first and last lines appear on his grave). Magee had been born in Shanghai of an American father and an English mother who were missionaries. He was educated at Rugby and at a school in Connecticut. The sonnet was written on the back of a letter to his parents which stated, 'I am enclosing a verse I wrote the other day. It started at 30,000 feet, and was finished soon after I landed.' The parents were living in Washington D.C. at the time of his death and, according to the Library of Congress book *Respectfully Quoted*, the poem came to the attention of the Librarian of Congress, Archbald MacLeish, who acclaimed Magee as the first poet of the war.

'High Flight' was published in 1943 in a volume called *More Poems from the Forces* (which was 'Dedicated to the USSR'). Copies of the poem — sometimes referred to as 'the pilot's creed' — were widely distributed and plaques bearing it were sent to all R.C.A.F. airfields and training stations. It became very much the pilot's poem the world over. The lines became even more famous when President Reagan quoted them on 28 January 1986 in his TV broadcast to the nation on the day of the space shuttle *Challenger* disaster.

Two footnotes: in his lyrics for the English version of the musical *Les Misérables* (1985), Herbert Kretzmer blended Magee's words with something from Evelyn Waugh's *Brideshead Revisited* ('to know and love another human being is the root of all wisdom') to produce the line: 'To love another person is to see the face of God.' Magee's original words are curiously reminiscent of Oscar Wilde's lines prefixed to his *Poems* (Paris edition, 1903):

Surely there was a time I might have trod
The sunlit heights, and from life's dissonance
Struck one clear chord to reach the ears of God.

Maguire, William H.
American sailor (1890–1953)

2 *Praise the Lord and pass the ammunition!*

Said in 1941, and subsequently used as the title of a song by Frank Loesser (1942), the authorship of this saying is disputed. It may have been said by an American naval chaplain during the Japanese attack on Pearl Harbor. Lieutenant Howell M. Forgy (1908–83) is one candidate. He was on board the US cruiser *New Orleans* on 7 December 1941 and encouraged those around him to to keep up the barrage when under attack. His claim is supported by a report in the *New York Times* (1 November 1942).

Another name mentioned is that of Captain W.H. Maguire. At first Captain Maguire did not recall having used the words but a year later said he might have done. Bartlett favours Maguire and makes no mention of Forgy. Either way, the expression actually dates from the time of the American Civil War.

Major, John
British Conservative Prime Minister (1943–)

3 *The harsh truth is that if the policy isn't hurting it isn't working. I know there is a difficult period ahead but the important thing is that we cannot and must not fudge the determination to stop inflation in its tracks.*

Major had to deliver this speech at Northampton (27 October 1989) on suddenly becoming Chancellor of the Exchequer following the resignation of Nigel Lawson. It had probably been written for his predecessor.

Adlai Stevenson said in his speech accepting the Democratic Presidential nomination (26 July 1952): 'Let's talk sense to the

American people. Let's tell them the truth, that there are no gains without pains.' 'No pains, no gains' is, indeed, a proverb more commonly known in the US.

1 Well — who would have thought it?

What Major is alleged to have said when opening his first Cabinet meeting following his sudden elevation to the Prime Minister-ship following the fall of Margaret Thatcher (in December 1990) was early evidence of his trademark mundanity. Following publication of the quotations awareness survey (see the Introduction to this dictionary), Nicholas Watt discussed the apparent unquotability of modern British politicians in *The Times* (5 October 1992). He wrang out of Lord Healey the reason for this Prime Minister's inability to deliver colourful quotes: 'John Major's not exactly a ball of fun. Anyway, the government is rather shell-shocked.' Lord Archer was quoted as saying of Major, 'He is every bit as eloquent as Callaghan and Healey.' Lord Hailsham came up with the fairly perceptive observation that: 'People remember quotes only after they have repeated them many times. We must wait and see about John Major. At the time people didn't think that Harold Macmillan's quotes were as memorable as they have become.'

But, invariably, bathos is the hallmark of Major's sayings — as in, 'Gentlemen, I think we had better start again, somewhere else', which is what he said after an IRA mortar-bomb attack on Downing Street had caused a large explosion during a Cabinet meeting in February 1991. He also has a verbal mannerism, 'Oh, yes . . . oh, yes.'

2 Fifty years on from now, Britain will still be the country of long shadows on county [cricket] grounds, warm beer, invincible green suburbs, dog lovers and — as George Orwell said — old maids bicycling to Holy Communion through the morning mist.

In a speech on 22 April 1993 to the Conservative Group for Europe, Major sought to show that though the future of Britain lay within Europe, the character of Britain would survive 'unamendable in all essentials'. As his speechwriter acknowledged (for one finds it hard to think that Major spotted it himself), one of Major's lyrical certainties was derived from George Orwell's essay, 'The Lion and the Unicorn:

Socialism and the English Genius: Part 1: England Your England', published in *Horizon* (December 1940). The socialist Orwell was, rather, talking about specifically *English* civilization — actually 'old maids *biking* to Holy Communion through the mists of the autumn morning' — which was 'somehow bound up with solid breakfasts and gloomy Sundays, smoky towns and winding roads, green fields and red pillar-boxes'. Orwell also talked rather of the beer being bitterer, the grass greener, and mentioned 'the queues outside the Labour Exchanges' which, for some reason, Major forbore to do.

Mallory, George Leigh
English mountaineer (1886–1924)

3 Because it's there.

Mallory disappeared in 1924 on his last attempt to scale Mount Everest. The previous year, during a lecture tour of the US, he had frequently been asked why he wanted to achieve this goal. On one such occasion he replied: 'Because it's there.'

In 1911, at Cambridge, A.C. Benson had urged Mallory to read Carlyle's life of John Sterling — a book that achieved high quality simply 'by being *there*'. Perhaps that is how the construction entered Mallory's mind. On the other hand, Tom Holzel and Audrey Salkeld in *The Mystery of Mallory and Irvine* (1986) suggest that 'the four most famous words in mountaineering' may have been invented for the climber by a reporter named Benson in the *New York Times* (18 March 1923). A report in the *Observer* (2 November 1986) noted that Howard Somervell, one of Mallory's climbing colleagues in the 1924 expedition, declared forty years later that the 'much-quoted remark' had always given him a 'shiver down the spine — it doesn't smell of George Mallory one bit'. Mallory's niece, Mrs B.M. Newton Dunn, claimed in a letter to the *Daily Telegraph* (11 November 1986) that the mountaineer had once given the reply to his sister (Mrs Newton Dunn's mother) 'because a silly question deserves a silly answer'.

The saying has become a catchphrase in situations where the speaker wishes to dismiss an impossible question about motives and also to express his acceptance of a challenge that is in some way daunting or maybe foolish. In September 1962 President Kennedy said: 'We choose to go to the moon in this decade, and do the other things, not because they are easy but because they are hard; because that goal will serve to organize and measure the best of our energies and skills . . . Many years ago the great British explorer George Mallory, who was to die on Mount Everest, was asked why did he want to climb it, and he said, "Because it is there." Well, space is there, and . . . the moon and the planets are there, and new hopes for knowledge and peace are there.'

There have been many variations (and misattributions). Sir Edmund Hillary repeated it regarding his own attempt on Everest in 1953.

Malory, Sir Thomas
English writer (d 1471)

1 Hic jacet Arthurus, rex quondam rexque futurus [Here lies Arthur, the once and future king].

This is what, according to Malory in Le Morte d'Arthur (1469–70), was written on the tombstone of the legendary King Arthur. (Hence the title of T.H. White's Arthurian romance, The Once and Future King, 1958.) On the other hand, if a King Arthur did exist (in the sixth century AD, if at all), there is a notice in the ruins of Glastonbury Abbey, Somerset, which claims to mark the site of his tomb.

Mankiewicz, Joseph L.
American film producer and writer (1909–93)

2 My native habitat is the theatre. I toil not, neither do I spin. I am a critic and a commentator. I am essential to the theatre — as ants to a picnic, as the boll weevil to a cotton field.

Spoken by George Sanders as the critic 'Addison de Witt' in the film All About Eve (1950). The allusion in the second sentence is to Matthew 6:28: 'Consider the lilies of the field, how they grow; they toil not, neither do they spin.'

Manning, Olivia
English novelist (1908–80)

3 Fortunes of War.

Manning's Balkan trilogy of novels and her Levant trilogy form a single narrative with this overall title, and the BBC TV adaptation of the six books was called Fortunes of War (1985). The earliest citation in OED2 for the phrase 'fortunes of war' is 1880, but it had long been known in the singular: 'After uncertain fortune of war, on both sides' was written by John Selden in 1612; Charles Dickens, Sketches by Boz, Chap. 12 (1833-6) has this cry from a street game: 'All the fortin of war! this time I vin, next time you vin'; the war memorial at the cemetery of El Alamein (following the battle of 1942) is dedicated 'to whom the fortune of war denied a known and honoured grave'.

Mao Zedong
(Mao Tse-tung)
Chinese revolutionary and Communist leader (1893–1976)

4 I hope that everybody will express his opinions openly. It's no crime to talk, and nobody will be punished for it. We must let a hundred flowers bloom and a hundred schools of thought contend and see which flowers are the best and which school of thought is best expressed, and we shall applaud the best blooms and the best thoughts.

Mao's statement at a meeting of officials and party leaders in May 1956 invited intellectual criticism of the regime and outlined an experiment allowing freedom of dissent. A period of self-criticism was duly launched on 27 February 1957 in a major speech to an audience of 1,800 influential Chinese. It had the title 'On the Correct Handling of Contradictions Among the People', but Mao found that his proposal did not have the support of the whole party and the press. When the official text was published on 19 June in the People's Daily, the horticultural image was given a sinister and revealing twist: 'Only by letting poisonous weeds show themselves above ground can they be uprooted.'

The campaign ran from 1 May, but so great was the amount of criticism stirred up that it was ended by 7 June and reprisals taken against some of those who had spoken out. These people were attacked as bourgeois rightists. Leaders of student riots were executed. Understandably, therefore, the passage about 'flowers blooming' is not included in the little red book of Quotations from Chairman Mao Tse-tung (1966).

1 *'He who is not afraid of death by a thousand cuts dares to unhorse the emperor' — this is the indomitable spirit needed in our struggle to build socialism and communism.*

Mao appears to be drawing on a proverbial saying in this English translation of his *Quotations* (1966). An eastern source for the phrase may be hinted at in what Jaffar the villainous magician (Conrad Veidt) says in the 1940 film version of *The Thief of Baghdad*: 'In the morning they die the death of a thousand cuts.' The film comedy *Carry on Up the Khyber* (1968) has the phrase, too. Now, the phrase 'death of/by a thousand cuts' is used to mean 'the destruction of something by the cumulative effect of snipping rather than by one big blow'.

2 *People of the world, unite and defeat the US aggressors and all their running dogs!*

In a 'Statement Supporting the People of the Congo Against US Aggression' (28 November 1964), Mao provided a vivid weapon in the coinage 'running dogs', for use against the 'lackeys' of the US during the Vietnam War. Edgar Snow had earlier recorded him using the term in 1937.

3 *Don't be a gang of four.*

Apparently, on one occasion, Mao gave this warning to Jiang Qing, his unscrupulous wife, and her colleagues. They became labelled as the Gang of Four in the mid-1970s when they were tried and given the death sentence for treason and other crimes (later commuted to life imprisonment). The other three members were Zhang Chunqiao, a political organizer in the Cultural Revolution; Wang Hogwen, a youthful activist; and Yao Wenyuan, a journalist.

Marie-Antoinette
Queen of France (1755–93)

4 *Let them eat cake.*

This remark is commonly ascribed to Marie-Antoinette, an Austrian disliked by the French people, after she had arrived in France to marry King Louis XVI in 1770. More specifically she is supposed to have said it during the bread shortage of 1789, though no evidence exists to prove that she did.

The saying is to be found in Book 6 of Rousseau's *Confessions*, published posthumously in 1781–8 but written during the 1760s. Rousseau's version, referring to an incident in Grenoble about 1740, goes: 'At length I recollected the thoughtless saying of a great princess who, on being informed that the country people had no bread, replied, "Let them eat cake [*Qu'ils mangent de la brioche*]".' The *ODQ* (1979) notes that Louis XVIII in his *Relation d'un Voyage à Bruxelles et à Coblentz en 1791* (published 1823) attributes to Marie-Thérèse (1638–83), wife of Louis XIV, 'Why don't they eat pastry? [*Que ne mangent-ils de la croûte de pâté?*]'

Burnam (1975) adds that Alphonse Karr, writing in 1843, recorded that a Duchess of Tuscany had said it in 1760 or before. Later, it was circulated in order to discredit Marie-Antoinette. Similar remarks are said to date back to the thirteenth century, so if Marie-Antoinette did ever say it, she was quoting.

Marks, Leo
English bookseller and cryptographer (1920–   )

5 *The life that I have is all that I have,*
And the life that I have is yours.
The love that I have of the life that
*   I have*
Is yours and yours and yours.

A sleep I shall have
A rest I shall have,
Yet death will be but a pause,
For the peace of my years in the long
*   green grass*
Will be yours and yours and yours.

'Code Poem for the French Resistance'. The poem was of the type written to be used as the basis for codes used by Special Operations Executive agents in the Second World War. It could also be used as an *aide-mémoire* for those codes and was specifically written for use by Violette Szabo, the British wartime spy. Hence its use in the biographical film *Carve Her Name With Pride* (1958). Leo is the son of the owner of Marks & Co., the booksellers featured in Helene Hanff's book *84, Charing Cross Road* (1971).

Marlborough, Sarah Duchess of
English wife of the 1st Duke (1660–1744)

1 *His Grace returned from the wars today and pleasured me twice in his top-boots.*

I included the interesting remark in this form in my book *Quote . . . Unquote 2* (1980). The previous year, the *ODQ* had put, 'The Duke returned from the wars today and did pleasure me in his top-boots', acknowledging 'oral trad. Attr. in various forms'. When and where the remark first appeared in print is impossible to say. One earlier source is I. Butler, *Rule of Three* (1967). Another is James Agate, *Ego 4* (for 28 July 1938) who, talking of pageants, writes: 'How can yonder stout party hope to be Sarah, Duchess of Marlborough — "His Grace returned from the wars this morning and pleasured me twice in his top-boots" — when we know her to be the vicar's sister and quite unpleasurable?'

Marlowe, Christopher
English playwright (1564–93)

2 *Was this the face that launch'd a thousand ships?*

Referring to Helen of Troy, Marlowe's mighty line occurs in *Dr Faustus* (c 1594). Earlier, he had said something similar in *Tamburlaine the Great* (1587): 'Helen, whose beauty . . . drew a thousand ships to Tenedos.' Accordingly, Shakespeare must have been alluding to Marlowe's line when in *Troilus and Cressida* (c 1601) he wrote of Helen:

> Why she is a pearl
> Whose price hath launch'd above a
> thousand ships.

He also alludes to it in *All's Well That Ends Well.* The consistent feature of these mentions is the figure of a 'thousand', which was a round number probably derived from the accounts of Ovid and Virgil. Burnam (1975) quotes from Lucian's 'The Dialogues of the Dead' (c 190AD): 'This skull is Helen . . . Was it then for this that the thousand ships were manned from all Greece?'

Much alluded to and played upon. Chips Channon records (23 April 1953) in the House of Commons: '[Aneurin] Bevan looked at poor, plain Florence Horsburgh [Independent MP for the Combined English Universities] and hailed her with the words "That's the face that sank a thousand scholarships".' To Jack de Manio, the broad-caster, is attributed a more recent version. Of Glenda Jackson, the actress, he is alleged to have said, in the 1970s: 'Her face could launch a thousand dredgers.'

3 *My men, like satyrs grazing on the lawns,*
Shall with their goat feet dance an antic hay.

From Marlowe's *Edward II* (1593). Antic hay = a grotesque country dance. Hence the title of Aldous Huxley's novel *Antic Hay* (1923).

4 *Fair blows the wind for France.*

Also from *Edward II*. A little later in 'The Ballad of Agincourt' (1606) by Michael Drayton there is: 'Fair stood the wind for France/When we our sails advance.' Presumably it is from Drayton rather than Marlowe that H.E. Bates took the title of his story *Fair Stood the Wind for France* (1944).

5 *Whoever lov'd that lov'd not at first sight?*

A 'saw' (saying) from Marlowe's poem *Hero and Leander*, which was published in 1598, though probably written in 1593, the year of his death. Phebe, the shepherdess in Shakespeare's *As You Like It* (probably written in 1598), quotes the line (III.v.82).

See also SPRING-RICE 317:3.

Marshall, Arthur
English writer and entertainer (1910–89)

6 *It's all part of life's rich pageant.*

The origin of this happy phrase — sometimes 'pattern' or 'tapestry' is preferred to 'pageant' — was the subject of an inquiry by Michael Watts of the *Sunday Express* in 1982. The earliest he came up with was from a record called 'The Games Mistress', written and performed by Marshall *c* 1935. The monologue concludes: 'Oh My! Bertha's got a bang on the boko. Keep a stiff upper lip, Bertha dear. What, knocked a tooth out? Never mind, dear — laugh it off, laugh it off. It's all part of life's rich pageant.' Consequently, Marshall called his autobiography, *Life's Rich Pageant* (1984), but it seems a touch unlikely that he really originated the phrase. In 1831, Thomas Carlyle had talked of 'the fair tapestry of human life'.

Marshall, Thomas R.
American Democratic Vice-President
(1854–1925)

1 *What this country needs is a really good five cent cigar.*

Said to John Crockett, the chief clerk of the Senate, during a tedious debate in 1917 and quoted in the *New York Tribune* (4 January 1920). Another version is that it was said to Henry M. Rose, assistant Secretary of State. The remark is mentioned in a caption in *Recollections of Thomas R. Marshall* (1925). At about that time, 'Owls' cigars cost six cents and 'White Owls', seven cents.

Marston, John
English poet and playwright (1576–1634)

2 *'My kingdom for a horse' — look thee I speak play scraps.*

From his play *What You Will* (1607) — a clear example of quotation by a contemporary of Shakespeare. Marston's play is thought to have appeared in 1601 and Shakespeare's *Richard III* in 1591. ('What You Will' is also, of course, the subtitle of Shakespeare's *Twelfth Night*, written in 1601.)

Marx, Chico
American comedian (1886–1961)

3 *You can't fool me. There ain't no Sanity Clause!*

Florelo (Chico) replies thus, in Christmassy fashion, when Otis B. Driftwood (Groucho Marx) says in the film *A Night at the Opera* (1935): 'If any of the parties participating in this contract is shown not to be in their right mind, the entire agreement is automatically nullified. That's what they call a sanity clause.' Chico says he is the manager of a tenor whom Groucho would like to sing with the New York Opera Company and they go through the contract in this fashion.

Marx, Groucho
American comedian (1895–1977)

4 *Please accept my resignation. I don't care to belong to any club that will have me as a member.*

Zeppo Marx recalled that this was about The Friars Club, a theatrical organization, for which his brother did not have much use. Hector Ace added that Groucho had some misgivings about the quality of the members — 'doubts verified a few years later when an infamous card-cheating scandal erupted there'. The wording varies, but the one here is taken from Arthur Sheekman's introduction to *The Groucho Letters* (1967). The actual letter unfortunately does not survive. In *Groucho and Me* (1959), he himself supplied a version: 'PLEASE ACCEPT MY RESIGNATION. I DON'T WANT TO BELONG TO ANY CLUB THAT WILL ACCEPT ME AS A MEMBER.'

5 *I've been around so long, I knew Doris Day before she was a virgin.*

So ascribed to Groucho in 1980, but in Oscar Levant's *Memoirs of an Amnesiac* (1965) we find: '*Romance on the High Seas* was Doris Day's first picture; that was before she became a virgin.' I suspect it was Levant's remark, rather than a simple case of two men with but a single thought.

6 *My regiment leaves at dawn.*

A line spoken by Groucho in the film *Monkey Business* (1931), preceded by the words, 'Come, Kapellmeister, let the violas throb!' Presumably this is a cliché of operetta, but no precise example has been traced. It was certainly the situation in many romantic tangles, even if the line itself was not actually spoken.

7 *There'll always be a lamp in the window for my wandering boy.*

A line spoken by Groucho in the film *Horse Feathers* (1932). What is it? Probably a bringing together of two clichés from popular fiction and parlour poetry. 'Where is my wand'ring boy tonight?' is the first line of a poem/song written and composed by the (presumably American) Revd R. Lowry in 1877. Under the title 'Where Is Your Boy Tonight?' it is No. 303 in Ira D. Sankey's *Sacred Songs and Solos*. No mention of a lamp in the window, however.

Putting a light or lamp in a window is a traditional sign of devotion to or of showing support for a cause. In a speech in Scotland on 29 November 1880 Lord Rosebery said of Gladstone: 'From his home in Wales to the Metropolis of Scotland there has been no village too small to afford a crowd to greet him — there has been no cottager so humble that could not find a light to put in his window as he passed.' Groucho Marx returned to the theme in *At the Circus* (1939). About to become a ring-master, he is being helped by Chico into a tail-coat which he finds rather tight. 'You'd have to be a wizard to get into this coat,' he says. Chico: 'That's-a-right, it belonged to a wizard.' At this point, a pigeon flies out of the tail pocket. Chico: 'It's a homing pigeon.' And Groucho says: 'Then there'll always be a candle burning in my pocket for my wandering pigeon.'

Marx, Karl
German political theorist (1818–83)

1 *History repeats itself — the first time as tragedy, the second time as farce.*

In *The Eighteenth Brumaire of Louis Napoleon* (1852). Marx provides the context: 'Hegel says somewhere that all great events and personalities in world history reappear in one fashion or another. He forgot to add: the first time as tragedy, the second as farce.' Hence, the title of a book on the theatre (1988), by the playwright David Edgar, *The Second Time As Farce.*

2 *From each according to his ability, to each according to his needs.*

Usually attributed to Marx, but not from either *Das Kapital* or *The Communist Manifesto*. The slogan appears in his *Critique of the Gotha Programme* (1875) in which he says that after the workers have taken power, capitalist thinking must first disappear. Only then will the day come when society can 'inscribe on its banners: from each according to his ability, to each according to his needs'.

John Kenneth Galbraith commented in *The Age of Uncertainty* (1977): 'It is possible that these . . . twelve words enlisted for Marx more followers than all the hundreds of thousands in the three volumes of *Das Kapital* combined.'

There is some doubt whether Marx originated the slogan or whether he was quoting Louis Blanc, Morelly or Mikhail Bakunin. The latter wrote: 'From each according to his faculties, to each according to his needs' (declaration, 1870, by anarchists on trial after the failure of their uprising in Lyons).

Also, Saint-Simon (1760-1825), the French reformer, had earlier said: 'The task of each be according to his capacity, the wealth of each be according to his works.' And, much earlier, Acts 4:34-35 had: 'Neither was there any among them that lacked: for as many as were possessors of lands or houses sold them, and brought the prices of things that were sold, and laid them down at the apostles feet: and distribution was made unto every man according as he had need.'

3 *Prominent because of the flatness of the surrounding countryside.*

This aspersion is to be found cast against John Stuart Mill, the English philosopher and social reformer, in *Das Kapital*, Vol. 1, Chap. 16 (1867). After having demolished one of Mill's arguments, Marx says: 'On a level plain, simple mounds look like hills; and the insipid flatness of our present bourgeoisie is to be measured by the altitude of its "great intellects".'

4 *Workers of all lands unite. . . . The philosophers have only interpreted the world in various ways. The point however is to change it.*

Marx, though German-born, lived in London from 1849 onwards. He was buried in Highgate Cemetery on 17 March 1883. His ill-kept grave remained in a far corner of the cemetery until 1956 when the Soviet Communist Party paid for a monolithic black marble block to be installed, with these two quotations inscribed upon it. The grave is surmounted by a massive cast-iron head of Marx and bears an extract (at the top) from his closing words to *The Communist Manifesto* (1848), written originally in German: 'The workers have nothing to lose in this [revolution] but their chains. They have a world to gain. Workers of the world, unite!' The second quotation is from his *Theses on Feuerbach* (1888).

Mary I
English Queen (1516–58)

5 *When I am dead and opened, you shall find Calais lying in my heart.*

'Bloody Mary' or 'Mary Tudor', who ruled 1553-8, reputedly said this, according to *Holinshed's Chronicles* (1577). She was referring to the re-capture by the French of Calais in 1558, a notable defeat for the English, as the town had been an English possession for more than two hundred years and was its last territory in France. In the cod history book *1066 and All That* by Sellar and Yeatman (1930), we find: 'The cruel Queen, Broody Mary, died and a postmortem examination revealed the word "CALLOUS" engraved on her heart.'

Mary
British Queen, Consort of George V
(1867–1953)

1 *Well, Prime Minister, here's a pretty kettle of fish.*

Queen Mary's eldest son reigned for less than a year as Edward VIII. He abdicated in order to marry the American divorcee, Wallis Simpson. For most of 1936, the British public was kept in ignorance of the manoeuvres going on behind the scenes to resolve this crisis. The Prime Minister, Stanley Baldwin, steered matters to their conclusion. He subsequently told his daughter of a meeting he had had with Queen Mary as the storm grew: 'I had a tremendous shock. For, instead of standing immobile in the middle distance, silent and majestic, she came trotting across the room *exactly like a puppy dog*: and before I had time to bow, she took hold of my hand in both of hers and held it tight. "Well, Prime Minister," she said, "here's a pretty kettle of fish".' (Quoted in Frances Donaldson, *Edward VIII*, 1974).

Years later, meeting Queen Mary at a dinner party, Noël Coward boldly asked, 'Is it true, Ma'am, that you said, "Here's a pretty kettle of fish?"' She replied, 'Yes, I think I did.' (Cole Lesley, *The Life of Noël Coward*, 1978.)

In the form, 'This is a nice kettle of fish, isn't it?', the Queen's remark was noted on 17 November 1936 in the diary of Nancy Dugdale whose husband was Baldwin's Parliamentary Private Secretary. Extracts from the diary were published in the *Observer* (7 December 1986).

Maschwitz, Eric
English songwriter (1901–69)

2 *The sigh of midnight trains in empty stations . . .*
The smile of Garbo and the scent of roses . . .
These foolish things
Remind me of you.

From the song, 'These Foolish Things' (1936), once cited by John Betjeman as

evidence of poetry in popular culture. The song was originally published as by 'Holt Marvell' (with music by Jack Strachey) because Maschwitz had to conceal his identity as a BBC executive. This has led to such oddities as the *PDMQ* (1980) crediting the whole song to Strachey alone. In the *ODQ* (1992), it is still credited to 'Holt Marvell', as also in the *ODMQ* (1991), where the music credit is shared between Jack Strachey and 'Harry Link', whoever he might be.

3 *A Nightingale Sang in Berkeley Square.*

Title of a song first sung in the revue *New Faces* (1940). Music by Manning Sherwin. As Maschwitz acknowledged in his autobiography *No Chip on My Shoulder* (1957), the title was derived from a short story called 'When the Nightingale Sang in Berkeley Square' in Michael Arlen's *These Charming People* (1923). Nightingales are last reported to have sung in Berkeley Square in 1850 (according to Victoria Glendinning, *Trollope*, 1992).

Masefield, John
English Poet Laureate (1878–1967)

4 *I must down to the seas again.*

In Masefield's poem 'Sea-Fever' (1902), this line — without any 'go' — was apparently as he originally intended it, though the original manuscript is lost. An early draft of the poem has 'I must down' — indeed, it pursues a different course, beginning, 'I must down to the roads again, to the vagrant life.' The repeated line was 'I must down' in the first published version of *Salt Water Ballads* in 1902. Heinemann Collected Editions of Masefield's poetry had 'down' (in 1923, 1932 and 1938) but changed to 'go down' in 1946. *Selected Poems* in 1922 and 1938 both had 'go down'. No one knows why this divergence occurred, but the pull of Psalm 107 ('They that *go down to the sea* in ships, that do their business in great waters') may have been a factor. John Ireland's musical setting of the poem has the 'go'. Some editions also have a singular 'sea'. Curiously, the *ODQ* suggests that the 1902 original 'I must down to the seas' was 'possibly a misprint'.

Most of this information is drawn from an article by Agnes Whitaker in *The Times* (5 December 1980). She comments on 'the inspired economy' of 'I must down' and adds: 'It is disconcerting that standard editions, and works of reference which we treat almost like sacred texts, should contradict each other, especially over such an immensely well-known poem.'

Mathew, Sir James
Irish judge (1830–1908)

1 *In England, Justice is open to all, like the Ritz hotel.*

This remark was attributed to Mathew by R.E. Megarry in *Miscellany-at-Law* (1955). However, the thought is old enough. In *Tom Paine's Jests* (1794) there is: 'A gentleman haranguing on the perfection of our law, and that it was equally open to the poor and rich, was answered by another, "So is the London Tavern".' In William Hazlitt's *The Spirit of the Age* (1825), this jest was specifically ascribed to the radical politician John Horne Tooke (1736-1812).

Matthews, A.E.
English actor (1869–1960)

2 *I always wait for* The Times *each morning. I look at the obituary column, and if I'm not in it, I go to work.*

His own obituary appeared on 26 July 1960. This remark was included in my book *Quote . . . Unquote 2* (1980), though the source has been lost. Several people have used the line subsequently. In the *Observer* (16 August 1987), William Douglas-Home, the playwright, was quoted as saying: 'Every morning I read the obits in *The Times*. If I'm not there, I carry on.'

Maugham, W. Somerset
English novelist and short-story writer (1874–1965)

3 *The Moon and Sixpence.*

Maugham took the title of his 1919 novel from a review of an earlier book — *Of Human Bondage* (1915) — in *The Times Literary Supplement*. It had said that the main character was: 'Like so many young men . . . so busy yearning for the moon that he never saw the sixpence at his feet.'

[*Source*: Ted Morgan, *Somerset Maugham*, 1980.]

4 *I stand in the very first row of the second-raters.*

Said by *The Oxford Companion to English Literature* (1985) to be in his autobiography

The Summing Up (1938), this view has not been found there. Compare the similar self-estimation of Arnold Bennett (quoted in *The Lyttelton Hart-Davis Letters* for 18 January 1956), 'My work will never be better than third-rate, judged by the high standards, but I shall be cunning enough to make it impose on my contemporaries', and the view of Maugham as 'a good writer of the second rank' put forward by Karl G. Pfeiffer in his *Somerset Maugham, a Candid Portrait* (1959).

5 *To eat well in England, all you have to do is take breakfast three times a day.*

This oft-quoted view appears in Ted Morgan, *Somerset Maugham* (1980) as the response to a friend's statement that he 'hated the food in England': 'What rubbish. All you have to do is eat breakfast three times a day.'

6 *At a dinner party one should eat wisely but not too well, and talk well but not too wisely.*

An elusive quotation — but one that is to be found in Maugham's *A Writer's Notebook* (1949)

See also DAVIS 115:1.

Maxton, Jimmy
Scottish Independent Labour Party politician (1855–1946)

7 *If my friend cannot ride two horses — what's he doing in the bloody circus?*

Said of a man who had proposed disaffiliation of the ILP from the Labour Party and quoted in G. McAllister, *James Maxton* (1935). Maxton had been speaking in a debate at a Scottish Conference of the ILP in 1931 and been told he could not be a member of two parties — or ride two horses — at the same time. Hence the more general expression, 'If you can't ride two horses at once, you shouldn't be in the circus'.

Melbourne, 2nd Lord
English Whig Prime Minister (1779–1848)

8 *[Of the Prime Ministership] A damned bore.*

We have only Charles Greville's word for it, but when William IV offered the Prime Ministership to Melbourne in 1834, 'He thought it a damned bore and was in many minds what he should do — be minister or no'. His secretary urged him to accept, however, with the words: 'Why damn it, such a position was never occupied by any Greek or Roman, and if it only last two months, it is well worth while to have been Prime Minister of England.' The words were quoted by Clement Attlee while ironically congratulating Anthony Eden on becoming Prime Minister (in 1955) when an election was imminent.

[*Source*: Robert Blake in *The Prime Ministers*, Vol. 2, 1975.]

Mencken, H.L.
American journalist and linguist (1880–1956)

1 *No one ever went broke underestimating the intelligence of the American people.*

In fact what Mencken wrote (about journalism) in the *Chicago Tribune* on 19 September 1926, was: 'No one in this world, so far as I know . . . has ever lost money by underestimating the intelligence of the great masses of the plain people.'

2 *If after I depart this vale you ever remember me and have thought to please my ghost, forgive some sinner and wink your eye at some homely girl.*

Mencken suggested this epitaph for himself in *The Smart Set* (December 1921). After his death, it was inscribed on a plaque in the lobby of the offices of the Baltimore *Sun* newspapers (with which he had been associated most of his working life).

Mendelssohn, Felix
German composer (1809–47)

3 *Calm Sea and Prosperous Voyage.*

The pleasing title of this overture was taken from two poems by Goethe, with whom Mendelssohn was personally acquainted. One '*Meeresstille*', the other, '*Glückliche Fahrt*'. (Beethoven also made a choral and orchestral setting of these poems.) Nowadays one might wish a 'calm sea and a prosperous voyage' to a friend off on a sea cruise, but *Meeresstille* refers to that more sinister prospect for anyone on a vessel with sails — a becalmed sea.

Metternich, Prince
Austrian statesman (1773–1859)

4 *When Paris sneezes, Europe catches cold.*

Untraced. This comment, said to date from 1830, cannot be found in his *Mémoires*, for example. Another form is: 'When France has a cold, all Europe sneezes.'

5 *Italy is a geographical expression* [Italien ist ein geographischer Begriff].

Discussing the Italian question with Palmerston in 1847 (also in a letter dated 19 November 1849). Victor Emmanuel II was not proclaimed King until 1861, when Italy was indeed no more than a group of individual states.

Michaelis, John
American general (1912–85)

6 *You're not here to die for your country. You're here to make those so-and-sos die for theirs.*

A famous rallying cry to the 27th Infantry (Wolfhound) Regiment, which Michaelis commanded during the Korean War (and quoted by *Time* Magazine, 11 November 1985).

Miller, Arthur
American playwright (1915–)

7 *For a salesman, there is no rock bottom to the life . . . He's a man way out there in the blue, riding on a smile and a shoeshine . . . A salesman is got to dream, boy. It comes with the territory.*

From the 'Requiem' at the end of Miller's play *Death of a Salesman* (1948). Since at least 1900, 'territory' has been the American term for the area a salesman covers. Miller's use may, however, be a possible origin for the late twentieth-century expression, 'It comes/goes with the territory', meaning 'it's all part and parcel of something, what is expected'. From the *Washington Post* (13 July 1984): '[Geraldine Ferraro as prospective Vice-President] will have to be judged on her background, training and capacity to do the job. That goes with the territory.' In the film *Father of the Bride* (1991), Steve Martin says: 'I'm a father. Worrying comes with the territory.' From the London

Evening Standard (17 February 1993): 'Why go on about the latest "award-winning documentary maker"? If you get a documentary on television, you win an award: it goes with the territory.'

1 *Roslyn: 'How do you find your way back in the dark?' Gay nods, indicating the sky before them: 'Just head for that big star straight on. The highway's under it; take us right home.'*

From Miller's novel *The Misfits* (1961). In his screenplay (in the same year), the last line of the film, spoken by Clark Gable, becomes: 'The highway's under it. It'll takes us right home.' This is sometimes given as Gable's own 'last line', as he died shortly after the filming was completed.

Miller, Max
American journalist (1899–1967)

2 *I Cover the Waterfront.*

Miller was a 'waterfront reporter' on the *San Diego Sun* during the late 1920s and early 1930s. His book (1932) about his experiences led to a film (1933) about a journalist who exposes a smuggling racket. Hence, 'cover' is in the journalistic sense. The song with the title (by Johnny Green and Ed Heyman), sung notably by Billie Holiday, was originally unconnected with the film — written merely to cash in on the association — and sounds as if it might be about laying paving stones or some other activity. However, so successful was it that it was subsequently added to the soundtrack. Since the film, the phrase 'to cover the waterfront' has meant 'to cover all aspects of a topic' or merely 'to experience something'. A woman going in to try a new nightclub in the film *Cover Girl* (1944) says: 'This is it. We cover the waterfront.' In *The Wise Wound* (1978) by Penelope Shuttle and Peter Redgrove, 'she's covering the waterfront' is listed among the many slang expressions for menstruation.

Mills, Nat and Bobbie
English entertainers (1900–93) and (*d* 1955)

3 *Let's get on with it!*

Mr and Mrs Mills were a variety act that flourished in the 1930s and 1940s portraying 'a gumpish type of lad and his equally gumpish girlfriend'. Nat recalled (in 1979):

'It was during the very early part of the war. We were booked by the BBC to go to South Wales for a *Workers' Playtime*. Long tables had been set up in front of the stage for the workers to have lunch on before the broadcast. On this occasion, a works foreman went round all the tables shouting, "Come on, let's get on with it", to get them to finish their lunch on time. I was informed he used this phrase so many times, the workers would mimic him among themselves. So I said to Bobbie, "You start the broadcast by talking to yourself and I'll interject and say, 'Let's get on with it'". Lo and behold it got such a yell of laughter we kept it in all our broadcasts. Even Churchill used our slogan to the troops during the early part of the war.'

Milne, A.A.
English writer (1882–1956)

4 *Worraworraworraworraworra.*

This is the noise ('not a growl, and it isn't a purr') made by Tigger, the bouncy tiger, in Milne's *The House at Pooh Corner* (1928). However, 'wurrawurrawurra' also occurs in Thackeray's *The Rose and the Ring*, Chap. 15 (1856). Here it seems to denote eating noises — but from the same corner of the animal kingdom. Count Hogginarmo jumps into a circus ring, and then: 'Wurra wurra wurra wur-aw-aw-aw!!! In about two minutes, the Count Hogginarmo was GOBBLED UP by those lions: bones, boots and all, and there was an end of him.' Earlier still, on 26 January 1788, when Captain Arthur Phillip's fleet landed at what would later be called Sydney Harbour in Australia, it was greeted by Aborigines crying, '*Warra, warra!*' (meaning, 'Go away!')

Milton, John
English poet (1608–74)

5 *All hell broke loose.*

A popular descriptive catchphrase came originally from Milton's *Paradise Lost*, Bk 4, l.917 (1667), when the Archangel Gabriel speaks to Satan:

> Wherefore with thee
> Came not all hell broke loose.

As an idiomatic phrase it was already established by 1738 when Swift compiled his *Polite Conversation*. When there is 'A great Noise below', Lady Smart exclaims: 'Hey, what a clattering is there; one would think Hell was broke loose.'

1 *Unmoved,*
  Unshaken, unseduced, unterrified,
  His Loyalty he kept, his Love, his Zeal;
  Nor number, nor example with him
     wrought
  To swerve from truth, or change his
     constant mind.

A quotation to be found on the memorial tablet to the Liberal Prime Minister, H.H. Asquith, in Westminster Abbey. The lines, taken from *Paradise Lost* (Bk V, l.898), were chosen 'after much thought by his family', according to Asquith's biographer, Roy Jenkins.

2 *Tomorrow to fresh fields and*
  pastures new.

Should read, 'Tomorrow to fresh *woods* and pastures new' whether or not one is aware that Milton's *Lycidas* (1637) is being quoted. The misquotation probably gained hold because of the alliteration — always a lure in phrase-making. There may be tautology in the fields and pastures, but how likely is it that a shepherd would lead his flock into a wood where the sheep would be liable to get lost, lose their wool on bushes, eat poisonous plants and so on?

3 *Sabrina fair,*
  Listen where thou art sitting
  Under the glassy, cool, translucent
     wave,
  In twisted braids of lilies knitting
  The loose train of thy
     amber-dropping hair.

Billy Wilder's 1954 film *Sabrina*, based on a play by Samuel Taylor, was about the daughter (Audrey Hepburn) of a chauffeur who gets wooed by both the two brothers who employ her father. Known simply as *Sabrina* in the US, the film was released as *Sabrina Fair* in Britain. This could have been because the distributors thought that English cinema-goers would relish an allusion to the poetic name for the river Severn, as applied to the nymph in Milton's masque *Comus* (1634). On the other hand, the distributors might have been sending them a message that the film had nothing at all to do with Sabrina, a busty (41–18–36) model, who was at that time featured on TV shows with Arthur Askey, the comedian.

Alas, this second theory does not fit, as Norma Sykes (her real name) did not start appearing until 1956 and, in fact, took her stage-name from the title of the film. So, it must have been the allusion to Milton.

4 *A good book is the precious life-blood*
  of a master spirit, embalmed and trea-
  sured up on purpose to a life beyond
  life.

From *Areopagitica* (1644). A sentiment used for many years to promote the Everyman's Library series of classic reprints. Compare ANONYMOUS SAYINGS 12:2 and SIDNEY 311:2.

5 *Blest pair of sirens, pledges of*
     heav'n's joy,
  Sphere-born harmonious sisters.

In 'At a Solemn Music' (1645), the sirens are 'Voice' and 'Verse'. Notably set to music (1887) by Sir Hubert Parry.

Minney, R.J.
English writer (1895–1979)

6 *Carve Her Name With Pride.*

As Michael Powell comments in *Million-Dollar Movie* (1992), the title of Minney's book (1956, filmed UK, 1958), 'sounds like a quotation, and probably is'. But I think not. Minney makes no reference to the title in his somewhat soupy biography of Violette Szabo, the wartime agent who was executed by the Germans and became the first British woman to receive the George Cross (gazetted posthumously in 1946). The notion of carving an epitaph is, of course, an old one. Robert Browning has 'If ye carve my epitaph aright' in his poem 'The Bishop Orders His Tomb' (1845).

Mitchell, Margaret
American novelist (1900–49)

7 *Gone With the Wind.*

The title of Mitchell's famous novel (1936; filmed US, 1939) comes from Ernest Dowson's poem '*Non Sum Qualis Eram*' (1896): 'I have forgot much, Cynara! Gone with the wind.' It refers to the southern United States before the American Civil War, as is made clear by the on-screen prologue to the film: 'There was a land of Cavaliers and Cotton Fields called the Old South. Here in this patrician world the Age of Chivalry took its last bows. Here was the last ever seen of the Knights and their Ladies fair, of Master and Slave. Look for it only in books, for it is no more than a dream remembered, a Civilization gone with the wind.'

1 Scarlett: *Where shall I go? What shall I do?*
Rhett: *Frankly, my dear, I don't give a damn.*

In the last scene of the film, Scarlett O'Hara is finally abandoned by her husband, Rhett Butler. Although Scarlett believes she can win him back, there occurs the controversial moment when Rhett replies to her entreaty with these words. They were allowed on to the soundtrack only after months of negotiation with the Hays Office which controlled film censorship. In those days, the word 'damn' was forbidden in Hollywood under Section V (1) of the Hays Code, even if it was what Mitchell had written in her novel (though she hadn't included the 'frankly' — 'My dear, I don't give a damn', simply). Sidney Howard's original draft was accordingly changed to: 'Frankly, my dear, I don't care.' The scene was shot with both versions of the line, and the producer, David Selznick, argued at great length with the censors over which was to be used. He did this not least because he thought he would look a fool if the famous line was excluded. He also wanted to show how faithful the film was to the novel. Selznick argued that the *Oxford Dictionary* described 'damn' not as an oath but as a vulgarism, that many women's magazines used the word, and that preview audiences had expressed disappointment when the line was omitted. The censors suggested 'darn' instead. Selznick finally won the day — but because he was technically in breach of the Hays Code he was fined $5000. The line still didn't sound quite right: Clark Gable, as Rhett, had to put the emphasis unnaturally on 'give' rather than on 'damn'.

2 *After all, tomorrow is another day.*

The last words of the film, spoken by Vivien Leigh as Scarlett O'Hara, are: 'Tara! Home! I'll go home, and I'll think of some way to get him back. After all, tomorrow is another day!' The last sentence is as it appears in Mitchell's novel, but the idea behind it is proverbial. In John Rastell's *Calisto and Melebea* (c 1527) there occurs the line: 'Well, mother, tomorrow is a new day'.

Mitford, Nancy
English author (1904–73)

3 *Abroad is unutterably bloody.*

In *The Pursuit of Love* (1945), Mitford wrote (in the character of 'Uncle Matthew'): 'I loathe abroad, nothing would induce me to live there' and 'Frogs . . . are slightly better than Huns or Wops, but abroad is unutterably bloody and foreigners are fiends.' This no great opinion of foreigners is put down to his four years in France and Italy between 1914 and 1918. In W.H. Auden's anthology, *A Certain World* (1970), King George VI is quoted as saying, 'Abroad is bloody'.

4 *Love in a Cold Climate.*

The novel (1949) with this title caused Evelyn Waugh to write to Mitford (10 October): '[It] has become a phrase. I mean when people want to be witty they say I've caught a cold in a cold climate and everyone understands.' The title was suggested by Bennett Cerf, the book's American publisher. Earlier, Robert Southey, the poet, writing to his brother Thomas (28 April 1797) had said: 'She has made me half in love with a cold climate.'

Mola, Emilio
Spanish Nationalist general (1887–1937)

5 *The fifth column* [La quinta columna].

In October 1936, during the Spanish Civil War, Mola was besieging the Republican-held city of Madrid with four columns. He was asked in a broadcast whether this was sufficient to capture the city and he replied that he was relying on the support of the *quinta columna* [the fifth column], which was already hiding inside the city and which sympathized with his side. Hence the term 'fifth columnists' meaning 'traitors, infiltrators'. It was also the title of Ernest Hemingway's only play (1938).

Mondale, Walter
American Democratic Vice-President (1928–   )

6 *Where's the beef?*

A slogan borrowed by Mondale in 1984, when he was seeking the Democratic Presidential nomination, to describe what he saw as a lack of substance in the policies of his rival for the nomination, Gary Hart. Hence, a classic example of an advertising slogan turning into a political catchphrase. The Wendy International hamburger chain promoted its wares in the US, from 1984, with TV commercials, one of which showed elderly women eyeing a small hamburger on a huge bun – a Wendy competitor's product. 'It certainly is a big bun,' asserted one. 'It's a very big fluffy bun,' the second agreed. But the third asked, 'Where's the beef?' Mondale took it from there.

Montagu, Lady Mary Wortley
English writer (1689–1762)

1 *It has all been very interesting.*

Lady Mary's wonderful 'dying words' (as in *BDPF*, 1975, for example) have, unfortunately, not been authenticated. Robert Halsband in his *Life of Lady Mary Wortley Montagu* (1956) remarks that 'they are nowhere unequivocally recorded' and notes that the source – Iris Barry's *Portrait of Lady Mary Montagu* (1928) – is 'clearly fictitious'.

Montgomery, Bernard
(later 1st Viscount Montgomery of Alamein)
English field marshal (1887–1976)

2 *Here we will stand and fight; there will be no further withdrawal . . . We are going to finish with this chap Rommel once and for all. It will be quite easy. There is no doubt about it. He is definitely a nuisance. Therefore we will hit him a crack and finish with him.*

One of the most effective exhortations of the war was given by Montgomery as he took command of the Eighth Army on 13 August 1942. Two months before the Battle of El Alamein, he electrified his officers with a private pep talk. A recording of the speech was made after the war and was based on shorthand notes made at the time.

3 *Consider what the Lord said to Moses – and I think he was right.*

For a long time, it seemed that this was something that Montgomery – that blushing violet – had *actually* said. Then it was traced to a line in a sketch called 'Salvation Army' performed by Lance Percival as an

army officer but *with a Montgomery accent* on BBC TV's *That Was the Week That Was* (1962–3). Hence, it is simply a joke, though totally in character.

Compare *The Lyttelton-Hart-Davis Letters* (Vol. 4: relating to 1959), where exactly the same joke occurs in the form, 'Did you hear of the parson who began his sermon: "As God said – and rightly . . .".' No mention of Montgomery. Compare also a remark made by Donald Coggan, Archbishop of Canterbury, on 7 June 1977, during a sermon for the Queen's Silver Jubilee service at St Paul's Cathedral: 'We listened to these words of Jesus [St Matthew 7:24] a few moments ago.' Then he exclaimed: 'How right he was!'

One is reminded irresistibly of Lorenz Hart's stripper's song 'Zip' from *Pal Joey* (1940):

I was reading Schopenhauer last night,
And I think that Schopenhauer was right.

Compare, yet further, what William Jackson, Bishop of Oxford, once preached (according to *The Oxford Book of Oxford*, 1978): 'St Paul says in one of his Epistles – and I partly agree with him.'

Morgan, J.P., Jr
American banker (1867–1943)

4 *If you have to ask the price you can't afford it.*

Morgan Jr succeeded his father as head of the US banking house of Morgan. The story has it that a man was thinking of buying a yacht similar to Morgan's and asked him how much it cost in annual upkeep. Morgan replied with words to the effect: 'If you have to ask, you can't afford it.' Compare the remark of John Paul Getty (1892–1976): 'If you can actually count your money, you are not really rich.'

Morris, Jan
(formerly James Morris)
English writer (1926–)

5 *Farewell the Trumpets.*

Some book, film and programme titles are quasi-quotations or are, rather, quasi-poetic in sound – titles like *By the Sword Divided*, *Carve Her Name With Pride*, *To Serve Them All My Days*, *A Horseman Riding By*, *God Is an Englishman* and so on. (All of these are dealt with elsewhere in the text.) Morris has admitted that, having thought up the title *Farewell the Trumpets* (1978) for the final volume of her *Pax Brittanica* trilogy, she then wrote a poem to quote it from. The poem duly appears as the book's epigraph:

Say farewell to the trumpets!
You will hear them no more.
But their sweet and silvery echoes
Will call to you still
Through the half-closed door.

Morrison, Herbert
(later Lord Morrison of Lambeth)
English Labour politician (1888–1965)

1 Go to it!

On 22 May 1940 Morrison, as the Minister of Supply, concluded a radio broadcast calling for a voluntary labour force with these words. They echoed the public mood after Dunkirk and were subsequently used as a wall-poster slogan — in vivid letters — in a campaign run by the S.H. Benson agency (which later indulged in self-parody on behalf of Bovril, with 'Glow to it' in 1951–2).

'Go to it', meaning 'to act vigorously, set to with a will', dates from the early nineteenth century at least. In Shakespeare, *King Lear* (IV.vi.112), of course, it means something else:

Die for adultery! No:
The wren goes to't, and the small
    gilded fly
Does lecher in my sight.

Morrison, Herbert
American broadcaster (1905–89)

2 It is in smoke and flames now! Oh, the humanity!

'Toward us, like a great feather . . . is the *Hindenburg*. The members of the crew are looking down on the field ahead of them getting their glimpses of the mooring mast . . .' On 6 May 1937 radio commentator Morrison was describing the scene at the Naval airbase in Lakenhurst, New Jersey, as the German airship made its first arrival there that year (having made ten round trips to the US the previous year). 'It is starting to rain again . . . the back motors of the ship are just holding it just enough to keep it from — It's burst into flames! . . . It's crashing, terrible! . . . Folks, this is terrible, this is one of the worst catastrophes the

world ever witnessed . . . It's a terrific sight, ladies and gentlemen, the smoke and the flames now. And the plane is crashing to the ground . . . Oh, the humanity! All the passengers! . . . I can't talk, ladies and gentlemen . . .' (transcribed from a recording).

A few seconds later, Morrison managed to continue describing what *Time* Magazine called 'the worst and most completely witnessed disaster in the history of commercial aviation'. Although the *Hindenburg* was completely destroyed (virtually ending airships as a commercial venture), there were some survivors.

Mortimer, John
English author, playwright and lawyer (1923–   )

3 The shelf life of the modern hardback writer is somewhere between the milk and the yoghurt.

Quoted in the *Observer* (28 June 1987) and picked up by *ODMQ* (1991). As he had, in fact, said at the time, Mortimer was quoting the American humorous columnist Calvin Trillin (1935–   ).

4 Champagne socialist.

The *ODQ* (1992) attributes to Mortimer this description of himself and, indeed the *Sunday Telegraph* (3 July 1988) stated that 'he once described himself as a "champagne socialist"'. The phrase might, it is true, have been coined with Mortimer in mind — he likes a bottle or two, goes around calling everyone 'darling' and doesn't see why the good things in life should be denied him just because he is a 'bit Left' — but to what extent he has applied the phrase to himself, if at all, is not totally clear. From the *Independent* (2 September 1991): '[On the set of his latest television serial *Titmuss Regained*] Mortimer relaxed in the catering bus with a bottle of Moët (apparently determined not to disappoint those who think of him as a champagne socialist).'

The earliest use of the phrase found to date is in connection with that other larger-than-life character, the late tycoon and criminal, Robert Maxwell. From *The Times* (2 July 1987): 'Robert Maxwell, *Daily Mirror* newspaper tycoon and possibly the best known Czech in Britain after Ivan Lendl, has long been renowned for his champagne socialist beliefs.' At around that time, the phrase was also applied to socialist figures such as Clive Jenkins and Derek Hatton.

But maybe the phrase has even earlier beginnings: a similarly alliterative phrase was applied to a more admirable and larger-than-life socialist, Aneurin Bevan. Randolph Churchill (who was something of a champagne Conservative) recalled in the *Evening Standard* (8 August 1958), how Brendan Bracken had once 'gone for' Bevan: ' "You Bollinger Bolshevik, you ritzy Robespierre, you lounge-lizard Lenin," he roared at Bevan one night, gesturing, as he went on, somewhat in the manner of a domesticated orangutang. "Look at you, swilling Max's champagne and calling yourself a socialist".'

1 *Clinging to the wreckage.*

The origin of the title of Mortimer's autobiography (1982) is explained in an epigraphic paragraph or two: 'A man with a bristling grey beard [a yachtsman, said:] "I made up my mind, when I bought my first boat, never to learn to swim . . . When you're in a spot of trouble, if you can swim you try to strike out for the shore. You invariably drown. As I can't swim, I cling to the wreckage and they send a helicopter out for me. That's my tip, if you ever find yourself in trouble, cling to the wreckage!" ' Mortimer concludes: 'It was advice that I thought I'd been taking for most of my life.'

Morton, J.B.
('Beachcomber')
British humorous writer (1893–1979)

2 *Wagner is the Puccini of music.*

The *PDMQ* (1971) attributed this to Beachcomber and Rupert Hart-Davis concurs, saying that this announcement 'summed up the jargon-bosh of art-and music-critics beautifully' (*The Lyttelton Hart-Davis Letters* for 5 February 1956). But no precise source is available. On the other hand, James Agate in *Ego 6* (for 13 October 1943) has: 'I do not doubt the sincerity of the solemn ass who, the other evening, said portentously: "Wagner is the Puccini of music!" ' As Agate was addressing a group of 'school-marms' and as he generally had an after-dinner speaker's way with attribution, I am inclined to believe it was a Beachcomber line. If nothing else, we now have an earlier dating for the observation.

Mountbatten of Burma, Earl
British Royal, military commander and Viceroy (1900–79)

3 *In my experience, I have always found that you cannot have an efficient ship unless you have a happy ship, and you cannot have a happy ship unless you have an efficient ship. That is the way I intend to start this commission, and that is the way I intend to go on — with a happy and efficient ship.*

From Mountbatten's initial address to the crew of HMS *Kelly* after he became the destroyer's Captain in 1939. When Noël Coward wrote the script of his film *In Which We Serve* (1942), based on Mountbatten's association with HMS *Kelly* and its sinking during the Battle of Crete, the speech was adopted *verbatim*. Coward delivered it, too.

Moynihan, Daniel Patrick
American Democratic politician (1927–   )

4 *The time may have come when the issue of race could benefit from a period of 'benign neglect'.*

As a counsellor to President Nixon, Moynihan quoted the phrase in a memorandum dated 2 March 1970 and leaked to the *New York Times*. The inevitable furore ensued, though all Moynihan was suggesting was that racial tensions would be lessened if people on both sides were to lower their voices a little. He was quoting an 1839 remark by an Earl of Durham to Queen Victoria regarding Canada. She had done so well 'through a period of benign neglect' by the mother country that she should be granted self-government.

Mozart, Wolfgang Amadeus
Austrian composer (1756–91)

5 *I write [music] as a sow piddles.*

Quoted by Laurence J. Peter in *Quotations for Our Time* (1977). Source untraced, but using imagery of which Mozart was typically fond. Compare John Aubrey's memoir of Dr Kettle who, 'was wont to say that "Seneca writes, as a boare doth pisse", scilicet, by jirkes' (*Brief Lives*, from c 1690).

1 *Didn't I say before that I was writing this* Requiem *for myself?*

The last recorded words of Mozart concern the *Requiem* which he left unfinished when he died. He certainly seems to have said this on his last day alive, according to the biography (1828) by Georg Nikolaus Nissen based on that by Franz Xaver Niemetschek (1798) for which Mozart's widow Constanze supplied much material.

Muggeridge, Kitty
English writer (1903–94)

2 [Of David Frost] *He rose without trace.*

A notable remark, made *c* 1965. Curiously delighting in it, Frost provides the context in the first volume of his autobiography (1993). Malcolm Muggeridge (Kitty's husband) had predicted that after *That Was the Week That Was*, Frost would sink without trace. So she said, 'Instead, he has risen without trace'.

Münster, Count Georg
Hanoverian diplomat (1794–1868)

3 *Despotism tempered by assassination.*

So replied Lord Reith, the BBC's first Director-General, when asked by Malcolm Muggeridge in the TV programme *Lord Reith Looks Back* (1970) what he considered the best form of government. The phrase was not original. For example, *Quotations for Speakers and Writers* (1970) quotes the remark of a Russian noble *to* Count Münster on the assassination of Emperor Paul I in 1800: 'Despotism tempered by assassination, that is our Magna Carta.' The ODQ (1992) prefers a direct quote from Count Münster's *Political Sketches of the State of Europe, 1814–1867* (1868): 'An intelligent Russian once remarked to us, "Every country has its own constitution; ours is absolutism moderated by assassination".' Bartlett (1980) attributes 'Absolutism tempered by assassination' direct to the earlier Ernst Friedrich Herbert von Münster (1766–1839).
The dates are rather important. How else is one to know whether Thomas Carlyle in his *History of the French Revolution* (1837) was alluding to the saying, when he wrote: 'France was long a despotism tempered by epigrams'? In a speech to the International

Socialist Congress (Paris, 17 July 1889), the Austrian, Victor Adler, followed up with: 'The Austrian government . . . is a system of despotism tempered by casualness.'

Murray, Sir James
Scottish lexicographer (1837–1915)

4 *Knowledge is power.*

The first editor of what became *The Oxford English Dictionary* wrote this on the flyleaf of Cassell's *Popular Educator* — according to Elizabeth Murray, *Caught in the Web of Words* (1977).

5 *The traditional practice of dictionary makers is 'to copy shamelessly from one dictionary to another'.*

When *The Century Dictionary* (1889) seemed to plagiarize Murray's work, it was his friends who reminded him of the above. He did not necessarily subscribe to it himself. (Quoted in Elizabeth Murray, as above.)

6 *Have thy tools ready. God will find thee work.*

According to Elizabeth Murray, this was his favourite text. It supposedly came from Charles Kingsley, and Murray hung it in his bedroom.

Murrow, Edward R.
American broadcaster (1908–65)

7 *Anyone who isn't confused doesn't really understand the situation.*

Ascribed to Murrow on the subject of Vietnam by Walter Bryan, *The Improbable Irish* (1969). Then applied to the situation in Northern Ireland. There were a number of such sayings. An anonymous Belfast citizen was quoted in 1970: 'Anyone who isn't confused here doesn't really understand what's going on.'

Mussolini, Benito
Italian fascist leader (1883–1945)

8 *I will make the trains run on time and create order out of chaos.*

Efficiency may be the saving grace of a fascist dictatorship, but did Mussolini ever actually make this boast? Or did he merely claim afterwards that this is what he had done? One of his biographers (Giorgio Pini, 1939) quotes Mussolini exhorting a station-master: 'We must leave exactly on time . . . From now on everything must function to perfection.' The improvement was being commented on by 1925. In that year, HRH Infanta Eulalia of Spain wrote in *Courts and Countries after the War* that 'the first benefit of Mussolini's direction in Italy' is when you hear that 'the train is arriving on time'. Quite *how* efficient the trains really were, is open to doubt. Perhaps they just ran *relatively* more on time than they had done before. But they had managed all right for the famous 'March on Rome' (October 1922) which — despite its name — was largely accomplished by train.

N

Nansen, Fridtjof
Norwegian explorer (1861–1930)

1 *The cold of the polar regions was nothing to the chill of an English bedroom.*

Quoted in *The Laughing Diplomat* (1939) by Daniele Varè. Nansen made several voyages in the Arctic regions. He was also the first Norwegian ambassador to London (1906–8), which is when he presumably acquired his knowledge of the bedrooms.

2 *The difficult is what takes a little time; the impossible is what takes a little longer.*

Quoted — as said by Nansen — in *The Listener* (14 December 1939). Bartlett (1980) places this slogan specifically with the US Army Service Forces, but the idea has been traced back to Charles Alexandre de Calonne (1734–1802), who said: '*Madame, si c'est possible, c'est fait; impossible? cela se fera* [if it is possible, it is already done; if it is impossible, it will be done]' — quoted in J. Michelet, *Historie de la Révolution Française* (1847). Henry Kissinger once joked: 'The illegal we do immediately, the unconstitutional takes a little longer' (quoted in William Shawcross, *Sideshow*, 1979).

Napoleon I
French Emperor (1769–1821)

3 *England is a nation of shopkeepers* [L'Angleterre est une nation de boutiquiers].

Most of Napoleon's attributed sayings are, like Abraham Lincoln's, impossible to verify now. This remark was quoted by Barry E. O'Meara in *Napoleon in Exile* (1822).

Earlier, however, Samuel Adams, the American Revolutionary leader, *may* have said in his *Oration in Philadelphia* (1 August 1776): 'A nation of shop-keepers are very seldom so disinterested.' In the same year, Adam Smith was writing in *The Wealth of Nations*: 'To found a great empire for the sole purpose of raising up a people of customers, may at first sight appear a project fit only for a nation of shopkeepers.'

4 *Every soldier has the baton of a field-marshal in his knapsack.*

This is the anglicized form of a saying frequently attributed to Napoleon. E. Blaze in *La Vie Militaire sous l'Empire* (1837) has it thus: '*Tout soldat français porte dans sa giberne le bâton de maréchal de France*' (which should be more accurately translated as, 'Every French soldier carries in his cartridge-pouch the baton of a marshal of France'). This was how the saying first appeared in English in 1840. The meaning is: 'Even the lowliest soldier may have leadership potential.'

Mencken ascribes the saying to Louis XVIII (1755–1824) and, indeed, the French king who reigned after Napoleon said in a speech to cadets at Saint-Cyr (9 August 1819): 'Remember that there is not one of you who does not carry in his cartridge-pouch the marshal's baton of the Duke of Reggio; it is up to you to bring it forth.'

5 *An iron hand in a velvet glove.*

Napoleon is supposed to have said, 'Men must be led by an iron hand in a velvet glove', but this expression is hard to pin down as a quotation. Thomas Carlyle wrote in *Latter-Day Pamphlets* (1850): 'Soft speech and manner, yet with an inflexible rigour of command . . . "iron hand in a velvet glove", as Napoleon defined it.' The Emperor Charles V (1519–56) may have said it earlier. Sometimes an iron 'fist' rather than 'hand' is evoked. Either way, the image is of unbending ruthlessness or firmness covered by a veneer of courtesy and gentle manners.

1 *From the sublime to the ridiculous there is but one step.*

Nowadays most often used as a phrase without the last five words. The proverbial form most probably came to us from the French. Napoleon is said to have uttered on one occasion (possibly after the retreat from Moscow in 1812): '*Du sublime au ridicule il n'y a qu'un pas.*'

However, Thomas Paine had already written in *The Age of Reason* (1795): 'The sublime and the ridiculous are often so nearly related, that is difficult to class them separately. One step above the sublime, makes the ridiculous; and one step above the ridiculous, makes the sublime again.'

2 *Not tonight, Josephine.*

Napoleon did not, as far as we know, ever say the words that have become popularly linked with him. The idea that he had had better things to do than satisfy the Empress Josephine's famous appetite, or was not inclined or able to do so, must have grown up during the nineteenth century. There was also a saying, attributed to Josephine, apparently, '*Bon-a-parte est Bon-à-rien* [Bonaparte is good for nothing]', which may be relevant.

A knockabout sketch filmed for the Pathé Library in *c* 1932 has Lupino Lane as Napoleon and Beatrice Lillie as Josephine. After signing a document of divorce (which Napoleon crumples up), Josephine says, 'When you are refreshed, come as usual to my apartment.' Napoleon says (as the tag to the sketch), 'Not tonight, Josephine,' and she throws a custard pie in his face.

The film *I Cover the Waterfront* (US 1933) has been credited with launching the phrase, though it merely popularized it. A British song with the title had appeared in 1915 (sung by Florrie Forde and written by Worton David and Lawrence Wright) and an American one probably earlier. Indeed, the catchphrase may have been established in music hall and vaudeville by the end of the previous century.

3 *[Women] belong to the highest bidder. Power is what they like — it is the greatest of all aphrodisiacs.*

Attributed to Napoleon by Constant Louis Wairy (his valet) in *Mémoires de Constant, premier valet de l'empereur* (1830–1). Compare KISSINGER 205:9.

4 *In victory you deserve it: in defeat you need it.*

A saying of Napoleon's (unverified) on the subject of champagne.

5 *Plans are nothing, but planning is everything.*

Attributed to Napoleon, but as yet unsourced. He does, however, appear to have said: 'Unhappy the general who comes on the field of battle with a system.' This is said to be included in his *Maxims 1804–15*.

6 *France — armée — tête d'armée — Joséphine.*

Napoleon died on St Helena in 1821 saying either this (Tristan de Montholon, who reported it, says he heard Napoleon say it twice) or '*Mon Dieu! La nation Française. Tête d'armée* [My God! The French nation. Head of the army].'

Nasby, Petroleum V.
(David Ross Locke)
American humorist (1833–88)

7 *The late unpleasantness.*

A euphemism for the previous war or recent hostilities, this phrase was introduced by Locke in *Ekkoes from Kentucky* (1868). As 'Petroleum V. Nasby', he referred to the recently ended Civil War as 'the late onpleasantniss' and the coinage spread. It still survives: 'Here, for instance, is Dan Rather, America's father-figure, on the hot-line to Panama during the late unpleasantness [an invasion]' (*Independent*, 20 January 1990).

Nash, Ogden
American poet (1902–71)

8 *Every Englishman is convinced of one thing, viz.*
That to be an Englishman is to belong to the most exclusive club there is.

From 'England Expects', *I'm a Stranger Here Myself* (1938). Possibly the first expression of a frequently used format. Compare the similar views expressed about membership of the British Parliament. Mr Twemlow in Charles Dickens, *Our Mutual Friend*, Bk II, Chap. 3 (1864–5) says of the House of Commons: 'I think . . . that it is the best club in London.' And Winston Churchill called it 'the best club in Europe' (quoted in Leon Harris, *The Fine Art of Political Wit*, 1965).

Nathan, George Jean
American drama critic (1882–1958)

1 *The test of a real comedian is whether you laugh at him before he opens his mouth.*

In *American Mercury* (September 1929). Now a cliché. Fred Lawrence Guiles said of Stan Laurel in *Stan* (1980): 'Very early on in his stage career Stan had made an interesting discovery: he found that audiences laughed at him before he ever said or did anything.' In November 1987 Robert McLennan of the SDP said of Barry Humphries as Sir Les Patterson: 'Like all great comic creations, he makes you laugh before he opens his mouth.'

Naughton, Bill
British playwright (1910–92)

2 *It seems to me if they ain't got you one way then they've got you another. So what's it all about, that's what I keep asking myself, what's it all about?*

From *Alfie* (1966), the film script of his stage and radio play. The phrase 'What's it all about, Alfie?' was chiefly popularized by Burt Bacharach and Hal David's song. This was not written for the film, which had a jazz score, with no songs, by Sonny Rollins, but Cher recorded it and this version was added to the soundtrack for the American release of the picture. Cilla Black then recorded it in Britain and Dionne Warwick in the US.
When Michael Caine, who played Alfie in the film, published his autobiography in 1992, it was naturally entitled *What's It All About?*

Nelson, Horatio
(Viscount Nelson)
English Admiral (1758–1805)

3 *The Nelson touch.*

Denoting any action bearing the hallmark of Horatio Nelson, his quality of leadership and seamanship, this term was coined by Nelson himself before the Battle of Trafalgar (1805): 'I am anxious to join the fleet, for it would add to my grief if any other man was to give them the Nelson touch.' The *Oxford Companion to Ships and the Sea* (1976) describes various manoeuvres to which the term could be applied, but adds: 'It could have meant the magic of his name among officers and seamen of his fleet, which was always enough to inspire them to great deeds of heroism and endurance.' The British title of the film *Corvette K-225* (US, 1943) was *The Nelson Touch*.

4 *I owe all my success in life to having been always a quarter of an hour before my time.*

I.e. early. Chiefly in sea battles rather than in private life, one expects. We have this statement by courtesy of Samuel Smiles in *Self-Help* (1859). In *The Dictionary of War Quotations* (1989) the wording is: 'I have always been a quarter of an hour before my time, and it has made a man of me.'

5 *Before this time tomorrow I shall have gained a peerage, or Westminster Abbey.*

Nelson said this at the Battle of the Nile (1798). Earlier, at the Battle of Cape St Vincent (1797), he is reported to have said: 'Westminster Abbey or victory!' Both of these echo Shakespeare, *Henry VI, Part 3* (II.ii.174): 'And either victory, or else a grave.'

6 *I really do not see the signal.*

At the Battle of Copenhagen in 1803, Nelson 'put the telescope to his blind eye', as the modern allusion would have it — that is to say, he made sure he did not see what he did not want to see (a signal ordering him to desist from action) and had a decisive victory. His exact words, according to Robert Southey's *Life of Nelson* (1813) were: 'I have only one eye — I have a right to be blind sometimes . . . I really do not see the signal!'
Alan Watkins, writing in the *Observer* (27 June 1993): 'Mr [John] Major then indulged in some misquotation of his own involving Lord Nelson, who is supposed to have said at the Battle of Copenhagen: "I really do not see the signal," though the more popular version is: "Danger? I see no danger." Mr

Major took the latter version and replied, referring to the press: "Assault? I see no assault".' (Is Watkins right about the popularity of the 'danger' version?)

1 England expects that every man will do his duty.

At 11.30 a.m. on 21 October 1805 the British Fleet approached Napoleon's combined French and Spanish fleets before the Battle of Trafalgar. Nelson told one of his captains: 'I will now amuse the fleet with a signal.' At first, it was to be, 'Nelson confides that every man will do his duty'. But it was suggested that 'England' would be better than 'Nelson'. Flag Lieutenant Pasco then pointed out that the word 'expects' was common enough to be in the signal book, whereas 'confides' would have to be spelt out letter by letter and would require seven flags, not one.

When Admiral Lord Collingwood saw the signal coming from HMS *Victory*, he remarked: 'I wish Nelson would stop signalling, as we all know well enough what we have to do.'

Mencken found an American saying from 1917 during the First World War 'England expects every American to do his duty.' In Britain, at about the same time, there was a recruiting slogan: 'England Expects that Every Man will Do His Duty and Join the Army Today.'

2 Kiss me, Hardy.

What exactly did Nelson say as he lay dying on HMS *Victory* at Trafalgar in 1805, having been severely injured by a shot fired from a French ship? It has been asserted that, according to the Nelson family, he was in the habit of saying 'kismet' (fate) when anything went wrong. It is therefore not too unlikely that he said, 'Kismet, Hardy' to his Flag Captain, and that witnesses misheard, but there is no real reason to choose this version.

In fact, the recording angel had to work overtime when Nelson lay dying, he said so much. The first reliable report of what went on was by Dr Beatty, the ship's surgeon, included in *Despatches and Letters of Lord Nelson* (ed. Nicholas, 1846):

> Captain Hardy now came to the cockpit to see his Lordship a second time. He then told Captain Hardy that he felt that in a few minutes he should be no more, adding in a low tone, 'Don't throw me overboard, Hardy.' The Captain

answered, 'Oh, no, certainly not.' Then replied his Lordship, 'You know what to do. Take care of my dear Lady Hamilton. Kiss me, Hardy.' The Captain now knelt and kissed his cheek, when his Lordship said, 'Now I am satisfied. Thank God I have done my duty.'

This seems to be quite a reasonable description and, if Hardy did actually kiss him (a gesture that surely couldn't be mistaken), why should Nelson not have asked him to? Was there something wrong with a naval hero asking for this gesture from another man? Robert Southey in his *Life of Nelson*, published earlier, in 1813, also supports the 'kiss me' version (his account is almost identical to Beatty's). In Ludovic Kennedy's *On My Way to the Club* (1989), he recalls his own investigations into the matter: 'I was delighted to receive further confirmation from a Mr Corbett, writing from Hardy's home town of Portesham [in 1951]. He said that Nelson's grandson by his daughter Horatia had recently paid him a visit, at the age of over ninety. "He told me he had asked his mother what exactly had happened when Nelson was dying. She said she herself had asked Hardy, who replied, 'Nelson said, "Kiss me, Hardy" and I knelt down and kissed him'".'

Nerval, Gérard de
French poet (1808–55)

3 Well, you see, he doesn't bark and he knows the secrets of the sea.

Explaining his penchant for taking a lobster for a walk in the gardens of the Palais Royal, Paris, on a long blue leash (or pink lead, in some versions). Théophile Gautier, *Portraits et Souvenirs Littéraires* (1875), has an elaborate version of the explanation, which translates as: 'Why should a lobster be any more ridiculous than a dog? Or any other animal that one chooses to take for a walk? I have a liking for lobsters; they are peaceful, serious creatures; they know the secrets of the sea; they don't bark, and they don't gnaw upon one's *monadic* privacy like dogs do. And Goethe had an aversion to dogs, and he wasn't mad.' An unanswerable conclusion, surely?

Nevins, Allan
American writer and teacher (1890–1971)

4 Too little, too late.

Nevins wrote in an article for *Current History* (May 1935): 'The former allies had blundered in the past by offering Germany too little and offering even that too late, until finally Nazi Germany had become a menace to all mankind.' That was where the phrase began. On 13 March 1940 the former Prime Minister David Lloyd George said in the House of Commons: 'It is the old trouble — too late. Too late with Czechoslovakia, too late with Poland, certainly too late with Finland. It is always too late, or too little, or both.' From there the phrase passed into more general use, though usually political. From the *Notting Hill & Paddington Recorder* (25 January 1989): 'Junior Transport Minister, Peter Bottomley, came to West London last week to unveil plans for a £250 million relief road that will cut a swathe through the heart of the area . . . But Hammersmith and Fulham councillors are furious about the government consultation exercise which they claim is "too little too late".'

From the *Guardian* (30 January 1989): 'The Home Office is preparing a video to warn prisoners of the dangers [of AIDs] — but is it too little, too late?'

Newbolt, Sir Henry
English poet (1862–1938)

1 *The Island Race.*

The characterization of Britain as an 'island race' understandably reached its apogee in the Second World War, but at big patriotic moments there has always been a tendency to draw attention to the fact of Britain being an island, from John of Gaunt's 'sceptr'd isle' in Shakespeare's *Richard II* onwards. Winston Churchill said, 'We shall defend our Island, whatever the cost may be' in his 'We shall fight on the beaches' speech of 4 June 1940. The flag-waving film *In Which We Serve* (1942) refers specifically to the 'island race'. Churchill used the phrase as the title of Bk 1, Vol. 1 of his *History of the English-Speaking Peoples* (1956). In his *History of the Second World War*, Vol. 5 (1952) he also quotes the 'island story' phrase from Tennyson's 'Ode on the Death of the Duke of Wellington' (1852):

Not once or twice in our rough island story
The path of duty was the way to glory.

The first prominent appearance of 'island race' appears, however, to have been as the title of a poem by Newbolt in 1898.

See also O'REILLY 258:3 *and* TENNYSON 326:6.

Newton, Sir Isaac
English scientist (1642–1727)

2 *O Diamond! Diamond! thou little knowest the mischief done!*

To his dog who is said to have knocked over a candle and set fire to Newton's papers, thus destroying the labour of many years. Probably apocryphal, though recounted by 1772. Another version renames the dog: 'Ah, poor Fidele, what mischief hast thou done!'

3 *If I have seen further it is by standing on the shoulders of giants.*

In a letter to Robert Hooke (5 February 1676). Hooke had claimed to have discovered first the gravitational law of inverse squares, and Newton was attempting to conciliate him. Long' before, in 1159, Bernard of Chartres, the French philosopher, had been quoted as saying, 'We are like dwarfs on the shoulders of giants, so that we can see more than they . . . not by virtue of any sharpness of sight on our part . . . but because we are carried high and raised up by their giant size.' The proverbial expression 'A dwarf on a giant's shoulders sees the further of the two' appears to have been established by the fourteenth century.

Newton, John
English hymnwriter (1725–1807)

4 *Amazing grace! how sweet the sound,*
  That saved a wretch like me!
I once was lost, but now am found,
  Was blind, but now I see.

Most people are familiar with 'Amazing Grace' from the great popular success it had when sung and recorded by Judy Collins in the early 1970s, but it is quite wrong for record companies to label the song 'Trad.' — as, for example, on the CD 'Amazing Grace' (Philips 432–546–2), by Jessye Norman. It was a hymn written in the seventeenth century by Newton, a reformed slave-trafficker. He (together with the poet William Cowper), wrote the Olney Hymnbook of 1779, and this is but one example from that work.

The slightly complicated thing is that the tune to which 'Amazing Grace' now gets sung is a traditional tune — it is an old American one — but that is hardly any excuse for denying Newton his credit for the words. (Some people say that before it was an anonymous American tune, however, it was an anonymous Scottish tune.)

New York Sun
(see *Sun, The*)

Nicholas, Saint
Christian prelate (*fl.* 350)

1 *God be glorified!*

One of the numerous legends associated with St Nicholas, patron saint of Greece and Russia, and popularly known as 'Santa Claus', concerns his birth. It is said that he leapt from his mother's womb and cried out, 'God be glorified!' In Benjamin Britten's cantata *St Nicholas* (1948), which has a libretto by Eric Crozier, he can be heard saying it.

Nicholson, Vivian
English football pools winner (1936–)

2 *I'm going to spend, spend, spend, that's what I'm going to do.*

Nicholson and her husband Keith, a trainee miner, were bringing up three children on a weekly wage of £7 in Castleford, Yorkshire. Then, in September 1961, they won £152,000 on Littlewoods football pools. Arriving in London by train to collect their prize (recounted in her autobiography *Spend, Spend, Spend*, 1977), she made this off-the-cuff remark to reporters. It made newspaper headlines and was used as the title of a TV play. The win was the prelude to misfortune. Keith died in a car crash and Viv worked her way through a succession of husbands until the money had all gone.

Niemöller, Martin
German Protestant pastor and theologian (1892–1984)

3 *When Hitler attacked the Jews . . . I was not a Jew, therefore, I was not concerned. And when Hitler attacked the Catholics, I was not a Catholic, and therefore, I was not concerned. And when Hitler attacked the unions and the industrialists, I was not a member of the unions and I was not concerned. Then, Hitler attacked me and the Protestant church — and there was nobody left to be concerned.*

Attributed to Niemöller by the *Congres-*

sional Record (14 October 1968), though it has not been documented. Niemöller did, however, speak out against Hitler until he was silenced in 1937. The following year he was put in Sachsenhausen Concentration Camp, and then sent to Dachau. He spent four years in solitary confinement before being liberated by the Allies in 1945. Sometimes a version is given which begins: 'In Germany they came first for the Communists, and I didn't speak up because I wasn't a Communist . . .'

Nixon, Richard M.
American Republican 37th President (1913–94)

4 *Would you buy a used car from this man?*

Although attributed by some to Mort Sahl and by others to Lenny Bruce, and though the cartoonist Herblock denied that he was responsible (*Guardian*, 24 December 1975), this is just a joke and one is no more going to find an origin for it than for most such. As to *when* it arose, this is Hugh Brogan, writing in *New Society* (4 November 1982): 'Nixon is a double-barrelled, treble-shotted twister, as my old history master would have remarked; and the fact has been a matter of universal knowledge since at least 1952, when, if I remember aright the joke, "Would you buy a second-hand car from this man?" began to circulate.' It was a very effective slur and, by 1968, when the politician was running (successfully) for President, a poster of a shifty-looking Nixon with the line as caption was in circulation.

One might use the phrase now about anybody one has doubts about. The *Encyclopedia of Graffiti* (1974) even finds: 'Governor Romney — would you buy a *new* car from this man?' In August 1984, John de Lorean said of himself — after being acquitted of drug-dealing — 'I have aged 600 years and my life as a hard-working industrialist is in tatters. Would you buy a used car from me?'

5 *Regardless of what they say about it, we are going to keep it . . . I don't believe I ought to quit because I am not a quitter.*

From a TV address (23 September 1952). Nixon was defending himself, when running as a Vice-Presidential candidate, against charges that he had been operating a secret fund. He denied that any of the money had been put to his personal use: every penny had gone on campaign expenses. Then he proceeded to throw dust in the eyes of viewers by mentioning a dog called 'Checkers' that had been given to his daughters. Was that a politically acceptable gift? He rejected any idea of disappointing his daughters by returning it. Never mind that the problem was not the dog but the 'secret fund', the so-called 'Checkers' speech saved the day for Nixon.

1 *Just think about how much you're going to be missing. You won't have Nixon to kick around any more, because, gentlemen, this is my last press conference.*

To the press, on losing the California gubernatorial election (7 November 1962), following his two terms as Eisenhower's Vice-President. Nixon was reluctant to appear and concede defeat before newsmen, feeling that they had given him a tough time during the campaign. But he did, and bade them what turned out to be a temporary farewell. President Kennedy's comment was that Nixon must have been 'mentally unsound' to make this statement: 'Nobody could talk like that and be normal.' In 1982 John Ehrlichman attributed the Nixon performance to a 'terrible hangover'.

2 *I see another child tonight. He hears a train go by. At night he dreams of faraway places where he'd like to go. It seems like an impossible dream.*

In his speech accepting the Republican Presidential nomination at Miami on 8 August 1968, Nixon suddenly switched to the third person. He told of a boy growing up with limited prospects in a small town in southern California. The climax came when Nixon let the audience know that he was that small boy whose 'impossible dream' had become a reality. William Safire, then a Nixon speechwriter, recalled how proud his boss was of that ending, and what Nixon had had to say about it: 'I'd like to see [Rockefeller] or Romney or Lindsay do a moving thing like that "impossible dream" part, where I changed my voice. Reagan's an actor, but I'd like to see him do it' (quoted in the *Washington Post*, 6 May 1984).

The phrase was taken from a song, 'The Impossible Dream', in the 1965 musical *Man of La Mancha* about Don Quixote (lyrics by Joe Darion, music by Mitch Leigh, based on Dale Wasserman's play):

To dream the impossible dream,
To fight the unbeatable foe,
To bear with unbearable sorrow,
To run where the brave dare not go.

3 *This is the greatest week in the history of the world since the Creation.*

On the USS *Hornet* welcoming the Apollo XI astronauts home from the first moon landing on 24 July 1969, Nixon greeted them with these words. Dr Billy Graham, the evangelist, told him shortly afterwards: 'Mr President, I know exactly how you felt, and I understand exactly what you meant, but, even so, I think you may have been a little excessive.'

4 *The great silent majority of my fellow Americans.*

Still trying to extricate the US from Vietnam, Nixon gave a TV address on 3 November 1969 designed to show it would be wrong to end the war on less than honourable terms or to be swayed by anti-war demonstrations. He himself wrote some paragraphs calling for the support of a particular section of American opinion. The notion of a large unheard body of opinion — sometimes called the 'silent centre' or 'Middle America' — was not new but Nixon's appeal ushered in a period of persecution of the 'vocal minority'.

Ironically, the phrases 'silent majority' and 'great majority' were used in the nineteenth century to describe *the dead*. *Harper's New Monthly* Magazine had 'The silent majority' as a heading in September 1874. The dying words of Lord Houghton in 1884 were: 'Yes, I am going to join the Majority and you know I have always preferred Minorities.' Compare BROWNE 71:4.

5 *I feel it could be cut off at the pass.*

One of the milder sayings to have emerged from the transcripts of the Watergate tapes (published as *The White House Transcripts*, 1974) was 'to cut something/someone off at the pass'. This was a recycled phrase from Western films where the cry would be uttered, meaning 'to intercept, ambush' (sometimes in the form 'head 'em off at the pass'). As said by President Nixon it meant simply 'we will use certain tactics to stop them'. The phrase occurred in a crucial exchange in the White House Oval Office on 21 March 1973 between the President and his Special Counsel, John Dean:

RN: You are a lawyer, you were a counsel . . . What would you go to jail for?

JD: The obstruction of justice.

RN: The obstruction of justice?

JD: That is the only one that bothers me.

RN: Well, I don't know. I think that one . . . I feel it could be cut off at the pass, maybe, the obstruction of justice.

1 *I don't give a shit what happens. I want you all to stonewall it, let them plead the Fifth Amendment, cover-up or anything else, if it'll save it, save the plan.*

On the Watergate cover-up this conversation (22 March 1973) was revealed in one of the transcripts of recordings Nixon himself had ordered to be made of his day-to-day conversations. These enabled the world to know that the holder of the highest office, a head of state, could talk like a sleazy racketeer.

2 *This country needs good farmers, good businessmen, good plumbers, good carpenters . . .*

Even in his rambling, maudlin farewell address to White House staff on 9 August 1974, Nixon seemed unable to resist an inept reference to 'plumbers', a code word for those who had broken into the Watergate building to 'plug leaks' and had started off the whole tawdry affair. Presumably, Nixon did not realize what he was saying.

North, Christopher
(Professor John Wilson)
Scottish literary critic (1785–1854)

3 *The empire upon which the sun never sets.*

The phrase refers to the British Empire, which was so widespread at its apogee that the sun was always up on some part of it. North wrote in *Noctes Ambrosianae* (April 1829) of: 'His Majesty's dominions, on which the sun never sets.' Earlier, the idea had been widely applied to the Spanish Empire. In 1641 the English explorer and writer Captain John Smith (of Pocahontas fame) asked in *Advertisements for the Unexperienced* . . .: 'Why should the brave Spanish soldier brag the sun never sets in the Spanish dominions, but ever shineth on one part or other we have conquered for our king?'

See also ANONYMOUS SAYINGS 15:5.

Northcliffe, 1st Viscount
British newspaper proprietor (1865–1922)

4 *News is what someone, somewhere doesn't want published . . . all the rest is advertising.*

Unquestionably Northcliffe's view, but unverified. Compare the comment of journalist Hannen Swaffer (1879–1962) in conversation with Tom Driberg (c 1928): 'Freedom of the press in Britain is freedom to print such of the proprietor's prejudices as the advertisers don't object to' (recalled in Driberg's *Swaff*, 1974. Driberg suspected that Swaffer began to take this view in c 1902).

Novello, Ivor
Welsh-born composer and actor (1893–1951)

5 *Blaze of lights and music calling,*
Music weeping,
rising, falling, Like a rare & precious diamond
His brilliance still lives on.

Lines on Novello's memorial tablet in the crypt of St Paul's Cathedral, London, were written by Lynn S. Maury of the Ivor Novello Memorial Society, which mounted an eight-year campaign to have a plaque placed in the cathedral. Her monogram is attached to the words.

See also BURROUGHS 76:5.

O

Oates, Captain Lawrence Edward 'Titus'
English explorer (1880–1912)

1 *I am just going outside, and I may be some time.*

Oates walked to his death on Captain R.F. Scott's 1912 polar expedition. Beaten to the South Pole by the Norwegian explorer Roald Amundsen, the small party fell victim to terrible weather conditions on the return journey to its ship. One man died, and Oates, suffering from scurvy, from an old war wound and from frostbitten and gangrenous feet, realized that he would be next. He presumably thought that without him slowing them down, the remaining three members of the party might stand a better chance of survival. He did not bother to spend the couple of hours' painful effort needed to put on his boots. He made his classic stiff-upper-lip understatement, went out in his stockinged feet and did not return.

It was inevitable in time that iconoclasts would review the evidence and wonder, in the light of Oates's expressed criticisms of Scott, whether his action was truly voluntary or whether it was the result of silent hints from the expedition leader. As the only record of what Oates said was contained in Scott's diary (published as *Scott's Last Expedition*, 1923), it has been suggested that the words were Scott's invention. But opinion suggests that it was an act perfectly in character and there would have been no need for any invention.

Not only did Oates define courage for a generation, he unwittingly provided a joke expression or catchphrase to be used when a person is departing from company for whatever reason. When Trevor Griffiths came to write a TV drama series about Scott's expedition called *The Last Place on Earth* (1985), he accordingly substituted the line: 'Call of nature, Birdie.'

2 *Hereabouts died a very gallant gentleman.*

Scott wrote in his diary: 'We knew that poor Oates was walking to his death, but though we tried to dissuade him, we knew it was the act of a brave man and an English gentleman.' Oates's actual epitaph, composed later by E.L. Atkinson and Apsley Cherry-Garrard (and recorded in the latter's *The Worst Journey in the World*, 1922) took up this theme and was placed on a cairn marking the spot from where he walked. The epitaph continues: 'Captain L.E.G. Oates of the Inniskilling Dragoons. In March 1912, returning from the Pole, he walked willingly to his death in a blizzard, to try and save his comrades, beset by hardship. This note is left by the Relief Expedition. 1912.'

Ochs, Adolph S.
American newspaper proprietor (1858–1935)

3 *All the news that's fit to print.*

This slogan was devised by Ochs when he bought the *New York Times*, and it has been used in every edition since — at first on the editorial page, on 25 October 1896, and from the following February on the front page near the masthead. It became the paper's war-cry in the battle against formidable competition from the *World*, the *Herald* and the *Journal*. It has been parodied by Howard Dietz as 'All the news *that fits* we print' — which, at worst, sounds like a slogan for the suppression of news. However, no newspaper prints everything.

O'Connor, Edwin
American novelist (1918–68)

1 *The Last Hurrah.*

The title of a novel (1956; film US, 1958) about an ageing Boston-Irish politician making his last electoral foray. Hence the expression 'last hurrah' for a politician's farewell.

O'Keeffe, Patrick
American advertising practitioner (1872–1934)

2 *Say it with flowers.*

This slogan was originally devised for the Society of American Florists and invented in 1917 for its chairman, Henry Penn of Boston, Massachusetts. Major Patrick O'Keefe, head of an advertising agency, suggested: 'Flowers are words that even a babe can understand' — a line he had found in a poetry book. Penn considered that too long. O'Keefe, agreeing, rejoined: 'Why, you can say it with flowers in so many words.' Later came several songs with the title.

O'Reilly, P.J.
British lyricist (*fl.* 1910)

3 *Drake is going west, lads.*

Not to be confused with 'Drake he's in his hammock' or any other line from Sir Henry Newbolt's poem 'Drake's Drum' (1897). This comes from the song 'Drake Goes West', written by O'Reilly to music by Wilfrid Sanderson in 1910. In Noël Coward's song 'There Are Bad Times Just Around the Corner' (1950s) occur the lines: 'In Dublin they're depressed, lads,/Maybe because they're Celts/For Drake is going West, lads,/And so is everyone else.'

Orwell, George
(Eric Blair)
English novelist and journalist (1903–50)

4 *All animals are equal, but some are more equal than others.*

A fictional slogan from George Orwell's novel *Animal Farm* (1945), which was a commentary on the totalitarian excesses of Communism. It had been anticipated: Hesketh Pearson recalled in his biography of the actor/manager Sir Herbert Beerbohm

Tree (1956) that Tree wished to insert one of his own epigrams in a play called *Nero* by Stephen Phillips (1906). It was: 'All men are equal — except myself.' In Noël Coward's *This Year of Grace* (1928) there is the exchange: Pellet: 'Men are all alike' Wendle: 'Only some more than others'.

The saying alludes, of course, to Thomas Jefferson's 'All men are created equal and independent', from the Preamble to the American Declaration of Independence (1776). It has the makings of a formula phrase in that it is more likely to be used to refer to humans than to animals. Only the second half of the phrase need actually be spoken, the first half being understood: 'You-Know-Who [Mrs Thatcher] is against the idea [televising parliament]. There aren't card votes at Westminster, but some votes are more equal than others' (*Guardian*, 15 February 1989).

5 *Big Brother is watching you.*

Another fictional slogan comes from Orwell's novel *Nineteen Eighty-Four* (1948). In a dictatorial state, every citizen is regimented and observed by a spying TV set in the home. The line became a popular catchphrase following the sensational BBC TV dramatization of the novel (1954). Aspects of the Ministry of Truth in the novel were derived not only from Orwell's knowledge of the BBC (where he worked) but also from his first wife Eileen's work at the Ministry of Food, preparing 'Kitchen Front' broadcasts during the Second World War (*c* 1942–4). One campaign used the slogan 'Potatoes are Good for You' and was so successful that it had to be followed by 'Potatoes are Fattening'.

6 *There's a thin man inside every fat man.*

See CONNOLLY 105:5.

Osborne, Charles
Australian-born writer and arts administrator (1927–)

7 *If a third of all the novelists and maybe two-thirds of all the poets now writing dropped dead suddenly the loss to literature would not be great.*

Osborne was thus quoted in the *Observer* (3 November 1985) from remarks he had made at a (British) Arts Council press conference. It was only later — as he confirmed to me in 1991 — that Osborne became aware that

Rebecca West had uttered a similar sentiment at the 1962 Edinburgh Festival Writers' Conference: 'It would be no loss to the world if most of the writers now writing had been strangled at birth' (a remark recorded, for example, in Stephen Spender, *Journals 1939–83*, 1985).

O'Shaughnessy, Arthur
English poet (1844–81)

1 *We are the music makers,*
We are the dreamers of dreams . . .
We are the movers and shakers
Of the world for ever, it seems.

From his 'Ode' (1874), set to music by Edward Elgar as *The Music Makers* (1912). Hence, the modern expression 'movers and shakers' to describe people of power and influence. From J.F. Burke's novel, *Death Trick* (1975): 'Beniamino Tucci was known as the Little Godfather of the Upper West Side. A mover and shaker with many interests.' From *The Economist* (7 November 1987): 'Many of the advertised movers and shakers [in President Reagan's administration] soon resign in disgust, or bolt back to the private sector once their Washington experience can be cashed in.'

Owen, David
(later Lord Owen)
English Labour then Social Democrat politician (1938–)

2 *We are fed up with fudging and mudging, with mush and slush.*

'To fudge and mudge', meaning 'to produce the appearance of a solution while, in fact, only patching up a compromise', was a verb that often arose in discussions of the Social Democratic Party and the Liberal Party in Britain during the 1980s. Owen, one of the SDP's founders, had used it earlier in his previous incarnation, as a member of the Labour Party. He said the above to Labour's Blackpool Conference (2 October 1980).

P

Paine, Tom

English-born American revolutionary and
political theorist (1737–1809)

1 *We have it in our power to begin the
world over again.*

From *Common Sense*, originally published
in 1776. The words were quoted by Ronald
Reagan, first at the end of his 'Evil empire'
speech (at Orlando, Florida, 8 March
1983), then in a televised Presidential campaign debate with his challenger, Walter
Mondale (7 October 1984).

Possibly they were also alluded to in
Reagan's 'Farewell Address to the Nation'
(11 January 1989): 'Once you begin a great
movement, there's no telling where it will
end. We meant to change a nation, and
instead, we changed a world.'

Paine's words were also quoted by
Margaret Thatcher on a visit to the White
House in November 1988. An odd choice of
quotation, when Paine had done his best to
end any possibility of a 'special relationship'
between Britain and America. The passage
continues: 'Independence is the only bond
that can tie and keep us [Americans]
together . . . Let the names of Whig and
Tory be extinct.'

Pankhurst, Emmeline and Christabel

English suffragette leaders (mother
and daughter) (1858–1928) and
(1880–1958)

2 *Votes for Women.*

Both Pankhursts, founders of the Women's
Social and Political Union, have described
how this battle-cry emerged. This is a syn-
thesis of their recollections. In October 1905

a large meeting at the Free Trade Hall, Manchester, was to be addressed by Sir Edward
Grey, who was likely to attain ministerial
office if the Liberals won the forthcoming
general election. The WSPU was thus keen
to challenge him in public on his party's
attitude to women's suffrage in Britain: 'The
question was painted on a banner in large
letters . . . How should we word it? "Will
you give women suffrage?" – we rejected
that form, for the word "suffrage" suggested
to some unlettered or jesting folk the idea of
suffering. "Let them suffer away!" – we
had heard the taunt. We must find another
wording and we did!

'It was so obvious and yet, strange to say,
quite new. Our banners bore this terse
device: "WILL YOU GIVE VOTES FOR
WOMEN?" ' The plan had been to let down
a banner from the gallery as soon as Grey
stood up to speak. Unfortunately, the
WSPU had failed to obtain the requisite
number of tickets. It had to abandon the
large banner and cut out the three words
which would fit on a small placard. 'Thus
quite accidentally came into existence the
slogan of the suffrage movement around the
world.'

Alas, Sir Edward Grey did not answer the
question and it took rather more than this
slogan – hunger-strikes, suicide, the First
World War – before women got the vote in
Britain in 1918. In the US, the Nineteenth
Amendment, extending female franchise on
a national scale, was ratified in time for the
1920 elections.

Other uses to which the slogan was put:
a newspaper with the title *Votes for Women*
was launched in October 1907. At a meeting
in the Royal Albert Hall, someone boomed
'Votes for Women' down an organ pipe. The
International Labour Party used to refer to
it as 'Votes for Ladies'. In due course, some
feminists were to campaign with the slogan
'Orgasms for women'.

Parker, Dorothy
American writer (1893–1967)

1 *Pearls before swine.*

When Clare Booth Luce, going through a swing-door with Parker used the customary phrase 'Age before beauty', Parker, ushering her ahead, said, 'Pearls before swine'. Mrs Luce described this account as completely apocryphal in answer to a question from John Keats, Parker's biographer, as reported in his *You Might as Well Live* (1970).

2 *How can they tell?*

In 1933, when told that President Calvin Coolidge had died, Parker produced this, one of her two or three most quoted remarks. It is given, however, as 'How do they know?' in Malcolm Cowley, *Writers at Work*, Series 1 (1958). In that form it is also attributed to Wilson Mizner (Alva Johnston, *The Legendary Mizners*, 1953). The lack of contemporary sources and its omission, for example, from the Keats biography (as above) makes one wonder if the remark has drifted to Parker from Mizner.

See also TYNAN 338:4.

Parkinson, C. Northcote
British author and historian (1909–93)

3 *It is a commonplace observation that work expands so as to fill the time available for its completion.*

First promulgated in *The Economist* (19 November 1955), what later became known as 'Parkinson's Law' was concerned with the pyramidal structure of bureacratic organizations. A pre-echo may be found in the eighteenth-century Lord Chesterfield's letters: 'The less one has to do, the less time one finds to do it in.'

Pascal, Blaise
French philosopher and mathematician (1623–62)

4 *All the troubles of men are caused by one single thing, which is their inability to stay quietly in a room.*

From the French, '*Tous le malheur des hommes vient d'une seule chose qui est de ne savoir pas demeurer en repos dans une chambre*' (*Pensées*, 1670). I once saw the last word translated as 'bedroom', which put a rather different complexion on the idea.

Paterson, 'Banjo'
Australian poet (1864–1941)

5 *Waltzing Matilda.*

Paterson's song (written in 1894 but not published until 1903) has the status of an unofficial Australian national anthem. The title 'Waltzing Matilda' comes from the Australian phrase for carrying your 'Matilda' or back-pack as a tramp does. The *Macquarie Dictionary* (1981) suggests a derivation from the German *walzen*, to move in a circular fashion 'as of apprentices travelling from master to master', and German *Mathilde*, a female travelling companion or bed-roll (from the girl's name). Hence the first verse goes:

Oh! there once was a swagman
     camped in a Billabong
Under the shade of a Coolabah tree;
And he sang as he looked at his old
     billy boiling,
'Who'll come a-waltzing Matilda with
     me?'

[Swagman = itinerant labourer carrying his swag, or bundle; Billabong = dead water, backwater; billy = cooking-pot].
Australians can get quite abusive when discussing the meaning of this song. The above lines are as shown in *The Dictionary of Australian Quotations* (ed. Murray-Smith, 1984). Note, however, this different transcription in *ODQ* (1992):

Once a jolly swagman camped by a
     bill-abong,
Under the shade of a coolibah tree;
And he sang as he watched and waited
     till his 'Billy' boiled:
'You'll come a-waltzing, Matilda, with
     me.'

Paul, Leslie
Irish social philosopher (1905–85)

6 *Angry Young Man.*

Any writer from the mid-1950s who showed a social awareness and expressed dissatisfaction with conventional values and with the Establishment — John Osborne, Kingsley Amis and Colin Wilson among them — was likely to be labelled with this phrase. Paul had called his autobiography *Angry Young*

Man in 1951, but the popular use of the phrase stems from *Look Back in Anger*, the 1956 play by John Osborne, which featured an anti-hero called Jimmy Porter. Other earlier uses of phrases like it, though not necessarily with precisely this sense, include, by H.G. Wells, *Brynhild* (1937): 'I am Angry Man . . . almost professionally'; by Rebecca West in *Black Lamb and Grey Falcon* (1941): 'The angry young men run about shouting'; by J.B. Priestley, *Magicians* (1954): 'He's the contemporary Angry Little Man.'

The phrase did not occur in Osborne's play but was applied to the playwright by George Fearon in publicity material from the Royal Court Theatre, London. Fearon later told the *Daily Telegraph* (2 October 1957): 'I ventured to prophesy that this generation would praise his play while mine would, in general, dislike it . . . "if this happens," I told [Osborne], "you would become known as the Angry Young Man". In fact, we decided then and there that henceforth he was to be known as that.'

In Osborne's *Almost a Gentleman* (1991), he pours the inevitable scorn on Fearon, and quotes him as saying, 'I suppose you're really — an angry young man . . . aren't you?', and comments: 'He was the first one to say it. A boon to headline-writers ever after.'

Peniakoff, Vladimir
Belgian-born soldier and writer (1897–1951)

1 *Spread alarm and despondency.*

Meaning, 'have a de-stabilizing effect, purposely or not'. During the Second World War, Lieutenant-Colonel Peniakoff ran a small raiding and reconnaissance force on the British side which became known as 'Popski's Private Army'. In his book *Private Army* (1950), he wrote: 'A message came on the wireless for me. It said "Spread alarm and despondency" . . . The date was, I think, May 18th, 1942'. When a German invasion was thought to be imminent at the beginning of July 1940, Winston Churchill had issued an 'admonition' to 'His Majesty's servants in high places . . . to report, or if necessary remove, any officers or officials who are found to be consciously exercising a disturbing or depressing influence, and whose talk is calculated to spread alarm and despondency'. Prosecutions for doing this did indeed follow. The phrase goes back to the Army Act of 1879: 'Every person subject to military law who . . . spreads reports calculated to create unnecessary alarm or despondency . . . shall . . . be liable to suffer penal servitude.'

Pepys, Samuel
English civil servant and diarist (1633–1703)

2 *And so to bed.*

Pepys's famous signing-off line for his diary entries occurs first on 15 January 1660. However, on that occasion, these are not quite his last words. He writes: 'I went to supper, and after that to make an end of this week's notes in this book, and so to bed'. Then he adds: 'It being a cold day and a great snow, my physic did not work so well as it should have done.' Usually, the phrase is the last thing he writes, though sometimes he just puts, 'So to bed.' The fame of the phrase 'And so to bed' is in part due to its use as the title of a play by J.B. Fagan (1926), which was turned into a musical by Vivian Ellis (1951).

Both Mencken (1942) and Bartlett (1980) give the date of its first appearance as 22 July 1660 (when the phrase in fact is just 'So to bed'); the *ODQ* (1992) also has, misleadingly, 20 April 1660. The reason for this confusion is that these books *may* have been dealing with incomplete or inaccurate transcriptions of Pepys's shorthand that were superseded by the Latham/Matthews edition of 1970–83.

Indeed, the first time I read the diaries — in an old Dent's Everyman's Library edition (1906, revised 1953) — I was more than a little surprised that the full phrase 'And so to bed' was *nowhere* to be found. It couldn't have been excised on the grounds of taste, could it?

Percival, Horace
English actor (*d* 1961)

3 *Don't forget the diver!*

This — of all the many catchphrases sired by BBC radio's *ITMA* show — is the one with the most interesting origin. It was spoken by Percival as 'the Diver' and was derived from memories that the star of the show, Tommy Handley, had of an actual one-legged man who used to dive off the pier at New Brighton, Merseyside, in the 1920s. 'Don't forget the diver, sir, don't forget the diver,' the man would say, collecting money. 'Every penny makes the water warmer, sir.' The radio character first appeared in 1940 and no lift/elevator descended for the next few years without somebody using the Diver's main catch-phrase or his other one, 'I'm going down now, sir!'

But who was the original diver? James Gashram wrote to *The Listener* (21 August 1980):

My grandfather McMaster, who came from a farm near the small village of Rathmullen, in Co. Donegal, knew Michael Shaughnessy, the one-legged ex-soldier, in the late 1890s, before he left for the Boer War and the fighting that cost him his leg. About 1910, Shaugh-nessy, then married to a Chester girl, settled in Bebington on the Wirral penin-sula . . . Before the internal combustion engine, [he] used to get a lift every week-day from Bebington to New Brighton in a horse-drawn bread-cart owned by the Bromborough firm of Bernard Hughes. The driver of that cart, apparently, was always envious of the 'easy' money Shaughnessy got at New Brighton — sometimes up to two pounds a day in the summer — and would invariably say to him on the return to Bebington, 'Don't forget the *driver*'. Shaughnessy rarely did forget. It was many years later, some time in the early 1930s, that, remember-ing the phrase so well, he adapted it to his own purposes by changing it to 'Don't forget the diver', and shouted it to the people arriving from Liverpool.

As for 'I'm going down now, sir', bomber pilots in the Second World War are said to have used this phrase when about to make a descent. From *ITMA*'s VE-Day edition:

Effects: Knocking
Handley: Who's that knocking on the tank?
The Diver: Don't forget the diver, sir — don't forget the diver.
Handley: Lumme, it's Deepend Dan. Listen, as the war's over, what are you doing?
The Diver: I'm going down now, sir.
Effects: Bubbles.

Perelman, S.J.
American humorist (1904–79)

1 *I've got Bright's Disease. And he's got mine.*

Caption to a cartoon in *Judge* (16 November 1929). This disease of the kidneys was first described in 1827 by Dr Richard Bright, who is not to be blamed for the intrinsic humour in naming diseases after specific people. Hence, I have heard 'Parkinson's Disease' interpreted as an affliction from which Michael Parkinson, the one-time British TV chat-show host, was said to suf-fer. Its chief sympton was supposedly a tendency to do less and less work the more one was paid — a quite unjustified slur in his case.

2 *'Oh, son, I wish you hadn't become a scenario writer!' she sniffed.*
'Aw, now, Moms,' I comforted her, 'it's no worse than playing the piano in a call house.'

From Perelman's piece entitled 'Strictly from Hunger' which later became the title of his second book (1937). A common enough comparison at the time. Flexner (1976) has as a saying from the Depression: 'Don't tell my mother I'm in politics — she thinks I play the piano in a whorehouse.'

Perkins, Frances
American politician (1882–1965)

3 *Call me madam.*

The phrase that became the title of Irving Berlin's musical, first performed on Broad-way in 1950, starring Ethel Merman as a woman ambassador appointed to represent the US in a tiny European state. It was inspired by the case of Pearl Mesta, the society hostess, whom President Truman had appointed as ambassador to Luxem-bourg, and the title arose from a kind of mis-quotation. When Perkins was appointed Secretary of Labor by President Roosevelt in 1933, she became the first US woman to hold Cabinet rank. It was said that when she had been asked *in Cabinet* how she wished to be addressed, she had replied: 'Call me Madam.' She denied that she had done this, however. It was *after* her first Cabinet meeting that reporters asked how they should address her. The Speaker-elect of the House of Representatives, Henry T. Rainey, answered for her: 'When the Secretary of Labor is a lady, she should be addressed with the same general formalities as the Secretary of Labor who is a gentleman. You call him "Mr Secretary". You will call her "Madam Secretary". You gentlemen know that when a lady is presiding over a meeting, she is referred to as "Madam Chairman" when you rise to address the chair' (quoted in George Martin, *Madam Secretary – Frances Perkins*, 1976). Some of the reporters put this ruling into Perkins's own mouth and that presumably is how the misquotation occurred.

Pertwee, Boscoe
English poet and wit (*fl.* seventeenth century, if at all)

1 *I used to be indecisive, but now I'm not so sure.*

M.M. Harvey of Andover sent this quotation to BBC Radio *Quote . . . Unquote* in 1977, but it has proved impossible to verify either the source or the existence of its author. Compare, however, from Christopher Hampton's play, *The Philanthropist* (1970): '*Philip (bewildered):* I'm sorry. (*Pause.*) I suppose I am indecisive. (*Pause.*) My trouble is, I'm a man of no convictions. (*Longish pause.*) At least, I think I am.'

Pétain, Henri Philippe
French Marshal and politician (1856–1951)

2 *They shall not pass.*

The phrase '*Ils ne passeront pass*' was popularly supposed to have been coined by Pétain, the man who defended Verdun with great tenacity in 1916. He is said to have uttered it on 26 February that year. However, the first official record of the expression appears in the Order of the Day for 23 June 1916 from General Robert Nivelle (1856–1924) to his troops at the height of the battle. His words were '*Vous ne laisserez pas passer*' [You will not let them pass]. Alternatively, Nivelle is supposed to have said these words to General Castelnau on 23 January 1916. To add further to the mystery, the inscription on the Verdun medal was '*On ne passe pas*'. One suspects that the slogan was coined by Nivelle and used a number of times by him but came to be associated with Pétain, the more famous 'Hero of Verdun'.

The slogan saw further service. Later, as '*No pasarán*, it was used on the Republican side during the Spanish Civil War.

Philip, Prince
(Duke of Edinburgh)
Greek-born Consort of Queen Elizabeth II (1921–)

3 *Just at the moment we are suffering a national defeat comparable to any lost military campaign and, what is more, it is self-inflicted . . . I think it is time we pulled our finger out.*

This kind of remark (made to businessmen on 17 October 1961) helped give the Queen's husband a reputation for plain speaking, which contrasted with the customary anodyne statements put into royal mouths by cautious courtiers.

4 *I never see any home cooking – all I get is fancy stuff.*

When this 1962 remark appeared in the *PDMQ* (1971) it had to be corrected, at the Prince's request, lest it reflect badly on the Buckingham Palace chefs. He said he had been referring to meals consumed away from the Palace.

5 *The* Daily Express *is a bloody awful newspaper.*

Said at a 1962 press reception in Rio de Janeiro, this view was later qualified in answer to a question from Willie Hamilton (in the MP's book, *My Queen and I*, 1975): 'I was having a private conversation with a journalist who claimed that the *Daily Express* was a splendid newspaper. My reply was spontaneous and never intended for publication . . . I can say that the reasons [for my remark] no longer exist.'

Pitkin, William
American teacher (1878–1953)

6 *Life begins at forty.*

In 1932 Pitkin, who was Professor of Journalism at Columbia University, published a book called *Life Begins at Forty* in which he dealt with 'adult reorientation' at a time when the problems of extended life and leisure were beginning to be recognized. Based on lectures Pitkin had given, the book was a hearty bit of uplift: 'Every day brings forth some new thing that adds to the joy of life after forty. Work becomes easy and brief. Play grows richer and longer. Leisure lengthens. Life's afternoon is brighter, warmer, fuller of song; and long before shadows stretch, every fruit grows ripe . . . Life begins at forty. This is the revolutionary outcome of our new era . . . TODAY it is half a truth. TOMORROW it will be an axiom.' It rapidly became a well-established catchphrase. Helping it along was a song with the title by Jack Yellen and Ted Shapiro (recorded by Sophie Tucker in 1937).

Pitt, William
British Prime Minister (1759–1806)

1 *Yes, I know I am young and inexperienced but it is a fault I am remedying every day.*

In a 1987 election broadcast, James Callaghan quoted this response in support of Neil Kinnock, the then leader of the British Labour Party. It remains untraced, though 'Pitt the Younger', becoming Britain's youngest Prime Minister at the age of twenty-four undoubtedly did have to justify himself. Another version is that when King George III commented on his extraordinary youth, Pitt replied: 'Time, Your Majesty, will take care of that.' His father, the Earl of Chatham ('Pitt the Elder') had similarly had to justify his own youth (though he was not to become Prime Minister until in his late forties). In a House of Commons speech (6 March 1741) he replied to Sir Robert Walpole: 'The atrocious crime of being a young man, which the honourable gentleman has, with such spirit and decency, charged upon me, I shall neither attempt to palliate nor deny; but content myself with wishing that I may be one of those whose follies cease with their youth, and not of those who continue ignorant in spite of age and experience.'

2 *Oh, my country! how I leave my country!*

Pitt's last recorded words refer to the breaking up of the English coalition in the wake of the defeat of Austro-Russian forces by Napoleon at the Battle of Austerlitz in 1805. Often given as ' . . . how I love my country!' In the 1862 edition of Stanhope's life of Pitt it is 'love'; in the 1879 edition, 'leave'. Alternatively, popular tradition has it that his actual last spoken words may have been 'I think I could eat one of Bellamy's veal pies'.

Pompadour, Madame de
Mistress of Louis XV of France (1721–64)

3 *Après nous le déluge [After us, the flood].*

The Marquise de Pompadour's celebrated remark to Louis XV was made on 5 November 1757 after Frederick the Great had defeated the French and Austrian armies at the Battle of Rossbach. It carries with it the suggestion that nothing matters once you are dead and has also been interpreted as a premonition of the French Revolution. Bartlett notes that this 'reputed reply' by the King's mistress was recorded by three authorities, though a fourth gives it to the King himself. Bartlett then claims the saying was not original anyway but was 'an old French proverb'. However, the ODP has as an English proverb, 'After us the deluge', deriving from Mme de Pompadour. Its only citation is Burnaby's 1876 *Ride to Khiva*: 'Our rulers did not trouble their heads much about the matter. "India will last my time . . . and after me the Deluge".' Metternich, the Austrian diplomat and chancellor, may later have said '*après moi le déluge*', meaning that everything would grind to a halt when he stopped controlling it. The deluge alluded to in both cases may be a dire event like the Great Flood or 'universal deluge' of Noah's time.

Ponte, Lorenzo da
Italian librettist (1749–1838)

4 Così fan tutte.

The title of Mozart's opera (1790) means 'that's what all women do' (*or* 'women are like that'). The phrase had appeared earlier in Da Ponte's text for *Le nozze di Figaro* (1778). In that opera, Don Basilio sings, '*Così fan tutte le belle, non c'è alcuna novità* [That's what all beautiful women do, there's nothing new in that]'.

Pope, Alexander
English poet (1688–1744)

5 *Leather and prunella.*

An expression meaning something to which the speaker is entirely indifferent. In George Eliot's *Middlemarch*, Chap. 43 (1871–2), Lydgate says, 'Ladislaw is a sort of gypsy; he thinks nothing of leather and prunella', suggesting that he cares nothing for social rank. The phrase is a misinterpreation of lines in Pope's *An Essay on Man* (1733):

> Worth makes the man, and want of it, the fellow:
> The rest is all but leather or prunella

in which Pope distinguishes between a cobbler (hence, the leather) and a parson (prunella is the material from which clerical gowns were made).

1 *Who breaks a butterfly upon a wheel?*

Meaning 'who goes to great lengths to accomplish something trifling?', the expression comes from Pope's 'Epistle to Dr Arbuthnot' (1735). As 'Who Breaks a Butterfly on a Wheel', it was famously used as the headline to a leading article in *The Times* (1 July 1967) when Mick Jagger, the pop singer, was given a three-month gaol term on drugs charges.

2 *Hard as thy heart and as thy birth obscure.*

Also in the 'Epistle to Dr Arbuthnot' occur Pope's self-justificatory lines:

> Let the two Curls of Town and Court, abuse
> His father, mother, body, soul, and muse.
> Yet why? that Father held it for a rule,
> It was a sin to call our neighbour fool.

In a series of pamphlets Edmund Curll had depicted Pope's father as being, variously, a lowly 'Mechanic, a Hatter, a Farmer, nay a Bankrupt'. Further, 'the following line, "Hard as thy Heart, and as thy Birth obscure" had fallen from a . . . Courtly pen, in certain *Verses to the Imitator of Horace*'. Pope's eighteenth-century editors went to some trouble in footnotes to show that, on the contrary, Pope's father was 'of a Gentleman's family in Oxfordshire' and not to be sneered at. The 'Courtly pen' was probably that of Lord Hervey (1696–1743), though he may have been joined in the attack by Lady Mary Wortley Montagu who by this time had fallen out with Pope.

3 *The moving toyshop.*

Edmund Crispin's detective thriller with this title (1946) begins with the apparent disappearance of a toyshop in Oxford. It refers to Pope's comment on women in *The Rape of the Lock* (1714):

> With varying vanities, from ev'ry part,
> They shift the moving toyshop of the heart.

Porter, Cole
American composer and lyricist
(1891–1964)

4 *And when they ask us, how dangerous it was,*
Oh, we'll never tell them, no, we'll never tell them:
We spent our pay in some café
And fought wild women night and day,
'Twas the cushiest job we ever had.
And when they ask us, and they're certainly going to ask us,
The reason why we didn't win the Croix de Guerre,
Oh, we'll never tell them, oh, we'll never tell them
There was a front, but damned if we knew where.

These words became famous during the First World War and were brought to a new audience in the stage show *Oh What a Lovely War* (1963; filmed UK, 1969). As such, they were a parody of the song 'They Didn't Believe Me' by Jerome Kern and Herbert Reynolds (M.E. Rourke) (1914):

> And when I told them how beautiful you are
> They didn't believe me, they didn't believe me.
> Your lips, your arms, your cheeks, your hair,
> Are in a class beyond compare,
> You're the loveliest girl that one can see.
> And when I tell them, and I'm certainly goin' to tell them,
> That I'm the man whose wife one day you'll be
> They'll never believe me, they'll never believe me,
> That from this great big world you've chosen me.

The parody was thought to be anonymous until Robert Kimball, editor of the *Complete Lyrics of Cole Porter* (1983), was going through the composer's voluminous papers and came across the words in the 'oldest compilation Porter had preserved of his works, a set of typed miscellaneous lyrics'.

In fact, Porter's version is slightly different from the one given above — e.g. line 2 is 'We never will tell them, we never will tell them'; line 5, "'Twas the wonderfulest war you ever knew', etc. So, we do not have 100 per cent proof that Porter wrote the parody, but it is an intriguing possibility. Note how the words 'night and day', which he was to couple in his most famous song in 1932, make an early appearance together here.

1 *You're the nimble tread of the feet of Fred Astaire,*
 You're Mussolini,
 You're Mrs Sweeny,
 You're Camembert.

Porter's 'list' song 'You're the Top' (from the show *Anything Goes*, 1934) has understandably had to be revised since it was first published. Of this segment, in due course, Mussolini was topped rather than the tops, and Mrs Charles Sweeny (as she had been since 1933), became the infamous Margaret, Duchess of Argyll (who died in July 1993).

Potter, Dennis
English TV playwright (1935–94)

2 *Vote, Vote, Vote, for Nigel Barton.*

Potter was a frequent borrower for the titles of his plays — *Blue Remembered Hills* (from A.E. Housman), *Pennies from Heaven, Where the Buffalo Roam, Follow the Yellow Brick Road, Cream in My Coffee* and *Lipstick on My Collar* (all from songs). See also CORY 107:3. But the title of this BBC 'Wednesday Play' (1965) about a Labour politician is possibly less obvious. It echoes the election song (usually sung by children to the tune of 'Tramp, tramp, tramp, the boys are marching' and known by 1880):

 Vote, vote, vote for (Billy Martin),
  Chuck old (Ernie) out the door —
 If it wasn't for the law
  I would punch him on the jaw,
 And we don't want (Ernie) any more.

According to Iona and Peter Opie, *The Lore and Language of Schoolchildren* (1959), Sir Anthony Eden said in 1955: 'I remember how in the old days the boys used to go round singing in chorus:

 'Vote, vote, vote for So-and-so;
 Punch old So-and-so in the eye;
 When he comes to the door,
 We will knock him on the floor,
 And he won't come a-voting any more!'

Potter, Stephen
English humorist (1900–69)

3 *'Yes, but not in the South', with slight adjustments will do for any argument about any place, if not about any person.*

From *Lifemanship* (1950), the second volume of Potter's not solely humorous exploration of the art of 'One-Upmanship', which he defined as 'how to make the other man feel that something has gone wrong, however slightly'. In discussing ways of putting down experts while in conversation with them, Potter introduces the above 'blocking phrase' with which to disconcert, if not totally silence, them. In a footnote, he remarks: 'I am required to state that World Copyright of this phrase is owned by its brilliant inventor, Mr Pound' — though which 'Pound' he does not reveal. Indeed, the blocking move was known before this. Richard Usborne wrote of it in a piece called 'Not in the South' included in *The Pick of 'Punch'* (1941). He introduced a character called Eustace who had found a formula 'for appearing to be a European, and world, pundit. It was a formula that let me off the boredom of finding out facts and retaining knowledge.' It was to remark, 'Not in the South.'

Powell, Anthony
English novelist (1905–)

4 *Books Do Furnish a Room.*

Whence the title of the tenth volume (1971) of Powell's novel sequence, *A Dance to the Music of Time*? According to the blurb on the dust-jacket of the first edition: 'The book's title is taken to some extent from the nickname of one of the characters, Books-do-furnish-a-room Bagshaw, all-purpose journalist and amateur of revolutionary theory, but the phrase also suggests an aspect of the rather bleak post-war period — London's literary world finding its feet again.'

The notion of books being looked upon as furniture — and the consequent taunt to people who regard them as such — is an old one. Lady Holland in her *Memoir* (1855) quotes the Revd Sidney Smith as joking: 'No furniture so charming as books.' And Edward Young in *Love of Fame: The Universal Passion*, Satire II (1725–8) has: 'Thy books are furniture.'

1 A Dance to the Music of Time.

The overall title of Powell's novel sequence (published 1951–75 and giving a panoramic view of postwar Britain) is given in the first novel, *A Question of Upbringing*. The narrator, Nicholas Jenkins, looking at workmen round a bucket of coke in falling snow, is put in mind of the painting with this title by Nicolas Poussin, which hangs in the Wallace Collection, London. There it is known as *Le 4 stagioni che ballano al suono del tempo* — a title bestowed by Giovanni Pietro. Sometimes, however, the painting is known, less interestingly, as '*Ballo della vita humana* [The Dance of Human Life]'.

Powell, Enoch
English Conservative, then Ulster Unionist politician (1912–   )

2 As I look ahead, I am filled with foreboding. Like the Roman, I seem to see 'the River Tiber foaming with much blood'.

With these words, on 20 April 1968, Enoch Powell, the Conservative Opposition Spokesman for Defence, concluded a speech in Birmingham on the subject of immigration. The next day, he was dismissed from the Shadow Cabinet for a speech 'racialist in tone and liable to exacerbate racial tensions'. What became known as the 'Rivers of Blood' speech certainly produced an astonishing reaction in the public, unleashing anti-immigrant feeling that had been largely pent up until this point. Later, Powell said that he should have quoted the remark in Latin to emphasize that he was only evoking a classical prophecy of doom and not actually predicting a bloodbath. In Virgil's *Aeneid* (VI:87) the Sibyl of Cumae prophesies: '*Et Thybrim multo spumantem sanguine cerno.*'

But 'Rivers of blood' was quite a common turn of phrase in English before Powell made it notorious. Thomas Jefferson in a letter to John Adams (4 September 1823) wrote: 'To attain all this [universal republicanism], however, rivers of blood must yet flow, and years of desolation pass over; yet the object is worth rivers of blood, and years of desolation.' Speaking on European unity (14 February 1948), Winston Churchill said: 'We are asking the nations of Europe between whom rivers of blood have flowed, to forget the feuds of a thousand years.'

3 Milk is rendered immortal in cheese.

In a broadcast talk in 1967, I quoted Powell as having said this but have no idea where I got it from. If, indeed, Powell did say this, he had been anticipated by Clifton Fadiman (*b* 1904) in *Any Number Can Play* (1957), where he wrote of: 'Cheese, milk's leap toward immortality.'

Pressburger, Emeric
Hungarian-born screenwriter (1902–88)

4 Killing a Mouse on Sunday.

Pressburger's novel (1961) was about a survivor from the Spanish Civil War who comes out of retirement twenty years afterwards to kill a brutal police chief. The title is from Richard Braithwaite, *Barnaby's Journal* (1638), describing Banbury, 'the most Puritan of all Puritan towns':

To Banbury came I, O profane one!
Where I saw a Puritane one
Hanging of his cat on Monday
For killing of a mouse on Sunday.

When the novel was filmed, the title became, less obscurely, *Behold a Pale Horse* (1964 – see BIBLE 60:1). In *Million-Dollar Movie* (1992), Michael Powell, Pressburger's long-time film collaborator, describes how 'the title was certainly no help . . . Emeric had discovered that great tempter, *The Oxford Dictionary of Quotations* . . . I was worried about the title. I said so . . . "It is a cat and mouse story, Michael." "Great! . . . why not call it *Cat and Mouse?*" "I have called it *Killing a Mouse on Sunday*, Michael".'

Priestley, J.B.
English novelist and playwright (1894–1984)

5 Let the People Sing.

The title of a novel by Priestley and written so that it could first be broadcast by the BBC in (of all months) September 1939. The story, about people fighting to save a village hall from being taken over by commercial interests, was later made into a film (1942). Characters in the story write a song that goes:

Let the people sing,
And freedom bring
An end to a sad old story.
Where the people sing,
Their voices ring
In the dawn of the people's glory.

In December 1939 another song was recorded with this title (music by Noel Gay, lyrics by Ian Grant and Frank Eyton) and featured in the 1940 revue *Lights Up*. Later, ENSA, the forces' entertainment organization, used it as its signature tune. On 1 April 1940 the BBC started a long-running series of programmes — again with this title — featuring 'songs of the moment, songs of the past, songs of sentiment, songs with a smile, songs with a story, songs of the people'. The phrase almost took on the force of a slogan. Angus Calder in *The People's War* (1969) wrote of Ernest Bevin, the Minister of Labour from October 1940: 'Bevinism in industry was symbolized by the growing understanding of the value of music and entertainment in helping people to work faster . . . There were the BBC's *Workers' Playtime* and *Music While You Work* which "progressive" management relayed over loudspeakers several times a day . . . "Let the People Sing", it might be said, was the spiritual essence of Bevinism.' The phrase appears to have originated with Priestley, though one might note the similarity to the hymns 'Let all on earth their voices raise' and 'Let all the world in every corner sing'.

1 *The Admass.*

I.e. the public to which advertisers address themselves. The term was coined by Priestley in *Journey Down a Rainbow* (written with Jacquetta Hawkes, 1955): 'This is my name for the whole system of an increasing productivity . . . plus high-pressure advertising and salesmanship, plus mass communication, and the creation of the mass mind, the mass man.'

Profumo, John
English Conservative politician
(1915–)

2 *There was no impropriety whatsoever in my acquaintanceship with Miss Keeler.*

When rumours surfaced of a relationship between the Secretary of State for War and Christine Keeler, a 'model' who had also been sharing her favours with a Soviet military attaché in London, Profumo made a statement to the House of Commons on 22 March 1963. It later became clear that there *had* been 'impropriety' (apart from adultery, there was the possibility of a security risk) and Profumo resigned. For many, his 'misleading' of (or 'lie' to) the House was con-

sidered a worse crime than anything else he had done.

3 *I shall not hesitate to issue writs for libel and slander if scandalous allegations are made or repeated outside the House.*

From the same statement. Subsequently, the phrase, 'I shall not hesitate to issue writs' became, through the offices of *Private Eye* Magazine, a catchphrase associated with Harold Wilson who became British Prime Minister in 1964. He was famously ready to say he would have recourse to the law, though he did not always do so.

Pudney, John
English poet (1909–77)

4 *Do not despair
For Johnny-head-in-air;
He sleeps as sound
As Johnny underground . . .*

From the poem 'For Johnny' (1942), said to have been written by Pudney on the back of an envelope during the Blitz. The lines were subsequently used in the film *The Way to the Stars* (1945) in which they were recited following the death of their 'author', an RAF pilot.

The character 'Johnny Head-in-Air' originally appeared in English translations of *Struwwelpeter* (1845), the collection of verse tales by Heinrich Hoffmann.

Punch
London-based humorous weekly periodical (1841–1992)

5 *Advice to persons about to marry, — Don't.*

What is probably the most famous of all *Punch* jokes appeared on the January page of the 1845 Almanack. R.G.C. Prices in his history of the magazine, wonders whether it is perhaps 'the most famous joke ever made' and remarks that 'it needs an effort to realise how neat, ingenious and profound it must have seemed at the time'. It was based on an advertisement put out by a house furnisher of the day and was probably contributed by Henry Mayhew, better known for his serious surveys of *London Labour and the London Poor*, though others also claimed to have done so.

1 Collapse of stout party.

A catchphrase that one might use as the tagline to a story about the humbling of a pompous person. It has long been associated with the magazine *Punch* and was thought to have occurred in those wordy captions that used to be given to its cartoons. But, as Ronald Pearsall explains in his book *Collapse of Stout Party* (1975): 'To many people Victorian wit and humour is summed up by *Punch* when every joke is supposed to end with "Collapse of Stout Party", though this phrase tends to be as elusive as "Elementary, my dear Watson" in the Sherlock Holmes sagas.'

At least the *OED2* has managed to find a reference to a 'Stout Party' in the caption to a cartoon in the edition of *Punch* dated 25 August 1855.

2 Peccavi.

'*Peccavi*' is the Latin phrase for 'I have sinned'. The *OED* sees it as part of the expression 'to cry *peccavi*', an acknowledgement or confession of guilt. The earliest citation given by the *OED* is Bishop John Fisher's Funeral Sermon at St Paul's for Henry VII (1509): 'King David that wrote this psalm, with one word speaking his heart was changed saying *Peccavi*.' This refers to Psalm 41:4: 'I said, Lord, be merciful unto me: heal my soul, for I have sinned against thee.'

But the phrase occurs in a number of other places in the Bible, mostly in the Old Testament — for example, 'And Saul said unto Samuel, I have sinned' (1 Samuel 15:24.)

The Latin word is often thought to have furnished a famous pun. Here is Charles Berlitz's version in *Native Tongues* (1982): 'Sir Charles Napier, a British officer in India, was given command of an expedition to annex the kingdom of Sind in [1843] . . . To announce the success of his mission, he dispatched to the headquarters of the British East India Company a one-word message, the Latin word *peccavi*, which means "I have sinned".'

Alas, Napier did no such thing. It was *Punch* on 18 May 1844 which suggested that Caesar's '*Veni, vidi, vici*' was beaten for brevity by 'Napier's dispatch to Lord Ellenborough, *Peccavi*.' *ODQ* credits the joke to Catherine Winkworth. She was a young girl, so it was sent into *Punch* on her behalf. It seems, however, that the joke was soon taken as genuine, even at *Punch* itself. On 22 March 1856, the magazine (confusing sender and receiver in the original) included the couplet:

> '*Peccavi* — I've Scinde,' wrote Lord Ellen, so proud.
> More briefly Dalhousie wrote — '*Vovi* — I've Oude.'

3 Bang goes/went sixpence!

A lightly joking remark about one's own or another person's unwillingness to spend money. The origins of this lie in a *Punch* cartoon of 5 December 1868. A Scotsman who has just been on a visit to London remarks: 'Mun, a had na' been the-ere abune twa hoours when — *Bang* — went *Saxpence!*' The saying was repopularized by Sir Harry Lauder, the professional stage Scotsman.

4 Dropping the Pilot.

Meaning 'to dispense with a valued leader', this phrase comes from the caption to a *Punch* cartoon which appeared on 29 March 1890 and showed Kaiser Wilhelm II leaning over the side of a ship as his recently disposed-of Chancellor, Otto von Bismarck, dressed as a pilot, walked down the steps to disembark. Bismarck had been forced to resign following disagreements over home and foreign policy. The phrase was also used as the title of a poem on the same subject. From the *Independent* (12 May 1990): 'Kenneth Baker, the Conservative chairman, yesterday called on Tories to stop idle speculation about the party leadership . . . "We have moved through difficult waters . . . We should not, we must not, we will not drop the pilot".'

5 Like the curate's egg.

Meaning 'patchy, good in parts', the phrase comes from the caption to a *Punch* cartoon, Vol. cix (1895) in which a Bishop is saying: 'I'm afraid you've got a bad egg, Mr Jones.' The nervous young curate, keen not to say anything at all critical, flannels: 'Oh no, my Lord, I assure you! Parts of it are excellent.'

6 Since when I have used no other.

Pears' soap was advertised in the 1880s and 1890s with a picture of a grubby tramp penning a testimonial letter and the handwritten caption: 'Two years ago I used your soap *since when* I have used no other!' This was taken, with permission, from a *Punch* cartoon by Harry Furniss which appeared on 26 April 1884. The original caption was: 'GOOD ADVERTISEMENT. I used your soap two years ago; since then I have used no other.'

Pears' soap also used a signed testimonial (with picture) from Lillie Langtry, the actress and mistress of King Edward VII (when he was Prince of Wales). Hers read: 'Since using Pears' Soap for the hands and complexion *I have discarded all others*.' This advertisement is undated but may possibly predate the *Punch cartoon*.

1 *It isn't as funny as it used to be.*

People have said this about *Punch* apparently almost since it began. F.C. Burnand, editor 1880–1906, was asked why *Punch* wasn't as funny as it used to be. 'It never was,' he said.

2 *Noah's wife was called Joan of Ark.*

Listed as one of 'British children's answers to church school questions' in a US publication called *Speaker's Idea File* (1993). But how old did the compilers think it to be? About as old as the Ark itself is the fact of the matter. *Punch*, Vol. cxxii (29 January 1902) has this:

A LITTLE LEARNING
Teacher And who was JOAN OF ARC?
Scholar Please, sir, NOAH's wife.

3 *Look here, Steward, if this is coffee, I want tea; but if this is tea, then I wish for coffee.*

This was the caption to a cartoon by G.D. Armour in *Punch*, Vol. cxxiii (23 July 1902). Frequently misascribed. On BBC Radio *Quote . . . Unquote*, if I recall correctly, a panellist ascribed it to Charles de Gaulle. Robert Byrne in *The 637 Best Things Anybody Ever Said* (1982) gives it to Abraham Lincoln.

4 *One of my ancestors fell at Waterloo./ Which platform?*

Let us journey backwards through the history of this joke — we may actually have a rock-solid 'first use': *The Best of Myles* reprints as an overheard, this from Flann O'Brien's Dublin newspaper column [early 1940s]: 'D'you know that my great-grandfather was killed at Waterloo . . . Which platform?'

A.L. Rowse writes of Lord David Cecil in *Friends and Contemporaries* (1989): 'Anything for a laugh — simplest of jokes. I think of him now coming into my room [at Christ Church in the early 1920s], giggling and sputtering with fun. Someone had said, "My grandfather was killed at Waterloo" "I'm so sorry — which platform?"'

And then we find this cartoon by F.H. Townsend from *Punch*, Vol. cxxix (1 November 1905):

MR BINKS: 'ONE OF MY ANCESTORS FELL AT WATERLOO.'
LADY CLARE: 'AH? WHICH PLATFORM?'

To the old joke is often added the further response, 'Ha, ha! As if it mattered which platform!'

5 *What is that lady/gentleman for?*

This remark, out of the mouth of a not-quite babe or suckling, is a convenient stick with which to beat anyone the speaker wishes to reduce in importance. It is particularly useful when taunting politicians. For example, 'It was an anonymous little girl who, on first catching sight of Charles James Fox, is supposed to have asked her mother: "what is that gentleman for?" One asks the same question of Mr [Douglas] Hurd. Why is he where he is in this particular government? He has never been wholly in sympathy either with Mrs Thatcher or with her version of Conservatism.' — Alan Watkins, the *Observer* (29 May 1988).

Compare 'I am reminded of the small boy who once pointed at Hermione Gingold and asked, "Mummy, what's that lady for?"' — Michael Billington (possibly quoting Kenneth Tynan) in the *Guardian* (21 July 1988).

'"What," a little girl is supposed to have asked her mother, pointing at Sir John Simon, a pre-war Chancellor, "is that man for?" What, she might now ask, pointing at the Labour faithful assembling in Brighton today, is that party for?' — editorial, the *Independent on Sunday* (29 September 1991).

Is it possible to say where the taunt originated? The remark about Fox would seem to have evolved from what the young Viscount Eversley (born 1794) is reported to have said on hearing Fox speak in Parliament: 'What is that fat gentleman in such a passion about?' This was recorded by G.W.E. Russell in *Collections and Recollections* (1898). If that is the origin, the remark has undergone a considerable shift in meaning.

Much more likely is that the saying dates from a *Punch* cartoon (in the edition of 14 November 1906, vol. cxxxi). Drawn by F.H. Townsend, who was art editor of the magazine at the time, it shows the remark being said by a small boy to his mother about a man carrying a bag of golf clubs. The caption is 'MUMMY, WHAT'S THAT MAN FOR?'

1 *Sometimes I just sits and thinks and sometimes I just sits.*

Until recently this well-known saying did not feature in any dictionary of quotations. So where did it originate? On first being asked about it, people would invariably say, 'Oh, that's what my father used to say'. Pressed as to its possible origin, they would come up with a bewildering variety of suggestions — Lewis Carroll, Laurel and Hardy, Winnie-the-Pooh, Uncle Remus (it could certainly be made to sound southern American), Mark Twain. One person thought it could be found 'in Chapter 8, probably' of *Pickwick Papers* by Charles Dickens [concerning Joe, 'the fat boy'], but it could not. Several others were absolutely positive that it came from that little American book *The Specialist* (1930) by Charles Sales, the one about a man who specializes in the building of outdoor privies. The connection with sitting and thinking seemed highly likely, but, no, it does not rate a mention.

A woman, aged 50 [in 1987], remembered seeing, as a child, a china ornament made to look like a shed. When you looked in the door, you saw a little curly-headed black boy sitting on the lavatory with his trousers round his knees. And 'Sometimes I just sits . . .' was written underneath.

Even more correspondents knew for certain that the saying had been used as the caption for a picture postcard drawn by Mabel Lucie Atwell in the 1930s, but no one was able to turn up the picture in question, though one had 'thrown it out last week, as it happens'. From the same decade came memories of advertising slogans along the lines of 'Sometimes I just sits . . . and sometimes I sits and drinks a cup of Mazawattee Tea', and 'Sometimes I just sits . . . and listens to my Philco [radio]'.

Then came a reference to the novel *Anne of the Island* (1915) by L.M. Montgomery, the Canadian writer who had earlier written *Anne of Green Gables*. At one point in the book, an old woman who drives a mail-cart remarks: 'O' course it's tejus [tedious]. Part of the time I sits and thinks and the rest I jest sits.' Was this the first outing for what was clearly to become a much used and popular saying? No, it was not. Such evidence-sifting probably seems a shade preposterous . . . not least because the answer (when you know it) is a very obvious one.

On 24 October 1906 *Punch* carried a cartoon which showed a vicar's wife talking to an old, somewhat rustic gentleman who has been laid up with an injured foot. She is sympathizing with him and saying: 'Now that you can't get about, and are not able to read, how do you manage to occupy the time?' He replies: 'Well, mum, sometimes I sits and thinks and then again I just sits.' Headed, 'CHANGE OF OCCUPATION', the cartoon was by Gunning-King.

Puzo, Mario
American novelist (1920–   )

2 *He's a businessman. I'll make him an offer he can't refuse.*

Puzo's 1969 Mafia novel *The Godfather* gave to the language a new expression which, as far as one can tell, was Puzo's invention. Johnny Fontane, a singer, desperately wants a part in movie and goes to see his godfather, Don Corleone, seeking help. All the contracts have been signed and there is no chance of the studio chief changing his mind. Still, the godfather promises Fontane he will get him the part, with these words. In the 1971 film, the exchange was turned into the following dialogue:

> *Corleone:* In a month from now this Hollywood big shot's going to give you what you want.
> *Fontane:* Too late, they start shooting in a week.
> *Corleone:* I'm going to make him an offer he can't refuse.

3 *A lawyer with his briefcase can steal more than a thousand men with guns.*

In *The Godfather Papers* (1969) Puzo singled out this as the most quoted line from the novel. 'I've had people in France, Germany and Denmark quote that line to me with the utmost glee,' he said. 'And some of them are lawyers.' Puzo mentioned it to the head of the studio, the producer, director and everyone on the film, but the line did not get spoken in it.

Pym, Barbara
English novelist (1913–80)

1 *Some Tame Gazelle.*

The terribly English novelist has a coterie following for her stories of quiet lives lived in a narrow band of middle-class society. She was one of those writers who in most cases use quotations for their titles. Sometimes it was indicated in the book what the source was: *The Sweet Dove Died* (1978) (John Keats), *A Glass of Blessings* (1958) (George Herbert), *Less Than Angels* (1955) (Alexander Pope), *Civil to Strangers* (unpublished) (John Pomfret), and the short story 'So, Some Tempestuous Morn' (Matthew Arnold). At other times Pym kept mum. The short story 'Across a Crowded Room' is presumably Oscar Hammerstein II, of all people, but very 1950s. *A Few Green Leaves* (1980) could be anything or nothing, as also *Excellent Women* (1952).

Some Tame Gazelle (1950) replaced 'Some Sad Turtle' and apparently derives from a poem called 'Something to Love' by Thomas Haynes Bayly (1797–1839), a minor English poet:

> Some tame gazelle, or some gentle dove:
> Something to love, oh, something to love!

2 *No Fond Return of Love.*

Behind the title of this novel (1961) is an interesting story, which is related in Hazel Holt's memoir of Pym. Rejecting 'A Thankless Task' Pym decided she needed a title with 'love' in it, so sat down and worked her way through *The Oxford Book of English Verse* until she came to 'Prayer for Indifference' by the eighteenth-century poet Fanny Greville. She adapted the first line of:

> I ask no kind return of love,
> No tempting charm to please;
> Far from the heart those gifts remove
> That sigh for peace and ease.

3 *Perhaps in retirement . . . a quieter, narrower kind of life can be worked out and adopted. Bounded by English literature and the Anglican Church and small pleasures like sewing and choosing material for this uncertain summer.*

From Pym's diary entry for 6 March 1972, when one of her novels had been rejected (Pym is famous for having fallen out of favour and for then being rediscovered). The phrase 'this uncertain summer' is quintessential Pym and sounds as if it ought to have served her as a title. The phrase had been used by Sir James E. Smith in *The English Flora* (1824–8): 'It may be observed that our uncertain summer is established by the time the Elder is in full flower.' Compare *Uncertain Glory*, the title of a film (US, 1944) and taken probably from Shakespeare's *Two Gentlemen of Verona* (I.iii.85): 'O, how this spring of love resembleth/The uncertain glory of an April day.'

R

Rabelais, François
French writer (c 1494–c 1553)

1 Nature abhors a vacuum.

Rabelais quotes the maxim in its original Latin form 'natura abhorret vacuum' in Gargantua (1535). Galileo (1564–1642) asserted it as the reason mercury rises in a barometer. 'Nature abhors a straight line' was a saying of the garden landscaper, Capability Brown (1715–83). (Clare Boothe Luce, 1903–87, said, 'Nature abhors a virgin'.)

2 The comedy is ended.

The dying words of Rabelais are supposed to have been: 'Je m'en vais chercher un grand peut-être; tirez le rideau, la farce est jouée [I am going to seek a grand perhaps; bring down the curtain, the farce is played out].' The attribution is made, hedged about with disclaimers, in Jean Fleury's Rabelais et ses oeuvres (1877) (also in the life of Rabelais by Motteux, who died in 1718). In Lermontov's novel A Hero of Our Time (1840), a character says: 'Finita la commedia'. At the end of Ruggiero Leoncavallo's opera Il Pagliacci [The Clowns] (1892), Canio exclaims: 'La commedia è finita [the comedy is finished/over].'

3 Fais/Fay ce que voudras.

Meaning 'do what you will/do as you please', this is an appealing motto and one that has been adopted by more than one free-living soul. It appears first in Book I of Gargantua and Pantagruel (1532) by Rabelais. Then, in the eighteenth century it was the motto of the Monks of Medmenham, better known as the Hell Fire Club. Sir Francis Dashwood founded a mock Franciscan order at Medmenham Abbey in Buckinghamshire in 1745, and the members of the Club were said to get up to all sorts of disgraceful activities, orgies, black masses and the like. The politician John Wilkes was of their number. The motto was written up over the ruined door of the abbey.

Aleister Crowley (1875–1947), the satanist, who experimented in necromancy and the black arts, sex and drugs, also picked up the motto. Newspapers called him the 'Wickedest Man in the World', though he fell short of proving the claim. Of his 'misunderstood commandment', Germaine Greer comments in The Female Eunuch (1970): 'Do as thou wilt is a warning not to delude yourself that you can do otherwise, and to take full responsibility for what you do. When one has genuinely chosen a course for oneself it cannot be possible to hold another responsible for it.'

4 Farewell baskets, the grapes are gathered.

One of those peculiar lines that get turned into catchphrases. 'Adieu paniers, vendanges sont faites' occurs in Gargantua when Friar Jean des Entommeurs is exhorting his fellow monks to stop praying and repel the soldiers who are vandalizing their vineyard – a call to arms.

Raleigh, Sir Walter
English explorer and courtier (c 1552–1618)

5 But true love is a durable fire
In the mind ever burning;
Never sick, never old, never dead,
From itself never turning.

From Raleigh's poem 'Walsingham' (undated). A Durable Fire was the title given to a volume of the letters of Duff and Diana Cooper 1913–50 (published 1983).

1 *Give me my scallop-shell of quiet,*
My staff of faith to walk upon,
My scrip of joy, immortal diet,
My bottle of salvation,
My gown of glory, hope's true gage,
And thus I'll take my pilgrimage.

From 'The Passionate Man's Pilgrimage' or 'His Pilgrimage' (1604). There is some doubt about the authorship. The scallop shell was the emblem worn by pilgrims to identify themselves as such. More particularly, it was the emblem of St James of Compostela and was adopted, according to Erasmus, because the seashore was close to the end of the pilgrimage route to the saint's shrine.

Rattigan, Sir Terence
English playwright (1911–77)

2 *Aunt Edna.*

During the revolution in English drama of the 1950s this term was used by the new wave of angry young dramatists and their supporters to describe the more conservative theatre-goer — the type who preferred comfortable three-act plays of the Shaftesbury Avenue kind. Ironically, the term had been coined in self-defence by Rattigan, one of the generation of dramatists they sought to replace. In the preface to Vol. II of his *Collected Plays* (1953) he had written of: 'A nice, respectable, middle-class, middle-aged maiden lady, with time on her hands and the money to help her pass it . . . Let us call her Aunt Edna . . . Now Aunt Edna does not appreciate Kafka . . . She is, in short, a hopeless lowbrow . . . Aunt Edna is universal, and to those who may feel that all the problems of the modern theatre might be solved by her liquidation, let me add that . . . she is also immortal.'

Ratushinskaya, Irina
Ukrainian poet (1954–)

3 *Grey is the Colour of Hope.*

This is the title of a book (1988) and refers to the colour of the author's uniform as an inmate of a Soviet labour camp. On her twenty-ninth birthday, Ratushinskaya was sentenced to seven years in the camp, to be followed by five years' internal exile. Her 'crime' was her poetry. She was released (after intensive campaigning) in 1986, just prior to the Reykjavik summit meeting between Presidents Reagan and Gorbachev.

Ray, John
English botanist and paroemiologist (1627–1705)

4 *Misery loves company.*

Bartlett (1992) lists this proverb, along with five others, under Ray's name. This is surely misleading as the whole point of any proverb book — not least Ray's own *A Collection of English Proverbs* (1670) — is that it represents the traditional expression of wisdom rather than an individual's. Of course, some proverb collectors and scholars (notably Benjamin Franklin) did coin proverbs and slip them into their collection, but there is no reason to believe that Ray did so.

The *ODP* does not include this proverb, anyway, though *CODP* finds earlier citations *c* 1349 and 1578.

Raymond, Ernest
English novelist (1888–1974)

5 *Tell England, ye who pass this*
monument,
We died for her, and here we rest
content.

From Raymond's novel *Tell England*, Bk II, Chap. XII (1922): 'We had walked right on to the grave of our friend. His name stood on a cross with those of six other officers, and beneath was written in pencil the famous epitaph . . . The perfect words went straight to Doe's heart. "Roop," he said, "if I'm killed you can put those lines over me".'

The book (filmed UK, 1931) was about a group of English public school boys who end up at Gallipoli. Quite where the epitaph originated is hard to say. In *Farewell the Trumpets* (1978) James Morris finds it on a memorial from the Boer War at Wagon Hill, Ladysmith, in the form:

Tell England, ye who pass this
monument,
We, who died serving her, rest here
content.

Presumably, this memorial was erected *before* the First World War and *before* Raymond's book popularized the couplet.

Whatever the case, the words clearly echo the epitaph by the ancient Greek poet Simonides (*c* 556–*c* 468BC) on the Spartans who died at Thermopylae (delaying the vastly greater Persian army at the cost of their own lives): 'Tell the Spartans, stranger, that here we lie, obeying their orders.' Indeed, Diana Raymond, the novelist's widow, wrote in 1992: 'I (and all the family) always understood from Ernest that he had taken the lines from the epitaph for the Spartans who died at Thermopylae, substituting "England" for "Sparta" and making his own translation. This leaves the problem of the Boer War memorial at Ladysmith. Either two people had the same idea; or else Ernest had somewhere at the back of his mind without realising it a memory of this. I rather think the first answer is the right one; he was very accurate in his references.'

Reade, Charles
English novelist (1814–84)

1 *Make 'em laugh, make 'em cry, make 'em wait.*

This was a suggested recipe for writing novels to be published in serial form (as done by Charles Dickens and many others in the nineteenth century). Charles Reade who wrote *The Cloister and the Hearth* (1861) came up with it.

Reagan, Ronald
American film actor, Republican Governor and 40th President (1911–)

2 *Randy — where's the rest of me?*

In the film *King's Row* (1941), Reagan played the part of Drake McHugh, and Ann Sheridan appeared as Randy Monaghan. A famous moment occurs when Drake, on waking to find that his legs have been amputated by a sadistic doctor, poses this pained question. *Where's the Rest of Me?* was used by Reagan as the title of an early autobiography (1965).

3 *Win this one for the Gipper!*

Bridging his film and political careers, this Reagan slogan refers to George Gipp, a character he had played in *Knute Rockne — All-American* (1940). Gipp was a real-life football star who died young. At half-time in a 1928 army game, Rockne, the team coach, had recalled something Gipp had said to him: 'Rock, someday when things look real tough for Notre Dame, ask the boys to go out there and win one for me.' Reagan used the slogan countless times. One of the last was at a campaign rally for Vice-President George Bush in San Diego, California, on 7 November 1988. Reagan's peroration included these words: 'So, now we come to the end of this last campaign . . .

And I hope that someday your children and grandchildren will tell of the time that a certain President came to town at the end of a long journey and asked their parents and grandparents to join him in setting America on the course to the new millenium . . . So, if I could ask you just one last time. Tomorrow, when mountains greet the dawn, would you go out there and win one for the Gipper? Thank you, and God bless you all.'

4 *[On Government] An alimentary canal with a big appetite at one end and no responsibility at the other.*

The sixteenth edition of Bartlett (in 1992) came under particular attack for its treatment of President Reagan, the erstwhile 'Great Communicator'. While noting two of Reagan's many borrowings in footnotes ('Go ahead, make my day' and 'Evil empire'), it listed only *three* original sayings. Adam Meyerson, raising the topic in the *Washington Post* (14 February 1993), thought the choice of only three Reaganisms (compared with *twenty-eight* apiece for John F. Kennedy and Franklin Roosevelt) was politically motivated and intended to diminish the former President. Supporters of Bartlett responded with the suggestion that Reagan relied so much on borrowings from old movie scripts and on the scribblings of speechwriters like Peggy Noonan that his famous lines did not deserve Bartlett's form of immortality. But neither Kennedy nor Roosevelt produced his mighty lines unaided and the rule of thumb in compiling such dictionaries should always be to recognize the person who actually went out there and spoke the lines (however arrived at) — in other words the person who popularized them. For the record: the *Oxford Dictionary of Quotations* (1992) includes *five* Reaganisms (completely different from Bartlett's). *Chambers Dictionary of Modern Quotations* (1993) contains *fifteen* entries under 'Reagan', together with four cross-references to his borrowings.

In *Speaking My Mind* (1989), the book of Reagan's selected speeches, there is not a single mention of Peggy Noonan or any other speechwriter. The drafts which are reproduced in the book — spattered with emendations in the President's own hand — seem designed to convince that he really was 'speaking his own mind'.

Of the three sayings Bartlett did include, the above is a gag dating from 1965, when Reagan was campaigning for Governor of California. Bartlett gives no indication that this *may* be no more than a gag-writer's re-working of the definition of a baby long ascribed to Ronald Knox in the form 'a loud voice at one end and no sense of responsibility at the other'. It was so ascribed in the 1976 BBC Reith Lectures, though Frank S. Pepper's *Handbook of 20th Century Quotations* (1984) gives the 'baby' version to 'E. Adamson'.

1 A shining city on a hill.

In a speech on 14 October 1969 Reagan quoted Governor Winthrop of the Massachusetts Bay Colony who told new settlers in 1630: 'We shall be as a city upon a hill, the eyes of all people are upon us.' It was meant as a warning as much as a promise. Winthrop did not use the word 'shining'. A writer in the *Observer* (8 March 1987) recalled Reagan using it as early as 1976 when he had just lost the Republican nomination to Gerald Ford. He told his supporters he would be back, they would win in the end and once again America would be a 'shining city on a hill'. Later, when President, Reagan was often to use the image to describe the US as a land of security and success. He used the phrase particularly during his bid for re-election as President in 1984. In return, at the Democratic Convention, New York Governor Mario Cuomo remarked that a shining city might be what Reagan saw 'from the veranda of his ranch' but he failed to see despair in the slums. 'There is despair, Mr President, in the faces that you don't see, in the places that you don't visit in your shining city . . . This nation is more a tale of two cities than it is just a shining city on a hill.'

If anything, the image is biblical. Matthew 5:14 has: 'A city that is set on a hill cannot be hid . . . Let your light so shine before men that they may see your good works'; the 'holy hill' of Zion is a 'sunny mountain' according to one etymology; the New Jerusalem is the jewelled city lit by the glory of God in Revelation.

[*Source*: A letter to the *Observer* from Alan Mac-Coll, University of Aberdeen, 15 March 1987.]

2 Don't you cut me off. I am paying for this microphone.

Just prior to a broadcast debate at Nashua, New Hampshire, during the Presidential primary there in 1980, Reagan turned the tables on George Bush (then also a challenger) by insisting that the other Republican candidates be allowed to participate.

Reagan won the dispute over who should speak in the debate by declaring 'Don't you cut me off, I am paying for this microphone, Mr Green!' Never mind that the man's name was actually 'Breen', the line in the form, 'Don't you shut me off, I'm paying for this broadcast' had earlier been delivered by Spencer Tracy in the film *State of the Union* (1948). This borrowing was pointed out by Christoper J. Matthews writing in the *Washington Post* (6 May 1984), and by *Time* Magazine (8 February 1988).

3 There is no limit to what a man can do and where he can go if he doesn't mind who gets the credit.

The propensity for American Presidents to clutter their desks with plaques bearing uplifting messages dates back to the days of Harry S Truman at least. His 'the buck stops here' motto was apparently of his own devising. Jimmy Carter either retrieved the original or had a copy made and displayed it near his own desk when he was in the Oval Office. Enter Ronald Reagan. According to the *Daily Mail* (18 April 1985): 'Besides a calendar, a pen set, a clock and a horseshoe, the First Desk is now home to no fewer than eight inspirational messages. They range from the consoling "Babe Ruth struck out 1,330 times", through the boosting "Illegitimi Non Carborundum" . . . to the altruistic "there is no limit . . ."'

4 Congressional Medal of Honor, posthumously awarded.

Reagan told a meeting (undated) of the Congressional Medal of Honor Society about an aircraft gunner who couldn't leave his post when his plane was crashing. He was told by his commanding officer that he would win a 'Congressional Medal of Honor, posthumously awarded'. No such incident happened in real life, though it did in the film *Wing and a Prayer* (1944). In 1985, Michael Rogin, a Professor of Political Science at Berkeley, explored Reagan's other borrowings of film lines in a presentation entitled 'Ronald Reagan: The Movie'.

5 Evil empire.

The Soviet Union was so described by President Reagan in a speech to the National Association of Evangelicals at Orlando, Florida (8 March 1983): 'In your discussions of the nuclear freeze proposals, I urge you to beware the temptation of pride — the temptation blithely to declare yourselves above it all and label both sides equally at fault, to ignore the facts of history and the aggressive impulses of an *evil empire*.' The inspiration for this turn of phrase was made clear later the same month (23 March) when Reagan first propounded his 'Star Wars' proposal as part of a campaign to win support for his defence budget and arms-control project. The proposal, more properly known by its initials SDI (for Strategic Defence Initiative), was to extend the nuclear battleground into space. The President did not use the term 'Star Wars' but it was an inevitable tag to be applied by the media, given his own fondness for adapting lines from the movies. The film *Star Wars* and the sequel *The Empire Strikes Back* had been released in 1977 and 1980, respectively.

In the controversy over Reagan's poor showing in Bartlett (1992) (see above), it was argued that Bartlett was wrong in ascribing the phrase 'evil empire' to George Lucas, the creator of *Star Wars*. Apparently, in that film it appears only in the form 'evil galactic empire'. Compare from the *Independent* (19 May 1990): 'Frank Salmon, an East End protection racketeer who built an "evil empire" on violence and fear, was yesterday jailed for 7½ years at the Old Bailey.'

1 Where do we find such men?

In 1984, on the fortieth anniversary of the D-Day landings, President Reagan visited Europe and made a speech in which he eulogized those who had taken part in the event. 'Where do we find such men?' he asked. On a previous occasion he had said: 'Many years ago in one of the four wars in my lifetime, an admiral stood on the bridge of a carrier watching the planes take off and out into the darkness bent on a night combat mission and then found himself asking, with no one there to answer — just himself to hear his own voice — "Where do we find such men?"' But the very first time he had used the line he had made it clear where it came from and that it was fiction. The line comes from James Michener's novel *Bridges at Toko-Ri*, later filmed (1954) with William Holden who asks, 'Where do we get such men?' Over the years, fiction became fact for Reagan. Perhaps he could not, or was unwilling to, distinguish between the two.

[*Source:* Rogin, as above.]

2 It's morning again in America.

This slogan for Reagan's 1984 re-election campaign was apparently coined by Hal Riney (*b* 1932), an American advertising executive

[*Source: Newsweek*, 6 August 1984.]

3 Do we get to win this time?

So says John Rambo (a hunk bringing home American prisoners left behind in the Vietnam War) in the film *Rambo: First Blood Part Two* (US, 1985 — a sequel to *First Blood*, 1982). The terms 'Ramboesque', 'Rambo-like' and 'Ramboism' were rapidly adopted for mindless, forceful heroics. When Reagan quoted this line in a speech (undated), he did have the grace to credit it for once rather than pass it off as one of his own.

4 We are not going to tolerate these attacks from outlaw states run by the strangest collection of misfits, looney tunes, and squalid criminals since the advent of the Third Reich.

So President Reagan commented on the hijacking of a US plane by Shi'ite Muslims, in a broadcast (8 July 1985). Meaning 'mad person' or, as an adjective, 'mad', the phrase 'looney tune' refers to the cinema cartoon comedies called Looney Tunes, which have been produced by Warners since the 1940s. The phrase was already established and had been used in the Mel Brooks film *High Anxiety* (1977).

5 He lived by the sea, died on it, and was buried in it.

In his TV broadcast following the *Challenger* space shuttle disaster on 28 January 1986, Reagan said: 'There's a coincidence today. On this day 390 years ago, the great explorer Sir Francis Drake died aboard ship off the coast of Panama. In his lifetime the great frontiers were the oceans, and a historian later said, "He lived by the sea, died on it, and was buried in it." Well, today we can say of the *Challenger* crew: Their dedication was, like Drake's, complete.' The identity of the historian remains untraced. However, G.M. Trevelyan is supposed to have said of *Nelson* that he was, 'Always in his element and always on his element.' Compare what Mencken (1942) has as a 'Japanese proverb': 'If you were born at sea, you will die on it.'

1 *There is nothing better for the inside of a man than the outside of a horse.*

When *Time* Magazine quoted President Reagan as saying this (28 December 1987), it received many letters from readers saying such things as: 'This quotation bears a striking resemblance to a remark made by the California educator and prep school founder Sherman Thacher: "There's something about the outside of a horse that's good for the inside of a boy"'; and, 'Rear Admiral Grayson, President Woodrow Wilson's personal physician put it . . . "The outside of a horse is good for the inside of a man"'; and, 'Lord Palmerston said it.'

Time sensibly replied (19 January 1988): 'Everyone is right. The origin of the saying is unknown. It is one of the President's favorite expressions.'

See also MAGEE 231:1.

Rees-Mogg, Lord
English journalist (1928–)

2 *The arts are to Britain what sunshine is to Spain.*

'Sayings of the Week' in the *Observer* credited this to Sir William (as he then still was and Chairman of the Arts Council of Great Britain) on 31 March 1985. On 22 September the same year, it gave the credit for it to Luke Rittner, Secretary-General of the same organization. Clearly a popular saying in-house.

Reger, Max
German composer (1873–1916)

3 *I am sitting in the smallest room of my house. I have your review before me. In a moment it will be behind me.*

In 1906 Reger wrote what might appear to be the original of a famous type of abusive remark in a letter to the music critic Rudolph Louis. It is quoted in N. Slonimsky, *Lexicon of Musical Invective* (1953), having been translated from the German. Ned Sherrin, in *Theatrical Anecdotes* (1991), reports the similar reply from Oscar Hammerstein (grandfather of the lyricist) to a creditor: 'I am in receipt of your letter which is now before me and in a few minutes will be behind me.' (In the *Evening Standard*, 30 January 1992, Milton Shulman ascribed it to Noël Coward . . .) There seems every

chance that the real originator of the remark was John Montagu, 4th Earl of Sandwich. N.A.M. Rodger in *The Insatiable Earl* (1993) suggests that when William Eden (later Lord Auckland) defected from Sandwich in 1785 he wrote him a letter: 'Contemporaries repeated with relish Sandwich's terse reply . . . "Sir, your letter is before me, and will presently be behind me".' Rodger gives his source as J.H. Jesse, *George Selwyn* (1843–4) and adds, helpfully, 'Manufactured lavatory paper was not known in the eighteenth century.'

Remarque, Erich Maria
German novelist (1897–1970)

4 *All Quiet on the Western Front.*

This is the title given to the English translation of Remarque's novel *Im Westen Nichts Neues* [Nothing New in the West] (1929; film US, 1930). 'All Quiet on the Western Front' had been a familiar phrase of the Allies in the First World War, used in military communiqués and newspaper reports and also taken up jocularly by men in the trenches to describe peaceful inactivity. Partridge/*Catch Phrases* hears in it echoes of 'All quiet on the Shipka Pass' — cartoons of the 1877–8 Russo-Turkish War, which Partridge says had a vogue in 1915–16, though he never heard the allusion made himself. For no very good reason, Partridge rules out any connection with the US song 'All Quiet Along the Potomac'. This, in turn, came from a poem called 'The Picket Guard' (1861) by Ethel Lynn Beers — a sarcastic commentary on General Brinton McClellan's policy of delay at the start of the Civil War. The phrase (alluding to the Potomac River which runs through Washington D.C.) had been used in reports from McLellan's Union headquarters and put in Northern newspaper headlines.

Repington, Lieutenant-Colonel Charles à Court
English soldier and journalist (1858–1925)

5 *The First World War.*

Repington's book entitled *The First World War 1914–18* was published in 1920. Presumably this helped popularize the name for the war, ominously suggesting that it was merely the first of a series. Indeed, it was thought to be a shocking title because it presupposed another war.

Known at first as the 'European War', the conflict became known quite rapidly as the 'Great War'. By 10 September 1918, as he later described in his book, Repington was referring to it in his diary as the 'First World War', thus: 'I saw Major Johnstone, the Harvard Professor who is here to lay the bases of an American History. We discussed the right name of the war. I said that we called it now *The War*, but that this could not last. The Napoleonic War was *The Great War*. To call it *The German War* was too much flattery for the Boche. I suggested *The World War* as a shade better title, and finally we mutually agreed to call it *The First World War* in order to prevent the millennium folk from forgetting that the history of the world was the history of war.'

The *OED2* finds 'Great War' in use by 1914 (though earlier in 1887), but does not find 'First World War' until 1931.

Reuther, Walter
American labour leader (1907–70)

1 *If it looks like a duck, walks like a duck and quacks like a duck, then it just may be a duck.*

Usually ascribed to Reuther during the McCarthyite witch-hunts of the 1950s. He came up with it as a test of whether someone was a Communist. Then it came to be applied elsewhere — but usually in politics: 'Mr Richard Darman, the new [US] Budget director, explained the other day what "no new taxes" means. He will apply the duck test. "If it looks like a duck, walks like a duck and quacks like a duck, it's a duck"' — (*Guardian*, 25 January 1989). Curiously, it has also been attributed to Cardinal Cushing.

Revere, Paul
American patriot (1735–1818)

2 *The British are coming! The British are coming!*

Doubt has been cast on Revere's reputed cry to warn people of approaching British troops during the American War of Independence. On his night ride of 18 April 1775, from Boston to Lexington, it is more likely that he cried 'The regulars are out'. Hence, however, *The Russians Are Coming, The Russians Are Coming* (US film, 1966).

Rhodes, Cecil
British-born South African colonialist (1853–1902)

3 *Remember that you are an Englishman, and have consequently won first prize in the lottery of life.*

The source for this statement (much quoted as above by Sir Peter Ustinov — in *Dear Me*, 1977, for example) is a book called *Jottings from an Active Life* (1928) by Colonel Sir Alexander Weston Jarvis. Jarvis wrote of Rhodes: 'He was never tired of impressing upon one that the fact of being an Englishman was the greatest prize in the lottery of life, and that it was the thought which always sustained him when he was troubled.'

Hence, Tom Stoppard's attribution of the words to Kipling (quoted in 1989) is probably incorrect.

4 *So much to do, so little done, goodbye, God bless you.*

From 'Dr Robinson's sermon at Westminster' (presumably at a memorial service) comes this report of Rhodes's dying words. The gist of what he said before he breathed his last on 26 March 1902 was indeed 'So much to do, so little done', though this is sometimes quoted with the phrases reversed. It was a theme that had obviously preoccupied him towards the end of his life. He said to Lord Rosebery: 'Everything in the world is too short. Life and fame and achievement, everything is too short.'

Tennyson had already anticipated him. *In Memoriam* (1850) has these lines in section lxxiii:

So many worlds, so much to do,
So little done, such things to be.

The actual last words of Rhodes were much more prosaic: 'Turn me over, Jack.'

Rice, Grantland
American sports journalist and poet (1880–1954)

5 *For when the One Great Scorer comes*
To write against your name,
He marks — not that you won or lost —
But how you played the game.

From 'Alumnus Football' (1941). In Alan Bennett's parody of an Anglican sermon in the revue *Beyond the Fringe* (1961), the line is (deliberately?) misascribed to that 'Grand old Victorian poet, W.E. Henley' (who wrote, rather, 'It matters not how strait the gate . . . I am the master of my fate').

See also THE BIBLE 50:2 *and* DE COUBERTIN 116:3.

Rice, Sir Stephen
Irish lawyer and politician (1637–1715)

1 *I will drive a coach and six horses through the Act of Settlement.*

Rice, a Roman Catholic Chief Baron of the Irish Exchequer used the courts in Dublin to get his own back on an act of settlement (1662) and was quoted as having said this by W. King, *The State of the Protestants of Ireland* (1672). It is presumably the origin of the expression 'to drive a coach and horses through something', meaning 'to overturn something wantonly, and to render it useless'. In 1843, Charles Dickens wrote in *A Christmas Carol*: 'You may talk vaguely about driving a coach-and-six up a good old flight of stairs, or through a bad young Act of Parliament . . .' (which might seem to allude to the Rice example).

Rice-Davies, Mandy
British 'model and show girl' (1944–   )

2 *Well, he would, wouldn't he?*

An innocuous enough phrase but one still used allusively because of the way it was spoken by Rice-Davies during the Profumo Affair in 1963 (Secretary of State for War John Profumo carried on with Rice-Davies's friend Christine Keeler who was allegedly sharing her favours with the Soviet military attaché). The *ODQ* (1992) describes Rice-Davies as a 'courtesan', which is rather quaint. She was called as a witness when Stephen Ward, was charged under the Sexual Offences Act. During the preliminary Magistrates Court hearing on 28 June 1963, she was questioned about the men she had had sex with. When told by Ward's defence counsel that Lord Astor — one of the names on the list — had categorically denied any involvement with her, she replied, chirpily: 'Well, he would, wouldn't he?'
The court burst into laughter, the expression passed into the language and is still resorted to because — as a good catchphrase ought to be — it is bright, useful in various circumstances and tinged with innuendo.
'Oscar Wilde said the Alps were objects of

appallingly bad taste. He would, wouldn't he?' wrote Russell Harty in *Mr Harty's Grand Tour* (1988).

Richelieu, Cardinal
French prelate and statesman (1585–1642)

3 *If you give me six lines written by the hand of the most honest of men, I will find something in them which will hang him.*

Usually ascribed to Richelieu but it may have been said, rather, by one of his agents (according to an 1867 French source).

See also BULWER-LYTTON 73:4.

Riis, Jacob
Danish-born American journalist (1849–1914)

4 *How the Other Half Lives.*

The title of Riis's book (1890) describing the conditions in which poor people lived in New York City might appear to have given us the expression meaning 'how people live who belong to different social groups (but especially the rich)'. The expression seems basically to have referred to the poor but has since been used about any 'other half'. Riis alluded to the saying in these words: 'Long ago it was said that "one half of the world does not know how the other half lives".' *OED2* finds this proverb in English (by 1607), and in French, in *Pantagruel* by Rabelais (1532). Alan Ayckbourn entitled a play (1970) *How the Other Half Loves*.

Ripley, Robert Leroy
American journalist (1893–1949)

5 *Believe it or not!*

This exclamation was used as the title of a long-running syndicated newspaper feature, and radio and TV series in the US. Ripley created and illustrated a comic strip, *Ripley's Believe It or Not* (in c 1923), but one feels the phrase must have existed before, though citations are lacking.

Roberts, Allan
American songwriter (1905–66)

6 *You Always Hurt the One You Love.*

The title of a song (1944) written to music by Doris Fisher (1915–   ) crystallizes an age-old concept. Compare Oscar Wilde, *The Ballad of Reading Gaol* (1898): 'Yet each man kills the thing he loves.'

Roche, Sir Boyle
Irish politician (1743–1807)

1 *Mr Speaker, I smell a rat; I see him forming in the air and darkening the sky; but I'll nip him in the bud.*

Attributed remark in the Irish Parliament. In an untraced book — Wills, *The Irish Nation* — it is conceded that the Chamberlain to the Vice-Regal court (in Dublin), as Roche later became, had a 'graceful address and ready wit', but, additionally, 'it was usual for members of the cabinet to write speeches for him, which he committed to memory, and, while mastering the substance, generally contrived to travesty the language and ornament with peculiar graces of his own'. Could this be the reason for Roche's peculiar sayings?

The *Dictionary of National Biography* adds that 'he gained his lasting reputation as an inveterate perpetrator of "bulls" [i.e. ludicrous, self-contradictory propositions, often associated with the Irish]'.

2 *How could the sergeant-at-arms stop him in the rear, while he was catching him at the front? Could he like a bird be in two places at once?*

Supposedly said in the Irish parliament. This version is from *A Book of Irish Quotations* (1984). *BDPF* suggests that he was quoting from 'Jevon's play *The Devil of a Wife*' (untraced) and that what he said was, 'Mr Speaker, it is impossible I could have been in two places at once, unless I were a bird' — adding that the phrase was probably of even earlier origin.

3 *What has posterity done for us?*

Said in the Irish parliament? Benham (1948), claiming that it is 'erroneously attributed' to Roche, notes that the words occur in John Trumbull's poetic work *McFingal* (1775) and that Mrs Elizabeth Montagu had earlier written in a letter (1 January 1742): 'The man [Roche?] was laughed at as a blunderer who said in a public business "We do much for posterity; I would fain see them do something for us".' Even earlier, as Benham points out, Sir Richard Steele [in fact, it was Joseph Addison] had written in

The Spectator (No. 583; 1714): 'We are always doing, says he, something for Posterity, but I would fain see Posterity do something for us.' This obviously predates Roche.

The version given in *A Book of Irish Quotations* (1984) is: 'Why should we put ourselves out of our way to do anything for posterity; for what has posterity done for us? *(Laughter).* I apprehend you gentlemen have entirely mistaken my words, I assure the house that by posterity I do not mean my ancestors but those who came immediately after them.'

Rockefeller, Nelson
American Republican Governor and Vice-President (1908–79)

4 *The brotherhood of man under the fatherhood of God.*

When Governor Rockefeller was competing against Barry Goldwater for the Republican Presidential nomination in 1964, reporters latched on to a favourite saying of the candidate and rendered it with the acronym 'BOMFOG'. In fact, according to Safire (1978), they had been beaten to it by Hy Sheffer, a stenotypist on the Governor's staff who had found the abbreviation convenient for the previous five or six years.

The words come from a much-quoted saying of John D. Rockefeller II (1874–1960), the Governor's father: 'These are the principles upon which alone a new world recognizing the brotherhood of man and the fatherhood of God can be established . . .' Later, 'BOMFOG' became an acronym for any pompous, meaningless generality and was also used by feminists to denote use of language that demeaned women by reflecting patrician attitudes. The individual phrases 'brotherhood of man' and 'fatherhood of God' do not appear before the nineteenth century.

Roddenberry, Gene
American film producer and writer (1921–91)

5 *Space — the final frontier. These are the voyages of the starship* Enterprise. *Its five year mission: to explore strange new worlds, to seek out new life and new civilizations, to boldly go where no man has gone before.*

From the introductory voice-over commentary to the TV science-fiction series *Star Trek* (1966–9). Though short-lived, the show nevertheless acquired a considerable after-life through countless repeats (not least in the UK) and through the activities of 'Trekky' fans. In one of the feature films (1988) that belatedly spun off from the series, the split infinitive remained but feminism, presumably, had decreed that it should become 'to boldly go where no *one* has gone before'.

1 *Beam me up, Scotty!*

In fact, 'Beam us up, Mr Scott' appears to be the nearest thing to this catchphrase ever actually spoken in the series (in an episode called 'Gamesters of Triskelion'). According to 'Trekkers', Captain Kirk (William Shatner) never actually said to Lieutenant Commander 'Scotty' Scott, the chief engineer, 'Beam me up, Scotty!' — meaning that he should transpose body into matter, or some such thing. Another actual phrase that has been used is, 'Enterprise, beam us up' and, we are told, that in the fourth episode, 'Scotty, beam me up' *may* have been said. Somebody has probably written a doctoral thesis on all this.

Rogers, Will
American humorist-philosopher (1879–1935)

2 *I never met a man I didn't like.*

The folksy American 'cowboy comedian' of the 1920 and 1930s suggested this epitaph for himself (by 1926). It is a little more believable in context: 'When I die, my epitaph or whatever you call those signs on gravestones is going to read: "I joked about every prominent man of my time, but I never met one I dident [sic] like." I am so proud of that I can hardly wait to die so it can be carved. And when you come to my grave you will find me sitting there, proudly reading it.'
According to Paula McSpadden Love, *The Will Rogers Book* (1972), the utterance was first printed in the *Boston Globe* (16 June 1930). However, the *Saturday Evening Post* (6 November 1926) had: 'I bet you if I had met him [Trotsky] and had a chat with him, I would have found him a very interesting and human fellow, for I never yet met a man that I didn't like.'

Rohe, Ludwig Mies van der
German-born architect (1886–1969)

3 *Less is more.*

A design statement meaning that less visual clutter makes for a more satisfying living environment. It was quoted at his death in the *New York Herald Tribune*. Robert Browning had used the phrase in a different artistic context in 'Andrea del Sarto' (1855).

4 *God is in the details.*

The architect's obituary in *the New York Times* (1969) attributed this saying to Mies but it also appears to have been a favourite of the German art historian Aby Warburg (though E.M. Gombrich, his biographer, is not certain that it originated with him). In the form *Le bon Dieu est dans le détail*, it has also been attributed to Gustave Flaubert (1821–80).

Roland, Madame
Wife of French statesman (1756–93)

5 *O Liberty! how many crimes are committed in thy name!*

Mme Roland was about to be executed by the guillotine during the French Revolution (on 8 November 1793). According to Robert Chambers, *Book of Days* (1864), she addressed her remark to a gigantic statue of Liberty erected near it.

Rooney, Mickey
American film actor (1920–   )

6 *Let's put on a show!*

These are often taken to be staple lines from the films that the young Mickey Rooney made with Judy Garland from 1939 onwards. The expression apparently had several forms — 'Hey! I've got it! Why don't we put on a show?'/'Hey kids! We can put on the show in the backyard!'/'Let's do the show right here in the barn!' — though it is difficult to give a precise citation.
In *Babes in Arms* (1939) Rooney and Garland play the teenage children of retired vaudeville players who decide to put on a big show of their own. Alas, they do not actually say any of the above lines, though they do express their determination to 'put on a show'. In *Strike Up the Band* (1940), Rooney has the line: 'Say, that's not a bad idea. We could put on our own show!' —

though he does not say it to Garland. In whatever form, the line has become a film cliché, now used only with amused affection.

Roosevelt, Franklin D.
American Democratic 32nd President (1882–1945)

1 *I pledge you, I pledge myself to a New Deal for the American people.*

So said Roosevelt to the 1932 Democratic Convention that had just nominated him. The 'New Deal' slogan became the keynote to the election campaign, but it was not new to politics. In Britain, David Lloyd George had talked of a 'New deal for everyone' in 1919. Woodrow Wilson had had a 'New Freedom' slogan, and Teddy Roosevelt had talked of a 'Square Deal'. Abraham Lincoln had used 'New deal' on occasions. The FDR use was engineered by either Samuel Rosenman or Raymond Moley. 'I had not the slightest idea that it would take hold the way it did,' Rosenman said later, 'nor did the Governor [Roosevelt] when he read and revised what I had written . . . It was simply one of those phrases that catch public fancy and survive.' On the other hand, Moley claimed: 'The expression "new deal" was in the draft I left at Albany with Roosevelt . . . I was not aware that this would be the slogan for the campaign. It was a phrase that would have occurred to almost anyone.'

2 *Let me assert my firm belief that the only thing we have to fear is fear itself.*

Roosevelt took the Presidential oath of office on 4 March 1933 and then delivered his first Inaugural address. The classic sentence did not appear in Roosevelt's first draft but appears to have been inserted by him the day before the speech was delivered. As for inspiration: a copy of Thoreau's writings was with him at this time containing the line 'Nothing is so much to be feared as fear'. Raymond Moley asserted later, however, that it was Louis Howe who contributed the 'fear' phrase, having picked it up from a newspaper advertisement for a department store.

In fact, any number of precedents could be cited — the Duke of Wellington ('the only thing I am afraid of is fear'), Montaigne, Bacon, the Book of Proverbs — but in the end what matters is that Roosevelt had the wit to utter it on this occasion.

3 *He is the Happy Warrior of the political battlefield.*

Alfred E. Smith, the Democrat politician, had this nickname bestowed on him by Roosevelt in 1924. Smith ran against Herbert Hoover for the Presidency in 1928 but did not win. He subsequently fell out with Roosevelt when the latter became President. The phrase comes from William Wordsworth's 'Character of the Happy Warrior' (1807):

Who is the happy Warrior? Who is he
That every man in arms should wish
    to be?

4 *And while I am talking to you mothers and fathers, I give you one more assurance. I have said this before, but I shall say it again and again and again: Your boys are not going to be sent into any foreign wars.*

From a campaign speech delivered in Boston, Massachusetts (30 October 1940). In a sense, Roosevelt kept his promise. American boys were never sent into any foreign wars. The US went to war in December 1941 after the Japanese attack on Pearl Harbor and only later were American forces sent to Europe and elsewhere. Compare Lyndon Johnson (broadcast address on Vietnam, 21 October 1964): 'We are not about to send American boys nine or ten thousand miles away from home to do what Asian boys ought to be doing for themselves.'

5 *And who voted against the appropriations for an adequate national defense? MARTIN, BARTON and FISH.*

From election speeches, 1940. A slogan for crowd repetition. Seeking to blame Republicans for US military unpreparedness, Roosevelt cited three Congressmen — Joseph Martin, Bruce Barton (later of the advertising agency Batten, Barton, Durstine & Osborn) and Hamilton Fish. The speech in which the phrase first arose was written by Judge Samuel I. Rosenman and Robert E. Sherwood, the dramatist. Crowds loved to join the rhythmic line echoing 'Wynken, Blynken and Nod'.

6 *Sail on, Oh Ship of State!*
Sail on, Oh Union, strong and great.
Humanity with all its fears,
With all the hope of future years,
Is hanging breathless on thy fate!

On 20 January 1941, before the US had entered the Second World War, Roosevelt sent a letter to the British Prime Minister, Winston Churchill, containing this extract (with minor differences in spelling and punctuation) from an 1849 poem 'The Building of the Ship' by Longfellow. He commented: 'I think this verse applies to your people as it does to us.' (For Churchill's response, see 95:1.)

1 *Yesterday, December 7th 1941, a date which will live in infamy, the United States of America was suddenly and deliberately attacked by naval and air forces of the Empire of Japan.*

Thus Roosevelt began his address to Congress, the day after Pearl Harbor. In the draft it had said, 'a date which will live in world history' and 'simultaneously'. With such strokes did he make his speech seeking a declaration of war against Japan the more memorable. However, *Quotations in History* (1976) has 'date that shall live in infamy'. *The Dictionary of 20th-Century Allusions* (1991) has 'day that will live in infamy'.

Roosevelt, Theodore
American Republican 26th President (1858–1919)

2 *I wish to preach not the doctrine of ignoble ease but the doctrine of the strenuous life.*

In a speech at the Appomattox Day celebration of the Hamilton Club (Chicago, 10 April 1899) which helped swell Roosevelt's reputation and swept him into the Vice-Presidency in the election of 1900, and then into the White House following the assassination of President McKinley.

3 *There is a homely adage — 'Speak softly and carry a big stick — you will go far'.*

In 2 September 1901, just a few days before the assassination of President McKinley, Roosevelt said this at Minnesota State Fair. He went on, 'If the American nation will speak softly and yet build and keep at a pitch of the highest training a thoroughly efficient navy, the Monroe Doctrine [which sought to exclude European intervention in the American continent] will go far.' Note that he did not claim the 'adage' to be original.

4 *I am strong as a bull moose.*

After two terms as President, Roosevelt withdrew from Republican politics and then, in 1912, unsuccessfully tried to make a come-back as a Progressive ('Bull Moose') candidate. The popular name stemmed from a remark Roosevelt had made when he was standing as Vice-President in 1900. Writing to Mark Hanna, he said, 'I am strong as a bull moose and you can use me to the limit.'

5 *Good . . . to the last drop.*

Visiting Joel Cheek, perfector of the Maxwell House coffee blend, in 1907, the President drank a cup and passed this comment. The slogan has been in use ever since, despite those who have inquired, 'What's wrong with the last drop then?' Professors of English have considered the problem and ruled that 'to' can be inclusive and need not mean 'up to but not including'.

Rose, Billy
American impresario and songwriter (1899–1966)

6 *Does the Spearmint Lose Its Flavour on the Bedpost Overnight?*

The 1924 song with this title is usually credited to Marty Bloom and Ernest Breuer 'with assistance from' Rose. 'Chewing-gum' was substituted for 'Spearmint' when the song was revived in Britain in 1959, lest it seem to be advertising a particular brand.

7 *The Night is Young (and You're So Beautiful).*

Title of a song by Rose with Irving Kahal (1936). The previous year 'The Night Is Young (And So Are We)' had been written by Oscar Hammerstein II and Sigmund Romberg and included in the film *The Night is Young*. Hence, presumably, the expression, 'The night is young!' — the sort of thing one would say when attempting to justify another drink. From Frank Brady, *Citizen Welles* (1989): 'At three in the morning, when a few people decided to leave, Orson, stepping into the role of clichéd host from a Grade B movie, would not hear of it: "You're not leaving already, my friends. The night is still young. Play, Gypsies! Play, play, play!"'

Rosebery, 5th Earl of
British Liberal Prime Minister
(1847–1929)

1 *I have three ambitions in life: to win the Derby, marry an heiress, and become Prime Minister.*

A legend grew up that Rosebery had said this. Robert Rhodes James commented in *Rosebery* (1963) that, 'although it is quite possible that he did once make such an observation, it is extremely unlikely that it was meant seriously'. Rhodes James also quotes Algernon Cecil in *Queen Victoria and Her Prime Ministers* (1953) as saying: 'At London dinner-parties half a century ago it was rare for Rosebery to be mentioned without some allusion being made to his three declared ambitions . . . Aprocryphal or not, it gives if not Rosebery's measure of a man, yet certainly the measure of him given by the men of his time.'

Nevertheless, he achieved his ambitions in the sense that he did win the Derby thrice (twice while Prime Minister), he married Hannah Rothschild, an heiress, and — managing to overcome his aristocratic disdain for accepting almost anything that was offered him — he succeeded Gladstone as Prime Minister in 1894. But the Liberal Party was falling apart anyway, Rosebery was prey to insomnia and inaction, and he was out of office after a year. He was forty-eight and, despite his undoubted personal qualities, never held high office again.

2 *To your tents, O Israel!*

A famous — and possibly apocryphal — story concerns Rosebery saying this one evening when he felt his Rothschild relatives had kept him up long enough. The phrase was later used by G.B. Shaw as the title of a diatribe in *The Fortnightly Review* (November 1893), expressing Fabian disillusion with Gladstone's Liberal Party on such radical matters as Irish Home Rule. Michael Holroyd in *Bernard Shaw* (Vol. 1) calls it 'the Biblical call to revolt'. It is a quotation from 1 Kings 12:16.

3 *I am leaving tonight; Hannah and the rest of the heavy baggage will follow later.*

Rhodes James (as above) describes this as one of Rosebery's 'alleged *mots*'.

4 *I must plough my furrow alone.*

Rosebery said this in a speech (19 July 1901) on breaking away from his Liberal Party colleagues. A famous declaration of independence, but it seems likely that the expression had been used by others before him. He added: 'Before I get to the end of that furrow it is possible that I may find myself not alone . . . If it be so, I shall remain very contented in the society of my books and my home.' So it was to be.

Ross, Harold
American editor of *The New Yorker*
(1892–1951)

5 The New Yorker *will not be edited for the little old lady from Dubuque.*

When Ross founded the magazine in 1925, he made this declaration. Dubuque, Iowa, thus became involved in another of those yardstick phrases on account of its being representative of Middle America (like 'It'll play in Peoria', see 130:5). A man called 'Boots' Mulgrew who lived there used to contribute squibs to the Chicago *Tribune* signed 'Old Lady in Dubuque'. Ross, presumably, had heard of this line and consciously or otherwise developed it to describe the sort of person he was not creating the magazine for. (On the other hand, Malcolm Muggeridge once quoted a writer on the *Daily Express* who explained the huge readership of Beaverbrook newspapers in the UK by saying, 'I write for one little old reader'.)

6 *Who he?*

James Thurber in *The Years with Ross* (1959), describes how Ross would customarily add this query to manuscripts (though not for publication) on finding a name he did not know in an article (sometimes betraying his ignorance). He said the only two names everyone knew were Houdini and Sherlock Holmes. The phrase echoes the Duke of Wellington's peremptory 'Who? Who?' on hearing the names of ministers in Lord Derby's new administration (1852).

Re-popularized by *Private Eye* in the 1980s, this editorial interjection after a little-known person's name showed some signs of catching on: 'This month, for instance, has been the time for remembering the 110th anniversary of the birth of Grigori Petrovsky. Who he?' — *New Statesman*, 26

February 1988. A book with the title *Who He? Goodman's Dictionary of the Unknown Famous* was published in 1984.

Rotten, Johnny
(John Lydon) British pop singer (1957–   )

1 *Love is two minutes fifty-two seconds of squishing [or squelching] noises. It shows your mind isn't clicking right.*

Of recent *bons mots*, one of the most quoted – but variously so – is the opinion of Johnny Rotten, who was at one time with the notorious punk group, the Sex Pistols. Jonathon Green's *Dictionary of Contemporary Quotations* (1982) has the version: 'Love is two minutes fifty-two seconds of squishing noises. It shows your mind isn't clicking right.' But, in the previous year, my *Graffiti 3* had had a photograph taken in London (1980) of a wall bearing the legend: 'Love is three minutes of squelching noises. (Mr J. Rotten).'

Auberon Waugh in *Private Eye* (18 November 1983) settled for 'two and a half minutes of squelching' but provided the interesting gloss that, in an interview with Christena Appleyard in the *Mirror*, Rotten had wished to amend his aphorism: 'It is more like five minutes now, he says, because he has mastered a new technique.' McConville and Shearlaw in *The Slanguage of Sex* (1984) claim that as a result of Rotten's statement, 'squelching' became an expression for sexual intercourse. They suggest that he had referred to 'two minutes of squelching noises' in *New Musical Express* in 1978.

Routh, Dr Martin
English scholar (1755–1854)

2 *Always verify your references.*

In 1949 Winston Churchill gave an innaccurate account to the House of Commons of when he had first heard the words 'unconditional surrender' from President Roosevelt. Subsequently, in his *The Second World War*, Vol. 4 (1951), Churchill wrote: 'It was only when I got home and searched my archives that I found the facts as they have been set out here. I am reminded of the professor who in his declining hours was asked by his devoted pupils for his final counsel. He replied, "Verify your quotations".'

Well, not exactly a 'professor', and not exactly his dying words, and not 'quota-

tions' either. Martin Routh was President of Magdalen College, Oxford, for sixty-three years. Of the many stories told about Routh, Churchill was groping towards the one where he was asked what precept could serve as a rule of life to an aspiring young man. Said Routh: 'You will find it a very good practice *always to verify your references, Sir!*'

This story was first recorded in this form in 1878, as Churchill and his amanuenses might themselves have verified. James Morris in *Oxford* (1965) has it that Routh gave the advice to John Burgon, later a noted Dean of Chichester (indeed, it is in Burgon's *Lives of Twelve Good Men*, 1888 ed.). Perhaps Churchill was recalling instead the Earl of Rosebery's version, given in a speech on 23 November 1897: 'Another confirmation of the advice given by one aged sage to somebody who sought his guidance in life, namely, "Always wind up your watch and verify your quotations".'

Rubin, Jerry
American 'yippie' leader (1938–   )

3 *Don't trust anyone over thirty.*

Quoted in Flexner (1982). Actually, this appears to have been first uttered by *Jack Weinberg* at Berkeley in 1964–5 during a free speech demonstration. Bartlett (1992) finds Weinberg (1940–   ) saying in an interview on the free speech movement, 'We have a saying in the movement that we don't trust anybody over thirty'. In 1970 Weinberg told the *Washington Post* (23 March) that he did not actually believe the statement but had said it in response to a question about adults manipulating the organization.

Rushdie, Salman
Indian-born novelist (1947–   )

4 *Naughty but nice.*

Before achieving fame and misfortune as a novelist, Rushdie worked as a freelance advertising copywriter in London. It is often said that he was the inspiration behind the use of the phrase 'Naughty but nice' to promote fresh cream in cakes for the National Dairy Council in 1981–4. Advertisements being collaborative efforts, agencies – in this case Ogilvy & Mather – are reluctant to concede creative triumphs to particular individuals. Whatever his contribution on this one, however, Rushdie certainly did not coin the phrase 'Naughty but nice'. A 1939 US film had the title. It was about a professor of classical music who accidentally wrote a popular song. Curiously, *ODMQ* (1991) gives the coinage of the phrase to Jerry Wald and Richard Macaulay, writers of the film, on this basis. But Partridge/*Slang* glosses it as 'a reference to copulation since *c* 1900 ex a song that Minnie Schult sang and popularized in the USA, 1890s'. Indeed. There have since been various songs with the title, notably one by Johnny Mercer and Harry Warren in *The Belle of New York* (film, 1952). Compare also the similarly alliterative, 'It's Foolish But It's Fun' (Gus Kahn/Robert Stolz) sung by Deanna Durbin in *Spring Parade* (1940).

Rusk, Dean
American Democratic politician (1909–)

1 *We're eyeball to eyeball and the other fellow just blinked.*

In the missile crisis of October 1962, the US took a tough line when the Soviet Union placed missiles on Cuban soil. After a tense few days, the Soviets withdrew. Secretary of State Rusk was speaking to an ABC news correspondent, John Scali, on 24 October and said: 'Remember, when you report this, that, eyeball to eyeball, they blinked first.' Columnists Charles Bartlett and Stewart Alsop then helped to popularize this in the above form (though sometimes 'I think' is inserted before 'the other fellow').
   'Eyeball to eyeball' is a black American serviceman's idiom. Safire (1978) quotes a reply given by the all-black 24th Infantry Regiment to an inquiry from General MacArthur's HQ in Korea (November 1950) – 'Do you have contact with the enemy?' 'We is eyeball to eyeball.'

Ruskin, John
English art critic (1819–1900)

2 *There was a rocky valley between Buxton and Bakewell . . . divine as the vale of Tempe; you might have seen the gods there morning and evening, – Apollo and the sweet Muses of the Light . . . You enterprised a railroad . . . you blasted its rocks away . . . And now, every fool in Buxton can be at Bakewell in half-an-hour, and every fool in Bakewell at Buxton.*

An early attack on the pointlessness of much travel. This comes from *Praeterita* (1885–9).

3 *I have seen, and heard, much of Cockney impudence before now; but never expected to hear a coxcomb ask two hundred guineas for flinging a pot of paint in the public's face.*

On Whistler's painting 'The Falling Rocket, or Nocturne in Black and Gold', in a letter (18 June 1877) and included in *Fors Clavigera: Letters to the Workers and Labourers of Great Britain*. Whistler (an American) brought an action for libel and was awarded a farthing in damages. He was bankrupted by his legal costs; Ruskin could not pay his own either and had to be helped by friends.
   Whistler's reply to the question, 'For two days' labour, you ask two hundred guineas?' was 'No, I ask it for the knowledge of a lifetime'.

[*Source:* D.C. Seitz, *Whistler Stories*, 1913.]

Russell, Bertrand
(3rd Earl Russell)
English mathematician and philosopher (1872–1970)

4 *Better Red than dead.*

A slogan used by some (mainly British) nuclear disarmers. *Time* Magazine (15 September 1961) gave 'I'd rather be Red than dead' as a slogan of Britain's Campaign for Nuclear Disarmament. Russell wrote in 1958: 'If no alternative remains except Communist domination or the extinction of the human race, the former alternative is the lesser of two evils'. The counter-cry 'Better dead than red' may also have had some currency. (In the film *Love With a Proper Stranger* (US, 1964) Steve McQueen proposed to Natalie Wood with a picket sign stating 'Better Wed Than Dead'.)

Russell, Sir William Howard
British journalist (1820–97)

5 *The ground flies beneath their horses' feet; gathering speed at every stride, they dash on towards that thin red streak topped with a line of steel.*

So Russell wrote in a report dated 25 October and published in *The Times* (14

November 1854) when describing a Russian charge repulsed by the British 93rd Highlanders. This was the first stage of the Battle of Balaclava in the Crimean War (the Charge of the Light Brigade followed a few hours later). The *ODQ* (1979, 1992) has 'tipped' here instead of 'topped'.

By the time he wrote his book *The British Expedition to the Crimea* (1877), Russell was putting: 'The Russians dashed on towards *that thin red line tipped with steel* [his italics]. Thus was created the jingoistic Victorian phrase 'the thin red line', standing for the supposed invincibility of British infantry tactics.

Compare Kipling's poem 'Tommy' from *Departmental Ditties* (1890) which goes: 'But it's "Thin red line of 'eroes" when the drums begin to roll.'

S

Sabatini, Rafael
Italian-born novelist
(1875–1950)

1 *Born with the gift of laughter and a sense that the world was mad.*

Over the inside gate at Yale University's Hall of Graduate Studies is inscribed this slight variation of the first line from Sabatini's popular novel *Scaramouche* (1921), though understandably Yale savants did not immediately recognize it as such. How this not very highly-regarded literary figure came to have his work dispayed in such an illustrious setting was subsequently explained in a letter to *The New Yorker* (8 December 1934) from a young architect, John Donald Tuttle. He had chosen the line, he said, as a form of protest against the neo-gothic he had been forced to use on the building. 'As a propitiatory gift to my gods for this terrible thing I was doing, and to make them forget by appealing to their sense of humour, I carved the inscription over the door' (quoted in Burnam, 1980).

Sacks, Oliver
British-born neurologist
(1933–   )

2 *The Man Who Mistook His Wife for a Hat.*

A book (1985) by Sacks, a neurologist working in the US, describes various instances of brain disorders. The title refers to a case in which the patient could not recognize everyday objects. Also the title of an opera (1991) by Michael Nyman (based on the book).

Sackville-West, V.
English novelist and poet
(1892–1962)

3 *They rustle, they brustle, they crackle, and if you can crush beech nuts under foot at the same time, so much the better. But beech nuts aren't essential. The essential is that you should tramp through very dry, very crisp, brown leaves — a thick drift of them in the Autumn woods, shuffling through them, kicking them up . . . walking in fact 'through leaves'.*

In a BBC radio talk 'Personal Pleasures' (1950) Sackville-West explained the origin of an expression 'through leaves', used in her family to express pure happiness. That is, the sort of happiness enjoyed by young children shuffling through drifts of dry autumn leaves.

Saki
(H.H. Munro)
English writer
(1870–1916)

4 *Women and elephants never forget an injury.*

From 'Reginald on Besetting Sins' in *Reginald* (1904). The basic expression 'an elephant never forgets' is what one might say of one's self when complimented on remembering a piece of information forgotten by others. As such, it is based on the view that elephants are supposed to remember trainers, keepers and so on, especially those who have been unkind to them. A song with the title 'The Elephant Never Forgets' was featured in the play *The Golden Toy* by Carl Zuckmayer (London, 1934) and recorded by Lupino Lane. *Stevenson's Book of Proverbs, Maxims and Familiar Phrases* (1949) has that the modern saying really derives from a Greek proverb: 'The camel [sic] never forgets an injury' — which is exactly how Saki uses it.

Salinger, J.D.
American novelist (1919–   )

1 *The Catcher in the Rye.*

The title of Salinger's 1951 novel (about the emergent seventeen-year-old Holden Caulfield) may initially seem rather baffling. As explained in Chapter 22, however, it comes from a vision that Holden has of standing in a field of rye below a cliff where he will catch any children who fall off. He wishes to protect innocent children from disillusionment with the world of grown-ups.

Salisbury, 5th Marquess of
British Conservative politician (1893–1972)

2 *Too clever by half.*

To say that someone is 'too clever by half' is to show that you think they are more clever than wise and are overreaching themselves. As such, this is a fairly common idiom. However, the most notable political use of the phrase was by the 5th Marquess of Salisbury, a prominent Conservative, about another such, Iain Macleod. In a speech to the House of Lords in 1961, he said: 'The present Colonial Secretary has been too clever by half. I believe he is a very fine bridge player. It is not considered immoral, or even bad form to outwit one's opponents at bridge. It almost seems to me as if the Colonial Secretary, when he abandoned the sphere of bridge for the sphere of politics, brought his bridge technique with him.'

The remark seems to run in the family. The 3rd Marquess (later Prime Minister) had anticipated him in a debate on the Irish Church Resolutions in the House of Commons on 30 March 1868, when he said of an amendment moved by Disraeli: 'I know that with a certain number of Gentlemen on this side of the House this Amendment is popular. I have heard it spoken of as being

very clever. It is clever, Sir; it is too clever by half.'

Rodney Ackland's version of an Alexander Ostrovsky play was presented as *Too Clever by Half* at the Old Vic, London, in 1988.

Of Dr Jonathan Miller, the polymath, in the mid-1970s, it was said, 'He's too clever by three-quarters.'

Sandburg, Carl
American poet (1878–1967)

3 *Sometime they'll give a war and nobody will come.*

The origin of this light joke appears to lie in Sandburg's epic poem *The People, Yes* (1936). It became popular in the 1960s — especially as a graffito — at the time of protests against the Vietnam War. Charlotte Keyes (1914–   ) wrote an article in *McCall's* Magazine (October 1966), which was given the title 'Suppose They Gave a War, and No One Came?' A US film (1969) was called *Suppose They Gave a War and Nobody Came?*

It is also well known in German as '*Stell dir vor, es gibt Krieg, und keiner geht hin* [Suppose they gave a war and nobody came]'. Ralf Bülow in the journal *Der Sprachdienst*, No. 27 (1983) traced it back not only to Sandburg but also to Thornton Wilder. They both lived in Chicago in the early 1930s. Bülow recounts a Wilder anecdote which Sandburg may have picked up. In the same edition of *Der Sprachdienst*, Reinhard Roche comments on how German journalists and others have ascribed the remark to Bertolt Brecht because of his poem '*Wer zu Hause bleibt, wenn der Kampf beginnt* [Who will be away from home when the war begins?]' and argues that 'much more philological caution is needed before assigning certain popular expressions to literary figures'.

Sayers, Dorothy L.
English novelist and translator (1893–1957)

4 *The Nine Tailors.*

In the Sayers novel with this title (1934), 'Tailor Paul' is the name of one of the church bells of Fenchurch St Paul which play a significant part in the plot. The saying 'Nine Tailors Make A Man' is quoted on the last page of the novel. So what we have in the title is a blend of various elements. In bell ringing it was possible to indicate the sex of the dead person for whom the bells were being tolled. 'Nine tailors' or 'nine tellers' (strokes) meant a man. The bellringing use of the phrase does, however, echo an actual proverb, 'It takes nine tailors to make a man', which apparently came from the French, *c* 1600. The meaning here would seem to be that a man should buy his clothes from various sources. Or it was something said in contempt of tailors (in that they were so feeble that it would take nine of them to equal one normal man).

G.L. Apperson, the proverb collector, showed in 1929 that, until the end of the seventeenth century, there was some uncertainty about the number of tailors mentioned. In *Westward Hoe* by John Webster and Thomas Dekker (1607) it appeared as three.

Schroeder, Patricia
American Democratic politician (1940–)

1 *After carefully watching Ronald Reagan, he is attempting a great breakthrough in political technology — he has been perfecting the Teflon-coated Presidency. He sees to it that nothing sticks to him.*

From her speech in the US House of Representatives (2 August 1983). 'Teflon' is the proprietary name for polytetrafluoroethylene (first produced 1938, US patent 1945), a heat-resistant plastic chiefly known as the name given to a range of cookware coated with it that 'won't scratch, scar or mar' (1965). Hence, when President Reagan exhibited an ability during his first term of office (1981–85) to brush off any kind of 'dirt' or scandal that was thrown at him (chiefly through the charm of his personality), this was the epithet to apply to him. *Time* Magazine wrote (7 July 1986): 'Critics say that he is coated with Teflon, that no mess he makes ever sticks to him. That is perfectly true.' As his second term wore on, however, and as happens with an old nonstick frying-pan, the story was a little different.

Schroeder made the observation first, but it turned into a political cliché used by many.

Schulberg, Budd
American writer (1914–)

2 Terry (to Charley): *I coulda had class! I coulda been a contender! I coulda been somebody — instead of a bum, which is what I am! Let's face it. It was you, Charley!*

From the film *On the Waterfront* (US, 1954). Schulberg's script was performed by Marlon Brando as Terry and Rod Steiger as Charley, his brother. It has become a much-quoted line, not least because of the way in which Brando delivered it. Brando plays a dockyard worker fighting corruption. In this speech, he laments what has happened to his former career as a boxer and blames it on his brother's betrayal: 'Whadda I get? A one-way ticket to Palookaville.'

Schultz, Charles
M. American cartoonist and creator of 'Peanuts' strip (1922–)

3 *Good grief, Charlie Brown!*

A stock phrase from the 'Peanuts' strip. The behaviour of 'Charlie Brown' frequently elicits this exclamation from other characters.

4 *It was a dark and stormy night . . .*

The title of one of Schultz's books (date unknown). In it, the line is given to the character Snoopy in his doomed attempts to write the Great American Novel. As a scene-setting, opening phrase, this appears to have been irresistible to more than one story-teller over the years and has now become a joke. It was used in all seriousness by the English novelist Edward Bulwer-Lytton at the start of *Paul Clifford* (1830). At some stage, the phrase also became part of a jokey children's 'circular' story-telling game, 'The tale without an end'. Iona and Peter Opie in *The Lore and Language of Schoolchildren* (1959) describe the workings thus: 'The tale usually begins: "It was a dark and stormy night, and the Captain said to the Bo'sun, 'Bo'sun, tell us a story,' so the Bo'sun began . . ." And such is any child's readiness to hear a good story that the tale may be told three times round before the listeners appreciate that they are being diddled.'

Schumacher, E.F.
German-born British economist (1911–77)

1 *Small is Beautiful. A study of economics as if people mattered.*

Full title of the book (1973), the first phrase of which provided a catchphrase and a slogan for those who were opposed to the expansionist trend in business and organizations that was very apparent in the 1960s and 1970s and who wanted 'economics on a human scale'. However, it appears that Schumacher very nearly did not bother with the phrase. According to his daughter and another correspondent (*Observer*, 29 April and 6 June 1984), the book was going to be called 'The Homecomers'. His publisher, Anthony Blond, suggested 'Small*ness* is Beautiful', and then Desmond Briggs, the co-publisher, came up with the eventual wording.

Scott, C.P.
British newspaper editor (1846–1932)

2 *Comment is free, but facts are sacred.*

Scott was the influential editor of the *Manchester Guardian* for more than fifty-nine years — the longest editorship of a national newspaper anywhere in the world. In a signed editorial on 5 May 1921, marking the paper's centenary, he wrote: 'The newspaper is of necessity something of a monopoly, and its first duty is to shun the temptations of monopoly. Its primary office is the gathering of news. At the peril of its soul it must see that the supply is not tainted. Neither in what it gives, nor in what it does not give, nor in the mode of presentation, must the unclouded face of truth suffer wrong. Comment is free, but facts are sacred.' This passage was seized upon fairly quickly by politicians and journalists who, broadly speaking, held Scott in high regard. A man of forthright ideas and integrity, he is said to have expressed surprise when it was suggested to him that not all readers immediately turned to the leader page first of all.

Scott, Paul
English novelist (1920–78)

3 *The Jewel in the Crown.*

It would be reasonable to suppose that the 1984 television adaptation of Paul Scott's 'Raj Quartet' of novels had something to do with the popularity of this phrase, now meaning, 'a bright feature, an oustanding part of anything'. The first of Scott's novels was called *The Jewel in the Crown* (1966) and gave its name to the whole TV series. 'The Jewel in *Her* Crown' [my italics] is the title of a 'semi-historical, semi-allegorical' picture referred to early on in the book. It showed Queen Victoria, 'surrounded by representative figures of her Indian Empire: Princes, landowners, merchants, moneylenders, sepoys, farmers, servants, children, mothers, and remarkably clean and tidy beggars . . . An Indian prince, attended by native servants, was approaching the throne bearing a velvet cushion on which he offered a large and sparkling gem.' (In fact, Victoria, like Disraeli, who is also portrayed, never set foot in India.)

Children at the school where the picture was displayed had to be told that 'the gem was simply representative of tribute, and that the jewel of the title was India herself'. The picture must have been painted *after* 1877, the year in which Victoria became Empress of India. It was probably an actual picture, though the painter's name is untraced.

The *OED2* refers only to the 'jewels of the crown' as a rhetorical phrase for the colonies of the British Empire, and has a citation from 1901. The specifying of India as *the* jewel is understandable. The Kohinoor, a very large oval diamond of 108.8 carats from India, had been part of the British crown jewels since 1849.

Many writers have used the phrase in other contexts. In *Dombey and Son*, Chap. 39 (1846–8), Charles Dickens writes: 'Clemency is the brightest jewel in the crown of a Briton's head.' Earlier, in *The Pickwick Papers*, Chap. 24 (1836–7), he has (of Magna Carta): 'One of the brightest jewels in the British crown.' In the poem 'O Wert Thou in the Cauld Blast', Robert Burns has: 'The brightest jewel in my crown/Wad be my queen, wad be my queen.'

Scott, Captain Robert Falcon
English explorer (1868–1912)

4 *Great God! This is an awful place and terrible enough for us to have laboured without the reward of priority.*

Scott contrived masterly epitaphs for himself and his companions by keeping at his diary as he slowly froze to death. All these jottings were quickly published in

Scott's Last Expedition: Journals (1913). The above was written on reaching the South Pole and finding that the Norwegian explorer, Roald Amundsen, had beaten him to it.

1 *Had we lived, I should have had a tale to tell of the hardihood, endurance, and courage of my companions which would have stirred the hearts of every Englishman. These rough notes and our dead bodies must tell the tale.*

Towards the end, he addressed this 'Message to the public'.

2 *It seems a pity, but I do not think I can write more. R. SCOTT. For God's sake look after our people.*

The last entry in the diary, with the writing tapering away, was for 29 March 1912.

Scott, Sir Walter
Scottish novelist and poet (1771–1832)

3 *I offered Richard the services of my Free Lances.*

In *Ivanhoe* (1820) Scott writes this — and coins the word 'freelance', redolent of the Middle Ages when an unattached soldier for hire — a mercenary — would have been appropriately called a 'free lance'. Thus what is a nineteenth-century invention came to be used to describe the self-employed, especially writers or journalists.

4 *My own right hand shall do it.*

In his journal for 22 January 1826 Scott is reflecting on the fact that he has just been saddled with thousands of pounds worth of debts. He is going to raise the money by writing and not by involving anyone else. On another occasion (recorded in Cockburn, *Memorials*) he said, 'This right hand shall work it all off'. And so he did.

5 *When I want to express a sentiment which I feel strongly, I find the phrase in Shakespeare or thee [Robert Burns]. The blockheads talk of my being like Shakespeare — not fit to tie his brogues.*

Characteristic modesty, from his journal for 11 December 1826.

Segal, Erich
American writer (1937–   )

6 *Love means never having to say you're sorry.*

This saying was used in the film *Love Story* (1970) and as a promotional tag for it. Ryan O'Neal says it to Ray Milland, playing his father-in-law. He is quoting his student wife (Ali MacGraw) who has just died. Segal, who wrote the script, also produced a novelization of the story in which the line appears as the penultimate sentence, in the form 'Love means not ever having to say you're sorry'. A graffito (quoted 1974) stated: 'A vasectomy means never having to say you're sorry'; the film *The Abominable Dr Phibes* (UK, 1971) was promoted with the slogan: 'Love means never having to say you're ugly.'

Selfridge, H. Gordon
American-born store owner (1858–1947)

7 *The customer is always right.*

Selfridge was an American who, after a spell with Marshall Field & Co, came to Britain and introduced the idea of the monster department store. It appears that he was the first to say 'the customer is always right' and many other phrases now generally associated with the business of selling through stores. The hotelier César Ritz (1850–1918) was being quoted by 1908 as saying, '*Le client n'a jamais tort* [The customer is never wrong]'. *CODP*'s earliest citation is from Carl Sandburg's *Good Morning, America* (1928), introduced by the words, 'Behold the proverbs of a nation'.

8 *There are — shopping days to Christmas*

This may have been coined by Selfridge. At least, when he was still in Chicago he sent out an instruction to heads of departments and assistants at the Marshall Field store there: 'The Christmas season has begun and but twenty-three more shopping days remain in which to make our holiday sales record.' Another similar coinage was 'The Bargain Basement', also originally at Marshall Field's and then (from 1912) in London.

[*Source:* A.H. Williams, *No Name On The Door*, 1957.]

1 *Complete satisfaction or money cheer-
fully refunded.*

Another of his slogans, quoted in *ibid*.
Selfridge apparently made it the text of one
of his staff sermons and added: 'If a customer wants to try on fourteen pairs of
gloves and then decides not to buy — why,
that's all right by me.'

2 *This famous store needs no name on the
door.*

Slogan. In about 1925 Selfridge removed
the name-plates from his Oxford Street,
London, store (opened in 1909). His publicity director, George Seal, thought up this
rhyme and it was used on the firm's note-
paper as a caption to a picture of the
building. There was no other heading.

3 *'Business as usual' must be the order of
the day.*

From a speech (26 August 1914). In the context of the early days of the First World War,
the traditional store-keeper's slogan (as
might be used after a fire or similar) was first
used by H.E. Morgan, an associate of
Selfridge's. Winston Churchill also took
up the cry. It was used until it was shown
to be manifestly untrue and hopelessly
inappropriate.

Seneca
Roman philosopher and poet (*c* 4BC-AD65)

4 *Behold a thing worthy of a God, a brave
man matched in conflict with adversity*
[Ecce par Deo dignum, vir fortis cum
mala fortuna compositus].

From *De Providentia*, Sect. 4. An oft-
alluded to and variously rendered remark.
Robert Burton's *Anatomy of Melancholy*
(1621) has: 'Seneca thinks the gods are well
pleased when they see great men contending
with adversity.' Oliver Goldsmith's *The
Vicar of Wakefield* (1766) has: 'The greatest
object in the universe, says a certain philosopher, is a good man struggling with adversity; yet there is a still greater, which is the
good man that comes to relieve it.' The Revd
Sydney Smith's 'Sermon on the Duties of the
Queen' (preached in St Paul's Cathedral,
undated but possibly *c* 1837) has: 'A wise
man struggling with adversity is said by
some heathen writer to be a spectacle on
which the gods might look down with
pleasure.' It is ignored by Bartlett and *ODQ*.

Shackleton, Sir Ernest
Irish explorer (1874–1922)

5 *Men wanted for hazardous journey.
Small wages, bitter cold, long months
of complete darkness, constant danger,
safe return doubtful. Honour and recognition in case of success.*

Nominated by Julian L. Watkins in his book
The 100 Greatest Advertisements (Chicago,
1949/59) for the simplicity and 'deadly
frankness' of its copy is this small advertisement, said to have appeared in London
newspapers in 1900, signed 'Ernest Shackleton'. Watkins reports Shackleton as saying:
'It seemed as though all the men in Great
Britain were determined to accompany
me, the response was so overwhelming.'
Shackleton led three expeditions to the
Antarctic in 1907–9, 1914–17 and 1921–
22. His biographer, Roland Huntford, suggests that the advertisement would have
been published before the 1914 expedition
but casts doubt on it ever appearing.
Shackleton had no need to advertise for
companions, he says.

Shakespeare, William
English playwright and poet (1564–1616)

All's Well That Ends Well

6 *All's Well That Ends Well.*

The Revd Francis Kilvert's diary entry for 1
January 1878 has: 'The hind axle broke and
they thought they would have to spend the
night on the road . . . All's well that ends
well and they arrived safe and sound.' So, is
the allusion to the title of Shakespeare's play
(*c* 1603) or to something else? In fact, it was
a proverbial expression before Shakespeare.
CODP finds, 'If the ende be wele, than is alle
wele' in 1381, and points to the earlier form,
'Wel is him that wel ende mai'.

A curious footnote is that the title was
very nearly also bestowed on Leo Tolstoy's
War and Peace (1863–9). According to
Henry Troyat's biography, Tolstoy did not
decide on a title until very late. '*The Year
1805* would not do for a book that ended
in 1812. He had chosen *All's Well That
Ends Well*, thinking that would give the
book the casual, romantic tone of a long
English novel.' Finally, the title was 'borrowed from Proudhon' — *La Guerre et la
Paix* (1862).

1 'Twere all one
That I should love a bright particular
star
And think to wed it, he is so above
me.

Although one can see the point of Michael
Coveney entitling his biography of the
actress Dame Maggie Smith, A Bright Particular Star (1993), in the play the words are
said by a woman (Helena) about a man (Ber-
tram) (I.i.83).

Antony and Cleopatra

2 I have yet
Room for six scotches more.

Scarus's apparently jocular remark (IV.vii.9)
is quite the reverse. A 'scotch' is a cut, or
small incision, so when he meets Antony on
the battlefield he is boasting of his bravery.

As You Like It

3 And so from hour to hour, we ripe
and ripe,
And then, from hour to hour, we rot
and rot:
And thereby hangs a tale.

As a storytelling device, 'thereby hangs a
tale' is still very much in use to indicate that
some tasty titbit is about to be revealed. It
occurs a number of times in Shakespeare. In
As You Like It (II.vii.28) Jaques, reporting
the words of a motley fool (Touchstone),
says the above.
    Other examples occur in The Merry Wives
of Windsor (I.iv.143) and The Taming of
the Shrew (IV.i.50). In Othello (III.i.8),
the Clown says, 'O, thereby hangs a tail',
emphasizing the innuendo that may or may
not be present in the other examples.

4 A poor thing but mine own.

In 1985 the painter Howard Hodgkin won
the £10,000 Turner prize for a work of
art called 'A Small Thing But My Own'. It
was notable that he chose the word 'small'
rather than 'poor'. Nevertheless, he was
presumably alluding to Touchstone's line in
V.iv.57: 'A poor virgin, sir, an ill-favoured
thing, sir, but mine own.' Here Touchstone
is not talking about a work of art but about
Audrey, the country wench he woos. The
line is nowadays more likely to be used (in
mock-modesty) about a thing rather than a
person.

5 Whoever lov'd that lov'd not at first
sight?

(III.v.82) See MARLOWE 235:5.

Coriolanus

6 The gods look down, and this
unnatural scene
They laugh at.

(V.iii.184) The Gods (or God) laughing is a
phenomenon frequently to be observed in
many areas of literature. In the first book of
Homer's Iliad there is a scene in the gods'
dwelling on Olympus which has the gods
roaring with laughter. This was caused by
the spectacle of the crippled god of fire and
metallurgy, Hephaestus, with his bobbing
gait carrying round the wine-cup to serve
them. Homer says that this caused 'uncon-
trollable laughter' among the gods. This
passage gave rise to the expression 'Homeric
laughter', meaning an irresistible belly laugh
which is cosmically dominant. That is to
say, the laughter is epic rather than of the
sort that Homer might have produced. It is
interesting that here the laughter is directed
at a cripple, reminding us that, even among
the gods, there is very little laughter that is
not cruel.
    The Jewish God also laughs. A book
called The Day God Laughed (1978) by
Hyam Maccoby contains the story about
Rabbi Eliezer disputing with the Sages who
refuse to accept any sign that God approves
his interpretation of Jewish law. The prophet Elijah comments on God's involvement
in this dispute: 'He was laughing, and saying, "My children have defeated me, my
children have defeated me".' Maccoby adds
that this story was dismissed as one of the
imbecilities of the Talmud in the medieval
Disputation of Paris, when the Talmud was
put on trial by Christians.
    The Christian God laughs lots of times —
not least in the works of G.K. Chesterton,
especially in his poem 'The Fish':

For I saw that finny goblin
    Hidden in the abyss untrod;
And I knew there can be laughter
    On the secret face of God.

Blow the trumpets, crown the sages,
    Bring the age by reason fed!
('He that sitteth in the heavens,
    he shall laugh' — the prophet said.)

Then there is the poem by Sir Laurence
Jones, 'Lines to a Bishop who was shocked
(A.D. 1950) at seeing a pier-glass [mirror]

in a bathroom'. When the Bishop sees his nakedness, the poem ends:

> You shrink aghast, with pained and puzzled eyes,
> While God's loud laughter peals about the skies.

The poem 'Ducks' by F.W. Harvey (1888–1957) ends:

> Caterpillars and cats are lively and excellent puns:
> All God's jokes are good — even the practical ones!
> And as for the duck, I think God must have smiled a bit
> Seeing those bright eyes blink on the day he fashioned it.
> And He's probably laughing still at the sound that came out of its bill!

Laughter in Paradise was the title of a 1951 film about a dead man's revenge on the beneficaries of his will. In 1987 Liza Minelli quoted a proverb 'Man plans and God laughs', though this has not been recorded since.

The original idea (as in the headword quotation) also occurs in a Cole Porter song 'I Love Him But He Didn't Love Me' (1929), whose verse begins:

> The gods who nurse
> This universe
> Think little of mortals' cares.
> They sit in crowds
> On exclusive clouds
> And laugh at our love affairs.

Additionally, a song of the 1940s called 'Tonight' (also known as 'Perfidia'), written by Milton Leeds to music by Alberto Dominguez, has: 'While the Gods of love look down and laugh at what romantic fools we mortals be.' There is here a more obvious allusion to the situation in Shakespeare's *A Midsummer Night's Dream* (III.ii.115) when the sprite Puck says to Oberon, King of the Fairies:

> 'Lord, what fools these mortals be!'

It is but a short step from this to *The Stars Look Down*, the title of the novel (1935, filmed UK, 1939) by A.J. Cronin.

Cymbeline

1 *Heaven's gate.*

(II.iii.20) See BLAKE 63:4.

Hamlet

2 *Alas, poor Yorick . . . I knew him well, Horatio.*

When the gravedigger produces the skull of Yorick, the late King's jester, the Prince's actual words are: 'Alas, poor Yorick. I knew him, Horatio, a fellow of infinite jest, of most excellent fancy' (V.i.178). To make it easier to quote, presumably, the form 'I knew him *well*' crept into popular use.

3 *And all for nothing!*
For Hecuba!
What's Hecuba to him, or he to her,
That he should weep for her?

The sorrows of Hecuba are depicted in several Greek tragedies and, as Hamlet discusses with the players what play they might perform to catch his uncle out, the Prince reflects on an aspect of the actor's craft (II.ii.551). Acting can make the other actors (and the audience weep) but what is the point of doing so? He, Hamlet, has a much better motive for using the art. Michael MacLiammoir, the Irish actor, reduced the words to *All for Hecuba*, the title of a volume of memoirs (1946).

4 *They say the owl was a baker's daughter.*

So says Ophelia, mystifyingly (IV.v.43). The reference is to an old English legend about Christ going into a baker's shop and asking for something to eat. A piece of cake is put in the oven for Him, but the baker's daughter says it is too large and cuts it in half. The dough swells up to an enormous size, she exclaims 'Woo! Woo!' and is turned into an owl.

5 *Buzz, buzz!*

James Agate, the drama critic, gave this title to a collection of his reviews (1918). Why? Because it is what Hamlet says (II.ii.389) when told by Polonius, 'The actors are come hither, my lord'. One commentator describes it as 'a contemptuous exclamation dismissing something as idle gossip or (as here) stale news'.

6 *Caviare to the general.*

A famously misunderstood phrase meaning 'of no interest to common folk'. It has *nothing* to do with giving expensive presents of caviare to unappreciative military gentlemen. Lord Jenkins, Chancellor of Oxford University, apparently committed this solecism in an obituary of Lord Zuckerman in the *Independent* (2 April 1993): 'Solly

Zuckerman's taste was sharp and astringent, "Caviare for the general" (on the whole he liked generals in spite of his scepticism for conventional military wisdom), but once acquired it never palled.'

In *Hamlet* (II.ii.434), the Prince refers to a play which — he recalls — 'pleased not the million, 'twas caviare to the general' (in other words, the general public). The Arden Shakespeare notes that *c* 1600, when the play was written, caviare was a novel delicacy. It was probably inedible to those who had not yet acquired a taste for it.

1 Hamlet: *Lady, shall I lie in your lap?*
Ophelia: *No, my lord.*
Hamlet: *I mean, my head upon your lap.*
Ophelia: *Ay, my lord.*
Hamlet: *Do you think I meant country matters?*
Ophelia: *I think nothing, my lord.*
Hamlet: *That's a fair thought to lie between maids' legs.*

An exchange from III.ii.115. Shakespeare's bawdy is sometimes obscure, but few can miss that 'country matters' means physical love-making or fail to note the pun in the first syllable — which also occurs in John Donne's poem 'The Good-Morrow' (1635), and William Wycherley's *The Country Wife* (1675). *Country Matters* was the title of a British TV drama series (ITV, 1972) presenting an anthology of stories by H.E. Bates and A.E. Coppard, linked only by their setting in the English countryside. One presumes that the producers knew what they were doing in calling it this.

2 *It is a custom*
More honour'd in the breach than in the observance.

Usually taken to mean that whatever custom is under consideration has fallen into sad neglect. But in I.iv.16 the Prince is telling Horatio that the King's drunken revelry is a custom that would be *better* 'honour'd' if it were not followed at all.

3 *Each actor on his ass.*

Hamlet says this (II.ii.395) to Polonius who has just announced the arrival of the actors. It is thought that Shakespeare might have been quoting a line from a ballad. Michael MacLiammoir, the Irish actor, used the phrase as the title of one of his volumes of memoirs (1960).

4 *For this relief much thanks.*

Francisco to Barnardo, the two sentinels at the very beginning of the play (I.i.8). 'Relief' here in the sense of relieving another person of guard duty, nothing lavatorial. In *The Lyttelton Hart-Davis Letters* (for the 1960s), reference is made to the phrase being used as the title of a book about a Victorian sanitary engineer (Thomas Crapper, presumably) but if any such volume was published, it remains untraced.

5 *Like quills upon the fretful porpentine.*

'His face was flushed, his eyes were bulging, and . . . his hair was standing on end — like quills upon the fretful porpentine, as Jeeves once put it when describing to me the reactions of Barmy FotheringayPhipps on seeing a dead snip, on which he had invested largely, come in sixth in the procession at the Newmarket Spring Meeting.' So says Bertie Wooster in *The Code of the Woosters* (1938) by P.G. Wodehouse, using one of his favourite Shakespearean images (from *Hamlet*, I.v.20 — though Wooster probably wasn't aware of this). In the original, it is the Ghost of Hamlet's father who is telling the Prince he 'could a tale unfold' which would make 'each particular hair to stand on end/Like quills upon the fretful porpentine' (i.e. porcupine). In 1986 some of the more literate regulars of the Porcupine pub in Charing Cross Road, London, would talk of repairing to 'the Fretters'.

6 *The glass of fashion and the mould of form.*

Ophelia is lamenting Hamlet's apparent madness and decline (III.i.155). This is what he once was: a person upon whom others modelled themselves and who dictated what fashion should be. *The Glass of Fashion* was used as the title of a play by Sydney Grundy, first staged at the Globe, London, in the 1880s; also as the title of book (1954) by Cecil Beaton.

7 *Hamlet, revenge!*

The title of a detective novel (1937) by Michael Innes comes not from Shakespeare's play but from an earlier one (which is lost to us) on the same theme. Thomas Lodge saw it in 1596 and noted the pale-faced 'ghost which cried so miserably at the theatre, like an oyster-wife, Hamlet, revenge'.

1 *He that plays the king shall be welcome.*

Hamlet is talking to Rosencrantz (II.ii.318) and obviously toying with the idea of having the actors play out recent events at Elsinore. *He That Plays the King* was used as the title of a book of theatre criticism (1950) by Kenneth Tynan. The thriller *To Play the King* (1992) by Michael Dobbs, concerning a clash between a British Prime Minister and a King, might seem to allude to this, but probably owes more to 'playing the king' in chess or cards. Shakespeare quite frequently uses the 'play the —' formula, and not just about kings.

2 *Hoist with his own petard.*

Meaning 'to be caught in one's own trap', the origin of this phrase has nothing to do with being stabbed by one's own knife (poniard/poignard = dagger) or hanged with one's own rope. The context in which Hamlet uses it (at III.iv.209) makes the source clear:

> For 'tis the sport to have the engineer
> Hoist with his own petard.

A petard was a newly invented device in Shakespeare's day, used for blowing up walls, and so on with gunpowder. Thus the image is of the operative being blown up into the air by his own device. Compare the more recent expression 'to score an own goal'.

3 *A was a man, take him for all in all;
I shall not look upon his like again.*

The Prince is talking of his late father (I.ii.187). The second line gives us the 'we shall not see his like again' cliché of obituaries. In *Joyce Grenfell Requests the Pleasure* (1976) the actress recalls being rung up by the United Press for a comment on the death of Ruth Draper, the mono-logist: 'My diary records: "I said we should not see her like again. She was a genius." Without time to think, clichés take over and often, because that is why they have become clichés, they tell the truth.'

4 *The lady doth protest too much, methinks.*

Gertrude's line (at III.ii.225) is often evoked to mean, 'There is something suspicious about the way that person is complain-ing more than is natural'. However, what Hamlet's mother is actually doing is giving her opinion of 'The Mousetrap', the play-within-a-play. What she means to say is

that the Player Queen is promising more than she is likely to be able to deliver. Gertrude uses the word 'protest' in the sense of 'state formally' not 'complain'.

5 *For thine especial safety.*

The motto on the safety curtain at the Theatre Royal, Drury Lane, London, comes from IV.iii.40. A bright use for the phrase, but the original context is rather different. King Claudius says, 'Hamlet, this deed, for thine especial safety . . ./ . . . must send thee hence/With fiery quickness' — meaning that the commission or document sending him to England is for his own safety (iron-ically: as it turns out, Hamlet is supposed to be killed on the journey).

6 *Rosencrantz and Guildernstern are dead.*

The title of a play (1966) by Tom Stoppard, concerning two of the minor characters in *Hamlet*, is actually a quotation from Shake-speare's play. The line is spoken (V.ii.376) by one of the English ambassadors after Hamlet has arranged for the killing of his two old student friends (who had been set up by his uncle Claudius to kill *him*).

7 *There is method in my/his/her madness.*

This expression has evolved from, 'Though this be madness, yet there is method in it', which is said as an aside by Polonius about Hamlet (II.ii.205).

8 *This above all: to thine own self be true.*

Polonius, verging on the pompous, at I.iii.78. It would appear to have provided the somewhat unlikely title *This Above All* for a film (UK, 1942) based on a novel by Eric Knight.

9 *To be or not to be, that is the question.*

Hamlet's soliloquy beginning thus (at III.i.56) is one of the most quoted passages in all literature (though see the Introduction to this book). It is constantly alluded to, especially in the titles of works by other writers. A small selection: *To Be Or Not To Be* was used as the title of a film comedy (US, 1942, 1983) about Polish actors under the Nazis. *Slings and Arrows* was a post-Second World War revue in London, with Hermione Gingold. *Outrageous Fortune* was the title of a film (US, 1987), loosely about rival actresses aspiring to be in a production of

Hamlet. *Perchance to Dream* was the title of a musical by Ivor Novello (1945). *Mortal Coils* was the title of a collection of short stories (1922) by Aldous Huxley. A thriller by Cyril Hare was entitled *With a Bare Bodkin* (1982). There is a natural history book by John Hay called *The Undiscovered Country* (1982), and that title was also used for Tom Stoppard's 1980 adaptation of a play by Arthur Schnitzler. Graham Greene had a novel *The Name of Action* (1930).

1 *Very like a whale.*

Polonius says this (III.ii.373) to Hamlet when the Prince is teasing him about the shape of a cloud. It is 'like a camel' or 'backed like a weasel', and Polonius humours him by saying it is 'very like a whale'. John Osborne's 1980 TV play *Very Like a Whale* was about a captain of industry in emotional turmoil.

Henry IV, Part 1

2 *Discretion is the better part of valour.*

At V.iv.119 Falstaff cynically reinterprets an old maxim and this is how the words are still used, as well as in this form. What he precisely says is, 'The better part of valour is discretion'.

3 *Minions of the moon.*

Meaning 'night-time robbers'. In 1984, a French film was released in the English-language market with the title *Favourites of the Moon*. It was a quirky piece about Parisian crooks, petty and otherwise, whose activities overlapped in one way or another, but the English title hardly seemed relevant to the subject. Not surprisingly, as it was a translation back into English. The original French title was *Les Favoris de la Lune* and, as a caption made clear, this was a French translation of *Henry IV, Part 1* (I.ii.25), Falstaff saying to Prince Hal: 'Let not us that are squires of the night's body be called thieves of the day's beauty: let us be Diana's foresters, gentlemen of the shade, minions of the moon.'

4 *The turkeys in my panier are quite starved.*

As the events of the play cannot have occurred later than 1413 (when King Henry IV died), it was anachronistic of Shakespeare to have had anyone mention turkeys (II.i.26). These were not discovered until 1518 in

Mexico, from whence they were introduced to Europe. However, the term 'turkey-cock' had been in known in England since the Crusades (referring to what we now called guinea-fowl), so perhaps this is not an error after all. And yet, the earliest *OED2* citation for 'turkey-cock' is 1541 and it is not apparent whether this term was abbreviated to 'turkey' in 1597, when *Henry IV, Part I* was first performed.

5 *Would it were bedtime and all were well.*

This is how the phrase came to be used — as in Oliver Goldsmith, *She Stoops to Conquer*, I.ii (1773) — but when Falstaff says it to Prince Hal at V.i.125, before the battle of Shrewsbury, the form is: 'I would 'twere bed-time, Hal, and all were well.'

Henry IV, Part 2

6 *Under which king, Besonian? Speak or die!*

Pistol exclaims this (V.iv.110) to Justice Shallow who has just said he has some special authority under the King. Besonian literally means 'raw recruit', but here means 'ignoramus'.

Henry V

7 *Nay, sure, he's not in hell: he's in Arthur's bosom, if ever man went to Arthur's bosom.*

The Hostess (former Mistress Quickly) is talking of the dead Falstaff (II.iii.9). Her malapropism is for *Abraham's* bosom, meaning the place where the dead sleep contentedly. From Luke 16:23: 'And it came to pass, that the beggar died, and was carried by the angels into Abraham's bosom.' The person alluded to is Abraham, the first of the Hebrew patriarchs.

8 *A-babbled of green fields.*

One of the most pleasing touches to be found in all of Shakespeare may not have been his at all. At II.iii.17, the Hostess, continuing to relate the death of Falstaff, says: 'A' parted ev'n just between twelve and one, ev'n at the turning o' th' tide: for after I saw him fumble with the sheets and play with flowers and smile upon his fingers' end, I knew there was but one way; for his nose was as sharp as a pen, and a'babbled of green fields.' The 1623 Folio of Shakespeare's plays renders the last phrase as 'and a Table of green fields', which makes no sense, though some editors put 'as sharp as a pen, on a table of green field' (taking 'green field' to mean green cloth.)

The generally accepted version was inserted by Lewis Theobald in his 1733 edition. As the 1954 Arden edition comments: ' "Babbled of green fields" is surely more in character with the Falstaff who quoted the Scriptures . . . and who lost his voice hallooing of anthems. Now he is in the valley of the shadow, the "green pasture" of Psalm 23 might well be on his lips.'

Shakespeare may well have handwritten 'babld' and the printer read this as 'table' — a reminder that the text of the plays is far from carved in stone and a prey to mishaps in the printing process as are all books and newspapers.

1 *'Tis not the balm, the sceptre and the ball,*
The sword, the mace, the crown imperial.

'Crown Imperial' was the title given to Sir William Walton's march, which was composed for the Coronation of King George VI in 1936. 'Orb and Sceptre' followed for that of Queen Elizabeth II in 1953. In a television interview, Walton said that if he lived to write a march for a third coronation it would be called 'Sword and Mace'. The key to these titles lies in the above passage at IV.i.266, with the King himself speaking.

Oddly enough, the orchestral parts of 'Crown Imperial' bear a different quotation: 'In beauty bearing the crown imperial' from the poem 'In Honour of the City' by William Dunbar. This is what Walton must have begun with, subsequently discovering the Shakespeare sequence.

Henry VI, Part 2

2 Commons. (Within): *[i.e. a rabble off-stage] An answer from the King, or we will all break in!*
King: *Go, Salisbury, and tell them all from me, I thank them for their tender loving care.*

When people use the expression 'tender loving care' nowadays, it is a pretty fair bet that they are not quoting Shakespeare. However, he does use the three words in the same order (III.ii.277-9). In its modern sense, the *OED2* recognizes the phrase as a colloquialism

denoting, 'especially solicitous care such as is given by nurses' and cites *The Listener* (12 May 1977): 'It is in a nurse's nature and in her tradition to give the sick what is well called "TLC", "tender loving care", some constant little service to the sick.' But there is a much earlier use of the phrase, in this sense, in the final chapter, 'T.L.C. TREATMENT', of Ian Fleming's novel *Goldfinger* (1959). James Bond says to Pussy Galore, 'All you need is a course of TLC.' 'What's TLC?' she asks. 'Short for Tender Loving Care Treatment,' Bond replies. 'It's what they write on most papers when a waif gets brought in to a children's clinic.' This may point to an American origin. Indeed, a correspondent in the US recalls being told in the 1940s that there was a study done in foundling hospitals where the death rate was very high, which showed that when nurses picked up the babies and cuddled them more frequently, the death rate went down. This led to the prescription, 'TLC *t.i.d.*' (three times a day).

Julius Caesar

3 *Peace! count the clock.*
The clock hath stricken three.

(II.i.192) An anachronism, as mechanical clocks were not invented until the thirteenth century.

King John

4 *To gild the lily.*

Meaning, 'to attempt to improve something that is already attractive and risk spoiling it'. In quoting (IV.ii.11) this should be as in Salisbury's speech:

Therefore, to be possess'd with double pomp,
To guard a title that was rich before,
To gild refined gold, to paint the lily,
To throw a perfume on the violet,
To smooth the ice, or add another hue
Unto the rainbow, or with taper-light
To seek the beauteous eye of heaven to garnish,
Is wasteful and ridiculous excess.

Arden notes that 'to gild gold' was a common expression in Shakespeare's time.

King Lear

5 *Child Rowland to the dark tower came,*
His word was still 'Fie, foh, and fum,
I smell the blood of a British man'.

301

(III.iv.179). This is Edgar mouthing snatches of verse in his assumed madness. Shakespeare, in turn, was quoting a line from an older ballad (a 'child(e)' was a candidate for knighthood). In certain Scottish ballads of uncertain date, Childe Roland is the son of King Arthur who rescues his sister from a castle to which she has been abducted by fairies. In the *Chanson de Roland* (French, twelfth century) and other tellings of the legend, he is the nephew of Charlemagne. Shakespeare probably combined material from two completely different sources — the first line from a ballad about Roland, the second two from the old story of Jack the Giant-killer.

Later, Shakespeare's use was quoted by Robert Browning in the poem 'Childe Roland to the Dark Tower Came' (1855) which concludes with the lines:

Dauntless the slughorn to my lips I set,
And blew. 'Childe Roland to the Dark
Tower came.'

1 *The wheel has turned full circle.*

This modern cliché probably derives from what Edmund the Bastard says at V.iii.173: 'The wheel is come full circle'. He is referring to the Wheel of Fortune, being at that moment back down at the bottom where he was before it began to revolve. A modern example of the phrase in use: Chips Channon writes in his diary (13 October 1943): 'I turned on the wireless and heard the official announcement of Italy's declaration of war on Germany. So now the wheel has turned full circle.'

Love's Labour's Lost

2 *HONORIFICABILITUDINITATIBUS.*

The longest word in Shakespeare occurs at V.i.37 and appears to be a schoolmasterly joke, not original to him. The context allows it no meaning, just length, though it has something to do with honourableness. The *OED2* does not list it as a headword, preferring 'honorificabilitudinity' (honourableness). Samuel Johnson noted that it was 'often mentioned as the longest word known'. At twenty-seven letters it was overtaken, in time, by 'antidisestablishmentarianism' with twenty-eight, and by 'floccipaucinihilipilification', with twenty-nine, meaning, 'the action of estimating as worthless', which was first used in 1741, and is the longest word actually in the *OED2*. Scientific words of forty-seven and fifty-two letters have also

been invented, but don't really count.

Those seeking to prove that Francis Bacon wrote Shakespeare's plays claimed that the twenty-seven letter word was, in fact, an anagram — 'Hi ludi, F Baconis nati, tuiti orbi [These plays, born of F Bacon, are preserved for the world] — which surely deserves some sort of prize for ingenuity, if nothing else.

3 *Infants of the Spring.*

This was the title of Vol. I (1976) of Anthony Powell's autobiography *To Keep the Ball Rolling*. Powell does not indicate a source, but it is probably from *Love's Labour's Lost* (I.i.101):

Berowne is like an envious sneaping frost
That bites the first-born infants of the
spring

or, possibly, from *Hamlet* (I.iii.39):

The canker galls the infants of the spring
Too oft before their buttons be disclos'd.

Macbeth

4 *If you can look into the seeds of time,*
And say which grain will grow, and
which will not,
Speak then to me.

Banquo is talking to the witches (I.iii.58). Demons were said to have the power of predicting which grain would grow and which will not. *The Seeds of Time* was used by John Wyndham as title of a collection of short stories (1969).

5 *To-morrow, and to-morrow, and*
to-morrow,
Creeps in this petty pace from day to
day,
To the last syllable of recorded time;
And all our yesterdays have lighted fools
The way to dusty death. Out, out,
brief candle!
Life's but a walking shadow; a poor
player,
That struts and frets his hour upon
the stage,
And then is heard no more: it is a tale
Told by an idiot, full of sound and fury,
Signifying nothing.

Almost every phrase from Macbeth's speech at V.v.22 seems to have been used as title material. A slight exaggeration, but *Tomorrow and Tomorrow* was a film in 1932; *All*

Our Yesterdays was the title of Granada TV's 1960-73 programme devoted to old newsreels and *All My Yesterdays* of the actor Edward G. Robinson's memoirs (1974); *The Way to Dusty Death* was the title of a novel by Alastair Maclean (1973); *Brief Candles* was the title of a novel (1930) by Aldous Huxley; *Told By an Idiot* was a novel by Rose Macaulay (1923); 'full of sound and fury' is echoed in the title of William Faulkner's novel *The Sound and The Fury* (1929).

1 *I am tied to the stake and bear-like I must stand the course.*

Whence the line which Peter Black [TV critic of the *Daily Mail*] once applied so aptly to Gilbert Harding, pioneer [1950s] TV celebrity and professional boor? The *ODQ* gives it thus, except that 'bear-like' is missing. As such it is from *King Lear* (III.vii.54) and is spoken by Gloucester shortly before his eyes are put out. But right at the end of *Macbeth* (V.vii.2) there is:

> They have tied me to the stake, I cannot fly,
> But, bear-like, I must fight the course.

Either way, this is a brilliant choice of quotation to describe that grizzled name of yesteryear, trapped within the awful snare of professional celebrity.

2 *Cribbed, cabined and confined.*

Strictly speaking this should be, 'But now, I am cabin'd, cribb'd, confin'd, bound in / To saucy doubts and fears' — Macbeth to the First Murderer (at II.iv.23).

3 *Lead on, Macduff.*

Strictly speaking, the lines at V.iii.33 are:

> *Lay on*, Macduff;
> And damn'd be he that first cries,
> 'Hold enough!'

It would be interesting to know at what stage people started saying 'Lead on, Macduff' to mean, 'You lead the way, let's get started.' Partridge / *Catch Phrases* has an example from 1912, but it probably started long before then. There has been a change of meaning along the way. Macbeth uses the words 'lay on' as defined by *OED2* as: 'to deal blows with vigour, to make vigorous attack, assail.' The shape of the phrase was clearly so appealing that it was adapted to a different purpose.

The Merchant of Venice

4 *All that glitters is not gold.*

Meaning, 'appearances can be deceptive'. When quoting II.vii.65 this should be: 'All that *glisters* is not gold, / Often have you heard that told.' The proverb was common by Shakespeare's time. *CODP* quotes a Latin version — '*Non omne quod nitet aurum est* [not all that shines is gold]' — and also an English one, in Chaucer. The now obsolete word 'glisters', rather than 'glitters' or 'glistens', was commonly used in the saying from the seventeenth century onwards. In poetic use, Thomas Gray, for example, used 'glisters' in his 'Ode on the Death of A Favourite Cat drowned in a tub of Gold Fishe' (1748).

Pearson (1937) has Spenser, 'Gold all is not that doth golden seem', then Shakespeare, then Middleton 'All is not gold that glisteneth' and Dryden 'All . . . that glitters is not gold'.

5 *The devil can cite scripture for his own purposes.*

Meaning 'an ill-disposed person may turn even good things to his advantage', and in this precise form, this an allusion to Antonio at I.iii.93, where he says this because Shylock has just been doing so.

A Midsummer Night's Dream

6 *Our true intent is all for your delight.*

These words were written over the entrance to the first Butlin's holiday camp to be opened, at Skegness, in 1936. One wonders how many of the campers who passed under it recognized it as a great 'unspoken' line from Shakespeare? When Quince reads the prologue of the play within-a-play at V.i.113, he mispunctuates: 'We do not come, as minding to content you, / Our true intent is. All for your delight, / We are not here . . .'

It is also a motto that has cropped up on the programmes of countless British repertory theatres.

Much Ado About Nothing

7 Don Pedro: *You were born in a merry hour . . .*

Beatrice: *A star danced, and under that I was born.*

(II.i.316) The actress Gertrude Lawrence entitled her autobiography *A Star Danced* (1945).

Othello

1 *Put money in thy purse*

Iago to Rodrigo (I.iii.340). Michael Mac-Liammoir, the Irish actor, took the phrase for a volume of his diaries (1952), recounting the time he spent playing Iago to Orson Welles's Othello, in the 1951 film.

2 *Excellent wretch! Perdition catch my soul,*
But I do love thee, and when I love thee not,
Chaos is come again.

Othello on Desdemona (III.iii.91). Hence, the title of the rock musical *Catch My Soul* (1970), based on the play.

3 *Nay, we must think*
Men are not gods.

Desdemona speaks (III.iv.146). In 1936, a film about an actor playing Othello who nearly strangles his wife was called *Men Are Not Gods*.

4 *O farewell . . .*
Pride, pomp, and circumstance of glorious war!

(III.iii.360) Hence, 'Pomp and Circumstance', the title of five marches by Sir Edward Elgar (composed 1901–7, 1930).

Richard III

5 *Now is the winter of our discontent.*

See SUN 323:2.

6 *The bloody deed is/was done.*

The provenance of this phrase is not obvious. All that the *OED2* has to offer is from L.A.G. Strong's *Swift Shadow* (1937): 'Standing by like gawps to see bloody murder done'. A correspondent, G.W. Bullard, thought he had found it in Thomas Hood's 'The Dream of Eugene Aram' (1829):

Two sudden blows with a ragged stick,
    And one with a heavy stone,
One hurried gash with a hasty knife –
    And then the deed was done;
There was nothing lying at my foot
    But lifeless flesh and bone!

Bullard suspected bowdlerization – the dash at the end of line 3, the leaden 'and then' rather than 'the bloody' in line 4 – but, no, the first edition is as here.

In Shakespeare, of course, the phrase 'bloody deed' occurs several times and what with Macbeth's 'I have done the deed' and the almost immediate references to 'blood', not to mention Rosse's 'Is't known who did this more than bloody deed?' (II.iv.22), might have produced this conflation. The nearest one gets is *Richard III* (IV.iii.1): 'The tyrannous and bloody act is done' – which is what Tyrrel says about the murder of the Princes in the Tower. As with 'the bloody dog is dead' from the end of the same play (V.v.2), we are almost there, but the exact words remain untraced.

7 *A horse! a horse! My kingdom for a horse!*

The actual Richard III's last words when he met Henry Tudor at the Battle of Bosworth on 23 August 1485 were, 'I will die King of England. I will not budge a foot . . . Treason! treason!' That was how it was reported by John Rowe, who presumably picked it up from someone who had actually been at the battle, for he was not. Evidently, Richard then rushed on the future Henry VII and was killed.

Shakespeare's memorable, twice-repeated cry (V.iv.7/13) may have been inspired by lines in other plays written about the time he wrote his (c 1591). The only indication that Richard III might have had a similar concern at the actual battle is contained in the book of Edward Hall's chronicle called 'The tragical doynges of Kyng Richard the thirde' (1548) where it states: 'When the loss of the battle was imminent and apparent, they brought to him a swift and light horse to convey him away.'

See also CIBBER 99:6.

Romeo and Juliet

8 *The strangers all are gone.*

Spoken by the Nurse at I.v.143. Hence, the title of Vol. IV (1982) of Anthony Powell's autobiography *To Keep the Ball Rolling*.

9 *O Romeo, Romeo, wherefore art thou, Romeo?*

In this famous – and famously misunderstood – line (II.ii.33), 'wherefore' does not mean 'where'. Juliet is not *looking for* Romeo from her balcony. It means 'for what reason'.

Sonnets

1 *From you I have been absent in the spring.*

(Sonnet 98) *Absent in the Spring* was used as the title of a thriller (1948), written by Agatha Christie under the name Mary Westmacott.

The Tempest

2 *Suffer a sea-change into something rich and strange.*

When Ariel sings of a sea-change (I.ii.401) he does actually mean a change *caused by the sea*. Now, invariably, the expression is used simply as a grandiloquent way of saying 'change'.

3 *The stuff that dreams are made on.*

If one is quoting Prospero's words from IV.i.156 — 'We are such stuff/As dreams are made on' — it is definitely 'on' not 'of' (though Shakespeare did use the 'of' form elsewhere).

So, well done, the writer of the *Guardian* headline (9 May 1988): 'Stuff that dreams are made on' and, rather less well done, Humphrey Bogart as Sam Spade in *The Maltese Falcon* (1941): 'What is it?' he is asked before speaking the last line of the picture, and replies: 'The stuff that dreams are made of.' Absolutely no marks to the cast of the 1964 Cambridge Footlights revue, *Stuff What Dreams Are Made Of.*

Troilus and Cressida

4 *Launch'd above a thousand ships.*

See MARLOWE 235:2.

Twelfth Night

5 *Does thou think, because thou art virtuous, there shall be no more cakes and ale?*

Sir Toby Belch's remark to Malvolio at II.iii.114. The Arden Shakespeare comments that cakes and ale were 'traditionally associated with festivity, and disliked by Puritans both on this account and because of their association with weddings, saints' days, and holy days'. In due course, 'cakes and ale' became a synonym for enjoyment, as in the expression 'Life isn't all cakes and ale' (or 'beer and skittles', for that matter).

On 4 May 1876, Francis Kilvert wrote in his diary: 'The clerk's wife brought out some cakes and ale and pressed me to eat and drink. I was to have returned to Llysdinam to luncheon . . . but as I wanted to see more of the country and the people I decided to let the train go by, accept the hospitality of my hostess and the cakes and ale which life offered, and walk home quietly in the course of the afternoon' — a neat demonstration of the literal and metaphorical uses of the phrase.

Hence, also, the title of a novel (1930) by W. Somerset Maugham.

The Winter's Tale

6 *Our ship hath touch'd upon The deserts of Bohemia.*

(III.iii.1) A supposed geographical error on Shakespeare's part. Bohemia (now part of the Czech Republic) does not have a coast. However, at certain points in history it *did* have an outlet on the Adriatic.

7 *Exit pursued by a bear.*

A famous stage direction from III.iii.58. It refers to the fate of Antigonus who is on the sea coast of Bohemia (see above). Most of Shakespeare's stage directions are additions by later editors, but this one may be original. The bear used could have been a real one (as bear-baiting was common in places adjacent to Shakespeare's theatres) or portrayed by a man in costume.

8   GOOD FREND FOR IESUS SAKE
FORBEARE,
TO DIGG THE DUST ENCLOASED
HEARE:
BLESTE BE YE MAN [THA]T
SPARES THES STONES,
AND CURST BE HE [THA]T
MOVES MY BONES.

Inscription on Shakespeare's grave on the north side of the chancel in Holy Trinity church, Stratford-upon-Avon. The playwright was buried in this privileged position as he had become a 'lay rector' in 1605. Although he is buried with other members of his family, his grave, rather curiously, does not actually bear his name.

According to S. Schoenbaum, *William Shakespeare: A Documentary Life* (1975), several seventeenth-century sources suggest that Shakespeare wrote his own epitaph. However, perhaps the point is rather that he may have *chosen* it rather than *composed* it.

In the mid-eighteenth century the gravestone was so worn that it was replaced. In the nineteenth century Halliwell Phillips was curtly dismissing this 'wretched doggerel', but James Walter in *Shakespeare's True Life* (1890) was asking, 'Who dares question the words being those of the great dramatist himself?' Walter seemed to accept that because the words were 'there chiselled when the great one was laid in his grave', they must, therefore, have been written by him.

Hesketh Pearson in his biography (1949) argues that Shakespeare chose to phrase his wish simply and clearly, and not 'in the words of a King Lear', because of a very real fear that his remains would be removed. As Brian Bailey notes in *Churchyards of England and Wales* (1987): 'The charnel-house at Stratford, demolished in 1799, was reached from inside the church by a door in the north wall of the chancel, [near Shakespeare's tomb. Hence] . . . a plea that his bones should not be thrown in the charnel-house when subsequent burials uncovered them, as was the custom; but the curse prevented his widow being buried in the same grave, as she had wished, because no one dared disturb it.'

Shanks, Edward
English poet (1892–1953)

1 *O memory, take and keep*
All that my eyes, your servants,
bring you home!

These lines appear twice in a poem called 'Memory' by Edward Richard Buxton Shanks who edited *Granta* at Cambridge, served in the First World War, wrote novels and criticism and was the first winner of the Hawthornden Prize for Poetry. The full text is in *Poems of Today* (2nd Series), an anthology popular in schools, especially in the 1920s.

Shaw, George Bernard
Irish playwright and critic (1856–1950)

2 *What if the child inherits my beauty and your brains?*

There may be some truth in the story that Shaw was once approached by a woman who thought herself to be a fine physical specimen and suggested that they combine to make a baby, saying: 'You have the greatest brain in the world and I have the most beautiful body; so we ought to produce

the most perfect child.' His reply: 'Yes, but fancy if it were born with my beauty and your brains?'

Alas, this was not said to Isadora Duncan or any of the other women who have been woven into the tale. Hesketh Pearson in *Bernard Shaw* (1942) said the request came from 'a woman in Zurich', though no trace of a letter containing it has ever been found.

3 *Two countries separated by a common language.*

See WILDE 354:2.

4 *A man who never missed an occasion to let slip an opportunity.*

This was said of Lord Rosebery presumably in the 1890s when he was briefly Liberal Prime Minister, though it remains untraced. Robert Rhodes James in *Rosebery* (1963) has the slightly different 'man who never missed a chance of missing an opportunity' which, he says, expresses the point of view of 'the political extrovert who turns aside with contempt from hesitation, pusill-animity, and doubt'.

5 *You see things; and you say 'Why?' But I dream things that never were; and I say 'Why not?'*

A saying that has often wrongly been ascribed to both John and Robert Kennedy (because they both used it in numerous political speeches) is, in fact, also from Shaw. It is spoken by The Serpent, in an attempt to seduce Eve, in the play *Back to Methuselah* (1921). President Kennedy quoted it correctly (and acknowledged Shaw) in his address to the Irish Parliament in Dublin in June 1963. Robert's version tended to be: 'Some men see things as they are and say "Why?" I dream things that never were and say, "Why not?"' In this form it was attributed to Robert (Shaw going unmentioned) in the address delivered by Edward Kennedy at his brother's funeral in 1968.

So frequently was the saying invoked by Robert Kennedy as a peroration that, on the campaign trail, the words 'As George Bernard Shaw once said . . .' became a signal for reporters to dash for the press bus. Once he forgot to conclude with the Shaw quote, according to Arthur M. Schlesinger in *Robert Kennedy and His Times* (1979), and several reporters missed the bus. On another occasion it came on to rain and Kennedy told the crowd: 'It's silly for you to be standing in the rain listening to a politician . . . As George Bernard Shaw once said, "Run for the buses".'

1 Freddy: *Are you walking across the Park, Miss Doolittle? If so —*
Liza: *Walk! Not bloody likely. (Sensation). I am going in a taxi.*

Shaw's play *Pygmalion* (1914) is about the conversion of an illiterate, ill-spoken flower girl (Eliza Doolittle) by a professor of phonetics (Henry Higgins). It uses the same theme as part of Tobias Smollett's novel *Peregrine Pickle* (1751) in which Pickle trains a girl and then introduces her into exclusive and elegant circles. From Chap. XCV: 'One evening, being at cards with a certain lady, whom she detected in the very fact of unfair conveyance, she taxed her roundly with the fraud, and brought upon herself such a torrent of sarcastic reproof, as overbore all her maxims of caution, and burst open the floodgates of her own natural repartee, twanged off with the appellations of b***** and w*****, which she repeated with great vehemence . . . to the terror of her antagonist and the astonishment of all present: nay, to such an unguarded pitch was she provoked, that starting up, she snapt her fingers, in testimony of disdain, and, as she quitted the room, applied her hand to that part which was the last of her that disappeared, inviting the company to kiss it, by one of its coarsest denominations.'

Here, obviously, is the origin of the celebrated tea-party scene in Act III of Shaw's play. Audience anticipation for the first performance in London on Saturday 11 April 1914 had been whipped up by that morning's edition of the *Daily Sketch*: 'PYGMALION MAY CAUSE SENSATION!! Mr Shaw introduces a certain forbidden word. WILL MRS PATRICK CAMPBELL SPEAK IT? Has the censor stepped in or will the word spread? If he does not forbid it then anything might happen!! It is a word which the *Daily Sketch* cannot possibly print and tonight it is to be uttered on the stage.'

When the phrase was finally uttered, the audience gasped — 'their intake of breath making a sound that could have been mistaken for a protracted hiss,' according to Shaw's biographer, Hesketh Pearson (1942). 'This never happened again because all future audiences knew what was coming and roared with laughter.' Then there was laughter which continued for a minute and

a quarter according to the stage manager's stopwatch.

Although the play was well received by the critics, the press rumbled on about the language it used. *The Times* in its review (13 April 1914), said: 'O, greatly daring Mr Shaw! You will be able to boast you are the first modern dramatist to use this word on the stage! But really, was it worth while? There is a whole range of forbidden words in the English language; a little more of your usage and we suppose that they will be heard, too. And then goodbye to the delights of really intimate conversation.'

The *Daily Mirror* sought the view of a number of bishops. Sydney Grundy, theatre critic of the *Daily Mail*, said there was no harm in Shaw's 'incarnadine adverb' when informed by genius but 'on his pen it is poison'.

The Theatrical Managers' Association wrote to Sir Herbert Beerbohm Tree, who was presenting the play as well as playing Professor Higgins, saying that a member had complained of the phrase and that 'with a view to retaining the respect of the public for the theatre' they wanted him to omit the words. He declined. A revue opened at the Alhambra shortly afterwards with the title *Not ****** Likely*. In time, the euphemistic alternative 'Not Pygmalion likely!' emerged.

Shaw concluded: 'By making a fashionable actress use bad language in a fashionable theatre, I became overnight more famous than the Pope, the King, the Kaiser and the Archbishop of Canterbury.'

Pygmalion was filmed with Wendy Hiller in 1938, and thus the word 'bloody' was heard for the first time in the cinema. By the time *My Fair Lady* — the musical version — was filmed in 1964, the shock effect of 'bloody' was so mild that Eliza was given the line 'Come on, Dover, move your ruddy arse!' in the Ascot racing sequence. Which takes us right back to *Peregrine Pickle* . . .

2 Liza: *My aunt died of influenza: so they said . . . But it's my belief (as how) they done the old woman in.*

The words 'as how' were inserted by Mrs Patrick Campbell in her performances as Eliza Doolittle and were also incorporated in the 1938 film.

3 *Where the devil are my slippers, Eliza?*

Last words (spoken by Higgins) of the 1938 film version (and of the musical adaptation

My Fair Lady — in the order 'Eliza, where the devil are my slippers?') but not in Shaw's original stage text. The intention appears to be for Higgins to hint at some romantic interest in Eliza. Shaw always opposed this. Even his published text of the film script (1941) shuns the line. And although Higgins ask for his slippers twice during the course of Act IV of the original play, the words are not addressed to Eliza.

1 *All Americans are blind and deaf — and dumb.*

A whopping journalistic misquotation dating from the 1930s. Shaw *did* meet Helen Keller, the American writer who heroically overcame deafness and blindness. According to Hesketh Pearson's biography of Shaw (1942), he rather paid her the compliment: 'I wish all Americans were as blind as you.'

2 *The trouble Mr Goldwyn, is that you are only interested in art and I am only interested in money.*

Telegraphed version of the outcome of a conversation between Shaw and the film producer Sam Goldwyn. It appears to have been recounted first in Alva Johnson, *The Great Goldwyn* (1937).

3 G.K. Chesterton: *To see you, Mr Shaw, one would think there was a famine in the land.*
   G.B. Shaw: *And looking at you, Mr Chesterton, one would know who to blame.*

This celebrated fat man/thin man exchange was the subject of a letter to the *Guardian* from a Mr Robert Turpin of Plymouth (14 May 1985): 'I first heard the story from a great-uncle of mine who knew both Shaw and Chesterton and actually attended the meeting at which the exchange took place.' (If so, the great-uncle was privileged to be one of those rare people to have been present at the cracking of an immortal joke.)
   Caution immediately sets in, however — especially as the paper also carried a letter from Peter Black, the journalist, saying he had first encountered the story in Australia involving the portly Prime Minister, Sir Robert Menzies. The *PDMQ* (1980) meanwhile, had cast Lord Northcliffe, the well-built press baron, in the Chesterton role.
   The most reliable version must surely be that which appears in *Thirty Years With*

GBS (1951) by Blanche Patch, Shaw's secretary: 'One look at you, Mr Shaw, and I know there's famine in the land.' 'One look at you, *Mr Hitchcock*, and I know who caused it.' This was, of course, Alfred Hitchcock, the film director.

4 *Youth is too precious/important to be wasted on the young.*

The Treasury of Humorous Quotations (Nicolas Bentley's revision of Evan Esar's book, 1951) has this from Shaw in the form, 'Youth is a wonderful thing; what a crime to waste it on children.' But where is it to be found in all of Shaw?
   Later, in Sammy Cahn's lyrics for the song 'The Second Time Around' (1960; music by Jimmy Van Heusen) there is what is presumably no more than a quotation:

> It's that second time you hear your
>   love song sung,
> Makes you think perhaps, that
> Love like youth is wasted on the
>   young.

5 *Nobel Prize money is a lifebelt thrown to a swimmer who has already reached the shore in safety.*

Attributed to Shaw, but unverified. Shaw won the Nobel prize for Literature in 1925. Here he is merely paraphrasing Samuel Johnson's pointed remark to Lord Chesterfield: 'Is not a Patron, my Lord, one who looks with unconcern on a man struggling for life in the water, and, when he has reached ground, encumbers him with help?' (Letter, 7 February 1755).

6 *He who can, does. He who cannot, teaches.*

From Shaw's 'Maxims: Education' published with *Man and Superman* (1903). A development of this thought was popular as a graffito (reported, for example, from Middlesex Polytechnic in 1979): 'and those who can't teach lecture on the sociology of education degrees.'
   Yet a further development is encompassed by A.B. Ramsay in 'Epitaph on a Syndic' from his *Frondes Salicis* (1935):

> No teacher I of boys or smaller fry,
> No teacher I of teachers, no, not I.
> Mine was the distant aim, the longer
>   reach,
> To teach men how to teach men how
>   to teach.

Shawcross, Sir Hartley
(later Lord Shawcross)
English jurist and Labour politician
(1902–   )

1 *We are the masters now!*

It might have seemed in poor taste for a Labour minister to crow this. After all, it had been into the mouth of an imperialist that George Orwell had earlier put these words in his novel *Burmese Days* (1934): 'No natives in this Club! It's by constantly giving way over small things like that that we've ruined the Empire . . . The only possible policy is to treat 'em like the dirt they are . . . We've got to hang together and say, "We are the masters, and you beggars . . . keep your place".'

So quite why Shawcross, the Attorney-General in Britain's first post-war Labour Government, did say something like it bears some examination. For a start, it was not said, as one might expect, on the day new Labour MPs swarmed into the House of Commons just after their sweeping election victory in 1945. It was said on 2 April 1946, almost nine months later. Then again, what Shawcross said was, 'We are the masters at the moment', though understandably the more pungent variant has passed into the language. A look at Hansard reveals precisely why he chose this form of words. He was winding up for the Government in the third reading of the Trade Disputes and Trade Unions Bill and drew attention to what he saw as the Conservative Opposition's lack of support for a measure it had promised to introduce if it won the election:

> [We made this an issue at the election] when he invited us to submit this matter to the verdict of the people . . . I realise that the right hon. Member for Woodford [Winston Churchill] is such a master of the English language that he has put himself very much in the position of Humpty-Dumpty in *Alice* . . . 'When I use a word,' said Humpty-Dumpty, 'it means just what I intend it to mean, and neither more nor less.' 'But,' said Alice, 'the question is whether you can make a word mean different things.' 'Not so,' said Humpty-Dumpty, 'the question is which is to be the master. That's all.'
>
> We are the masters at the moment, and not only at the moment, but for a very long time to come, and as hon. Members opposite are not prepared to implement the pledge which was given by their leader in regard to this matter at the

General Election, we are going to implement it for them.

At the end of the debate, the votes cast were: Ayes 349; Noes 182. When the House met again after the 1950 General Election — at which the Conservatives just failed to oust Labour — Churchill commented: 'I like the appearance of these benches better than what we had to look at during the last four and a half years. It is certainly refreshing to feel, at any rate, that this is a Parliament where half the nation will not be able to ride rough-shod over the other half . . . I do not see the Attorney-General in his place, but no one will be able to boast "We are the masters now".'

So, by this time, the popular version of the words had already emerged.

Shelley, Percy Bysshe
English poet (1792–1822)

2 *The cemetery is an open space among the ruins, covered in winter with violets and daisies. It might make one in love with death, to think that one should be buried in so sweet a place.*

On Keats's burial place in the English cemetery in Rome. Shelley, whose own remains were to be buried, in due course, not far away from his fellow poet's, wrote of it in his preface to *Adonais* (1821), his elegy on the death of Keats.

Sheridan, Philip Henry
American general (1831–88)

3 *The only good Indian is a dead Indian.*

Sheridan, mostly a cavalry commander on the Federal side in the American Civil War, is supposed to have said this at Fort Cobb in January 1869, but exhaustive study by Wolfgang Mieder (in *The Journal of American Folklore*, No. 106; 1993) has shown that this particular racial slur may already have been proverbial and have been wished on Sheridan unjustly. For example, the previous year, during a debate on an 'Indian Appropriation Bill' in the House of Representatives (28 May 1868), James Michael Cavanaugh (1823–79), a congressman from Montana, had said: 'I will say that I like an Indian better dead than living. I have never in my life seen a good Indian (and I have seen thousands) except when I have seen a dead Indian.'

Mieder adds that, though Sheridan was

known as a bigot and Indian hater, Charles Nordstrom's account of the Fort Cobb incident in 1869 is of questionable authenticity: 'A chief of the Comanches, on being presented to Sheridan, desired to impress the General in his favor, and striking himself a resounding blow on the breast, he managed to say: "Me, Toch-a-way; me good Injun." A quizzical smile lit up the General's face as he set those standing by in a roar by saying: "The only good Indians I ever saw were dead".'

Sheridan repeatedly denied having made any such a statement, but, whatever the case, an imperishable formula had been devised: 'The only good X is a dead X' is still with us.

Sherman, William T.
American general (1820–91)

1 Hold the fort, for I am coming.

The phrase 'hold the fort' has two meanings: 'Look after this place while I'm away' and 'Hang on, relief is at hand'. In the second sense, there is a specific origin. In the American Civil War, General Sherman signalled words to this effect to General John M. Corse at the Battle of Allatoona, Georgia (5 October 1864). What he actually semaphored from Keneshaw Mountain was: 'Sherman says hold fast. We are coming' (Mencken, 1942) or 'Hold out. Relief is coming' (Bartlett, 1980).

The phrase became popularized in its present form as the first line of a hymn or gospel song written by Philip Paul Bliss *c* 1870 ('Ho, My Comrades, See the Signal!' in *The Charm*). This was introduced to Britain by Moody and Sankey during their evangelical tour of the British Isles in 1873 (and not written by them, as is sometimes supposed):

'Hold the fort, for I am coming,'
Jesus signals still;
Wave the answer back to heaven,
'By thy grace we will.'

More recently, perhaps thanks to a pun on 'union' (as in the American 'Union' and as in 'trade union'), the song has been adapted as a trade union song in Britain:

Hold the fort, for we are coming
Union men be strong
Side by side keep pressing onward.
Victory will come.

2 War is hell.

All he may have said in a speech at Columbus, Ohio (11 August 1880) was: 'There is many a boy here today who looks on war as all glory, but, boys, it is all hell.'

3 I will not accept if nominated, and will not serve if elected.

His words to the Republican national Convention in 1884. They were sent in a telegraph message to General Henderson when Sherman was being urged to stand as the Republican candidate for the US Presidency. This version was recalled by Sherman's son in an addendum to his father's *Memoirs* (4th edition, 1891). Perhaps most usually rendered in the form: 'If nominated, I will not run. If elected, I will not serve.'

Sherriff, R.C.
English playwright (1896–1975)

4 Journey's End.

The title of Sherriff's play (1929), set in the trenches of the First World War, might seem to nod towards Shakespeare — 'Journeys end in lovers meeting' (*Twelfth Night*, II.iii.44) or 'Here is my journey's end' (*Othello*, V.ii.268) — or towards Dryden, 'The world's an inn, and death the journey's end' ('Palamon and Arcite'). But it is impossible to be certain. In his autobiography, *No Leading Lady* (1968), Sherriff wrote of the titles he rejected, like 'Suspense' and 'Waiting', and then adds: 'One night I was reading a book in bed. I got to a chapter that closed with the words: "It was late in the evening when we came at last to our Journey's End". The last two words sprang out as the ones I was looking for. Next night I typed them on a front page for the play, and the thing was done.' He does not say what the book was.

Sickert, Walter
German-born English painter (1860–1942)

5 Come again when you can't stay so long.

As a young man, Denton Welch paid a visit to Sickert and later wrote a description of the oddities he had encountered. The great man persecuted and terrified him and, during tea, danced in front of him wearing boots such as deep sea divers wear . . . 'to see how Denton would react to the experience' (in Edith Sitwell's phrase). As Welch left the house, Sickert said the above to him. Welch's 'Sickert at St Peter's' appeared in *Horizon*, Vol. vi, No. 32 (1942). In *Taken*

Care of (1965), Edith Sitwell comments on the article but gives the tag as 'Come again — when you have a little less time'. Either way, this farewell was not originated by Sickert. Indeed, Welch ends his article by saying, 'And at these words a strange pang went through me, for it was what my father had always said as he closed the book, when I had finished my bread and butter and milk, and it was time for bed'.

Sidney, Sir Philip
English soldier and poet (1554–86)

1 *Thy necessity is yet greater than mine.*

Wounded at the Battle of Zutphen (1586), Sidney was 'thirsty with excess of bleeding' and called for something to drink. As he was putting the bottle to his lips, he saw a poor soldier who eyed it enviously. 'Which Sir Philip perceiving, took the bottle from his head, before he drank, and delivered it to the poor man with these words' — a story reported by Fulke Greville, Lord Brooke (1554–1628).

2 *A tale which holdeth children from play, and old men from the chimney corner.*

One of the quotations used to promote the Everyman's Library series of classic reprints. It is from *The Defense of Poetry* (1595): 'With a tale forsooth he [the poet] cometh unto you, with a tale which . . .' Compare ANONYMOUS SAYINGS 12:2 and MILTON 242:4.

Sieyès, Emmanuel Joseph
French prelate and revolutionary leader (1748–1836)

3 *I survived* [J'ai vécu].

When the Abbé Sieyès, who played an important part in the French Revolution and then lapsed into 'philosophic silence', was asked *c* 1795 what he had done during the Reign of Terror, this was his reply. Recorded by 1836.

Simenon, Georges
Belgian novelist (1903–89)

4 *I have made love to ten thousand women.*

Simenon's best-known remark arose parenthetically in an interview *he* was conducting

with an old friend Federico Fellini to publicize the latter's new film *Casanova*. Not in a calculated, premeditated or publicity seeking way, he suddenly said: 'You know, Fellini, I think that in my life I have been even more of a Casanova than you. I did the sum a year or two ago and since the age of 13 and a half I have had 10,000 women. It was not at all a vice, I suffer from no sexual vice, but I have a need to communicate. And even the 8,000 prostitutes who must be included in this total of 10,000 women were human beings, female human beings.' The interview was published in *L'Express* (21 February 1977) and the claim attracted worldwide publicity. Later, his second wife Denyse said: 'The true figure is no more than twelve hundred.' Patrick Marnham in *The Man Who Wasn't Maigret* (1992) calls this 'Simenon's last publicity coup . . . and in some ways his greatest coup of all'.

Simon, Paul
American songwriter (1942–)

5 *The mother and child reunion is only a motion away.*

From the song 'Mother and Child Reunion' (1972). Professor Simon Frith of the University of Strathclyde confidently stated in the *Independent* (22 January 1993) that this was a reference to abortion. Lesley Bennett responded the following day: 'Paul Simon told me (in 1968 or 1969) that "Mother and Child Reunion" was the name of a dish he had eaten in Chinatown in San Francisco. The dish was a combination of chicken with egg; the reunion, presumably, happened when they were eaten and digested together.'

Sims, George R.
English journalist and playwright (1847–1922)

6 *It is Christmas Day in the Workhouse.*
  And the cold bare walls are bright
  With garlands of green and holly,
  And the place is a pleasant sight.

The poem 'In the Workhouse — Christmas Day' (1879) became a popular late-Victorian recitation. It tells of a pauper rising up to challenge the 'guardians' who have come to watch the Christmas feast. He chides them for turning away a dying woman the previous year — his wife. Nowadays it is probably better known as the result of several parodies. One from the First World War (and included in the stage show *Oh What a Lovely War*, 1963) goes:

It was Christmas day in the cookhouse,
The happiest day of the year,
Men's hearts were full of gladness
And their bellies full of beer,
When up spoke Private Shorthouse,
His face as bold as brass,
Saying, 'We don't want your Christmas pudding
You can stick it up your . . .'
Tidings of comfort and joy, comfort and joy,
Oh, tidings of comfort and joy!

Hence, the further version performed by the music-hall comedian, Billy Bennett (*d* 1942).

It was Christmas Day in the cookhouse.
The troops had all gone to bed.
None of them had any Christmas pudding
'Cause the sergeant had done what they said.

Sitwell, Sir Osbert
English writer (1892–1969)

1 *Great Morning.*

The title of one of his volumes of memoirs (1947) may derive from fox-hunting. Compare Shakespeare, *Troilus and Cressida* (IV.iii.1): 'It is great morning; and the hour prefix'd / For her delivery to this valiant Greek'; and *Cymbeline* (IV.ii.61): 'It is great morning' – in both of which cases, the meaning is 'broad daylight'. Compare the title of J.B. Priestley's 1946 novel, *Bright Day*.

Skelton, Noel
British Conservative politician (1880–1935)

2 *To state as clearly as may be what means lie ready to develop a property-owning democracy, to bring the industrial and economic status of the wage-earner abreast of his political and educational, to make democracy stable and four-square.*

From an article in *The Spectator*, 19 May 1923. The phrase 'property-owning democracy' was later popularized by Anthony Eden and Winston Churchill (*c* 1946) and came to be associated with them, though Skelton undoubtedly coined the phrase.

Smith, Adam
Scottish philosopher and economist (1723–90)

3 *The real tragedy of the poor is the poverty of their aspirations.*

Unverified.

Smith, Alfred E.
American politician (1873–1944)

4 *Nobody shoots at Santa Claus.*

In American politics, this is sometimes said about about the folly of attacking government benefit programmes. Former Governor Smith said in 1933: 'No sane local official who has hung up an empty stocking over the municipal fireplace is going to shoot Santa Claus just before a hard Christmas.' Later Santa Claus came to represent the free lunch, the government handout, the something-for-nothing – and again, any politician had to take his courage in both hands to knock it.

5 *UNPACK.*

The *ODQ* (1992) has this as a telegraph message in 1932 to the Pope whom Smith had hoped would come to live in the United States, in the event of Smith's campaign for the Presidency proving successful. Rather it was a joke told *about* Smith, as in the form, 'What did Al Smith telegraph to the Pope after he lost the election?' 'Unpack.' As Smith stood for the Presidency in 1928 (and lost to Herbert Hoover), it seems that this joke took a little time to emerge.

6 *No matter how thin you slice it, it's still baloney.*

Said by Smith about Roosevelt's New Deal during campaign speeches in 1936. Roosevelt had supported him in 1928 but they fell out when Roosevelt himself ran for the presidency. The *PDMQ* (1980), on the other hand, has Brendan Gill, *Here at the New Yorker* (1975), ascribing the remark to Rube Goldberg.

See also ROOSEVELT 284:3.

Smith, Edward
English sea captain (*d* 1912)

7 *Be British, boys, be British.*

Smith's reputed last words were said to his crew some time in the hours between the

Titanic hitting the iceberg and his going down with the ship. Michael Davie in his book on the disaster describes the evidence for this as 'flimsy', but obviously the legend was well established by 1914 when the statue to him in Lichfield was erected. It has 'Be British' as part of the inscription.

See also WRIGHT 364:1.

Smith, F.E.
(1st Earl of Birkenhead)
British Conservative politician and lawyer (1872–1930)

1 *The world continues to offer glittering prizes to those who have stout hearts and sharp swords.*

From a Rectorial Address at Glasgow University (7 November 1923) in which he suggested that the only way to preserve the peace was to prepare for war. His subject was 'Idealism in International Politics'. John Campbell in his biography of Birkenhead (1983) comments that 'for ever after, his career was seen, as it still is, as exemplifying the single-minded pursuit of "glittering prizes", from cups and scholarships to office, wealth and fame. This was not at all the context in which F.E. coined the phrase.' Campbell states additionally that there were other instances of the phrase — 'but it seems clear from [an earlier] Montreal speech that F.E. was neither plagiarizing not consciously coining an epigram.'

Hence, *The Glittering Prizes*, the title of a BBC TV drama series (1976) by Frederic Raphael, about the fortunes of a group of Cambridge graduates.

Smith, Logan Pearsall
American writer (1865–1946)

2 *Thank heavens, the sun has gone in, and I don't have to go out and enjoy it.*

These are sometimes quoted as though they were Logan Pearsall Smith's last (dying) words as in *A Dictionary of Famous Quotations* (1962), for example. They are not, though the misunderstanding is understandable. They appear in a work called *Last Words* (1933). Smith did not die until 1946 when, according to James Lees-Milne, *Caves of Ice* (1983), his actual last words were, 'I must telephone to the Pope-Hennessys'.

Smith, Stevie
English poet (1902–71)

3 *A Good Time Was Had By All.*

Title of a collection of her poems (1937). Eric Partridge asked her where she had taken the phrase from and she duly replied, from parish magazines where reports of church picnics or social evenings invariably ended with the phrase.

4 *And do you think I bred you up to*
  live a life of shame
  To live a life of shame my boy as you
  are thinking to
  Down south in Kingston-upon-Hull
  a traveller in glue?

From the poem 'Correspondence Between Mr Harrison in Newcastle and Mr Sholto Peach Harrison in Hull', date unknown.

5 *Not Waving, But Drowning.*

Title of poem (1957), hence the modern proverbial expression used to describe any sort of situation where a gesture may be misinterpreted.

Smith, The Revd Sydney
English clergyman, essayist and wit (1771–1845)

6 *My idea of heaven is eating* pâté de foie gras *to the sound of trumpets.*

The source for this famous remark is Hesketh Pearson, *The Smith of Smiths* (1934). The *ODQ* (1979) put it in Chapter 10 and gave it as '— —'s idea of heaven . . .', as though Smith were quoting another. By 1992 the *ODQ* was putting it in Smith's own mouth but still finding it in Pearson's Chapter 10. Presumably Pearson found it in one of the little books of Smith's wit and wisdom published in the nineteenth century.

Compare this from Benjamin Disraeli's novel *The Young Duke* (I.10): 'All paradise opens! Let me die eating ortolans to the sound of soft music.' That was published in 1831.

Smollett, Tobias
Scottish novelist (1721–71)

7 *The Great Cham (of Literature).*

Smollett's nickname for Dr Samuel Johnson occurred in a letter to John Wilkes in 1759.

'Cham' is a form of 'khan' (as in Genghis Khan) meaning 'monarch' or 'prince'.

Snow, C.P.
(later Lord Snow)
English novelist and scientist (1905–80)

1 *Corridors of Power.*

This phrase was reasonably well established for the machinations of government, especially the bureacrats and civil servants of Whitehall, by the time Snow used it for the title of a novel (1964), but he undoubtedly popularized it. Earlier, he had written in his novel *Homecomings* (1956): 'The official world, the corridors of power, the dilemmas of conscience and egotism — she disliked them all.'

2 *Two Cultures and the Scientific Revolution.*

For a time, the title of Snow's 1959 Rede Lecture at Cambridge on the gap between science and literature and religion gave another much used phrase to the language. 'The Two Cultures' became a catchphrase in discussions of the inability of the two camps to speak a common language or, indeed, to understand each other at all.

Snowden, Philip
(1st Viscount Snowden)
English politician (1864–1937)

3 *This is not Socialism. It is Bolshevism run mad.*

An early political sensation on British radio was made in a broadcast during the 1931 general election. On 17 October Snowden, who had been Chancellor of the Exchequer in the 1929 Labour Government and who now held the same post in the National Government, said this of the Labour Party's plans. He also said: 'I hope you have read the Election programme of the Labour Party. It is the most fantastic and impracticable programme ever put before the electors.' The plans were, of course, similar to the ones he had himself devised in 1929. He later commented: 'My effort was universally believed to have had great influence on the result of the Election. The Labour Party gave me the credit, or, as they put it, the discredit of being responsible for the tragic fate which overtook them.'

Solon
Athenian statesman and poet
(c 640–c 556BC)

4 De mortuis nil nisi bonum [*Of the dead, speak kindly or not at all*].

Sometimes ascribed to Solon (in about 600BC), 'Speak not evil of the dead' was also a saying of Chilo(n) of Sparta (one of the Seven Sages, also sixth century BC). Later Sextus Propertius (*d* 2AD) wrote: '*Absenti nemo non nocuisse velit* [Let no one be willing to speak ill of the absent].' Sometimes simply referred to in the form '*de mortuis . . .*', it is a proverb which appears in some form in most European languages.

Somoza, Anastasio
Nicaraguan dictator (1925–80)

5 *Indeed, you won the elections, but I won the count.*

Quoted in the *Guardian*, 17 June 1977. Ironically, this remark had been anticipated by Tom Stoppard in his play *Jumpers* (1972): 'It's not the voting that's democracy, it's the counting.'

Sondheim, Stephen
American songwriter (1930–   )

6 *Everything's coming up roses.*

The title of a song in *Gypsy* (1959), music by Jule Styne. But did the expression exists before this? It is possibly adapted from the expression, 'to come out smelling of roses', but there do not seem to be any examples even of *that* before the date of the Sondheim coinage.

7 *Send in the Clowns.*

The title of a song in *A Little Night Music* (1973), words and music by Sondheim. The tradition that the 'show must go on' grew out of circus. Whatever mishap occurred, the band was told to go on playing and the cry went up 'send in/on the clowns' — for the simple reason that panic had to be avoided, the audience's attention diverted, and the livelihood of everybody in the circus depended on not having to give the audience its money back. Perhaps 'send in' was right for the circus, 'send on' for the stage?

Similarly, 'the show must go on' seems primarily a circus phrase, though no one seems able to turn up a written reference much before 1930. In 1950, the phrase was spoken in the film *All About Eve* and, in the same decade, Noël Coward wrote a song which posed the question 'Why Must the Show Go On?'

1 *Sunday in the Park with George.*

The title of Sondheim's 1983 musical is derived from that of a painting 'Sunday on the Island of La Grande Jatte' and the name of the painter, Georges Seurat, who first exhibited it at the 1886 Impressionist Exhibition.

Sophocles
Greek playwright (c 496–406BC)

2 *To die would be good, but never to have been born would be better.*

From the play *Oedipus at Colonus*, but sometimes remembered in a German translation. Friedrich Hölderlin quoted the words on the title page of his novel *Hyperion* (1797). They occur also at the end of Heinrich Heine's poem 'Morphine' (*'Gut ist der Schlaf, der Tod ist besser — freilich Das beste wäre, mie geboren sein'*). Friedrich Nietzsche wrote similarly in *The Birth of Tragedy* (1872), attributing the words to Silenus, the companion of Dionysus.

[*Source: The Times*, 8 April 1980.]

Sparrow, John
English academic (1906–92)

3 *Never lend a book; never give a book away; never read a book.*

The 'book collector's caveat', which Sparrow was fond of quoting, according to his obituary in the *Independent* (4 February 1992).

4 *This stone with not unpardonable pride,*
Proves by its record what the world denied:
Simon could do a natural thing — he died.

Suggested epitaph for Sir John (later Viscount) Simon (1873–1954), lawyer and Liberal politician. 'Lord Simon has died . . . John Sparrow wrote this epitaph many years ago . . . But then John Simon helped John Sparrow to become Warden of All Souls,

and the latter came to regret his epigram' — *Harold Nicolson's Diaries and Letters 1945–1962* (entry for 11 January 1954). In Sparrow's *Grave Epigrams and Other Verses* (1981), 'Simon' is replaced by *'Nemo'*.

5 *Without you, Heaven would be too dull to bear,*
And Hell would not be Hell if you are there.

Epitaph for Sir Maurice Bowra (1898–1971), first published in *The Times Literary Supplement* (23 June 1972) as a poem, 'C.M.B.' It was reprinted, in this altered form, in Sparrow's *Grave Epigrams and Other Verses* (1981):

Send us to Hell or Heaven or where you will,
Promise us only, you'll be with us still:
Heaven, without you, would be too dull to bear,
And Hell will not be Hell if you are there.

Bowra was a noted Oxford personality and Warden of Wadham. Sparrow was part of his circle, the Warden of All Souls, and a connoisseur of inscriptions and epitaphs. Bowra's actual grave in St Cross churchyard bears his name in suitably bold letters but no epitaph.

Spector, Phil
American record producer (1940–)

6 *To Know Him Is To Love Him.*

This song title has an interesting history. In *The Picture of Dorian Gray* (1890), Oscar Wilde had: 'To see him is to worship him, to know him is to trust him.' Blanche Hozier wrote to Mabell, Countess of Airlie, in 1908: 'Clementine is engaged to be married to Winston Churchill. I do not know which of the two is more in love. I think that to know him is to like him.'

Thus the format existed, but as 'To Know Him Is To Love Him', it became the title of a song, written by Spector in 1958. The words have a biblical ring to them, but whether Spector was ever aware of the words of No. 3 in *CSSM Choruses* (3rd ed., 1928, by the Children's Special Service Mission, London) we may never know. Written by R. Hudson Pope, it goes:

All glory be to Jesus
The sinner's only Saviour . . .
To know Him is to love Him,
To trust him is to prove Him.

Robert Burns (1759–96) came very close to

the phrase on a couple of occasions —
in 'Bonnie Lesley': 'To see her is to love
her/And love but her for ever', and in
'Ae Fond Kiss': 'But to see her was to
love her,/Love but her, and love for ever.'
Besides, the words have often been used in
an epitaph context. Fitz-Greene Halleck
(1795–1867) wrote 'On the death of J.R.
Drake':

Green be the turf above thee,
    Friend of my better days;
None knew thee but to love thee
    Nor named thee but to praise.

Samuel Rogers (1763–1855) wrote of
'Jacqueline':

Oh! she was good as she was fair.
None — none on earth above her!
As pure in thought as angels are,
To know her was to love her.

It appears that Spector acquired the title of
his song from the gravestone of his father, a
suicide.

Spencer, Herbert
English philosopher (1820–1903)

1 To play billiards well is the sign of a
misspent youth,

Under Spencer, the ODQ (1979) had: 'It
was remarked to me by the late Mr Charles
Roupell . . . that to play billiards was a sign
of an ill-spent youth.' On the other hand, in
the archives of the Savile Club in London it
is recorded that Robert Louis Stevenson,
who was a member from 1874 to 1894, propounded to Spencer that "proficiency in this
game [note: probably billiards, because it
was said in the Savile billiards room] is a sign
of a misspent youth' (mentioned in 'Words',
the Observer, 4 May 1986).

Other clubs also claim the honour and
some people would supply the word
'snooker' or 'bridge' instead of 'billiards'. A
keen billiards player, Spencer was dis-
pleased when the saying kept being ascribed
to him in newspapers. He had quoted it from
someone else. So he dictated a denial to
Dr David Duncan, who edited his Life and
Letters (1908) from which the ODQ quotation was taken. ODQ (1992) puts the
remark under Roupell and describes him as
an 'official referee of the British High Court
of Justice'.

Benham (1948) notes that a similar view
had earlier appeared in Noctes Ambrosianae
in March 1827.

2 The survival of the fittest.

Spencer wrote in Principles of Biology
(1864–7): 'This survival of the fittest which
I have here sought to express in mechanical
terms is that which Mr Darwin has called
"natural selection, or the preservation of
favoured races in the struggle for life".'

In other words, Spencer, in talking of
evolution, was pointing to the survival of
the most suitable, not of the most physically
fit.

Spenser, Edmund
English poet (c 1552–99)

3 Sweet Thames, run softly, till I end my
song.

In Handbook of 20th Century Quotations
(ed. Frank S. Pepper, 1984) this line is
attributed to T.S. Eliot in The Waste Land
(1922). As with ELIOT 133:4, this is another
example of Eliot's magpie-like use of quotation misleading readers who do not plunge
in among his fairly copious notes. Eliot
quotes it at his l. 176. The line is repeated
at the end of each verse of Spenser's Pro-
thalamion (1596).

4 Sleep after toyle, port after stormie seas,
Ease after warre, death after life, does
    greatly please.

From Spenser's The Faerie Queen, Bk 1,
c.ix.xl (1590–6), this text is popular as a
gravestone inscription. It was put, for example, on the bronze statue of Admiral Robert
Blake (1599–1657) at Bridgwater, Somerset.
It also appears on the tombstone of the
Polish-born novelist Joseph Conrad (1857–
1924) in the cemetery of St Thomas's
Roman Catholic Church, Canterbury. The
quotation had been used by Conrad as the
epigraph to his last complete work, The
Rover.

5 What wee gave, wee have;
What wee spent, wee had;
What wee left, wee lost.

This is the epitaph on Edward Courtenay,
Earl of Devon (d 1419) and his wife, at
Tiverton. Compare, 'That we spent, we
had:/That we gave, we have:/That we
left, we lost' — the epitaph of 'the Earl
of Devonshire' as quoted by Spenser in
The Shepheardes Calendar, 'May', l.70
(1579).

Spooner, The Revd William
English clergyman and academic
(1844–1930)

1 *Kinquering congs their titles take.*

Spoonerism, the accidental transposing of
the beginnings of words, is named after a
former Warden of New College, Oxford,
and the term had been coined by 1900.
Many of Spooner's reported efforts must be
apocryphal. 'In a dark glassly' and 'a half-
warmed fish' are two of the more likely ones.
'Kinquering congs . . .' — announcing the
hymn in New College Chapel (1879) —
sounds reasonable (it was reported in the
Oxford *Echo*, 4 May 1892), but 'Sir, you
have tasted two whole worms; you have
hissed all my mystery lectures and been
caught fighting a liar in the quad; you will
leave Oxford by the next town drain', seems
utterly contrived. Had he been an ornitho-
logist, Spooner might well have described
himself as a word-botcher.

2 *Was it you or your brother who was
killed in the war?*

A joke well-established at New College by
1963 was that Spooner had once inquired of
an undergraduate (*c* 1918), 'Now, tell me,
was it you or your brother who was killed
in the war?' Frank Muir in *The Oxford Book
of Humorous Prose* cites this from John
Taylor's *Wit and Mirth* (1630): 'A noble-
man (as he was riding) met with a yeoman
of the country, to whom he said, "My
friend, I should know thee. I do remember
I have often seen thee." "My good lord," said
the countryman, "I am one of your honour's
poor tenants, and my name is T.I." "I
remember thee better now" (saith my lord)
"There were two brothers but one is dead.
I pray thee, which of you doth remain
alive?"'

Spring-Rice, Sir Cecil
British diplomat and poet (1859–1918)

3 *And there's another country, I've
heard of long ago —
Most dear to them that love her,
most great to them that know.*

The title of *Another Country*, the play
(1981; film UK, 1984) by Julian Mitchell,
showing how the seeds of defection to Soviet
Russia were sown in a group of boys at an
English public school, might seem at first
glance, to be taken from the celebrated line
in Christopher Marlowe's *The Jew of Malta*
(*c* 1592):

> Fornication: but that was in another
> country;
> And besides the wench is dead.

But no. As the playwright has confirmed to
me, it comes from the second verse of
Spring-Rice's patriotic 'Last Poem' (1918),
which begins 'I vow to thee, my country' and
continues as above. In this original context,
the 'other country' is Heaven, rather than
the Soviet Union, of course. *Another Country* was also used as the title of a novel
(1962) by James Baldwin.

Stalin, Joseph
Soviet Communist leader (1879–1953)

4 *He who is not with us is against us.*

A view popularly ascribed to the Soviet
leader. *Time* Magazine (11 August 1986)
also noted a corollary attributed to the
Hungarian Communist Party leader, Janos
Kadar (1912-89): 'He who is not against us
is with us.' In fact, Stalin was quoting Jesus
Christ who said: 'He that is not with me is
against me' (Luke 11:23) and Kadar was
also quoting Christ who provided the corollary: 'He that is not against us is for us'
(Luke 9:50). It is not surprising that Stalin
quoted Scripture. He went from a church
school at Guri to the seminary at Tiflis to
train for the Russian Orthodox priesthood.

5 *The trouble with free elections is, you
never who is going to win.*

This has been attributed to Leonid Brezhnev,
but not traced. It is, however, just the kind
of thing Stalin might have said at the
Potsdam Conference in 1945 when Winston
Churchill's fate in the British General Election hung in the balance. Molotov has also
been suggested.

Stanley, Sir Henry Morton
British explorer and journalist (1841–1904)

6 *Dr Livingstone, I presume?*

The most famous greeting was put by
Stanley to the explorer and missionary
Dr David Livingstone at Ujiji, Lake
Tanganyika, on 10 November 1871.
Stanley had been sent by the *New York
Herald* to look for Livingstone who was
missing on a journey in central Africa. In

How I Found Livingstone (1872), Stanley described the moment: 'I would have run to him, only I was a coward in the presence of such a mob — would have embraced him, only, he being an Englishman, I did not know how he would receive me; so I did what cowardice and false pride suggested was the best thing — walked deliberately to him, took off my hat and said: "Dr Livingstone, I presume?" "YES," said he, with a kind smile, lifting his cap slightly.'

One unhelpful suggestion is that Stanley was making a tongue-in-cheek reference to a moment in Sheridan's *School for Scandal* (V.i) in which, after much mutual confusion, two of the main characters finally get to meet with the line, 'Mr Stanley, I presume.' But, really, it was not such a remarkable salutation after all. In the American Civil War, General Robert E. Lee, when he entered Maryland at Williamsport on 25 June 1863, was greeted by the spokesman of a women's committee of welcome with the words, 'This is General Lee, I presume?'

In the 1960s, when Robert F. Kennedy was campaigning south of Atlanta, he said to one of the rare white men he met: 'Dr Livingstone, I presume.'

1 *Through the Dark Continent. Through Darkest Africa.*

In 1878, Stanley published *Through the Dark Continent* and followed it, in 1890, with *Through Darkest Africa*. It is presumably from these two titles that we get the expressions 'dark continent' and 'darkest — —' to describe not only Africa but almost anywhere remote and uncivilized. Flexner (1982) suggests that 'In darkest Africa' was a screen subtitle in a silent film of the period 1910–14.

Stanton, Colonel Charles E.
American soldier (1859–1933)

2 *Lafayette, we are here.*

Nine days after the American Expeditionary Force landed in France, Stanton, a member of General Pershing's staff, stood at the tomb of Lafayette in the Picpus cemetery in Paris, and declared, 'Here and now, in the presence of the illustrious dead, we pledge our hearts and our honour in carrying this war to a successful issue. Lafayette, we are here!' This graceful tribute to the Marquis de Lafayette (1757–1834) who enlisted with the American revolutionary armies in 1777 and forged a strong emotional link between

the United States and France, was delivered by Stanton on 4 July 1917 and repeated on 14 July. As Bartlett (1968 and 1980) points out, the remark has also been attributed to General Pershing though he disclaimed having said 'anything so splendid'. There is evidence, however, that he may have pronounced the phrase before Stanton and that Stanton merely picked it up.

Stanton, Frank L.
American journalist and poet (1857–1927)

3 *Sweetes' li'l feller,*
Everybody knows;
Dunno what to call him,
But he's mighty lak' a rose!

From the song 'Mighty Lak' a Rose' (1901), music by Ethelbert Nevin. By 1991, when the singer Elvis Costello was entitling one of his albums (but no title song) 'Mighty Like a Rose', the southern American intonation of the original had clearly been dispensed with. Is there not also a parody?

Sweetest little feller,
Wears his sister's clothes.
Don't know what to call him,
But we think he's one of those.

Steffens, Lincoln
American journalist (1866–1936)

4 *I have seen the future and it works.*

Steffens was a muck-raking journalist who paid a visit to the newly formed Soviet Union as part of the William C. Bullitt diplomatic mission of 1919. As did a number of the first visitors to the new Soviet system, he returned with an optimistic view. His phrase for it was this. However, in his *Autobiography* (1931), he phrases it a little differently. ' "So you've been over into Russia?" said Bernard Baruch, and I answered very literally, "I have been over into the future, and it works".' Bullitt said Steffens had been rehearsing this formula even before he went to the Soviet Union. Later, he tended to use the shorter, more colloquial form himself.

Stein, Gertrude
American poet (1874–1946)

5 *Rose is a rose is a rose is a rose.*

Stein's poem 'Sacred Emily' is well-nigh impenetrable to most readers, but somehow it has managed to give a format phrase to the language. If something is incapable of explanation, one says, for example, 'a cloud is a cloud is a cloud'. What Stein wrote, however, is frequently misunderstood. She did not say 'A rose is a rose is a rose', but 'Rose is a rose is a rose is a rose' (i.e. upper case R and no indefinite article at the start and three not two repetitions). The Rose in question was not a flower but an allusion to the English painter, Sir Francis Rose, 'whom she and I regarded,' wrote Constantine Fitzgibbon, 'as the peer of Matisse and Picasso, and whose paintings — or at least painting — hung in her Paris drawing-room while a Gauguin was relegated to the lavatory.' (Letter to the *Sunday Telegraph*, 7 July 1978). Stein also refers to 'Jack Rose' (not a 'Jack' rose) earlier in the poem.

In John Malcolm Brinnin, *The Third Rose* (1959), Stein is quoted as saying: 'Now, listen! I'm no fool. I know that in daily life we don't go around saying "is a . . . is . . . is . . ." Yes, I'm no fool; but I think that in that line the rose is red for the first time in English poetry for a hundred years.' Note: *ODMQ* (1991) and *ODQ* (1992) have: 'Rose is a rose is a rose is a rose, is a rose.'

1 I Love You Alice B. Toklas.

The film comedy (US, 1968) with this title was about a lawyer (Peter Sellers) amid the Flower People of San Francisco in the 1960s. Alice B. Toklas (who came, as it happens, from San Francisco) was Stein's secretary and lover, for whom Stein 'ghosted' *The Autobiography of Alice B. Toklas* (1933). *The Alice B. Toklas Cookbook* (1954) — a mixture of memoirs and culinary hints — was, however, written by Toklas herself. Popular in the 1960s — perhaps in an 'alternative' edition — it seems to have contained recipes for marijuana cookies, hash brownies and such like.

2 The lost generation.

This phrase refers to the large number of promising young men who lost their lives in the First World War, and also, by extension to those who were not killed in the war but who were part of a generation thought to have lost its values. Stein recorded and popularized the remark made by a French garage owner in the Midi just after the war. Rebuking an apprentice who had made a shoddy repair to her car, he said: 'All you young people who served in the war' are from 'a lost generation' [*une génération*

perdue']. Ernest Hemingway used this as the epigraph to his novel *The Sun Also Rises* (1926) and referred to it again in *A Moveable Feast* (1964).

Steinem, Gloria
American feminist writer (1934–)

3 A woman without a man is like a fish without a bicycle.

The *ODQ* (1992) ascribes this saying to Steinem but gives no hint as to why it makes such a very dubious attribution, though it is reasonable to assume that the words must have crossed Ms Steinem's lips at some stage. It is, after all, probably the most famous feminist slogan of recent decades. Bartlett (1992) lists it anonymously as a 'feminist slogan of the 1980s'. I first quoted it on BBC Radio *Quote . . . Unquote* in July 1977 when it had been spotted by a listener as a graffito written up in German at the University of Birmingham. Indeed, the chances are that the saying originated in West Germany in the form '*Eine Frau ohne Mann ist wie ein Fisch ohne Velo!*'

Sterne, Laurence
Irish novelist and clergyman (1713–68)

4 A cock-and-bull story.

This phrase for a long, rambling, unbelievable tale, is used notably in Sterne's *Tristram Shandy* (1760–7). Indeed, the last words of the novel are: ' "L—d!" said my mother, "what is all this story about?" — "A cock and a bull," said Yorick, "And one of the best of its kind, I ever heard." '

Other suggested origins are that the phrase comes from: old fables in general which have animals talking, going right back to Aesop — confirmed perhaps by the equivalent French phrase '*coq à l'âne*' (literally, 'cock to donkey') — someone who hated having to listen to such fables was probably the first to dub them as such; Samuel Fisher's 1660 story about a cock and a bull being transformed into a single animal — which people may have thought pretty improbable; somehow from the Cock and Bull public houses, which are but a few doors apart in Stony Stratford, Buckinghamshire; generally confused tales told first in one pub, the Cock, and then retold in another, the Bull.

The *OED2*'s earliest citation of the precise form as it is now used comes (later than

Sterne) from the Philadelphia *Gazette of the United States* (1795): 'A long cock-and-bull story about the Columbianum' (a proposed national college).

1 *This world surely is wide enough to hold both thee and me.*

See JAMES I 188:4.

2 *God tempers the wind to the shorn lamb.*

In Sterne's *Sentimental Journey* (1768), we find: 'How she had borne it . . . she could not tell — but God tempers the wind, said Maria, to the shorn lamb.' That is to say, God arranges matters so as not to make them unduly harsh for the unfortunate. As such, this is possibly one of the most preposterously untrue of all proverbial sayings. For a proverb it is, not an original remark of Sterne's, as is sometimes supposed, though Sterne's wording is how it is now used. *CODP* finds a French version in 1594.

Winston Churchill in *My Early Life* (1930) (in the chapter entitled 'The Fourth Hussars') remembers a widely read colonel who could not pronounce his r's: 'When, for instance, on one occasion I quoted, "God tempers the wind to the shorn lamb", and Brabazon asked "Where did you get that fwom?" I had replied with some complacency that, though it was attributed often to the Bible, it really occurred in Sterne's *Sentimental Journey*.'

BDPF (1989) points out that Sterne erred in putting 'lamb' where earlier it had said 'sheep' — lambs are never shorn.

Stevenson, Adlai
American Democratic politician
(1900–1965)

3 *Eggheads of the world unite; you have nothing to lose but your yolks.*

Attributed. In a speech at Oakland (1 February 1956) he said, rather, 'Eggheads of the world, arise — I was even going to add that you have nothing to lose but your yolks.' 'Egghead' as a synonym for 'intellectual' had been popularized by the columnist Joseph Alsop during the 1952 US Presidential campaign.

4 *Dragged kicking and screaming into the twentieth century.*

For a well-known phrase, this is curiously little documented and has proved impossible to track to source. The earliest example found in this precise form comes from an article by Kenneth Tynan written in 1959 and collected in *Curtains* (1961): 'A change, slight but unmistakable, has taken place; the English theatre has been dragged, as Adlai Stevenson once said of the Republican Party, kicking and screaming into the twentieth century.'

Tony Benn said during a by-election in May 1961: 'It is given to Bristol in this election to wrench the parliamentary system away from its feudal origins, and pitchfork it kicking and screaming into the twentieth century.' Nobel prize winning chemist, Sir George Porter, said in a speech in September 1986: 'Should we force science down the throats of those that have no taste for it? Is it our duty to drag them kicking and screaming into the twentieth century? I am afraid it is.'

Obviously, it is a 'format' phrase that lends itself to subtle modification. From the *Daily Telegraph* (11 September 1979): 'Mr Ian McIntyre, whose ambition was to bring Radio 4 kicking and screaming into the 1970s'; from the *Washington Post* (19 January 1984): 'All [President Reagan] said before he was dragged kicking and screaming into the East Room was that he wouldn't call the Soviet Union an "evil empire" any more'; and from the same paper (19 December 1988): 'Still, Jones and Hawke, prodded by other corporate-minded partners, have dragged Arnold & Porter — sometimes kicking and screaming — into a 21st century mode of thinking, which they believe will position the firm to compete with firms that already have more than 1,000 lawyers.'

The nascent form can be found in a 1913 article by J.B. Priestley in *London Opinion*: '[By listening to ragtime] he felt literally dragged out of the nineteenth into the twentieth century.' (His use of 'literally' suggests that the idea of dragging from one century to another was already an established one.)

5 *I will make a bargain with the Republicans. If they will stop telling lies about the Democrats, we will stop telling the truth about them.*

Presidential campaign remark (10 September 1952), but apparently this was originated by Republican Senator Chauncey Depew about the *Democrats* earlier in the century.

1 *A heartbeat away from the Presidency.*

The traditional description of the position of the US Vice-President and, as Safire (1978) puts it, 'a reminder to voters to examine the shortcomings of a Vice-Presidential candidate'. The earliest use of the phrase Safire finds is Stevenson beginning an attack on Richard Nixon in 1952 with, 'The Republican Vice-Presidential candidate, who asks you to place him a heartbeat from the Presidency'. Jules Witcover entitled a book on Vice-President Spiro Agnew's enforced resignation in 1973, *A Heartbeat Away*. The phrase was much in evidence again when George Bush selected Dan Quayle as his running-mate in 1988.

2 *Someone asked me . . . how I felt, and I was reminded of a story that a fellow-townsman of ours used to tell — Abraham Lincoln . . . he [a boy in Lincoln's story] said that he was too old to cry, but it hurt too much to laugh.*

So, Stevenson after his electoral defeat on 5 November 1952. The actual Lincoln remark appeared in *Frank Leslie's Illustrated Weekly* (22 November 1862) after a defeat in the New York elections: '[I feel] somewhat like the boy in Kentucky who stubbed his toe while running to see his sweetheart. The boy said he was too big to cry, and far too badly hurt to laugh.'

3 *A politician is a person who approaches every subject with an open mouth.*

Another of those quotations that floats continually in search of a definite source and could have been said by anyone and everybody. Was it Oscar Wilde? Or Adlai Stevenson? Or Arthur Goldberg? The first two sources are given by different contributors to *Kindly Sit Down*, a compilation of after-dinner speeches by politicians (1983) collected by Jack Aspinwall. The second two sources are given in *PDMQ* (1980). In the absence of any hard evidence, one feels inclined to award the palm to Stevenson.

4 *She would rather light a candle than curse the darkness, and her glow has warmed the world.*

An eloquent tribute paid by Stevenson to Eleanor Roosevelt when the former First Lady died in November 1962. However, he was merely quoting the motto of the Christopher Society, which came, in turn, from a Chinese proverb.

Stevenson, Robert Louis
Scottish writer (1850–94)

5 *Steel-true and blade-straight*
The great artificer
Made my mate.

From Stevenson's poem 'My Wife' in *Songs of Travel* (1896). Rather curiously, it is quoted as:
STEEL TRUE
BLADE STRAIGHT
on the grave of Sir Arthur Conan Doyle (1859–1930), the creator of Sherlock Holmes, in All Saints churchyard, Minstead, Hampshire. Presumably, the widow — who was a spiritualist, if that is relevant — chose the epitaph.

6 *Under the wide and starry sky*
Dig the grave and let me lie.
Glad did I live and gladly die,
And I laid me down with a will.

This be the verse you grave for me:
Here he lies where he longed to be;
Home is the sailor, home from the sea
And the hunter home from the hill.

Stevenson's gravestone on Mount Vaea, Samoa, wrongly transcribes his poem 'Requiem' (1887), as above. The penultimate line should read 'Home is the sailor, *home from sea*', without the definite article. But this is a common quotation error.

7 *To travel hopefully is a better thing than to arrive, and the true success is to labour.*

From *Virginibus Puerisque*, 'El Dorado' (1881). But Stevenson had voiced much the same thought earlier in *Travels With a Donkey* (1879): 'For my part, I travel not to go anywhere, but to go. I travel for travel's sake. The great affair is to move.' Subsequently, the thought emerged in the form 'the journey not the arrival matters' (an expression used as the title of an autobiographical volume by Leonard Woolf, 1969). 'Getting there is half the fun' may have been used to advertise Cunard steamships in the 1920s and 1930s. It was definitely used to promote the Peter Sellers film *Being There* (1980) in the form: 'Getting there is half the fun. Being there is all of it.' In *Up the*

Organisation (1970), Robert Townshend opined of getting to the top: 'Getting there isn't half the fun — it's all the fun.'

Stone, Irving
American novelist (1903–89)

1 *The Agony and the Ecstasy.*

The title of Stone's novel (1961; film, US 1965), about Michelangelo and the Sistine Chapel, appears to be an original coinage. Compare what William Faulkner said in his speech accepting the Nobel Prize for Literature (10 December 1950): whatever was 'worth the agony and the sweat' was worth writing about.

Stoppard, Tom
British playwright (1937–   )

2 *If I knew, I'd go there.*

In answer to the journalists' clichéd question 'Where do you get your ideas from?' Source? I think a *Guardian* interview. But compare what Joyce Grenfell wrote in *Joyce Grenfell Requests the Pleasure* (1976). She stated that this was her reply to the question, 'Where do you get the ideas for your monologues?' The novelist Terry Pratchett was profiled in the *Observer* (8 November 1992): ' "Where do you get your incredible ideas from?" asked a boy. (Someone always does.) "There's this warehouse called Ideas Are Us," Pratchett replied.'

Story, Jack Trevor
British novelist (1917–   )

3 *Live Now, Pay Later.*

Title of a screenplay (1962) based on the novel *All on the Never Never* by Jack Lindsay. As a simple graffito, the same line was recorded in Los Angeles (1970) in *The Encyclopedia of Graffiti* (1974). The same book records a New York subway graffito on a funeral parlour ad: 'Our layway plan — die now, pay later.' 'Book now, pay later' was used in an advertisement in the programme of the Royal Opera House, Covent Garden, London, in 1977.

Back to 1962: in that year, Daniel Boorstin in *The Image* made oblique reference to travel advertisements using the line, 'Go now, pay later'. Was Hire Purchase ever promoted with 'Buy now, pay later'? It seems likely. These lines — in the US and UK — seem to be the starting point for a construction that has been much used and adapted since.

Stowe, Harriet Beecher
American novelist (1811–96)

4 *I s'pect I growed. Don't think nobody ever made me.*

From *Uncle Tom's Cabin* (1852), in which the slave girl, Topsy, who asserts that she has no mother or father, replies thus, on being asked who made her. Hence the rephrased expression: 'Like Topsy — she just growed.'

Strachey, Lytton
English biographer (1880–1932)

5 *I would try to get between them.*

During the First World War Strachey had to appear before a military tribunal to put his case as a conscientious objector. He was asked by the chairman what, in view of his beliefs, he would do if he saw a German soldier trying to violate his sister. With an air of noble virtue, the homosexual Strachey replied, 'I would try to get between them'. A correspondent suggests that it was much more likely that Strachey would have said something more grandiloquent — 'I would interpose my body' or some such — but the source for this anecdote is Robert Graves in *Goodbye To All That* (1929) and his version is the one given above.

Sultan Salman Al-Saud, Prince
Saudi Arabian air force pilot (1956–   )

6 *From space the world has no boundaries.*

The Prince was the first Arab in space: he flew as a member of the American *Discovery* shuttle crew in June 1985. He recited the Koran, spoke to his uncle King Fahd from the space craft and made the above observation, which was variously reported. The *Washington Post* (12 July 1985) had: 'Prince Sultan, who just went up in the space shuttle and made the statement about no boundaries in space.' The *Daily Telegraph* (6 July 1985) quoted his less crisp actual words. When asked about the Beirut hostage crisis, he had replied: 'Looking at it from up here, with trouble all over the world, not just in the Middle East, it looks very strange as you see the boundaries and borderlines disappearing. Lots of people who are causing some of these problems ought to come up here and take a look.'

Sun, The
American New York-based newspaper, founded 1833

1 *If you see it in the* Sun, *it's so.*

In 1897 a New York girl called Virginia O'Hanlon wrote a letter to the *Sun* which went, in part: 'Dear Editor: I am 8 years old. Some of my little friends say there is no Santa Claus. Papa says, "If you see it in the *Sun* it's so." Please tell me the truth, is there a Santa Claus?' The newspaper replied, in a famous piece, 'Your little friends are wrong . . . there is a Santa Claus . . . Not believe in Santa Claus! You might as well not believe in fairies!' After his death in 1906, it was revealed that Francis P. Church had written the editorial.

Sun, The
British London-based newspaper, founded 1964

2 *WINTER OF DISCONTENT. Lest we forget . . . the* Sun *recalls the long, cold months of industrial chaos that brought Britain to its knees.*

This was the headline to a feature (30 April 1979) in the run-up to the general election which swept Margaret Thatcher and the Conservatives to power and was probably the first major use of this phrase to characterize the industrial unrest of the winter of 1978–9. It alludes to Shakespeare's *Richard III* (I.i.1) which begins, famously, with Gloucester's punning and original metaphor:
> Now is the winter of our discontent
> Made glorious summer by this son of York;
> And all the clouds that lour'd upon our House
> In the deep bosom of the ocean buried
even if the editor of the Arden Shakespeare does describe the entire image as 'almost proverbial'. Probably made all the more memorable by Laurence Olivier's delivery of these lines in the 1955 film, the phrase 'winter of discontent' suffered the unpleasant fate of becoming a politician's and journalist's cliché following the winter of 1978–9 when British life was disrupted by all kinds of industrial protest against the Labour Government's attempts to keep down pay rises.

Most notably, rubbish remained uncollected and began to pile up in the streets and a gravediggers' strike in one area reportedly left bodies unburied.

This 'winter of discontent' (as it is still referred to many years later) may perhaps have contributed to the Conservative victory at the May 1979 general election. The question has been asked, who first referred to it as such? Mrs Margaret Thatcher, opening her election campaign on TV (2 April 1979) said, 'We have just had a devastating winter of industrial strife — perhaps the worst in living memory, certainly the worst in mine', which is almost it, but not quite. The first example found in a far-from-exhaustive search through the files is in the *Observer* (9 September 1979). The subtitle to an article is, 'Do we face a winter of discontent? Adrian Hamilton and Robert Taylor report on the union and employer mood.' The actual piece begins: 'To listen to the speeches at the annual conference of the Trades Union Congress at Blackpool this week was to believe that Britain is in for a winter of endless discontent and disruption.' At the end of that month, on the 26th, the *Daily Express* began a report of a speech by Mrs Thatcher at Milton Keynes, thus: 'STRIKE AT YOUR PERIL! Maggie spells out price of conflict this winter. Mrs Thatcher yesterday put a price on another winter of discontent. It would be lost jobs, she said.' As far as one can make out, at this distance, she did not actually use the phrase itself. It was probably a journalistic imposition and, as with the *Observer* use, it is interesting to note that the 'winter' referred to is the forthcoming one of 79–80 rather than the previous one. The *Observer* was still ringing changes on the original on 7 February 1982: 'WHY FOOTBALL MUST SURVIVE ITS WINTER OF PENURY AND DISCONTENT.'

The *Sun*'s earlier use of the phrase was, thus, the crucial one. (Sir) Larry Lamb, editor at the time, recalled in a Channel 4 TV programme *Benn Diaries II* (29 October 1989) that he introduced the phrase 'in a small way' during the winter itself (it was imitated by others), then 'in a big way' during the election. James Callaghan, the Prime Minister who was destroyed by the phrase, seems to have claimed that he used the phrase first (recalled in a TV programme, December 1991).

There is little new under the *Sun*, of course. J.B. Priestley, writing of earlier, much harder times in *English Journey* (1934) ended his fourth chapter with: 'The delegates have seen one England, Mayfair in the season. Let them see another England next time, West Bromwich out of season. Out of all seasons except the winter of discontent.'

1 GOTCHA!

This was how the *Sun* 'celebrated' the sinking of the Argentine cruiser *General Belgrano* during the Falklands war (front-page headline, 4 May 1982). But it was retained for the first edition only. Other 'gung-ho' *Sun* headlines of the time included: 'STICK IT UP YOUR JUNTA' (20 April) — its attitude towards a negotiated settlement — and 'THE SUN SAYS KNICKERS TO ARGENTINA' and 'UP YOURS, GALTIERI', which sound so unlikely they must have appeared. The *Sun* posture was memorably parodied at the time by *Private Eye*, which suggested the headline: 'KILL AN ARGIE AND WIN A METRO.'

Swaffer, Hannen
English journalist (1879–1962)

2 Yes and No — *No!*

A comedy by Kenneth Horne with the title *Yes and No* featuring Steve Geray and Magda Kun opened at the Ambassadors Theatre, London, in the autumn of 1938. It occasioned probably the shortest theatrical notice of all time. Swaffer wrote: '*Yes and No* (Ambassadors) — *No!*' (Source: a letter from Bill Galley of London WC1 in the *Sunday Telegraph*, 24 March 1970).

On BBC Radio *Quote . . . Unquote* (1993), Tony Hawks ascribed something similar to Dorothy Parker about the André Charlot musical show *Yes!* which was presented in London in 1923. Her one-word review had apparently been 'No!' — though I suspect this joke has been foisted upon her.

See also NORTHCLIFFE 256:4.

Swift, Dr Jonathan
Anglo-Irish writer and clergyman (1667–1745)

3 *Great fleas have little fleas*
Upon their backs to bite 'em,
And little fleas have lesser fleas,
And so ad infinitum.
And the great fleas themselves in turn

Have greater fleas to go on,
While these again have greater still,
And greater still, and so on.

This comes from *A Budget of Paradoxes* by Professor Augustus de Morgan (1806–71), but the first verse is based on Swift's *On Poetry, a Rhapsody* (1733), in which he was referring to literary critics ('thus every poet in his kind/Is bit by him that comes behind').

4 *Many a true genius appears in the world — you may know him by this sign, that the dunces are all in confederacy against him.*

From *Thoughts on Various Subjects* (1706). Hence, *A Confederacy of Dunces*, the title of a novel (1980) by John Kennedy Toole.

5 *Instead of dirt and poison we have rather chosen to fill our hives with honey and wax; thus furnishing mankind with the two noblest of things, which are sweetness and light.*

From the Preface to *The Battle of the Books* (1704). In *The Lyttelton Hart-Davis Letters* (for 25 January 1956) it is stated that Matthew Arnold said this conjunction was the *sine qua non* of all real civilization ('The pursuit of perfection, then, is the pursuit of sweetness and light . . . He who works for sweetness and light united, works to make reason and the will of God prevail' — *Culture and Anarchy*, 1869).

6 *Here lies the body of Jonathan Swift, Professor of Holy Theology, for thirty years Dean of this cathedral church, where savage indignation can tear his heart no more. Go, traveller, and if you can imitate one who with his utmost strength protected liberty. He died in the year 1745, on the 19th of October, aged seventy-eight.*

'Swift sleeps under the greatest epitaph in history,' said W.B. Yeats. He wrote it for himself and it may be found on a tablet in St Patrick's Cathedral, Dublin, where he lies buried and where he served as Dean 1713–45. The inscription (which is in Latin) includes the key phrase: '*Ubi saeva indignatio ulterius cor lacerare nequit*'.

T, U

Talleyrand, Charles Maurice de
French statesman
(1754–1838)

1 *It is not an event, it is an item of news*
[C'est une nouvelle, ce n'est pas un évènement].

Remark when the news of Napoleon's death at St Helena in 1821 reached Europe. Ignored by Bartlett and the *ODQ*, this quotation does, however, appear in Benham (1907). Quoting the 5th Earl of Stanhope's *Conversations with the Duke of Wellington* (for 1 November 1831), Elizabeth Longford, *Wellington: Pillar of State* (1972) places the remark at 'a Parisian party . . . at Mme Craufurd's . . . [and] Wellington and Talleyrand were there to hear the startled cries'.

Taylor, Ann and Jane
English writers (1782–1866) and (1783–1824)

2 *Who ran to help me when I fell,*
And would some pretty story tell,
Or kiss the place to make it well?
My Mother.

One of the verses from 'My Mother' *Original Poems for Infant Minds* (1804). Sometimes this is attributed to Ann Taylor only. A parody that was widely known by at least 1978, goes:

> Who took me from my bed so hot
> And placed me shivering on the pot,
> Nor asked me whether I should or not?
> My Mother!

See also CARROLL 87:1.

Tebbit, Norman
(later Lord Tebbit)
English Conservative politician
(1931–   )

3 *On your bike.*

Having just been appointed British Employment Secretary, Tebbit addressed the Conservative Party Conference on 15 October 1981. He related how he had grown up in the 1930s when unemployment was all around and commented: '[My father] did not riot. He got on his bike and looked for work. And he kept on looking till he found it.' This gave rise to the pejorative catchphrase 'on your bike' or 'get on your bike' from the lips of Mr Tebbit's opponents, and gave a new twist to a saying Partridge/ *Slang* dates from *c* 1960, meaning 'go away' or 'be off with you'. Tebbit later pointed out that he had not been suggesting that the unemployed should literally get on their bikes.

4 *Nobody with a conscience votes Conservative.*

When Tebbit had this view ascribed to him by the *Guardian* in January 1987, he extracted 'substantial damages' from the newspaper. But it often proves difficult to bury such remarks and remove them completely from the record. When *The New Statesman* repeated the attribution in error in the summer of 1992, Lord Tebbit, as he had now become, received further libel damages.

5 *Strangled by the old school tie.*

The *OED2*'s oldest citation for the very British phrase 'old school tie' — symbolizing the supposed freemasonry among those who have been educated at public (i.e. private) schools in Britain — dates from 1932 (in a piece by Rudyard Kipling). The strangulation element appears to have crept in more recently. *The Times* (27 September 1986) had: '[Trevor Howard] broke new ground, away from the English studio stereotypes of silly-ass eccentrics or decent but wooden chaps strangled by a combination of old school tie and stiff upper lip.'

But the key use of the term (though not, of course, its coining) appeared in Tebbit's autobiography, as quoted in the *Independent* (14 October 1988): 'Some thought my willingness to stand toe to toe against the more thuggish elements of the Labour Party and slug it out blow for blow rather vulgar. Others, especially in the country at large, seemed delighted at the idea of a Tory MP unwilling to be strangled by the old school tie.'

Tennyson, Alfred
(1st Baron Tennyson)
English Poet Laureate (1809–92)

1 *Did your mother call you early, dear?*

When Tennyson entered the Sheldonian Theatre in Oxford to receive an honorary degree of DCL, his long hair was in poetic disorder, dishevelled and unkempt. A voice cried this out to him, alluding to his poem 'The May Queen' (1832) which begins: 'You must wake and call me early, call me early, mother dear' (recounted by Julian Charles Young in a diary note, 8 November 1863).

2 *Having known me, to decline . . .*

This curious unattributed fragment is a quotation that gets interrupted in Anthony Hope's novel *The Dolly Dialogues*, Chap. 22 (1894). Clearly, it must have been something that was known to any well-read person of the 1890s. Indeed. It comes from Tennyson's 'Locksley Hall', l.43 (1842).

3 *Saw the Vision of the world, and all the wonder that would be.*
Saw the heavens fill with commerce, argosies of magic sails,
Pilots of the purple twilight, dropping down with costly bales;
Heard the heavens fill with shouting, and there rain'd a ghastly dew
From the nations' airy navies grappling in the central blue.

Sir John Colville's published diaries of his time as Winston Churchill's private secretary (*The Fringes of Power*, paperback editions 1986–7) reveal the wartime Prime Minister quoting 'Tennyson's prescient lines about aerial warfare' (19 March 1941) without saying what the lines are. They are to be found in 'Locksley Hall', at l.119 (probably written 1837–8). A rejected lover returns to his one-time home by the sea and, among other things, complains of the modern world of steamships and railways. He also makes a prediction of commerce and warfare being extended to the skies.

4 *Dark and true and tender is the North.*

From a song added to *The Princess* in 1850. Sometimes used, semi-humorously, to emphasize the qualities of those from the North of England or Scotland. If anything, however, the contrast is really between the North and the South of *Europe*. 'O Swallow, Swallow, flying, flying South', the poet instructs, 'tell her . . . that thou knowest each, / That bright and fierce and fickle is the South, / And dark and true and tender is the North.' The poet wishes it indicated that he does 'but wanton in the South, / But in the North long since my nest is made.'

5 *A nobler office on the earth*
Than valour, power of brain, or birth,
Could give the warrior kings of old.

G.K. Chesterton quotes these lines anonymously in *The Napoleon of Notting Hill* (1904). Preceded by the line, 'Revered, beloved — you that hold . . .' they constitute the first verse of Tennyson's 'To the Queen' — the new Poet Laureate's first poem to his sovereign in March 1851.

6 *Not once or twice in our rough island story*
The path of duty was the way to glory.

The probable origin of the 'island story' phrase. It comes from Tennyson's 'Ode on the Death of the Duke of Wellington' (1852). *Our Island Story, a child's history of England* (c 1910) by H.E. Marshall (stories and fables from King Arthur to Queen Victoria, addressed to two Australian children) was an immensely popular history book in the early twentieth century.

Compare NEWBOLT 253:1.

1 *Someone had blundered.*

The Charge of the Light Brigade at Balaclava, near Sebastopol, took place on 25 October 1854, during the Crimean War. Owing to a misunderstood order, 247 officers and men out of 637 were killed or wounded. Tennyson's famous poem about it was published in the *Examiner* newspaper on 9 December that same year. The second stanza runs:

> 'Forward the Light Brigade!'
> Was there a man dismay'd?
> Not tho' the soldier knew
> Someone had blundered.
> Their's not to make reply,
> Their's not to reason why,
> Their's but to do and die:
> Into the valley of Death
> Rode the six hundred.

['Their's' is as written.] According to Christopher Ricks's edition of the poems, Tennyson wrote this on 2 December 1854, 'in a few minutes, after reading . . . *The Times* in which occurred the phrase *someone had blundered*, and this was the origin of the metre of his poem'. In fact, *The Times* had spoken rather (in a leader on 13 November) of 'some hideous blunder'. Advised to be careful because controversy would offend the War Office, Tennyson allowed the 'someone had blundered' line to be deleted when his next collection of poems was published (*Maud, and Other Poems*, 1855). But when he heard that the Society for the Propagation of the Gospel intended to circulate this *revised* poem to the troops, he had copies of the *uncut* version printed and sent to the Crimea.

2 *Chalk and alum and plaster, are sold to the poor for bread.*

From *Maud*, I.i.x (1855). As with this line, it is extraordinary how frequently Tennyson turns out to be the author of 'lost quotations' and half-remembered bits of verse.

3 *For why is all around us here*
As if some lesser god had made the world,
But had not force to shape it as he would.

From 'The Passing of Arthur' (l.1315) in *Idylls of the King* (1859). Hence, *Children of a Lesser God*, the title of Marc Medoff's play (1979; film US, 1986), about a relationship between a deaf girl and her speech therapist. Medoff's suggestion, presumably, is that people with a disability like deafness could be said to be the work of a 'lesser god'.

4 *The old order changeth, yielding to the new,*
And God fulfils himself in many ways,
Lest one good custom should corrupt the world.

From 'The Passing of Arthur' in *Idylls of the King*, l.407 (1859). The meaning of the third line has puzzled some readers. Tennyson himself indicated that what he meant was 'e.g. chivalry, by formalism of habit or by any other means'.

5 *Lord of language.*

In *Ego 8* (for 2 May 1945), James Agate discusses a passage in *De Profundis* in which Oscar Wilde says of himself, 'I summed up all systems in a phrase and all existence in an epigram'. Agate writes: 'The boast about being "a lord of language". Wilde was that very different thing — the fine lady of the purple passage.' Whence, however, the 'lord of language'? In Tennyson's poem 'To Virgil' (1882) — 'written at the request of the Mantuans for the nineteenth centenary of Virgil's death' — the Mantuan poet is described, in a rush of alliteration, as 'landscape-lover, lord of language'.

The second phrase would also appear to be the original of one or two other complimentary phrases like 'master of language' and, in particular, 'lord of words'. The latter was used, for example, to describe the broadcaster, Sir Huw Wheldon, and the playwright, Samuel Beckett, at their deaths in 1986 and 1989, respectively. Other citations are lacking.

Teresa of Avila, Saint
Spanish mystic (1515–82)

6 *Let nothing disturb thee,*
Let nothing affright thee,
All passeth away,
God alone will stay,
Patience obtaineth all things.
Who God possesseth, is lacking in nothing
God alone sufficeth.

In *The Art of the Possible* (1971), R.A. Butler recalled how he quoted all but the last two of these lines to Winston Churchill when the Prime Minister retired in 1955, adding 'This, like St Augustine, I have learned'. But, no, this is commonly known as 'St Teresa's prayer', and Stephen Clissold in his biography of her (published in 1979) tells of the circumstances in which it was written.

Thatcher, Sir Denis (Bart.)
English businessman and husband of Margaret Thatcher (1915–)

1 *I like everything my beloved wife likes. If she wants to buy the top brick of St Paul's, then I would buy it.*

This statement appeared in the *Observer* 'Sayings of the Week' column on 7 April 1985 and may have been taken from an interview in the *Sunday Express*. Partridge/ *Slang* suggests that the phrase 'to give someone the top brick off the chimney' means 'to be the acme of generosity, with implication that foolish spoiling, or detriment to the donor would result, as in "his parents'd give that boy the . . ." or "she's that soft-hearted, she'd give you . . .".' Partridge's reviser, Paul Beale, who inserted this entry, commented that he had heard the phrase in the early 1980s but that it was probably in use much earlier.

Indeed, when Anthony Trollope was standing for Parliament in 1868, he described a seat at Westminster as 'the highest object of ambition to every educated Englishman' and 'the top brick of the chimney'. In *Nanny Says*, Joyce Grenfell's and Sir Hugh Casson's collection of nanny sayings (1972) is included, 'Very particular we are — it's top brick off the chimney or nothing'. Presumably, Denis Thatcher was reworking this saying for his own ends. Unconsciously, he may have been conflating it with another kind of reference, such as is found in Charles Dickens, *Martin Chuzzlewit*, Chap. 38 (1844): 'He would as soon as thought of the cross upon the top of St Paul's Cathedral taking note of what he did . . . as of Nadgett's being engaged in such an occupation.'

Thatcher, Margaret
(later Baroness Thatcher)
British Conservative Prime Minister (1925–)

2 *The Iron Lady.*

On 19 January 1976 Mrs Thatcher said in a speech 'The Russians are bent on world dominance . . . the Russians put guns before butter'. Within a few days the Soviet Defence Ministry newspaper *Red Star* (in an article signed by Captain Y. Gavrilov) had accused the 'Iron Lady' of seeking to revive the Cold War. The article wrongly suggested that she was popularly known by this nickname in the UK at that time, though a headline over a profile by Marjorie Proops in the *Daily Mirror* of 5 February 1975 had been 'The Iron Maiden'.

On 31 January, Mrs Thatcher made the phrase her own in a speech in her Finchley constituency: 'Ladies and gentlemen, I stand before you tonight in my green chiffon evening gown, my face softly made up, my fair hair gently waved . . . the *Iron Lady* of the Western World. Me? A cold war warrior? Well, yes — if that is how they wish to interpret my defence of values, and freedoms fundamental to our way of life.'

3 *Out of some long, bad dream that makes her mutter and moan, Suddenly, all men rise to the noise of fetters breaking.*

Mrs Thatcher was a great quoter — Kipling was top of her source list — though sometimes she misquoted, twisted or ignored the fact that she was speaking someone else's lines. When a newspaperman queried the source of the above lines, which Mrs Thatcher used to indicate how things were going in her 1979 election campaign, it was duly reported that the Prime-Minister-to-be had recalled his request in the small hours of the morning and taken the trouble to write him a note explaining their provenance: 'The Dawn Wind' (1911).

4 *Let us make this a country safe to work in. Let us make this a country safe to walk in. Let us make it a country safe to grow up in. Let us make it a country safe to grow old in. And [the message of the 'other' Britain] says, above all, may this land of ours, which we love so much, find dignity and greatness and peace again.*

In the peroration to a televised party political broadcast on 30 April 1979 (the eve of her first election win), Thatcher smuggled in an unacknowledged quote from Noël Coward's play *Cavalcade* (1931). In the original, the toast is: 'That one day this country of ours, which we love so much, will find dignity and greatness and peace again.' The hand of Sir Ronald Millar, the playwright and her principal speechwriter, may presumably be detected in this.

1 *There is no easy popularity in that [harsh economic measures already set in train by the government] but I believe people accept there is no alternative.*

From a speech to the Conservative Women's Conference, London, on 21 May 1980, came a famously nannyish phrase that became a rallying cry of the Thatcher government: 'there is no alternative'. It provides a good example of how it can be more difficult tracing the origins of recent quotations than of older ones. By the early 1980s, everyone in Britain knew the phrase, but how had it arisen? If she had said it in the House of Commons it would have been possible to search through the parliamentary record *Hansard* (the electronic version makes computer-searching very simple). But she had not, apparently. So one was faced with searching through newspapers for a mention of the phrase, except that most British newspapers were not being transferred on to computer databases until the mid-1980s.

Perhaps she had said it at one of her meetings with Parliamentary lobby correspondents? But these occasions are never directly reported (hence the obscurity surrounding the coining of Harold Wilson's famous observation 'a week is a long time in politics', see 358:2), and if she had said it at one, the political correspondents consulted were unable to remember.

In 1984 Dr David Butler, the psephologist, approached me regarding the phrase because he was revising his *British Political Facts*. Some more asking around was done and no progress was made. Patrick Cosgrave, an adviser to Mrs Thatcher before she became Prime Minister, suggested that, perhaps, the phrase had not actually been coined by her, but simply picked up, in the way she had of seizing on ideas that she fancied.

Butler wrote to Downing Street and received a letter from Mrs Thatcher's then political secretary espousing a similar view: 'I am not sure that the Prime Minister ever actually used the phrase . . . and my suspicion, shared by others, is that TINA was coined by those who were pressing for a change of policy.'

This only took us further away than ever from a satisfactory conclusion. Then, in 1986, and in the time-honoured fashion, I happened to stumble upon a report of

Mrs Thatcher speech to the Conservative Women's Conference, marking the end of her first year in office, as above. So, there, she *had* said it, and publicly, too. I don't know whether this was the first time — in fact, I think she may well have said it at some stage in 1979 — but at last here was a reference.

A correspondent suggested a comparison with the old Hebrew catchphrase '*ain breira*' ('there is no choice'). The acronym 'TINA', said to have been coined by Young Conservatives, was flourishing by the time of the Party Conference in September 1981.

2 *To those waiting with bated breath for that favourite media catchphrase, the U-turn, I have only one thing to say. You turn if you want to. The lady's not for turning.*

In a speech to the Conservative Party Conference at Brighton (11 October 1980), Mrs Thatcher came up with what is, in a sense, her best remembered formally spoken 'line'. While not convincing the hearer that she could have alluded unaided to the title of the play *The Lady's Not for Burning* (1948) by Christopher Fry, the cry had the curiously insidious memorability that most effective slogans need to have. Again, one detects the hand of Sir Ronald Millar in all this. Indeed, in the *Sunday Times* (23 November 1980), he confirmed that he had coined the phrase, but also reported that he would have 'preferred his friend the prime minister to have said "the lady's not for turning" with an elided " 's" exactly as in the original title of Christopher Fry's play.' Which is odd, because any recording of the speech will confirm that she did not say, 'The lady is not', but 'the lady's not . . .' (just as she was told).

3 *As the poet said, 'One clear morn is boon enough for being born', and so it is.*

Here Mrs Thatcher is relying on that old standby, 'As the poet said . . .' to disguise forgetfulness or genuine ignorance of the source. The occasion was a BBC Radio interview with Pete Murray on 7 March 1982 when, tearfully, she described her fears while it had seemed that her son Mark was lost on a Trans-Sahara car rally. She realized then, she said, that all the little things people worried about really were not worth it . . . 'As the poet said . . .'

I was puzzled by the quotation and wrote to Downing Street for illumination, my letter plopping on the mat just as the Falklands War broke out. When that little difficulty was resolved, I received back a photocopy of an anonymous poem which had presumably been carried about in the Thatcher handbag for many a year. Subsequently, in *Woman's Own* (17 November 1984), it was revealed that the poem had been taken from something called 'Love's Tapestry Calendar 1966':

Life owes me nothing:
    One clear morn
Is boon enough
    for being born;
And be it ninety years
    or ten,
No need for me
    to question when.
While life is mine,
    I'll find it good
And greet each hour
    with gratitude.

1 *Failure? Do you remember what Queen Victoria once said? 'Failure? — the possibilities do not exist.'*

At the start of the war in the Falklands, Mrs Thatcher gave a TV news interview (5 April 1982) in which she evoked the spirit of Queen Victoria with the remark that had been made at the end of 'Black Week' in 1899, during the Boer War: 'We are not interested in the possibilities of defeat; they do not exist.' *Time* Magazine (December 1982) ascribed the words to Mrs Thatcher as though they were not a quotation.

See also VICTORIA 341:1.

2 *Just rejoice at that news and congratulate our forces and the Marines. Goodnight. Rejoice!*

On the recapture of South Georgia, to newsmen outside 10 Downing Street (25 April 1982). Wording confirmed by TV recordings made at the time. Usually rendered as 'Rejoice, rejoice!' From the *Daily Telegraph* (26 April 1982): 'A triumphant Prime Minister declared "Rejoice, rejoice" last night . . .'. Much later, this is Julian Critchley MP writing in the *Observer* (27 June 1993): 'Shortly after Mrs Thatcher's defenestration in November 1990, I ran into [Sir Edward] Heath in a Westminster corridor. I quoted a Spanish proverb: if you wait by

the river long enough, the body of your enemy will float by. Heath broke into a broad grin: "Rejoice, rejoice", was his reply.'

Either way, can one detect signs of her Methodist upbringing? Although 'Rejoice, rejoice!' is quite a common expression, each verse of Charles Wesley's hymn 'Rejoice! the Lord is King' ends: 'Rejoice, again I say, rejoice' (a hymn played at the 1983 Conservative Party Conference). There was also a nineteenth-century hymn (words by Grace J. Frances), 'Rejoice, Rejoice, Believer!' The refrain of 'O Come, O Come Emmanuel' (a hymn translated by J.M. Neale) goes, 'Rejoice! Rejoice! Emmanuel/Shall come to thee, O Israel'.

3 *Victorian values . . . those were the values when our country became great, not only internationally but at home.*

In the general election of 1983 and thereafter, Margaret Thatcher and other Cabinet ministers frequently commended the virtue of a return to Victorian values. The phrase appears to have been coined by Brian Walden in a TV interview with Mrs Thatcher on ITV's *Weekend World* on 17 January 1983. It was he who suggested to her that she was trying to restore 'Victorian values'. She replied: 'Very much so. Those were the values when our country became great. But not only did our country become great internationally, also much advance was made in this country — through voluntary rather than state action.' Mrs Thatcher also said in an LBC radio interview on 15 April: 'I was brought up by a Victorian grandmother. We were taught to work jolly hard. We were taught to prove ourselves; we were taught self-reliance; we were taught to live within our income . . . You were taught that cleanliness is next to godliness. You were taught self-respect. You were taught always to give a hand to your neighbour. You were taught tremendous pride in your country. All of these things are Victorian values. They are also perennial values.' On 23 April the *Daily Telegraph* quoted Dr Rhodes Boyson, the Minister for Schools, as saying: 'Good old-fashioned order, even Victorian order, is far superior to illiterate disorder and innumerate chaos in the classroom,' and Neil Kinnock, then Chief Opposition Spokesman on Education, as saying: 'Victorian Britain was a place where a few got rich and most got hell. The "Victorian values" that ruled were cruelty, misery, drudgery, squalor and ignorance.'

1 Some say Maggie may, or others say Maggie may not. I can only say that when the time comes, I shall decide.

'Maggie May' is a character in a Liverpool song, dating from at least 1830. She is a prostitute who steals sailors' trousers, but, as the song goes on to relate: 'A policeman came and took that girl away./For she robbed a Yankee whaler,/She won't walk down Lime Street any more.'

A number of groups (including the Beatles) revived the song at the time of Liverpool's resurgence in the early 1960s. Lionel Bart and Alun Owen wrote a musical based on her life and called *Maggie May* in 1964. Margaret Thatcher unwisely alluded to the song in April 1983 when wishing to appear coy about whether she would be calling a General Election soon.

2 Oh, the Right Honourable Gentleman is afraid of an election is he? Afraid, afraid, afraid, frightened, frit, couldn't take it, couldn't stand it!

Mrs Thatcher's challenge to the prominent Labour minister, Denis Healey, occurred in the House of Commons on 20 April 1983. He had suggested that she was preparing to 'cut and run' regarding a general election. 'Frit', as an abbreviation for 'fright/frightened' is still widely-used in the North Midlands — including Grantham where she was born. The first recorded use of the word was by the Northamptonshire poet, John Clare. In 'The Village Minstrel' (1821), he wrote:

> The coy hare squats nesting in the corn,
> Frit at the bow'd ear tott'ring over her head.

3 We had to fight the enemy without in the Falklands. We always have to be aware of the enemy within which is more difficult to fight and more dangerous to liberty.

From a speech to the 1922 Committee (19 July 1984). The expression 'enemy within' refers to an internal rather than external threat. It has been suggested that it is a shortened version of 'the enemy/traitor within the gate(s)' — 'one who acts, or is thought to act, against the interests of the family, group, society, etc. of which he is a member' — but, whatever the case, it is a phrase with a long history. In 1940 Winston Churchill said of the BBC that it was 'an enemy within the gates, doing more harm than good'. A 1957 film had a title *The Enemy Below* and a 1978 TV film *The Enemy at the Door*.

On 22 January 1983 *The Economist* wrote of the industrial relations scene in Britain: 'The government may be trusting that public outrage will increasingly be its ally. Fresh from the Falklands, Mrs Thatcher may even relish a punch-up with the enemy within to enhance her "resolute approach" further.'

Seven months later, Mrs Thatcher was using exactly the same phrase and context regarding the British miners' strike. She 'told Tory MPs that her government had fought the enemy without in the Falklands conflict and now had to face an enemy within . . . she declared that the dockers and pit strikers posed as great a threat to democracy as General Galtieri, the deposed Argentine leader' (*Guardian*, 20 July 1984).

Earlier, in 1980, Julian Mitchell had used the phrase as the title of a play about anorexia. It was also the title of a Tony Garnett BBC TV play in 1974 and of a stage play by Brian Friel in 1962. A book (1960) by Robert F. Kennedy about 'organized corruption' in the US labour movement had the title, as did one by John Watner during/about the Second World War (untraced). The earliest *OED2* citation dates from 1608: 'The enemy within . . . sporteth herself in the consumption of those vital parts, which waste and wear away by yielding to her unpacifiable teeth' — Edward Topsell, *The Historie of Serpents*.

4 In church on Sunday morning — it was a lovely morning and we haven't had many lovely days — the sun was coming through a stained glass window and falling on some flowers, falling right across the church. It just occurred to me that this was the day I was meant not to see.

Mrs Thatcher expressed her feelings on having escaped death in an IRA bomb explosion at Brighton. In a TV interview she referred to Sunday, 14 October 1984. The *Observer* (21 October) reported the final phrase as 'the day I was not meant to see'. The *Daily Telegraph* (17 October) had already affirmed that 'the day I was meant not to see' was the correct version, adding: 'Since they are words which may well enter future anthologies, we should get the record straight.'

1 *Stop being moaning minnies.*

On 11 September 1985 Mrs Thatcher paid a visit to Tyneside and was reported as accusing those who complained about the effects of unemployment of being 'Moaning Minnies'. In the ensuing uproar, a Downing Street spokesman had to point out that it was the reporters attempting to question her, rather than the unemployed, upon whom Mrs Thatcher had bestowed the title.

As a nickname, it was by no means an original coinage. Anyone who complains is a 'moaner', and a 'minnie' is a word that can be used to describe a lost lamb which finds itself an adoptive mother. From the *Observer* (20 May 1989): 'Broadcasters are right to complain about the restrictions placed on them for the broadcasting of the House of Commons . . . But the Moaning Minnies have only themselves to blame.'

The original 'Moaning Minnie' was something quite different. In the First World War a 'Minnie' was the slang name for a German *minenwerfer*, a trench mortar or the shell that came from it, making a distinctive moaning noise. In the Second World War the name was applied to air-raid sirens which also made that noise.

2 *The tumult and the shouting dies;*
The Captains and the Kings depart:
Still stands Thine ancient sacrifice
An humble and a contrite heart.

Mrs Thatcher had a seemingly inexhaustible supply of quotations — never more so than when she had just returned in triumph to 10 Downing Street. Here she was quoting Rudyard Kipling's 'Recessional' (1897), on being re-elected for a third term in June 1987. So much did she enjoy it that she repeated the words at that year's Conservative Party Conference.

3 *There is no such thing as Society. There are individual men and women, there are families.*

Reported remark, in *Woman's Own* (31 October 1987).

4 *Home is where you come to when you have nothing better to do.*

The meaning of this observation from an interview given to *Vanity Fair* (May 1991) was disputed. Her view was that she had spoken as if addressing her children — this was the traditional attitude of children

towards their homes — and had not been describing her own feelings about home. All she had meant to say was that the children's home was always there. Compare FROST 148:3.

See also DRAKE 124:7; FRANCIS OF ASSISI 144:3.

Thomas à Kempis
German religious writer (1379–1471)

5 *Man proposes and God disposes.*

When Thomas à Kempis included the saying '*Nam homo proponit, sed Deus disponit*' in *De Imitatione Christi* (*c* 1420), it was the first appearance of the idea in this form. It derives from an old proverb found in Greek, Hebrew and Latin. Proverbs 16:9 in the Bible has it in the form: 'A man's heart deviseth his way; but the Lord directeth his steps.'

'Man Proposes, God Disposes' was the title of an extraordinary painting (1864) by Sir Edwin Landseer, showing two polar bears amid the wreckage of a ship caught in Arctic ice. In 1987, Liza Minnelli said 'Man plans and God laughs' in a TV interview, which sounds like a modern development of the old proverb.

6 Sic transit gloria mundi.

The phrase meaning 'so passes away the glory of the world' — now mostly used ironically, in the Latin, when something has failed — is an allusion to *De Imitatione Christi* in which Thomas à Kempis has '*O quam cito transit gloria mundi* [O, how quickly the world's glory passes away]'. It is used at the coronation ceremony of Popes when a reed surmounted with flax is burned and a chaplain intones: '*Pater sancte, sic transit gloria mundi*' to remind the new Holy Father of the transitory nature of human vanity. *ODQ* (1992) says, however, that it was used at the crowning of Alexander V at Pisa in July 1409, and is of earlier origin, which, if so, would mean that it was à Kempis who was doing the quoting.

7 *Everywhere I have sought rest and not found it, except sitting in a corner by myself with a little book.*

Quoted by Allen Andrews in *Quotations for Speakers and Writers* (1969), but unverified. Benham (1948) has that, 'according to his biographer', Thomas à Kempis inscribed these words in his books: '*In omnibus requiem quaesivi, et nusquam invei nisi in een hoecksken met een boecksken, id est angello cum libello* [In all things have I sought rest and have never found it except in a little nooklet with a booklet, that is in a small corner with a small book].'

Thomas, Dylan
Welsh poet (1914–53)

1 *And Death Shall Have No Dominion.*

The title of Thomas's notable poem (1936) on immortality is a straightforward allusion to Romans 6:9: 'Christ being raised from the dead dieth no more: death hath no more dominion over him.'

2 *Not for the proud man apart*
From the raging moon I write
On these spindrift pages.

From his poem 'In my craft or sullen art' (1945). The phrase 'raging moon' may be an original coinage to Thomas. The nearest the *OED2* gets is 'raging *noon*'. In 1970, *The Raging Moon* was given to the title of a film (from a novel by Peter Marshall) about physically disabled people.

3 *I've had eighteen straight whiskies. I think that's the record.*

Thomas made this dying boast to his girlfriend, Liz Reitell, after a drinking bout in New York. These were not his last words, although he went into a coma shortly afterwards and died. His biographers have subjected the bout to much scrutiny and have watered it down to a mere four or five whiskies. He often exaggerated.

Thompson, Francis
English poet (1859–1907)

4 *Look for me in the nurseries of heaven.*

This is the text chosen for Thompson's grave in the Roman Catholic annexe to Kensal Green Cemetery, London. The quotation was carved by Eric Gill and is from Thompson's poem 'To My Godchild Francis M.W.M.' (1913).

Thompson, William Hale 'Big Bill'
American politician (1867–1944)

5 *I'd punch him in the snoot.*

On what he would do if King George V were ever to set foot in Chicago. No direct quotation exists of whatever it was he said when running for a third term in 1927 — 'poke in the snoot', 'bust in the snoot' are other reported versions — but his Anglophobia is not in question.

Thomson, James
Scottish poet (1700–48)

6 *Rule, Britannia,*
Britannia rules the waves.
Britons never, never, never
Shall be slaves.

Of the several recordings of the famous patriotic song 'Rule, Britannia' few can match that by Cilla Black (on PCS 7103). I suspect it was recorded when Swinging London was at its height and the Union Jack flag was plastered patriotically over everything from mini-skirts to tea-mugs. Anyway, the above is what she is heard to sing. The words for what is now known as 'Rule, Britannia' were written by Thomson for *Alfred: a Masque* (1740) (which had another author called Mallet, but Thomson is thought to have written this bit.) The music was by Dr Thomas Arne. Thomson's words, in their original form, are these (my italics):

When Britain first, at Heaven's
  command,
Arose from out the azure main,
This was the charter of the land,
And guardian angels sung this strain:
'Rule, Britannia, *rule* the waves;
Britons never *will* be slaves.'

Of course, Cilla Black is not alone in preferring to sing 'rules' and 'shall'. Annually, at the Last Night of the Proms, several hundred other people can be heard singing her version — and drowning out those who may feel like sticking to Thomson.
  There is a difference, however, between a poetic exhortation — 'rule' — and a boastful assertion in — 'rules'. As for the difference between 'will' and 'shall', life is really too short to go on about that at any length. But an interesting defence of the Cilla Black reading comes from Kingsley Amis and James Cochrane in *The Great British Songbook* (1986): 'When what a poet or lyric-writer wrote differs from what is habitually sung, we have generally preferred the latter . . . Britons never "shall" be slaves here, not "will" as James Thomson, a Scot following Scottish usage, naturally had them.'

Thoreau, Henry David
American writer (1817–62)

1 *If a man does not keep pace with his companions, perhaps it is because he hears a different drummer. Let him step to the music which he hears, however measured or far away.*

From *Walden* (1854). Hence, presumably: *Different Drummer*, a ballet (1984) choreographed by Kenneth MacMillan; *The Different Drum* (1987), a work of popular psychotherapy by M. Scott Peck; and *Different Drummer*, a BBC TV series (1991) about eccentric American outsiders.

Thorpe, Jeremy
English Liberal politician (1929–)

2 *Bunnies* can *(and* will*) go to France. Yours affectionately, Jeremy. I miss you.*

Thorpe was a flamboyant politician who became leader of the Liberal Party but then had to resign in 1976 because a former male model called Norman Scott spread rumours that the two of them had had a homosexual affair. It was further alleged that Thorpe had plotted to have Scott murdered, though this charge was overturned at the Old Bailey in 1979.

In an earlier bid to defuse the situation, Thorpe had allowed publication of a letter he had written to Scott on 13 February 1961. It ended as above. Scott explained the 'bunnies' as referring to Scott as a frightened rabbit — this was how Thorpe had described him on the night he had seduced Scott. The saying became part of the folklore surrounding the scandal.

Times, The
British London-based newspaper, founded 1788

3 *At social gatherings he was liable to engage in heated and noisy arguments which could ruin a dinner party, and made him the dread of hostesses on both sides of the Atlantic. The tendency was exacerbated by an always generous, and occasionally excessive alcoholic intake.*

From the obituary of Randolph Churchill (7 June 1968). *Times* obituaries are traditionally unsigned but this one — which, not before time, pushed forward the boundaries of what it was possible to say about the recently dead — is generally believed to have been written by Malcolm Muggeridge.

4 *But the truth is that when it comes to the heat [sic] of the matter, to the courage that supports a nation, Lord George-Brown drunk is a better man than the Prime Minister [Harold Wilson] sober.*

After Brown announced that he was quitting the Labour Party and after an incident in which he was photographed falling in the gutter outside the Houses of Parliament, *The Times* commented thus in a leading article on 4 March 1976. *The Times* Magazine (23 May 1993), while mentioning that Woodrow Wyatt claimed to have made the remark earlier — in 1963 — also revealed that William Rees-Mogg had actually come up with the sentence, as editor, in 1976: 'I wrote it. I remember it well. Bernard Levin was sitting in my outer office. I showed it to Bernard and said: "I don't really think I can print that, do you?" Bernard replied: "If you *don't* print it, I shall never speak to you again." Perhaps Woodrow's memory is playing him up.'

Compare what Andrew Bonar Law is reported to have said: 'Asquith, when drunk, can make a better speech than any of us when sober' (Longman, *Guide to Political Quotations*, 1985). Also the story told by John Beevers in the *Sunday Referee* (19 February 1939): 'About ten years ago there was a famous scene in the House. Mr Jack Jones was speaking. Lady Astor entered and sat down opposite him. He stopped speaking, turned to her and said: "I am not drunk. I have had so many insults from this lady I resent it. She does not talk to me straight. She talks under her breath." The Deputy Speaker then said how glad he would be if the honourable lady would keep quiet. Mr Jones continued: "It is a common thing for the honourable lady to talk under her breath about drunkenness when I am speaking. I will tell her straight in her teeth that I am a better man when I am drunk than she is when I am sober." And the House laughed its head off.'

See also POPE 266:1.

Toplady, Augustus Montague
English clergyman (1740–78)

1 *Rock of Ages, cleft for me,*
Let me hide myself in Thee.

From a hymn first published in *The Gospel Magazine* (1775). BDPF (1989) recounts two stories of its composition: one, that it was written while seated by a great cleft in the rock near Cheddar, Somerset; two, that it was written on the ten of diamonds between two rubbers of whist at Bath.

The phrase 'rock of ages' is said to be the actual meaning in Hebrew of the words 'everlasting strength' at Isaiah 26:4.

Train, Jack
English actor (1902–66)

2 *I don't mind if I do!*

The immortal reply of the character 'Colonel Chinstrap' (played by Train) whenever a drink was even so much as hinted at, in the BBC radio wartime comedy hit *ITMA*. The catchphrase first appeared on the programme during 1940–1 in the form, 'Thanks, I will!' The Colonel was based on an elderly friend of the announcer, John Snagge. He was a typical ex-Indian Army type, well-pleased with himself. The phrase had existed before, of course. *Punch* carried a cartoon in 1880 with the following caption:

> *Porter:* Virginia Water!
> *Bibulous old gentleman (seated in railway carriage):* Gin and water! I don't mind if I do!

ITMA, however, secured the phrase a place in the language, as the Colonel doggedly turned every hint of liquid refreshment into an offer:

> *Tommy Handley:* Hello, what's this group? King John signing the Magna Carta at Runnymede?
> *Chinstrap:* Rum and mead, sir? I don't mind if I do!

Tree, Sir Herbert Beerbohm
English actor-manager (1853–1917)

3 *A committee should consist of three men, two of whom are absent.*

Committees generally have come in for a good deal of ribbing from the phrase-makers. The above remark is attributed to Lord Mancroft (1914–87) in some anthologies, but Hesketh Pearson gives it to Tree in the 1956 life of the great actor-manager. On the other hand, *The Treasury of Humorous Quotations* (1951) has E.V. Lucas (1868–1938) saying, 'The best committee is a committee of two when one is absent.' Hendrik Van Loon wrote in *America* (1927): 'Nothing is ever accomplished by a committee unless it consists of three members, one of whom happens to be sick and the other absent.' All of which goes to show how hard it is to keep a good joke out of other people's mouths.

To J.B. Hughes (untraced) is attributed the remark, 'If Moses had been a committee the Israelites would still be in Egypt'. (Or, 'never would have got across the Red Sea' in a remark attributed (1965) to General Booth, founder of the Salvation Army.)

The anonymous observation, 'A camel is a horse designed by a committee' (quoted, for example, in American *Vogue*, 1958) bears an interesting resemblance, surely, to 'A donkey is a horse translated into Dutch' — which Georg Christoph Lichtenberg (1742–99) had in his *Aphorisms*.

John Le Carré included in the novel *Tinker, Tailor, Soldier, Spy* (1974), the observation, 'A committee is an animal with four back legs'. Anon. said: 'A committee of one gets things done.'

Trenet, Charles
French singer and songwriter (1913–)

4 Baisers Volés *[Stolen Kisses].*

The title of a film (France, 1968) by François Truffaut is taken from a phrase in the song, '*Que Reste-t-il de Nos Amours*' (1943), written and performed by Trenet (and which is featured in the film). In English, there had earlier been the song 'A Stolen Kiss' (1923) by R. Penso; also a ballad, undated, by F. Buckley, 'Stolen Kisses are the Sweetest'.

Trinder, Tommy
English comedian (1909–89)

5 *Overpaid, overfed, oversexed and over here.*

On American troops in Britain during the Second World War (quoted in the *Sunday Times*, 6 January 1976). This was Trinder's full-length version of a popular British expression of the early 1940s. He certainly did not invent it although he may have done much to popularize it. Partridge/*Catch Phrases* makes no mention of Trinder and omits the 'overfed'.

As 'over-sexed, over-paid and over here' it is said also to have been a popular expression about American troops in Australia 1941–5 (according to *The Dictionary of Australian Quotations*, 1984) and to have been revived there during the Vietnam War.

Trotsky, Leon
Russian revolutionary (1879–1940)

1 *Go where you belong from now on — the dustbin of history.*

This is Trotsky's phrase (sometimes 'dust-heap' or 'scrapheap' is put instead). Was it with reference to the fate of the decrees emanating from Kerensky's Provincial Government in the Winter Palace in 1917? Or was it to the fate of his opponents (as suggested by E.H. Carr in his *Socialism in One Country* (1958)? The latter, in fact, and specifically referring to the Mensheviks (the moderates who opposed Lenin and the Bolsheviks' call for the overthrowing of Tsar by revolution). The phrase appears in Trotsky's *History of the Russian Revolution*, Vol. 3, Chap. 10 (1933): 'You [the Mensheviks] are pitiful, isolated individuals; you are bankrupts; your role is played out. Go where you belong from now on — into the dustbin of history!'

Earlier, in a similar coinage, Charles Dickens reflected on Sir Robert Peel's death in 1850: 'He was a man of merit who could ill be spared from the Great Dust Heap down at Westminster.' Augustine Birrell, politician and writer (1850–1933), wrote of 'that great dust-heap called "history"' in his essay on Carlyle.

Truman, Harry S
American Democratic 33rd President (1884–1972)

2 *If you can't stand the heat, get out of the kitchen.*

Looking back in 1960, Truman said: 'Some men can make decisions and some cannot. Some men fret and delay under criticism. I used to have a saying that applies here, and I note that some people have picked it up.'

When Truman announced that he would not stand again as President, *Time* Magazine (28 April 1952) had him give a 'down-to-earth reason for his retirement, quoting a favourite expression of his military jester Major General Harry Vaughan', namely, 'If you can't stand the heat, get out of the kitchen'. The attribution is usually given to Truman himself but it may not be what he said at all. 'Down-to-earth' is not quite how I would describe this remark, whereas 'If you can't stand the stink, get out of the shit-house' would be. I have only hearsay evidence for this, but given Truman's reputation for salty expressions, it is not improbable.

Bartlett (1980) quotes Philip D. Lagerquist of the Harry S Truman Library as saying, 'President Truman has used variations of the aphorism . . . for many years, both orally and in his writings' (1966). Note the 'variations'.

3 *The buck stops here.*

Truman had a sign on his desk bearing these words, indicating that the Oval Office was where the passing of the buck had to cease. It appears to be a saying of his own invention. 'Passing the buck' is a poker player's expression. It refers to a marker that can be passed on by someone who does not wish to deal. Later, Jimmy Carter restored Truman's motto to the Oval Office. When President Nixon published his memoirs (1978), people opposed to its sale went around wearing buttons which said, 'The book stops here'.

4 *The son of a bitch isn't going to resign on me, I want him fired.*

Truman's language was notably salty for the period. His wife had to reprimand him for frequent recourse to 's.o.b.'s'. In 1951 he sacked General Douglas MacArthur from his command of UN forces in Korea for repeatedly criticizing the administration's policy of non-confrontation with China. Truman added this remark, lest the General hear of the decision and jump the gun.

Turner, J.M.W.
English painter (1775–1851)

5 *The Fallacies of Hope.*

Turner liked not only to give titles to his pictures — 'The Fighting Téméraire', 'Slavers throwing overboard the dead and dying —

typhoon coming on', and so on — but to append portions of verse as citations or captions. As one of his biographers, Jack Lindsay, explained (1966): 'He wanted the extra heightening of consciousness which the verses provided.' However, if the verses did not quite fit his ideas, he happily rewrote them, be they by Shakespeare or Gray or whoever. He also wrote his own poetry so that he could quote from it in these captions, including a work which survives only in fragments, 'The Fallacies of Hope' (c 1812). There are some who believe that the poem never actually existed. Kenneth Clark used the phrase as the title of one of the parts of his TV series *Civilisation* (1969) and explained how Ruskin had said of Turner that he was indeed 'without hope' — especially in the face of Nature's cruelty and indifference. Turner also wrote: 'Hope, hope, fallacious hope, where is thy market now?' Unfortunately, Turner was considerably less of a poet than he was a painter. Under his painting 'Queen Mab's Grotto', he appended supposed lines from *A Midsummer Night's Dream* — 'Frisk it, frisk it, by the moonlight beam' (which appear nowhere in Shakespeare) and from his own 'Falacies of Hope' — 'Thy orgies, Mab, are manifold'. That should give sufficient flavour of his written art.

Twain, Mark
(Samuel Clemens)
American writer (1835–1910)

1 Cheer up! The worst is yet to come.

Partridge/*Catch Phrases* manages no more than 'a US c.p. of ironic encouragement since *c* 1918'. The most usual attribution, though, is to the American writer Philander Johnson (1866–1939) in his *Shooting Stars* (*c* 1920). I have found the expression earlier, however, in *The Love Letters of Mark Twain* — in a letter from Twain to his wife (1893–4). Twain also uses the expression in *Those Extraordinary Twins* (1894).

The similar expression, 'Cheer up . . . you'll soon be dead!' appears in several British entertainments in the period 1909–18. The original non-ironic line, 'The worst is yet to come', occurs in Tennyson's *Sea Dreams* (1864). The worst pun on the phrase concerns the man who was eating a German meal but was encouraged to continue with the words, 'Cheer up, the *wurst* is yet to come!'

2 When I was a boy of fourteen, my father was so ignorant I could hardly stand to have the old man around. But when I got to be twenty-one, I was astonished at how much he had learned in seven years.

As Burman (1980) points out, if Twain ever said this (or words to the effect: it is untraced), there was more than a hint of poetic licence about it. His own father died when Samuel Clemens (Twain) was eleven.

3 Everybody talks about the weather but nobody does anything about it.

Was this said by Twain or by Charles Dudley Warner (1829–1900)? It first appeared in an unsigned editorial in the *Hartford Courant* (24 August 1897) in the form — 'A well-known American writer said once that, while everybody talked about the weather, nobody seemed to do anything about it' — but the quip has often been assigned to Twain who lived in Hartford, Connecticut, at the time. In 1993 Henry McNulty, an Associate Editor and the Reader Representative on the *Courant* (which is 'the Oldest Newspaper of Continuous Publication in America') guided me through the minefield of attribution: 'For many years the *Courant*, quite understandably, has taken the position that Warner, not Twain, made this remark. (Example: a 1947 *Courant* article on the subject was headlined, "Sorry, Mark, But Charlie Really Said It".) But after studying what various experts have had to say, I am now in favour of attributing it to Twain until new evidence turns up.

'As far as I know, the "weather" remark has not been found in any of Twain's writings, so I suppose it's fair to say that *in print*, the *Courant* is the original source. But who wrote the *Courant* editorial? Then, as now, they were unsigned. In 1897, Warner was the *Courant*'s editor, so it is certain that the editorial was approved (or at least seen) by him; but did he actually write it? No one knows, and there is no way to tell for sure today.

'Assuming that Warner wrote the editorial, one possibility is that the reference was to himself. He certainly was well-known at the time; he was a prolific writer; and the phrase "Politics makes strange bedfellows" is one from one of his eighteen books. It's not impossible that this was just a further quip, a wink to his friends. But if not, the most likely suspect would be Mark Twain.

Warner and Twain were friends, neighbors and literary collaborators (they wrote *The Gilded Age*). Again, the "well-known American writer" phrasing would very likely be an in-joke, since of course every *Courant* reader would be familiar with Twain.

'Some years later, several people indeed attributed the remark to Warner. Charles Hopkins Clark, editor of the *Courant* after Warner's death in 1900, is reported to have said, "I guess it's no use. They still believe Mark Twain said it, despite all my assurances that it was Warner." That seems conclusive, but could his statement be colored both by the passage of time and by the fact that he and Warner were friends and colleagues?

'In July 1989, the New York State Bar Journal addressed the problem in a column entitled "Legal Lore". The Bar Journal decided to attribute the remark to both men. "Mark Twain . . . probably did make the oral comment first to his billiard companion, Charles Dudley Warner," it said. "But . . . Warner deserves the credit for having first put into writing this well-weathered statement.

'In the absence of any genuinely new historical evidence, this seems to me to be the best solution. I suppose one can't blame the *Courant* for insisting for all these years that Warner, not Twain, was the sole author of the quip, but I'm afraid that owes more to chauvinism than to scholarship.'

1 *Golf is a good walk spoiled.*

So attributed by Laurence J. Peter in *Quotations for Our Time* (1977) but otherwise unverified.

2 *The report of my death was an exaggeration.*

Twain's reaction to a false report, quoted in the *New York Journal* (2 June 1897). Frequently over-quoted and paraphrased ever since, this has become the inevitable remark to invoke when someone's death has been wrongly reported (most usually one's own). It is also now employed in the sense of, 'You thought I was finished, but look at me now' (for example, by George Bush in February 1988 regarding the decline in his political fortunes). Variations include: 'Reports of my death have been greatly exaggerated' or 'are premature'. A headline from the *Independent* (13 November 1993): 'Reports

of Queen Mother's death exaggerated Down Under'.

See also DISRAELI 123:3.

Tynan, Kenneth
English critic (1927–80)

3 *The bland leading the bland.*

'They be blind leaders of the blind. And if the blind lead the blind, both shall fall into the ditch' — Matthew 15:4 (see 56:10). This famous observation from the gospels seems to cry out to be tampered with. And so it has been. I incorrectly believed Kenneth Tynan had said about Sir Ralph Richardson that, in a certain play, he was guilty of being 'the bland leading the bland'. Not so, as I am reminded by Kathleen Tynan's *Life of Kenneth Tynan* (1987). Her husband had in fact been talking of *The New Yorker* Magazine which he had been about to join as drama critic in 1958. He told a journalist before leaving England, 'They say *The New Yorker* is the bland leading the bland. I don't know if I'm bland enough.'

What Tynan *did* say about Ralph Richardson on one occasion was, 'What is the word for that voice? Something between bland and grandiose: blandiose, perhaps' (in a review of *Flowering Cherry* in the *Observer*, 1957).

At about the same time, J.K. Galbraith was writing in *The Affluent Society* (1958): 'These are the days when . . . in minor modification of the scriptural parable, the bland lead the bland.'

4 *Verlaine was always chasing Rimbauds.*

Come to think of it, the 'bland leading the bland' sounds just the sort of thing Dorothy Parker might have said about *The New Yorker* in *her* later years. Perhaps Tynan was quoting her? He had done so before. For example, it was she who, apparently, first delivered the 'chasing Rimbauds' line. Tynan purloined it in his very early days as a (schoolboy) critic. It earned him a rebuke from James Agate (recounted in *Ego* 8, for 20 July 1945), who wrote: 'To say that "Verlaine was always chasing Rimbauds" is just *common*. Like cheap scent.'

5 *Oh! Calcutta!*

The title of Tynan's sexually explicit stage revue (1969) derives from a curious piece of word play, being the equivalent of the French '*Oh, quel cul t'as* [Oh, what a lovely bum you've got]'. French *cul* is derived from the Latin *culus* 'buttocks' but, according to the context, may be applied to the female vagina or male anus. In her *Life of Kenneth Tynan* (1987), Kathleen Tynan states that she was writing an article on the surrealist painter Clovis Trouille, one of whose works was a naked odalisque lying on her side to reveal a spherical backside. The title was 'Oh! Calcutta! Calcutta!': 'I suggested to Ken that he call his erotic revue *Oh! Calcutta!*. . . . I did not know at the time that it had the further advantage of being a French pun.'

1 The Sound of Two Hands Clapping.

A collection of Tynan's critical writings was published with this title in 1975. As he acknowledged, it derives from a Zen koan ('a riddle used in Zen to teach the inadequacy of logical reasoning'): 'We know the sound of two hands clapping. But what is the sound of one hand clapping?' This koan is said to appear as the epigraph of J.D. Salinger's *For Esmé — With Love and Squalor* (1953), though not in all editions.

Upton, Ralph R.
American engineer? (*fl.* 1912)

2 Stop; look; listen.

As a notice at US railroad crossings, this slogan was devised by Upton in 1912, according to R. Hyman, *A Dictionary of Famous Quotations* (1967). This rather esoteric piece of information stayed with me for many years, until suddenly confirmation started flooding in. The date was confirmed by Meredith Nicholson in *A Hoosier Chronicle* (1912): 'Everybody's saying "Stop, Look, Listen!" . . . the white aprons in the one-arm lunch rooms say it now when you kick on the size of the buns.' The originator was confirmed by *Notes and Queries*, 195:174 (1950) saying that it was devised by Upton to replace the former 'Look out for the locomotive'. And any number of allusions testify to its popularity. A show with the title *Stop! Look! Listen!* (with music by Irving Berlin) opened on Broadway (27 December 1915); in 1916, George Robey introduced one of his greatest popular songs, 'I Stopped, I Looked, I Listened' in *The Bing Boys Are Here*, in London; a 1936 cheesecake advertisement for a New York supplier of artists' materials had the slogan 'Stop, Look and Kiss 'em.'

V

Vandiver, Willard D.
American politician
(1854–1932)

1 *I come from a state that raises corn and cotton and cockleburs and Democrats, and frothy eloquence neither convinces nor satisfies me. I am from Missouri. You have got to show me.*

Vandiver was a representative in Congress from Columbia, Missouri, from 1897 to 1905. When he was a member of the House Naval Committee and was inspecting the Navy Yard at Philadelphia in 1899, he good-humouredly made the above statement when speaking at a dinner. 'I'm from Missouri' quickly became a way of showing scepticism and demanding proof. Missouri, accordingly, became known as the 'Show Me' state. The date of the speech is sometimes given as 1902, the speaker's name as 'Vandiner'.

Veblen, Thorstein
American economist
(1857–1929)

2 *The outcome of any serious research can only be to make two questions grow where one question grew before.*

In the *University of California Chronicle* (1908), 'Evolution of the Scientific Point of View'. Veblen was clearly alluding to Jonathan Swift's 'A Voyage to Brobdingnag' in *Gulliver's Travels* (1726): 'And he gave it for his opinion, that whoever could make two ears of corn or two blades of grass to grow upon a spot of ground where only one grew before, would deserve better of mankind, and do more essential service to his country than the whole race of politicians put together.'

3 *Conspicuous consumption of valuable goods is a means of reputability to the gentleman of leisure.*

In *The Theory of the Leisure Class* (1899). Veblen coined the term 'conspicuous consumption' to describe the extravagant use of expensive goods to display status. Compare the term 'conspicuous waste' (the *OED2*'s only citation is from 1969), a Marxist term to denote much the same thing but more critically.

Victoria
British Sovereign
(1819–1901)

4 *I will be good.*

These pious words were not said by Queen Victoria on her accession to the throne in 1837, but six years earlier when she was a mere twelve years of age. It was casually revealed precisely what lay in store for her, and this is what she said.

5 *We are not amused.*

Did she ever utter this famous put-down or didn't she? The subject was raised in the 1919 *Notebooks of a Spinster Lady* written by Miss Caroline Holland (1878–1903): '[The Queen's] remarks can freeze as well as crystallize . . . there is a tale of the unfortunate equerry who ventured during dinner at Windsor to tell a story with a spice of scandal or impropriety in it. "We are not amused," said the Queen when he had finished.'

The equerry in question appears to have been the Hon. Alexander Yorke. Unfortunately, the German he had told the story to laughed so loud that the Queen's attention was drawn to it. Another contender for the snub is Admiral Maxse whom she commanded to give his well-known imitation of her which he did by putting a handkerchief on his head and blowing out his cheeks.

Interviewed in 1978, Princess Alice, Countess of Athlone, said she had once questioned her grandmother about the phrase — 'I asked her . . . [but] she never said it' — and affirmed what many have held, that Queen Victoria was 'a very cheerful person.'

1 *We are not interested in the possibilities of defeat.*

During one week of the South African War in December 1899 — 'Black Week', as it came to be called — British forces suffered a series of setbacks in their fight against the Boers. Queen Victoria 'braced the nation in words which have become justly famous' (W.S. Churchill, *A History of the English-Speaking Peoples*, Vol. 4). 'Please understand,' she told A.J. Balfour, who was in charge of the Foreign Office, 'that there is no one depressed in *this* house. We are not interested in the possibilities of defeat. They do not exist.'

Margaret Thatcher quoted these words in her first television interview during the Falklands War (5 April 1982), having seen them as a motto on Winston Churchill's desk in his Second World War bunker beneath Whitehall: 'Do you remember what Queen Victoria once said? "Failure — the possibilities do not exist". That is the way we must look at it. I'm not talking about failure. I am talking about supreme confidence in the British fleet, superlative troops, excellent equipment.' So she was reported in *Time* Magazine (19 April 1982), though she might have been surprised to find the quote being attributed directly to her by *Time* in December of that year.

See also THATCHER 330:1.

2 *Bertie!*

It might be thought that the Queen's dying word was an entirely-to-be-expected reference to her late and long-lamented consort, Prince Albert. Rather, it was the name of her son and heir, Albert Edward, who took the title of King Edward VII.

Vidal, Gore
American novelist and critic (1925–   )

3 *It is not enough to succeed. Others must fail.*

This was quoted as 'the cynical maxim of a clever friend' by the Revd Gerard Irvine during his 'anti-panegyric' for Tom Driberg (Lord Bradwell) after a requiem mass in London on 7 December 1976.

'It's not enough that I should succeed — others should fail,' was attributed to David Merrick, the Broadway producer, in Barbara Rowes, *The Book of Quotes* (1979).

Villiers De L'Isle Adam, Philippe-Auguste
French writer (1838–89)

4 *Living? The servants will do that for us [Vivre? les serviteurs feront cela pour nous]*.

From *Axël* (1890). This has given rise to a number of joke variations, of which 'Sex? Our servants do that for us' is probably the best-known. In the film comedy *Carry on Up the Khyber* (UK, 1968), Kenneth Williams as the Khasi of Kalabar says to Joan Sims as Lady Ruff-Diamond, 'I do not make love . . . I am extremely rich. I have servants to do everything for me.' Which only goes to show how old this version must have been even then, for it to have been included in a *Carry On*.

When the film actor Victor Mature was told that he looked as though he had slept in his clothes, he is said to have replied: 'Don't be ridiculous. I pay someone to do that for me.'

Virgil
Roman poet (70–19BC)

5 *Amor vincit omnia [Love conquers all].*

One of the best known proverbial expressions of all comes from Virgil's *Eclogues*, (No. 10, l.69). Chaucer's Prioress had it on her brooch, as mentioned in 'The General Prologue' to *The Canterbury Tales*.

6 *Arma virumque cano [I sing of arms and the man].*

The first line of Virgil's *Aeneid* has given us the poet's phrase 'I sing . . .'. Robert Herrick in *Hesperides* (1648) begins: 'I sing of brooks, of blossoms, birds, and bowers'. William Cowper begins 'The Sofa' in *The Task* (1785):

I sing the Sofa. I who lately sang
Truth, Hope and Charity, and touch'd with awe
The solemn chords . . .
Now seek repose upon a humbler theme.

Titles of poems by Walt Whitman include, 'One's Self I Sing', 'For Him I Sing' and 'I Sing the Body Electric'.

It also gives us the title of a play *Arms and the Man* (1894) by George Bernard Shaw — or, rather, it does so via Dryden's translation of the same: 'Arms, and the man I sing'. This version had earlier been cited by Thomas Carlyle in *Past and Present* (1843) when he wrote: 'For we are to bethink us that the Epic verily is not *Arms and the Man*, but *Tools and the Man*, — an infinitely wider kind of epic.'

1 Decus et tutamen.

The inscription found on the rim of the British pound coin, which replaced the banknote in 1983. The same words, suggested by John Evelyn the diarist, had appeared on the rim of a Charles II crown of 1662–3 (its purpose then was as a safeguard against clipping). Translated as 'an ornament and a safeguard' — referring to the inscription rather than the coin — the words come from Virgil's *Aeneid* (Bk V) '*Decus et tutamen in armis*'. In its full form, this is the motto of the Feltmakers' Company (incorporated 1604).

2 Facilis descensus Averni *[It is easy to go down into Hell]*.

From Virgil's *Aeneid* (VI.126), this phrase is employed when wanting to suggest that man is readily inclined towards evil deeds. Avernus, a lake in Campania, was a name for the entrance to Hell. The epic poem continues with:

Noctes atque dies patet atri ianua Ditis;
Sed revocare gradum superasque evadere ad auras,
Hoc opus, hic labor est.

[Night and day, the gates of dark Death stand wide; but to climb back again, to retrace one's steps to the upper air — there's the rub, that is the task.]

3 Beware Greeks bearing gifts.

A warning against trickery, this is an allusion to the most famous Greek gift of all — the large wooden horse which was built as an offering to the gods before the Greeks were about to return home after besieging Troy unsuccessfully for ten years. It was taken within the city walls of Troy, but men leapt out from it, opened the gates and helped destroy the city. Virgil in the *Aeneid* (II.49) has Laocoon warn the Trojans not to admit the horse, saying '*timeo Danaos et dona ferentes* [I fear the Greeks, even when they offer gifts]'.

Voltaire
French writer and philosopher (1694–1778)

4 I disapprove of what you say, but will defend to the death your right to say it.

A remark attributed to Voltaire, notably by S.G. Tallentyre in *The Friends of Voltaire* (1907). But Tallentyre gave the words as a free paraphrase of what Voltaire wrote in his *Essay on Tolerance*: 'Think for yourself and let others enjoy the privilege to do so, too'. So what we have is merely Tallentyre's summary of Voltaire point of view.

Then along comes Norbert Guterman to claim that what Voltaire *did* write in a letter of February 1770 to a M. Le Riche was: 'Monsieur l'Abbé, I detest what you write, but I would give my life to make it possible for you to continue to write.' So, whether or not he used the precise words, at least Voltaire believed in the principle behind them.

5 If – – – did not exist it would have to be invented.

This format phrase originated in Voltaire's remark: '*Si Dieu n'existait pas, il faudrait l'inventer* [If God did not exist, it would be necessary to invent him]' — *Epîtres*, xcvi (1770). Other examples include: 'If Austria did not exist it would have to be invented' (Frantisek Palacky, *c* 1845); 'If he [Auberon Waugh, a literary critic] did not exist, it would be unnecessary to invent him' (Desmond Elliott, literary agent, *c* 1977); 'What becomes clear is that Olivier developed his own vivid, earthy classical style as a reaction to Gielgud's more ethereal one . . . So if Gielgud did not exist would Olivier have found it necessary to invent himself?' (review in the *Observer*, 1988); 'If Tony Benn did not exist, the old Right of the Labour Party would have had to invent him' (*Observer*, 15 October 1989).

1 *In this country [England] it is thought well to kill an admiral from time to time to encourage the others.*

From Voltaire's novel *Candide* (1759). This was a reference to the case of Admiral Byng who, in 1756, was sent to relieve Minorca which was blockaded by a French fleet. He failed and, when found guilty of neglect of duty, he was condemned to death and shot on board the *Momarque* at Portsmouth.

2 *God is always on the side of the big battalions.*

Voltaire did not say this, though he did refer to the idea. In this form it has been attributed to the French Marshal, the Vicomte de Turenne (*d* 1675) and to Roger, Comte de Bussy-Rabutin (in a letter to the Comte de Limoges, 18 October 1677) — the latter adding, 'and against the small ones'.

What Voltaire wrote in a letter to Le Riche (6 February 1770) was: '*They say that God is always on the side of the big battalions*', obviously referring back. Earlier, in what are called his 'Piccini Notebooks' (*c* 1735–50), Voltaire had, in fact, written: 'God is on the side not of the heavy battalions, but of the best shots.'

Vreeland, Diana
American fashion journalist (*c* 1903–89)

3 *I love London. It is the most swinging city in the world at the moment.*

The coming together of the words 'swinging' and 'London' for the first time may have first occurred publicly in an edition of the *Weekend Telegraph* Magazine on 30 April 1965 in which Vreeland's words were quoted. In addition, a picture caption declared, 'London is a swinging city'. Almost exactly one year later, *Time* Magazine picked up the angle and devoted a cover-story to the concept of 'London: The Swinging City' (edition dated 15 April 1966).

4 *The beautiful people.*

Coinage of this term is credited to Vreeland in *Current Biography* (1978). Whether she deserves this or not is open to question. The earliest *OED2* citation with capital letters for each word is from 1966, though there is a *Vogue* use from 15 February 1964 which would appear to support the link to Vreeland. The *OED2* makes the phrase refer primarily to 'flower people' and 'hippies', though I would prefer the 1981 *Macquarie Dictionary's* less narrow definition of: 'Fashionable social set of wealthy, well-groomed, usually young people.' The Lennon and McCartney song 'Baby You're a Rich Man' containing the line 'How does it feel to be one of the beautiful people?' was released in July 1967.

William Saroyan's play *The Beautiful People* had been performed long before all this, in 1941, and Oscar Wilde in a letter to Harold Boulton (December 1879), wrote: 'I could have introduced you to some very beautiful people. Mrs Langtry and Lady Lonsdale and a lot of clever beings who were at tea with me.'

W

Walker, James J.
American politician (1881–1946)

1 *Will you love me in December as you do in May?*

A song with this title (music by Ernest R. Ball) was written by Walker, a future Mayor of New York, in 1905. Possibly it had some influence on the coinage of the expression 'A May/December romance' or 'Spring/winter romance' to describe a union between a younger person and an older one. Compare this, from 'To the most Courteous and Fair Gentlewoman, Mrs Elinor Williams' by Rowland Watkyns (*d* 1664): 'For every marriage then is best in tune,/When that the wife is May, the husband June.'

Wallace, W.R.
American poet (*d* 1881)

2 *A mighty power and stronger*
Man from his throne has hurled,
For the hand that rocks the cradle
Is the hand that rules the world.

From his poem 'What rules the world' (1865) — a tribute to motherhood, first appearing in *John O'London's Treasure Trove. The Hand That Rocks the Cradle* was the title of a film (US, 1992).

Walpole, Horace
(4th Earl of Orford)
English writer (1717–97)

3 *This world is a comedy to those that think, a tragedy to those that feel.*

So Walpole wrote to the Countess of Upper Ossory on 16 August 1776, and it is to him that the observation is usually credited. However, Blaise Pascal (1623–1662) is reported to have said earlier: '*La vie, c'est une tragédie pour celui qui sent, mais une comédie pour celui qui pense.*' This is unverified.

4 *These . . . were what filled me with disgust, and made me quit that splendid theatre of pitiful passion.*

So said Walpole of his retirement in 1767 from the House of Commons when he came to write his *Memoirs of the Reign of King George III* (published posthumously). He was trying not to pass off his anecdotes as a history of England but hoped that they contained 'the most useful part of all history, a picture of human minds'.

Compare the theatrical imagery used by two American politicians a few years later: 'You retire from the great theatre of action with the blessings of your fellow citizens' (the President of Congress's remarks — probably penned by Thomas Jefferson — at the resignation of George Washington as Commander in Chief, 23 December 1783); 'Having now finished the work assigned me, I retire from the great theatre of action' (George Washington's own remarks on that occasion).

5 *Everything's at sea — except the Fleet.*

Said to have been a reflection of Walpole's on the state of England. Presumably he meant that the country's affairs were (as we would now say) 'all at sea'. This was quoted by Malcolm Muggeridge on BBC Radio *Quote . . . Unquote* in 1978, but remains untraced.

6 *Lie down, I think I love you.*

Considered a sufficiently well-established, smart, jokey remark to be listed by the *Sun* (10 October 1984) as one of its 'Ten top chat-up lines'. I have a feeling it may also have been used in a song or cartoon just a little before that. Indeed, there was a song entitled 'Lie Down (A Modern Love Song)' written and performed by the British group Whitesnake in 1978. Earlier, 'Sit Down I Think I Love You', written by Stills, was performed by the Mojo Men in 1967. An article 'Down with sex' was published in collected form (1966) by Malcolm Muggeridge in which he wrote: 'I saw scrawled on a wall in Santa Monica in California: "Lie down! I think I love you." Thus stripped, sex becomes an orgasm merely.'

And then again, there was the Marx Brothers' line from *The Cocoanuts* (1929), 'Ah, Mrs Rittenhouse, won't you . . . lie down?' As ever, there is nothing new under the sun. Walpole, in a letter to H.S. Conway on 23 October 1778, wrote: 'This sublime age reduces everything to its quintessence; all periphrases and expletives are so much in disuse, that I suppose soon the only way to making love will be to say "Lie down".'

Walpole, Sir Robert
(1st Earl of Orford)
English Whig Prime Minister (1676–1745)

1 *[The gratitude of place-expectants] is a lively sense of future favours.*

Ascribed to Walpole by Mencken (1942), who apparently found it in William Hazlitt, *Lectures on the English Comic Writers* (1819), 'On Wit and Humour'. By this century, the *Dictionary of American Proverbs* has, as simply proverbial, 'Gratitude is a lively expression of favours yet to come.' Prior to Walpole, La Rochefoucauld had said, 'The gratitude of most men is merely a secret desire to receive greater benefits' *Maxims*, No. 298 (1678).

2 *The balance of power.*

An expression used by Walpole in the House of Commons (13 February 1741) which has now come to mean the promotion of peace through parity of strength in rival groups. The *ODQ* (1979) gave it as though Walpole had coined the phrase, but dropped it in 1992. Safire (1978) states that the phrase was being used in international diplomacy as early as 1700. Initially, the phrase appears to have been 'the balance of power in Europe'. In 1715, Alexander Pope wrote a poem with the title 'The Balance of Europe': 'Now Europe's balanc'd, neither

side prevails;/For nothing's left in either of the scales.'

3 *As to the conduct of the war: as I am neither admiral nor general, as I have nothing to do with either our Navy or Army, I am sure I am not answerable for the prosecution of it.*

As Prime Minister in 1741. Untraced.

Warhol, Andy
American artist (1927–87)

4 *In the future everyone will be famous for fifteen minutes.*

The phrase 'to be famous for fifteen minutes' means to have transitory fame of the type prevalent in the twentieth century. It comes from the celebrated saying to be found in a catalogue for an exhibition of Warhol's work in Stockholm (February–March 1968). The artist actually wrote: 'In the future everyone will be world-famous for fifteen minutes.' It is often to be found used allusively — 'He's had his fifteen minutes.' *Famous for Fifteen Minutes* was the title of a series of, naturally, fifteen-minute programmes on BBC Radio 4 in 1990 in which yesterday's headline-makers were recalled from obscurity.

Washington, Booker T.
American educationist (1856–1915)

5 *The dignity of labour.*

A phrase, referring especially to manual labour, which has proved hard to trace. The *OED2*'s earliest citation is only in 1948. Washington comes close in *Up from Slavery* (1901): 'No race can prosper till it learns that there is as much dignity in tilling a field as in writing a poem.'

The similar 'honest toil' is almost as elusive. Thomas Gray in his 'Elegy' (1751) spoke of the *'useful* toil' of the 'rude forefathers' in the countryside. *Useful Toil* was the title of a book comprising 'autobiographies of working people from the 1820s to the 1920s' (published 1974). The *OED2* finds 'honest labour' in 1941. Thomas Carlyle spoke of 'honest work' in 1866. 'Honourable toil' appears in the play *Two Noble Kinsmen* (possibly by John Fletcher and William Shakespeare, published 1634).

Washington, George
1st American President (1732–99)

1 *Father, I cannot tell a lie. I did it with my little hatchet.*

A version of the words attributed to Washington when asked, as a boy, by his father, how a certain cherry tree had come to be cut down. A tale almost certainly invented by Mason Locke Weems, Washington's first popular biographer. In *The Life of George Washington: With Curious Anecdotes Equally Honorable to Himself and Exemplary to His Young Countrymen* (1800), Weems wrote: 'Looking at his father with the sweet face of youth brightened with the inexpressible charm of all-conquering truth, he bravely cried out. "I can't tell a lie. I did cut it with my hatchet".'

See also WALPOLE 344:4.

Waugh, Evelyn
English novelist (1903–66)

2 *Up to a point, Lord Copper.*

A phrase used when disagreeing with someone it is not prudent to differ with comes from Waugh's novel about journalists, *Scoop* (1938): 'Mr Salter's side of the conversation was limited to expressions of assent. When Lord Copper [a newspaper proprietor] was right he said, "Definitely, Lord Copper'; when he was wrong, "Up to a point".' An example from the *Independent* (4 April 1990): 'We are told that [Norman Tebbit] was only trying to help . . . he was out to "stop Heseltine". Well, up to a point, Lord Whitelaw'.

3 *I have been here before.*

From Waugh's *Brideshead Revisited*, Chap.1 (1945) where Charles Ryder says it about Brideshead (hence the 'revisited'). *I Have Been Here Before* had earlier been the title of a 'Time' play (1937) by J.B. Priestley.

4 *As I took the cigarette from my lips and put it in hers, I caught a thin bat's squeak of sexuality, inaudible to any but me.*

Charles Ryder of Lady Julia in *Brideshead Revisited*, Chap. 3 (1945). A later use of 'bat's squeak', not otherwise much recorded: at the Conservative Party Conference in 1981, a then upwardly rising politician called Edwina Currie was taking part in a debate on law and order. To illustrate some point, she held aloft a pair of handcuffs. Subsequently, the Earl of Gowrie admitted to having felt 'a bat's squeak of desire' for Mrs Currie at that moment.

5 *I pray that the church is not struck by lightning.*

This was the gist of a telegram said to have been sent by Waugh to Tom Driberg MP on the occasion of the latter's marriage (to a woman). The occasion was remarkable — and not only to Waugh — because Driberg was a notorious and active homosexual. According to Alan Watkins, *Brief Lives* (1982), Waugh in fact wrote — rather than telegraphed — to the effect: 'I will think of you intently on the day and pray that the church is not struck by lightning.' The letter is not, alas, included in Waugh's published correspondence. Watkins adds: 'This sentence in this same connection is, oddly enough, attributed to Aneurin Bevan and Winston Churchill also.'

Webb, Sidney
(later Lord Passfield)
English socialist (1859–1947)

6 *Once we face the necessity of putting our principles first into Bills, to be fought through committee clause by clause; and then into the appropriate machinery for carrying them into execution from one end of the kingdom to the other . . . the inevitability of gradualness cannot fail to be appreciated.*

From his presidential address to the Labour Party Conference (26 June 1923). The phrase 'the inevitability of gradualness' was taken to mean that, for Labour, electoral success would come gradually but certainly, and by evolution not revolution.

7 *Nobody told us we could do this.*

This was Webb's comment when the new National Government came off the Gold Standard in 1931. The outgoing Labour Government had failed to deal with a financial crisis in this manner.

Weber, Max
German economist (1864–1920)

8 *The Protestant work ethic.*

An attitude towards business, based on the teachings of Calvin and the analysis of

Weber, which suggests that it is one's duty to be successful through hard work. Weber's original article had the title *'Die protestantische Ethik und der Geist des Kapitalismus* [The Protestant Ethic and the Spirit of Capitalism]' (1904–5).

Weldon, Fay
English novelist and playwright (1931–   )

1 Go to work on an egg.

Hardly a profile of Weldon goes by without mention of her time as an advertising copywriter (compare RUSHDIE 287:4) and her coining of this slogan for the British Egg Marketing Board in 1957. She did indeed work for the Mather & Crowther agency, but in 1981 she poured a little cold water on the frequent linking of her name with the slogan: 'I was certainly in charge of copy at the time "Go to work on an egg" was first used as a slogan as the main theme for an advertising campaign. The phrase itself had been in existence for some time and hung about in the middle of paragraphs and was sometimes promoted to base lines. Who invented it, it would be hard to say. It is perfectly possible, indeed probable, that I put those particular six words together in that particular order but I would not swear to it.'

Weller, Charles E.
American journalist (*fl.* 1867)

2 Now is the time for all good men to come to the aid of the party.

This typewriter exercise was possibly originated by Charles E. Weller, a court reporter in Milwaukee (1867) to test the efficiency of the first practical typewriter, which his friend, Christopher L. Scholes, had made. However, in his book *The Early History of the Typewriter* (1918), Weller does not claim credit for the coinage. In the Muir & Norden *My Word* stories (1973), the line is stated to be found in 'The Typewriter's Song' by Edwin Meade Robinson — though I suspect this is merely a quotation of it.

Whoever was responsible did not do a very good job because the phrase contains only eighteen letters of the alphabet. 'The quick brown fox jumps over the lazy dog', on the other hand, has all twenty-six. This was once thought to be the shortest sentence in English containing all the letters of the alphabet but it was superseded by: 'Pack my box with five dozen liquor jugs' (which is three letters

shorter overall) and 'Quick blowing zephyrs vex daft Jim' (which is even shorter). Even more concise 'pangrams' have been devised but they are also shorter on sense and memorability.

Welles, Orson
American film director and actor (1915–85)

3 This is the biggest electric train set a boy ever had!

Remark on learning how to use a Hollywood studio. Frank Brady in *Citizen Welles* (1989) suggests that this was just prior to the filming of *Citizen Kane* in about 1939.

4 Dear Wheeler, you provide the prose poems. I'll provide the war.

In the film *Citizen Kane* (1941), which Welles wrote in some form of collaboration with Herman J. Mankiewicz, Kane is shown a war correspondent's message, 'Could send you prose poems about scenery but . . . there is no war in Cuba', and suggests this as his reply. This is based on an 1898 exchange between the newspaper artist Frederic Remington and his proprietor, William Randolph Hearst. Remington asked to be allowed home from Cuba because there was no war for him to cover. Hearst cabled: 'Please remain. You furnish the pictures and I will furnish the war.' Hearst was, of course, the model for Kane.

5 You know what the fellow said — in Italy, for thirty years under the Borgias, they had warfare, terror, murder and bloodshed, but they produced Michelangelo, Leonardo da Vinci and the Renaissance. In Switzerland, they had brotherly love; they had five hundred years of democracy and peace and what did that produce? The cuckoo clock.

So says Harry Lime (played by Welles) in Carol Reed's film *The Third Man* (1939). It soon got around that Welles had added this speech to the basic script which was written by Graham Greene and Carol Reed. Indeed, it appears only as a footnote in the published script of the film. In a letter, dated 13 October 1977, Greene confirmed to me that it *had* been written by Welles during shooting: 'What happened was that during the shooting of *The Third Man* it was found necessary for the timing to insert another sentence and the speech you mention was put in by Orson Welles.'

Whether the idea was original to Welles is another matter. After all he introduces the speech with, 'You know what the fellow said . . .' Welles apparently later suggested that the lines came originally from 'an old Hungarian play'. In *This Is Orson Welles* (1993), Welles is quoted as saying: 'When the picture came out, the Swiss very nicely pointed out to me that they've never made any cuckoo clocks — they all come from the Schwarzwald in Bavaria!'

Wellington, 1st Duke of

Irish-born soldier and politician
(1769–1852)

1 The battle of Waterloo was won on the playing fields of Eton.

This view was first ascribed to the 1st Duke of Wellington in Count Charles de Montalembert's *De L'Avenir Politique de l'Angleterre* in 1856. The Frenchman stated that the Duke returned to Eton in his old age and, recalling the delights of his youth, exclaimed: 'It is here that the battle of Waterloo was won' (i.e. he made no mention of playing fields).

Burnam (1980) suggests that Sir Edward Creasy built on this in *Memoirs of Eminent Etonians* (though as this was published in 1850, and the French book not until 1856, this must have been difficult). Anyhow, Creasy had the Iron Duke passing the playing fields in old age and saying, 'There grows the stuff that won Waterloo'.

Then in 1889, a third writer, Sir William Fraser, in *Words on Wellington*, put together Montalembert's remark with Creasy's playing fields to produce the popularly known version. The 7th Duke tried to pour more cold water on the matter in letters to *The Times* sometime prior to his death in 1972:

> During his old age Wellington is recorded to have visited Eton on two occasions only and it is unlikely that he came more often. He attended the funeral of his elder brother in College Chapel in October 1842 and he accompanied the Queen when she came to Eton with Louis Philippe in October 1844. On the first occasion, he attended the ceremony only and went away when it was over: and, on the second, he is hardly likely to have talked about the battle of Waterloo. Wellington's career at Eton was short and inglorious and, unlike his elder brother,

he had no particular affection for the place . . . Quite apart from the fact that the authority for attributing the words to Wellington is of the flimsiest description, to anyone who knows his turn of phrase they ring entirely false. It is, therefore, much to be hoped that speakers will discontinue using them either, as is generally the case, in order to point out their snobbishness, which is so alien to ideas generally now held, or else to show that Wellington was in favour of organized games, an assumption which is entirely unwarranted.

Perhaps the nearest the 1st Duke came to any sort of compliment about the effect his old school had on him was, 'I really believe I owe my spirit of enterprise to the tricks I used to play in the garden' [of his Eton boarding-house] quoted in Vol. 1 of Elizabeth Longford's biography (1969).

But the saying, however apocryphal, still exerts its power. One H. Allen Smith (*b* 1906) said: 'The battle of Yorktown was lost on the playing fields of Eton' (Yorktown, in Virginia, was the scene of the surrender of British forces at the end of the War of Independence, 1781). George Orwell (an Old Etonian himself) averred: 'Probably the Battle of Waterloo *was* won on the playing fields of Eton, but the opening battles of all subsequent wars have been lost there' (*The Lion and the Unicorn*, 1941).

2 A damn close-run thing.

As with most of Wellington's alleged remarks, this was not quite what he said, but it is how it is remembered. What he told the memoirist Thomas Creevey (on 18 June 1815) about the outcome of the Battle of Waterloo, was: 'It has been a damned serious business. Blücher and I have lost 30,000 men. It has been a damned nice thing the nearest run thing you ever saw in your life.' The *Creevey Papers*, in which this account appears, was not published until 1903. Somehow out of this description a conflated version arose, with someone else presumably supplying the 'close-run'.

3 I don't care a twopenny damn what becomes of the ashes of Napoleon Bonaparte.

Attributed, but unverified. James Morris in *Pax Britannica* (1968) comments: 'a dam was a small Indian coin, as Wellington knew when he popularized the phrase "a twopenny dam".' *BDPF* (1989) says: 'The derivation . . . from the coin, a dam, is without foundation.'

1 Publish and be damned!

Wellington's comment in 1842 to a blackmailer called Stockdale who offered not to publish anecdotes of the Duke and his mistress, Harriet Wilson, in return for payment. Legend has it that the Duke scrawled this response in bright red ink across Stockdale's letter and sent it back to him. Hence, the title of a book about the press (1955) by Hugh Cudlipp. Richard Ingrams declared on several occasions (c 1977) that a suitable motto for *Private Eye*, of which he was editor, would be: 'Publish and Be Sued'.

2 The scum of the earth.

Wellington's description of his men in a despatch to Lord Bathurst, the War Minister, in 1813, requires a hefty footnote. Harold Whelan supplied it in a letter to the *Sunday Times* on 23 June 1985: 'The words "We have in the service the scum of the earth as common soldiers" were said in July 1813, after the battle of Vittoria, when Wellington's troops ("our vagabond soldiers") were "totally knocked up" after a night of looting.'

On more than one occasion Wellington spoke in complimentary terms about the common soldiers under his command. *The Scum of the Earth* is the title of a novel by Arthur Koestler (1941). The expression predates Wellington. Dr John Arbuthnot in *John Bull*, III.vi.25 (1712) has 'Scoundrels! Dogs! the Scum of the Earth!'

3 I don't know what effect these men will have upon the enemy, but, by God, they frighten me.

This referred to some of his generals, and not to his regimental officers or to the rank and file, as is made clear from the text of the despatch to Sir Colonel Torrens, military secretary at the Horse Guards, written 29 August 1810. There Wellington said, rather: 'As Lord Chesterfield said of the generals of his day, "I only hope that when the enemy reads the list of their names, he trembles as I do".'

4 Up Guards and at 'em!

At the Battle of Waterloo, Wellington is supposed to have said, 'Up Guards and at them *again*', and so it was reported in a letter from a certain Captain Batty of the Foot Guards

four days later on 22 June 1815, though the saying is popularly rendered in this shorter form.

Benham (1980) has this: 'In A. Tels guidebook, *Excursions to the Lion of Waterloo* (2nd ed. 1904), a Belgian publication, this is improved as follows: "Wellington cried, 'Upright, guards! prepare for battle'." In *The Times* (15 October 1841), appeared an "anecdote which may be relied on" quoted from *Britannia*, to the effect that lately the Duke had sat for his bust to "one of the most distinguished of living sculptors," who stated "that it would be popular and effective if it could represent his Grace at the moment when he uttered the memorable words . . . at Waterloo. The Duke laughed very good-humouredly at this observation and said 'Ah! the old story. People will invent words for me . . . but really I don't know what I said. I saw that the moment for action was come, and I gave the command for attack. I suppose the words were brief and homely enough, for they ran through the ranks and were obeyed on the instant, . . . but I'm sure I don't recollect them, and I very much doubt whether anyone else can'."'

Again, in 1852, the Duke commented to J.W. Croker: 'What I must have said and probably did say was, Stand up, Guards! and then gave the commanding officers the order to attack.' The following year, *Notes & Queries* was already puzzling over the matter.

5 Sir, if you believe that, you will believe anything.

When Wellington was accosted in Pall Mall by a minor government official who raised his hat and said: 'Mr Jones, I believe', the Duke replied the above. It is said that there *was* a Mr Jones who bore a striking resemblance to Wellington — George Jones, a military painter. Was what Wellington said original, however?

Wells, H.G.
English novelist and writer (1866–1946)

6 The war to end wars.

On the afternoon of 11 November 1918, David Lloyd George announced the terms of the Armistice to the House of Commons and concluded: 'I hope we may say that thus, this fateful morning, came to an end all wars.' Wells had popularized the notion of the 'war to end wars' in a book he had brought out in 1914 with the title *The War That Will End War*. This, however, was not an original cry:

it had been raised in other wars. Later, Wells commented ruefully: 'I launched the phrase "the war to end war" and that was not the least of my crimes.'

Sometimes it is is said — for example, in the *Observer* Magazine (2 May 1993) — that it was a phrase of the 1930s and that there is no evidence the words were used at the time of the First World War. Clearly not the case.

1 *In the country of the blind the one-eyed man is king.*

This saying has become associated with Wells because of its use by him in the story he wrote with the title *The Country of the Blind* (1904) — though he quite clearly labelled it as an 'old proverb'. Indeed, it is that and occurs in the proverbs of many languages (as shown by the *CODP*, 1982.) An early appearance is in a book of *Adages* by Erasmus (*d* 1536): '*In regione caecorum rex est luscus.*' Other sixteenth-century uses of the saying include John Palsgrave's translation of Fullmin's *Comedy of Acolastus* and John Skelton's 'An one eyed man is Well syghte when he is amonge blunde men' (1522).

2 *The New World Order.*

In an exchange of New Year's greetings with President Bush in January 1991, President Gorbachev of the Soviet Union spoke of the serious obstacle posed to a 'new world order' by the Iraqi invasion of Kuwait. After the allied victory in the Gulf War, Bush himself proclaimed a New World Order based on law and human rights. Always a rather vague concept, Wells had used the phrase as the title of a book in 1940. 'New Order' had previously been the name given to programmes of Hitler's regime in Germany in the 1930s and of a Japanese Prime Minister in 1938.

Wertenbaker, Timberlake
Anglo-French-American playwright (1928–)

3 *Our Country's Good.*

Wertenbaker's 1988 play about Australian convicts putting on a production of Farquhar's *The Recruiting Officer* in the 1780s takes its title from George Barrington's prologue for the opening of the Sydney Play House in 1796 (when, also, the actors were principally convicts). The first play to be staged there was, however, Dr Young's tragedy,

The Revenge. Barrington's words — which Wertenbaker puts in her play — include:

> True patriots we; for be it understood,
> We left our country for our country's
>   good . . .
> And none will doubt but that our
>   emigration
> Has proved most useful to the British
>   nation.

4 *Three Birds Alighting on a Field.*

The title of this play (1991) about the modern art market might appear to be one of those apparently arbitrarily applied titles fixed to paintings ('Cornfield with Crows' is a well-known Van Gogh one). In fact, as the play's original director, Max Stafford-Clark, explained on BBC Radio *Quote . . . Unquote* (1993), Wertenbaker took the title from an interview with Francis Bacon when he described the process of painting. He said how he started drawing a figure and how the figure became less and less important, ending up being about 'three birds alighting on a field'. 'And in the play,' Stafford-Clark added, 'Wertenbaker reverses that. The painter has fallen in love with the woman and he says, "I started off painting this picture about three birds alighting on a field but you've taken over this canvas".'

Bacon's own paintings include works with such titles as 'Figure in a Landscape', 'Three Figures in a Room' and 'Landscape with Car'.

Wesker, Arnold
English playwright (1932–)

5 *Chips with Everything.*

Title of a play about class attitudes in the RAF during National Service, first performed by the English Stage Company at the Royal Court Theatre, London, in 1962. It alludes to the belief that the working classes tend to have chips as the accompaniment to almost every dish. Indeed, the play contains the line: 'You breed babies and you eat chips with everything.' Partridge/*Catch Phrases* dates it *c* 1960 and says the phrase has 'been applied to that sort of British tourist abroad which remains hopelessly insular'.

It has a wider application than just to tourists, however, and Wesker was popularizing a phrase that had already been coined. In an essay, published as part of *Declaration* (1957), the film director Lindsay Anderson stated: 'Coming back to Britain is always something of an ordeal. It ought not to be, but it is. And you don't have to be a snob to feel it. It isn't just the food, the sauce bottles on the cafe tables, and the *chips with everything*. It isn't just saying goodbye to wine, goodbye to sunshine . . . We can come home. But the price we pay is high.'

Wesley, John
English evangelist and founder of Methodism (1703–91)

1 *Cleanliness is next to Godliness.*

Although this phrase appears in Wesley's Sermon 88 'On Dress', within quotation marks, it is without attribution. *BDPF* (1989) claims that it is to be found in the writings of Phinehas ben Yair, a rabbi. In fact, the inspiration appears to be the Talmud: 'The doctrines of religion are resolved into carefulness . . . abstemiousness into cleanliness; cleanliness into godliness.' So the saying is not from the Bible, as might be supposed.

Thomas J. Barratt, one of the fathers of modern advertising, seized upon it to promote Pears' Soap, chiefly in the UK. On a visit to the US in the 1880s, he sought a testimonial from a man of distinction. Shrinking from an approach to President Grant, he ensnared the eminent divine, Henry Ward Beecher. Beecher happily complied with Barratt's request and wrote a short text beginning: 'If cleanliness is next to godliness . . .' and received no more for his pains than Barratt's 'hearty thanks'.

2 *I look upon the whole world as my parish.*

The expression meaning 'I am knowledgeable about many peoples and places; I look upon the world as my oyster' derives from a letter Wesley wrote to the Revd James Hervey (and which was included in Welsey's diary for 11 June 1739). In it, he defended himself against charges that he had invaded the parishes of other clergymen: 'You . . . ask, How is it that I assemble Christians, who are none of my charge, to sing psalms and pray and hear the Scriptures expounded? and think it hard to justify doing this in other men's parishes, upon catholic principles . . . Seeing I have now no parish of my own, nor probably ever shall . . . Suffer me now to tell you my principles in this matter. I look upon all the world as my parish . . . This far I mean, that, in whatever part of it I am, I judge it meet, right, and my bounden duty

to declare unto all that are willing to hear the glad tidings of salvation'.

3 *God buries his workmen, but carries on his work.*

Wesley and his hymn-writing brother Charles are commemorated by a wall plaque in Westminster Abbey. This bears three sayings: 'The best of all is, God is with us' (what John Wesley 'said emphatically' the day before he died), 'I look upon all the world as my parish' (as above) and this one. Where does it come from? There is no mention of it in *Wesley Quotations* (1990) by Betty M. Jarboe, a former reference librarian at the University of Indiana.

West, Mae
American vaudeville and film actress (1893–1980)

4 *Beulah — peel me a grape!*

A catchphrase expressing dismissive unconcern, which was first uttered by West to a maid in the film *I'm No Angel* (1933). A male admirer has just stormed out on her. It has had some wider currency since then but is almost always used as a quotation.

5 *Come up and see me some time.*

West had a notable stage hit on Broadway with her play *Diamond Lil* (first performed 9 April 1928). When she appeared in the 1933 film version entitled *She Done Him Wrong*, what she said to a very young Cary Grant (playing a coy undercover policeman) was: 'You know I always did like a man in uniform. And that one fits you grand. Why don't you come up some time and see me? I'm home every evening.' As a catchphrase, the words have been rearranged to make them easier to say. And that is how W.C. Fields says them *to* Mae West in the film *My Little Chickadee* (1939). She herself took to mouthing them in the easier-to-say form.

White, Andrew D.
American academic (1832–1918)

6 *I will not permit thirty men to travel four hundred miles to agitate a bag of wind.*

White was the first President of Cornell University (1867–85). With these words he forbade Cornell's first intercollegiate football game with the University of Michigan at

Cleveland, Ohio, in 1873. Quoted by Flexner (1982).

White, Elwyn Brooks
American humorist (1899–1985)

1 I say it's spinach.

From a caption devised by White for a cartoon by Carl Rose which appeared in the issue of *The New Yorker* dated 8 December 1928. The cartoon shows a mother at table saying: 'It's broccoli, dear.' Her little girl replies: 'I say it's spinach, and I say the hell with it.' Harold Ross, then editor of the magazine, remembered that when White asked his opinion of the caption the writer was clearly uncertain that he had hit on the right idea. 'I looked at the drawing and the caption and said, "Yeh, it seems okay to me", but neither of us cracked a smile.' The use of the word 'spinach' to mean nonsense (mostly in the US) stems from this — as in the title of Irving Berlin's song 'I'll Say It's Spinach' from the revue *Face the Music* (1932) and as in the book title *Fashion is Spinach* by Elizabeth Dawes (1933).

Whitelaw, William
(later Viscount Whitelaw)
British Conservative politician (1918–   )

2 Harold Wilson is going around the country stirring up apathy.

Whitelaw is a British Conservative politician (holder of the office of Deputy Prime Minister until ill-health forced him to retire in 1988) famous for his informal sayings. The essence of these 'Whitelawisms' or 'Willieisms' is a touching naivety which may conceal a certain truth.

The most notable is his description of the then Prime Minister, Harold Wilson, during the 1970 General Election going 'around the country stirring up apathy'. On the face of it, a nonsensical remark, but conveying, oddly, just what Wilson was doing. In the *Independent* (14 July 1992), Whitelaw told Hunter Davies: 'It's a strange thing. I did say those words, but the real meaning has been lost. For a start, I meant to say "spreading apathy" not "stirring it up" . . . Wilson was so sure of victory that he was going round the country calming people down, telling everyone not to worry, leave it all to him. I was really attacking him for encouraging people not to want a change, not saying people were apathetic to him.'

3 A short, sharp, shock.

In a speech at the Conservative Party Conference (10 October 1979), Whitelaw, as Home Secretary, outlined a new method of hard treatment for young offenders. This expression had apparently been used by other Home Secretaries before him and is a quotation from W.S. Gilbert, *The Mikado* (1885):

> To sit in solemn silence in a dull, dark, dock,
> In a pestilential prison, with a life-long lock,
> Awaiting the sensation of a short, sharp, shock,
> From a cheap and chippy chopper on a big black block.

Whitman, Walt
American poet (1819–92)

4 When Lilacs Last in the Dooryard Bloom'd.

This is the title of a poem written by Whitman a few weeks after the April 1865 assassination of President Lincoln, which it commemorates. Whitman also wrote a prose description of the assassination which was included in his *Memoranda During the War* (1875) and reprinted in *The Faber Book of Reportage* (1987). This might give the impression that he was actually present but he was away from Washington D.C. at the time. In it, however, he says: 'I find myself always reminded of the great tragedy of that day by the sight and odour of these blossoms.'

5 Out of the cradle, endlessly rocking.

A silent film subtitle occurring in the epic *Intolerance* (1916), written and directed by D.W. Griffith. It accompanies a shot of Lillian Gish rocking a cradle and is repeated many times during the course of the long film. The words come from the title of a Whitman poem (1859).

6 I sing the body electric.

Lest any reader has seen the film *Fame* (1980) and wondered why it is that a pupil of the New York High School for the Performing Arts calls a rather grand composition 'I Sing the Body Electric', well, the title comes from Walt Whitman. Whitman certainly can't be blamed for the lyrics beyond that: 'I sing the body electric . . . /I celebrate the "me" yet to come/And toast to my own reunion/When I become one with the sun.'

Whittington, Robert
English teacher (c 1480–c 1530)

1 *A man for all seasons.*

Robert Bolt's title for his 1960 play about Sir Thomas More (filmed UK, 1967) has provided a popular phrase for an accomplished, adaptable, appealing person — also a cliché, whereby almost anything can be described as 'a — — for all seasons'. From Laurence Olivier, *On Acting* (1986): '[Ralph Richardson] was warm and what the public might call ordinary and, therefore, quite exceptional. That was his ability, that was his talent; he really was a man for all seasons.' Jean Rook wrote of Margaret Thatcher in the *Daily Express* (in 1982–3): 'She has proved herself not the "best man in Britain" but the Woman For All Seasons".'

Bolt found his play title in a description of More (1478–1535) by his contemporary Whittington: 'More is a man of angel's wit and singular learning; I know not his fellow. For where is the man of that gentleness, lowliness and affability? And as time requireth, a man of marvellous mirth and pastimes; and sometimes of as sad a gravity: as who say a man for all seasons.'

Whittington wrote the passage for schoolboys to put into Latin in his book *Vulgaria* (c 1521). It translates a comment on More by Erasmus — who wrote in his preface to *In Praise of Folly* (1509) that More was *'omnium horarum hominem'*.

Wilcox, Ella Wheeler
American poet (1855–1919)

2 *Laugh and the world laughs with you; Weep and you weep alone.*

Lines from Wilcox's poem 'Solitude' (1883) and, as *CODP* points out, an alteration of the sentiment expressed by Horace in his *Ars Poetica*: 'Men's faces laugh on those who laugh, and correspondingly weep on those who weep.' Another alteration is: 'weep, and you sleep alone'. In this form it was said to the architectural historian James Lees-Milne and recorded by him in his diary on 6 June 1945 (published in *Prophesying Peace*, 1977).

Wilde, Oscar
Irish playwright, poet and wit (1854–1900)

3 *I have invented an invaluable permanent invalid called Bunbury, in order that I may be able to go down into the country whenever I choose.*

Hence, the name 'Bunbury' for an imaginary person who is invoked in order to furnish an excuse not to do something. Invented by Algernon in Wilde's *The Importance of Being Earnest* (1895). The activity is accordingly known as 'Bunburying'. Bunbury is the name of an actual village in Cheshire.

4 *The dance of the seven veils.*

Salome so beguiled Herod by her seductive dancing that he gave her the head of St John the Baptist, as she requested. In neither Matthew 14:6 nor Mark 6:22 is she referred to by name — only 'as the daughter of Herodias' — nor is the nature of her dancing described. The name Salome was supplied by Josephus, the second century Jewish historian. By the time of Richard Strauss's opera *Salome* (1905), based on Wilde's one-act tragedy *Salomé* (1894), the Dance of the Seven Veils is referred to as such. One of Wilde's stage directions is '*Salomé dances the dance of the seven veils*' and one must assume, therefore, that the idea originated with him.

5 Mrs Allonby: *They say, Lady Hunstanton, that when good Americans die they go to Paris.*
Lady Hunstanton: *Indeed? And when bad Americans die, where do they go to?*
Lord Illingworth: *Oh, they go to America.*

The originator of the remark 'Good Americans, when they die, go to Paris' was Thomas Gold Appleton (1812–84). He was quoted by Oliver Wendell Homes in *The Autocrat of the Breakfast Table* (1858) and by Wilde in *The Picture of Dorian Gray* (1890). Wilde then proceeded to build upon it as above in his play *A Woman of No Importance* (1893).

6 *No good deed goes unpunished.*

This is a consciously ironic rewriting of the older expression 'No *bad* deed goes unpunished' and has been attributed to

Wilde, but remains unverified. Joe Orton recorded it in his diary for 13 June 1967: 'Very good line George [Greeves] came out with at dinner: "No good deed ever goes unpunished".' James Agate in *Ego 3* (for 25 January 1938) states: '[Isidore Leo] Pavia was in great form today: "Every good deed brings its own punishment.'

1 *Please do not shoot the pianist. He is doing his best.*

Wilde reported having seen this notice in a bar or dancing saloon in the US Rocky Mountains ('Leadville' from *Impressions of America*, c 1882–2). Hence, the film *Tirez Sur Le Pianiste* (France, 1960), translated as 'Shoot the Pianist/PianoPlayer' and Elton John's 1972 record album, 'Don't Shoot Me, I'm Only the PianoPlayer'.

2 *[Of the UK and the US] Two nations separated by a common language.*

The 'origin request' most frequently received. Sometimes the inquirer asks, 'Was it Wilde or Shaw?' The answer appears to be: both. In *The Canterville Ghost* (1887), Wilde wrote: 'We have really everything in common with America nowadays except, of course, language' However, the 1951 *Treasury of Humorous Quotations* (Esar & Bentley) quotes Shaw as saying: 'England and America are two countries separated by the same language', but without giving a source. The quote had earlier been attributed to Shaw in *Reader's Digest* (November 1942).

Much the same idea occurred to Bertrand Russell (*Saturday Evening Post*, 3 June 1944): 'It is a misfortune for Anglo-American friendship that the two countries are supposed to have a common language', and in a radio talk prepared by Dylan Thomas shortly before his death (and published after it in *The Listener*, April 1954) — European writers and scholars in America were, he said, 'up against the barrier of a common language'.

Inevitably: 'Winston Churchill said our two countries were divided by a common language' (*The Times*, 26 January 1987; *European*, 22 November 1991.)

3 *[Of G.B. Shaw] He hasn't an enemy in the world — and none of his friends like him.*

Shaw himself quoted this remark in *Sixteen Self Sketches* (1949). An early appearance

occurs in Irvin S. Cobb, *A Laugh a Day Keeps the Doctor Away* (1921), in which someone says of Shaw, 'He's in a fair way to make himself a lot of enemies.' 'Well,' replies Wilde, 'as yet he hasn't become prominent enough to have any enemies. But none of his friends like him.'

4 *Children begin by loving their parents. After a time they judge them. Rarely, if ever, do they forgive them.*

This is sometimes quoted as 'First they love us, then they judge us'. It comes from Wilde's play *A Woman of No Importance* (1893).

5 *The love that dare not speak its name.*

I.e. homosexual love, particularly between men. This expression is so much bound up with the Wilde case that it is sometimes assumed that he coined it. Not so. It was the person who had helped land him in his predicament, Lord Alfred Douglas (1870–1945), who wrote the poem 'Two Loves', which concludes with the line, 'I am the love that dare not speak its name.'

In both his trials, Wilde was asked about the poem. In the second (April–May 1895) he was asked to explain the line and gave a spontaneous explanation: 'In this century [it] is such a great affection of an elder for a younger man as there was between David and Jonathan, such as Plato made the very basis of his philosophy, and such as you find in the sonnets of Michelangelo and Shakespeare. It is that deep, spiritual affection that is as pure as it is perfect . . . It is in this century misunderstood, so much misunderstood that it may be described as the "Love that dare not speak its name", and on account of it I am placed where I am now.' Wilde's words produced an outburst of applause from the gallery which inevitably rattled the judge.

6 *Feasting with Panthers.*

At the 1981 Chichester Festival there was a play with this title, devised and directed by Peter Coe, about Wilde's trials. The phrase comes from *De Profundis* (1905), in a passage about his life before he was sent to Reading gaol for homosexual offences: 'People thought it dreadful of me to have entertained at dinner the evil things of life, and to have found pleasure in their company. But then, from the point of view through which I, as an artist in life, approach them they were delightfully suggestive and stimulating. It was like feasting with panthers; the danger was half the excitement.'

1 *I am dying, as I have lived, beyond my means.*

So said Wilde as he called for champagne when he was approaching death in 1900, but they were not his 'dying words'. He lived for another month. Similarly, his remark about the furnishings in his room, 'This wall paper'll be the death of me — one of us'll have to go' was indeed said by Wilde, but not *in extremis*. The jest was first recorded, apparently, in R.H. Sherard's *Life of Oscar Wilde* (1906).

Wilder, Billy
American film director and writer (1906–)

2 *He has Van Gogh's ear for music.*

Appearing on BBC Radio *Quote . . . Unquote* in 1977, Kenneth Williams came up with a rather good showbiz story. He quoted the above as what Orson Welles had reputedly said of the singing of Donny Osmond (then a popular young star).

In fact, Orson Welles did not say it, nor was it about Donny Osmond, but the reasons why the joke had been reascribed and redirected are instructive. It was in fact Billy Wilder, the film director, who made the original remark. He has a notably waspish wit but is, perhaps, not such a household name as Orson Welles. He lacks, too, Welles's Falstaffian stature and his, largely unearned, reputation in the public mind for having said witty things. And Wilder said it about *Cliff* Osmond, an American comedy actor who had appeared in the film director's *Kiss Me Stupid*, *The Fortune Cookie* and *The Front Page*. As far as one knows, he is not related to Donny Osmond but, apparently, he had to be replaced in the anecdote because he lacked star status. The correct attribution was given in Gary Herman, *The Book of Hollywood Quotes* (1979).

Wilhelm II
German Emperor (1859–1941)

3 *We have fought for our place in the sun and won it. Our future is on the water.*

So spoke Kaiser Wilhelm in a speech at Elbe in 1901, echoing the phrase for German colonial ambitions in East Asia, which had

been coined by Count Bernard von Bülow (1849–1929), the German Chancellor, in a speech to the Reichstag in 1897: 'In a word, we desire to throw no one into the shade, but we also demand our own place in the sun [*Platz an der Sonne*].' Subsequently, the notion was much referred to in the run-up to the First World War. Hence, probably, *A Place in the Sun* — the title given to the 1951 film of Theodore Dreiser's *An American Tragedy*. A much earlier appearance occurred in the *Pensées* of Blaise Pascal (Walker's translation, 1688): 'This Dog is mine, said those poor Children; That's my place in the Sun. This is the beginning and Image of the Usurpation of all the Earth'. The phrase is now hardly ever used in this precise sense, but simply to indicate a rightful piece of good fortune, a desirable situation, for example: 'Mr Frisk could bring Aintree punters their place in the sun' (headline from the *Independent on Sunday*, 1 April 1990).

4 *A contemptible little army.*

The greatest canard of the First World War was that Kaiser Wilhelm had described the 1914 British Expeditionary Force as 'a contemptibly little army' — referring to its size rather than to its quality. The British Press was then said to have mistranslated this so that it made the Kaiser appear to have called the B.E.F. 'a contemptibly little army'. Rank and file thereafter happily styled themselves 'The Old Contemptibles'.

The truth as revealed by Arthur Ponsonby in *Falsehood in War-Time* (1928) is that the whole episode was a propaganda ploy masterminded by the British. The B.E.F. Routine Orders for 24 September 1914 contained what was claimed to be a copy of orders issued by the German Emperor on 19 August: 'It is my Royal and Imperial command that you concentrate your energies for the immediate present upon one single purpose, and that is that you address all your skill and all the valour of my soldiers to exterminate first, the treacherous English [and] walk over General French's contemptible little army.'

The Kaiser's alleged words became widely known but an investigation during 1925 in the German archives failed to produce any evidence of the order ever having been issued. The ex-Kaiser himself said: 'On the contrary, I continually emphasized the high value of the British Army, and often, indeed, in peace-time gave warning against underestimating it.' It is now accepted that the phrase was devised at the War Office by Sir Frederick Maurice.

1 Hang the Kaiser!

During the Versailles Peace Conference and for some time afterwards, Britain's Northcliffe newspapers and others kept up this cry. Candidates at the 1918 General Election are said to have lost votes if they did not subscribe to the policy. The Allies committed themselves to try the ex-Kaiser in the Treaty of Versailles (28 June 1919), but the Government of the Netherlands refused to hand him over for trial in June 1920. Arthur Ponsonby (as above) argued that casting the Kaiser as villain of the piece had been a put-up job anyway: 'When, as months and years passed, it was discovered that no responsible person really believed, or had ever believed, in [his] personal guilt, that the cry "Hang the Kaiser" was a piece of deliberate bluff, and that when it was over and millions of innocent people had been killed, he, the criminal, the monster, the plotter and initiator of the whole catastrophe, was allowed to live comfortably and peacefully in Holland, the disillusionment to simple, uninformed people was far greater than ever realized.' The ex-Kaiser died in 1941.

Wilkes, John
English politician (1727–97)

2 Earl of Sandwich: 'Pon my soul, Wilkes, I don't know whether you'll die upon the gallows or of the pox.
Wilkes: That depends, my Lord, whether I first embrace your Lordship's principles, or your Lordship's mistresses.

A famous exchange which made an early appearance in Sir Charles Petrie, The Four Georges (1935), but is quite likely apocryphal. Where did Petrie get it from, and where had it been for the intervening two centuries?

It is frequently misapplied. George E. Allen in Presidents Who Have Known Me (1950) has it between Gladstone and Disraeli. It is difficult to imagine the circumstance in which either Disraeli or Gladstone could have made either of the remarks.

William, Captain Lloyd S.
American soldier (fl. 1918)

3 Retreat? Hell, no! We just got here!

An attributed remark, made when advised by the French to retreat, shortly after his arrival at the Western Front in the First World War. Or, specifically referring to the retreat from Belloar (5 June 1918), quoted in Partridge/Catch Phrases. Untraced and unverified. Margaret Thatcher quoted it at a Confederation of British Industry dinner in 1980.

Williams, Tennessee
American playwright (1911–83)

4 Cat On a Hot Tin Roof.

The title of Williams's play (1955; film US, 1958) derives from the (mostly US) expression 'as nervous as a cat on a hot tin roof', which derives, in turn, from the common English expression 'like a cat on hot bricks', meaning 'ill-at-ease, jumpy'. John Ray in his Collection of English Proverbs (1670–8) had: 'to go like a cat upon a hot bake stone'. An expression 'nervous as cats' appeared in Punch's Almanack for 1903. In the play, the 'cat' is Maggie, Brick's wife, 'whose frayed vivacity', wrote Kenneth Tynan, 'derives from the fact that she is sexually ignored by her husband'.

5 Blanche Dubois: I have always depended on the kindness of strangers.

Her last words in the play, A Streetcar Named Desire (1947). Blanche is about to be taken off to an institution. Hence, the frequent use of the phrase 'the kindness of strangers' as the title of: Donald Spotto's biography of Williams (1990), Bernard Braden's autobiography (1990), John Boswell's account of 'the Abandonment of Children in Western Europe from Late Antiquity to the Renaissance' (1988) and so on.

Not to be confused with the film titles The Comfort of Strangers (1990, based on Ian McEwan's novel) and The Company of Strangers (1991).

Wilson, Charles E.
American Republican politician (1890–1961)

6 What's good for General Motors is good for the country.

President Eisenhower wished to appoint Wilson as Secretary for Defense. At hearings of the Senate Committee on Armed Services in January 1953, the former President of General Motors was asked about any possible conflict of interest, as he had accepted several million dollars worth of General Motors shares. When he was asked whether he would be able to make a decision against the interests of General Motors and his stock, what Wilson in fact replied was not the above, but: 'Yes, sir, I could. I cannot conceive of one because for years I thought what was good for our country was good for General Motors, and vice versa. The difference did not exist.'

Wilson was finally persuaded to get rid of his stock, but he never quite lived down his (misquoted) remarks.

1 *[It gives] a bigger bang for a buck.*

Wilson said this of the new type of H-bomb tested at Bikini in 1954 (and is so quoted in Safire, 1978). *PDMQ* (1980) misinterprets a passage in David Halberstam, *The Best and the Brightest* (1973) and attributes the remark to President Eisenhower.

Wilson, Harold
(later Lord Wilson of Rievaulx)
English Labour Prime Minister (1916–)

2 *The school I went to in the north was a school where more than half the children in my class never had any boots or shoes to their feet. They wore clogs, because they lasted longer than shoes of comparable price.*

From a speech as President of the Board of Trade at Birmingham in July 1948. Newspaper reports wrongly suggested he had claimed that when he was at school some of his classmates had gone *barefoot*. A former teacher at the school, reacting to the abbreviated report, denied that any of Wilson's schoolmates had ever gone barefoot and soon the politician was being widely reported as having said that he himself had had to go barefoot to school. This gave rise to the jibe by Ivor Bulmer-Thomas (see 73:3). The incident was the first of many misunderstandings between Wilson and the press.

3 *The gnomes of Zurich.*

A term used to disparage the tight-fisted methods of speculators in the Swiss financial capital who questioned Britain's creditworthiness and who forced austerity measures on Wilson's Labour Government when it came to power in 1964. George Brown, Secretary of State for Economic Affairs, popularized the term in November of that year and it is often associated with him. Wilson himself had, however, used it long before in a speech to the House of Commons (12 November 1956), referring to 'all the little gnomes in Zurich and other financial centres'. In 1958, Andrew Shonfield wrote in *British Economic Policy Since the War*: 'Hence the tragedy of the autumn of 1957, when the Chancellor of the Exchequer [Peter Thorneycroft] adopted as his guide to action the slogan: I must be hard-faced enough to match the mirror-image of an imaginary hard-faced little man in Zurich. It is tough on the Swiss that William Tell should be displaced in English folklore by this new image of a gnome in a bank at the end of a telephone line.'

4 *I have always deprecated — perhaps rightly, perhaps wrongly — in crisis after crisis, appeals to the Dunkirk spirit as an answer to our problems because what is required in our economic situation is not a brief period of inspired improvisation, work and sacrifice, such as we had under the leadership of the Rt Hon. Member for Woodford [Winston Churchill], but a very long, hard prolonged period of reorganization and redirection. It is the long haul, not the inspired spirit that we need.*

Wilson said this in the House of Commons on 26 July 1961. No sooner had he become Prime Minister than he said in a 'hastily compiled' speech to the Labour Party Conference on 12 December 1964: 'I believe that the spirit of Dunkirk will once again carry us through to success'. Neatly pointed out by Paul Foot in *The Politics of Harold Wilson* (1968).

5 *The white heat of the technological revolution.*

What Wilson actually told the Labour Party Conference in Scarborough on 1 October 1963 was: 'We are redefining and we are restating our socialism in terms of the scientific revolution . . . the Britain that is going to be forged in the white heat of this revolution will be no place for restrictive practices or outdated methods on either side of industry.'

1 *What I think we are going to need is something like what President Kennedy had when he came in after years of stagnation in the United States. He had a programme of a hundred days — a hundred days of of dynamic action.*

From a Labour Party political broadcast (15 July 1964). In fact, Kennedy had specifically ruled out a 'hundred days', saying in his Inaugural Address that his programmes could not be carried out even in a thousand days (compare KENNEDY 200:3).

2 *A week is a long time in politics.*

In 1977 I asked the recently retired Prime Minister when he had first uttered his most-quoted dictum. Uncharacteristically, he was unable to remember. For someone who used to be able to cite the column numbers of *Hansard* in which his speeches appeared, this was a curious lapse. Inquiries among political journalists led to the conclusion that in its present form the phrase was probably first uttered at a meeting between Wilson and the Parliamentary lobby in the wake of the sterling crisis shortly after he first took office as Prime Minister in 1964. However, Robert Carvel, then of the London *Evening Standard*, recalled Wilson at a Labour Party Conference in 1960 saying, 'Forty-eight hours is a long time in politics'.

Apart from dating, there has been some dispute as to what precisely the dictum means. Most would take it to be along the lines of, 'Just give a problem time and it will solve itself', 'What a difference a day makes', 'Wait and see', and 'Don't panic, it'll all blow over'. But when I consulted Wilson in 1977, he challenged the accepted interpretation. 'It does not mean I'm living from day to day,' he said. 'It was intended as a prescription for long-term strategic thinking and planning, ignoring the day-to-day issues and pressures which may hit the headlines but which must not be allowed to get out of focus while longer term policies are taking effect.'

The phrase caught on: from the late 1980s, Channel Four TV has carried a weekly review with the title *A Week in Politics*, clearly alluding to Wilson's phrase. From the *Independent* (19 May 1989), on the outgoing editor of the TV programme *Forty Minutes*: 'His successor will have to work hard, though, to keep the for-

mula fresh. 2,400 seconds is a long time in television.'

When Wilson took his peerage, he chose as his motto: '*Tempus Rerum Imperator*' — 'timing is everything'.

3 *Weeks rather than months.*

Now an idiom meaning 'sooner rather than later', this echoes Wilson's use of the phrase at the Commonwealth Prime Ministers' Conference (12 January 1966). Wilson had first used it in an unreported speech on that day and it was later included in the final communiqué: 'In this connection [the use of military force in Rhodesia] the Prime Ministers noted the statement by the British Prime Minister that on the expert advice available to him, the cumulative effect of the economic and finanical sanctions [against Rhodesia] might well bring the rebellion to an end within a matter of weeks rather than months'. As was to be discovered, this was a little wide of the mark.

4 *It is difficult for us to appreciate the pressures which are put on men I know to be realistic and responsible, not only in their executive capacity but in the highly organized strike committees in the ports, by this* tightly knit group of politically motivated men *who, as the last General Election showed, utterly failed to secure acceptance of their views by the British electorate, but who are now determined to exercise backstage pressures, forcing great hardship on the members of the union and their families, and endangering the security of the industry and the economic welfare of the nation.*

Wilson said this to the House of Commons on 22 June 1966, during the sixth week of a national seamen's strike. He later explained: 'I did not use the word "Communist", though no one in the House or in the press . . . had any doubts whom I had in mind.' Compare this with what his namesake Woodrow in the US had said earlier about Senate isolationists who filibustered a bill to allow the arming of merchant vessels (4 March 1917): 'A little group of wilful men representing no opinion but their own, has rendered the great government of the United States helpless and contemptible.'

1 *From now on the pound abroad is worth 14 per cent or so less in terms of other currencies. That doesn't mean, of course, that the pound here in Britain, in your pocket or purse or in your bank, has been devalued.*

After a devaluation of the pound, Wilson gave a broadcast address on 19 November 1967. In *The Labour Government 1964–70* (1971), he said this was the only part of the Treasury draft speech he had incorporated in his final version — 'Though I was cautioned by a civil service adviser, I was reinforced by the words of one of my own staff whose maiden aunt had telephoned to express concern that her Post Office Savings Bank holdings had been slashed by three shillings in the pound.'

The following evening, the Opposition leader, Edward Heath, quoted Wilson's reference to the 'pound in your pocket' as a misleading pledge that prices would not rise as a result of devaluation. The charge was taken up by many others.

2 *Get your tanks off my lawn, Hughie.*

According to Peter Jenkins, *The Battle of Downing Street* (1970), Wilson made this remark to Hugh Scanlon, the trade union leader, at Chequers, the prime ministerial residence, in June 1969 during the battle between the Government and the trade unions over reform. Scanlon was head of Britain's second largest union, the engineers'. Jenkins reports that Wilson was enraged at the intransigence and arrogance of Scanlon and Jack Jones, another union leader. In an exchange of views, Scanlon said, 'Prime Minister, we don't want you to become another Ramsay Macdonald' (that is, betraying the Labour movement). Wilson replied, 'I have no intention of becoming another Ramsay Macdonald. Nor do I intend to become another Dubček. Get your tanks off my lawn, Hughie!' As such, this is the first recorded use of a political metaphor for 'back off, don't threaten me'. Subsequently it has entered the lexicon of British politics and journalism. From the *Financial Times* (6 November 1982) on the Harrods/Lonrho dispute: 'If this is your idea of a game, please play somewhere else in the future . . . To make it absolutely clear: get your tanks off my lawn.' From the *Observer* (14 April 1991): 'It is true, of course, that the Home Secretary does not park his tanks on [BBC Director-General] Checkland's lawn . . . That is not the British way.' From a speech made by John Major to the Conservative Party Conference, 8 October 1993: 'Let me say to some of our European colleagues, "You're playing with fire [on GATT world free trade talks], or to put it more bluntly, "Get your tractors off our lawn".'

3 *You can't guarantee being born a Lord. It is possible — you've shown it — to be born a gentleman.*

When President Nixon came to dinner with Wilson at Downing Street in 1969, the first year of his Presidency, he had to sit down at table with John Freeman, the British Ambassador to Washington. So far Nixon had managed to ignore the man who had once written of him as 'a man of no principle whatsoever except a willingness to sacrifice everything in the cause of Dick Nixon'. As it turned out, Nixon proposed a toast and graciously said he hoped all that was behind them. As Henry Kissinger recorded in his *Memoirs* (1979), Wilson scribbled the above note to Nixon on a menu card.

Compare what King James I is reputed to have said: 'I can make a Lord, but only God Almighty can make a gentleman.'

4 *I see myself as the big fat spider in the corner of the room. Sometimes I speak when I'm asleep. You should both listen. Occasionally when we meet I might tell you to go to the Charing Cross Road and kick a blind man standing on the corner. That blind man may tell you something, lead you somewhere.*

A bizarre picture of himself that Wilson gave to two BBC reporters, Barrie Penrose and Roger Courtior, in the mid-1970s. He was convinced that there was a massive South African plot afoot to discredit leading British politicians and summoned the reporters to help them expose it. The remark was included in *The Pencourt File* (1978).

Wilson, Woodrow
American Democratic 28th President (1856–1924)

5 *The world must be made safe for democracy.*

In 1917, Wilson took the US into the First World War. His address to Congress on

2 April asking for a declaration of war included the words: 'The world must be made safe for democracy. Its peace must be planted upon trusted foundations of political liberty.' The words might never have been remembered had not Senator John Sharp Williams of Mississipi started clapping and continued until everyone joined in. In 1937, James Harvey Robinson commented: 'With supreme irony, the war to "Make the world safe for democracy" ended by leaving democracy more unsafe in the world than at any time since the collapse of the revolutions of 1848.'

Windsor, Duchess of
(formerly Mrs Wallis Simpson)
American-born wife of the Duke of Windsor (1896–1986)

1 *I married him for better or worse, but not for lunch.*

This rather pleasing play on the words from the Anglican marriage service was reported in an article by Ludovic Kennedy in the *Observer* (2 December 1979), based on *The Windsor Story* by J. Bryan III and Charles J.V. Murphy, in the context: '[The Duke of Windsor] usually lunched alone on a salad while the duchess went out ("I married the Duke for better or worse but not for lunch").'

But Partridge/*Catch Phrases* (1977) has it listed as an 'Australian catchphrase used by a woman whose husband has retired, works at home or comes home for his midday meal', dating it from the 1940s and 'familiar to Britons since at least the latish 1960s'.

Wister, Owen
American writer (1860–1938)

2 *When you call me that, smile.*

This is how the phrase is usually remembered and how it appears in Chap. 2 of Wister's novel, *The Virginian* (1902): 'Therefore Trampas spoke. "You bet, you son-of-a—". The Virginian's pistol came out, and . . . he issued his orders to the man Trampas:— "When you call me that, smile!"'

However, in the film version (1929) — based on the play and the novel by Wister — what Gary Cooper says, standing up to Walter Huston, is: 'If you want to call me that, smile'. (*Halliwell's Film Guide*, 1987, has the cliché as 'Smile when you say that'.)

Wolfe, Tom
American novelist and writer (1931–   )

3 *The Right Stuff.*

Referring to the qualities needed by test-pilots and would-be astronauts in the early years of the US space programme, this was the title of Wolfe's 1979 book (filmed US, 1983). But the 'right (sort of) stuff' had been applied much earlier to qualities of manly virtue, of good officer material and even of good cannon fodder. Partridge/*Slang* has an example from the 1880s. In this sense, the phrase was used by Ian Hay as the title of a novel — 'some episodes in the career of a North Briton' — in 1908.

It is now a handy journalistic device. An *Independent* headline over a story about the ballet *Ondine* (13 May 1988) was, 'The Sprite Stuff'; the same month, the London *Magazine* had 'The Right Stuff' as the title of an article on furnishing fabrics; in 1989, there was an ITV book programme called *The Write Stuff*.

It has also been used as an expression for alcohol (compare 'the hard stuff').

4 *The Bonfire of the Vanities.*

The title of Wolfe's 1987 novel is derived from Savonarola's 'burning of the vanities' in Florence, 1497. The religious reformer — 'the puritan of Catholicism' — enacted various laws for the restraint of vice and folly. Gambling was prohibited and Savonarola's followers helped people burn their costly ornaments and extravagant clothes.

5 *A liberal is a conservative who has been arrested.*

In two places in *The Bonfire of the Vanities*, Wolfe quotes this, but is clearly referring to an established saying. In the Fall 1993 issue of the American *Policy Review*, James Q. Wilson is credited with a similar observation: 'There aren't any liberals left in New York. They've all been mugged.'

Wolsey, Thomas
English prelate (c 1475–1530)

6 *I see the matter against me how it is framed. But if I had served God as diligently as I have done the King, he would not have given me over in my grey hairs.*

Cardinal Wolsey's remark was made to Sir William Kingston, Constable of the Tower of London, when Wolsey was under arrest for high treason, in November 1530. These were not his actual 'last words', as is sometimes suggested, though they were spoken on his deathbed. His last words appear to have been: 'Master Kingston, farewell. My time draweth on fast. Forget not what I have sent and charged you withal. For when I am dead you shall, peradventure, understand my words better.' Wolsey was not executed but died in Leicester on his way to the Tower. Shakespeare in *Henry VIII* (III.ii.455) takes the report of Wolsey's death in Raphael Holinshed's *Chronicle* (1587) — which is more or less as in the first paragraph above — and comes up with slightly different wording for Wolsey's exit from the play. To Cromwell, his servant, he says:

> Had I but serv'd my God with half the zeal
> I serv'd my king, he would not in mine age
> Have left me naked to mine enemies . . .
> Farewell
> The hopes of court, my hopes in heaven do dwell.

Wolstenholme, Kenneth
English sports commentator (1920–)

1 They think it's all over . . . It is now!

Commentating for BBC Television on the World Cup Final at Wembley between England and West Germany on 30 July 1966, Wolstenholme ad-libbed what has come to be regarded as the 'most famous quote in British sport'. After a disputed third goal, the England team was 3–2 in the lead as the game continued in extra time. 'Some people are on the pitch,' Wolstenholme began before the final whistle, 'They think it's all over.' Then Geoff Hurst scored England's fourth goal (and his third) and decisively won the game. So that was why Wolstenholme added, 'It is now!'

It took until the 1990s for the phrase really to catch on. By 1992, a jokey BBC Radio sports quiz had the title *They Think It's All Over*. Some accounts have the commentator saying, '*Well*, it is now. It's four.' According to the *Guardian* (30 July 1991), Wolstenholme himself used to complain if the 'well' was omitted but then a replay of his commentary showed that he had not said the word after all.

Wood, Mrs Henry
English novelist (1814–87)

2 Dead! . . . and never called me mother!

This line is recalled as typical of the three-volume sentimental Victorian novel, yet nowhere does it appear in Wood's *East Lynne* (1861) where it is supposed to. Nevertheless, it was inserted in one of the numerous stage versions of the novel (that by T.A. Palmer in 1874) which were made between publication and the end of the century. Act III has, 'Dead, dead, dead! and he never knew me, never called me mother!' Mrs Wood's obituary writer noted in 1887: 'At present, there are three dramatic versions of *East Lynne* nightly presented in various parts of the world. Had the author been granted even a small percentage on the returns she would have been a rich woman . . . The adapters of *East Lynne* grew rich and Mrs Henry Wood was kept out of their calculations.' Thus did *East Lynne* become 'a synonym for bad theatrical melodrama' (Colin Shindler, *The Listener*, 23–30 December 1982).

The line arises in a scene when an errant but penitent mother who has returned to *East Lynne*, her former home, in the guise of a governess, has to watch the slow death of her eight-year-old son ('Little Willie') unable to reveal her true identity. Whether the line was carried through to any of the various film versions of the tale, I do not know, but expect so.

Woodrooffe, Tommy
English radio commentator (1899–1978)

3 The Fleet's lit up.

Woodrooffe committed the most famous British broadcasting boob on the night of 20 May 1937. He had been due to give a fifteen-minute BBC radio description of the illumination of the Fleet on the night of the Coronation Naval Review at Spithead. What he actually said, in a commentary that was faded out after less than four minutes, began like this: 'At the present, the whole Fleet's lit up. When I say "lit up", I mean lit up by fairy lamps. We've forgotten the whole Royal Review. We've forgotten the whole Royal Review. The whole thing is lit up by fairy lamps. It's fantastic. It isn't the Fleet at all. It's just . . . it's fairyland. The whole Fleet is in fairyland.'

He concluded: 'I was talking to you in the middle of this damn — in the middle of this

361

Fleet. And what's happened is the Fleet's gone, disappeared and gone. We had a hundred, two hundred, warships all around us a second ago and now they've gone. At a signal by the morse code — at a signal by the Fleet flagship which I'm in now — they've gone . . . they've disappeared. There's nothing between us and heaven. There's nothing at all.' (Text checked against the BBC recording.)

Eventually, an announcer said: 'The broadcast from Spithead is now at an end. It is eleven minutes to eleven, and we will take you back to the broadcast from the Carlton Hotel Dance Band.' That familiar BBC figure, A. Spokesman, commented later: 'We regret that the commentary was unsatisfactory and for that reason it was curtailed.' Naturally, many listeners concluded that Woodrooffe himself had been 'lit up' as the result of too much hospitality from his shipmates on board HMS *Nelson*. But he denied this: 'I had a kind of nervous blackout. I had been working too hard and my mind just went blank.' He told the *News Chronicle*: 'I was so overcome by the occasion that I literally burst into tears . . . I found I could say no more.'

The phrase 'The fleet's lit up' became so famous that it was used as the title of a 'musical frolic' at the London Hippodrome in 1938 and of a song by Vivian Ellis within that show.

The *ODQ* (1979) misspells Woodrooffe's surname, states that he said, 'The Fleet *is all* lit up', which he did not, and describes the occasion as his 'first live outside broadcast', which it most certainly was not. The 1992 edition repeats the first and last of these errors.

Woollcott, Alexander
American writer (1887–1943)

1 *For all his reputation [he] is not a bounder. He is every other inch a gentleman.*

R.E. Drennan in *Wit's End* (1973) quotes Woollcott as having said this of Michael Arlen. The same remark has also been attributed to Rebecca West (by Ted Morgan in *Somerset Maugham*, 1980) about the same subject. *Every Other Inch a Lady* was the title of the autobiography (1973) of Beatrice Lillie, the actress who was Lady Peel in private life. The basic expression 'every inch a gentleman' occurs, for example, in William Thackeray, *Pendennis*, Chap. 54

(1848–50), and Shakespeare, *King Lear* (IV.vi.107) has 'Every inch a king'.

2 *All the things I really like to do are either illegal, immoral, or fattening.*

So Woollcott wrote in *The Knock at the Stage Door* (1933). Hence, presumably, the song, 'It's Illegal, It's Immoral Or It Makes You Fat' by Griffin, Hecht and Bruce, and popularized in the UK by the Beverley Sisters (1950s).

Wordsworth, Christopher
British journalist and critic (*fl.* 1977)

3 Travels *by Edward Heath is a reminder that* Morning Cloud's *skipper is no stranger to platitude and longitude.*

From a book review in the *Observer* (18 December 1977). The conjunction had been made earlier by Christopher Fry in his play *The Lady's Not For Burning* (1949): 'Where in this small-talking world can I find/A longitude with no platitude?'

Wordsworth, William
English poet (1770–1850)

4 *I wander'd lonely as a cloud*
That floats on high o'er vales and
hills.
When all at once I saw a crowd,
A host, of golden daffodills;
Beside the lake, beneath the trees,
Fluttering and dancing in the breeze.

From 'I wandered lonely as a cloud', also known as 'The Daffodils' (1815). In her journal for 15 April 1802, the poet's sister Dorothy described a windy walk she had taken with him from Eusemere during which they had encountered a huge number of daffodils. She wrote: 'We saw that there was a long belt of them along the shore, about the breadth of a country turnpike road. I never saw daffodils so beautiful. They grew among the mossy stones about and about them; some rested their heads upon these stones as on a pillow for weariness; and the rest tossed and reeled and danced, and seemed as if they verily laughed with the wind, that blew upon them over the lake; they looked so gay, ever glancing, ever changing.'

It is interesting that William's poem makes direct use of phrases from this description, though always enhancing them. Dorothy's 'a long belt' becomes 'a crowd, a host'; her 'tossed and reeled and danced' becomes 'tossing their heads in sprightly dance'. This is not to suggest that William in any way 'stole' his ideas from Dorothy's diary. He recognized how often his poems originated in her own vivid experiences:

She gave me eyes, she gave me ears;
And humble cares, and delicate fears.

But she jotted down descriptions which more than once were used by William as a reminder of experiences. Colette Clark in her comparison of the poems with the journal, *Home at Grasmere* (1960), asks: 'Was it Dorothy or William who first spoke the phrases which seem so spontaneous in the Journal and then reappear in the poems? Sometimes we know it to be Dorothy . . . Such a lively chronicle close at hand would have been irresistible to any poet, and William seems to have used it again and again. It was not until two years after that heavenly walk from Eusemere that he wrote "The Daffodils", but there is no doubt that he first re-read Dorothy's account and tried to recapture the joy and delight of her description in his own poem.'

Wotton, Sir Henry
English diplomat and poet (1568–1639)

1 *An ambassador is . . . sent to lie abroad for . . . his country.*

Wotton was England's envoy to Venice in the reign of King James I. His punning view of the diplomat's calling very nearly cost him his job. As Izaak Walton recounted in his *Life*, Wotton had managed to offend a Roman Catholic controversialist called Gasper Scioppius. In 1611 Scioppius produced a book called *Ecclesiasticus*, which abused James I and related an anecdote concerning Wotton: on his way out to Italy in 1604, Wotton had stayed at Augsburg where a merchant, Christoper Fleckmore, invited him to inscribe his name in an album. Wotton wrote: '*Legatus est vir bonus peregre missus ad mentiendum Reipublicae causa*' — 'which he would have been content should have been thus Englished: An ambassador is an honest man, sent to lie abroad for the good of his country.' Scoppius, on the basis of this joke, accused James I of sending a confessed liar to represent him abroad.

According to the *Dictionary of National Biography*, 'Wotton's chances of preferment were ruined by the king's discovery of the contemptuous definition of an ambassador's function . . . James invited explanations of the indiscreet jest. Wotton told the king that the affair was "a merriment," but he was warned to take it seriously, and he deemed it prudent to prepare two apologies.'

James said that one of these 'sufficiently commuted for a greater offence', but the joke had done its damage, and, although Wotton was later to be given further diplomatic work and become Provost of Eton, he continued to suffer for it.

2 Hic jacet hujus sententiae primus author disputandi pruritus, ecclesiarium scabies. Nomen alias quaere.

'Here lies the first author of the sentence: The Itch of Disputation will prove the Scab [or Leprosy] of the Churches. Inquire his name elsewhere.' Wotton left instructions that his epitaph should contain this wording. The 'sentence' occurs in his 'Panegyric to King Charles'. A.W. Ward in *Sir Henry Wotton* (1898) comments: 'What I take it he meant to imply by his farewell aphorism was the principle that in the controversies about the non-essentials is to be found the bane of the religious life which it is the one Divine purpose of the Churches to advance.' Accordingly, the epitaph (in Latin, as above) is on his grave, now to be found on one of the stones leading into the Choir of Eton College Chapel. Wotton was Provost of Eton at his death.

Wren, Sir Christopher
English architect (1632–1723)

3 *LECTOR, SI MONUMENTUM REQUIRIS, CIRCUMSPICE . . .*

'Reader, if you seek his monument, look around': the last two lines of Wren's epitaph on a wall tablet by his burial place in the crypt of St Paul's Cathedral, London, which he designed. His actual gravestone has a factual description. The famous epitaph was reputedly composed by his son.

Horace Smith (1779–1849) commented drily that it would 'be equally applicable to a physician buried in a churchyard'.

Wright, Lawrence
(also wrote as Horatio Nicholls)
English music publisher and songwriter (1888–1964)

4 *Are we downhearted? — no!*

A phrase connected with the early stages of the First World War had political origins before that. Joseph Chamberlain (1838–1814) said in a 1906 speech: 'We are not downhearted. The only trouble is, we cannot understand what is happening to our neighbours.' The day after he was defeated as candidate in the Stepney Borough Council election of 1909, Clement Attlee, the future Prime Minister, was greeted by a colleague with the cry, 'Are we downhearted?' (He replied, 'Of course, we are.')

On 18 August 1914, the *Daily Mail* reported: 'For two days the finest troops England has ever sent across the sea have been marching through the narrow streets of old Boulogne in solid colums of khaki . . . waving as they say that new slogan of Englishmen: "Are we downhearted? . . . Nooooo!" "Shall we win? . . . Yessss!"' Wright merely incorporated the phrase in a song.

1 *Be British! was the cry as the ship went down,*
Ev'ry man was steady at his post,
Captain and crew, when they knew the worst:
Saving the women and children first,
Be British! was the cry to ev'ry one,
And though fate had prov'd unkind
When your country to you pleaded,
You gave freely what was needed,
To those they left behind.

'Be British' was written and composed by Wright with Paul Pelham in 1912 to commemorate the sinking of the *Titanic*. It is in march tempo and, if nothing else, demonstrates that it was believed very soon after the event that Commander Smith had said 'Be British' (see 312:7).

Wright, Peter
British intelligence officer (1916–   )

2 *I have loved justice and hated iniquity: therefore I die in exile.*

Wright was author of a book on the security services — *Spycatcher* — which the British Government tried and failed to ban in 1986. Wright had already gone to live in Australia, where he quoted this remark, made originally by Hildebrand, Pope Gregory VII, on his deathbed in May 1085. Hildebrand died at Salerno after a long struggle with the Holy Roman Emperor, Henry IV, over the rival claims of spiritual and temporal powers.

Wyndham, George
English politician (1863–1913)

3 *Over the construction of Dreadnoughts . . . What the people said was, 'We want eight, and we won't wait.'*

From a speech in Wigan (27 March 1909). The policy of the Liberal Government had reduced defence expenditure to pay for the introduction of social services and the Welfare State. Construction of only eight new Dreadnought destroyers was to be spread over two years but news of the threatening German shipbuilding programme caused a popular outcry, encapsulated in the slogan. As is clear, Wyndham (who had briefly been in the Conservative Cabinet in 1902) was merely quoting it, not coining it.

X, Y, Z

Xenophon
Greek historian (c 428–c 354BC)

1 Thalatta, thalatta *[the sea, the sea]*.

In *Anabasis* (IV.vii.24) Xenophon tells how Greek mercenaries retreated to the Black Sea following their defeat in battle (401BC). When they reached it, the soldiers gave this cry. Hence, *The Sea, The Sea* — the title of a novel (1978) by Iris Murdoch.

The Chevalier Sigmund Neukomm (*d* 1858) also wrote a song with this title, which was parodied in H.J. Byron's version of *Aladdin*, with reference to tea-clippers, in 1861:

The Tea! The Tea!
Refreshing Tea.
The green, the fresh, the ever free
From all impurity.

Yeames, W.F.
British painter (1835–1918)

2 *And When Did You Last See Your Father?*

It was in 1878 that Yeames first exhibited the painting with this title at the Royal Academy; the original is now in the Walker Art Gallery, Liverpool. There can be few paintings where the title is as important as (and as well known as) the actual picture. This one was even turned into a tableau at Madame Tussaud's where it remained until 1989. In Roy Strong's book *And When Did You Last See Your Father? — The Victorian Painter and British History* (1978), he notes: 'The child . . . stands on a footstool about to answer an inquiry made by the Puritan who leans across the table towards him . . . To the left the ladies of the house . . . cling to each other in tearful emotion. They,

it is clear, have not answered the dreaded question.'

All Yeames himself recalled of the origin of the painting was this: 'I had, at the time I painted the picture, living in my house a nephew of an innocent and truthful disposition, and it occurred to me to represent him in a situation where the child's outspokenness and unconsciousness would lead to disastrous consequences, and a scene in a country house occupied by the Puritans during the Rebellion in England suited my purpose.'

The title of the painting is often remembered wrongly as 'When Did You . . . ?' but has become a kind of joke catchphrase, sometimes used nudgingly, and often allusively — as in the title of Christopher Hampton's 1964 play *When Did You Last See My Mother?* and the 1986 farce by Ray Galton and John Antrobus, *When Did You Last See Your . . . Trousers?*

Yeats, W.B.
Irish poet (1865–1939)

3 *The Celtic twilight.*

This phrase came to be used (by others) to describe the atmosphere and preoccupations of Celtic Britain — particularly in the sense that they were on the way out (compare the phrase 'twilight of empire'). It derives from the title of a collection of stories by Yeats on Celtic themes (1893).

4 *Things fall apart; the centre cannot
   hold;*
*Mere anarchy is loosed upon the
   world . . .*
*The best lack all conviction, while the
   worst
Are full of passionate intensity.*

Of all the quotations used by and about politicians, the most common by far in recent years in Britain is this of lines from Yeats's 'The Second Coming' (1921). The trend was probably started by Kenneth Clark, the art historian, at the conclusion of his TV series *Civilisation: a Personal View* (1969). Roy Jenkins in his BBC TV Dimbleby Lecture of 23 November 1979 (which pointed towards the setting up of the centrist Social Democratic Party) followed suit. In *The Listener* (14 December 1979), Professor Bernard Crick threatened to horsewhip the next politician who quoted the poem. On the very next page, Neil Kinnock (later to become Labour Party leader) could be found doing so. The threat has had no lasting effect, either.

1 *Stop babbling, man! How much?*

On being told over the telephone that he had been awarded the Nobel Prize for Literature in 1923. Untraced and unverified.

2 *Under bare Ben Bulben's head*
  In Drumcliff churchyard Yeats is
  laid . . .
On limestone quarried near the spot
By his command these words are cut:

Cast a cold eye
On life, on death.
Horseman, pass by!

Yeats's epitaph is to be found on his grave in Drumcliff churchyard, Co. Sligo, Ireland, and was written by himself. The wording and the proposed place of burial were described in 'Under Ben Bulben', written on 4 September 1938, a few months before the poet's death. (Ben Bulben is the mountain above Drumcliff.) Yeats died in France and because of the Second World War his remains were not brought back for burial at the designated spot until 1948.

Young, George W.
English poet (1846–1919)

3 *Your lips, on my own, when they*
  printed 'Farewell',
Had never been soiled by the
  'beverage of hell';
But they come to me now with the
  bacchanal sign,
And the lips that touch liquor must
  never be mine.

A temperance poem, written *c* 1870, which became a favourite for recitation. A similar verse is attributed to Harriet Glazebrook and dated 1874. Mencken (1942) has it as anonymous, *c* 1880, and first published in *Standard Recitations* (1884).

Zola, Émile
French novelist (1840–1902)

4 *J'accuse.*

See CLEMENCEAU 101:1.

Index

In the Index quotations are represented in capsule form under keyword headings drawn from the one or two main or most significant words in the quotation. The keywords may also reflect *mis*quotations.

anguish: howls of a., 173:6
animals: all a. are equal, 258:4
annus horribilis, 134:4
another country, 317:3
answer is in the plural, 223:4
  soft a. turneth away wrath, 52:7
ant: with patience elephant screws a., 29:3
antic: dance an a. hay, 235:3
anything can go wrong, 15:3
apathy: stirring up a., 352:2
aphrodisiac: power is greatest a., 250:3
  power is ultimate a., 205:9
  writer is an a., 46:1
appalling frankness, 40:2
appeal: last a. to reason, 181:5
appealing: so different so a., 169:5
appetite: big a. at one end, 276:4
apple: eat a. through tennis racquet, 109:1
approaches every subject with open mouth,
  321:3
après nous le déluge, 265:3
April is cruellest month, 133:2
Arabs: fold their tents like the A., 219:2
  Jews are A. on horseback, 123:1
Arcadia: et in A. ego, 11:4
archaeologist is the best husband, 92:2
are you now or have you ever been, 31:1
armed conflict, 128:3
arms: I sing of a. and the man, 341:6
army: contemptible little a., 355:4
a-roving: go no more a., 80:1
arrest several of these vicars, 204:1
arrive: better than to a., 321:7
arrogance of power, 149:2
ars longa vita brevis, 180:4
arse: kick him up the a. Alfred, 98:3
art: clever but is it a., 205:3
  only interested in a., 308:2
  remarkable example of modern a., 99:1
Arthur: in A.'s bosom, 300:7
  speak for England A., 4:3
artists in august occasions, 148:4
arts are to Britain as sunshine to Spain, 279:2
ashes of Napoleon Bonaparte, 348:3
ask not what your country can do for you,
  200:4
asphalt jungle, 75:2
aspirations: poverty of their a., 312:3
Asquith, H.H., epitaph, 242:1
ass: each actor on his a., 298:3
  law is an a., 121:2
assassination: despotism tempered by a., 247:3
astonish me, 119:1
astonished: you are a., 193:4
ate a hearty breakfast, 10:1
Atlantic: cheaper to lower A., 162:7
attempt great things for God, 6:5
attitudes: Anglo-Saxon a., 87:5
Attlee, Clement, taxi, 97:6
auld lang syne, 75:5
aunt Edna, 275:2
Australia: advance A. fair, 226:1
autumn: mists of the a. morning, 232:2
avenged: south is a., 66:8
awareness: more positive signs of a., 64:1
awful place, 293:4
awkward squad, 76:4

B
babbled: a-b. of green fields, 300:8
baby: dream on b., 10:5
  is you ain't my b., 195:5
  with loud voice at one end, 276:4
Babylon: by waters of B., 66:5
Bach: now B. is decomposing, 158:3
back to the drawing board, 33:1
  to square one, 6:6
back-rooms: boys in the b., 43:3
backs to the wall, 169:1
backwards: only understood b., 203:2
badly: thing worth doing b., 91:4
baggage: Hannah and the rest of b., 286:3
baker: owl was b.'s daughter, 297:4
balance of power, 345:2
  redress b. of the old, 85:3
bald: go up thou b. head, 51:2
  men fighting over comb, 66:9
Balfour: Mr B.'s poodle, 156:1
ball: Hitler has only got one b., 15:1
Balliol men distinguished from lesser souls, 33:4
baloney: it's still b., 312:6
banality of evil, 30:6
banana: have a b., 88:5
bananas: yes we have no b., 103:4
bang: bigger b. for a buck, 357:1
  goes sixpence, 270:3
  kiss kiss b. b., 197:1
bank: cried all the way to the b., 214:5
banner with a strange device, 219:1
Barabbas: now B. was a publisher, 79:5
  now B. was a robber, 58:3
barbarians at the gates, 157:1
barbaric but it's home, 122:1
barbarism to degeneration, 101:3
bark: doesn't bark and knows secrets of the sea,
  252:3
Basingstoke: like B., 158:1
baskets: farewell b., 274:4
bastard: knocked the b. off, 179:4
bat: thin b.'s squeak of sexuality, 346:4
bath: female llama surprised in b., 96:1
  whether needed or not, 146:2
baton of field-marshal in knapsack, 249:4
battalions: God on side of big b., 343:2
battle: France has lost a b., 116:4
  of Britain about to begin, 94:3
  sent language into b., 200:6
battles: mother of b., 185:5
BBC not impartial, 165:6
be: to b. or not to b., 299:9
  prepared, 38:3
beach: life's a b., 19:1
beaches: fight on the b., 94:1
beam me up Scotty, 283:1
bear: exit pursued by b., 305:7
bear-like must stand the course, 303:1
beard: singeing king of Spain's b., 125:1
beast: fit night out for man nor b., 139:5
beat generation, 202:2
beautiful people, 343:4
  small is b., 293:1
beauty: England home and b., 67:4
because it's there, 232:3
bed: and so to b., 262:2
  never go to b. with woman, 4:1

should have stayed in b., 188:3
went to b. with man, 92:4
bedpost: on the b. overnight, 285:6
bedroom: cold of English b., 249:1
beds: double b. versus single, 17:1
bedtime: would it were b., 300:5
beef: where's the b., 243:6
been there done that, 82:2
Beethoven: sonata in B by B., 119:5
before: I have been here b., 346:3
beginning: end of the b., 95:2
  in my b. is my end, 133:7
behind every great man, 7:1
  get thee b. me, 57:2
  it will be b. me, 279:3
behold a pale horse, 60:1
believe: if you b. that, 349:5
  it or not, 281:5
  only half what you see, 7:2
bell, book and candle, 7:3
  for whom the b. tolls, 124:1
Bella's knees were made to bend, 192:1
Bellman and True, 164:3
bells of hell go ting, 44:4
benefit: for the b. of Mr Kite, 212:1
benevolent: I believe in b. dictatorships, 68:4
benign neglect, 246:4
Berkeley: nightingale in B. Square, 238:3
Berliner: Ich bin ein B., 201:1
Bertie, 341:1
Besonian: under which king, B., 300:6
best and the brightest, 169:2
  friends won't tell you, 12:1
  he is doing his b., 354:1
  only mediocre always at b., 22:2
  prime minister we have, 78:3
  swordsman in all France, 7:4
  why not the b., 87:6
best-regulated: accidents happen in b. families,
  119:4
betray: guts to b. my country, 143:6
better: far far b. thing, 121:5
  getting b. and b., 107:5
  he is not b. he is much the same, 36:3
  hole, 38:5
  the chill blast of winter, 8:1
  things were done b., 202:1
  with Christ which is b., 59:1
Beulah peel me a grape, 351:4
beware Greeks bearing gifts, 342:3
bias against understanding, 61:3
Bible: Africans had the B., 201:8
bid ben bid bont, 82:4
Big Brother is watching you, 258:5
  too b. for boots, 73:3
bigger bang for a buck, 357:1
bike: on your b., 325:3
biking: old maids b. to Communion, 232:2
billiards: to play b. well is sign, 316:1
bimetallist: sallowest b. in Cheshire, 91:2
biography adds new terror, 70:2
bird in two places at once, 282:2
  is on the wing, 10:4
  mugwump is sort of b., 20:6
  what wonderful b. the frog are, 28:3
birds of the air, 56:8
  three b. alighting, 350:4

birth: as thy b. obscure, 266:2
birthday: happy b. to you, 179:2
bitch: life's a b., 19:1
bites: man b. dog, 65:3
black: any colour as long as b., 143:1
  I'm b. and I'm proud, 70:3
black-coated workers, 179:1
blade on the feather, 107:3
blade-straight: steel-true and b., 321:5
blame: know who to b., 308:3
bland leading the b., 338:3
blast: better chill b. of winter, 8:1
blaze of lights and music calling, 256:5
bless: God b. 'im, 12:5
blessing in disguise, 97:2
blest pair of sirens, 242:5
blind: all Americans b. and deaf, 308:1
  halt and the b., 57:7
  in country of the b., 350:1
  leading the b., 56:10
blinked: other fellow just b., 288:1
blood and iron, 61:4
  half world deep trenched in b., 28:4
  libel, 44:3
  sweat and tears, 93:2
  Tiber foaming with much b., 268:2
bloody: abroad is unutterably b., 243:3
  and thirsty, 162:4
  awful newspaper, 264:5
  deed is done, 304:6
  not b. likely, 307:1
  wrong with b. ships, 43:1
bloom: let hundred flowers b., 233:4
  make the desert b., 54:7
bloomed: last in the dooryard b., 352:4
blow: knock-out b., 156:2
blunder: it's a b., 17:2
blundered: someone had b., 327:1
body: I sing the b. electric, 352:6
  like an old book, 145:3
  politic, 85:5
Bognor: bugger b., 155:2
Bohemia: deserts of B., 305:6
boidies: where dem b. is, 10:4
boldly go where no man has gone before, 282:5
boldness has genius power magic, 160:4
Bolshevism run mad, 314:3
BOMFOG, 282:4
bones: cursed be he that moves my b., 305:8
bonfire of the vanities, 360:4
book: bell, b. and candle, 7:3
  good b. is the precious life-blood, 242:4
  like the cover of an old b., 145:3
  never lend a b., 315:3
  sitting with a little b., 332:7
  your servants to read, 166:4
books do furnish a room, 267:4
  were read, 45:3
boon enough for being born, 329:3
boots: children had no b., 357:2
  too big for b., 73:3
  truth is putting on her b., 83:3
bore: prime ministership a damned b., 239:8
born: boon enough for being b., 329:3
  never to have been b. better, 315:2
  sucker b. every minute, 41:3
  with gift of laughter, 290:1

cat on hot tin roof, 356:4
 that walks alone, 43:2
catch a falling star, 123:8
 first c. your hare, 44:2
 my soul, 304:2
catch–22, 175:2
catcher in the rye, 291:1
cause: rebel without a c., 217:3
caveat: I'll have to c. my response, 168:3
caviare to the general, 297:6
Celtic twilight, 365:3
centre cannot hold, 365:4
 of consciousness of universe, 159:4
Ceylon: soft o'er C.'s isle, 175:1
chalk and alum and plaster, 327:2
cham: great c. of literature, 313:7
champagne for your real friends, 24:6
 is deserved in victory, 250:4
 socialist, 245:4
change: point is to c. world, 237:4
 wind of c. is blowing, 230:3
changes: there'll be some c., 135:1
channel storms, 8:5
charge: in c. at the White House, 168:2
 who's in c. of clattering, 43:4
chariots of fire, 63:1
Charlie: chase me C., 108:6
 good grief C. Brown, 292:3
chase me Charlie, 108:6
chastity and continency but not yet, 36:1
Chatterley: like Lady C., 106:1
che sera sera, 9:1
cheap: potent c. music, 108:3
cheer up worst is yet to come, 337:1
cheerful: being so c., 170:5
cheers: cup that c., 109:4
cheese: milk rendered immortal in c., 268:3
 246 different kinds of c., 116:6
chemistry: sexual c., 147:5
cheque: have you brought the c. book, 79:4
Cheshire: sallowest bimetallist in C., 91:2
chestnut: under the spreading c. tree, 220:2
chew: can't fart and c. gum, 193:1
chewing gum for the eyes, 71:1
 lose its flavour, 285:6
chicken in every pot, 176:5
 kinky when use whole c., 213:2
chienlit: la c. non, 117:3
child: I hear a c. weeping, 126:6
 give us c. for eight years, 211:2
 inherits my beauty, 306:2
Childe Roland to dark tower came, 301:5
children: hates c. and dogs, 139:1
 in class had no boots, 357:2
 make sure c. are frightened, 155:1
 of a lesser god, 327:3
 parents last people to have c., 44:6
 rarely forgive parents, 354:4
Chile: small earthquake in C., 103:3
chill blast of winter, 8:1
chimney: old men from c. corner, 311:2
China: great wall of C., 152:1
 oil for lamps of C., 182:2
chips with everything, 350:5
chivalry: age of c. is past, 74:6
Christ: bowels of C., 110:3
 with C. which is better, 59:1

Christmas Day in the workhouse, 311:6
 do they know it's C., 154:3
 shopping days to C., 294:8
 war ends C. day, 142:5
chuck it Smith, 91:5
church of England is Tory party at prayer, 122:3
 not pillar of c., 99:3
 pray c. not struck by lightning, 346:5
 waiting at the c., 84:1
Churchill, Randolph, obituary, 334:3
cigar: good c. is a smoke, 204:4
 good five cent c., 236:1
 is just a c., 146:4
circle: wheel turned full c., 302:1
circumstance: pomp and c., 304:4
circus: what's he doing in bloody c., 239:7
citizen of the world, 161:3
city: have not here a lasting c., 59:5
 most swinging c., 343:3
 rose-red c., 74:4
 shining c. on hill, 277:1
civilization: without interval of c., 101:3
clapping: sound of two hands c., 339:1
clattering: in charge of c. train, 43:4
clause: no sanity c., 236:3
clean teeth in the dark, 190:1
cleanliness is next to godliness, 351:1
clever but is it art, 205:3
 too c. by half, 291:2
cliché: between c. and indiscretion, 228:4
 every c. except, 96:3
clinging to the wreckage, 246:1
clock hath stricken three, 301:3
clockwork orange, 73:6
close: far away is c. at hand, 164:4
 moving peacefully to close, 115:2
 your eyes and think of England, 180:1
close-run: damn c. thing, 348:2
closed: but New Zealand was c., 18:1
clothes: out of wet c., 46:2
clothing: sheep in sheep's c., 98:1
cloud no bigger than man's hand, 51:1
clowns: send in the c., 314:7
club: Englishman belongs to c., 250:8
 not belong to c. have me as member, 236:4
co-existence: peaceful c., 149:3
coach: drive c. and horses through, 281:1
coast of Coromandel, 210:1
cock and bull story, 319:4
cod: piece of c. passeth, 223:3
coffee: if this is c. I want tea, 271:3
coitum: post c. animal triste est, 24:2
cold: love in a c. climate, 243:4
 of English bedroom, 249:1
 war, 41:6
collapse of stout party, 270:1
colour: any c. as long as black, 143:1
 grey is the c. of hope, 275:3
column: fifth c., 243:5
 to a c. in the Evening Standard, 187:4
coma: state of resentful c., 209:1
comb: bald men fighting over a c., 66:9
come again when you can't stay, 310:5
 on down, 111:1
 up and see me some time, 351:5
 with me to the Casbah, 67:3

facts are sacred, 293:2
fade: merely f. away, 224:2
fail: others must f., 341:3
failure possibilities do not exist, 330:1
fair blows the wind for France, 235:4
  day's wages, 121:4
  my f. lady, 213:5
fais ce que voudras, 274:3
faith: break f. with us who d., 227:3
faithful unto death, 59:6
fake: if you can f. that, 75:3
Falklands: the F. thing was a fight, 66:9
fall: pride goeth before a f., 52:8
fallacies of hope, 336:5
fame: nothing can cover high f., 141:3
families: accidents happen in best-regulated f., 119:4
family: selling off f. silver, 230:5
famine in the land, 308:3
famous for fifteen minutes, 345:4
far away is close at hand, 164:4
  bridge too f., 72:2
  f. better thing, 121:5
  from a f. country, 52:9
  from the madding crowd, 165:1
farce: second time as f., 237:1
farewell: and so we say f., 141:1
  baskets, 274:4
  the trumpets, 244:5
Farnham: our F. which art in Hendon, 23:1
fart: can't f. and chew gum, 193:1
farted: when f. where he pissed, 174:5
fashion: glass of f., 298:6
  true to you in my f., 124:4
fat: imprisoned in every f. man, 105:5
  till the f. lady sings, 22:3
  white woman, 106:7
  who's your f. friend, 72:3
father learned much in seven years, 337:2
  Lloyd George knew my f., 156:4
  priest is man called F., 24:5
  the F., the Son and the pigeon, 12:3
  war is f. of all, 182:1
  when did you last see your f., 365:2
fathers: victory finds hundred f., 99:5
fattening: illegal immoral or f., 362:2
faults: women's f. are many, 30:1
favour: looks with f. upon, 40:4
favours: lively sense of future f., 345:1
fay ce que voudras, 274:3
fear: have to f. is f. itself, 284:2
  in a handful of dust, 133:5
  never negotiate out of f., 200:2
feast: moveable f., 176:1
  spectre at the f., 119:2
feasting with panthers, 354:6
feather: blade on the f., 107:3
feet: better to die on your f., 187:2
fence: grass greener other side of f., 13:2
fences: good f. make good neighbours, 148:1
fetters: noise of f. breaking, 328:3
few and far between, 85:2
  owe by so many to so f., 95:6
fiction: stranger than f., 74:5
field: corner of a foreign f., 69:3
  never in f. of human conflict, 95:6
fields: a-babbled of green f., 300:8

killing f., 18:3
  were the essence of the song, 99:7
fifteen: famous for f. minutes, 345:4
fifth column, 243:5
fifty million Frenchmen, 166:5
fight and f. and f. again, 151:2
  here we will stand and f., 244:2
  in no circumstances f., 163:1
  on the beaches, 94:1
film is battleground emotion, 149:5
filthy lucre, 59:3
final: face f. curtain, 5:6
  solution of Jewish problem, 181:3
find: where do we f. such men, 278:1
finest hour, 94:4
  swordsman in all France, 7:4
finger: put f. in dike, 8:3
  time we pulled our f. out, 264:3
  whose f. on trigger, 113:4
finish: nice guys f. last, 126:4
fire and ice, 148:6
  chariots of f., 63:1
  don't let awkward squad f., 76:4
  next time, 39:2
  true is durable f., 274:5
fired: I want him f., 336:4
first catch your hare, 44:2
  loved not at f. sight, 235:5
  nothing ever done for f. time, 107:1
  of May, 15:2
  world war, 279:5
firstest with the mostest, 143:2
fish without a bicycle, 319:3
fishing: hours spent in f., 13:1
fittest: survival of the f., 316:2
Flanders: in F. fields the poppies blow, 227:2
flashed from his bed, 36:3
flatness of surrounding countryside, 237:3
flavour: does Spearmint lose its f., 285:6
flea: after a f., 50:6
  between a louse and a f., 195:2
fleas: great f. have little f., 324:3
fleet: everything's at sea except the f., 344:5
  f.'s lit up, 361:3
flesh: world, the f. and the devil, 65:6
fleshpots of Egypt, 50:4
flew: he pushed and they f., 218:3
fling: youth must have its f., 158:2
flinging pot of paint, 288:3
flood: after us the f., 265:3
floor: golden f., 184:7
floreat Etona, 41:4
flower: where I thought a f. would go, 217:1
flowers: let hundred f. bloom, 233:4
  say it with f., 258:2
fly in the ointment, 53:7
  needs f. into my eye, 188:4
  said the spider to the f., 185:2
foe was folly, 159:2
fog in channel, 8:5
  night and f., 181:2
fold their tents like the Arabs, 219:2
folk-dancing: incest and f., 42:7
folk that live on hill, 5:4
follow: I must f. them, 210:4
  them as leader, 209:2

lines: know your l., 108:1
lion shall lie down with lamb, 54:4
lions led by donkeys, 223:1
lips are sealed, 40:1
  read my l., 77:4
  that touch liquor, 366:3
liquor: lips that touch l., 366:3
listening: actor's a guy who's not listening, 68:3
lit: fleet's l. up, 361:3
  not l. again in our lifetime, 166:3
literary: claim to l. fame, 48:3
literature: great cham of l., 313:7
  loss to l. not great, 258:7
little: does L. Nell die, 121:1
  Jack Horner, 19:2
  local difficulties, 229:1
  old lady from Dubuque, 286:5
  so l. done, 280:4
  too l. too late, 252:4
live: folk that l. on hill, 5:4
  if I'd known I'd l. this long, 62:2
  in hearts we leave behind, 85:1
  long l. kind, 18:4
  now pay later, 322:3
  want to l. for ever, 114:2
Liverpool centre of universe, 159:4
  pool of life, 196:3
lives: how the other half l., 281:4
liveth: name l. for evermore, 56:2
living: servants will do that, 341:4
  world owes me a l., 121:6
Livingstone: Dr L. I presume, 317:6
llama: like female l. in bath, 96:1
Lloyd George knew my father, 156:4
lobster doesn't bark, 252:3
lobsters: change l. and dance, 87:3
local: little l. difficulties, 229:1
log cabin to White House, 153:3
London: swinging L., 343:3
  when man is tired of L., 193:6
lonely: none but the l. heart, 218:1
long: how l. O Lord, how l., 54:3
  hot summer, 138:1
longitude: platitude and l., 362:3
look: not l. upon his like again, 299:3
  stranger, 35:2
looney tunes and squalid criminals, 278:4
lord: consider what L. said to Moses, 244:3
  L.'s prayer, 23:1
  no guarantee born l., 359:3
  nor privy, nor seal, 38:4
  O L. if I forget thee, 34:4
  of language, 327:5
Lorraine: Cross of L. is heaviest, 95:3
lose: don't l. it again, 113:3
  you l., 106:4
losing: fights when sure of l., 132:2
lost generation, 319:2
  he who hesitates is l., 2:5
  I've l. my little Willie, 226:2
  matters not how won or l., 280:5
  no love l. between us, 161:6
lot: not a l., 114:3
lottery: first prize in l. of life, 280:3
Louis: drop the gun L., 64:1
louse: between a l. and a flea, 195:2
love: always hurt the one you l., 281:6

conquers all, 341:5
greater l. hath no man, 58:1
him for the enemies he made, 102:1
I l. you Alice B. Toklas, 319:1
in a cold climate, 243:4
in l. with death, 309:2
is like the measles, 60:6
is two minutes of squishing, 287:1
know him is to l. him, 315:6
lie down I think I l. you, 344:6
made l. to 10,000 women, 311:4
me love my dog, 47:7
make l. to every woman, 47:4
means never having to say sorry, 294:6
no fond return of l., 273:2
no l. lost between us, 161:6
support of woman I l., 130:3
that dare not speak name, 354:5
that I have of the life, 234:5
that makes world go round, 87:2
time to l. and to die, 53:4
treated like a l. affair, 20:3
true l. is durable fire, 274:5
we must l. one another or die, 35:4
wilder shores of l., 63:5
will you l. me in December, 344:1
loved: these I have l., 69:2
  whoever l. that l. not at first, 235:5
lover: all world loves a l., 135:3
  high-bouncing l., 140:6
  sighed as a l., 157:3
lovesome: garden is a l. thing, 71:3
loving: tender l. care, 301:2
lower than vermin, 48:3
lowest depth is journalist, 203:1
lucky Jim, 5:1
lucre: filthy l., 59:3
lugger: once aboard the l., 186:2
lunch: no such thing as free l., 146:5
  not married for l., 360:1
lying low and saying nuffin, 172:1

M
Macduff: lead on M., 303:3
machine: desiccated calculating m., 48:5
  house is m. for living, 210:3
mad as hell, 90:2
  don't get m. get even, 201:5
  sense that world was m., 290:1
madam: call me m., 263:3
madding: far from m. crowd, 165:1
made: here's one I m. earlier, 14:1
madness: method in his m., 299:7
Maggie may, 331:1
magnanimity: in victory m., 96:4
magnifique: c'est m. mais ce n'est pas la guerre, 67:1
Mahomet: mountain won't come to M., 38:1
maids: old m. biking to Communion, 232:2
mail must get through, 19:3
Maine: as M. goes, 137:2
mairzy doats and dozy doats, 20:1
majority: great silent m., 255:4
  one is a m., 93:1
  to join great m., 71:4
make my day, 127:1
maker: ready to meet my m., 99:4

rain: into each life some r. must fall, 219:3
neither r. nor snow, 178:1
wedding-cake left out in r., 35:3
Welsh are Italians in r., 28:1
random harvest, 180:3
Randy, where's the rest of me, 276:2
rape, how to deal with, 322:5
when r. is inevitable, 28:5
rare Ben Jonson, 195:4
rashers: pounds of r. of ham, 24:4
rat: I smell a r., 282:1
you dirty r., 81:4
raven like a writing desk, 86:6
read: book your servants to r., 166:4
he who runs may r., 55:3
his books were r., 45:3
my lips, 77:4
never r. a book, 315:3
rather praise than r., 194:1
reader: common r., 193:3
reading: lose no time in r., 123:4
real pain for your sham friends, 24:6
reap: that shall he also r., 58:8
reappraisal: agonizing r., 126:1
rears: sex r. ugly head, 4:2
reason: last appeal to r., 181:5
will know the r. why, 173:1
rebel without a cause, 217:3
red: better r. than dead, 288:4
thin r. line, 288:5
references: verify your r., 287:2
reform result in exact opposite, 6:4
yes, 117:3
refuse: offer he can't r., 272:2
wretched r. of teeming shore, 209:6
regiment leaves at dawn, 236:6
rejoice, r., 330:2
rejoicing: went on his way r., 58:4
relationship: special r., 96:5
relief: for this r. much thanks, 298:4
relieve: opportunity to r. yourself, 154:5
remedies: require desperate r., 138:3
remedying youth and inexperience, 265:1
remember: we will r. them, 61:1
report of my death an exaggeration, 338:2
requiem: writing r. for myself, 247:1
research: dignified by name of r., 209:1
outcome of serious r., 340:2
resign: son of bitch isn't going to r., 336:4
responsibility: no sense of r. at other end, 276:4
power without r., 39:5
rest: everywhere I have sought r., 332:7
Randy, where's the r. of me, 276:2
retreat hell no, 356:3
return: I shall r., 224:1
no fond r. of love, 273:2
reunion: mother and child r., 311:5
revenge: Hamlet r., 298:7
review: I have your r. before me, 279:3
revolt into style, 167:1
revolutions: make r. by halves, 211:4
rhyme: Pears was put to r. with stairs, 210:2
rib: Adam's r., 49:5
rich are different, 175:6
don't make r. poorer, 216:4
life's r. pageant, 235:6
made Gay r. and R. gay, 153:6

man in his castle, 3:4
man's joke always funny, 71:2
man's plaything, 169:5
man to enter kingdom of God, 57:3
poor little r. girl, 108:2
rid me of this turbulent priest, 176:7
ride: if my friend can't r. two horses, 239:7
riders: ourselves r. on the earth, 227:5
rides in the whirlwind, 2:4
ridiculous: from sublime to r., 250:1
position r., 90:4
rien, 221:5
rift: loads every r. with ore, 198:4
right: country r. or wrong, 116:2
customer is always r., 294:7
do the r., 227:6
I think the Lord was r., 244:3
my own r. hand shall do, 294:4
stuff, 360:3
Rimbauds: Verlaine always chasing R., 338:4
ring: return the r., 151:1
round the moon, 30:3
rises: sun also r., 53:2
rising of the moon, 166:1
Ritz: justice open like R. hotel, 239:1
river: cross over the r., 188:1
who passed the r., 164:1
road less travelled, 148:7
people in middle of r., 48:4
yellow brick r., 42:3
roareth: what is this that r. thus, 160:1
robbed: we was r., 188:2
robber: now Barabbas was a r., 58:3
robe: seamless r., 58:2
rock of ages, 335:1
rocket: risen like r., 173:3
rocking: cradle endlessly r., 352:5
rocks: hand that r. the cradle, 344:2
Roland: Childe R. to dark tower, 301:5
role: not yet found a r., 1:1
rolls: how money r. in, 8:4
Romeo: wherefore art thou R., 304:9
Rommel is definitely a nuisance, 244:2
roof: cat on hot tin r., 356:4
roof-top: friend fall from r., 105:2
room at the top, 68:1
books do furnish a r., 267:4
inability to be quiet in r., 261:4
slipped away into next r., 182:4
smoke-filled r., 114:5
Roosevelt, F.D., mush, 221:1
rose is a r. is a r., 318:5
mighty like a r., 318:3
money is r. of evil, 59:4
name of the r., 128:1
never promised a r. garden, 165:5
without trace, 247:2
rose-red city, 74:4
Rosencrantz and Guildernstern are dead, 299:6
roses: days of wine and r., 124:3
everything's coming up r., 314:6
rough island story, 326:6
seas make tough sailors, 24:7
round: ring r. the moon, 30:3
rowed: all r. fast, 103:5
rugged individualism, 184:2

survived: I s., 311:3
suspension: willing s. of disbelief, 104:4
suspicion: Caesar's wife above s., 81:1
Sussex by the sea, 205:6
sweat: blood, s. and tears, 93:2
Sweeny: you're Mrs S., 267:1
sweet: there is a lady s. and kind, 31:2
sweetness and light, 324:5
swimmer who has already reached shore, 308:5
swine: pearls before s., 261:1
swinging: most s. city, 343:3
Switzerland: in S. they had brotherly love, 347:5
sword: by the s. divided, 173:2
  pen is mightier than the s., 73:4
swordsman: best s. in France, 7:4
swore: by the nine gods he s., 225:3

T

tailors: nine t., 291:4
take: not going to t. this any more, 90:2
tale, dead bodies must tell t., 294:1
  thereby hangs a t., 296:3
  which holdeth children, 311:2
talk: we have ways of making you t., 27:4
  well but not too wisely, 239:6
tall: trees are t., 98:4
tame: some t. gazelle, 273:1
tanks: get your t. off my lawn, 359:2
tap your heels three times, 42:6
Tarzan: me T. you Jane, 76:5
taste: ghastly good t., 48:2
taxes: no new t., 77:4
  only little people pay t., 175:3
taxi: empty t. arrived, 97:6
  I'm going in a t., 307:1
tea: if this is coffee I want t., 271:3
  pound of t. at one and three, 24:4
teaches: he who cannot t., 308:6
tears, blood sweat and t., 93:2
technological: white heat of t. revolution, 357:5
teeth: clean t. in the dark, 190:1
  skin of my t., 51:5
Teflon-coated presidency, 292:1
television is chewing gum for the eyes, 71:1
tell: best friends won't t. you, 12:1
  England ye who pass, 275:5
  how can they t., 261:2
  it not in Gath, 50:7
tempers: God t. wind to shorn lamb, 320:2
tender loving care, 301:2
tends: all power t. to corrupt, 1:3
tennis: anyone for t., 64:3
  eat apple through t. racquet: 109:1
tent: stripped, washed and brought to t., 90:3
tents: fold their t. like the Arabs, 219:2
  to your t. O Israel, 286:2
termino nobis donet in patria, 91:7
terminological inexactitude, 92:3
territory: dream comes with t., 240:7
terror: adds new t. death, 70:2
testimony: human t. should err, 185:3
Texas the place where there are most cows, 26:2
thalatta, t., 365:1
Thames: sweet T. run softly, 316:3
thanks: for this relief much t., 298:4

Thatcher, Margaret, re-elected, 204:2
theatre: and they fill the t., 190:4
  great t. of action, 189:3
  splendid t. of pitiful passion, 344:4
there: because it's there, 232:3
thereby hangs a tale, 296:3
these I have loved, 69:2
thin man wildly signalling, 105:5
  red line, 288:5
thing: do your own t., 135:7
  poor t. but mine own, 296:4
  the distinguished t., 189:1
  worth doing badly, 91:4
  worthy of God, 295:4
  vision t., 77:3
things: attempt great t., 6:5
  fall apart, 365:4
  I've done for England, 177:2
  that will destroy us are, 26:3
  were done better in my day, 202:1
think: close eyes and t. of England, 180:1
  it's all over, 361:1
  of Shakespeare, 46:6
thinks: sometimes I just sits and t., 272:1
thirty: don't trust anyone over t., 287:3
thistle: always plucked a t., 217:1
thou: loaf of bread and t., 140:2
thought: who would have t. it, 232:1
  with but a single t., 169:4
thousand: death by t. cuts, 234:1
  face that launched t. ships, 235:2
  first one t. days., 200:3
  in a t. generations, 204:3
  night has a t. eyes, 67:2
  picture is worth t. words, 23:2
  points of light, 77:5
  years of history, 151:3
three birds alighting on field, 350:4
  fine days and thunderstorm, 11:3
  screaming popes, 38:2
through leaves, 290:3
thumb: put in his t., 19:2
thunderstorm: three fine days and t., 11:3
Thursday: man who was T., 91:3
thus far shalt thou go, 51:6
Tiber foaming with much blood, 268:2
ticket at Victoria station, 49:4
tie: old school t., 325:5
tiger-shooting: not man to go t., 174:1
tightly-knit group of politically men, 358:4
time: dance to the music of t., 268:1
  do we get to win this t., 278:3
  fire next t., 39:2
  fool the people all the t., 215:1
  for all good men to come to aid of party, 347:2
  good t. was had by all, 313:3
  half as old as t., 74:4
  has come the Walrus said, 87:4
  I may be some t., 257:1
  is now, 26:4
  nothing ever done for first t., 107:1
  peace for our t., 89:2
  seeds of t., 302:4
  to love and t. to die, 53:4
  week is long t. in politics, 358:2
  work expands to fill t., 261:3